Research Methods
for Counseling

Counseling and Professional Identity

Richard Parsons & Naijian Zhang – Series Editors

COUNSELING and
PROFESSIONAL IDENTITY

Research Methods
for Counseling

An Introduction

Robert J. Wright
Widener University

Los Angeles | London | New Delhi
Singapore | Washington DC

Los Angeles | London | New Delhi
Singapore | Washington DC

FOR INFORMATION:

SAGE Publications, Inc.
2455 Teller Road
Thousand Oaks, California 91320
E-mail: order@sagepub.com

SAGE Publications Ltd.
1 Oliver's Yard
55 City Road
London EC1Y 1SP
United Kingdom

SAGE Publications India Pvt. Ltd.
B 1/I 1 Mohan Cooperative Industrial Area
Mathura Road, New Delhi 110 044
India

SAGE Publications Asia-Pacific Pte. Ltd.
3 Church Street
#10-04 Samsung Hub
Singapore 049483

Acquisitions Editor: Kassie Graves
Editorial Assistant: Elizabeth Luizzi
Production Editor: Laura Barrett
Copy Editor: Paula L. Fleming
Typesetter: C&M Digitals (P) Ltd.
Proofreader: Jennifer Thompson
Indexer: Jeanne Busemeyer
Cover Designer: Candice Harman
Marketing Manager: Lisa Sheldon Brown
Permissions Editor: Karen Ehrmann

Printed in the United States of America

Library of Congress Cataloging-in-Publication Data

Wright, Robert J., 1945-

Research methods for counseling : an introduction / Robert J. Wright, Widener University.

pages cm
Includes bibliographical references and index.

ISBN 978-1-4522-0394-2 (pbk.)

1. Counseling—Research—Methodology. I. Title.

BF636.6.W75 2013
158.3072—dc23   2012039563

This book is printed on acid-free paper.

13 14 15 16 17 10 9 8 7 6 5 4 3 2 1

Contents

Detailed Table of Contents

5   Qualitative Research II—Processes   90

6   Action Research Methods   121

SECTION III: DESCRIPTIVE STATISTICS AND CORRELATION 151

7 Nature of Variables and Data 152

8   Concordance and Correlation   201

SECTION IV: INFERENTIAL STATISTICS AND HYPOTHESIS TESTING   231

9   Sampling and Sampling Error   233

10 Scientific Method and Hypothesis Testing

13 Instrument Development and Survey Research 358

SECTION VI: ORGANIZING AND APPLYING RESEARCH SKILLS 391

14 Organizing Valid Research 393

15 Mixed Methods Research 426

16 Approaches for Evaluation 455

17 Writing Research Proposals and Reports 485

Editor's Preface

Counseling is a developing discipline and as such we who claim professional identities as counselors must be informed consumers of the research and findings that give shape to our profession as well as become effective contributors to that knowledge base. While no single text will make one an expert in research methodology *Research Methods for Counselors,* by Robert J. Wright, Ph.D. provides the essential foundation for just such practice.

This text, as you will soon come to experience, provides not only a comprehensive analyses of the nature, the need and the value of research methodology for counselors but does so in a way that actively engages you , as reader and fosters your development as a Counselor and practitioner-researcher. *Research Methods for Counselors* is unique among similar text in that it is an essential part of Sage Publication's series for counselor, entitled: *Counseling and Professional Identity in the 21st Century*. Collectively the books in this series provide readers with the fundamental knowledge and skills necessary to become a professional counselor.

Counseling and Professional Identity in the 21st Century is a new-fresh – pedagogically sound series of texts targeting counselors in training. This series is NOT simply a compilation of isolated books matching that which is already in the market. Rather each book, with its targeted knowledge and skills, will be presented as but a part of a larger whole. The focus and content of each text serves as a single lens through which a counselor can view his/her clients, engage in his/her practice and articulate his/her own professional identity.

Counseling and Professional Identity in the 21st Century is unique not just in the fact that it 'packaged' a series of traditional text, but that it provides an *integrated* curriculum targeting the formation of the readers' professional identity and efficient, ethical practice. Each book, within the series, is structured to facilitate the ongoing professional formation of the reader. The materials found within each text are organized in order to move the reader to higher levels of cognitive, affective and psychomotor functioning, resulting in his/her assimilation of the materials presented into both his/her professional identity and approach to professional practice. While each text targets a specific set of core competencies (cognates and skills), competencies identified by the Council for Accreditation of Counseling & Related Educational Programs (CACREP) as essential to the practice of counseling (see inside front cover), each book in the series will emphasize each of the following:

a. the assimilation of concepts and constructs provided across the text found within the series thus fostering the reader's ongoing development as a competent professional;
b. the blending of contemporary theory with current research and empirical support;

c. a focus on the development of procedural knowledge with each text employing case illustrations and guided practice exercises to facilitate the readers ability to translate the theory and research discussed into professional decision making and application;
d. the emphasis on the need for and means of demonstrating accountability, and;
e. the fostering of the reader's Professional Identity and with it the assimilation of the ethics and standards of practice guiding the Counseling Profession.

We are proud to have served as co-editors of this series feeling sure that each will serve as a significant resource to you and your development as a professional counselor.

Richard Parsons, Ph.D.
Naijian Zhang, Ph.D.

Preface

GOALS AND MIND-SETS

It is no secret that graduate students in clinical programs in counseling generally see research courses as anxiety provoking. Classes in research design, statistics, and measurement methods are one part of the graduate curriculum put off as long as possible. It is as though some students feel the research requirements will just go away if they wait long enough. When students are finally forced to enroll in their required research or statistics classes, their fears interact with a curriculum filled with unfamiliar terminology and symbols. The result is a passive victim mind-set and a deep resentment of what is seen as an unnecessary exercise with irrelevant and boring material. The decontextualized nature of many textbooks' approach to this academic area only reinforces these feelings.

This text is my attempt to help students cast off this mind-set by demonstrating the relevancy of research to each counselor now entering the profession. I have placed the research concepts discussed in this book into the context of what is relevant for counselors to know and the ways that this information is helpful to practitioners.

This textbook was written to provide readers with an overview of the various approaches used by researchers in their efforts to expand our understanding of the field. As an overview, it describes and explains both qualitative-interpretative and quantitative-empirical approaches for research.

The principal goal of this book is to introduce graduate students to the worldview of researchers in the social sciences by bridging the gap between clinical skill and the ability to use the emerging knowledge of the profession. An assumption I have made in writing this text is that many graduate students do not intend to become researchers themselves. To that end, this book is designed to help graduate students become informed research consumers.

To value and understand research in the social sciences requires the ability to read with understanding scientific literature in clinical psychology and counseling. It means the research consumer can analyze and evaluate what is in journal articles and what is presented at meetings of professional associations. The development of this mind-set is empowering and liberating for all professionals in counseling, and it is now a core requirement of all professional associations and part of all licensing examinations.

PHILOSOPHICAL PERSPECTIVE

Research in the social and behavioral sciences is not a series of isolated procedures. It is an integrated process that includes a framework of knowledge and a methodological foundation focused on the task of improving understanding of the human condition and human behavior. No single approach to conducting research in counseling and counseling psychology can answer all questions or solve all problems. Therefore, the research consumer needs a practical understanding of various approaches and methods used by practitioner-researchers to explore the complex nature of the human psyche. In addition to this skill set for reading and understanding research, students working to become counselors should be able to evaluate what they read.

Prepared research consumers know how to find current and past published research in an area of professional interest. Once they have identified and reviewed it for quality, research consumers can organize this literature, summarize it, and write cogent literature reviews.

OVERVIEW AND ORGANIZATION

This book was developed and written to support a first-level course in research for counselors and related specializations in the social sciences. Therefore, the text is designed to develop students' understanding and interpretation of literature in the behavioral sciences. As a first-level overview of the domain of research methods and systems, the text does not present complex computational formulations or algorithms. The emphasis is on developing a practical understanding and ability to interpret and evaluate research. The focus of each chapter is on developing skills needed to read and evaluate research presented by others. Thus, this textbook presents explanations through the use of numerous examples from the literature. These excerpts from research articles are illustrative of the various research approaches. Over 170 excerpts from journals of counseling and related fields are included, each of which was selected to provide an example of the concepts being explained in the surrounding text.

Occasionally, individuals want a deeper or more elaborated description of the research described in this book. To address that need, SAGE supports a student website providing the technical and/or mathematical basis of various research models.

This first-level textbook provides wide coverage of issues and approaches from various research domains. This wide coverage is evident from the text's organization. The introductory section provides three chapters that examine questions of research philosophies, ethics, and the scientific literature of counseling. Here students also find guidance for developing a review of the literature.

This introductory section is followed by the three chapters in Section II. This section describes interpretative-qualitative approaches and models for research. Chapter 4 provides a description of the skills and tools of qualitative research, while Chapter 5 describes the models that have been developed for interpretative-qualitative studies. Chapter 6 presents and discusses action research as a collaborative form of qualitative research.

In Section III, Chapters 7 and 8 explain how researchers describe, summarize, and present data they collect. This discussion includes basic descriptive statistics and methods, and Chapter 8 describes ways to document the concordance among variables. Then Section IV, a three-chapter section (Chapters 9, 10, and 11), describes empirical methods for hypothesis testing.

The next segment, Section V, provides two chapters (Chapters 12 and 13) on psychological measurement and testing. These chapters explain psychological test scores and their interpretation, and they provide readers with information about where they can find independent reviews of published tests. The criteria for evaluating psychological tests are also elaborated in these chapters. Information is provided here about how to develop and employ questionnaires and client checklists.

The final part of this book, Section VI, presents four related chapters (Chapters 14–17) on how research is actually conducted. The first of these chapters describes how to evaluate the validity of the research approach employed in a study. Chapter 15 then introduces the emerging, highly pragmatic approach to research known as mixed methods research.

Chapter 16 brings together all the research areas and skills described in this book to explain the process of evaluating programs and systems. Evaluation skills are now invaluable in clinical settings because health care providers, third-party payers, federal and state agencies, and philanthropic foundations demand documentation of program effectiveness. This push for total accountability mandates proof of effectiveness for all clinical activities and operations, including the approaches used by therapists.

Chapter 17 meets a need many graduate students have if they are required to develop a research proposal. This chapter provides guidance for developing and writing a research proposal. In addition to writing methods and sources of research ideas, this chapter provides guidance for writing a full research report or article for publication.

DEDICATION

This text is affectionately dedicated to Jeanne, my wife, best friend, and indefatigable editor. It is her energy, dedication, and intellect that made it possible for me to complete this project.

SECTION I

Using and Valuing Counseling Research

"You cannot teach a man anything; you can only help him discover it in himself."

Galileo

This section of the book is divided into three chapters that introduce the need for professional counselors to become competent consumers of research. Here practitioners will find guidance for locating and using research evidence in their practices. This section also provides counselors-in-training with a background in the ethical standards and duties of those using research evidence to make data-based decisions with regard to their clients.

Chapter 1   describes the expectation of our society that practitioners will keep up with developments in the field and document the effectiveness of their professional contacts with clients. The expanding requirements of third-party agents for documentation and accountability are also explained. This chapter discusses mandates for research and assessment skills for all new practitioners and presents the specific requirements of each of the various professional organizations in counseling and counseling psychology.

Chapter 2   discusses the ethical standards governing the activities of practitioners who conduct research. This discussion describes past abuses and the rationale for the Nuremberg

Code of 1947. Abuses of research participants from populations of immature, disabled, and incarcerated individuals are described. The resulting Belmont Report in 1979 and its implications for researchers are also included in this chapter.

Chapter 3   describes various types of published research and how to identify and locate research evidence for counseling- or counseling psychology–related topics. It then discusses the process of writing integrated summaries of research.

The Research Consumer

"I always liked myself far better as a pure scientist."

Carl R. Rogers

OBJECTIVES

By reading and studying this chapter, you should acquire the competency to do the following:

- Understand and value the emphasis on research skill development in graduate programs for mental health professionals.
- Describe the research knowledge standards mandated by professional organizations for all new therapists seeking a professional license.
- Explain the role of a practitioner-researcher in terms of both accountability and improving clinical practice.
- Describe the three general research frameworks guiding the selection and organization of research methods in counseling and related social sciences.
- Describe sources of research ideas and problems to solve for the beginning practitioner-researcher.

INTRODUCTION AND MAJOR THEMES

This chapter is organized around the theme of the well-informed research consumer. The conceptualization here of the practitioner is a professional who has the skill and knowledge to consume research. A well-informed consumer of research can identify sources of technical literature addressing areas of concern, read and evaluate research articles, and organize summaries of the current state of the profession regarding a topic or issue. These researchers are able to identify interventions and therapeutic approaches supported by data. They are also able to conduct ongoing evaluations of the success of their therapeutic interventions.

This chapter is divided into three major sections. The first is a description of the social forces within our society that make it necessary for people in the helping professions to have research and accountability skills. This position is reinforced in the second section with statements from the major professional societies and licensing boards for the helping professions detailing their expectations and mandates for new practitioners.

The third section of the chapter describes steps that an effective practitioner-researcher follows in problem solving. Scholars and other researchers may frame their work using different philosophies, but a common thread links all researchers in the behavioral sciences.

That section also discusses the researcher's professional integrity and his or her commitment to the ethical use of evidence-based treatments. Practitioner-researchers have the ability to record and report findings of their own research and present those findings appropriately. Thus, they are conversant with various approaches for finding unbiased answers to clinical and other problems they encounter in their professional activities.

All too often, the development of clinical skills is divorced from the development of research skills. To borrow a metaphor from John Gray, it is as if "researchers are from Mars and therapists are from Venus." Researchers complain that practitioners ignore emerging models of effective practice, while practicing therapists complain that research results are often difficult to interpret and not relevant to real-world practice. This division represents more than a problem of translation from science to practice; it is reinforced by the guiding philosophies of academic departments responsible for providing the education and development of new professionals in counseling and related social sciences.

RESEARCH KNOWLEDGE AND SKILL MANDATES
FOR THERAPISTS' TRAINING

For the past two decades, professional societies for counseling and clinical psychology have moved to increase the knowledge base of new members in the areas of research, statistics, measurement, and evaluation. The knowledge and skills now being required of new practitioners exceed those required of previous generations. New curricular requirements are enforced both through the educational standards that university-based programs must meet and by the requirements of the examinations that must be passed to qualify for a license as a practitioner.

Background

The costs of providing medical and psychological therapies have come under careful scrutiny and oversight in the past 50 years. Yet the history of the need for practitioners to document the effectiveness of their therapeutic interventions and control costs can be traced to the era before World War II and the first cooperative health care models.

By 1929, a number of western cities and rural communities had formed health care cooperatives centered on the practice of a small group of physicians (Tufts Managed Care Institute, 1998). During the 1930s and 1940s, this movement spread along with a concept of prepaid health care. For example, workers on the construction of large infrastructure projects like the Hoover Dam project had 5 cents withheld from every dollar they were paid to cover medical expenses, including those from on-the-job injuries. These prepaid plans later became the health maintenance organizations (HMOs) of today. The late 1940s and 1950s saw this movement take another direction with the establishment of nonprofit group health insurance programs. At first, the American Medical Association opposed these efforts to make physicians employees of sponsoring organizations.

A great shift occurred in July of 1965 under the leadership of President Lyndon Johnson with the creation of Medicare and Medicaid programs within the Social Security Administration. Medicare and Medicaid began to include psychotherapy as covered services in 1990.[1]

Current Status

Paralleling Medicare and Medicaid's payments for psychological services, medical insurance companies also started providing payment for psychological therapies for covered individuals. With all third-party payment systems for psychotherapy, there is a need to follow treatment guidelines and accept negotiated payment levels. Also, providers of mental health care need to be able to document the effectiveness of their therapies and account for their activities.

Practitioners today work in an environment in which the mandates of health management systems and health insurers, led by the policies of Medicare and Medicaid, prescribe what are and are not covered treatments. To qualify for reimbursement, the therapy must be directed to help what health care managers define as a medically required condition. A clear diagnosis of the patient's condition must be made and coded in the medical records of the patient. Working within these parameters, the therapist has both the number and the nature of therapy sessions, which must use an approved approach to treatment, specified.

Health care providers have developed codes for organizing and billing for psychological services known as **Current Procedural Terminology (CPT)**.

Applications from the Literature

CPT Codes for Psychological Services

Note: The American Medical Association maintains a web page with all the per-hour reimbursement levels for the various states and regions of the United States: https://ocm.ama-assn.org/OCM/CPTRelativeValueSearch.do. Naturally, patients receiving an ethical treatment from a licensed therapist that is not on the list of codes can pay for the treatment from private funds.

Code	Description
90801	Psychological Diagnostic Interview Examination (includes report prep time 90885)
90802	Interactive Diagnostic Interview (with language interpreter or other mechanisms)
90816	Individual psychological psychotherapy, 20–30 minutes for Inpatient (Outpatient = 90804)

(Continued)

(Continued)

Code	Description
90818	Individual psychological psychotherapy, 45–50 minutes for Inpatient (Outpatient = 90806)
90821	Individual psychological psychotherapy, 75–80 minutes for Inpatient (Outpatient = 90808)
90847	Family psychotherapy with patient present (90846 without patient present; 90849 multiple-family group psychotherapy)
90853	Group psychotherapy
96101	Psychological testing, interpretation and reporting per hour by a psychologist (per hour)
96102	Psychological testing per hour by a technician (per hour)
96103	Psychological testing by a computer, including time for the psychologist's interpretation and reporting (per hour)
96105	Assessment of Aphasia
96111	Developmental Testing, Extended
96115	Neurobehavioral Status Exam (per hour)
96116	Chart Review, Scoring, and Interpretation of Instruments, Note Writing
96118	Neuropsychological testing, interpretation and reporting per hour by a psychologist
96119	Neuropsychological testing per hour by a technician
96120	Neuropsychological testing by a computer, including time for the psychologist's interpretation and reporting
96150	Health & Behavioral Assessment–Initial
96151	Reassessment
96152	Health & Behavior Intervention–Individual
96153	Health & Behavior Intervention–Group
96154	Health & Behavior Intervention–Family with Patient
96155	Health & Behavior Intervention–Family without Patient
97770	Cognitive Rehabilitation

Source: Grohol, J. M. (2012). CPT codes for psychology services. PsychCentral. Retrieved from http://psychcentral.com/lib/2007/cpt-codes-for-psychology-services

When a therapist disagrees with the decision of a third-party payer, he or she must be ready to prove, with current research, what the best standard for care is for the client and what therapies are most effective for achieving the treatment goals.

RESEARCH SKILL REQUIREMENTS IN PROFESSIONAL STANDARDS

Professional societies exist to provide a framework for highly educated individuals employed in a given occupation to maintain control and provide direction for the practice of others in that occupation. This includes setting standards for professional practice and establishing requirements for those entering the profession. The professional society takes responsibility for ensuring the efficacy of practice by its members while providing for the protection of the interests of the general public. This results in the public granting privileges and certain powers to members of the profession, including the power to receive a professional license from the state.

American School Counselor Association (ASCA)

In 2012, the ASCA published the third edition of its *National Model: A Framework for School Counseling Programs*. In this highly prescriptive framework, the ASCA has taken a new direction in defining skills that school counselors must bring to their professional positions. One large section of this reformed document specifies that school counselors have certain research skills.

Applications from the Literature

Specific School Counselor Competencies

Note: These research and evaluation competencies are a portion of the full statement of competencies for school counselors by the American School Counselor Association.

Skills and Attitudes

IV-B: An effective school counselor is able to accomplish measurable objectives demonstrating the following abilities and skills:.

   IV-B-2d: Reviews school data, school counseling program audits, and school counseling program goals with the [advisory] council.

   IV-B-3: Collects, analyzes, and interprets relevant data, including process, perception, and outcome data, to monitor and improve student behavior and achievement.

   IV-B-3a: Analyzes, synthesizes, and disaggregates data to examine student outcomes and to identify and implement interventions as needed.

(Continued)

(Continued)

IV-B-3b: Uses data to identify policies, practices, and procedures leading to success, as well as systemic barriers and areas of weakness.

IV-B-3c: Uses student data to demonstrate a need for systemic change in areas such as course enrollment patterns; equity and access; and the achievement, opportunity, and information gap.

IV-B-3d: Understands and uses data to establish goals and activities to close the achievement, opportunity, and information gap.

IV-B-3e: Knows how to use and analyze data to evaluate the school counseling program, research activity outcomes, and identify gaps between and among different groups of students.

IV-B-3f: Uses school data to identify and assist individual students who do not perform at grade level and do not have opportunities and resources to be successful in school.

IV-B-3g: Knows and understands theoretical and historical basis for assessment techniques.

IV-B-6: Designs and implements action plans aligning with school and school counseling program goals.

Action Plans: For every desired competency, there must be a plan outlining how the desired result will be achieved. Each plan should contain:

(1) competencies addressed

(2) description of the activity

(3) data driving the decision to address the competency

(4) timeline in which the activity is to be completed

(5) who is responsible for delivery

(6) means of evaluating student success

(7) expected results for students

IV-B-6a: Uses appropriate academic and behavioral data to develop school counseling core curriculum and closing-the-gap action plan and determines appropriate students for the target group or interventions.

IV-B-6f: Identifies data collection strategies to gather process, perception, and outcome data.

Knowledge

V-A: School counselors should articulate and demonstrate an understanding of:
    V-A-1: Basic concepts of results-based school counseling and accountability issues
    V-A-2: Basic research and statistical concepts to read and conduct research
    V-A-3: Using data to evaluate program effectiveness and to determine program needs
    V-A-4: Program audits and results reports

Abilities and Skills

V-B: The effective school counselor is able to accomplish measurable objectives demonstrating the following abilities and skills:

V-B-1: Uses data from results reports to evaluate program effectiveness and to determine program needs.

V-B-1a: Uses formal and informal methods of program evaluation to design and modify comprehensive school counseling programs.

V-B-1b: Uses student data to support decision making in designing effective school counseling programs and interventions.

V-B-1c: Measures results obtained from school counseling core curriculum and closing-the-gap activities.

V-B-1d: Works with members of the school counseling team and with the administration to decide how school counseling programs are evaluated and how results are shared.

V-B-1e: Collects process, perception, and outcome data.

V-B-1f: Uses technology in conducting research and program evaluation.

V-B-1g: Reports program results to professional school counseling community.

V-B-1h: Uses data to demonstrate the value the school counseling program adds to student achievement.

Attitudes

V-C: School counselors believe:

V-C-3: School counselors should use quantitative and qualitative data to evaluate their school counseling program and to demonstrate program results.

V-C-4: The results of the school counseling program should be analyzed and presented in the context of the overall school and district performance.

Source: American School Counselor Association (ASCA). (2012). *The ASCA national model: A framework for school counseling programs* (3rd ed.). Alexandria, VA: American School Counselor Association, pp. 148–159.

School Counselor Performance Standards

The school counselor's performance evaluation contains basic standards of practice expected of school counselors implementing a school counseling program. These performance standards provide both a basis for counselor evaluation and a means for counselor self-evaluation (ASCA, 2012)

Program Audit

The primary purpose for school counselors to collect information is to guide future action within the program and to improve future results for students. To meet this goal, the ASCA asks all school counselors to conduct an audit of their counseling program using a form published by the association: http://www.lehman.edu/deanedu/share/pdf/SSE_Program_Audit.pdf.

Association of State and Provincial Psychology Boards (ASPPB)

This central organization administers a widely used licensing examination in the United States and Canada, the *Examination for Professional Practice in Psychology* (EPPP). Most states and Canadian provinces set cutoff scores students must achieve on this test to qualify for a license to practice. This test has eight sections, two of which are focused on issues of research, statistics, and assessment. Those two sections account for 22 % of all items on the EPPP (ASPPB, 2011).

Canadian Counselling and Psychotherapy Association (CCPA)

The CCPA requires the following components be included in the curriculum of all Canadian universities providing graduate education in counseling (CCPA, 2003). Course material involves the use of relevant research data by faculty and students, including the following:

Assessment Processes, including

- Knowledge related to the evolution of the development of individual and group assessment instruments and processes.
- Knowledge of basic concepts of measurement theory, including reliability and validity and related statistical concepts.
- Knowledge and the ability to use a variety of assessment approaches, including standardized and non-standardized instruments, computer-based approaches, observational methods, etc.
- An understanding of the influences of issues of diversity regarding appraisal.
- An ability to appropriately select, apply, and interpret appraisal techniques and instruments within counselling and consultation processes.
- Ethical and legal issues related to assessment.

Research Methods, including

- Knowledge of basic principles of qualitative and quantitative research design, along with related processes of data analysis.
- An understanding of challenges involved in conducting counselling research.
- Knowledge of the influence of issues of diversity related to conducting research.
- Legal and ethical issues involved in research.

Program Evaluation, including an understanding of how to conduct needs assessments, specify program objectives and evaluate the impact of counselling programs. (CCPA, 2003, § III.B)

Commission on Accreditation for Marriage and Family Therapy Education (COAMFTE) of the American Association of Marriage and Family Therapy (AAMFT)

COAMFTE accreditation standards provide the following requirements for graduate programs preparing marriage and family therapists: a curriculum of graduate education including significant material on research in couples therapy. Graduate study will provide a focus on research methodology, data analysis, and the evaluation of research.

The content of the graduate curriculum will also include quantitative and qualitative research and their methods (COAMFTE, 2005).

Council on Rehabilitation Education (CORE)

New program standards have set the following requirements (areas of knowledge) for graduate programs in rehabilitation counseling: basic statistics and psychometric concepts, an understanding of research methodology and relevant statistics, and basic research methods involving the interpretation of quantitative and qualitative research articles in rehabilitation and related fields. Graduate programs must also teach students to apply research literature to practice (e.g., to choose appropriate interventions to plan assessments [CORE, 2011]).

Council for Accreditation of Counseling and Related Educational Programs (CACREP)

The CACREP section "Research and Program Evaluation" mandates that graduate programs require studies that provide an understanding of research methods, statistical analysis, needs assessment, and program evaluation. These are to include the importance of research in advancing the counseling profession, the use of research to inform evidence-based practice, and ethical and culturally relevant strategies for interpreting data (CACREP, 2009).

International Association of Counseling Services Inc. (IACS)

This accrediting body for campus-based counseling centers adopted a new set of standards for counseling centers seeking accreditation in 2005 (IACS, 2005). Two of those standards address research and evaluation skills needed by professional employees and interns of university-based centers.

Research: An integral responsibility of the counseling service is to conduct ongoing evaluation and accountability research, to determine the effectiveness of its services, and to improve the quality of services.

Services must adhere to the following:

a) Counseling services must abide by professional ethical standards as well as expectations developed by university groups responsible for overseeing research. Ultimate responsibility for the establishment and maintenance of accepted ethical practices shall reside with the individual researcher and the Director of the counseling service.

b) The counseling service should contribute to studies of student characteristics and follow-up studies of student progress in various programs.

c) Counseling services should be involved with students and faculty who wish to conduct individual research on student characteristics or on the influence of specific student development programs. Such activities must be in compliance with appropriate professional ethical standards as well as institutional research board requirements.

d) The counseling service should make every effort to contribute to the fields of counseling, psychology, and other relevant professions (e.g., student personnel services, social work, etc.) through research and other scholarly endeavors.

Program Evaluation: There must be a regular review of the counseling service based on data from center evaluation efforts. When possible it is desirable to include comparative data from other institutions in the evaluation process. (IACS, 2005, p. 5)

INFORMED RESEARCH CONSUMERS

"It is, I think, particularly in periods of acknowledged crisis that scientists have turned to philosophical analysis as a device for unlocking the riddles of their field. Scientists have not generally needed or wanted to be philosophers."

Thomas Samuel Kuhn

Research in Counseling and Related Professions

In 1776, our revolutionary forefathers held certain "truths to be self-evident." Unfortunately for those who had to engage in an 8-year war for independence, not every-one in Great Britain saw America's "truths" as being all that self-evident. What is evident is that what each of us knows, values, and believes may not be the same.

For example, many of us were taught and believe that our planet earth is 4.55 billion years old (Dalrymple, 1991).[2] And that all matter is composed of atoms (Dalton, 1808). Yet, we were not present when the earth was formed, and we have never seen an atom. The implication is that much of what we "know to be true" is what we have read or been taught and is simply our **assumed knowledge.** This type of knowledge is information generally agreed upon by others.

Empiricism, with its reliance on sensory experience and measurement, is another way to establish what we know. The difficulty with pure empiricism is that it involves actually seeing and recording what happened, operations not readily available for most occasions (Leob, 1981).[3]

In the mental health sciences, the overarching effort is to expand on what is generally agreed upon and to push back the frontiers and limitations of the conventional. In mental health professions, this effort takes many forms. It can be argued that all decisions about the direction of an intervention or treatment with a client are made using a form of research. The practitioner-researcher evaluates the information the client and others pro-vide. Next, he or she analyzes the meaning of those data and decides on a course of action. If the analysis is made using the therapist's interpretative skill, the focus of the effort is qualitative. However, if the analysis is based on numerical data and employs exact prob-abilities, it is quantitative. After either type of analysis, the therapist helps the client gain self-awareness and better resolve his or her problems. Finally, the practitioner-researcher takes careful note of the outcome of his or her efforts and evaluates what has occurred. From the evaluative summaries of outcomes, practitioner-researchers can meet the reporting requirements of most **managed health care** or **third-party fee-for-service insurance** programs.

Why Become a Practitioner-Researcher?

There are several reasons for graduate students in one of the counseling professions to be educated as practitioner-researchers. These include the following:

1. Professional accountability

2. Ability to meet the needs of clients

3. Literacy in one's own field

4. Professional development and improvement

5. Professional empowerment providing the ability to influence the profession

6. Ability to meet the standards of professional societies and demonstrate research knowledge and skills on licensing and certifying examinations (National Board of Certified Counselors, 2012; National Board of Professional Psychology, 2012).

Accountability

For the past 3 decades, the major professional societies have worked to make our fields true professions, requiring state licensure and having the ability to receive third-party payment for services (Virginia Association of Clinical Counselors, 2011).[4] By being part of a profession, practitioner-researchers are viewed by the public as having expertise acquired by advanced education and careful training. A related public assumption is that members of a profession share a common set of values and ethics and work from a defined core of knowledge.

These public perceptions of counselors and other mental health professionals have been accompanied by certain privileges, including the control of titles and a limitation of who may practice. It has also made third-party payment by managed health care agencies possible. Third-party payment for services requires that practitioners provide a diagnosis and a plan for treatment that fits within the managed health care system's guidelines, and **third-party agencies** require all treatments to be documented by evidence as to their efficacy.

In a very real sense, accountability in counseling and other mental health professions follows the money. This need for documentation and accountability is true not only to be reimbursed in a managed care system but also from public sources. For example, consider the growth in the number of older and or disabled adults qualified for Medicare and the inclusion of professional counseling and clinical psychology as components of Medicare health plans. For counselors to receive reimbursement, they must provide documentation of the value of services clients are receiving as well as the need for, and the appropriateness of, the interventions and/or therapy (Centers for Medicare and Medicaid Services, 2012;

Photo 1.1   Carl Rogers

Natalie Rogers Trust.

Henry J. Kaiser Family Foundation, 2011). This evidence-based proof of the effectiveness of interventions requires that practitioners be competent consumers of research and knowledgeable about research methods. Effectiveness documentation also requires the therapist to be competent in data management, analysis, and presentation.

The idea of basing decisions about treatment effectiveness on research evidence is as old as counseling and psychology. An enormous amount of behaviorally focused scientific literature supports behavior modification therapies. This literature began in American journals with the writings of John Watson (1913). Behavioral approaches for mental health interventions and treatment are easily adapted to quantitative data collection and reporting and are widely employed in clinics and practitioners' offices today.

Even Carl Rogers once proposed that research should be conducted as to the true value of client-centered therapies (Association for Humanistic Psychology, n.d.).[5] Contemporary counseling research journals regularly report on the effectiveness of interventions and other approaches for the provision of mental health care.

The need for accountability has forced a number of therapists to modify their approach for treatment. Much of what made up the "person-centered counseling" of Carl Rogers and his followers has been minimized in favor of what are considered more efficient and cost-effective approaches for providing mental health care (Harris, 2011; Whitbourne, 2011).

Data-Based Problem Solving

The second factor moving practitioners to become researchers is the need to assure ourselves that we have based our clinical decisions on the best possible evidence and that we have built in assessments of the success of our efforts.

In our new era of accountability, therapeutic approaches or procedures employed by practitioner-researchers should be selected because they are efficient, practical, and highly effective. This requires that treatment goals be set based on evidence. The term applied to this approach is *data-based decision making*. By this approach, diagnostic evidence is provided by the client and collected through a careful review of all that is known about the client's circumstances.

CASE IN POINT   1.1

During the 21st century, a new clinical education and service delivery approach for counselors in training has been adopted in a number of graduate programs. Central to this new approach is a formative evaluation and feedback system. The model assumes that there are differences in therapists' abilities. These differences in effectiveness become apparent early in the training process. It also assumes that beginning therapists performing poorly can improve when they learn to integrate client feedback into their work (Sparks, Kisler, Adams, & Blumen, 2011). Feedback provided from the client is at the heart of a committed alliance that nascent clinicians form with each individual they are helping. The feedback is provided in the form of one of two postsession measures, the Outcome Rating Scale (ORS; S. D. Miller, Duncan, Brown, Sparks, & Claud, 2003) and the Child Outcome Rating Scale (CORS; Duncan, Sparks, Miller, Bohanske, & Claud, 2006). In addition, the process of feedback involves the use of a semantic differential scale, the Session Rating Scale (SRS; S. D. Miller & Duncan, 2000). Items on this measure typically take the following form:

Please Place a Check Mark (✓) on the Line Nearest to How You Feel About Today's Session

My therapist does not value my concerns	|_____|	My therapist respects & understands my concerns
I feel like I am being lectured to	|_____|	My therapist listens to me

Statistical software is available that uses the outcome data from treatment sessions to track individual client progress while providing guidance to the developing therapist. One package that supports client-directed therapy is provided by Barry L. Duncan and his colleagues at the Heart & Soul of Change Project (http://heartandsoulofchange.com/).

Systems Evaluation

Finally, all clinics and practices, including the programs provided by school counselors, must be periodically evaluated with an eye to improvement. These evaluations are mandated by funding agencies and are built into virtually all applications for grants and **subventions.** They are also specified by the American School Counselor Association (2012). Most states require school districts to evaluate their system and file a strategic plan for improvement on a regular basis with the state's education secretary. These evaluations include close reviews of the school's counseling programs.

In Summation

The practitioner-researcher is a therapist empowered by the skills and knowledge base needed to be an able consumer of researcher. This empowerment makes it possible for the practitioner-researcher to assume a leading role in clinical practice or other therapeutic settings. It also allows the practitioner-researcher to serve as a valued consultant to his or her peers. For example, it is possible for the practitioner-researcher to assist teams of peers in developing grants or subventions for agency funding, as well as initiate new directions for programs and activities.

GETTING STARTED AS A PRACTITIONER-RESEARCHER

The public's perception of researchers has been badly distorted by many factors, including, among others, science fiction films and books, politicians who oppose the findings of science, and the seeming inability of scientists to agree upon a final single answer to questions. Adding to the public's confusion are the complex jargon used by some scholars and the seemingly impenetrable and undecipherable level of mathematics and other equations typically employed by quantitatively focused researchers.

Being a scientist is part of the fantasy life of many children below high school age (see Case in Point 1.2). During high school, however, romantic notions about science bump into the reality of learning scientific principles. All too many students are turned off during high school to all science and scientific scholarship. As undergraduates, too few students elect programs of study rich in science and mathematics. Counseling and psychology professional associations are addressing this unfortunate situation with new standards.

CASE IN POINT 1.2

A child I watched grow up pestered his parents and maternal grandmother (with whom the family was living) for a science kit. He knew he wanted to become a real scientist someday and wanted to get an early start. He became pestiferous until his parents bought a toy chemistry set. With these materials, he could visualize himself in a real laboratory making important discoveries. Unfortunately, he had no direction or goal, but that did not stop him from mixing various reagents to see what would happen. Today, he can look back on that year and know that those pseudo-experiments, while enthusiastically pursued, were not science but a form of symbolic child's play.

Philosophical Foundation for Counseling Research

No single orthodox approach or methodology is employed by practitioner-researchers engaged in the production and consumption of research in counseling. This reflects the existence in counseling and the related mental health professions of unresolved, philosophical issues. Philosophy provides a framework for doing research and a perspective for consumers of research. Unresolved issues lead researchers to adopt different points of view about the nature of knowledge and how reality is defined. Diverse perspectives have led to varying ways of identifying research questions and the development of different research tools for answering those questions. Yet the bottom line for each of the major philosophical approaches to research is answering questions about and improving the human condition and the practice of mental health care.

Empirical (Quantitative) Research in Human Services

What psychologists once considered the central set of beliefs at the core of psychology was established in the laboratories of Wilhelm Wündt in Germany at Leipzig

University (Ayer, 1952). From 1878 to World War I, Wündt chaired the dissertation research projects of 160 young psychologists from all over the world. These graduates of Leipzig set the direction of psychological science throughout Europe and North America (Farr, 1983).

The approach of Wündt was highly empirical and was based on the model for human understanding and learning during the 18th-century Enlightenment (Hume, 1748/1961). Wündt aligned the emerging discipline of psychology with the natural and physical sciences, and he adopted many of the emerging statistical methods being developed in other sciences. Through his graduate students, Wündt's influence spread to the universities of the United States, where the philosophy of **logical positivism** and the use of empirical methods quickly came to dominate American psychology.

A New Research Paradigm

A shift away from this empirical paradigm was driven by another German force in psychology. In Vienna during the late 19th century, the field of **psychoanalysis** began as a branch of neurology. Its independent influence soon spread throughout European universities. The primary centers for psychoanalytical training in the 1920s were Berlin and Vienna. The rise of German fascism in the 1920s and 1930s and the subsequent formation of a Nazi-dominated government in Germany in 1933 forced many psychoanalytically trained therapists to escape continental Europe and emigrate to Great Britain and the United States.[6]

These German and Austrian intellectuals had a major impact on numerous American psychologists and therapists (Kramer, 1995). For example, the **neo-Freudian,** Otto Rank, had a profound influence on Carl Rogers. Rogers was already well educated in empirical sciences and psychological testing when he met Otto Rank. Rogers saw in Rank's model for social work therapy a totally new approach that counseling psychologists could employ in forming therapeutic helping relationships. Rogers's approach, **client-centered counseling,** was initially presented during a professional meeting in 1948. What Carl Rogers proposed was a truly **humanistic** approach to counseling (Rogers, 1951).

Rogers also held several meetings with Abraham Maslow and other humanistic and **phenomenologically** oriented psychologists at a state park in Michigan in the1950s. (See Chapter 5 for a discussion of phenomenology.) From these discussions emerged a new organization. In 1961, these psychologists created the Association for Humanistic Psychology with its own journal, the *Journal of Humanistic Psychology* (Aanstoos, Serlin, & Greening, 2000). Ten years later, the American Psychological Association recognized the field of **humanistic psychology** and elevated it to divisional status as Division 32.

For the new discipline of humanistic psychology to grow, a new approach to conceptualizing research was needed. This new conceptualization became part of a worldview or **paradigm** that adopted interpretative research methods. These methods were first refined in the 1920s by anthropologists and then by sociologists who followed the **anti-positivist** movement of Max Weber. These humanistic psychologists deployed their research activities and data-gathering efforts away from the university laboratory. Such postpositive researchers, the antipositivists, brought their research to field settings where the individuals being studied lived and worked. The emerging collection of new data-gathering techniques based on fieldwork and focused on individuals was central to establishing this new direction in research.

These emerging research methods have been refined and now are used with one of several approaches for analysis and theory building. Collectively, these methods for data collection and the new methodologies for data analysis became known as **qualitative research** (Guba & Lincoln, 2005).

Contemporary philosophers providing the foundation for the new worldview have asserted that it is never possible to understand and describe a single universal reality. The postpositivists hold that all we believe to be true is evolving and can never provide a long-enduring absolute truism, only an approximation (Kuhn, 1996). This position is central to the interpretative approach to research and the worldview of those employing qualitative approaches to research.

Third Research Paradigm

More recently, another conceptual shift has been defining a third, highly pragmatic paradigm.[7] This new direction began with mandates for **standards-based assessment** and for **accountability** of those in the helping professions. The public demand for accountability is one product of the rising cost of service delivery. Use of public funds to support therapy programs combined with easy access to data about professional outcomes and costs make accountability both a necessity and feasible. These cost data are now accessible to the media, politicians, and the general public (Ganapathy, 2004).

This third research paradigm employs both major research paradigms: empiricism and phenomenology. They are combined into a highly pragmatic approach described as mixed-method research (Johnson, Onwuegbuzie, & Turner, 2007). (The methods and models of this third research paradigm are described in Chapter 16.)

Background Knowledge

The most effective practitioners are comfortable with the scientific literature in their field and develop a personal reading program focused on the literature of the mental health professions. A good rule of thumb is to invest between 60 and 90 minutes a week on professional reading and development. Once in a professional position, the practitioner will have many opportunities to identify areas in which he or she needs more knowledge. Such situations may arise when an unusual client presents or when an anomaly occurs.

Practitioner-researchers in private practice will occasionally be stumped by what a client reveals or does during therapy. An effective practitioner-researcher will know how to learn more about the issue and be able to access and understand current research findings on the topic. This capacity can also be applied to conducting action research from the clinical setting with the clients (see Chapter 6 for a discussion of action research). These background issues and concerns can easily lead to a research problem.

From Anomaly to Research Problem

The first step in all research is a felt problem or anomaly that the practitioner-researcher has noted. The next step is an examination of the background literature from previous related studies, followed by a synthesis of that literature to form a problem statement or **research question.** Subsequent steps relate to data collection and analysis and the development of meaningful conclusions. Research methods and approaches are the core content of this textbook.

Identifying Researchable Problems

The practitioner's own professional practice is a good source of researchable ideas. In addition, science builds upon itself, with each new finding becoming the starting point for other research efforts. Therefore, another excellent source of ideas for research is found in the last chapter of most doctoral dissertations, where the author provides a list of possible related ideas needing to be pursued. Ideas are also provided by the authors of the many research papers published in professional journals.

Applications from the Literature

Seven Ideas for Further Research from a Journal Article

Note: This study employed an empirical research design (randomized comparison groups) to investigate whether a simple institutional metacommunication intervention with clients had an effect on the development of a therapeutic alliance between client and counselor. This adjunctive instruction involved inviting therapy clients to take a proactive role in their treatment by encouraging feedback to their therapist about various aspects of the therapy process. In this study, 94 clients were randomly assigned to one of two conditions.

Discussion: There were various limitations of this study. First, the results of the present study should be replicated. Even though the sample size in the present study is adequate, this study represents an initial investigation of a potential promising area in psychotherapy research. Second, perhaps the adjunctive instruction prompted clients' responses that were based on social desirability. This is of concern, but even the group differences of the responses up to 24 sessions as well as "vindictive" clients who benefited from the adjunctive instruction counter this interpretation. If replicated, future studies should examine whether the present findings can be explained by client and/or therapist process characteristics. Third, future research should examine the impact of the adjunctive instruction on the trajectory of the therapeutic alliance in a therapeutic context other than a university outpatient clinic, where detailed quality management (i.e., precise case formulations, biweekly supervision, or the use of postsession reports) is available. Fourth, the present study does not include an active control group. Alternative adjunctive instructions (i.e., an unstructured phone call as attention control group) should be examined to determine whether there are comparable effects as found in this study. However, if a contrastive control group is designed, potential negative side effects should be considered. Fifth, from a methodological point of view, the analysis of a three-item scale may be adequate with respect to repeated session-by-session measurements using hierarchical linear models. However, the therapeutic alliance could be measured more comprehensively than by a repeated three-item session-by-session scale and could include perspectives other than the clients'. Sixth, further research should examine the role of adjunctive instruction in predicting outcome. Seventh, clinical significance of the present findings should be elaborated more precisely. From a clinical perspective, BPSR scores under 2 (2 = *yes*, 1 = *mostly yes*) represent an indication to take a more precise look at the case formulation with two questions: (a) Can the answer can be explained according to the client's plans/schemata? and (b) Should the therapy/therapist be more responsive on neglected aspects of the case formulation?

Source: Fluckiger, C., Del Re, A. C., Wampold, B. E., Znoj, H. C., & Franz, J. U. (2012). Valuing clients' perspective and the effects on the therapeutic alliance: A randomized controlled study of an adjunctive instruction. *Journal of Counseling Psychology, 59*(1), 18–26. doi: 10.1037/a0023648

Applications from the Literature
Future Research Ideas from a Dissertation

Note: The author selected a qualitative approach to learn about the development of a therapeutic alliance between clients and seven volunteer therapists certified by the Biofeedback Certification Institute of America. The seven were all practicing within a 50-mile radius of the university.

Future Studies: Because of the pilot nature of this study, the questionnaire broadly surveyed several areas lacking within the biofeedback literature. Nonetheless, the study clearly showed the disparity between real practice and written literature on biofeedback. Further, the study highlighted the need for an updated literature examining the integration of biofeedback and talk therapy. As such, future studies should address several topics in detail. Suggestions for areas of study include further research on how clinics integrate biofeedback with talk psychotherapy, including correlations linking treatment success measures to the type of integration used. In addition, studies should investigate whether one's verbal organization of the treatment alliance indicates a better use of this construct in practice. Research further investigating the treatment alliance in biofeedback and ways in which this differs from solely talk psychotherapy treatment is needed as well.

Source: Bhogal, K. R. (2008). *Integrating biofeedback and talk therapy: A focus on the relationship.* Doctoral dissertation, Widener University. ProQuest and UMI ID No. 3405248

SUMMARY

Providing individual psychotherapy is a highly labor intensive activity. Group design for therapy can help, but the cost of hiring a highly educated licensed professional is still significant. Therapy also requires considerable investment in overhead and support staff. As this book goes to press, the private practice price of all this is in the range of $165 an hour (depending on the practitioner's level of training and specialization and the location of the office). This figure is discounted by the Medicare/Medicaid contracts as well as by private insurers. The national average paid to licensed psychologists and counselors in 2012 by third parties was $82 per hour.[8] These expenses have ushered in mandates for accountability in counseling and psychotherapy. To be able to document the quality of service being delivered and meet accountability requirements, the professional associations have increased the research and evaluation training required of all new professionals entering the field.

Counselors can avail themselves of research models to answer research questions. These approaches include quantitative methods that encompass empirical research. These methods were derived from the physical sciences and are highly structured. Other approaches are more subjective and employ interpretative approaches to data analysis. These qualitative approaches to research are based on a humanistic paradigm.

In becoming a practitioner-researcher, the young scholar needs to become well-read in the professional journals. By reading journal articles, practitioners can improve their practice skills as well as answer questions that arise when treating individuals. The literature of the profession is also a superb source of inspiration and new research ideas.

DISCUSSION QUESTIONS

1. Use the Internet to learn the specific Medicare and Medicaid reimbursement rates for several therapeutic interventions paid in different areas in the United States.

2. Examine your graduate program's application for program approval from CACREP and in particular how the program meets the research standard.

3. Use the library's database to identify one article of interest to you from the *Qualitative Research Journal* and another from the *Journal of Educational Psychology*. Compare research methods and likely worldviews of the authors of the articles.

NOTES

1. To prevent the costs of long-term mental health care, particularly the hospitalization of individuals with chronic neurological and psychiatric impairments, from overwhelming the system, caps have been made part of the program. For example, in 1990 psychotherapy was provided with only 50% coverage. Under the Obama administration, the patient's share of psychotherapy costs was reduced to 20%.

2. Many conservative Christian believers follow and believe the estimate of Dr. John Lightfoot, a 17th-century Anglican clergyman, who pegged the creation of the earth as occurring in the year 4004 BCE.

3. One guiding research philosophy is logical positivism. This philosophy is associated with the empirical approach. An opposing framework for research is seen in psychoanalysis, which draws from the philosophy of "idealism" as developed by Hegel. Later it was neo-Freudian psychoanalysis that influenced the uniquely American concepts of client-centered therapy and humanistic psychology. Humanistic psychology has a framework that includes the **existential philosophies** of Soren Kierkegaard and Rollo May (May, 1994). Humanistic theories have provided a framework for qualitative research methods. A third approach is pragmatic and less doctrinaire. It sees research methods as tools needed to answer questions of worth and effectiveness. To document effectiveness, the researcher often selects a mix of research methods. .

4. The Commonwealth of Virginia was the first state to establish a licensing program for professional counselors in 1975.

5. Rogers followed a complex path toward realizing his professional identity and developing what became known as the **third force** in therapy (Bugental, 1964). Carl Rogers was raised in a strict home with highly committed Christian parents (Rogers, 1961). His choice for higher education was the Agriculture School of the University of Wisconsin, where he studied biological sciences. Later he decided to do graduate work at Union Theological Seminary in New York City. That also proved to be a false start, and Rogers entered Teachers College of Columbia University, where he studied child development and guidance with Leta Hollingworth (Thompson & Henderson, 2007).

6. Most of these highly educated German and Viennese therapists were Jewish and threatened with death by the anti-Semitic Nazi government. They included Sigmund and Anna Freud, Eric H. Erikson, Otto Rank, Karen Horney, Wilhelm Reich, Erich Fromm, Kurt Lewin, Harry Stack Sullivan, Alfred Adler, Kurt Goldstein, Wolfgang Kohler, Max Wertheimer, Kurt Koffka, and many others.

7. Thomas Kuhn was the originator of the term *paradigm-shift*.

8. In the 1970s, when I was working as a fellow in a rehabilitation hospital that was part of a large university medical center, the hospital billed my clients' insurers $10 per hour for my time, and my mentor billed at $15 per hour.

CHAPTER 2

Ethical Research Practices

"Having a strong ethical compass is paramount to being a good counselor."

Patrice Hinton Oswalt

OBJECTIVES

By reading and studying this chapter, you should acquire the competency to do the following:

- Describe the slow evolution of ethical principles for researchers before 1979.
- Discuss the history and importance of the Nuremberg Code.
- Explain core recommendations of the Belmont Report.
- Describe the makeup and role of an Institutional Review Board.
- Describe recent developments regarding the ethical use of laboratory animals.

INTRODUCTION AND MAJOR THEMES

A central theme of this chapter is the need to employ ethical methods when conducting research. This section examines the horrific past ethical errors leading to the Belmont Report and subsequent federal legislation to correct such abuses. The impact of the Belmont Report is discussed, as well as the application of its principles in actual practice. The emerging awareness of ethical research practice in the use of animals is also introduced. The chapter presents official positions on ethical practice in research approved by various professional societies, including the American Counseling Association (2005) and the American Psychological Association (2010a).

The last section in this chapter addresses the need for practitioner-researchers to always employ a high degree of ethical behavior when engaging in research. For professionals in the helping professions, ethical behavior is more than the ethical practice of clinical skills. It also involves ethical practice in both research and assessment.

RESEARCH ETHICS FOR PRACTITIONER-RESEARCHERS

Most practitioners in the mental health professions agree with Oswalt's statement that the embodiment of the ethical compass is the profession's code of ethics (Oswalt & Lebeau, 2011). Most of what is learned in undergraduate and graduate study provides a framework for future professionals to know how to do things right, whereas the study of ethics helps the practitioner-researcher to do the right thing (Shallcross, 2011).

Photo 2.1 Parents Rushing Their Child to a Hospital After She is Stricken With Poliomyelitis in 1948

Wikimedia Commons.

Codes of ethics are one hallmark of professional organizations. Ethics codes provide the general public with an assurance of the integrity of professionals practicing in the field. Likewise, practitioners adhering to the code of ethics of their profession know they are acting professionally. One assumption held by members of the public is that members of various mental health professions follow published canons of ethics to guide their practice and as the basis for all decisions involving research (Shallcross, 2011).

Various professional societies in this field have developed and adopted statements of ethical standards. These include statements by the American Psychological Association (APA; 2010a) and the American Counseling Association (ACA; 2005). (Published statements from the APA and ACA related to research are provided in Appendices B and C, respectively.)

At the start of the 20th century, death from diseases that are well controlled today killed and left disabled millions of people, including huge numbers of children. The public had a collective attitude that scientists should do something to make life better for all and that the niceties of ethical treatment of research subjects could be bypassed.

Ethics and American Researchers

A congress of physicians met in Philadelphia in 1847 and formed a new professional society, the American Medical Association. At that meeting, they approved a code of ethics for physicians to follow. The code never mentions medical research or experimenting on one's patients. The code did include reasonable guidelines such as the following:

§2. Every case committed to the charge of a physician should be treated with attention, steadiness and humanity. Reasonable indulgence should be granted to the mental imbecility and caprices of the sick. Secrecy and delicacy, when required by peculiar circumstances, should be strictly observed; and the familiar and confidential intercourse to which physicians are admitted in their professional visits, should be used with discretion, and with the most scrupulous, regard to fidelity and honor. The obligation of secrecy extends beyond the period of professional services; none of the privacies of personal and domestic life, no infirmity of disposition or flaw of character observed during professional attendance, should ever be divulged by him except when he is imperatively required to do so. The force and necessity of this obligation are indeed so great, that professional men have, under certain circumstances, been protected in their observance of secrecy, by courts of justice.

The full code is available at http://www.ama-assn.org/resources/doc/ethics/1847code.pdf.

The first psychology laboratory was established by G. Stanley Hall at Johns Hopkins University in 1879. Other universities soon followed, building vibrant psychology departments with well-equipped psychological research laboratories. However the American Psychological Association was not incorporated until 1892, and it did not publish a code of ethics until 1953. That document was the forerunner of today's American Psychological Association's *Ethical Principles of Psychologists and Code of Conduct* (2010a). The 1953 version included a small section on psychological research, placing the responsibility for judging the ethical standard of any research on the professional discretion of the researcher.

The American Counseling Association and its predecessor, the American Personnel and Guidance Association, was first chartered in 1952. The organization established an Ethical Practices Committee the following year. The publication of the first code of ethics followed a few years later in 1961. This document has been updated on a regular basis following about a 7-year cycle. The original document had 10 points relating to research and publication. The first was to "avoid causing any injurious effects or after-effects of the experiment upon his subjects" (American Personnel and Guidance Association, 1961, p. 208). There is no mention of informed consent, and a point is made that the research may include using a hoax with subjects, if necessary. There is no description of providing a dehoaxing counseling session for participants.

European Codes of Ethics for Researchers

The modern concept of medical ethics began in Great Britain at the dawn of the 19th century in the writings of a Manchester physician, Thomas Percival. In his 1803 publication, *Medical Ethics; or, a Code of Institutes and Precepts Adapted to the Professional Conduct of Physicians and Surgeons,* he proposed that the care and benefit of patients should be the paramount concern for physicians (see the Kellogg Health Sciences Library entry: http://www.library.dal.ca/kellogg/Bioethics/codes/codes.htm). From the Middle Ages through the era of the Enlightenment, the primary concern of physicians was their own reputations and welfare.

The British Association for Counselling and Psychotherapy was not organized until 1970 and then was a federation of related organizations. It did not accept individual members until 1977. In 2002, it published its first statement on ethics, the *Ethical Framework for Good Practice in Counselling and Psychotherapy.* This was most recently updated in 2010; see http://www.itsgoodtotalk.org.uk/assets/docs/BACP-Ethical-Framework-for-Good-Practice-in-Counselling-and-Psychotherapy_1276615182.pdf.

The Canadian Counselling and Psychotherapy Association began in 1965. The CCPA published a code of ethics in 1999, and a bilingual edition was published in 2007. See http://www.ccacc.ca/_documents/CodeofEthics_en_new.pdf.

Ethical Research With Infra-Human Animals

The American Psychological Association is one of the few professional societies that established a committee to design a statement of ethical policies related to research with animals, the Committee on Animal Research and Ethics (CARE). At the time of this book's publication, CARE was soliciting positions and opinions of professionals in the field as it drafted a new statement.

Cartoon 2.1

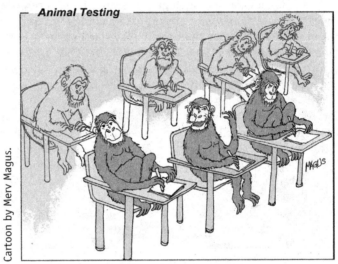

Cartoon by Merv Magus.

Animal Testing

"Did you figure out if we are in the treatment or control group?"

The US Department of Health and Human Services, National Institutes of Health, Office of Laboratory Animal Welfare (OLAW) has the power to enforce rules it has published for the protection of laboratory animals. Its policy is enunciated in federal legislation, the Health Research Extension Act of 1985 (Animals in Research Act, Pub. L. 99-158). The government enforces this law by controlling which laboratories and universities receive federal funding for psychological and biomedical research. This law, like most legislation, has been put into action via rules and regulations written by the designated agency of government, in this case the OLAW. One set of rules from OLAW is the "Public Health Service Policy on Humane Care and Use of Laboratory Animals" (2002). These rules provide a lengthy list of prescriptive requirements for using animals in research. The requirements vary by species; for example, there is one set of guidelines for primates, another for rodents, barnyard animals, bovine species, etc. The regulations cover many aspects of working with animals, including their housing and feeding and the disruption, suffering, and distress experimental animals may feel. One core principle that researchers using animals must address is the need for and

relevance of their research to human beings. These federal guidelines can be read at http://
grants.nih.gov/grants/olaw/references/phspol.htm#USGovPrinciples.

ETHICS PROBLEMS OF THE RECENT PAST

European Eugenics

In the late 1800s, Sir Francis Galton began a detailed study of what he believed to be the
genetic basis of many problems in society. His data were used by British scholars, including
Karl Pearson. Pearson used emerging statistical models to arrive at genetic explanations for
physical and cognitive differences between groups of people. He later was a leader in the
British **eugenics** movement.[1] This group, which had considerable influence, believed that
by selective breeding, it would be possible to improve the gene stock of white Englishmen.
In the United States and Germany, this movement took on a dark character with the forced
sterilization of those seen to be inferior members of the human species (Swan, 2010).

American Eugenics

One of the most influential American psychologists of this early era was James McKeen
Cattell, who left the United States to study with both Wündt and Galton (Boeree, 1999–2000).
While in London, he became fascinated with the application of statistical methods to the
study of individual differences. He also saw the logic of applying the "scientific use of sta-
tistics" in support of an American eugenics movement that had its start in England under
Sir Francis Galton.

The American Eugenics Society (AES) flourished between 1900 and 1946. Its role was,
among other things, to teach "race hygiene, race biology, the value of races, and the advantages and dangers of race crossing" (AES, cited in Mehler, 1988, p. 4). It also sought to
promote as a prophylactic task for public health agencies the prevention of the mentally
defective from ever becoming parents (Black, 2003). The eugenicists' drive was toward a
"better and fitter" race of Americans.

The organization encouraged states to pass sterilization laws, and it provided model
legislation that had been vetted by constitutional lawyers contracted by the AES. The result
was that 30 states passed laws to force the sterilization of individuals with a history of
criminality, including prostitutes, those convicted of a sex crime, the "feebleminded," individuals with inherited defects, and epileptics (O'Keefe, 1993).

Patently, these laws were written to keep "defective" individuals from reproducing amongst
themselves, thereby reducing the burden of "social dependents" needing to be supported in
a state institution. Another likely additional goal of the eugenics laws was to prevent individuals with mild retardation from reproducing with normal people. The possibility of a
"Forrest Gump and Jenny" was seen as dangerous and as potentially causing a contamination
of otherwise good genetic stock (Finerman, Tisch, & Newirth, 1994).[2]

The US Supreme Court supported forced sterilization in 1927. *Buck v. Bell,* 274 U.S. 200,
was about a mentally challenged young woman who was born to parents who were

Photo 2.2 Better Baby Contests Were Conducted by Eugenics Organizations to Celebrate Quality Human Genetic Examples

mentally challenged. At that time, Chief Justice Oliver Wendell Holmes wrote in the Court's opinion, "Three generations of imbeciles are enough." These laws remained in force into the 1970s, by which time over 60,000 men and women had been sterilized.

The AES also sponsored contests that celebrated racial quality. These included "Better Baby Contests."

To learn more about the eugenics movement in the United States, see the Cold Spring Harbor Laboratory DNA Learning Center's archive on the American eugenics movement (http://www.eugenicsarchive.org/eugenics/list_topics.pl).

Special Case of German Medicine

Prior to the 1940s, the concept of medical ethics only addressed how physicians and therapists treated one another. Professional ethics discussions centered on their financial agreements and fee structures (Rogers & Russell, 2002). There were no guidelines for using humans in medical research, and some researchers tested their ideas, treatments, and potions on readily available subjects such as those in insane asylums, orphanages, and prisons.

The German push to achieve superiority in science saw German universities require research-based dissertations of all persons becoming medical doctors. To gain academic promotion and tenure, it was necessary for faculty to take the lead with new biomedical research (Niethammer, 2004). The only ethical constraints on "professor-doctors" were limits imposed by some institutes and universities. For all intents and purposes, those restraints were removed in 1933 when the Nazi Party became the governing party of Germany. Between 1933 and 1945, researchers had access to a number of populations viewed as undesirables. Even peer-reviewed research grant applications in medicine and related fields made open descriptions of what we would consider today to be horrific (Swan, 2010). Researchers professionally supervised the euthanizing of over 100,000 mental patients and disabled children. One research team devised a portable gas chamber that was moved from one hospital to another to euthanize the "undesirable" population.

Using grant money, institutes and universities established new laboratories where thousands were killed in the name of science by the deliberate infection of human subjects. Researchers wrote careful descriptions of the subjects' deaths. These studies included deliberately wounding subjects (mostly women) to induce staphylococcus infections and sickening people with typhoid and malaria. The scientists inflicted harsh conditions on their subjects, including hypothermia, electrocution, and starvation, and studied the slow deaths that ensued. These victims were later autopsied, and specimens were preserved and carefully stored. The researchers took careful notes on thousands of killings and kept them for later publication.[3] Only after the fall of East Germany were the last of these specimens found and appropriately disposed.

Physicians of that era in Germany designed more efficient gas chambers and better chemical agents for death chambers used in concentration camps to bring about the "final solution." They even designed improved rifle munitions and instructed firing squad members on efficient methods to kill that used fewer bullets.

Nuremberg Code

The horrors perpetrated by German physicians who were freed of all restraints by the Nazi government after 1933 were reported in the press. These crimes were deemed so repulsive that a war crimes tribunal was called at Nuremberg after World War II. That tribunal saw the prosecution of some of the offending medical doctors. Advocates for human rights and dignity were disappointed at the outcome of what was called the "Doctors' Trial." Most of the medical researchers were not convicted of the worst charges. The court expressed an opinion that the research being conducted in concentration camps was not qualitatively different from the clinic- and university-based research that took place before the Nazi era began. Also, it was noted that no laws in any Western nation, including the United States and Great Britain, made such research practices illegal.

It should also be noted that the United States had captured Lt. General Shiro Ishii and the members of Japan's infamous medical experimentation unit, Imperial Army Unit 731. The US Command traded the research results and laboratory notes of the unit for the captives' freedom (Swan, 2010).

Ten Points: To the points made by prosecutors at Nuremberg, the justices added a few and wrote a 10-point code for medical researchers and others engaged in human experimentation. These points, in edited form were as follows:

1. Informed consent must be given by the subjects or guardians for their welfare to be part of the research. No forms of extortion or coercion may be used to gain the agreement to participate.

2. There must be a need for the research, and it must serve society in positive ways. The research must be only possible through the use of humans.

3. Preliminary studies with infra-human species must provide a model for the disease being studied and provide a natural history that indicates the likely outcome with humans.

4. The research should be conducted in a way that does no injury or harm (physical or psychological) to participants.

5. No experiment should be conducted where there is a prior reason to believe that death or disabling problems will occur, except in those experiments where the experimental physicians also serve as subjects.

6. The risk to be taken should never exceed the humanitarian importance of the problem to be solved.

7. The researcher must protect experimental subjects against even remote possibilities of injury, disability, or death.

8. The experiment should be conducted only by scientifically qualified persons.

9. A human subject should be at liberty to bring the experiment to an end if he or she has reached the physical or mental state where continuation of the experiment seems to be impossible.

10. During the course of the experiment, the scientist in charge has the responsibility to monitor the research activity and be prepared to terminate the research if it is likely to result in injury, disability, or death.

Outcome: The medical establishment in the Western nations was slow to accept responsibility for not having a code of ethics and slow to accept that some medical researchers were unethical. The **Nuremberg Code** was included by the World Medical Association in the **Declaration of Helsinki** in 1964, a full 17 years after Nuremberg. Yet not until 1979 did the US National Institutes of Health adopt the Nuremberg Code into the Belmont Report, America's first national medical research ethics policy.

Ethics and Research in the United States

Possibly the most egregious example of unethical research conducted in the United States is known as the Tuskegee Syphilis Study. Working with the Tuskegee Institute in 1932, the US Public Health Service (USPHS) lured 399 poor African Americans living in Alabama to receive "free medical care." What the subjects of the study did not know was that the USPHS was infecting them with syphilis. When the study began, there was no cure for the disease, and many people of all backgrounds died. The study was designed to chart and record the natural progression of slow-acting syphilis infections. In 1947, the antibiotic penicillin became available and was widely used as a cure for syphilis, but the "scientists" continued their study to see what course the untreated disease would follow. This abomination of a research study ended in 1972, and it was a major impetus for the Belmont Report. An out-of-court settlement was reached with survivors and victims' families, but an apology was never given by either the Tuskegee Institute or the USPHS. The final report of the USPHS (1996) was archived at the University of Virginia and can be read at http://www.hsl .virginia.edu/historical/medical_history/bad_blood/report.cfm.

Five more examples of misguided research follow in Cases in Point 2.1a–e.

CASE IN POINT   2.1A

On New York City's Staten Island, the Willowbrook State School was designed for 4,000 residential pediatric patients with mental disabilities. The facility was overpopulated by 2,000 children, badly underfunded, and inadequately staffed. In the 1960s, otherwise healthy residential children with significant mental disabilities were placed in an experiment involving live hepatitis viruses. Some children were orally infected, while others were injected with the virus. The study focused on the use of gamma globulin as a cure for the disease (Hevesi, 2010). Some members of the infected student population were treated, and others were used as nontreatment controls.[4]

CASE IN POINT   2.1B

In the 1940s, male inpatients of a state-run mental hospital in Ypsilanti, Michigan, were placed in an experimental study of a new flu vaccine. Most subjects were treated with the vaccine. All subjects were later deliberately infected with the flu. The subjects were so mentally disabled, they could not describe how they felt to researchers as they became ill with the influenza virus (Stobbe, 2011).

An interesting note is that the researcher in this study was Jonas Salk of the University of Michigan, School of Public Health. In 1955, he developed a new vaccine and was responsible for a worldwide program preventing the disabling and sometimes deadly disease poliomyelitis, or polio.

CASE IN POINT   2.1C

Following the Korean War (1950–1953), major pharmaceutical corporations found huge markets for patent medicines, cosmetics, soaps, and other personal cleansing agents. These corporations needed an inexpensive and highly controlled method for testing their products for safety and potential dangers. Product development laboratories along with the corporations' advertising agencies turned to the use of "volunteers" in state prisons. During the 1960s, half of the states passed legislation making it legal for private contractors to experiment on incarcerated men and women (Stobbe, 2011).

Photo 2.3   Solomon McBride, MD, Holmesberg Prison's Director of Human Research, Examining a Test Subject

Temple University Libraries Urban Archives.

The photograph with this Case in Point shows a scene from inside the Holmesberg State Penitentiary in Philadelphia. In this photo, a prisoner's back is covered in test sites where various chemicals and cosmetic items were being tested for possible adverse reactions. The physician in the photograph is Solomon McBride, MD, who was the penitentiary's director of human subject experimentation. This use of prisoners for experimental testing went on in Pennsylvania from 1951 to 1974.

CASE IN POINT 2.1D

In August of 1971, what was to be a 2-week psychological research study on how behavior patterns develop in prisons had to be cut short. Some subjects were selected to be "prisoners" and others "guards." The prisoners were actually stripped, sprayed for lice, and shackled before being placed in cells and incarcerated in a mock-up of a real prison block. The experiment had to end when some of the "prisoner" participants were in real psychological distress and most of the "prison staff" violated their core values and assumed roles in the mock prison that were antithetical to how they lived their lives (Zimbardo, 2007).

Photo 2.4 In the Stanford Prison Study of 1971, Students Played Guards and Prisoners in an Experiment That Continues to Generate Interest

Chuck Painter.

CASE IN POINT 2.1E

In 1961, Stanley Milgram conducted a series of psychological experiments supported by grants from the National Science Foundation in his laboratory at Yale University (Milgram, 1974). The focus of his research was the psychological variable **obedience**. He tested the following research question: "For how long will someone continue to give shocks to another person if they are told to do so, even if they thought they could be seriously hurting the subject?" In the first study, he recruited 40 men from New Haven, Connecticut, from varying backgrounds to serve as ersatz "lab assistants." These recruits were paid a stipend and were the real subjects of the experiment. Their job was to shock ersatz learners who failed to give a correct answer to the questions the "lab assistants" were instructed to ask. The shocks were fake; when activated, the device only made an electrical buzzing noise. The "learners being shocked" pretended to be slow to learn and to experience increasing levels of pain with the sequence of fake shocks. The "laboratory assistants" were told to increase the voltage each time an answer was missed.

Milgram's study is considered to be one of the best examples of unethical psychological research as measured by today's standards. To see the study being repeated in Great Britain, visit this 2009 BBC video clip: http://www.youtube.com/watch?v=BcvSNgOHZwk.

New Era and a New Direction

During the 1970s, public opinion was clearly opposed to these research practices, and new federal laws and regulations provided humane standards for human subject experimentation.

Even though the students used in the Stanford study were informed prior to their commitment to be part of the study, they did not know they would be treated without dignity and in psychologically harmful ways. In prison-based studies, researchers likely did not provide inmates with full insight into what could happen to them. It is also likely that the inmates' participation was coerced by the authority figures who managed most aspects of their lives. Likewise, the problem with using mental patients is similar: They are powerless to object and unable to understand what is being done to them. This is even more of a problem when children with mental disabilities are used in dangerous experiments.

Public opinion through the first half of the 20th century was influenced by the devastation that diseases brought with them. Every community, town, and city across the country was open to what seemed to be random devastation by crippling and/or deadly diseases. Pandemics of dangerous flu strains, polio, and illnesses of childhood (e.g., measles, whooping cough, chicken pox, diphtheria, and many others) brought with them the possibility of death, disfigurement, and permanent disability. Some entire towns would close themselves off completely to outsiders to prevent the spread of these diseases into their communities (Fanning, 2010). Thus, there was a sense of urgency for science to stop the devastation wrought by these diseases, even if it meant that ethical niceties such as the dictum "First of all, do no harm," were ignored.[5]

The change in attitude toward research ethics in the United States has led many biomedical researchers to conduct their studies in international locations where governmental agencies have little experience in clinical research and regulations and enforcement of ethical standards is lax (Stobbe, 2011). It is likely that today more than half of all human subject experimentation being conducted by American laboratories takes place offshore (Office of the Inspector General, 2001).

Belmont Report of 1979

In the 1970s, the federal government took steps to provide guidance for researchers working with human subjects. The result was the publication of a statement of ethical principles and standards for practice. Each component of the statement of ethical standards by the professional societies noted in Appendices B and C encompasses principles first spelled out in the **Belmont Report** issued in 1979.

The Belmont Report was developed to reflect a new public awareness and concern about the course that some researchers were following in their zeal to improve the human condition.

Ethical Principles From the Belmont Report

The principles of the Belmont Report have been incorporated into the ethical standards of American professional societies for scientists and practitioners studying human subjects. Its principles are also seen in the ethical statements from professional organizations in other advanced nations around the world.

Federal Policies and the Belmont Report: The National Research Act of 1974 (Pub. L. 93-348) mandated the formation of a commission to study and establish guidelines for behavioral and biomedical research. The commission viewed the Nuremberg Code, applied in the war crimes trials following World War II, as the basic prototype for the Belmont Report (National Commission for the Protection of Human Subjects of Biomedical and Behavioral Research, 1979).[6]

This document laid out three central principles for ethical research with human subjects: respect for persons, beneficence, and justice (Gabriele, 2003). Each of these was then applied in three dimensions: informed consent, assessment of risks and benefits, and selection of subjects. These points have been incorporated as central to the standards for ethical research adopted by the major professional societies in the mental health fields.

The Belmont Report is still a living and vital document. Gabriele (2003) argued that each new generation of scholars and practitioner-researchers should analyze and interpret its principles in terms of their own circumstances. This process of **hermeneutic analysis** of the principles espoused in the Belmont Report is something all graduate students should learn as they gain practical research skills.

Respect for Persons: This principle has two components. Researchers have a moral obligation to acknowledge and respect the autonomy of all individuals and to protect individuals with diminished autonomy.

In 1984, Karen S. Kitchener published an analysis of ethical practices for counseling practitioners.[7] Her model uses the term *autonomy* to describe the principle of ensuring that individuals have freedom of choice. Autonomous individuals operate in life, setting their personal goals, holding considered opinions, and making their own decisions. Researchers must always respect this autonomy and provide potential participants with an accurate understanding of what they are being asked to do and why. To gloss over risky possibilities or to use coercion is to show disrespect to the autonomous individual and commit an unethical act. Not all individuals are capable of autonomous self-determination and judgment, perhaps due to developmental status or a disabling condition. It is the responsibility of the researcher to protect those who are immature or incapacitated.

Beneficence: Two dicta are involved in this standard. One is from the teaching of Hippocrates of Cos (460–370 BCE): "First of all, do no harm." The second is to minimize risk factors and possible harm while maximizing the potential benefit to the subjects.

The dicta of beneficence mandates that individuals are never harmed irrespective of what benefits to others may accrue from that harm. Kitchener (1984) described a parallel issue, one she called "nonmaleficence." The point is to avoid activities and actions with the potential to cause harm. The catch here is that to know what is potentially harmful, the researcher may first need to challenge subjects with experimental treatments or conditions to determine if the treatments are potentially harmful. This can become a balancing problem. All research activity involves some degree of risk for the subjects as well as potential benefits. The goal is to avoid harm while optimizing possible benefits. In some forms of qualitative research, achieving this can be a complex task. For example, in action research (see Chapter 6), the determination of possible harm may not be possible. This is because research participants and researchers work together in a changing field setting while trying new activities and approaches.

The second point about the standard for beneficence means to focus on increasing the benefit brought by the research effort. Benefits may extend far beyond the subjects participating in the research. Literature on children's health and development is filled with research findings that optimize the quality of life for numerous children never involved in the original research.

Justice: The standard for justice addresses the need to ensure that all classes of individuals benefit equally and are burdened equally by the research enterprise. This is a standard mandating that diversity is honored and that all members of the population being studied are treated fairly. Injustice occurs when a burden is unduly imposed on a class of individuals or when a class is denied a benefit that is deserved. Another way of conceiving the principle of justice is that equals should be treated equally. Kitchener (1984) described justice as providing equal opportunity to equal individuals and providing opportunity to unequals equally as defined in proportion to their differences.

Additionally, practitioner-researchers must exhibit **multicultural competence** and be in compliance with the standards of the Association for Multicultural Counseling and Development (Sue, Arredondo, & McDavis, 1992). Competencies include having knowledge of the values and norms of the various cultural groups with which the practitioner-researcher is engaged. It also implies that the researcher has an open mind and a willingness to learn from others who have different backgrounds. This includes taking into account objections and concerns of clients and participants from diverse cultural communities. A third principle is that the practitioner-researcher must recognize and isolate his or her personal biases and assumptions about other cultures and ethnic groups (Sue, 2001).

In this regard, the selection of research subjects should be analyzed in terms of whether the researcher is using a class of subjects for study simply because they are convenient or available (e.g., undergraduate students, ethnic minorities, institutionalized persons, or persons receiving a social welfare intervention).

All advances and benefits from research funded with public tax monies should benefit all classes and individuals and not be limited to a select group who can afford the end products.

To these core principles of the Belmont Report, Kitchener added a fifth. She named *fidelity*. This principle obligates the practitioner-researcher to honor all commitments and follow through on all promises made to participants and institutions involved (Kitchener, 1984). If the researcher promised a complete debriefing, it must be provided. Or, if a written report was to be provided to the institution where the study was carried out, it must be written and distributed as promised.

Applications of the Principles of the Belmont Report

Principles guiding practitioner-researchers today are based on the ethical framework provided by the mandates of the Belmont Report.

Informed Consent

All subjects should be viewed as research volunteers who are invited to participate in the effort to expand scientific knowledge. This volunteerism cannot include coercion or improper or inappropriate rewards for participation. This volunteer principle can be employed whether there is a likely benefit for the subject or not. Potential participants should understand clearly the range of risk and the voluntary nature of their agreement to be part of the study. Voluntary participants must have the right to exit the study at any point in the process.

The special problem may arise (especially in behaviorally focused research) where a full disclosure of the nature of the study and its design to the volunteer-subject may hurt the validity of the study or compromise the outcome. This problem does not relieve the researcher from the responsibility of carefully answering all questions raised about the research by the participant. If the researcher must include a hoax to maintain the research effort's validity, the study must pose minimal potential for discomfort (mental or physical), and it must be followed by a complete debriefing and assistance for the voluntary participant.

Informed consent requires that the practitioner-researcher has fully explained the study and its potential risks and advantages to potential subjects. This requires that the explanation be in the appropriate language of the potential participant and presented without technical language or other confusing jargon. It must be geared to the cognitive capacity of the potential participant, and the researcher is obligated to assess the extent to which the explanation was comprehended. Parents, guardians, or a court-appointed third party (i.e., guardian ad litem) must be consulted for consent when the potential participant is a minor child, non compos mentis, or incapacitated in some way.

Applications from the Literature

Counselors' Compliance With Informed Consent Regulations

Note: In this study the authors report that many rehabilitation counselors assume that the clerk taking the intake information provides information needed to fully inform the client of possible negative consequences from the counselor-client relationship. Later in the article, the authors also document information about action taken against a number of counselors for unethical or unprofessional behaviors.

Professional disclosure is defined as the act of sharing the information needed to understand the nature and characteristics of the counseling process toward the goal of furthering informed autonomous decision making. Professional disclosure may also be understood as a combination of the concepts of informed consent and counseling best practices. . . . [according to] the results from a survey based on a **random sample** of 261 certified rehabilitation counselors regarding the content, circumstances, timing, and format of their disclosure. In brief, the survey results suggest that whereas many rehabilitation counselors appreciate the importance of professional disclosure, their actual practices do not always reflect full and adequate disclosure. Many types of information considered important—and, in some cases, critical—to ensuring fully informed consent are not generally included in the disclosure process. The study found that many rehabilitation counselors do not fully inform their clients about the limits on confidentiality at the outset of the rehabilitation counseling relationship, including the legal responsibility to report situations of potential harm (to self or others) and child or elder abuse. Furthermore, this study revealed that a number of rehabilitation counselors do not disclose limitations on confidentiality at any point during the entire counseling relationship. Failure to disclose such critical information may have far-reaching and deleterious effects on all parties, including destruction of the client's trust in the counselor, disruption of needed services, ethics violation charges, and malpractice litigation.

Source: Carlisle, J., & Neulicht, A. T. (2010). The necessity of professional disclosure and informed consent for rehabilitation counselors. *Rehabilitation Counseling Bulletin, 53*(4), 218–225. doi: 10.1177/0034355210368567

Assessment of Risks and Benefits: The possibility that a participant will benefit in some way by participation in a research effort is normally expressed in terms of probability. Benefits include relief of problems or illnesses or the resolution of critical issues in the life of the potential participant.

Risks express the potential harm that may occur for participants. The type of harm varies by the nature of the subject and the treatment the practitioner-researcher employs. Harm includes psychological damage, including a loss of self-esteem; economic loss, including lost time; social harm, including loss of social standing; and physical pain or injury.

The researcher must enumerate each of the risks and potential benefits and decide if the ratio is generally positive in that the potential for benefit outweighs the risk. Once that analysis has been completed, the researcher must explain all risks and possible benefits to the potential participants.

Selection of Subjects

Meeting the standard for justice requires that fair procedures be employed in the recruitment and assignment of research subjects. This requires researchers to avoid biased choices of who receives which treatment or which participants are exposed to the greatest risk.

Additionally, it is the researcher's responsibility to draw a distinction between classes of subjects who should be prioritized for research and those who should not be burdened by participation. For example, institutionalized patients have many problems to overcome, and unless the study is specific to them, institutionalized patients as a class should have a low priority. People who are less burdened should be the first class in the priority list for possible participation.

Institutional Review Board (IRB): Ethical research implies a need to have peers and other experts review the possible study **a priori,** provide advice, and decide whether to allow the effort to move ahead. This approval process is the task of a faculty committee known as the **Institutional Review Board (IRB).** The review board has the responsibility to protect all human subjects and enforce the ethical standards enumerated in the Belmont Report. Each institution's review board must be composed of no fewer than five members representing the various disciplines that conduct research at the institution (Code of Federal Regulations, 2009, § 46.107[a–c]). The IRB must be organized so as to have no conflicts of interest, and include at least one non-scientist.

Additionally the IRB's membership must be diverse and include members from all racial groups and be drawn from both genders. Results of the IRB review, including all recommendations, should be presented in writing to the principal researcher for the study soon after the board makes its decision. The original application and associated documents, along with the IRB's written decision, should be maintained in a file for a minimum of 3 years.

Publication houses, state funding agencies, and many large private philanthropic and charitable agencies require that all sponsored research be vetted by an appropriate IRB. Research conducted through any institution receiving federal aid or grants must be reviewed and approved by an IRB. Appendix D provides a sample of the application a practitioner-researcher may need to file with his or her institution's review board.

A number of exceptions or waivers may be employed to reduce the time frame of the IRB process. Remember that the IRB of a university may only meet once a month for a total of just eight or nine meetings during the academic year. IRBs may require several weeks to review the proposed research effort prior to making a decision on it. Thus, applications to conduct research must be submitted as soon as practicable. Also, note that research involving the researcher as a participant in the process with the individuals being studied may require several meetings with the IRB to fully elaborate and explain the proposed project.

Applications from the Literature

Discussion of Problems Associated With the IRB Process Faced by Practitioner-Researchers Employing Qualitative Methods

Note: The authors describe how institutional review boards have set new, more stringent standards for approval of projects by scholars proposing to use qualitative methods for data collection and analysis. This change has followed new federal rules for granting **subventions** giving preference to research in the social sciences and education that uses "scientific methods." The new rules require that priority for funding research be given to "scientifically based studies" that provide "scientifically based evidence." The federal policy revisions were part of the revisions encouraged by President George W. Bush and his advisers in 2002 and 2003.

Introduction: The issue of risk to research participants is not trivial. But as the AAUP (2001) pointed out, "This is not to suggest that risk-benefit analysis is inapplicable to social science research, but rather to emphasize a simple proposition: that different kinds of risks and benefits are associated with different kinds of research" (p. 61).[8] Medical experimentation runs rather different kinds of risks to patients; in such research, participants can and have died. Social research, however, poses different kinds of risks. Research participants may be embarrassed, humiliated, feel their dignity has been compromised, or experience very real invasions and violations of their privacy. They may feel that they have lost control over some portion of their lives (a loss of agency) or that they have been made fools of (as occasionally happens when participants have been deceived regarding the purposes of research, which deception is approved under certain circumstances by federal law). These are not inconsequential concerns residing in human subjects' protection, but it is clear that as the AAUP report parsed the issue, different kinds of research pose different kinds of risks; losing one's life appears to be rather more serious than losing one's dignity—although the individual research participants may not hold that view at the moment.

Taken in the light of campus concerns for the importance of externally funded research and development projects, the stance of some IRBs toward more interpretive social science projects would seem strange. In view of concerns surrounding the IRBs and academic freedom, the somewhat ambiguous powers granted to these boards, and because of recent attacks on qualitative research, it is slightly less bewildering or puzzling.

Source: Lincoln, Y. B., & Tierney, W. G. (2004). Qualitative research and institutional review boards. *Qualitative Inquiry, 10*(2), 219–234. doi: 10.1177/1077800403262361

An important exemption is provided for research involving publicly accessible, preexisting data; documents; specimens; or federal, state, or local governmental agency databases (Code of Federal Regulations, 2009, 46.101[4]). This regulation also mandates that to qualify for an exemption to the IRB process, these data must be employed in a manner that prevents subjects from ever being identified.

Graduate students may be granted waivers from the IRB process for research efforts if the research is conducted within an educational or academic environment, does not link individuals' identities with scores or individual results, and does not include elected officials or candidates for elected office (Code of Federal Regulations, 2005, 46.101[1]).

Researchers in private practice without access to an IRB may employ a peer review system that provides guidance to the practitioner-researcher. The American Psychological Association (2010a) has recommended that psychologists in private practice form peer consultation groups that meet on a periodic basis to discuss problems and issues arising in their practices. Such groups may also serve in the role of an IRB. Independent (fee-based) IRBs are also available for practitioner-researchers who are not linked to an agency or institution. Following are some examples of such independent IRBs:

- The Copernicus Group, http://www.cgirb.com/
- RCRC Independent Review Board, http://www.rcrc-irb.com/
- New England Institutional Review Board, http://www.neirb.com/

SUMMARY

Contemporary practitioners have been provided with a set of ethical codes that provide them with guidance that can ensure their integrity as researchers. These guidelines are relatively recent and are still evolving. In counseling, the ACA predecessor, the APGA, established a committee to study ethics and the practice of counseling in 1953, and it published its first code of ethical principles in 1961. The ethical codes from the ACA and other mental health related organizations all include principles first adopted in the Belmont Report of 1979.

Clearly, racism led to policies and pseudo-science during much of the 20th century leading up to World War II. This included the eugenics movement in England and the United States. Over 60,000 American citizens were forcibly sterilized under the eugenics laws. The "science of eugenics" reinforced racism and led to making marriage between members of different races illegal.

In retrospect, we can recognize the horrors of the "research" conducted on European Jews and other minority groups by Nazi scientists for the sadistic and inhuman activity it was. The conclusion of World War II brought about the Nuremberg Tribunal and the Nuremberg Code, which provided guidelines for research with humans.

In psychology laboratories during and after the war, expediency was the primary concern, and ethical codes and guidelines of the era let the researchers provide their own oversight. The result was a number of studies that did obvious harm to those who participated as subjects. In medical research, the disabled were infected with diseases. Prisoners were coerced and bribed to suffer drug and cosmetic product testing on their skin, in their eyes, and through their digestive tracts. The poor and uneducated were hoodwinked into being infected with a deadly disease so researchers could chart their suffering and eventual deaths.

By the 1970s, there was a change in public and professional opinion about the role of research and researchers. This culminated in the Belmont Report and subsequent federal legislation on ethical research practice. The Belmont Report itself included the principles espoused in the Nuremberg Code.

Starting in the 1980s, another set of concerns about the ethical treatment of research animals has emerged. The National Institutes of Health have developed federal guidelines for researchers using various species of animals in their work. The American Psychological Association is in the process of developing its own set of ethical principles for psychologists and others following the ethical standards of the APA.

DISCUSSION QUESTIONS

1. The modern ACA statement of ethics standards is included in Appendix C of this book. The original ACA statement of ethical standards (1961) in available at http://www.counseling.org/resources/library/ACA%20Archive/Code%20of%20Ethics%201961.pdf. After reading the research section of both, describe how they are different.

2. Some of the material included in medical textbooks today describing human anatomy, physiology, and pathology includes information collected by studying prisoners of the Nazi government in Germany between 1933 and 1945. The doctors who collected these data used what we would now describe as unethical and inhumane methods. They were responsible for tens of thousands of horrific and painful deaths of men, women, and children. The nature of this material is too horrific to ever be reproduced by newer, ethical methods. Despite its irreplaceable nature, should these materials be purged from the textbooks and databases used in today's medical education? Explain your position.

3. When a therapist enlists subjects for a study of smoking cessation interventions, he or she may consider using incarcerated individuals. This class of people is known to include smokers who could benefit from being able to stop. However, there is a real likelihood that some form of interpersonal pressure or coercion will be brought to bear on prisoners to participate. Discuss the ethical issues involved in making the decision to include or not include prisoners in this study.

4. Assume you are employed as a therapist in a US Department of Veterans Affairs outpatient clinic. What steps would you take in recruiting subjects to participate in an experiment on the impact of group process for the reduction of posttraumatic stress disorder among members of the National Guard returning home following a combat tour of duty in a war zone?

5. What is your position regarding the use of animals in psychological research? Explain your position and provide hypothetical examples to support your case.

6. Some university psychology departments dispose of living laboratory animals, usually rodents, by providing them to local zoos that use them to feed large reptiles. These reptiles will only consume live animals. Take and defend a position on this procedure. Is it appropriate? Explain why or why not.

NOTES

1. In 1912, Karl Pearson was quoted as stating, "The right to live does not connote the right of each man to reproduce his kind. . . . As we lessen the stringency of natural selection, and more and more of the weaklings and the unfit survive, we must increase the standard, mental and physical, of parentage" (in O'Connor & Robertson, 2003).

2. The concern was that the higher birth rate of people of "inferior stock" and those who were defective would outpace that of the better, fitter stock of white Americans. A similar position was expressed in a book by Pat Buchanan, the commentator who ran for the Republican Party presidential nomination in 1992. His concern was the legal and illegal immigration of Hispanics, who tend to have more children than non-Hispanics (Buchanan, 2011).

3. The medical faculty assumed that after the war, they would be able to use this material to continue their faculty status and with these new data advance in the profession.

4. Senator Robert Kennedy visited the Willowbrook State School in 1965 and saw firsthand the extreme overcrowding, lack of care, and squalor of the facility. He described the place as a "snake pit" (North Dakota Center for Persons with Disabilities, 2009).

5. The dictum, taught in medical and mental health education from the Latin "*Primum non nocere*," probably dates back to the teaching of Hippocrates (Duma, 1971).

6. The report's name reflects the location where many of the discussions were held leading to the document's final publication in 1979, the Belmont Conference Center in the Smithsonian Institution.

7. Karen S. Kitchener is the John Evans Professor of Education at the University of Denver and the American Personnel and Guidance Association's 1982 winner of the Ralph F. Berdie Memorial Research Award.

8. American Association of University Professors. (2001). Report: Protecting human beings: Institutional review boards and social science research. *Academe, 87*(3), 55–67.

CHAPTER 3

Using the Literature

"If I have seen further, it is only by standing on the shoulders of giants."

Isaac Newton

OBJECTIVES

By reading and studying this chapter, you should acquire the competency to do the following:

- Explain the concept of a fee-for-publication article.
- Compare and contrast primary and secondary source material.
- Describe the peer review process.
- Explain and provide examples of gray literature.
- Explain how to efficiently use online search engines.
- Evaluate the quality of published research papers in counseling.
- Describe the component parts of a research paper.

INTRODUCTION AND MAJOR THEMES

The literature of any professional field provides its foundation and documents its importance to society. The literature of all natural and social sciences is expanding at an incredible rate, estimated at 3.26% compounded annually (Bauerlein, Gad-el-Hak, Grody, McKelvey, & Trimble, 2010). This rate of expansion results in a doubling of the size of the literature holdings every 20 years. Growth reflects both an increase in the number of research scholars and an expanding number of options for publishing. While the numbers of published articles are climbing, however, the quality of what is being published is diminishing. Two of every five published articles are never cited by anyone in subsequent literature. The clear implication is that much of what is published is of poor quality and inconsequential.

A primary skill for a new practitioner-researcher is the ability to find, identify, and evaluate the professional literature of his or her field. This skill set also includes the capability to organize cogent literature related to a topic of interest, read and analyze that literature, and identify the central essence of the articles. Finally, this literature-reviewing ability also implies that the practitioner-researcher can integrate the cogent literature into a well-documented statement, position, or research question for investigation.

The Western tradition of sharing new scientific findings in published journals dates from the 17th century. Recently, the introduction of online search engines and published library databases have dramatically changed techniques for identifying the literature related to a topic. Scholars can now use a wireless hand-held computer to identify and have available research resources of an entire university library. The problem for researchers becomes one of evaluating and selecting the best and most on-target articles for developing their research ideas and writing reviews.

PROFESSIONAL LITERATURE

The professional literature of any field of study is presented in various formats and at different levels of complexity. Each of these formats and levels serves the need of a particular audience. Some literature within a profession is designed as a vehicle for sharing new developments and approaches with other members of the profession. Other forms of professional literature help interested scholars needing quick insight into trends and new developments. Another form of the literature serves the needs of the lay public and clients being served by members of the profession.

Applications from the Literature

Guidelines for Authors, *Journal of Counseling and Development*

Note: The Journal of Counseling and Development is one of many professional journals of the American Counseling Association (ACA). The ACA is just one of scores of professional associations in the human services professions publishing professional journals. Each of these journals has a statement as to what type of articles it publishes and a list of criteria required for a paper to be accepted for publication.

Guidelines: [*The Journal of Counseling and Development*] publishes articles that inform counseling practice with diverse client populations in a variety of settings as represented by the membership of the American Counseling Association (ACA). Articles should be scholarly; be based on existing literature; and include implications for practice and, when appropriate, implications for public policy related to the counseling profession. Manuscripts typically fall into one of the following categories, although other kinds of submissions may be appropriate for JCD readers.... Practice, Theory, Research, Assessment and Diagnosis, and Profiles.

Source: American Counseling Association. (2012). Guidelines for authors. *Journal of Counseling and Development, 90*(2), 249–250.

History of Publication of Professional Literature

The breadth and depth of publications by scholars throughout the world is enormous. A count made 10 years ago identified over 23,750 journals (Mabe, 2003). Those journals published over 1.5 million articles annually, adding to the growing total of over 50 million articles in the published knowledge base (Jinha, 2010). The modern era's scholarly knowledge base began in 1665 in France with the first publication of *Le Journal des Sçavans*[1] and in 1666 with the initial publication of the *Philosophical Transactions of the Royal Society* (Jinha).

Prior to scholarly journals, researchers of the Renaissance wrote their findings in letters posted among friends and others in the field known to the author. In the 17th century, the process of publishing scientific findings in journals reduced disputes among scholars over who was the originator and who was a follower. It also facilitated a rapid expansion of the knowledge base by making cutting-edge ideas and new findings available to any Latin-literate individual with access to the journals. (The international language of scholars in that era was Latin.) The invention of movable type and the printing press made it possible for the wealthy to establish private collections of books and copies of journals.

Primary Source Literature

Cartoon 3.1   Insider's Guide to Academic Writing

One hallmark of a professional society or organization is its commitment to expanding the base of knowledge about the field. Professional organizations also seek to share new developments and findings among their members. To achieve this goal, most organizations publish a journal to which members are encouraged to submit their new research findings and suggest possible revised practices or policies based on research findings. Articles in these journals are part of the **literature** of a field. These articles, written as a direct report by the person who actually collected and analyzed new research data, are referred to as **primary sources** of literature.

In addition to research-based articles, journals also publish articles that are reviews of previous scientific literature, information for improving practice, and new theories. In a recent edition of the *Journal of Counseling and Development,* two articles addressed counseling theory related to practice, one article addressed an issue of assessment and diagnosis, six were pure research articles, and five articles had an international focus. Even though they addressed different aspects of counseling, all are examples of primary research. For articles to qualify as primary sources, the authors must provide their analysis of their research findings, their interpretation of situations, and/or observations of developments.

From Word Processor to the Published Word

Articles are selected by journal editors for publication from among those submitted for consideration by prospective authors. Most journals have an ongoing and open call to all potential authors to submit articles for consideration for publication. In a similar way, research papers presented at national and regional conferences and conventions are selected for possible inclusion months in advance by the organizers of the research session.

If an article is selected for inclusion in a journal, the author is not paid for the effort, and the journal becomes the holder of the **copyright** on the article. Just being published is considered honorific and is viewed as enhancing the author's reputation.

The actual selection process for adopting an article for publication occurs in several steps. The first step involves the professional (paid) editor of the journal. That editor selects articles for further consideration that appear to fit one or more of the goals of the journal and are aligned with the theme the editor has in mind.

Next, the article is sent to about three independent, volunteer editors who are content and research methods experts in the field. College faculty members make up the largest component of this group of volunteer **guest editors.** A recent issue of the *Journal of Counseling Psychology* listed and thanked 63 volunteer guest editors for that issue, all of whom were college faculty members. Other journals, like the *Journal of Counseling and Development,* have an elected board of volunteer editors who each serve a 3-year term. Each year, 20 new peer editors start a term on that editorial board.

Applications from the Literature

Excerpt from the "Guidelines for Reviewing Manuscripts for the *Journal of Counseling Psychology"*

Note: This is a small part of the guidance provided to the volunteer peer reviewers. The full statement describes the "blind" reading process and ethics of reviewers. It also gives directions for providing editorial help to authors who have submitted flawed but salvageable manuscripts. The total set of guidelines covers 18 double-spaced pages and uses 5,500 words.

1. *Is the topic of the manuscript appropriate for JCP?* If the Editor believes that a manuscript is clearly outside the scope of the journal, it is rejected without peer review. However, you may receive a manuscript to review because the Editor has some question about its appropriateness for JCP. It is helpful for the Editor to have your opinion on this question. The standardized rating form contains an item assessing fit. You might also decide to address this question in your narrative. A statement describing the topics appropriate for publication in JCP is included inside the front cover of each issue. . . .

(Continued)

(Continued)

2. *Can the flaws in this manuscript be remedied in a revision?* We begin by recognizing that all research is inevitably flawed, and that despite an investigator's best efforts, flaws will remain in every published study. Although the initial version of a manuscript may contain many problems and would require extensive reworking, JCP Action Editors are encouraged to invite a revision if there is a reasonable chance that all the serious issues could be successfully addressed, and the revised manuscript has the potential to make a significant contribution to the literature. Conversely, a study that has been brilliantly executed except for one major problem will be rejected if the Editor believes this problem constitutes a "fatal flaw." The crucial point is that your recommendation to reject the manuscript or invite a revision should hinge primarily on your judgment about whether it is possible to address all the major flaws you have found in a revision. Even if you believe the process would be arduous (perhaps further data collection is required), or that the current version of the manuscript is very far from ideal, consider a recommendation to revise if you believe that there is a reasonable chance these issues could be eventually addressed.... Thus, an inappropriate choice of statistical analyses is never the sole basis for rejecting a manuscript if the data can be reanalyzed. However, an inappropriate choice of a measure to operationalize a key construct may be the sole basis to reject a manuscript, because this choice cannot be undone....

Source: American Psychological Association. (2006). *Guidelines for reviewing manuscripts for the* Journal of Counseling Psychology. Retrieved from http://www.jbo.com/jbo3/JCP_Reviewer_guidelines.pdf

Rejection Rates: Some journals publishing primary source material are provided with many more submissions than could ever be published in that journal. These popular journals need to enforce a high rejection rate. The more prestigious the journal, the more articles are submitted to it. In turn, the more articles that are submitted, the more selective the review process becomes, and the journal becomes even more prestigious. Some of the most prestigious journals in counseling and counseling psychology are published by the American Psychological Association. This is reflected in the levels of rejection for publication of articles submitted for publication in its journals (American Psychological Association, 2011).[2]

Fee-for-Publication Journals: Most journals published by professional organizations are fee-free; that is, the author is not asked to pay for the privilege of being published. This is not always the case. A number of journals have small circulations and need to charge authors by the page to be published. These are known as fee-journals. Some of these fee-journals are peer reviewed and have publication standards that appear similar to those of fee-free journals. Others have less oversight and can be described as vanity journals or journals of last resort.

Since the 1990s, the number of fee-based journals has been greatly expanded by the advent of open-source, online journal publication. Many reputable journals have begun to make their publications available online through academic databases without cost. Others

Table 3.1 Rejection Rates for Counseling-Related Journals of the American Psychological Association

The Counseling Psychologist	78%
Psychoanalytic Psychology	55%
Cultural Diversity & Ethnic Minority Psychology	79%
Journal of Counseling Psychology	81%
Journal of Educational Psychology	79%
Journal of Family Psychology	76%
Journal of Personality & Social Psychology	81%
Psychological Assessment	74%
Psychology of Addictive Behaviors	70%

Source: American Psychological Association. (2011). Summary Report of Journal Operations, 2010. *American Psychologist, 66*(5), 405–406. Retrieved from http://www.apa.org/pubs/journals/features/2010-statistics.pdf

are placed in databases that charge libraries, research centers, and even some individuals for a license to access the articles. More entrepreneurial models also exist online. Some new open-source journals, not affiliated with nonprofit organizations, charge the article's author a fee in the range of $50 to $75 per page to publish an article in their online pay-to-publish journal.

Occasionally, untenured college faculty members believe these fee-journals provide a shortcut to achieving a solid publication record. They publish in such journals in the hope of staying on their career path and moving ahead in academe. These journals are well known by administrators and senior colleagues, and many aspiring academics are disappointed in their effort.

National and Regional Meetings: National and regional meetings of professional associations follow a course similar to that of professional journals. The organization publishes a call for papers in its journals and in national newsletters such as *The Chronicle of Higher Education.* Abstracts are sent in digital form via the Internet to the appropriate conference session leaders by hopeful authors. The session chairperson or leader distributes the research abstracts to three peer reviewers, who critically read and evaluate each for possible inclusion in the conference program. Session coordinators or leaders and their peer reviewers are volunteers who are not paid for their efforts.

Based on the decision of the reviewers, a conference may invite the author of the paper to make a standard 10- to 20-minute presentation followed by a question and answer session with the audience. Other conference formats include the roundtable discussion, in which the author presents his or her study to interested conferees seated around a table. Perhaps the majority of research papers are now presented during national conferences via poster sessions. In a poster session, the author mounts his or her work on a 4-by-8-foot bulletin board and stands with it for an hour answering questions by conferees who approach the bulletin board.

CASE IN POINT   3.1

Poster sessions provide each author with a standard cork-covered bulletin board and a box of push pins to mount his or her research. This provides only 32 square feet for the display.

Each author is expected to stand near the display and discuss the research with conference attendees who approach the bulletin board. This small space is even more limiting, as the font type and print size must be clear and large enough to be read from a distance of about 10 feet (3 meters). Thus, the display of the research often takes the form of a large outline, something more like a huge PowerPoint presentation. Organizations usually schedule an hour for the poster session and 30 minutes between sessions to allow for setup and teardown time.

Selected articles submitted to the meeting coordinator are then independently vetted by several scholars (peer reviewers) with solid knowledge of the field being addressed in the paper. These "guest editors" also work on a *pro bono publico* basis. Their recommendations serve as the gatekeeper for acceptance and provide editorial ideas to improve the quality of the author's paper presentation.

Gray Literature: As scholarly publication becomes easier online, some researchers are bypassing the journal process with its lengthy review and edit phases. They simply post their paper as a draft on their personal or institutional web page. By calling the article a draft, technical report, e-print, or **working paper,** they cannot be criticized for research errors that come to light later. This form of literature is flexible, is quickly disseminated, and can provide far more detailed information than can be published in the usual research paper. It is produced by university faculty, university and medical center laboratories, governmental agencies and laboratories, and a number of associations (Outten, 2011). Because it avoids the usual bibliographic channels, **gray literature** is not available in the usual library database systems and is normally found by using Internet search engines.

As is the case with pay-to-publish journals, readers should employ caution in using gray literature. The reputation of the author and sponsoring institution should be taken into account when judging these publications. A large amount of gray literature is published by **think tanks**. Think tanks are often funded by outside philanthropies and private donors with their own agenda.[3]

Secondary Source Literature

Organizations supplement the publication of primary source journals with a number of different secondary source publications. A secondary source is a publication written by an author not involved in the collection or analysis of the original data that describes research findings. A secondary source article is published after the original primary sources that it uses. For example, this textbook, like most others, is a secondary source. It contains much information and many research examples, but it does not report original research by the author. Other examples are reviews of the literature written as part of most professional publications, dissertations, blogs, newsletters, grant applications, online encyclopedias, magazine articles, and many others. Thus, the *Journal of General Psychology* provides articles that are mostly primary source publications, while the magazine *Psychology Today* provides articles and feature stories that are mostly secondary source material.

Readers need to use caution when using secondary source material. The author of a secondary source selects which primary sources to include and then writes his or her own interpretation and summary of them. The process of writing a secondary source article is wide open to the bias, spin, or distortions of the author. For example, newspapers, news magazines, and broadcast news networks are secondary sources. Most news media, including newspapers, hire journalists who are theoretically without bias in their reporting. Yet, competing newspapers in the same town can have widely different perspectives on the same issue or incident being reported. Some television news networks are widely recognized for the biased coverage and interpretations of events they describe.

When using a secondary source, the reader should be diligent in finding out whether the author used a biased approach to writing. This can be done by examining the original literature cited by the author to check for the correctness of any interpretations and the secondary source author's summary. Also, the reader can conduct a literature search to see whether research with a different point of view was used in the secondary source.

Secondary source publications also include the newsletters of professional societies. Examples are newspaper-format publications such as the *Chronicle of Higher Education* and magazine-format publications such as *Monitor on Psychology*, *Counseling Today*, and *ASCA School Counselor*. Additionally, a broad spectrum of sources for information for counselors and psychotherapists can be found on hundreds of blogs now published on the Internet. Following are four examples:

- The American Counseling Association's blog is written by counselors in practice: http://my.counseling.org/.
- Wollongong University's (Australia) blog, *In the Room*, provides advice from counselors for counselors: http://gandalwaven.typepad.com/intheroom/.
- An independent blog from a Los Angeles social worker, *Where the Client Is*, provides features on the promotion and marketing of private practices, interviews with established clinicians, and links to practice-building resources: http://www .wheretheclientis.com/.
- The American School Counselor Association's *ASCA Scene* provides a networking site and meeting place for school counseling professionals to share and learn from each other: https://schoolcounselor.groupsite.com/main/summary/.

The best use of secondary source material is to gain a quick overview of a wide domain of knowledge. This can guide a researcher in finding an area of interest for further exploration and review. Secondary sources can also identify authors who are active and making important contributions to a field. Once identified, the significant author's name can be used as a keyword in an online search for primary source material. Also, secondary source material can also provide a retrospective view of what researchers of an earlier era were feeling and the nature of their worldviews.

BUILDING A FRAMEWORK OF KNOWLEDGE

Counseling and related fields, including psychotherapy, developmental psychology, and assessment/diagnostics, are adding new knowledge to the domain of mental health practice at an expanding rate. Recognizing the need to keep professionals up-to-date, state licensing boards mandate the ongoing continuing education of all licensed practitioners. Self-directed reading of the professional literature can be a central feature in a personal program for professional development. Professional journals often have self-administered questions associated with articles in their journals. By reading the article, completing the test, and scoring at a passing level, the reader can gain continuing education credit.

Professional Development Effort

Highly effective practitioners develop a personal reading program focused on the literature of their professions and related disciplines. During their graduate education programs, students have regular reading assignments set by their graduate faculty. However, once one enters clinical practice, it takes personal discipline to establish a personal development program that sets aside an hour or so each week for reading and reflecting on current professional literature.

Frequently during job interviews for counseling positions, candidates are asked to describe their personal development program and discuss recently read professional literature. This is not a "gotcha" question but one that all applicants should be ready to address.

Focus of a Personal Reading Program

The focus can be very broad, and reading programs may facilitate the general development and expansion of the professional's knowledge base. Conversely, a clearly focused reading program may provide an answer to a specific question that emerged during clinical practice. The questions that practitioners wish to answer assist in their evolution from being therapists to being informed consumers of research.

The first steps in the research process include the identification of a potential problem or anomaly. The next step is an examination of background literature from previous studies, followed by a synthesis of that literature to identify a solution or form a problem statement and research question. Subsequent steps in the process of expanding the knowledge base in counseling and other social sciences relate to data collection and analysis and the development of meaningful conclusions. (These topics are examined in the next 14 chapters of this textbook.)

Practitioners in private practice will occasionally be stumped by what a client presents during therapy. An effective counselor or therapist will know how to learn more about the issue and be able to access and understand current research findings on the topic. This capacity with research databases can also be applied to action research projects carried out in a clinical setting while working with clients (see Chapter 6 for a discussion of action research).

Isaac Newton noted in his "shoulders of giants" quip that science builds upon itself. Each new finding becomes the starting point for other research efforts. In this tradition, one excellent source of ideas for research is found in the last chapter of most doctoral dissertations, where the author provides a list of possible ideas needing to be pursued. Ideas are also provided in the discussion and conclusion sections of many published research papers.

Professional Literature and Quality Research

By belonging to professional societies and subscribing to their journals (printed copy or online form), the practitioner has the tools needed for his or her professional development.[4] University libraries can provide access to professional journals along with access to a wide literature collection. Almost all academic libraries sign agreements with governmental agencies to receive and house important documents. To receive these free documents, the library must provide access for members of the general public to read and use academic material.[5] To a real extent, the library on every campus houses "Newton's giants."

Searching the Scientific Literature

Hundreds of journals are publishing thousands of articles related to various fields and specializations of mental health. To find the appropriate articles during a literature search can be a daunting task. To facilitate the researcher's task, academic search systems have been developed and marketed to academic libraries. These systems identify articles that the user can read online. Most university libraries permit access to these search systems from off campus by registered students and faculty of the university.

One of the most widely employed university database and retrieval systems is EBSCOHost. This database provides access to over 350 separate databases, each containing a long list of journals and other forms of literature. These lists are focused on most fields of scholarship. One of the most useful of these EBSCOHost systems for the social science researcher is Academic Search Premier. EBSCOHost is not available for individual subscription but is available through many public libraries, public high school libraries, laboratories, and hospitals.

Additionally, a fee-based system ($22/month in 2013) provided by Questia.com can be used by any subscriber.[6] This system provides an integrated literature search functionality, including professional journals, textbooks, and magazine articles.

Major publishing houses, including Sage (http://online.Sagepub.com/), sell individual articles published in their journals from their websites. The Sage publication list of 650 journals is heavily weighted toward the social sciences. Perhaps the largest of the private online libraries is that of Wiley Online. The Wiley collection includes over 1,500 journals covering a broad spectrum of many disciplines.

Older and difficult-to-find journal articles can often be read online by using the JSTOR system (http://www.JSTOR.com/). This fee-based system stores and presents articles from 1,000 different journals. The JSTOR system is also available through most university-based academic libraries.

Online Search Engines

In addition to academic search engines, all-purpose search engines exist that are widely used by the general public. These search engines can find primary and secondary source publications, gray literature, blogs, books, and individual rants and opinions. Naturally, entrepreneurs try to influence the search process to make their products or opinions the prominent finding in an online search. Advertisers also buy space to place their products in the results of individual searches. Thus, links found via search engine vary widely in quality and usefulness.

Search engines from Internet service providers are powerful tools for collecting and reviewing large amounts of information on a topic of interest. For example, in a recent search for the words "mania and hypomania," the Google search engine provided over 1,030,000 entries with web links. Using the Yahoo! search engine for the same search revealed over 237,000 entries with links, and the Microsoft search engine, Bing, identified 14,700 entries with links. The Questia.com system identified 757 journal articles, 10,141 books, 10,967 newspaper stories, and 2,187 magazine articles on the topics of mania and hypomania.

Structuring Internet Searches for Professional Journals

In today's world of technology, it is easier than ever to find answers to research questions. The problem is how to evaluate what is revealed. With the huge amount of information that a search engine provides, the difficulty is in being able to read, analyze, and evaluate the quality of what is made available. To facilitate the reading and evaluating processes, and to winnow down the number of entries to review, the researcher can do another search with a more exacting description of the information sought. Thus, if one changes the Google search request from "mania and hypomania" to "college men, mania and hypomania" the number of results falls from over 1 million to 36,800. The result is a major drop, but still there are far too many results to review. The next search for "lithium-carbonate treatment, college men, mania and hypomania" cuts the list down to 16,400 entries. Finally, "lithium-carbonate treatment with group counseling, college men, mania and hypomania" produces fewer than 1,000 entries.

Internet search engines are powerful tools for gaining a background on a topic, but developing a context in which to interpret the results of such searches requires a depth of understanding that comes from regular reading of the literature and knowledge of research methodology. In the previous example, to structure a profitable database search, a researcher would need to know from background reading that bipolar affective disorder (mania and hypomania) are frequently treated with a cocktail of drugs including lithium-carbonate.

See the following box for a selected list of available journals in the mental health professions.

Applications from the Literature

Sampling of Journals in the Mental Health Professions

Selected Journals of the American Psychological Association (For a complete list, see http://search.apa.org/publications?query=&facet=subject:ClinicalPsychology&section=subject&pubtype=journals and then select the format for the listing preferred [e.g., by subject area].)

Developmental Psychology

This journal publishes articles that advance knowledge and theory about development across the life span. The journal includes significant empirical contributions as well as scholarly reviews and theoretical or methodological articles.

Journal of Counseling Psychology

Journal of Counseling Psychology publishes theoretical, empirical, and methodological articles on multicultural aspects of counseling, counseling interventions, assessment, consultation, prevention, career development, and vocational psychology and features studies on supervision and training.

Journal of Consulting and Clinical Psychology

This journal publishes studies from a variety of populations that have clinical interest, including but not limited to medical patients, ethnic minorities, persons with serious mental illness, and community samples. It also focuses on studies that have a cross-cultural or demographic focus and are of interest for treating behavior disorders.

Couple and Family Psychology: Research and Practice

Published quarterly by the Society of Family Psychology, Division 43, of the APA, its first issue was March of 2012. This new peer-reviewed journal is intended to be a forum for scholarly dialogue regarding the most important emerging issues in the field and a primary outlet for research, particularly as it impacts practice, and for papers regarding education, public policy, and the identity of the profession of family psychology.

Personality Disorders: Theory, Research, and Treatment

This journal publishes a wide range of cutting-edge research on personality disorders and related psychopathology from a categorical and/or dimensional perspective.

Psychological Assessment

Psychological Assessment is concerned mainly with empirical research on measurement and evaluation relevant to the broad field of clinical psychology.

Journal of Educational Psychology

The main purpose of this journal is to publish original, primary psychological research pertaining to education across all ages and educational levels. A secondary purpose is the occasional

(Continued)

(Continued)

publication of exceptionally important theoretical and review articles that are pertinent to educational psychology.

Journal of Psychotherapy Integration

This journal publishes original, peer-reviewed papers that move beyond the confines of single-school or single-theory approaches to psychotherapy and behavior change and that significantly advance our knowledge of psychotherapy integration.

Psychotherapy: Theory, Research, Practice, Training

Division 29 of the APA, Psychotherapy, publishes this journal to note recent innovations that help make research–practice integration feasible. Its articles consider how to break down the barriers to enhance researcher–practitioner dialogue, as well as how to make ongoing outcome assessment feasible for clinicians. Moreover, the articles address how to promote training in evidence-based practice and how to translate efficacy research into clinical practice and clinical insight into empirical study to better establish a two-way bridge between research and practice.

Psychological Services

Psychological Services publishes high-quality, data-based articles on the broad range of psychological services.

Journal of Abnormal Psychology

The *Journal of Abnormal Psychology* publishes articles on basic research and theory in the broad field of abnormal behavior, its determinants, and its correlates.

Professional Psychology: Research and Practice

This journal publishes articles on the application of psychology, including the scientific underpinnings of the profession of psychology.

International Journal of Play Therapy

International Journal of Play Therapy publishes original research, theoretical articles, and substantive reviews of topics germane to the play therapy modality.

Clinician's Research Digest: Briefings in Behavioral Science

A six-page monthly newsletter, *Clinician's Research Digest* reviews over 100 journals each month and summarizes the most relevant articles with an eye toward identifying the clinically relevant bottom line.

Psychoanalytic Psychology

Psychoanalytic Psychology serves as a resource for original contributions that reflect and broaden the interaction between psychoanalysis and psychology.

The Clinical Psychologist

Published by the Society of Clinical Psychologists, Division 12 of the APA, this journal is firmly committed to identifying and promulgating treatments that work. It strives to extend and improve the effectiveness of the research methods used and the constructs investigated by clinical researchers.

Selected Journals of the American Counseling Association (For full information on ACA journals, see http://www.counseling.org/Publications/Journals.aspx.)

Journal of Counseling and Development

The official journal of the American Counseling Association publishes articles on professional practice and new research on counseling-related topics.

Journal of Addictions and Offender Counseling

This journal focuses on prevention and treatment programs, the attitudes and behaviors of substance abuse professionals, tested techniques, treatment of adolescents and adults, and qualitative and quantitative studies. It is also open to literature focusing on the attitudes and behaviors of addictions and offender counselors.

Measurement and Evaluation in Counseling and Development

This journal is the official publication of the Association for Assessment in Counseling and Education (AACE). Articles found in this journal cover a wide range of the theoretical and practical problems faced by the measurement specialist, including those experienced by administrators, counselors, and personnel workers. It deals with data from schools and colleges, public and private agencies, business, industry, and government. All articles clearly describe implications for the counseling field and for practitioners in assessment, measurement, and evaluation.

Counselor Education and Supervision

This journal is dedicated to publishing manuscripts concerned with research, theory development, or program applications related to counselor education and supervision. It is the official publication of the Association for Counselor Education and Supervision (ACES).

Counseling and Values

This is the official journal of the Association for Spiritual, Ethical, and Religious Values in Counseling (ASERVIC). The journal promotes theory, research, and intellectual inquiry into the spiritual, ethical, religious, and values domains of counseling.

Professional School Counseling

This journal communicates the latest theory, research, practice, techniques, materials, and ideas to assist school counseling professionals at all levels in their professional development.

(Continued)

(Continued)

Career Development Quarterly (CDQ)

This is the official journal of the National Career Development Association (NCDA). Its goal is to publish articles fostering career development through the design and use of career interventions and to publish articles on career counseling, individual and organizational career development, work and leisure, career education, career coaching, and career management.

Journal of Addictions & Offender Counseling

This journal contains articles of interest to professionals in the field of addictions and offender counseling and focuses on descriptions of prevention and treatment programs.

Journal of Employment Counseling

The *Journal of Employment Counseling* publishes articles illuminating theory or practice in employment counseling and reporting professional experimentation or research.

Journal of Humanistic Counseling (JHC)

This journal focuses on humanistic counseling and development and asserts that humanity is responsible for its own destiny.

Journal of Multicultural Counseling and Development

This journal is concerned with research, theory, or program applications pertinent to multicultural and ethnic minority interests in all areas of counseling and human development.

Other Selected Journals

Action Research (AR)

This international, interdisciplinary, peer-reviewed, quarterly refereed journal is a forum for the development of the theory and practice of action research.

The Family Journal (TFJ)

This journal advances the theory, research, and practice of counseling with couples and families from a family systems perspective. Research articles include quantitative, qualitative, and evaluation designs.

Journal of Humanistic Psychology

This journal is published online and freely distributed by the Association for Humanistic Psychology at http://jhp.sagepub.com/content/early/recent/.

Journal of Humanistic Counseling, Education, and Development

This journal addresses issues and concerns affecting counselors and educators committed to developing humanistic education practices in schools.

Child Development

Child Development is the primary journal of the Society for Research in Child Development (SRCD). It has published articles, essays, reviews, and tutorials on various topics in the field of child development since 1930.

Journal for Specialists in Group Work

In addition to accepting manuscripts for traditional sections of the journal on practice, theory, training, and research, the *Journal for Specialists in Group Work* publishes research manuscripts.

Qualitative Research (QR)

This bimonthly peer-reviewed journal publishes original research and review articles on methodological diversity and provides a multidisciplinary focus on qualitative research.

Rehabilitation Counseling Bulletin (RCB)

This journal features articles important to rehabilitation counseling practitioners in counseling, education, or research settings. Each issue includes original empirical research, theoretical essays, comprehensive literature reviews, intensive case studies, research critiques, and media reviews.

CRITICAL READING

Any one article or research report only presents an author's understanding of what was done and/or seen. Other authors may not come to the same interpretation or conclusion based on similar research findings. Readers of research need to examine the slant that the author may take in reporting his or her work. The author's point of view may be identified in the article's literature review. When structuring a review of the literature, the practitioner-researcher may find other articles that take a different approach or work from a different perspective. (See Chapter 17 for a description of how to write a review of research literature, research reports, and proposals.)

Evaluating the Quality of a Review of the Literature

Practitioners have an obligation to evaluate the literature they review before employing it in their practices or disseminating it in their own writing. This implies that practitioners are prepared to identify biased interpretations and unreasonable claims (Lunsford & Lunsford, 1996).

Due Diligence

Reviewers need a critical eye when they read. Some research is sterling, presenting solid evidence that was carefully tabulated and analyzed. Unfortunately, high-quality research makes up a distinct minority of what is published in the social sciences (Bauerlein et al., 2010). Look for the following when evaluating published research:

- Quality research articles describe in detail the use of reputable methods and document the appropriateness of the methods used for the study.
- The article presents a case for its generalizability beyond the boundaries of the study.
- Quality researchers include a statement of the known limitations of their work and do not hide flaws in the procedures and processes used.
- Quality reviews include a variety of types of literature, including primary journal articles and gray literature (e.g., technical reports).
- Secondary sources such as Internet blogs, books, reference works, published reviews, fee-based journal articles, and commercial manuals are used in moderation and fully disclosed.
- While a variety of sources is best, information systems such as those provided by Ask.com and Wikipedia are written by anonymous authors and edited by other unidentified individuals. The point of view of these authors and editors may be tilted toward a particular bias on a topic.[7]
- All assertions are well documented with either new research evidence or references.
- Data and findings seem to be well linked and the analysis process completely described.
- All conclusions and recommendations are justified from the paper's findings.
- Quality research articles are carefully edited and free of referencing errors.

Writing Process

In research reviews, all assertions that are not **common knowledge** must be documented by an appropriate citation of a high-quality, primary source. Unless a historical point is being made, the citation should be to current primary literature. The mental health field is evolving, and there is an ongoing stream of emerging literature in most parts of the domain. Secondary sources such as textbooks can provide a good mapping system, showing the review author where the research has been and which important scholars are adding to current developments. Other secondary source material (e.g., editorial opinions) may be useful in a review of the literature to provide a point of emphasis. In general, however, the review of the literature should be built around primary sources.

Once a large area of literature has been read and evaluated, the reviewer is ready to create an outline. This outline will use the major themes found in the literature as the various divisional headings. In a research article, these themes should align perfectly with the research questions and goals for the study.

In a stand-alone review of the literature, the emergence of themes from the literature is the creative component of the process. Here the author, using his or her background knowledge of the field, sets and prioritizes themes for the written review to follow. Each theme or research question needs to be explored in the literature, and each provides a framework for further organizing the articles in the review.

Likewise, in an actual study, the primary literature related to the research method selected and the measurements employed must be explored and included in the review. Articles from the literature should be coded to indicate what theme(s) each addresses. Identified articles to be used for each theme then need to be sequenced so that their discussion fits together in a cohesive paragraph or two. The articles can be organized to provide a point-counterpoint sequence or to flow in a continuous chain of deductive reasoning. They can also be placed in a timeline or in any of a number of other sequences that support the author's goal for the review.

Once related research has been collected and organized by theme, the process of writing a review can begin. Having an outline and structural sequence for the articles helps the writing move along at a comfortable tempo and minimizes the occurrence of **writer's block.** The writing moves from theme to theme and seeks to integrate information within each theme. The conclusion of the review integrates the various themes that were explored into a final statement. In the case of an actual research project, this is typically where the hypothesis is spelled out.

During this integration and writing phase, holes in the collected literature will likely become evident. This discovery will send the author back to the library, where he or she should initiate more reading and analyzing. Likewise, some articles that have been identified, found, read, and analyzed will no longer be needed. Such excess material becomes evident during the outlining phase. Authors sometimes have difficulty discarding these articles; they can become the writer's pets and get shoehorned into the literature review, even though their presence is clearly awkward. Good writers learn to be their own editors and cut this unnecessary material from their work.

Components of Research Reports

Most research presentations and research articles have seven major parts: title, abstract, introduction, method, results, conclusions or discussion of the implications of the study, and references that were cited. (See Chapter 17 for a more detailed description of the parts of research articles as established by the American Psychological Association.)

The title provides readers with an idea of the issues being studied. Cute titles can mislead readers and are best avoided. The abstract is a 200- to 300-word paragraph that tells readers the concepts studied, the research question asked, and the salient outcome or findings from the study. Both the title and abstract of an article may have word limits imposed by the publisher of the journal or conference proceedings where the article appears.

The introduction can involve about a third of the narrative. With a few exceptions, it provides an unbiased review of the relevant research on the topic and a statement of the problem being studied. In the literature review, the author may identify a gap in what is already known on the topic. Qualitative research studies also provide detailed background literature on the research method that the author(s) plan to employ. In some approaches to qualitative research (e.g., grounded theory), the review of literature occurs after the data have been collected and the coding process to analyze the data has begun. (See Chapter 5 for more on this approach.)

Throughout this section, the author provides citations that reference previous research. These citations follow a particular format. Most journals in counseling and other helping professions use the format and style elaborated by the *Publication Manual of the American Psychological Association,* 6th edition (2010b).

With the exception of grounded theory research, the author normally provides a problem statement at the end of the literature review section. It may be tightly expressed as a scientific hypothesis or be a more general statement (see Chapter 17 for more on problem statements and research questions).

The methods section of research articles and presentations provides readers with a detailed description of what the author(s) did to answer the research question or resolve the research problem. This section includes a description of the subjects or participants in the study, the materials and procedures employed, a timeline including detailed information about data collection, the location of the study, and all measurement devices or assessment procedures employed with participants and/or subjects.

The method section is followed by a results section, which provides a short presentation of the findings. These results are usually presented as a series of statistical analyses. The tradition of empirical research is not to discuss or speculate on the results in this presentation of findings. In qualitative research involving an interpretative approach to data analysis, the results section can be quite lengthy and discuss interim findings as they occurred. In this section, the author may describe his or her personal philosophical and/or cognitive framework that is potentially impacting the interpretations of the data (see Chapter 5 for a discussion of "bracketing"). Qualitative-focused researchers also need to explain, usually with examples, the coding developed to organize the raw data into meaningful information that they interpreted.

The sixth component of a research presentation or article is the discussion section, which includes the author's conclusions and the research's possible implications. Critical readers of research should use due diligence with this section. When reading an author's conclusions, ask questions such as these:

- Were any unsupported conclusions presented?
- To what extent were the conclusions presaged by the introduction and literature review?
- Did the author only emphasize results that agreed with his or her point of view?
- Were the author's arguments logical? And did the conclusions follow logically from the results?

The final, seventh section of a research article provides an alphabetical list of materials cited in the presentation. These are exact references that correspond to the in-text citations, not a bibliography of related materials. One goal of the American Psychological Association is to provide a common template for researchers to use when presenting their studies for presentation and/or publication. The APA system also provides readers with an easy method to locate and access literature cited by the authors of articles, research presentations, and dissertations. Details of the APA reference format are far too complex to include in this chapter, and students should have their own copy of the APA's *Publication Manual* (2010b).

SUMMARY

In Western civilization, the printed record of scientific discovery has been recorded by scholars in professional journals for the past 350 years. The journal literature provides the framework for ongoing elaboration of new knowledge in counseling and the social sciences.

Literature written by the individual(s) who collected and analyzed the data is described as primary source material. Some primary source material is not published in a journal article. The alternative method is to simply print and post one's findings. This type of highly flexible publication has been named gray literature. A third outlet for publication of research is the fee-for-publication journals. These are not published by the professional associations and are often offered by entrepreneurial publishers. Like high-quality articles published in journals, high-quality research papers presented during conferences and the annual meetings of professional organizations are selectively chosen and peer reviewed by uncompensated fellow scholars.

A different type of information is provided by secondary source publications. Secondary sources are not written by the individual who collected and analyzed original data but by another author. Secondary sources include textbooks, magazines, newsletters and newspapers, online information sources, and blogs. Their questionable accuracy and potential for distortion make these resources less dependable than primary source material.

The rapid rate of growth of literature in counseling and other social sciences exceeds what an individual can fully read on any general subtopic. Academic search systems can uncover thousands of primary source materials on any issue, and commercial search engines can identify hundreds of thousands of primary sources for an issue. The most efficient method to organize a presentation of the literature is to search for keywords that narrow the scope of the research area.

An efficient system for writing a literature review is to identify themes and use them to outline the review. The outline should identify the specific articles that are to be included in each section of the review and their sequence. The goal is a well-integrated, definitive statement of what previous researchers have reported and what it means to the current circumstance.

DISCUSSION QUESTIONS

1. Select an esoteric area of mental health such as the "jumping Frenchmen of Maine disorder" or the "Windigo psychosis" and count how many entries you can find using three different search engines.

2. Some news publications have been accused of showing a liberal bias (e.g., *The Nation* magazine, *Mother Jones* magazine, and possibly the *New York Times*) and others a highly conservative bias (e.g., *The New Republic* magazine, the *Washington Times,* and the *New York Post*). Buy, or read online, a current copy of one of these publications. Select a story covering a national or international topic and compare how your local newspaper covers the story with either a liberal or conservative standard. Report your findings to class.

3. Describe your personal professional development program. What journals do you read without being required to do so? Do you make and file notes about what you read? Why or why not?

4. Critically read the review of the literature from any one of the following journal articles. They can be found on the Internet using their doi numbers. The serials collection librarian at your university can also help you find the original journal publication. While reading, take special note of how the literature review is organized and how it transitions from segment to segment. Write your findings for class presentation.

Beilock, S. L., & Carr, T. H. (2005). When high-powered people fail: Working memory and "chocking under pressure" in math. *Psychological Science, 16*(2), 101–105. doi:10.111/j.09567976.205.00789.x

Bianchi, A. J., & Lancianese, D. A. (2007). Accentuate the positive: Positive sentiments and status in task groups. *Social Psychology Quarterly, 70*(1), 7–26. doi:10.1177/019027250707000104

Page, R. M., Yanagishita, J., Suwanteerangkul, J., Zarco, E. P., Mei-Lee, C, & Miao, N. (2006). Hopelessness and loneliness among suicide attempters in school-based samples of Taiwanese, Philippine, and Thai adolescents. *School Psychology International, 27*(5), 583–598. doi:10.1177014303430607341

Sullivan, M., Bhuyan, R., Senturia, K., Shiu-Thornton, S., & Ciske, S. (2005). Participatory action research in practice: A case study in addressing domestic violence in nine cultural communities. *Journal of Interpersonal Violence, 20*(8), 977–995. doi: 10.1177/0886260505277680

Young, M. A., & Kleist, D. M. (2010). The relationship process in healthy couple relationships: A grounded theory. *The Family Journal: Counseling Therapy for Couples and Families, 18*(4), 338–343. doi: 10.1177/1066480710377740

NOTES

1. The journal was suspended from 1792 to 1816 due to the French Revolution and then by the Napoleonic Wars. When it was published again in 1816, it was named *Journal des Savants*.

2. The American Counseling Association does not publish the rejection rates for its journals.

3. Two extremely wealthy businesspeople holding well-defined political positions, Charles and David Koch, have provided funding to support the work of a number of research and policy institutes, including the Aspen Institute, the Cato Institute, and the Manhattan Institute.

4. Journal subscriptions are included with membership dues for professional associations.

5. There is no requirement for the academic library to extend full membership or borrowing privileges to the public; it need only grant the public access to read.

6. About 40 universities in the United States and Canada provide students with access to RefWorks.

7. In June of 2011, then-retired Alaska governor Sarah Palin, while visiting Boston, told a small crowd outside the Paul Revere House that it was "he who warned the British that they weren't gonna be takin' away our arms by ringin' those bells, and makin' sure as he's ridin' his horse through town to send those warning shots and bells that we were going to be sure and we were going to be free, and we were going to be armed" (Kellman, 2011).

As most historians know, this story is actually quite the opposite of everything Paul Revere did on the night of April 18, 1775. Facts notwithstanding, the enthusiastic supporters of Ms. Palin launched an attack on Wikipedia and edited the history of the midnight ride of Paul Revere to align with the revisionist history presented by the former governor. Palin doubled down the next day and told reporters that she was correct and Mr. Revere did ring bells and warn the British Army in Boston that Americans would not give up their guns.

SECTION II

Qualitative Approaches for Research

"Life at its best is a flowing, changing process in which nothing is fixed."

Carl Rogers

Three chapters describing interpretative research designs and methods are included in this section of the text. In many ways, the research model employed by practitioner-researchers is a reflection of the therapeutic communication process used in counseling with individual clients. Researchers collect data through direct observation and/or by analysis of expressed and written language. Once collected, data need to be organized in a meaningful way for the researcher to interpret, code, and evaluate.

Chapter 4   focuses on the tools used to conduct qualitative research in the human service professions. Also addressed in Chapter 4 is the question of how qualitative research is evaluated.

Chapter 5   focuses on six primary research methodologies employed in qualitative research efforts. It also provides guidance for preparing research reports employing qualitative designs.

Chapter 6   the last in this section, describes the theory and practice of action research. This chapter is built around the model first developed by Kurt Lewin.

CHAPTER 4

Qualitative Research I

Tools and Skills

"Merely fact-minded sciences make merely fact-minded people."

Edmund Gustav Albrecht Husserl

OBJECTIVES

By reading and studying this chapter, you should acquire the competency to do the following:

- Frame qualitative research questions.
- Describe and contrast four different forms of sampling used in most qualitative research.
- Describe and explain the use of the major tools used in qualitative research, including interviewing, observing, and transcript analysis.
- Describe qualitative research software options.

INTRODUCTION AND MAJOR THEMES

Goals for different approaches to behavioral research are similar despite differences in the underlying paradigms that frame the research and the methods that are followed. The patent differences between the various approaches to research lie in their assumptions, organization, data collection, and analysis. In this chapter, the tools used with an interpretative approach to researching issues in counseling, clinical psychology, and other social sciences are described.

This chapter presents the case that empirical research based on systematic measurement and probability models cannot provide adequate descriptions of complex human interactions and behaviors. Since the 1960s, many social scientists have adopted nonempirical research methods that can answer questions of what, how, and why and provide cogent insight into the most complex of all human activities and behaviors. These methods usually rely on interpretative analysis of data gained by the in-depth study of a few individuals.

Interpretivists believe that there is no universal common reality that can be objectively defined. They study how people construct their own perceptions of reality and how individuals, using these personal frames of reference, interact and cope with their environment. Interpretivist research methods have been described as qualitative, unlike the traditional empirical quantitative methods of the natural and physical sciences.

Case study practitioner-researchers and other qualitatively focused scholars rarely use large-scale data collection methods and statistical techniques for data analysis. The primary data-gathering instrument is the observant practitioner-researcher (Guba & Lincoln, 2005). Working with small, often self-selected groups, the researcher uses both clinical and research skills to develop an understanding of human activities and behaviors. This can be a slow process, and high-quality interpretative research tends to be labor-intensive and require copious amounts time.

Researchers employing quantitative methods argue that they should maintain a distance between themselves and participants in their projects to guarantee a measure of "scientific objectivity." Qualitative researchers, on the other hand, argue that close interaction between researcher and research participant is a prerequisite of a sound research approach. Quantitative researchers, employing "scientific methods," share a common language and model of scientific understanding, while qualitative researchers employ less structured methods and are free to be more creative and flexible in their approach. The classification *qualitative research* has been characterized as an umbrella term covering these less structured approaches and methods (Atkins, Coffey, & Delamont, 2001).

This chapter provides an overview of the principal tools available to practitioner-researchers engaged in qualitative research.

QUALITATIVE RESEARCH PRINCIPLES

Qualitative research is a distinctive and highly regarded approach to adding to the base of knowledge we have about human beings and our activities. Catherine Cassell and Gillian Symon (1994) have characterized qualitative research as

> a focus on interpretation rather than quantification; an emphasis on subjectivity rather than objectivity; flexibility in the process of conducting research; an orientation towards process rather than outcome; a concern with context— regarding behaviour and situation as inextricably linked in forming experience; and finally, an explicit recognition of the impact of the research process on the research situation. (p. 7)

Background

Historically, qualitative research has its roots in the philosophy of German idealism and phenomenology (Hegel, 1807/1979). The sciences of anthropology and sociology provide many tools for researchers following an interpretative research model. The Austrian-born economist Karl Raimund Popper (1985) proposed that what we know is composed of personal conjecture and that reality as we know it is constructed to match our beliefs, not an objective corporeality.

Marketing Research

Just as the academic debate about qualitative versus quantitative approaches to research was about to begin, an unexpected new pragmatic force entered the discourse on the side of social scientists endorsing qualitative methods. In the late 1950s, qualitative methodologies were widely adopted by advertising firms. These companies saw qualitative methods as providing effective and efficient techniques for the developing field of marketing research, and they gave well-paying consulting jobs to social scientists trained in interpretative forms of research.

A primary tool of these early market researchers was the **focus group**. Advertising agencies quickly adopted the use of these groups, as the firms realized that a well-run group can tell the manufacturer why some products sell and why others are not as appealing. By the 1960s, the focus group also became a tool for politicians and an essential way for some policy makers to make decisions (Fern, 2001). Naturally, this provided an easy target for critics. Much of the earliest qualitative research was described as not truly rigorous and was characterized as being journalistic (Holloway, 1997). However, focus groups are widely used today in marketing research, by political campaigns, and as a respected research method for social scientists.

Applications from the Literature

Example of Qualitative Research Using Focus Groups

Note: A total of 23 undergraduate students in an advanced case-management class participated in a service-learning experience at a residential treatment facility for troubled adolescents and elementary-age children. The residential facility was a locked psychiatric clinic. There were two phases to the qualitative research effort, one using an open-ended questionnaire and the second using focus groups.

Methods: As a qualitative research tool, focus groups offer significant benefits. By their very nature, they provide opportunities to collect data from a group of people simultaneously while at the same time allowing for observation of and interaction among participants. Generally lasting one to two hours, focus groups are particularly useful for several reasons. First, time is often limited for group meetings. To maximize focus group time, the moderator follows a semi-structured interview guide or identifies four to five questions around which to center the discussion, then keeps the discussion on topic. Interviewing several participants simultaneously also saves time and allows for exploration of multiple perspectives. Second, since people often feel more comfortable talking in a group, this format offers an opportunity for genuine interaction among interviewees "that is concentrated on attitudes and experiences which are of interest to the researcher." Third, interaction among participants may be more informative than individually conducted interviews.

Source: Diambra, J. F., Mcclam, T., Fuss, A., Burton, B., & Fudge, D. L. (2009). Using a focus group to analyze students' perceptions of a service-learning project. *College Student Journal, 43*(1), 114–122.

Social Science Research

In addition to focus group research, interpretative studies were widely used in criminology and sociology. Many of these research efforts involved large-scale case studies. These were often published as monographs and provided future researchers with models for the integration of observations and interviews in developing an understanding of a person or entity. Important examples include the sociological study of *Middletown in Transition: A Study in Cultural Conflicts* (Lynd & Lynd, 1937) and the criminological case study by Edward Sutherland, *The Professional Thief* (1937).

By the 1960s, the interpretative approach had been given a new set of research tools with the elaboration of **grounded theory** by Barney Glaser and Anselm Strauss (1967). The broad dimensions of qualitative research methods widely employed today were presented in that volume. Beginning in the late 1960s until his untimely death in 1982, James P. Spradley popularized the use of a research model from anthropology known as **ethnography** (Spradley, 1980). The ethnographic interview is an important research tool for collecting ethnographic data that is widely used in qualitative studies (Spradley, 1979).

Interpretative research designs are a natural extension of the skill set of a psychotherapist. The best counselors observe and listen to clients before organizing the client's themes and perceptions into a focus that is interpretable and understandable to both counselor and client. This same model of starting with data and working toward a meaningful explanation is the essence of grounded theory research.

Qualitative Advantage

Interpretivists normally do not use statistical inference and engage in formal hypothesis testing. Yet, B. G. Glaser (1992) was open to their use in his description of grounded theory research. Qualitative methods make it possible for researchers to study issues and problems in greater depth and detail than is possible using an empirical scientific approach (Patton, 2002). This capability of the qualitative approach has been described as providing a "thick description" of a phenomenon (Geertz, 1985; Klenke, 2008). For example, a practitioner-researcher can quantify the contact hours between a client and therapist, but the subtlety of the communication between client and therapist is not an easily quantified entity. How can moments of client insight, or the emotional release expressed as crying, or the client's sense of personal accomplishment be adequately explained by numbers?

The long-term impact of an intervention on the client is another dimension that defies description as a number. For these reasons, a different method for research is needed that fits with the context of ongoing therapy while assessing highly complex phenomena (Hill et al., 2005).

The researcher selects the research approaches and frames the study; therefore, the research method often directly reflects the researcher's values, educational background, and philosophy (Guba & Lincoln, 2005). The underlying framework and the model selected to guide the study should reflect the nature of the research problem. All too often, however, the choice is limited by the background and skills of the researcher (Holloway, 1997). A problem arises when researchers short-circuit the consideration of various research methods because they feel that one method is easier to do than another (Hill, Thompson, & Williams, 1997).

This nearsighted thinking misses the point that good research is difficult to do and that all research is labor intensive and will present many problems. To adapt an adage, the grass isn't greener in another person's paradigm.

Epistemology and Axiology for Interpretative Studies

At its core, the research framework employed by people using qualitative methods is phenomenological. Qualitative researchers hold the philosophical belief that each individual perceives phenomena experienced in the environment in unique ways. This belief in **multiple realities** is **constructionist,** implying that we each organize and interpret our experiences to construct our view of reality. How individuals construct an understanding of reality is informed by our **culture.**

Culture is composed of a set of beliefs learned and shared by members of a community. It also provides its members with a shared set of symbols and language. The symbols can include physical objects that are prized or that have special meaning to members of the group. These are also described as the **artifacts** of the culture. Each culture also has a set of rules and folkways guiding behavior in everyday life, and cultures provide a moral compass for their members in the form of **mores** (Thompson & Hickey, 2008).

Each culture has an established set of **values** that are stable but can be slowly modified over time. Values help each member of a cultural group share common conceptualizations guiding their judgments of value. Art, music, literature, and many other dimensions of social living are guided and interpreted by the values held by a culture's members. The American author Ernest Hemingway once quipped, "About morals, I know only that what is moral is what you feel good after and what is immoral is what you feel bad after" (Hemingway, 1932/1999, p. 2). In the social sciences, this hedonistic interpretation offered by Hemingway exceeds the framework of a common set of values shared by a culture.

The constructionist viewpoint is central to the **epistemology** of qualitative researchers. This is from the ancient Greek word *epistêmê* meaning knowledge. Today's word *epistemology* goes further and includes methods we use to know what we know (Williams, 2001). It is the scholar's epistemology that guides his or her work in the study of a cultural group. It is also an object of investigation. Much research with infants and young children, for example, is directed to observing and charting the ontogenetic changes in the developing individual's epistemology. Jean Piaget referred to this as the study of genetic-epistemology (Piaget, 1962).

Understanding qualitative data using an interpretative approach requires the researcher to break free of his or her own cultural background and see the world through the eyes of the research participant. To understand another's point of view, it is necessary to learn how others create their personal knowledge and belief systems. This understanding from the perspective of another is difficult to accomplish. It requires first being able to step outside one's own culture and belief system and, in a nonjudgmental way, see the environment from the perspective of the participants in the study. This approach, described as **emic,** implies the researcher has the capability to be a true insider and has access to the belief system and culture of participants (Rubin & Babbie, 2011).

The word **axiology** is a 20th-century term describing the values system of individuals. Axiology is a central concern for those using an interpretative approach to research. Qualitative researchers should take stock of the extent to which they infuse their work with their personal values and culture. Interpretative researchers strive to minimize the impact of their own values while valuing each participant's unique understanding of his or her **personal field** or reality (Hays & Wood, 2011). This qualitative research axiology of valuing the perspective of the research participant is what makes qualitative research possible. The researcher's axiology informs the choice of questions to be answered, selection of participants, methods used to collect and analyze data, and conclusions drawn about outcomes and observations.

In contrast, researchers employing a quantitative approach believe that there is a single reality and that controlled data collection methods can reveal universally valid findings explaining that reality. This view is based on the physical and natural science traditions that dominated the social sciences during the first half of the 20th century (Popper, 1935/2002). To achieve such **experimental validity,** quantitative researchers have developed a logical series of steps that are followed when answering research questions (D. T. Campbell & Stanley, 1963). (See Chapter 14 for a discussion of these methods.) The scientific approach employs a common language and a scientific research structure, and it strives to be **value-free** or **value-neutral** (Christians, 2005).

Researchers who have a qualitative focus do not believe being value-neutral is humanly possible. This belief is based on the observation that all researchers have their individual motivations and cognitive framework for interpreting the environment around them (Hertz, 1997). The researcher's values are evident in the literature chosen for review, the treatments and measures adopted for the study, the power levels of the statistics applied to the analysis, and the conclusions drawn from the data.

COMPONENTS AND TECHNIQUES OF QUALITATIVE RESEARCH

A number of qualitative research methods are available to the practitioner conducting an interpretative study. By only employing a single research approach or method and a single data source, the researcher limits his or her study and may miss important findings. The best approach for securing the findings is to **triangulate,** or use several different approaches to address the phenomena in question. The triangulation process is much like the use of a satellite-based global positioning system. If only one data source (single satellite) is locked on to the position, the location on the ground will be unreliable and may miss the mark by a wide margin. If two satellites are locked on to the ground target (your satellite transceiver), the location will be more accurately defined and the error margin greatly reduced. With three or more locked-on satellites, the position will be spot-on. This process of using several data sources to navigate is called triangulation. The same principle applies in research, whereby several independent data sources each leading to a common conclusion can strengthen the finding.

In interpretative studies, researchers know that their observations of events are deeply affected by the individuals involved in the study, including themselves (Berg, 2004). When different lines all converge on a common picture of that phenomenon, the researcher can have a degree of confidence not otherwise available when employing only a single method. The level of confidence a researcher can have in his or her findings has the parameter of the **triangle of error** framed by the various lines of sight obtained from the different research methods (Berg).

Framing Qualitative Research Problems

The qualitative research effort starts with a sensed problem, anomaly, or idea that a researcher decides to pursue. Most qualitative research endeavors start with an examination and careful reading of the background literature on the problem as well as dimensions related to the problem area. The exception to the rule is grounded theory (Glaser & Strauss, 1967). Grounded theory researchers attempt to be independent of all preknowledge about their data and allow the research data to be the source of new perspectives and theories. However, researchers usually study topics from fields to which they are sensitized and where they have a knowledge base derived from the literature and/or from experience (McGhee, Marland, & Atkinson, 2007).

With the possible exception of a study using grounded theory, the researcher's reading program from the associated literature should be supplemented by analysis of what is read along with the development of a series of syntheses of what is already known about the issue. By doing this reading and reflecting on the problem area, the researcher can pose an appropriate and worthwhile research question (Berg, 2004).

Questions guiding qualitative research should be open-ended, providing researchers with the opportunity to remain open-minded and for the emergence and development of new sub-questions (Farber, 2006). The research question must also be written to provide a theme and focus for the study and provide limits or guidelines (Creswell, 2007). The research question helps keep the researcher from running amuck. Without the discipline imposed by a well-structured research question, it is very easy for the enterprise of qualitative research to become multidirectional and unfocused in its goals.

The well-conceived research question also frames the population from which participants will be drawn, and it guides the researcher in selecting the most appropriate research method to employ in the effort. Research questions written for most qualitative studies involve the words *what, why,* or *how.* Here are some examples:

- How do sexual minority (GLBT) students living in undergraduate resident halls feel they are viewed by straight students with whom they live? What personal coping strategies do GLBT undergraduate students employ in living among straight peers?
- What are the core motivational factors of individuals running for a seat on the local school board?
- Why do some professional marriage counselors become divorced once they earn their licenses?
- What impedes some women from reporting a sexual assault?
- How do reality TV shows depict American women in the 21st century?

Applications from the Literature

Examples of Research Problems and Research Questions from Two Qualitative Research Studies

Example A: Study Without a Question Statement, While Including a Statement of Purpose

Note: Data for this qualitative study were collected through the use of in-depth interviews with seven adults, each with parents suffering progressive neurological impairments from Parkinson's disease.

The purpose of this phenomenological study was to explore, appreciate, and describe the experiences of adult children who have a parent with Parkinson's disease, and to then compare the findings to existing literature on other chronic illnesses, pointing out similarities and differences. Hopefully, the findings help to increase therapist and researcher sensitivity to issues and concerns expressed by the adult child about a disease for which no known etiology or cure is available.

Source: Blanchard, A., Hodgson, J., Lamson, A., & Dosser, D. (2009). Lived experiences of adult children who have a parent diagnosed with Parkinson's disease. *The Qualitative Report, 14*(1), 61–80.

Example B: Example With a Clear Research Question

Note: A purposeful sample of 25 young adults, all of whom had been diagnosed as having a learning disability and were provided with special education services while in school, were individually interviewed in this study.

Despite the presence of the ADA [Americans with Disabilities Act] in the American workplace, very little research pertaining to employees with learning disabilities has been conducted. Therefore, this inquiry focused on perceptions of employees with learning disabilities about the culture of the workplace. In essence, what are the issues for employees with learning disabilities in job acquisition, job advancement, self-disclosure, and experiences with employer attitudes and beliefs?

Source: Price, L., Gerber, P. J., & Mulligan, R. (2003). The Americans with Disabilities Act and adults with learning disabilities as employees. *Remedial and Special Education, 24*(6), 350–358. doi: 10.1177/07419325030240060601

Research questions are frequently followed by **nominal definitions** for ambiguous terms. Nominal definitions are working definitions. The term *graduate student* can be defined several ways, for example, as any student enrolled in one or more postgraduate classes. The definition may also be more specific, such as "any matriculated postgraduate student enrolled in at least 6 semester hours of graduate course work." In the previously noted study (Price, Gerber, & Mulligan, 2003) of former special education students in the workplace, the authors provided the following nominal definition for *an adult with a learning disability*:

All adults had been diagnosed as having learning disabilities under the criteria of the local school district, the state of New Jersey, and federal guidelines of both the

Individuals with Disabilities Education Act (IDEA) and Section 504 of the Vocational Rehabilitation Act of 1973. Community child study teams in New Jersey had classified the research participants as having specific learning disabilities, perceptual impairments, or neurological impairments while they were in K–12 settings. All had demonstrated average to above-average intelligence on standardized intelligence tests. All had difficulties that did not fall under the exclusionary clause in the federal definition of learning disabilities. All showed significant problems and delays in one or more of the following areas: written language, spoken language, reading comprehension, math calculation or comprehension, reading comprehension, word attack skills, and listening skills. (pp. 351–352)

Researchers may also clarify their terms by employing **operational definitions.** While more commonly used in empirical, or quantitative, research, operational definitions are also employed in some qualitative research. These definitions are normally employed to describe the participants or the population involved in the study. Operational definitions imply some form of measurement has been used in describing an object, variable, or phenomenon. This form of definition makes it clear to all readers, as well as to the researcher, exactly what form the study's data will take (Babbie, 1995). For instance, an operational definition for *problem drinking behavior* might be "a person who is inebriated through the consumption of alcohol 3 or more times a month or has occasional blackouts following excessive consumption of alcoholic drinks."

The fuzziness of the author's adjectives describing participants is removed by adding operational definitions. In counseling research, a large number of terms need to be explained or defined. Among these are *middle class, hypertensive, good sportsmanship, hostility, ardor* or *affection, creativity, impoverished, chronic illness, shyness, panic, extrovert, pestiferous, ethnic minority, middle school, blithesome, churlish, quality of life, aggressive, low self-esteem, impoverished, overweight, locus of control,* and many more.

Sampling and Participant Selection

Sampling from a large population to approximate the membership of that population is the model used in quantitative research, and occasionally it is the guiding principle for researchers employing qualitative methods. This type of sampling involves building a statistically accurate representation through techniques such as random sampling.

Applications from the Literature

Example of Random Sampling in a Qualitative Research Study

Note: In this 10-year longitudinal study of displaced Pennsylvania steel workers, a random selection from all laid-off hourly laborers who were the former employees of a steel plant were interviewed. A total of 87 of the original sample were interviewed again after 10 years.

Method: In 1987 I conducted in-person in-depth interviews with 102 randomly selected displaced steelworkers who resided in the Shenango Valley and had been employed as hourly blue-collar laborers at two steel fabrication plants that closed in 1983 and 1984. The sampling frame was a list compiled by the United Steelworkers of America of all hourly manufacturing workers at the plants. The interviews were conducted in the respondents' homes or in a community center, and the response rate was 86 percent. It is estimated that approximately 10 percent of the local steelworkers who were displaced in the 1980s relocated beyond a 60-mile radius of the valley to obtain employment, and another 20 percent traveled that distance to look for work but decided not to relocate (primarily because they could not find stable or high-paying employment).

Source: Zippay, A. (2002). Dynamics of income packaging: A 10-year longitudinal study. *Social Work, 41*(3), 291–300.

Convenience or Accidental Samples

We know more about the psychology and sociology of undergraduate students than any other group within the population. This reflects how convenient undergraduate students are for faculty and advanced graduate students in need of participants for their research studies. There are many sources of potential participants in and around academic institutions, clinics, group homes, outpatient facilities, special education centers, child guidance centers, shelters for the abused and/or homeless, and many others. By using participants that are readily accessible, the researcher can save time and money.

Using an accidental or **convenience sample** is not without shortcomings. There is an enhanced likelihood that data gained from participants that are in the environment around the researcher are influenced by the researcher. Also, by drawing participants from a convenient group, the researcher limits his or her study to one appropriate for the demographic characteristics of the available group (Rubin & Babbie, 2011).

Accidental samples are composed of participants who are representative of a phenomenon that is under study and are accidentally available to the researcher. For example, a researcher might want to conduct ethnographic interviews with family members who were rescued from their homes following a natural disaster, like the survivors of Hurricane Katrina in New Orleans (August 29, 2005). By being in situ at a federal evacuation center the week of August 28 to September 3, 2005, the researcher would have been able to locate and interview a good number of potential participants for the study. This group of available participants would have been brought together by accident and could have provided the researcher with a very convenient group for possible inclusion in the study.

A colleague once attended the 25th reunion of members of her undergraduate class. Her senior thesis involved interviewing and assessing a sample of women in that graduating class. She was able to repeat components of that original undergraduate study with her peers during the reunion. This was a clear case of using an accidental sample (Lawler, 1993).

Opportunistic Samples

When participants in a qualitative study are selected because they are part of an ongoing activity, the researcher is using a propitious circumstance to frame the research. These opportunities for doing field research are not unusual and can be planned in advance around a schedule of activities. For example, if a researcher is interested in learning about male bonding among freshmen, he or she may elect to follow a group of college men who are "rushing a fraternal social organization." In this type of theoretical study, both interviews and observations can be made with participants as the opportunities present themselves (Lehner, 1998).

Clinical studies of therapeutic impact often employ **opportunistic samples** of participants. It is difficult to imagine a circumstance when clients can be recruited to accept therapeutic treatments. A more common design for such research involves a sample of participants who have requested clinical therapy.

Applications from the Literature

Example of Opportunistic Sampling Employed in an Ethnographic Interview Research Study

Note: Participants in this study were new clients of a university-based marriage and family therapy (MFT) clinic run as part of the training of new therapists. During intake, all clients were told that the MFT clinic conducts research with therapists in training and therapy sessions in front of one-way mirrors through which the sessions were observed by faculty.

An interesting finding from this research is that the participants (members of 14 families in therapy) reported that the counseling sessions at the university's clinic improved the ability of parents to set rules and establish limits with their children, improved inter-spousal communications, and made family members better able to accept criticism.

Sample Selection: In Option 1, three couples, one family, and three individuals were interviewed twice over a 4-month period concerning their reactions to and perceptions of family therapy practice. In Option 2, three couples, two families, and two individuals were interviewed twice over the same 4-month period; overall, 14 clients were interviewed. As stated earlier, the term *client*, as used in this context, referred to a single unit (i.e., individual, marital, or family) but included all spouses, significant others, nuclear, blended, or extended members within that unit that arrived at the counseling session. Clients who requested counseling services at the clinic were informed about the research project by their counselor and were given a choice of whether or not to participate in the study.

Therapists included four doctoral students (one male and one female) from the school of social work, and one male and one female from a doctoral program in marriage and family therapy. The therapists' level of experience ranged from 1 to 6 years. Clients were selected using an opportunistic sampling strategy (Honigman, 1970).[1] Opportunistic sampling was well suited for this study because generalization to a population was not the research goal. Instead, the goal was to generate vivid descriptions of the effectiveness of family therapy practice within a single setting.

Source: Sells, S. P., Smith, T., E., & Moon, S. (1996). An ethnographic study of client and therapist perceptions of therapy effectiveness in a university-based training clinic. *Family Therapy, 22*(3), 321–342. doi: 10.1111/j.1752-0606.1996.tb00209.x

Purposeful Samples

Participants in many qualitative research efforts are purposefully selected because they match certain goals of the researcher (Rubin & Babbie, 2011). This may be accomplished by screening participants into or out of the group to be studied. Researchers employing qualitative methods often select participants who have special insight or information to share and are thought of as being **key informants.** For example, if a researcher was interested in learning about the coping strategies for stress reduction used by the **sandwich generation** of middle-age women, he or she would screen a large group of women in a population (e.g., members of the PTA at a school), looking for women with responsibilities for both their own family and for aging parents or in-laws. Once identified, these women could provide rich information about coping with duel caregiving responsibilities. Yet, this purposeful sample would not be a good representation of all American women, or even all mothers.

Purposeful sampling also is used when the goal of the research is to study deviant cases from a population that do not represent the norm (Rubin & Babbie, 2011). For example, important insights may result from interviews with otherwise successful young people who elect to live alone and not commit to a relationship with any other individual. (See Chapters 9, 13, and 17 for further discussion of sampling.)

Snowball Sampling

Some populations should be studied but are inaccessible to academic researchers. These hard-to-locate group members may be involved in illegal activities or be highly mobile. The term **snowball sample** is a metaphoric sobriquet describing how a small ball of snow grows in size when it is released and rolls down a steep, snow-covered hill. The process starts with the identification of a few members of the population or group to be studied. These participants are then encouraged to provide the names and access to others they know in the same group. This step often requires the practitioner engaged in research to build trust with the original participants. The process is not dissimilar to that used by many recent college graduates who network to find their first postgraduate employment.

Once the second tier of participants becomes part of the study, they can also be used to identify a third tier of individuals who could become participants. Snowball samples have been used in qualitative research to study such diverse topics as anomie among NFL professional football players (Carter & Carter, 2007), cocaine use (Macdonald, 1989), sadomasochism (Nichols, 2011), and prostitution (Scambler, 2007).

Applications from the Literature

Example of Snowball Sampling

Note: This qualitative, feminist research effort explored the prevailing construction of drug use and studied access and ethical considerations in doing research with a marginalized group.

(Continued)

(Continued)

The Research Design: I visited both agencies to describe my research and to hand out one-page information sheets on it. I included a phone number at which to contact me if any of their clients were interested
in doing an interview. However, I did not receive any calls. As I had suspected, unless the women talked
to me directly or were contacted through a friend or participant, there was no interest in participation.
Fortunately, the snowball sample broadened on its own and I made no further attempts to reach women
other than by word of mouth. However, I realized how handicapped social science researchers are in the
absence of historical contact with the individuals they wish to study. This may partially explain why the
majority of research on illegal drug users has been conducted through drug treatment centres and prisons, and why negative stereotypes prevail.

Source: Boyd, S. (2001). Feminist research on mothers and illegal drugs. *Resources for Feminist Research, 28*(3), 113–130.

Demographic Data

Demographic information describing a study's participants is essential for being able to
explain the meaning of a qualitative study to others. Answers to **demographic questions**
provide objective descriptive data about the participants. In designing demographic questions, the central rule is to never ask questions for which there is no need to know the
answer. Many new researchers will ask demographic questions not needed for the study
but out of personal curiosity. If the information is not involved in the research question, do
not ask it. Occasionally, participants who answer demographic questions before responding to other parts of the interview or questionnaire have a tendency to answer other items
in a stilted way. They have a need to align themselves with the identity they created up
front. Therefore, it may be a good idea to place demographic items at the end of the interview or questionnaire.

A caution about asking demographic questions is that what appears to be a straightforward human dimension may be highly convoluted and complex. Questions of race and
ethnicity are always difficult to phrase well. The increasing number of blended families
creates a complex problem for researchers concerned about race and ethnicity. For example, the category of "Hispanic" covers so many different cultures and regions around the
world as to make it an almost meaningless choice. Likewise the classification of "Asian"
covers a myriad of different nations, languages, and cultures. Yet, these categories are
employed by the US Census. Many demographic questionnaires and interviews ask about
ethnicity and race using the structure of the decennial Census survey:

Please specify your ethnicity.

___ Hispanic or Latino

___ Not Hispanic or Latino

Please specify your race.

___ American Indian or Alaska Native

___ Asian

___ Black or African American

___ Mixed or Combined Race

___ Native Hawaiian or Other Pacific Islander

___ White

Defining and describing the education level of a participant can lead to a huge list of possibilities. Asking an individual to answer an open-ended question may seem to be a simpler approach. The problem can be coding the answers later, with individuals having introduced many misleading variations on their educational backgrounds. Here is an example of a structured-format question:

What is the highest degree or level of school you have completed? If currently enrolled, mark the previous grade or highest degree received.

___ No schooling completed

___ Nursery school to 8th grade

___ 9th, 10th, or 11th grade

___ 12th grade, no diploma

___ High school graduate, diploma

___ High school diploma equivalent (for example: GED)

___ Some college credit, but less than one year

___ One or more years of college, no degree ___ Associate degree (for example, AA, AS)

___ Bachelor's degree (for example, BA, AB, BS)

___ Master's degree (for example, MA, MS, MEng, MEd, MSW, MBA)

___ Professional degree (for example, MD, DDS, DVM, LLB, PsyD, JD)

___ Doctorate degree (for example, PhD, EdD)

When a researcher wishes to determine the socioeconomic status (SES) of a minor child, a possible question to ask is whether that child received a free or reduced lunch at school. Adults are better able to answer questions of SES but may not always answer truthfully. College-age young adults may have been kept relatively clueless about their family's SES. (The measurement of demographic characteristics is covered in depth in Chapter 13.)

Cartoon 4.1

Cartoon by Merv Magus.

"The only portfolio that counts in life is a stock market portfolio, the ultimate report card of us all."

Interviewing

The ability to interview participants and collect critical data by interviewing others is a major skill of successful qualitative researchers. Researchers employ three formats with interview research: unstructured or ethnographic, structured, and semistructured (Zhang & Wildemuth, 2009).

Ethnographic Interviews

Unstructured interviews first appeared in the scientific journals of anthropology as an approach for learning the social reality of individual members of a community. In this approach, also described as **ethnographic interviewing,** neither the questions nor the answers are structured in advance. The process is similar to a conversational method. The interview process does not start with a hypothesis and central question but with a conversation in which the interviewer generates questions by listening to the participant's ongoing narration. The focus is on learning the social reality of the participant. Each person of a community providing answers to an unstructured interview is likely to create different patterns of response (Zhang & Wildemuth, 2009).

When an interview is conducted without an **interview protocol,** it has a freewheeling and unstandardized structure that allows the participant greater latitude and is in essence an ethnographic interview (Fontana & Frey, 2005). The researcher using an unstructured interview approach needs a clear knowledge base related to the topic of the interview. Without preset questions, the interviewer can develop appropriate questions and probes based on emerging issues identified during interactions with the interviewee (Berg, 2004). Detailed note taking and the production a copious amount of data during the interview process is very likely to interfere with the interview process. The open nature of this approach implies the need to record the interview and extract the meaning of the data later.

Totally open or unstructured interview recordings and transcripts are the most complex form of data to analyze. The researcher must invest significant time in examining the recording or transcript for what the participant was conveying and what the deeper meaning of the responses may be.

Structured Interviews

Interview research is also commonly used to report demographic data. Structured interviews are organized around a protocol of specific questions that participants answer using a list of alternative possibilities. These interviews, a verbal form of the survey questionnaire, are further described in Chapter 13. Structured interview questions or **prompts** are designed specifically to match the research goals and objectives and provide structure for the interviewing process.[2]

Once any semistructured or structured interview protocol has been developed, it needs to be vetted by other researchers to ensure its appropriateness and minimize possible research and researcher bias. The great advantage to structured interviews is the speed with which answers can be coded and analyzed.

Semistructured Interviews

Most qualitative researchers employ **semistructured interviews** that provide a set of questions to which the participant can respond openly (Fontana & Frey, 2005). Questions or prompts for semistructured interviews are normally organized on an interview protocol that the researcher develops and uses during the interview process. Collecting qualitative data through the use of semistructured interviews is a labor-intensive task. Structured and semistructured interviews require the development of interview questions that address aspects of the study's central research question without simply rephrasing the principal question.

Most semistructured interviews have two basic components: prompts and demographic questions. The interview with open-ended, semistructured questions can be recorded by hand or digitally recorded. Then the data are subjected to one of several analytical approaches. Making a digital recording of the responses has the advantage of providing more reliable data that others can review later.[3]

Interviewers should be carefully trained in the use of the protocol and the interview process. Interviewers also need to be shown, through demonstration, that the interview process should flow easily and never become confrontational. The senior researcher should train his or her interviewers by practicing the questions and process with them. A good approach for providing this training is through careful simulations. Later, a review of the process and training may be needed if the interviewers are asked to conduct many interviews. This review of the interview protocol and procedures reduces the likelihood of **interviewer drift.** The word *drift* describes the subtle shift in the data collection process that occurs over time with interviewers.

Participants need to be ethically recruited under the direction of the lead researcher. The interview process normally begins with introductions to the nature of the process and research goal. Participants need to be assured of the confidentiality of their responses and of the appreciation of the researcher for their time and interest in helping expand what is known on the topic or focus of the research.

Interview Protocol Development

Interviews can be used as a supplemental component or serve as the primary data-gathering tool of a qualitative research study. The semistructured interview process gains information from participants who respond to protocol items composed of open-ended questions and a series of supplemental or follow-up probes. Supplemental probes are used to help participants elaborate on their initial answers. These follow-up questions may take the form of "Please tell me a little more about that," or "You never mentioned . . . ," or "In what ways have you found that to be true for you?"

Applications from the Literature

Goal Statement and Research Methodology from an Interview-Based Qualitative Study

Note: The authors' use of *hegemonic femininity* describes the significant sociocultural pressures on American women to be thin and always appear to be physically fit. The authors aver that women today are constantly engaged in a process of "body-work." The sample included undergraduate women volunteers, seven of whom were interviewed in depth. Those interviews were used to construct an open-ended questionnaire that was taken by 32 undergraduate volunteers, including 12 men.

To answer the research question, the sample was interviewed with a series of questions such as these:

- What do you think is most attractive about yourself? Why?
- What do you like about your appearance? Why? How does this make you feel?
- What, if anything, do you dislike about your appearance? Why? How does this make you feel? Do you try to change this and, if so, how?

Research Purpose: In this study our main research objective is to contribute to the body of knowledge about college-age women's perceptions of femininity and related impact on body image. Our goal is to yield descriptive data that illustrates, problematizes, or refutes existing theoretical scholarship regarding the mind-body dichotomy and its relationship to female body image. A great deal of body image research focuses on women with eating disorders: However, body image can involve various dimensions of both satisfaction and dissatisfaction. Additionally, feminist research on the mind-body dichotomy is primarily theoretical. Therefore, there is little evidence of the ways in which hegemonic femininity, and its polarization of the mind and body, impacts women's body image development. Accordingly, we are interested in: (a) our participants' conceptions of femininity and masculinity, (b) how family, peers, and media transmit messages about femininity, and (c) our participants' perception of their body image attitudes and behaviors.

Research Methodology: In this study we combine qualitative in-depth interviews and open-ended surveys from which we also elicited qualitative data (structured as written interviews.) The second author conducted in-depth interviews with seven white female college students, who attend liberal arts colleges in the northeast, in order to learn about their body image as well as their ideas about femininity and masculinity. The second author conducted these interviews in order to share insider-status with the participants. Her status as a college student, coupled with shared age-gender-race traits, allowed her to quickly build rapport and use empathy during each of the interviews. The sampling method was that of convenience; we asked local students in their residence halls if they would be willing to be interviewed for a study about body image and gender. We did not ask any of the students if they had ever suffered from an eating disorder, nor did we provide any additional information other than explaining informed consent and confidentiality in a written letter to those who responded favorably to our initial query.

Source: Leavy, P., Gnong, A., & Ross, L. S. (2009). Femininity, masculinity, and body image issues among college-age women: An in-depth and written interview study of the mind-body dichotomy. *The Qualitative Report*, 14(2), 261–292. Retrieved from http://www.nova.edu/ssss/QR/QR14-2/leavy.pdf

Writing Semistructured Interviews: This approach also involves an interview protocol and list of possible follow-up probes. The interview questions are open-ended and more focused and linked with the research question under study. The choice of employing a semistructured method and probing questions should be guided by the goal of the research project. For example, if a researcher wishes to learn what the attitude of a hospital patient is to his or her health or to an upcoming surgery, a structured attitude survey instrument would be useful. If, however, the researcher wants to know the depth of anxiety or level of concern the patient and/or members of the patient's immediate family are experiencing, a better approach for the interview would involve open-ended questions.

Each probe on a protocol should be written using carefully crafted language designed for participant understanding. Likewise, the language should be at an appropriate complexity level and employ terms that all participants in the study will interpret in similar ways.

In a study of client satisfaction with personal counseling, a researcher may employ the following three questions as part of the interview protocol:

1. What was the primary problem that brought you to seek counseling?

   - Probe: Describe how that problem impacted you and those around you.
   - Probe: What did you expect counseling would provide for you?

2. Do you believe a change has occurred for you?

- Probe: Can you describe the change?
- Probe: How are your current interactions with others?

3. What techniques did you learn to improve your condition?

- Probe: Under what conditions do these skills work best?
- Probe: In what way did your therapist show he or she understood your problem?

In developing the questions for an interview protocol, researchers could use a team approach. When researchers work together in the development of a protocol's questions, it becomes possible to use creativity-enhancing methods, including **brainstorming,** the **reversal technique,** and the **random association method** (Baillie, 2003). The starting point in question development is to produce an inclusive list of all matters and individuals potentially related to the research question. For example, in a study of heterosexual couples who enjoy a mutually satisfying relationship, the following items may be on the list:

How the couple met

Why they committed to an exclusive relationship

Background communalities and differences

Perception of partner's personality style and tempo

Perception of personal personality style and tempo

Shared and individual activities

Role of friends in their relationship

Role of extended family in their relationship

Vision for the next 5 years

Each of these items on the list can be used to create several open-ended questions for the protocol. Developing three or more questions for each item allows the researcher to collect data that are stable and reliable.

Applications from the Literature

Description of a Semistructured Interview

Note: This pilot study of character development by athletic coaches took place in an exclusive 200-year-old New England boarding school. The upper school, where the ethnographic study took place, enrolled 300 students and employed 75 faculty, tutors, and coaches.

Data Gathering: Interviews were conducted with coaches in November, prior to the start of the [basketball] season, around a semistructured interview protocol designed to elicit maximum breadth across the character development topic. These interviews explored the coaches' own sport experience, including influential coaches and life experiences, their coaching philosophy, and their approach to various aspects of character development in sport. As a pilot study, the focus was directed primarily towards understanding character development from the coaches' perspective. Semistructured, postseason interviews, however, were also conducted with a purposeful sample of players (Patton, 1990)[4] at the close of the season to gain their perspective on the experience of team and individual character development. Interviews were recorded and transcribed for analysis.

Source: Davidson, M. L., & Moran-Miller, K. E. (2005). Character development in sport: An ethnographic study of character development in an elite prep-school basketball program. *Journal of Research in Character Education, 3*(1), 121–138.

Active Interviews

This format for a qualitative interview actively engages the interviewer and participant in a discussion of the research question. It has been argued that all interviews, including structured ones, use active interaction that is shaded by the individuals involved in the process (Holstein & Gubrium, 2004). The point is that all interviews are social encounters during which knowledge is actively constructed. The **active interview** facilitates knowing the process of meaning development, not just the surface content of the participant's thinking. Researchers employing an active interview approach consider the interviewer and interviewee as equal partners in constructing meaning around an interview event.

Active interviews can be guided by the list of related topics developed around the research question. An active interview takes the form of a conversation that may include challenging the participant's position by the interviewer and the participant challenging the assumptions of the researcher. This approach is best assisted by making a digital video recording the interview (Berg, 2004). Active interviews are best carried out in an informal environment conducive to self-disclosure and openness. This openness also extends to the interviewer, who poses the question and then facilitates the participant in exploring his or her perspective and ideas about the topic.

Observations as a Research Technique

Observational data can come from various places and be collected for a number of reasons. Observations can be conducted in a laboratory setting, as when researchers observe participants from behind a one-way mirror. This laboratory approach tends to be employed by quantitatively focused scholars. Qualitative researchers tend to use observations of participants in their natural settings. For example, anthropologists have used observational methods in a field setting to build the knowledge base for much of what we know about comparative human culture today.

Cartoon 4.2

Cartoon by Merv Magus.

"I'm going to be an anthropologist when I grow up, so I'm practicing field research with this small tribe."

Models for Field-Based Observational Research

There are a number of options for collecting field-based data. Field-based observations take two major forms. One is the ethnographic approach of being a participant-observer in the activity along with members of the group being studied. The other is being a nonparticipating observer. There are various ways to be a nonparticipating observer or, as some wags have called it, "a potted plant as researcher." This entails selecting a single location from which to make observations and attempting to be as unobtrusive as possible. For example, Michael Moffatt, after negotiating ethical access, moved into an undergraduate dormitory on the campus of Rutgers University and lived as a fellow student while collecting the data to write a powerful book on the socialization of American college students, *Coming of Age in New Jersey* (1989).

In this approach to making direct observations in the field, the researcher first secures the cooperation of the appropriate authorities to conduct the research. Failure to do this can lead to a bad result. For example, an unknown researcher taking field notes on children at play in a school's playground, even if observing from off campus, is likely to attracted unwanted attention.

In the process of collecting data by using assistants or by using questionnaires and interviews, the researcher may visit the location where the activity is occurring. When the researcher is in the field, it is possible to make firsthand observations (Patton, 2002). Observations can be used to supplement other dimensions of a qualitative research study. For example, Davidson and Moran-Miller studied character development in a preparatory school athletic program (excerpted above) and used observations of locker-room monologues by coaches as a source of data.

Also, in field-based research, a decision must be made as to whether the participants to be observed are to be informed and whether all participants must provide consent. This decision is complicated by the fact that people tend to behave differently when they know they are being watched (Mayo, 1949). (See Chapter 14 for a discussion of the observer or Hawthorne effect.)

In doing field-based observational research, it is best for researchers to keep their field notes private. If notes are taken by hand, they should to be carefully elaborated and marginal notations made on the clean copy within 1–2 hours of ending the observations. During the recopying process, the researcher should look for emerging themes and possible illustrative instances to plan to observe during future sessions in the field. For example, a colleague studied the culture of the middle managers of a large government-sponsored corporation in Tokyo by making field notes in his assigned office area each day. These were written unobtrusively on index cards. Later, during a long ride on the commuter train home, he recopied his notes, annotated them, cleaned them up, and made a list of what to try to observe the next day (Skinner, 1978). Field notes must be kept confidential and away from participants, as the participants may not like what the observations reveal about them or their group.

Nonparticipant observational research is detached and more clinical than is participant-observational research or ethnographic research. For that reason, nonparticipant observational research usually takes less time to complete than does ethnographic research. In both cases, the researcher can recognize when a point has come to close down the data-collecting phase. That point is known as the **saturation point.** Saturation occurs when the researcher recognizes that he or she has seen and heard all the unique information the participants have to contribute. Once the observations become redundant, it is time to end that phase of the research.

CASE IN POINT   4.1

Supervision of counselors during their internships frequently involves unobtrusive observation of graduate students working in their placements. These observations of the advanced student should occur when he or she is working both with a group and with single clients. Unobtrusive observations can be made by using either a video-recording process or by employing a one-way mirror observational booth.

Most supervisory observations employ a semistructured observational system. Using this format, supervisors have a list of categories of activities they are looking for, but they are also free to record observations of interactions or behaviors not on the observational protocol.

This approach to supervision has the potential to be influenced by a biasing effect. The nature of observation by the university's supervisor is highly **subjective** and based on the experience and professionalism of that individual. For that reason, most graduate programs strive to provide a highly trustworthy method for supervising interns. This process includes postobservation interviews by the supervisor with the student and his or her mentor in the field. In addition, more than one supervisor may observe the same counseling trainee or review the video of the counseling trainee with a client.

Qualitative Observation Research in Child Development

Observation is a central tool in the study of children. Sensitive, well-prepared psychologists and social workers have collected child development data that are now the framework for both the education and treatment of children. A priority of President Obama has been the expansion of early childhood education programs. The growth of these programs has added a new and growing field for professional counselors who work with the parents of children receiving special services.

CASE IN POINT 4.2

While best known as a naturalist and biologist, Darwin was an early proponent of a qualitative approach to child study. In the 19th century, he published a detailed description of his own children. His descriptions of neonatal reflexology and infant behaviors are compelling and considered to be medically precise. He wrote, for example, that

> a warm soft hand applied to the side of his face excited a wish to suck. This must be considered as a reflex or an instinctive action, for it is impossible to believe that experience and association with the touch of his mother's breast could so soon have come into play. (Darwin, 1877, pp. 285–286)

Observational research has been frequently employed in the study of the ontology of cognitive development during childhood. The use of careful observation in the scientific study of children provided the foundation for much of the writing in the development of human behaviors, motivations, language, and intellect (Piaget, 1932, 1952, 1955, 1960, 1962, 1965, 1967; Piaget & Inhelder, 1956; Piaget, Inhelder, & Szeminska, 1960).

In qualitative research, observations of young children are usually supported by digital recordings of the children interacting with the environment or other people. The following three examples are of this form of research:

- Albert Bandura's study of learned aggression by preschoolers:

  http://video.google.com/videoplay?docid=-4586465813762682933#

- Study of delay of gratification with 4-year-olds:

  http://www.youtube.com/watch?v=4CYr4FgMYGI&feature

- Study of stranger anxiety among infants:

  http://www.youtube.com/watch?v=i5MudJ7yxkE&feature

Transcription

In many qualitative studies where the nature of human interactions is of interest, a successful research technique may involve transcription (Lapadat & Lindsay, 1998).

Transcription appears to be a simple task, but appearances can deceive. Transcriptions are all about judgments on issues such as the detail to omit or include, the emotional nuances shown by a speaker, the pauses and thought breaks, and even the syntax and dialect of the language spoken (Bailey, 2008). Transcription is a central feature in interviewing.

With the possible exception of professional court recorders using stenograph machines, researchers cannot make an exact written transcript without first making a digital or magnetic recording of the action and later working to capture each word for the written record.

Researchers go about the task of transcribing in two principal ways. One involves **naturalism,** whereby every utterance is captured in as much detail as possible (Oliver, Serovich, & Mason, 2005). By this process, even the greeting and social chatter used to warm up the participant become part of the written record. The naturalistic transcript contains marginal notations for emotional responses, and it notes all pauses, gaps, and dialect use. In employing a naturalistic approach, the researcher minimizes the subjective nature of judgment calls about what is included and what is redacted.

Oliver et al. (2005) used the term **denaturalism** to describe transcribing only what is judged to be germane to the action that occurred. In summarizing research on the use of transcripted material, Davidson (2009) noted that transcripts composed of selected material are more useful as they have less information that is tenuous and confusing to others not present during the original verbal activity.

A very different point of view is held by researchers who feel naturalism is the most revealing approach for analysis. The primary tool for transcription used in discourse analysis and conversational analysis is the naturalistic method developed by Gail Jefferson (Potter & Hepburn, 2005). The Jeffersonian approach provides markers for making notations of all subtleties in the speech and language patterns of a person in conversation (Jefferson, 2004). A copy of the Jeffersonian notation system for transcription of spoken language can be reviewed at http://www.liso.ucsb.edu/Jefferson/Transcript.pdf.

Software Support for Qualitative Research

There are several software packages that support identifying categories and coding of text and transcripted material. These programs can be used with both written and voice material and assist in identifying reoccurring phrases, key words, and themes. Most universities have one or more of these packages available on the campus server for student and faculty use. Following are five that are commercially available for researchers:

1. NVivo 10 by QSR International, http://www.qsrinternational.com/products_nvivo.aspx

2. ATLAS_ti 7 by ATLAS_ti Scientific Software Development, http://www.atlasti.com/

3. CATPAC II by Galileo, http://www.galileoco.com/N_catpac.asp

4. MAXQDA by VERBI GmbH, http://www.maxqda.com/

5. Tropes by Semantic Knowledge, http://www.semantic-knowledge.com/tropes.htm

The American Evaluation Association maintains a web page listing more than 30 software products commercially available for purchase and/or license designed to provide fast and reliable qualitative analytics with text and voice data. This web page also provides purchase information and contacts for the programs. Many of these software packages are available for a free trial. To access this resource, see http://www.eval.org/Resources/QDA.asp.

Remember that good word processing software can also provide the researcher with a valuable tool for searching text material to find identified key words and phrases.

SUMMARY

Qualitative research methods are used with interpretative studies in which the focus is on the deep meaning of words and images rather than on empirical evidence. The qualitative approach can provide a deep level of insight into the nature of human motivation and behaviors. As an approach, it recognizes that we all have personal values and beliefs that provide a framework for our interpretation of experiences and the sensory input we receive. Qualitative researchers do not believe any research method can be truly value-free and strive instead to achieve trustworthy answers to research questions.

In this chapter, the major processes used for framing qualitative research—sampling, observing, interviewing (including transcribing), and using qualitative research software—are described. Sampling in qualitative studies is normally designed to collect information from a small group of participants who are not selected on a random basis.

Observations can be made either by becoming a participant-observer or by using a nonparticipant system for observing and collecting field notes. Interviews, a commonly employed qualitative research method, may be open-ended or may be more structured with questions developed to collect evidence on specific areas of research focus. Transcriptions may be written as exact transcripts of every word, gesture, solipsism, dialect, and emotion shown by the participant. They normally start as a digital recording of the interview or other spoken data that is then transcribed for analysis. Other transcript approaches (denaturalistic) are less exacting and focus on the central issues of the study only. Transcript analysis systems can be enhanced by use of software systems.

DISCUSSION QUESTIONS

1. Consider an undergraduate sports team. In a few paragraphs, describe how a qualitative researcher interested in how a team culture develops could go about conducting a meaningful study. Include how to approach the team, enter its domain of activity, and go about data collection.

2. In question 1, what qualitative approach to research would you select? Why would that be the optimal research method?

3. Devise a semistructured interview protocol that could be employed to assess the plans and concerns of unwed adolescent women preparing for their premier parturition.

NOTES

1. Honigman, J. J. (1970). Sampling in ethnographic fieldwork. In R. Naroll & R. Cohen (Eds.), *A handbook of method in cultural anthropology* (pp. 266–281). Garden City, NY: Natural History Press.

2. Structured interviews: A structured protocol of questions for the interview is a common instrument used to elicit objective facts and statistically reliable opinions. Models for statistical sampling and the development of reliable and valid opinion surveys/interviews are discussed in Chapter 13, "Instrument Development and Survey Research."

3. Recordings can be done using old-fashioned magnetic audio or video systems or by using digital recording. Digital recordings have the advantage of being less subject to wear and less likely to be unintentionally erased or distorted. Digital recording equipment is smaller and highly adaptable for storage in computer files. The danger of digital research material is its computer adaptability, which makes it easy for security to be compromised; digital interview files can be spread far and wide by file sharing and/or a social network.

4. Patton, M. Q. (1990). Humanistic psychology and qualitative research: Shared principles and processes. *Person-Centered Review, 5*(2), 191–202.

Qualitative Research II

Processes

"The outcome of any serious research can only be to make two questions grow where only one grew before."

Thorstein Bunde Veblen

OBJECTIVES

By reading and studying this chapter, you should acquire the competency to do the following:

- Compare and contrast the six principal research methodologies employed by qualitative researchers, including

  - phenomenology,
  - narrative inquires,
  - grounded theory,
  - ethnography,
  - case study, and
  - consensual qualitative research.

- Describe data collection techniques and approaches for data analysis used with the six qualitative research models.
- Explain how qualitative researchers account for the **reliability** of their work.
- Describe the factors contributing to the trustworthiness of a qualitative research study.
- Describe the elements normally elaborated in a qualitative research report.

INTRODUCTION AND MAJOR THEMES

A common thread in qualitative research is the central role played by the researcher. It is the clinical practitioner serving as a researcher who is the primary assessment instrument used to collect all data and also the means by which data are analyzed. While potential researcher bias is important to recognize and discuss, it is also assumed to be part and parcel of the research process. Special techniques have been developed that can improve the veracity of qualitative research findings by documenting their trustworthiness.

Various methods for conducting qualitative research have been identified since the 1950s. These methods all focus on interpreting the true meaning of the words and/or actions of individuals. The focus of interpretation is to uncover true meanings and reach an in-depth understanding of the nature of human activity and interpersonal interactions. Samples of participants in qualitative studies are typically (but not exclusively) small groups who are selected with a purpose in mind.

Qualitative methods use data collection and analysis approaches outlined in Chapter 4. These methods are frequently combined in a single research effort and can complement each other. This chapter describes six qualitative methods, including phenomenology, several forms of related narrative and text analyses, grounded theory, ethnographic research, various forms of case study research, and consensual qualitative research.

COMPARISON OF QUALITATIVE AND QUANTITATIVE RESEARCH MODELS

The scientific research model was first developed during the era of the Enlightenment (circa 1500–1800 CE) and refined by the empiricists of the 19th century (Comte, 1865/1988). As noted in Chapter 1, the discipline of psychology emerged from the study of "natural philosophy" by adopting the scientific methods of the physical and biological sciences. The scientific method has its own language to objectively describe observations and is highly objective, with a structured set of methods for defining and describing the "true nature of reality." The scientific method tests theories by creating hypotheses, systematically collecting data, and determining the statistical probability that the hypothesis is true.

Qualitative research method is a generic term that describes a series of rigorous approaches for collecting, analyzing, and interpreting data gathered in natural settings. Qualitative research methods emphasize an interpretative core. Practitioner-researchers using a qualitative strategy such as phenomenology or other interpretative methods do not normally use statistical decision making. Unlike empirical researchers, who use large probability samples, qualitatively focused researchers generally use a small number of participants. This sample of participants is often selected with a distinct purpose in mind and is not a randomly created group. The research process is subjective, and both the researcher and the participants engage in the research effort on a person-to-person basis. This involves the researcher's interpersonal skills and clinical capability. As in all interpretative/clinical methods, there is no shortcut, and the researcher should be prepared to invest the time and effort needed to produce a stellar final report.

Another point of comparison between the qualitative and quantitative approaches to research relates to issues of design **validity.** Quantitative researchers use research methods designed to ensure the **fidelity** of observed outcomes with the causal agent introduced by the researcher. In qualitative research, the researcher focuses on **trustworthiness** in lieu of the traditional concept of research validity. This construct is built on a foundation of **credibility, transferability, dependability, and confirmability.**

This chapter describes six major approaches used by those engaged in interpretative research. The final segment of the chapter provides a guide for writing and reporting the results of an interpretative research effort.

QUALITATIVE RESEARCH METHODOLOGIES

Qualitative research methodologies provide complex textual descriptions of the ways individuals in an identified local population experience an ongoing event or activity. Researchers using qualitative methods work to identify culturally specific information from which a deep description can be written to explain human behaviors and activities. Thus, the findings of qualitative research may be specific to a social context or phenomenon. Generalization to other contexts and populations is not guaranteed but is possible (Mack, Woodsong, MacQueen, Guest, & Namey, 2012).

Phenomenology

At the beginning of the 20th century, an ideological crisis occurred in Western philosophy, sciences, polity, and arts (Groenewald, 2004). With the exception of the most esoteric studies in particle physics, the science of the era was seen as sterile and limited by the confines of the philosophy of **positivism.** A prominent figure of the 1920s and 1930s was Edmund G. A. Husserl, a mathematician and philosopher. Professor Husserl developed a new, vibrant philosophical perspective and method designed to break free of the limitations and biases built into positivism. This philosophical framework arrived just as major shifts in approach and methodology were being developed in the arts and sciences. Husserl was the first to propose that objects in our external world may have an independent existence but that we can only be certain about how we perceive them in our conscious thinking. For Husserl, reality as we know it should always be treated as a phenomenon (Eagelton, 2008). This perspective, which has been called **Husserl reductionism,** was the philosophical basis for the development of phenomenological sciences.

CASE IN POINT   5.1

World-Changing Events

Three major disasters had a horrific impact on Europe early in the 20th century. The general malaise and sense of futility that arose from these events contributed to an emerging new philosophical perspective that would take hold in the later 20th century. These three disasters shook the foundation of what had always been assumed to be unchangeable. One was the First World War (1914–1918), which killed 10 million combatants and another 7 million civilians while wounding and maiming another 12 million persons. It reduced the European population by about 3.5% and the population of young men by about one fifth (Meyer, 2007).

The second was the disestablishment of the historic polity along with the loss of the social and political structures that had dominated Europe for a millennium. This involved the dissolution of empires and the impoverishment of the Central Powers of Europe (Austria-Hungry, Bulgaria, Empire of Germany, and Ottoman Empire). World War I, then called the Great War, also brought down hereditary monarchs, impoverished many of the ruling class, and saw the rise of populist governments.

The final major destructive loss was brought about by the Spanish influenza pandemic of 1918–1919, which killed off about 5% of the population of the planet. The pandemic was spread by troops returning home from the battlegrounds of the Great War, thus hitting young adults in the urban centers of Europe and North America especially hard.

Each of these disasters contributed to the upheaval in philosophical thinking and our assumptions about the true nature of mankind and the place of humans in the world. That which had always seemed knowable and immutable now was viewed as a phenomenon that existed only in human cognition.

Husserl had Jewish ancestors and became a problem for his protégé and student Martin Heidegger. Heidegger was an ardent Nazi, and as a party leader, he helped to enforce the "Jewish laws" of 1933. These laws banned Husserl from teaching and publishing and barred him from access to university and state libraries. Heidegger took over Husserl's professorship and in that position modified the concept of phenomenology so as to emphasize the central role of human language. He saw language as transcending mere communication and as being the "dimension in which human life moves." Heidegger believed that human language brings the world into being in the first place (Eagelton, 2008).

Photo 5.1 and 5.2   Photographs of Professors Heidegger (left) and Husserl (right)

Wikimedia Commons.

Wikimedia Commons

World War II brought another international upheaval and saw new philosophies begin where Husserl and Heidegger left off. The philosophical existentialism of Jean-Paul Sartre and Maurice Merleau-Ponty extended the language-centric phenomenological theory of Heidegger into a new philosophy that Thomas Kuhn (1996) described as the new world-view. Kuhn believed that, as a result of the emergence of this new worldview, a paradigmatic shift was taking place in scientific thinking. This new philosophical model gained acceptance in the latter half of the 20th century.

Sartre, a French intellectual and philosopher, built a new phenomenal perspective around the proposition that human consciousness is equivalent to freedom and beyond the causal effects of the world. Consciousness is what makes reality possible and is dynamic and self-motivated (Sartre, 2001).[1] The second great French philosopher of phenomenology, Maurice Merleau-Ponty (1945/1976), developed a phenomenological model for rejecting the mind-body dualism and offered a model for human perception. Later in his life, he ended his friendship with Sartre over what he thought to be Sartre's "ultra-Bolshevik beliefs" (Sartre, p. 2).

Clark Moustakas (1994) proposed a deemphasis of the role of the researcher in interpreting participant responses and focus instead on the participants' descriptions. The goal of this transcendental phenomenology is to bring together the descriptions of several participants of a shared phenomenon and draw out of the participants' descriptions the true essence of their shared phenomenological experience.

The ultimate goal of the researcher who works from a transcendental phenomenological perspective is that after reading a report, the reader will know the perspective of the participants about what it was truly like to experience the phenomena under study (Creswell, 2012). For example, a practitioner-researcher may write a phenomenological report based on therapeutic contact with parents who have lost a young child to a devastating illness (e.g., craniopharyngioma). The shared essence of their grief could be the focus of the phenomenological report.

Analysis of Phenomenological Data

The phenomenological research process of bringing together individual perceptions, and finding the core meaning and true essence of what they share, starts with the participants' statements. Next comes the data reduction step, including the identification through transcript analysis of core and shared statements. This leads to the identification of common themes and shared meanings. The resulting written report provides a statement of the phenomenon's essential, invariant, structure (Creswell, 2008).

Applications from the Literature

Excerpts from a Phenomenological Analysis of Interview Data

Note: The study focused on the lived experiences of nine mothers on their first child's initial day of kindergarten. The mothers were thought to have been marginalized when they were girls and in the lower grades. The mothers were all European Americans who had dropped out of junior or senior high school and who had a child while they were still in school. Each was paid $50 for volunteering to be interviewed.

What Mothers Were Like: Starting kindergarten means letting go—and that is hard. Although mothers talked about the experience of sending children to kindergarten as occurring over a long period of time, the first day of kindergarten was an event that precipitated strong emotional reactions. Here are the words of three mothers:

> *Mother # 1: I put Jason on that bus to go to his first day of kindergarten and I cried and I cried and I cried and I cried.*

> *Mother # 2: It was hard. In fact, I cried. I stood there and cried.*

> *Mother # 3: I cried. I cried, and I cried hard.*

Separation for the purpose of going to kindergarten was eagerly anticipated by some mothers. Even so, the separation on the first day of kindergarten was poignant and emotionally intense. The separation was short—maybe three hours until the mothers saw their children again. But the separation on the first day of kindergarten seemed to have been symbolic of loosening ties that bound mothers and children. They understood this to be a major step in the process of their children growing up.

The separation for kindergarten gave the mothers pause to consider how rapidly the preschool years had gone by. Their children were infants, then suddenly they were in kindergarten, and soon they would be out of high school. Time was going by so quickly, and with the passage of time, their separation from their children would increase.

Source: McClelland, J. (1995). Sending children to kindergarten: A phenomenological study of mother's experiences. *Family Relations, 44*(2), 177–183.

Narrative Inquiry

Research inquiry based on analysis of narrative material (written, spoken, and drawn) has been described as potentially involving various forms of science, history, and literature (Riessman, 1993). As a research method it is clearly interdisciplinary. This form of qualitative research can present one person's life story or the lived experiences of two or more individuals. Narratives include any discourse and/or written text material (Creswell, 2008). Most narratives in social science research take the form of stories giving an account of events and or actions.

Storytelling by individuals is a universal human activity and one of the first forms of discourse each of us learn as children (Riessman, 1993). In every culture, children go through several developmental phases in their story-development and telling ability. Storytelling is so natural that almost all reports of an event take the form of a story that is told in a temporal sequence of perceived occurrences composing the event. Riessman went on to make the point that research participants often attempt to hold the floor and create long answers in the form of a storyline in response to a researcher's open-ended question. One strategy commonly used to hold the floor is the use of the word *and* to link several clauses. This provides the speaker with a moment to mentally regroup and begin talking again.

Creswell (2008) described two primary forms for narrative inquiry. One, **analysis of narratives,** involves identifying and describing themes common across the stories of various individuals. The other, **narrative analysis,** occurs when the researcher collects descriptions of happenings and events and then organizes them into a storyline, or **restories** the recalled material.

A variation of narrative inquiry involves spoken descriptions of past events and activities by one or more individuals with firsthand experience. The remembered accounts provided by participants can be coded and organized into a meaningful restoried whole, providing the essence of what transpired and what the participants lived (Riessman, 1993). The resulting research report from the narrative analysis is described as an **oral history.**

CASE IN POINT   5.2

Oral history is widely employed today to preserve and document the historical record of important occurrences still in the memories of individual witnesses and participants. It is also the vehicle used to preserve the firsthand history of the atrocities of the recent past that some groups may want to repress.[2]

Oral history archives are housed in Holocaust museums around the United States and throughout much of the Western world. These archives preserve the stories of survivors of the horror that descended on Europe during the 1930s and 1940s—the 6 million deaths and untold suffering by millions more during the 13 years of the German Third Reich. It is an obligation of a civilized society to always maintain such records. When these records are not kept, future generations have a tendency to gloss over and eventually forget what once happened. It is the task of each generation to gather and preserve the record and oral history of such events. (The national archive of oral histories from the European Holocaust can be seen at http://www .ushmm.org/research/collections/oralhistory/.)

More recently, over 800,000 men, women, and children were killed in a genocide rarely discussed in the Western media. That slaughter occurred in the small African nation of Rwanda.

In the 21st century, genocide in the Horn of Africa is leading to the death and brutalization of non-Arab tribal peoples in southern Sudan and Darfur. The death toll before Sudan was divided into two nation-states was in the range of 300,000.[3]

Another direction for narrative research is provided by the Internet. A huge number of chatrooms, bulletin boards, and forums provide support for individuals. While many of these are designed to make a point or tout a product or politician, most are legitimate and potentially helpful for individuals. Issues covered on such forums and the give and take of comments by participants provide a rich source of data for social science researchers. The use of online dialogues requires special steps to maintain the appropriate level of ethical practice by the researcher. The extra steps involve obtaining permission from the host and webmaster of the page, as well as providing informed consent to and obtaining permission from all participants.

Applications from the Literature

Example of Online Narrative Research from an Online Support Group for Blended Families

Note: After obtaining permission from the webmaster and forum participants, the author monitored the postings on an Internet bulletin board support system for stepfamily members over a 2-month period. The postings were all from and to group members who were stepmothers.

Method: Data for this study were obtained from a website devoted to providing blended family support.... The website ... chat room called the "Forum" ... acts as an online support group for the members. The Forum is a message board on which the members can post and/or respond to a message. Responses are posted below the original message so that other members can differentiate easily between them. For the most part, the postings come from members of blended families dealing with difficult family issues. However, there are occasional announcements of good news as well. The narratives utilized in this study were found on the Forum; therefore, discussion of the results will focus on the Forum.... Many of the Forum members, however, displayed thorough knowledge of the other members' family situations, lives, etc. via their postings. When reading the postings, one sensed a genuine feeling of concern among the Forum's members about each other's issues. Because of these characteristics, the Forum stood out as characteristic of the criteria necessary for a successful support group, such as a place where members experience mutual support, engage in catharsis, and develop social networks....

In order to begin analysis of the postings on the Forum, the webmaster for the site was contacted to obtain permission to both post the study on the Forum and to inform participants of the author's intent to create an article based on the discussion themes on the Forum with the condition of anonymity of all Forum members....

All of the online postings were coded three times. During the first coding phase, the printouts of the ... postings were read and initial notes were made of the general themes that began to emerge. Next, all of the newly emergent themes were assigned a color. The postings were then read a second time to verify the existence and accuracy of the emergent themes, and statements were then highlighted (according to the appropriate color) as representatives of the emergent themes. Finally, index cards were created for quick reference that contained quotes and their themes. To most thoroughly code the narrative postings, the present study focused on both the manifest and the latent content of the postings, which are the most reliable means of uncovering the surface meaning as well as the underlying meaning of a participant's statement or narrative.

Source: Christian, A. (2005). Contesting the myth of the "wicked stepmother": Narrative analysis of an online stepfamily support group. *Western Journal of Communication, 69*(1), 27–47. doi: 10.1080/10570310500034030

Narrative Research Processes

Interpretative analysis is used in narrative studies to identify critical themes emerging from the spoken dialogue. This analysis examines the data for factors that enabled and constraints that limited the narrator's performance. In this analysis, several informative issues may surface, including how the narrators interpreted what occurred, what social resources helped and/or hindered them, and their cognitive strategy and approach to problem solving.

Steps for Interpretative Narrative Analysis: The idiosyncratic nature of narrative research resists being sequenced into a step-by-step process. Creswell (2008) provided five general tasks that are normally completed in narrative research.

1. Verify that narrative research can provide the best answer to the research problem.

2. Identification of a few select individuals with good memory of the events and who have good stories about their lived experience to tell. Over several interviews, collect and transcribe the participants' raw narrations. Search for diaries, correspondence, old photographs, and other artifacts associated with the individual that can assist in telling and interpreting what occurred.

3. Place the narrator and his or her story in the correct social, cultural, and historical context at the time the activity occurred.

4. Organize the narrator's stories into a framework that provides a sequence with a beginning, middle, and ending. This framework provides an understandable new storyline. This step is described by Creswell as restorying. The beginning of the new storyline provides the context and setting for the activities to follow. The middle identifies the problem or conflict, the antagonist(s), and the main character. Between the middle and the ending there may be a description of an epiphany that results in a dramatic change in the direction of the storyline. These moments of personal insight and growth are often found in biographies and autobiographies of important figures. For example, the conversion of Malcolm X to Islam changed his life from one dominated by identity confusion and petty crime to one of religious devotion (Haley, 1965). In another case, President Obama had an epiphany on a trip to visit relatives in Kenya before he began law school (Obama, 1995). Not all restories will provide a denouement; however, such a change in the storyline should be carefully analyzed and explained whenever it occurs.

5. Creswell's last task for narrative researchers is one that should occur throughout the narrative research activity. Researchers should work in close collaboration with participants and negotiate the interpretation and meaning of the narrated stories. The validity of the researchers' conclusions is enhanced when the narrative analysis is a collaborative endeavor.

Quantitative Analysis of Narrative Texts

Powerful new software provides researchers with a versatile quantitative tool for the analysis of text material. Evaluations provide clinical markers for possible themes in the text or transcript.

Semantic Text Analysis: A researcher can use the software to search and identify words and phrases that the researcher has coded. These codes can be selected through the interpretative analysis of narrative material or from a theoretical model. The software makes it possible for a single researcher to analyze tens of thousands of pages of transcribed written narratives and identify latent patterns within the data.

The meaning of a sentence is rarely revealed by its surface grammar. Semantic analytical tools are designed to identify the latent patterns of meaning that lie within a long narrative or across many shorter statements (Mehl, 2006). There are over two dozen programs available for use by practitioner-researchers. These are reviewed and described on the following web page by Professor Kimberly Neuendorf of Cleveland State University: http://academic.csuohio.edu/kneuendorf/content/cpuca/qtap.htm.

Hermeneutical Analysis: This form of narrative analysis is conducted to describe the deep or latent meaning of culture and human practices as revealed through the arts and/or written texts of a group of people. This type of analysis originally took its name from the ancient Greek god Hermes, son of Zeus and the nymph Maia, who was the eloquent herald and messenger among the various gods and between the gods and mankind[4] (Burkert, 1991).

The practice of **hermeneutics** involves wide reading of source material linked to the research question being explored. The analysis may involve texts and/or art or other creative products, including news editorials and even advertising copy. Hermeneutics is a research methodology designed to reach deep understanding of text material. This deep understanding is produced through a systematic interpretative process. The hermeneutic research process involves developing a **hermeneutic circle** (Schmidt, 1996).

Applications from the Literature

Excerpt from Study Using Hermeneutic Analysis

Note: Using a form of hermeneutic analysis, the authors studied transcripts from clients receiving long-term psychotherapy. This approach made it possible to reconcile the wide time frame and differing therapeutic dialogues.

Aggregation of Findings: This process of correction and elaboration can be considered as an answer to those who ask how qualitative research can be aggregated. Observations are aggregated by metamorphosis of the understanding rather than by simple accretion. Each new observation changes the previous understanding, but the new understanding must also encompass the previous observations. That is, the model is not static or fixed but continually growing, even though its name remains the same. This process has been described as the hermeneutic cycle. Having a name (i.e., assimilation model) for the evolving understanding underlines the continuity of this process.

Source: Stiles, W. B., & Angus, L. (2001). Qualitative research on client's assimilation of problematic experiences in psychotherapy. *Psychologische Beiträge, 43*(3), 112–117.

A hermeneutic circle or cycle describes how the understanding of a text or artwork as a whole can only be accomplished by understanding various parts or examples. This insight into the meaning of the parts is only possible by knowing the whole; thus one has a circle and a conundrum. To escape from the circle and find the true meaning of the whole body (corpus) of material, the researcher must have an understanding of the historical, cultural, political, and literary context of the era of the text.[5]

Discourse and Conversation Analysis[6]: Another variation of narrative analysis involves the study of human discourse and conversations. The discourse may be formal like a legal deposition, take the form of social conversation, or be drawn from a semistructured setting such as a focus group. The principles and methods of transcription and narrative analysis apply to the study of discourse.

Conversation analysis is usually done with the aid of a digital video recording of the communication among people as it occurs (Peräkylä, 2005). Collecting data can be as simple as setting up a digital video recorder in the room where a conversation takes place (Gee, 2010). James Gee even argued that video games and interactions individuals have with them also qualify for conversation analysis. He averred that video games require a form of interactive communication, albeit with a software program.

Tools of conversation analysis are multilayered. Three primary assumptions guiding discourse analysis include **gaze,** gestures, and action (Peräkylä, 2005). The tool kit for assessing the transcribed text version of verbal interactions includes speaker overlaps, rate of speaking, pitch and intensity, openings, turn taking, closings, laughter, reversals of position, and many others.

The assumption of gaze holds that the researcher is not a passive collector of words but has an informed way to gaze on the raw material being analyzed (Hausendorf & Bora, 2006). The researcher cannot escape the constructive process of selecting what is salient and what is not needed from the transcript. A second, more corporal interpretation of gaze deals with eye contact and is described with the assumption of action.

The assumption that talk is action includes hand movements, body positioning, and gaze. There is a significant cultural component to this assumption, and interpretations of speech actions must be made within the appropriate context. Hand gestures during conversation and discourse have been studied as being either manipulative or semaphoric. The semaphoric nature includes arm and hand gestures, while the manipulative gestures are the movements of the fingers with materials and objects (Quek et al., 2002).

The research process with discourse analysis starts with a transcript of the conversation. This running transcript is examined for salient components. Each of these central parts of the conversation can be matched with the video of the moment when the words were uttered. This facilitates linking observational data on actions with the words being spoken. (See the student website for an example of discourse analysis used to uncover latent dimensions in the personality of a "hardened criminal.")

Grounded Theory

The primary goal of grounded theory is the identification of higher-order concepts leading to the discovery or development of a theory. As the new theory is based on data collected in the field, it is described as being a theory grounded in data (B. G. Glaser & Strauss, 1967). As grounded theory starts with data and works toward the development of a theory, it does not begin with a hypothesis or even a finalized research question (Punch, 2005). Data from the field in a grounded study provide information about the social processes among participants and their actions, interactions, and reactions (Creswell, 2008).

Variations in Grounded Theory

There are several approaches to grounded theory beyond the original Glaser and Strauss model. One of these is an outcome of a debate between the two principals of the field, Barney Glaser and Anselm Strauss. The Glaserian model employs a more reflective approach to the development of codes for organizing the raw data into categories. The Strausian approach is more analytical than the grounded theory research proposed by Glaser. The Strauss approach uses substantive codes and appears less casual, focusing on causal relationships, intervening or moderating factors, and actions and consequences.

Another form of grounded theory, proposed by Kathy Charmaz (2006), rejects the structuralism of both the Glaserian and Strausian methods. She preferred a model for developing grounded theory with a constructivist perspective. The interpretative component of the research involves identifying words, phrases, and descriptions that are cogent to the participant (Creswell, 2008). As do proponents of other grounded theory approaches, Charmaz began by identifying participants who could provide a rich source of data. The process then involves coding and category and concept building, as it works to build a "suggestive" conclusion, not a firm theory.

Literature Reviews in Grounded Theory Studies

Unlike other forms of research, grounded theory does not expect the researcher to have a solid background in the scientific literature related to the topic of the study. If a theory and model for explanation already existed, there would be no need to do grounded theory research. The researcher attempts to have an open mind as he or she begins to collect and analyze the study's data (Punch, 2005). The following URL connects with a short lecture by Barney Glaser about the role of the literature review in grounded theory research: http://www.youtube.com/watch?v=7S1kJ0k3yHk.

Grounded Research Participants

The goal of grounded theory is to understand what is happening in a research situation (Dick, 2000). This approach involves using qualitative data to discover the guiding theory implicit within it. Grounded theory is truly an emergent approach in which the theory emerges from raw data (Glaser, 1992).[7] Grounded theory research begins with a general sense of a problem area for exploration. The topic of interest is one that does not already have a clear or evident theory or explanation. Next, the researcher identifies two or three potential participants, or informants, who are interviewed in depth. These participants are purposefully chosen to match a **theoretical sample** of interest to the researcher. Following the initial data gathering, subsequent small, purposeful samples of participants are then identified, and more data are collected. These participants add to the theoretical sample and enable the researcher to enhance the study's validity and potentially employ triangulation in the process of theory development.

For example, a theory of stress induced by examination anxiety built using a sample of residential undergraduates between the age of 18 and 23 years may not be appropriate for a group of returning adults working toward a degree while raising a family or to commuting students. By sampling from different groups and even in different settings, it is possible to build a meaningful database that can be analyzed with the potential for transferability.

Data Collecting

Any number of different qualitative data collection methods may be used, including interviews, informal conversation, group feedback, or other field-based activity that results in interpretable qualitative data (Dick, 2000). Glaser (1992) averred that researchers should avoid recording or note taking during the interviewing process. Bob Dick suggested doing critical-word note taking as well as audiotaping. Critical words can be used to cue the researcher as to where during the taped interview he or she should focus. Perhaps the best approach is to employ a "nanny cam." Once participants are informed and give their permission to have the interview recorded, these unobtrusive (almost hidden) video cameras can provide an exact record and not interfere with the interview process. Video recordings also have the advantage of showing the posture and body language participants use when being interviewed (Onwuegbuzie, Leech, & Collins, 2010).

Coding Process

Data collected during the first round of interviews are carefully analyzed to learn how the informants interpret the experience or phenomenon and identify the steps in its development. These data are organized by theme using **open coding** for the categories based on reoccurring words, phrases, and ideas. John Creswell (2008) argued that this initial list of coded themes should be limited to about 12 categories (codes). Codes may go beyond the manifest and easily observed and involve latent undercurrents in the data.

The first reading through the text materials and the formation of the initial collection of coded categories involves careful perusal. It also involves examining all source data for how those components of data address the overall research question (Corbin & Strauss, 2008). In this process, the reader makes marginal notes and reflects on what was found while reading. On a subsequent reading, the researcher edits and organizes categories to define them more clearly and verifies that the categories (codes) are all-inclusive for the elements of the data set. Finally, the categories must be mutually exclusive.

This initial exploration provides the basis for a return to the field for more interviews, cued with the previously developed conceptualization of the process from the first-round interviews. New data collection field trips are part of the recursive process. Data collection and analysis are ongoing and concurrent processes. With subsequent rounds of data collection using ever more refined open-ended questions and a continuing coding process, the open codes will become more clearly defined. This process has been described as the "constant comparative method" (Strauss & Corbin, 1990). This process ends when the researcher identifies a point of **saturation**. That point occurs when there is no longer a need for more interviews as no new information is being gained by the interview effort. Creswell (2008) suggested this point could be reached with anywhere between 20 and 60 interviews.

Figure 5.1   Coding and Theory Development

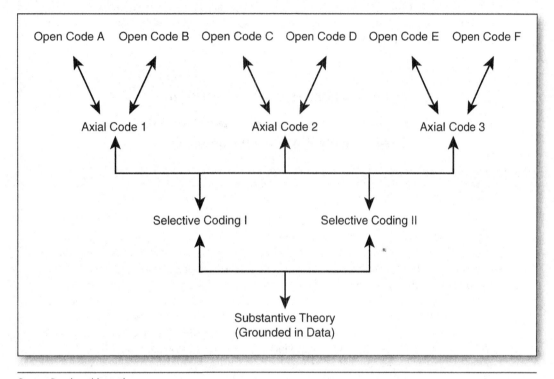

Source: Developed by author.

The coded data are then reorganized to provide a meaningful structure or organization. This involves identifying connections between categories. Connections may be in the form of concepts that are superordinate and subordinate to each other, or the concepts may form a continuum across the categories. New assigned codes are referred to as **axial codes.** The process of identifying axial codes considers the special conditions when categories interact and what the outcomes or consequences are for interactions with possible core phenomena. It also takes into consideration likely causal conditions and the strategies deployed by participants in the action. Researchers occasionally also collect artifacts, do direct observations, and gather other sources of information to assist in the identification and definition of the new structure created through axial coding.

Selective coding follows the open and axial coding phases of the research. The process provides the interpretative phase of the study. In selective coding, the researcher organizes a unified storyline or explanation that unites the axial coding and provides a testable statement of predictive relationships within the data. This process may be supplemented by the inclusion of a flowchart portraying the cause-effect linkages and identifying moderating influences on the identified relationships. The outcome of this final step is the development of a new theory. (See the student website for an example of grounded theory being used in the study of the relationship process with couples in healthy marriages.)

The ultimate value of a grounded theory is its clarity or understandability and its fit with new data. The new theory must be able to account for outcomes represented by data from new cases and in other venues.

Applications from the Literature

Example of Strausian Coding in a Grounded Theory Study With School Counselors

Note: The purpose of the study was to describe social justice strategies used by school counselors to promote change in their settings. The research question guiding the study was "What advocacy strategies do school counselors who self-identify as social justice advocates use to enact change within their school communities?"

Data Collection: Recursivity was built into each stage of the research process so that simultaneous data collection and analysis continuously informed each other and, in turn, the emerging grounded theory. After the first two interviews were transcribed, four research team members individually reviewed and coded the transcripts using an open coding process. Open coding involved analyzing each line or paragraph of the transcripts for codes reflecting each participant's experiences. More specifically, each discrete idea, event, or experience was given a name (e.g., "courage," "dialoguing," "student empowerment"). To create a codebook for the remaining interviews, researchers used constant comparison with their discrete codes to identify categories that related to a common overarching concept and to discern any discrepancies between their discrete codes.

After each interview was conducted, transcribed, and coded using this codebook, we utilized axial coding to examine the relationship between each of the preestablished categories.

Source: Singh, A. A., Urbano, A., Haston, M., & McMahon, E. (2010). School counselors' strategies for social justice change: A grounded theory of what works in the real world. *Professional School Counseling, 13*(3), 135–145.

Ethnographic Research

The central goal of **ethnographic research** is to develop a deep understanding of the culture of an identifiable group, business, organization, or community (Spradley, 1980). The research question is one that provides a general theme and direction for the study. Specific research questions may be developed later as the observational data are subjected to one of several analytical methods. While developing the research question, the ethnographer also reflects on his or her possible biases and records them for inclusion later in the research report.

Preparation for beginning an ethnographic study requires the researcher to become immersed in the history, religion, rituals, language, and norms of the group to be studied. This may involve learning a new dialect of the researcher's own language or mastering a completely new language.

The researcher almost always records data from ethnographic research by hand in his or her field notes. These notes are likely to cover a number of volumes before the study reaches the point of saturation. The notes themselves should start with a clear description of the setting and environment. Next, they should describe the actors who are participants in the study and their official and unofficial relationships with each other.

Field notes may also contain one-to-one and/or group interview data along with numerous other items, including anecdotal accounts, observations of social and ritualistic behaviors, media preferences and use of technology, digital photographs of scenes or items too difficult to describe, belief systems, totems and ancestral lineages, discourse among participants, and artifacts that are part of the culture. Raw field notes should be organized each day and recopied. Along with recopying, the ethnographer should make a marginal note of recurrent themes, commonalities of language meanings and intent, and ritualistic behaviors. Additionally, the field notes should have marginal notes recording the researcher's hunches about the possible meanings of what was observed.

Cartoon 5.1   "Unobtrusive Observations"

"I love having a snack outside, but I always have the feeling that we are being observed around here."

Cartoon by Merv Magus.

Ethnographic Research Method

The researcher's focus is on a total culture-sharing group. Thus, the ethnographic study normally involves 20 or more active participants. To develop an understanding of the group's culture, the research takes place where the participants live and/or work together. The **ethnographer** becomes a participant in the community and an observer of the interactions and activities of the participants (Creswell, 2008). The researcher eventually becomes part of the ongoing activity. One classification of ethnographic research is the **realistic approach** developed by cultural anthropologists in the early 20th century.

This realistic approach takes the form of an anthropologist (or other researcher) learning a tribal culture by assuming the role of another member of the community, such as the Inuit people of the far north, by participating in customs, struggles, and daily life as a member of the tribal group. In this case, the final report is a straightforward factual account of what occurred and how the researcher interpreted those activities (Creswell, 2008). It could also be a study of the peer culture in a drug rehabilitation facility for adolescents or of the culture of very old people living in an assisted-living community.

Getting In

Clearly, most practitioner-researchers cannot be convincing in role-playing a North Slope Inuit, a teenager, or a frail octogenarian. To obtain untainted field data, the researcher must develop a trusting relationship with the community. This process is described as **getting in.** It may begin by making friends of a few group members first who can serve as gatekeepers, opening a way for the ethnographer to get in.

There is a potential for ethical problems as a researcher gains access and collects data from a community. It may not be possible to sit down and explain the research and gain informed consent from all members of the group. That problem notwithstanding, it is never appropriate or ethical to gain access by using a ruse to secretly become part of the community. For example, a less ethical researcher could enter the rehabilitation facility in the guise of a volunteer staff member or as a custodial aid.

Permission to conduct research is needed first. This may be from a center's director or from a tribal council. Many group leaders may be flattered by the attention. However, if there has been a bad history of relationships with outsiders, the research may never get off the ground. The membership of the group also needs to provide their consent. This may occur during a meeting of the tribe or group with the researcher and the leadership that provided its permission. During this session, the emphasis should be on overcoming inhibitions and assuring group members of confidentiality and as much anonymity as is possible within the research model and the limits of laws. When community members believe in the researcher's good intent and his or her devotion to high ethical standards and to the project, access will be maximized (Hannan, 2006).

Critical Ethnography

Creswell (2008) proposed a second major type of ethnography, **critical ethnography,** which advocates for the needs of marginalized groups within the larger society. For example, a researcher may use ethnography to study the culture and socialization of adolescents attending a segregated academy in the Mississippi Delta or the culture of law enforcement officers working in US counties bordering Mexico. The ethnographic reports from critical ethnography tend to be value laden and advocate for change.

With either approach, a key to being a successful ethnographer is keeping clear, accurate, and updated field notes. The presence of a notebook or recording device can be off-putting and may shut down communication with some group members. One method researchers have used involves scribbling a word list on a small pad of sticky notes or on a small deck of note cards kept in a pocket. If asked, the researcher may reply that he or she must scribble an occasional personal "reminder." Another method is to send the brief reminder notes in a text message to a colleague. As soon as possible after leaving the field setting, the researcher's cryptic jottings must be elaborated and turned into a full set of field notes for the day.

Applications from the Literature

Two Examples from Methods Sections in Ethnographic Studies

Example A: Critical Ethnography

Note: Getting in is a term ethnographers use to refer to the process of establishing trust within a specific community or culture (Fetterman, 1989). In terms of this study, the first step in gaining acceptance was to participate in meetings of the Lesbian, Gay, and Bisexual Student Alliance (LGBSA), the formal organization that arguably forms the center of the gay and bisexual student subculture. The focus of the research was on the role of the LGB student culture in the decision of individuals to come out.

Methodology: Ethnographic techniques were used to explore the experiences of gay and bisexual college men at "Eastern University" during parts of the academic years from 1991 to 1993. For Geertz (1973),[8] ethnography seeks as its goal what he described as **"thick description,"** which most often is achieved through extensive and intensive involvement in the culture of a group under study (in this case a student subculture). Participant observation, formal and informal interviews, key informants, and document analysis were used as part of this study. The use of multiple data-collection methods provides opportunities for the ethnographer to cross-check one's findings—a process that [has been] discussed as "triangulation." The formal interviews followed methods for ethnographic interviewing suggested by Spradley (1979),[9] in which descriptive, structural, and contrast questions were developed. The interviews were tape-recorded and transcribed verbatim.

Source: Rhoads, R. A. (1997). A subcultural study of gay and bisexual males: Resisting developmental inclinations. *Journal of Higher Education, 68*(4), 460–482.

Example B: Realist Ethnography (Example of Sampling Employed in an Ethnographic Interview Research Study)

Note: Option 1 refers to having the therapist conduct an ethnographic interview with clients immediately following the therapy session. Option 2 involved having a different clinician conduct the interviews with the clients following their session with the therapist.

(Continued)

(Continued)

Sample Selection: In Option 1, three couples, one family, and three individuals were interviewed twice over a 4-month period concerning their reactions to and perceptions of family therapy practice. In Option 2, three couples, two families, and two individuals were interviewed twice over the same 4-month period; overall, 14 clients were interviewed. As stated earlier, the term *client*, as used in this context, referred to a single unit (i.e., individual, marital, or family) but included all spouses, significant others, nuclear, blended, or extended members within that unit that arrived at the counseling session. Clients who requested counseling services at the clinic were informed about the research project by their counselor and were given a choice of whether or not to participate in the study. Therapists included four doctoral students, [one male and one female] from the school of social work, and one male and one female from a doctoral program in marriage and family therapy. The therapists' level of experience ranged from 1 to 6 years. Clients were selected using an opportunistic sampling strategy. Opportunistic sampling was well suited for this study because generalization to a population was not the research goal. Instead, the goal was to generate vivid descriptions of the effectiveness of family therapy practice within a single setting. Sampling of new clients ended when theoretical saturation was reached within each category (Strauss & Corbin, 1990).[10] This meant that each new interview or observation yielded no new or relevant data regarding a particular category.

Source: Sells, S. P., Smith, T., E., & Moon, S. (1996). An ethnographic study of client and therapist perceptions of therapy effectiveness in a university-based training clinic. *Journal of Family Therapy, 22*(3), 321–342. doi: 10.1111/j.1752-0606.1996 .tb00209.x

Case Study

Case study is an approach used in qualitative research to explain or describe an individual, a community, a system, or an event. When focused on a single case, the study is described as a **within-site case study.** The case study report may describe more than one study and make comparisons or explain concordances between them in a process known as **multisite case study.** The latter approach provides outcomes that have more generalizability to other cases in other venues (Yin, 2008). Alternatively, the approach may focus on one case (e.g., an award-winning rowing club). Once underway, the researcher may elect to focus on three exemplar members of the men's coxed eight boat. This case study within a case study is described as a **nested design.** Each case should be studied in depth and over time to better understand the system, event, or people involved. When multiple case studies or nested case studies are included in one report, it is possible to make crossover comparisons and identify more reliable explanations and present deeper descriptions (Patton, 2002; Stake, 1995).

Case Selection

To select a case to study, the researcher must first decide the direction and focus the study will take. It could be to focus on just one issue and explain it in depth with a case study. This type of research, known as an **instrumental case** study, needs to identify one exemplar case (Creswell, 2008).

Researchers using an instrumental case study approach focus intensively on an individual or identifiable group known as a **bound group.** A bound group may be an individual person or an entire clinic's staff. Typically, cases that are normative or quotidian do not provide the best data for an instrumental case study. Informants in the environment may help the researcher identify stellar examples or cases that have a potential to be the most revealing and instructive for the analysis. In all systems, there are certain events and individuals that can provide a key to understanding a principle or developing a new conceptualization. For example, in conducting a case study of the motivations of therapists working in hospices, those recognized for their clinical skill by the families of individuals who have died could be considered key cases, whereas other clinical employees in the same centers may not be able to present similarly well-reasoned insights and knowledge.

If the goal of a case study is to explain an activity, phenomena, or issue, one bound group may be too limiting and unable to show various dimensions and variations. This may call for combining several case studies into a **multiple case study** by integrating their data. These case studies can be conducted either as a nested grouping or as several stand-alone exemplar cases.

Applications from the Literature

Example of a Case Description in a Case Study Research Study

Note: The focus of the study was on employing a therapeutic intervention for a 4-year-old who suffered posttraumatic stress disorder (PTSD). The approach involved engaging the child's guardian as a cotherapist working with the youngster.

Results: Alonzo (pseudonym), a Hispanic 4 year and 9 month old boy, presented with his grandmother, age 57 years, for treatment due to trauma-related symptoms (e.g., angry outbursts, difficulty sleeping, withdrawn, and encopresis). When Alonzo was 5-months-old, he was physically abused by his biological parents. Alonzo was removed from his biological parents and placed with his paternal grandparents, who then adopted him. Alonzo had recently started unsupervised visits with his biological parents. Three and a half months prior to treatment, Alonzo was visiting with his biological mother and father when he witnessed his biological father hit his paternal grandfather in the face and his biological mother and grandmother yelling at each other. The grandmother, who Alonzo calls his mother, reported that after Alonzo witnessed the fight, his mood and behavior significantly changed (e.g., not social, not as happy as he was, difficult time going to sleep, more aggressive). Also, Alonzo began having difficulty with his bowel movements and he began wearing diapers. Alonzo saw his pediatrician due to encopresis and the doctor recommended that Alonzo see a psychotherapist. Alonzo saw a psychologist for approximately five sessions, but the grandmother reported that there was no progress and they dropped out of treatment. However, due to worsening of Alonzo's behavior and encopresis, she sought treatment again and enrolled in the current study. Of note, the grandmother was college educated but was not working due to taking care of an elderly parent. The grandfather, a graduate of high school, had a landscape business and the annual household family income was $50,000.

Source: Salloum, A., & Storch, E. A. (2011). Parent-led, therapist-assisted, first-line treatment for young children after trauma: A case study. *Child Maltreatment, 16*(3), 227–232. doi: 10.1177/1077559511415099

Case Analysis

The bottom line is to write a case study report based on multiple sources of information drawn from the case. The problem is that case studies provide the researcher with a great amount of data that is often difficult to organize and interpret (Baxter & Jack, 2008). An easy trap for the researcher using the case study method to fall into is becoming distracted by superfluous, but nonetheless interesting, information. To avoid stepping into the minutia, researchers should continually relate findings to the stated research question or problem. Research questions guide the case study's data collection and analysis and provide limitations.

Researchers employing a case study method may employ a **holistic** interpretation of an entire case, including tracing and charting past events leading to the current scene, precipitant members of the group, and the current status of the case (Creswell, 2008). This may include summarized data from semistructured interviews. The final write-up may also include a description of the historical sequence of events leading to the current situation, a cross-check of facts and records, an examination and description of artifacts, and direct observations in the field by the researcher.

Alternatively, data interpretation may be completed by employing an **embedded analysis** of specific case dimensions. Case studies can be designed to portray the nature of the activities and functioning of several individuals embedded in the case. For example, a holistic case study of a college sorority's ability to support members and reduce the stress of college life can be enhanced by the addition of several embedded case studies such as intermember tutoring or of the annual recruiting of a new pledge class. Embedded case studies may include empirical data; in the study of the sorority, data might be included about the backgrounds of the members of the pledge class.

Embedded analyses, or **analyses-within-the-case,** include a number of areas for concern by the researcher, including the background of events precipitating the current scene, the environment and other individuals within it, and the social and/or political context in which the case and participants operate (Stake, 2005).

Case Report

One approach used in organizing the final case study report is a storytelling format (Baxter & Jack, 2008). This is much like high-quality investigative journalism and provides a way to tie the key elements into a description that readers can readily understand (Denny, 2011). In building the story of the case, the researcher draws together the various sources of data and, through a triangulation process, develops interpretative conclusions (Yin, 2008). In the interpretation process, it is important to refer to previous literature and link what was just learned with what was previously reported.

Behaviorally Focused Case Studies

A tool in the kit of all behaviorally focused counselors is the ability to make careful observations and cogent interpretations of behavior. Observations and their interpretations can be reliable or potentially flawed sources of information. To improve the reliability of unstructured observations, a counselor should have a clear idea of what is being observed and why. For example, an aggressive child's interactions with others may be the theme that guides observations.

Counselor observations can be made over a range of cognitive, motor, and social-emotional behaviors. Counselors should always be aware of their own biases and prejudices. These may reflect personal values, religious beliefs, ethnicity, and/or the social class with which the counselor identifies. Before interpreting observations, a counselor should examine himself or herself for biased notions about the client being observed. Another task for the observer is to be unobtrusive so as not to change the participant's natural behavior pattern simply by being present.

Time Sampling: One systematic observational technique is **time sampling.** This is one of three systems for organizing observations, the other two being **interval sampling** and **frequency sampling** (Repp, Roberts, Slack, Repp, & Berkler, 1976). Time sampling involves using an observational checklist and a time counter. First, the timer is set to a useful observation interval (e.g., 60 seconds). The observation is made and recorded on the checklist at the prescribed time interval. Observations continue for the duration of the observation session. Sessions should occur at different times during the time block set aside for observing.

Interval and Frequency Sampling: This method is employed to observe a simple target behavior (e.g., aggression toward a member of a therapy group). During specified time frames, the actual amount of time spent on one or the other condition is recorded and tabulated. Frequency sampling has the observer count how many unique incidences of a particular behavior occur over a time frame.

Event Sampling: Another observational approach is **event sampling.** This involves making periodic observations during a limited time frame (e.g., of patients in the dayroom of a residential rehabilitation facility) and determining in which activities the individual participates. The most efficient method is to make a digital video of the activity, then conduct observations later by using checklists for one or more clients being observed.

Data Recording: As the researcher observes many points of data for an individual client that are sequenced temporally, these behavioral case studies are occasionally described as **time series designs.** These observations can be charted to show how the client changes in his or her behavior over time. When a therapeutic intervention is initiated, the observations prior to the intervention constitute the **baseline** for the case study. The pattern of observations after the intervention depicts the effect of the treatment. These two elements are described in the behavioral science literature as an A–B design, with the A observations being the baseline and the B observations being the outcome.

Medical Case Studies

Case studies in counseling tend to be descriptive of the current situation and predictive of what may occur. Counseling psychologists are less likely to be retrospective in evidence gathering for individual cases (clients) than are those working within a medical context. Medical case studies are based on first diagnosing a patient's problem.[11] Medical specialists in mental health typically collect medical histories and probe to learn about past elements in a patient's life that may contribute to his or her present status.

Once a diagnosis is established and the individual has been admitted, hospitals change their focus. Case study methods are used to describe what is ongoing with patients, to chart progress, and to identify how to improve the patient's condition. This prospective process is usually attended by a psychologist and or social worker along with the medical staff. Data from each case study are presented and described during regular meetings known as **chart rounds.** When the medical case study is retrospective and focused on the causes of what occured, the process is described as a **mortality-morbidity (M&M) conference** (Deis et al., 2009).

Consensual Qualitative Research (CQR)

Consensual qualitative research is a semistructured approach to interviewing participants. The structure makes CQR more quantitative than other forms of qualitative research (Hill et al., 2005).

CQR could be described as "collaborative qualitative research" in that it involves a close collaboration among several researchers (Paulus, Woodside, & Ziegler, 2008). At its heart, CQR employs many of the processes of grounded theory with the added advantages of providing a method for reducing possible research bias and providing consistent and reproducible outcomes. A core goal of the CQR approach is to reduce the potential for systematic error that may arise when a single researcher works alone.

CQR also reduces the likelihood that groupthink will bias the final analysis. The method does this by adding one or more auditors to check the work of the primary CQR team of judges and verify the **core ideas** uncovered, **domains** recognized, and cross-analyses with the data. The CQR approach provides greater transparency and ensures rigor in the qualitative research project[12] (Hill et al., 1997).

CQR Research Methods

CQR research requires the development and deployment of semistructured, open-ended questions (e.g., interviews). The CQR process requires that all participants answer the same list of questions and probes. Several expert judges are employed throughout the data analysis process to assure consistency across all individuals while still facilitating in-depth examination and data analysis. The CQR process is primarily postmodern, and in the constructionist tradition including the development of open-ended questions and coding responses to them (Hill et al., 2005).

The interviewers are on a quest to learn what participants really believe. This is accomplished by using a standard protocol of questions along with an assortment of optional probes for exploring the participant's answers in greater depth. The CQR method is one that prizes objectivity while eschewing experimental designs and probability based hypothesis testing. It provides an objective summation of participants' words while avoiding the pure interpretative approaches such as grounded theory. The interactive nature of data collection gives the CQR process a postpositivist flair (Hill et al., 2005).

Consensus Building

Central to the CQR process is the building of a working consensus among the members (judges) of the research team. This process is built around mutual respect among the judges, shared power, and the committed involvement of all members of the CQR team (Hill et al., 1997). Reaching a consensus implies the team members actually like each other and have the interpersonal skills to openly discuss disagreements that inevitably arise in the CQR process.

Building a consensus is best accomplished face-to-face. The use of digital video conferencing is not as effective because subtle cues and nonverbal communication among and between team members may be missed. Face-to-face meetings make it possible for commonly held and minority opinions and interpretations to be fairly and openly expressed and evaluated.

Sampling for CQR

There are two dimensions to the question of sampling in CQR. The first is the question of the demographics of the researchers on the CQR team. The optimal team has a diversity of backgrounds and special abilities. Teams can range from 2 researchers and a 3rd individual serving as the auditor up to a team of 12 (Hill et al., 2005).

The typical sample used in CQR is randomly drawn from a homogeneous population of potential participants (Hill et al., 1997). This approach is not always followed, as some researchers use a form of purposeful sampling. That sampling can ensure that participants all have similar backgrounds or meet the needs of a theoretical sample specified by the CQR team.

The population framed for drawing a pool of participants should have knowledge of the dimension being studied. A group of between 8 and 15 participants is recommended (Hill at al., 1997). Samples this small ($n < 15$) are too small to be probability-based samples. As in most research, more participants ($n > 12$) will provide more data, which will result in greater stability for the findings. This is especially true when the sample of participants is heterogeneous in terms of what they know about the phenomena being studied.

Applications from the Literature

Example of CQR from the Literature

Note: The authors used a purposive sample of 40 same-sex couples (half male-male and half female-female). They were recruited from the gay, lesbian, and bisexual community of a midsized southern city and its surrounding counties. They employed individual interviews and traditional survey measures of relationship quality and experiences with their families of origin.

Data Analyses: **Randomly selected** transcripts (7 from the 20 female couples and 7 from the 20 male couples) formed the data set for qualitative analysis of the text addressing couples' perceptions of family support. Using the consensual qualitative research (CQR) method (Hill, Thompson,

(Continued)

(Continued)

& Williams, 1997),[13] data were subjected to a series of analyses by a primary research team of three coders and one external auditor. The primary research team members and external auditor were doctoral level graduate students. The primary team first identified all content relevant to the research question in the randomly selected transcripts and reached consensus regarding the text to be analyzed. Next, the primary team coded 4 of the transcripts to determine and reach consensus on the **domains**, or general topic areas, represented in the text. After determining the domains, two members of the primary team independently assigned the data from 12 of the 14 transcripts to the appropriate domains. During a consensus meeting, the two main coders, the third consulting coder, and a faculty advisor verified the results of this first level of coding. The coded material was then given to the external auditor who reviewed the coding and provided feedback to the primary team. The feedback was then discussed and incorporated as appropriate into revisions of the coding.

Source: Rostosky, S. S., Korfhage, B. A., Duhigg, J. M., & Stern, A. J. (2004). Same-sex couple perceptions of family support: A consensual qualitative study. *Family Process, 43*(1), 43–57.

Analysis of CQR Data

Data analysis in CQR research moves through several steps. Starting with the raw interview data, the first step is the identification of domains that can be used to organize and group the interview data. By starting with the data and allowing the domains to emerge, it is possible to reduce researcher bias due to preconceived notions about what was found. The domains should be identified individually by the members of the CQR team before the team meeting, where members work to define and clarify the domains to be used for data analysis. These domains are the common denominator across the various participants. The domains are then used to organize the information (words, phrases, and sentences) from each transcribed interview.

During the second step in CQR data analysis, the researcher reviews the various examples collected for each domain. Each example is clarified, and their commonality is summarized. For example, the transcript of an interview in one of the domains may read, "She can be, you know, like a real pit bull, totally nagging and bitching. I can, you know, like really hate her and wonder why I ever hooked up in the first place with her." This could be clarified and summarized by the CQR researcher as "Does not like his partner's assertiveness." Through these summaries, the essence of each domain can be revealed.

The last step in CQR research is **cross-analysis** to identify and agree on a common set of themes and on their wording. These themes reoccur across the participants' answers (Hill et al., 2005). This final analysis requires the CQR team to meet and hash out a true concensus on the wording of each.

QUALITY INDICATORS FOR QUALITATIVE RESEARCH

As was noted earlier, Lincoln and Guba (1985) introduced the concept of trustworthiness in lieu of the more traditional view of scientific validity for research. Being trustworthy is the key to excellent qualitative research. The elements of trustworthiness include credibility, transferability, dependability, and confirmability (Krefting, 1991).

Credibility

Credibility is a property decided upon by the reader of the qualitative study. To be credible to readers implies the researcher has established his or her bona fides as a knowledgeable and skilled qualitative researcher. The use of triangulation, using several approaches to answering the same research question, and the rigor and amount of time spent in the data collection phase of the study also contribute to credibility.

Additionally, the researcher using digital recording systems with interviews or in support of other analytical methods can improve the credibility of the data. Documentation provided by verbatim transcripts is another solid method and helps to establish the study's credibility.

Transferability

A principle of D. T. Campbell and Stanley's (1963) concept of **external validity** was that the study and its findings could be repeated by other researchers working in different venues. (External validity is described in Chapter 14.) This same need for transferability is a component of trustworthy qualitative research (Trochim & Donnelly, 2007). A detailed description of the study's participants, as well as all methods for conducting the study including time lines, note-taking methods, and criteria for choice of codes, is a key to transferability to other research settings.

Dependability

Dependability answers the question of whether the study and findings can be repeated. Research contexts change over time, and different researchers construct different perspectives regarding all aspects of the research they read. To assess the dependability of a qualitative study, the researcher should provide, or make available, the raw evidence and the coding models developed. Making these data available to other scholars can be facilitated by posting data to the Internet. To avoid an ethical lapse, researchers should always use artificial names for places and individuals.

Confirmability

Confirmability describes the degree to which data and findings can be corroborated by others. This may involve a study audit, including checking the coding against new data from participants not included in the original study. It may also require having some participants read the transcripts of the data they provided and checking for accuracy. The study may employ an expert in the field as an auditor or, more simply, have the other author work to identify negative instances that are contradictive of the first researcher's conclusions.

Self-Reflection or Bracketing

Qualitative research data are drawn from the participants of the study, but it is the researcher who decides what to collect and from whom and analyzes the data through the filter of his or her perspective. Qualitative researchers should work to reduce the potential for their work to be idiosyncratic.

The purpose of data analysis in qualitative research is to identify deep or latent meanings and provide linkages with other individuals or systems (Wolcott, 2009). As the researcher decides what data to collect and how to analyze it, biases and self-constructed mental frameworks of the researcher will influence what is found and reported. Paula Saukko (2005) has argued that bracketing, or reflexive meditation, makes awareness of the self and one's constructions of reality possible.

Being aware of those constructions does not mean the qualitative researcher should work to completely exorcize them from the research and the written report. Rather, he or she should examine them and decide if they are part of a meaningful interpretation of the products from the study. If those constructions are useful, they can be explained in the report (Wolcott, 2009).

REPORTING QUALITATIVE RESEARCH

In a qualitative research report or article, there is a need for careful referencing and citation of background material. Qualitative research reports must explain the study's methods and findings. The methods section of a research paper should also justify the qualitative technique chosen for data analysis.

Methods Section

One potentially problematic area for qualitative studies is the research methodology description section. Qualitative researchers must develop detailed, complex descriptions of how the research was carried out. The various approaches selected must be justified as appropriate and the philosophical premise behind the research explained and defended. Explaining and describing the coding steps and outcomes can be a challenging undertaking. Another issue arises when the researcher changes his or her approach or coding system midstudy. This need for change may be apparent to the qualitative researcher but may seem to be a convenient flip-flop to the reader.

Qualitative researchers should reflect on their research findings, report their own possible biases, and elaborate on how their biases may have interacted with data collection and analysis. Unless this issue is carefully clarified and elaborated, it can be a serious point of skepticism for readers.

Participant Description

One of the more difficult sections to write is the description of the participants and/or other data sources. The question of the sufficiency of the number of participants and data sources must be addressed. The small sample size and its select nature should be explained and elaborated upon. Related to this is proving to the reader that data saturation was reached in the study (Strauss & Corbin, 1998).

Data Analysis

When writing the data analysis section, the researcher should lay out a careful step-by-step description so readers can follow the logic of the approach. This section includes an explanation of how the research analysis took place, including the how and who of data transcription and coding and how the explanatory model was finalized. In this process, the researcher needs to discuss contradictions that occurred and how they were handled (Stenius, Mäeklä, Movsky, & Garbhelik, 2008). Simple descriptive statistics providing a picture of the participants are occasionally part of this presentation.

Where possible, researchers should use graphs and flowcharts to help readers understand the study and its findings. The flowchart should depict the working of the theory; it should not provide only a simple linear sequence. The complex interplay among variables and factors being studied should be clearly depicted.

Applications from the Literature

Qualitative Study's Outcome With Two Flowcharts

Note: The authors used interviews with 32 women over the age of 50 to determine the context in which adult women perceive violence in their communities and how their present fears of violence relate to their childhood experiences.

Figure 5.2   Flowchart of Hierarchical Code, "Generational Differences"

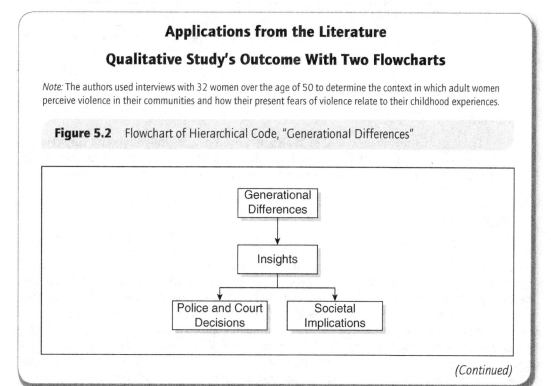

(Continued)

(Continued)

Figure 5.3 Flowchart of Hierarchical Code, "Safe Places"

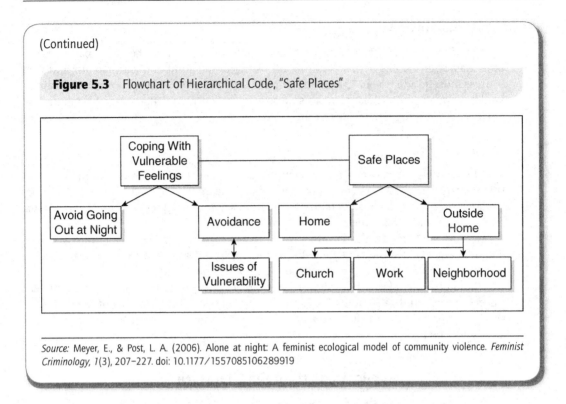

Source: Meyer, E., & Post, L. A. (2006). Alone at night: A feminist ecological model of community violence. *Feminist Criminology, 1*(3), 207–227. doi: 10.1177/1557085106289919

Limitations

Qualitative research reports should also describe possible limitations and concerns the author may have about the study and its trustworthiness. Finally, it should point future researchers toward other related studies for which this work has identified a need.

SUMMARY

The chapter describes six approaches to qualitative research. The common thread throughout these methods is the need to collect data from individuals that provide a deep description of the circumstance or perceptions of the individuals studied. One of the principal methods used in qualitative research is grounded theory. Using the three-tiered coding system of grounded theory, it is possible for researchers to identify the core or central phenomena represented by the data collected using the various qualitative methods and develop verifiable theories to describe human behavior, feelings, and emotions. Qualitative studies should be able to document their trustworthiness. In qualitative studies, the principal determinants of authenticity for the method and veracity of the results and conclusions are fourfold: credibility, transferability, dependability, and confirmability.

DISCUSSION QUESTIONS

1. Select one of the research vignettes included in Chapter 4 or 5 and locate and read the complete journal article. Conduct an analysis of the trustworthiness of the article. Include in your analysis a discussion of its credibility, transferability, dependability, and confirmability.

2. Identify a senior person in your life. This could include a grandparent or other relative, a senior faculty member or staff person who has a long history with a college department, a schoolteacher or administrator with at least 20 years of experience, or a clinic's senior therapist. Interview this person and develop an oral history of what he or she remembers experiencing, thinking, and feeling during an earlier time, such as his or her first year at work.

3. Assume that you will anonymously respond to several open-ended questions at the end of this course. Those questions will ask about your reaction to the course material and the instructional process. Take some time to self-reflect on your own constructed framework of thinking and how that may influence (bias) your answers. Write out these brackets and review them again after a day to ensure their trustworthiness.

NOTES

1. To listen to a half-hour lecture on Sartre and phenomenalism, visit the following URL: http://www.youtube.com/watch?v=3Evg21BiXzY, posted by Professor Rick Roderick.

2. An example of the loss of such a record and the resulting change to history can be seen in the genocide of Greek and other Christian minorities that occurred in the Ottoman Empire's final days. Between 1915 and 1922, 350,000 Greek Orthodox Christians of the Pontos in modern-day Hungary, and up to 1,500,000 Greek Orthodox Christians in territories formerly under the control of Mehmed VI, 36th Sultan of the Ottoman Empire and Caliph of the Faithful, were exterminated by forced death marches and the burning of farms and towns throughout Micra Asia on the coast of modern Turkey. This was done as part of a jihad declared by Mehmed's father, the 35th sultan. That jihad included a declaration of war against the allied entente powers, including France, Italy, the United States, and Great Britain and the many other allies. The word *holocaust* comes from the Greek word *olokaftoma* and means total consumption by fire. It was first applied to this slaughter by Turks, the first of the 20th-century genocides. Today, the secular government of Turkey refuses to acknowledge this history and passed a law in 2005 (Article 301) making it a crime punishable by up to 2 years in prison to comment publicly about the atrocities committed against the Greeks and other minorities by the Ottoman Empire.

3. The Sudan's Darfur region was divided, creating a semiautonomous state and safe zone for the displaced population of 2.7 million indigenous Africans chased away from their farms and villages by the Islamic-Arabic militia forces of Omar al-Bashir. The new state is led by a rebel group, Justice and Equality Movement (JEM), which opposes the apartheid policies toward and brutalization of African-Darfuri people.

4. The word *hermeneutic* appeared in Western literature in 1678 in a Latin language text as referring to literary interpretation. Later, in 1737, the term *hermeneutics* appears in theological literature in English as describing a method of biblical interpretation (*Oxford English Dictionary,* 2002).

5. There are other types of hermeneutics, including biblical hermeneutics in search of God's true meaning. This approach includes other related methods, including biblical numerology, which is used to search for the hidden meaning of numbers in the Bible.

6. A major debate is ongoing within the research community as to whether social conversation and more formal discourse can be studied using the same methods. Discourse analysis can be applied to a range of text sources, including conversations.

7. It is unfortunate that the name of method, grounded theory, is the same as the final product of using the method, a grounded theory.

8. Geertz, C. (1973). *The interpretation of cultures: Selected essays.* New York, NY: Basic Books.

9. Spradley, J. P. (1979). *The ethnographic interview.* Belmont, CA: Wadsworth, Cengage.

10. Strauss, A., & Corbin, J. (1990). *Basics of qualitative research: Grounded theory procedures and techniques.* Newbury Park, CA: Sage.

11. The current trend of requiring therapists to provide a diagnostic statement and treatment plan to a third party prior to receiving payment for services is making the medical approach far more common than the approach of traditional client-centered counseling.

12. A clause in the **No Child Left Behind Act** (NCLB; Pub. L. 107-110, 2002), inserted by the administration of President George W. Bush, was one reason for an expansion in the use of CQR. The clause stated that all research funded by the US Department of Education must follow rules of "**scientific inquiry**" and be based on proven scientific evidence. Scientific inquiry is described as including the use of control groups, carefully structured research designs, and analysis with inferential statistics. This rule calling for "**evidence-based**" scientific proof was repeated in the reauthorization for the **Individuals with Disabilities Education Act** (IDEA, Pub. L. 108-446, 2004). The law and the rules under it specifically excluded postpositive models of research from being supported by federal grants or subventions. CQR models can be structured with treatment and control groups, and outcome data can be statistically analyzed and fit under the "scientific evidence" requirement.

13. Hill, C. E., Thompson, B. J., & Williams, E. N. (1997). A guide to conducting consensual qualitative research. *The Counseling Psychologist, 25*(4), 517–572. doi: 10.1177/0011000097254001.

CHAPTER 6

Action Research Methods

"If you want to truly understand something, try to change it."

Kurt Lewin

OBJECTIVES

By reading and studying this chapter, you should acquire the competency to do the following:

- Describe the role of Kurt Lewin in the development of action research.
- List and discuss four areas of study commonly employing action research.
- Describe the dynamic use of participants in the research process.
- Discuss the major ethical concerns related to using action research.
- Write several examples of well-worded action research questions.
- Explain what goes on during the reconnaissance step in action research.
- Elaborate on the special issues action researchers face in achieving IRB approval for their studies.
- Describe the role that reflection plays in the action research process.
- Explain how a researcher can establish the validity of an action research project.
- Explain the steps involved in making the decision to initiate a second and other subsequent action research cycles.

INTRODUCTION AND MAJOR THEMES

Kurt Lewin was a member of the great immigration of scholars to the United States who escaped Nazi Germany before the onslaught of the Holocaust.[1] Lewin is credited with being the father of both modern group dynamics and action research (Greenwood & Levin, 2007). Lewin's approach to helping individuals and organizations was based on his theories of how reality is defined. Lewin was an early phenomenologist who assumed each individual defines a unique **lifespace** within his or her psychosocial field. This field is composed of perceptions, psychological state, and psychosocial experiences. Human behavior was described by Lewin as being the product of how individuals resolved their sense of self within a changing lifespace (Lewin, 1951/1975).

In the 1940s, Lewin published research covering a number of diverse problems in social psychology. One series of studies involved organizational team building and encouraging improved innovation by workers. Much of this research required employing a "naturalistic" approach for collecting and interpreting data. Lewin's research method had researchers working as collaborators and teammates with the participants to understand and improve the system. He coined the name *action research* (AR) to describe this participatory approach. A hallmark of AR is the central role of reflection in the process of data interpretation and identifying problem solutions (Lewin, 1948).

While Lewin believed that AR provided a method for identifying short-term solutions to social problems, others now see the process of AR as being a continuous process of improvement. In this approach, the results of a sequence of AR findings are woven together to provide an organization with a path to continuous development and improved quality (Greenwood & Levin, 2007).

For action research to work well, two types of knowledge need to come together in a problem-solving partnership. One type is the local knowledge held by individuals in the system or environment that is to be studied. This type of knowledge is built on what insiders know, their tacit understanding of how "things actually work," and the operational theories they have developed. Local theories are the product of long observation and innumerable discussions with fellow insiders. Local knowledge is brought to the study by the participants, who understand what makes it possible for people to work skillfully and effectively in their environments. Theories based on local knowledge are complex, dynamic, and effective for meeting local needs (Greenwood & Levin, 2007). Balancing this local knowledge is what the researchers bring—another type of knowledge that is professional and scientifically constructed. Scientific knowledge is the product of generations of descriptive and qualitative research studies.

Action research includes volunteer participants who are typically self-selected. Action research is generally viewed as an applied form of qualitative research.

Lewin and others since his time have argued that research in the social sciences needs to be a dialogue between the two types of knowledge, local and scientific. This is the essence of action research, a dialectical relationship between the two (Greenwood & Levin, 2007).

ACTION RESEARCH, AN APPROACH FOR ALL PRACTITIONERS

Psychology emerged as a distinct social science, clearly independent from philosophical analysis, in the 19th-century laboratories of Wilhelm Wündt (University of Leipzig) and Sir Francis Galton (University College, London). From that time forward, research in the social sciences has followed the lead of the physical sciences and focused on how **dependent variables** are influenced by **experimental (independent) variables** and how outcomes can be statistically predicted by carefully measured variables. The scientific model for the study of psychology and social sciences was rarely challenged during the 100 years following the publication of Wündt's first psychology text in 1874 (Wündt, 1874/1999). This empirical approach, based on the logic of positivism, has been challenged by the postpositivists, who employ a variety of qualitative research methods to construct models and theories for understanding cultures and social structures created by individuals and society. One of the first to challenge the dominance of empirical quantitative research was Kurt Lewin.

CASE IN POINT   6.1

Variables in Research

In the psychological and social sciences, the term *variable* describes any construct describing a dimension. The term implies that the property (construct being described) varies from case to case. Some variables are associated with physical properties such as height, socioeconomic status, weight, galvanic skin response level, etc. Others are associated with hypothesized dimensions such as intelligence, anxiety, greed, fear, empathy, etc. These hypothetical constructs can be measured indirectly through observations, interviews, and psychological assessment measures.

When a variable is introduced to research participants as a way to produce a change in the participants, that variable is an experimental or independent variable. The variable describing the dimension that is to change is the dependent variable. A dependent variable in one study may become the independent variable in another study. Thus, the researcher may study the effect of group counseling (independent or experimental variable) on client empathy levels (dependent variable). In another study, the experimental (independent) variable may be the empathy level of the counselor, and the dependent variable may be the client satisfaction level with the counselor.

Pure quantitative research approaches may be characterized as focusing on what has passed and as providing researchers with analysis about what occurred and why it happened (Chandler & Torbert, 2003). In a similar way, qualitative researchers focus on how past structures and conditions shape the perceptual field of participants and provide a framework for how individuals interpret their environments.

Both qualitative and quantitative methods are geared to provide generalizable conclusions and expand the base of human knowledge. To achieve this, quantitative researchers aggregate data about many individuals and variables. Qualitative researchers, on the other hand, work to develop in-depth, rich descriptions frequently supported with case study examples (Chandler & Torbert, 2003).

Action research (AR) goes beyond these core research techniques by not just explaining what occurred but bringing the focus of research into the present and working toward improving the future. Action research is focused on the ongoing dynamic character of the phenomenon being considered and the human interactions involved with its modification. AR also provides insight into the future by engaging researchers as coparticipants in the ongoing research effort where they help bring about change while at the same time assessing the impact of their actions.

Pragmatic Practitioners

As noted in Chapter 1, all professional associations related to counseling and the behavioral sciences have recently upgraded the research skill standards expected for professional therapists. This trend is likely to continue, with future generations of counselors and counseling psychologists possessing ever more advanced skills as practitioner-researchers. The various mandates for research skills reflect a critical need for counselors in this age of accountability (Bradbury, Mirvis, Neilsen, & Pasmore, 2007). The profession can be badly damaged if its membership is not able to document the positive role it plays in the lives of individuals and indeed the mental health of entire communities. Action research can provide proof of the efficacy of counseling.

Between Two Paradigms

In 1932, when Kurt Lewin arrived in the United States, the dominant research paradigm of American social scientists was scientific and based on experimental testing and statistical analyses. The worldview of most social scientists of that era has been described as positivistic and based on a scientific paradigm. Interpretative research methods were not yet a major force in the design and conduct of psychosocial research. Lewin's conceptualization of the action research model presaged much of what became part of the postmodern movement in research and the development of qualitative research in the social sciences.

Kurt Lewin and Field Theory

Lewin was greatly influenced by three other World War II–era émigrés into the United States: Kurt Koffka (Smith College), Wolfgang Köhler (Swarthmore College), and Max Wertheimer (New School for Social Research; Wertheimer, 1997). These fellow escapees from Nazi oppression were central figures in the development of Gestalt psychology and Gestalt therapy (W. D. Ellis, 1938/1999). The Gestalt theory holds that the human mind brings to all phenomena its own framework for interpreting and understanding the scene. Köhler once said, "The whole is different from the sum of its parts."[2] The easy analogue proving this point involves artistic productions. Music is more than just a series of notes; it is a whole that we experience and interpret as being either pleasing or not to our taste. The painter uses many simple brush strokes, the product of which we can see as a whole and interpret as such, yet no single brush stroke is a work of art. Rather, the holistic understanding viewers have of the composite of all the brush strokes makes the work a painting.

Kurt Lewin's concept of field theory as a basis for human psychology is steeped in the principles of Gestalt psychology (Lewin, 1951/1975). The individual's "field" is the totality of his or her mentally coexisting and interdependent realities. Dynamic internal tensions develop as the individual strives to define his or her personal self while resolving the stressors from the perceived social environment. Lewin proposed that to understand human behavior, it is necessary not only to consider the isolated behavior but also to include all the elements of the social environment in which the behavior occurs.

Figure 6.1 Example Based on Work of Gestalt Psychology[3]

In this picture, you may see a bald man with a white beard. Or you may see an old man walking with a cane and a young woman carrying a load of grain through an archway. A sleeping dog lies in the road, the face of a woman is to the left of the arch, and a man is seen on the right of the arch.

Applications of Action Research

As a social psychologist, Lewin believed in using research to expand our understanding of the human condition. He organized his exploration of the nature of social and psychological phenomena by employing an interactive approach in which he manipulated situational variables in the natural environment and examined outcomes with the participants. Lewin named this participatory form of research *action research*.

Action Research in Educational Settings

Today, several forms of action research are reported in the journals. Action research is widely practiced in schools and is frequently organized and carried out by professional school counselors. This application of action research, referred to as educational action research (EAR), is normally undertaken to improve the methods and approaches employed by educators and school counselors (Mertler, 2012; Mills, 2007; Wright, 2012).

Photo 6.1 Photograph of Kurt Lewin

Participatory Action Research

Another widely employed approach is known as participatory action research (PAR). This method has researchers fully engaged with those who are the focus of the study in a research-based problem-solving effort. The technical nouns *replicate* and *subject,* used in experimental research to describe individuals, are replaced with the noun *participant* by researchers employing PAR. This shift in terminology emphasizes the different role of those in the study, not subjects to which something happens or who are measured but participating volunteers and partners in the research effort (Coghlan & Brannick, 2010; Greenwood & Levin, 2007; McIntyre, 2008; Stringer, 2007).

Action Research in Evaluation

The third major application for action research is in program and system evaluation (Stringer, 2007). When stakeholders and evaluators work together to observe, collect data, reflect on the findings, and review what they have found, they are employing an action research approach to the tasks of evaluating. Evaluation action research involves sharing perceptions and interpretations and developing a clearly defined vision of a project's or program's strengths and challenges. This topic is presented in Chapter 16.

Action Research for Social Justice

Action research is widely employed in the pursuit of social justice (Greenwood, 2002). The social justice movement has its roots in the great struggle for civil rights for all people that was born in the 1950s and, in the United States, blossomed into federal legislation during the 1960s. The movement for social justice and equality is ongoing today and supported by most social scientists in the helping professions. Social justice as a movement often addresses the social hierarchy and challenges the status quo. Social justice is a many-faceted movement concerned with the need to eliminate racism, encourage feminism, provide equal rights for individuals with different sexual orientations, end ethnic discrimination, advocate for the needs of those with disabilities, and eliminate ageism.

Research for social justice can be directed toward learning the origins of social forces within institutions that perpetuate structural inequality and social inequity. Action research is an ideal method for researchers working with an agenda of social justice. Action researchers can employ a number of lenses to examine a range of social dimensions within the domain of the research effort. Different action research lenses can be focused on economic, political, social policy, cultural, and historical questions related to the human condition and the status of groups.

Applications from the Literature

Introduction Statement of a Feminist-Based Action Research Study

Note: A group of low-income women working in partnership with community agencies and a university formed a coalition they named Women Organizing Activities for Women. The original group of 80 was invited to participate in a feminist participatory action research effort to improve their life conditions. Twenty women from the original group remained active during the 2 years of the study.

Introduction: In response to this disjuncture we adopted a feminist participatory action research framework (FPAR) to inform our work with a group of women on low income. We defined FPAR as a conceptual and methodological framework that enables a critical understanding of women's multiple perspectives and works towards inclusion, participation, and action, while confronting the underlying assumptions researchers bring into the research process. Feminist participatory action researchers seek to facilitate building knowledge to change the conditions of women's lives, both individually and collectively, while reconstructing conceptions of power so that power can be used in a responsible manner.

FPAR is a tool, not a panacea, that involves a particular way of looking at the world and interacting with research participants to overcome the androcentrism that characterizes other types of research. FPAR blends participatory action research and critical feminist theory by advocating that women must be involved in all stages of the research process including identifying the problems to be explored, carrying out the research, and interpreting and acting upon the results. FPAR's goals include identifying changes of immediate benefit to research participants, analyses of the structural determinants of social problems, and action strategies.

In order to accomplish these goals, feminist participatory action researchers aim to engage in democratic inquiry where they collaborate with participants in an effort to understand and enact solutions to problems of major importance to a community of women.... This has resulted in a veiled assumption that researchers and community members share understandings about what constitutes action and have the capacity to enact action plans. This is problematic because expectations regarding action may differ considerably and smaller and achievable personal/local actions may go unrecognized given the emphasis placed in the literature on alleviating the broader and more elusive structural conditions that engender poverty, powerlessness, and poor health.

Source: Reid, C., Tom, A., & Frisby, W. (2006). Finding the 'action' in feminist participatory action research. *Action Research,* 4(1), 315–332. doi: 10.1177/1476750306066804

Ethics in Action Research

The central goal of action research efforts is not to provide a description or comparison but to initiate and evaluate changes to the ongoing system being studied. Additionally, as noted in the previous section, AR may examine dimensions for change through a number of lenses drawn from a number of different disciplines. This presents several ethical issues not usually faced by more traditional qualitative and quantitative approaches to research (Gelling & Munn-Giddings, 2011).

Seven potential ethical concerns have been identified by Gelling and Munn-Giddings (2011); in addition to these, Jack Whitehead and Jean McNiff added one more (2006). Ethical concerns for practitioners employing action research should be addressed prior to gaining approval of the institution's IRB committee. These ethical and ethics-related issues include the following:

- **Ongoing independent review.** The IRB process is one that became de rigueur following the Belmont Report of 1979. It was well structured to meet the needs of research following the quantitative, positivistic approach for human subject experimentation, but it is not well suited to provide good guidance for action researchers (Boser, 2007; DeTardo-Bora, 2004). The research assumption of many IRB committee members not trained in AR is that research should be carried out on strangers who are not true participants in the research process (C. Ellis, 2007). When an action research project is vetted by an IRB, little is known about how the project will proceed after the initial action and review phase. Therefore, subsequent steps in the effort will need to be revisited by the IRB or by a member of the committee assigned to provide periodic guidance for the researcher(s).

Cartoon 6.1   Institutional Review Board and the Action Research Proposal

The problems that action research projects often face with IRBs are similar to those that doctoral dissertations may encounter with their sponsoring committees. Both oversight committees may not approve studies that have the organic quality of changing as they go along. Much care must go into preparing action research proposals. Careful documentation of the research method may be necessary, and the researcher may need to identify resources for the action research approach. The following resources provide useful information for the proposal development process:

Ferrance, E. (2000). *Action research*. Providence, RI: US Department of Education, Northeast and Islands Regional Educational Laboratory at Brown University. Retrieved from http://www.lab.brown.edu/pubs/themes_ed/act_research.pdf

Riel, M. (2010). *Understanding action research*. Retrieved from Center for Collaborative Action Research, Pepperdine University, http://cadres.pepperdine.edu/ccar/define.html

Whitehead, J. (n.d.). *ActionResearch.net*. Retrieved from http://www.actionresearch.net/

Donato, R. (2003). *Action research*. Retrieved from University of Pittsburgh, Center for Applied Linguistics, http://www.cal.org/resources/digest/0308donato.html

CASE IN POINT   6.2

The College of Education at a large doctoral-granting university experienced problems with the university's Institutional Review Board approvals for doctoral dissertation and faculty research proposals employing participatory action research. The IRB was made up of eight senior faculty members in the fields of educational psychology and measurement, philosophy (ethics), medieval history, economics, law (an assistant dean from the law school), electrical engineering, nursing (oncology), and social work. This board experienced a number of contentious discussions over most action research proposals. The ongoing debate typically resulted in a 2 or 3-month delay before the decision to (a) approve, (b) require modifications, or (c) reject an action research proposal. Contention was often focused on the issue of how participants could be researchers and subjects at the same time. The related problem of parental approval with informed consent at each step of the process also became a blocking issue.

At the request of the college's curriculum and planning committee, the dean of education petitioned the university's senate for permission to establish another IRB that would function just within the College of Education. As this book goes to press, that decision has not yet been made. Other colleges on the campus, including the School of Social Work, are following the discussions closely.

- **Value.** Researchers have an obligation to document and be able to assure others that the research will be able to effect change and is needed. While based on the literature of what is already known, an AR proposal should also document that the participants and others (managers and other stakeholders) involved in the effort are supportive.
- **Risk-to-benefit ratio.** Researchers have an obligation to identify all potential risks and minimize them. Naturally, risks will arise that cannot be foreseen, especially as the AR cycles into ensuing phases in the research process. The risks raised by AR can be political in nature. Action research is often focused on improving social conditions and changing the status quo. Change frequently brings about resistance and evokes countermeasures.

Another consideration that should be addressed involves time and institutional resources. Do the potential outcomes justify taking professionals away from their primary tasks and using staff time and material resources?

CASE IN POINT 6.3

A good argument can be made that counselors and others doing research into the process of reconciliation between groups that have had a history of strife and animus must weigh the benefit-to-harm ratio carefully for participants in an AR project. When societies have been violently divided (e.g., Northern Ireland), all forms of research can prove to be distressing for participants. The distress is a function of the potential triggering of stressful events and of social ostracism for cooperating with outsiders. Participating in a study can even raise the possibility of physical harm befalling researchers and participants. A likely result of researchers charging pell-mell into the field to begin a study is that their behavior can cause a chilling effect with the population, negatively impacting all future research.

A model for doing action research in a community with a 400-year history of antagonism and strife was reported by two action researchers in the Ardoyne sector of Belfast in Northern Ireland[4] (Lundy & McGovern, 2006). One of the researchers was from the Ardoyne sector. That researcher returned to the Ardoyne as a researcher and became a member of an ongoing community of local residents working to create a commemorative book. That book was to be a repository of memories and thoughts from survivors of the era known simply as "the Troubles." By working within an existing community effort, and by providing full community control over what the direction of the project would follow, the researchers were able to study how such a project could facilitate reconciliation and healing.

- **Informed consent.** There is an absolute need to address the question of informed consent. This need is well stated in the Belmont Report of 1979 (see Chapter 2), and it is often a central consideration of members of IRBs. With action research, potential participants should be engaged in the actual design and structure of the study and understand each step in the research process. Additionally, participants should be informed of all possible risks and potential costs that may be involved in being part of the AR project.
- **Participant selection.** Participant action research requires the freely given participation of everyone involved. Individuals who are to be part of the study must volunteer and provide a signed consent form. The natural tendency for researchers to try to "tip the balance" with a potential subject through coercion or the use of peer pressure must be checked.
- **Respect for participants.** As stated in the Belmont Report of 1979, all researchers, including those using a participatory action research approach, must ensure the welfare and autonomy of all participants. This includes protecting the confidentiality of information about participants and permitting

participants to withdraw their cooperation at any point in the research effort. Once again, coercion must be avoided and the wishes of participants honored. A potential pitfall for practitioner-researchers is misusing a power relationship with potential participants to coerce cooperation. One method to avoid "selling" potential subjects on an action research program is to involve them in the planning process. When researchers work with a group of participants in the development of what it would mean to be part of an action research effort, cooperation will be optimized. The dictum of Hippocrates, "First of all, do no harm," must always be a guiding principle for the action researcher whenever participants may be at risk. The wishes of participants must be paramount.

- **Validity.** Since the time of Kurt Lewin, the development of the model for action research has been criticized as producing either research with little action or action with little research (Watkins, 1991). Kurt Lewin stressed the role of change in action research, but he was also open to employing scientific methods in natural settings where change could be scientifically assessed (Foster, 1972). It has been argued that the relevance of action research is based on its meaning to stakeholders and local collaborators in the research, not in the generalizability and universality of its findings (Riel & Lepori, 2011). Hilary Bradbury and Peter Reason (2006) took a different position, making the case that AR must be able to withstand scrutiny for validity and/or exhibit and document its trustworthiness. Their point is that even research that is "ethically good" must also be of high quality and valid. They enumerated several concerns to be addressed in assessing the validity and usefulness of action research:

1. Did the study facilitate the emergence of a new, long-lasting infrastructure?

2. Is the study worthy of the description "significant"?

3. Did the researchers employ appropriate research methods?

4. Did the study provide reflexive consideration and go beyond the purely intellectual?

5. Was it inclusive of various ways of knowing?

6. Was it designed to be relational and involve wide participation?

7. Do the findings exhibit conceptual-theoretical integrity?

- **Ensuring intellectual freedom.** Intellectual freedom is based on the assumption that all participants, as well as the researcher(s), are capable of independent thought and of being critically engaged in the research (Whitehead & McNiff, 2006). The researcher as a participant must honor and respect the contributions of all participants and avoid the natural tendency to push for consensus or employ power tactics to bend the AR to his or her way of thinking.

Applications from the Literature

Discussion of Intellectual Freedom and Respect in an Action Research Context

Note: This paper presents the practical and theoretical issues involved in applying participatory action research to concerns and problems in counseling psychology.

Disagreement and Constraint: The relationships that develop among members of participatory action research groups can develop difficulties. The researcher may be faced with a group that forms goals, research processes, and actions that are fundamentally different from those of the researcher. In some of these instances, researchers are faced with the question of whether or not they are willing to continue to facilitate a process to which they feel in opposition. Similarly, the participants may irrevocably disagree with one another, and the researcher may be unable to facilitate the development of group understanding and action. Cultural differences are likely to manifest in participants' views of the phenomenon under study, and constructive discussion is essential so as to minimize misunderstandings and come to agreements.

As debilitating as conflict and disagreement are a loss of motivation and commitment and a sense of resignation among participants. When the bulk of the work and energy comes only from one or a few people, the participatory action research process is fundamentally challenged. (In practice, at least at certain points of the project, this occurs more often than not and can be a constant struggle and source of frustration.)

In each of these instances, the researcher is tempted to fall back on a power imbalance to reestablish a project that may have involved a substantial commitment of time and energy and from which she or he may be reluctant to withdraw. Although quickly withdrawing may not be seen as an optimal response, as points of conflict may contain the potential for new knowledge generation that could better inform future actions, there are times when a project simply may not be feasible for any number of reasons. Finally, the participatory researcher must closely attend to a group process that appears to lack diversity and tension to guard against the potential problem that has been termed "consensus tyranny." In such instances, individual perspectives are silenced, and adverse social processes (e.g., groupthink, intimidation) can undermine true participation.

Source: Kidd, S. A., & Kral, M. J. (2005). Practicing participatory action research. *Journal of Counseling Psychology, 52*(2), 187–195. doi: 10.1037/0022-0167.52.2.187

ACTION RESEARCH CYCLE

The action research approach developed by Kurt Lewin provides for replanning and iterating modified plans until the problem is resolved or improvement is no longer possible (Ferrance, 2000). To demonstrate this concept, Lewin used a spiral with seven steps. Below is a modification of the original, designed around tasks of conducting research in a clinical environment. This model has been expanded to eight steps, including the

Figure 6.2   Model for Initial Action Research Cycle

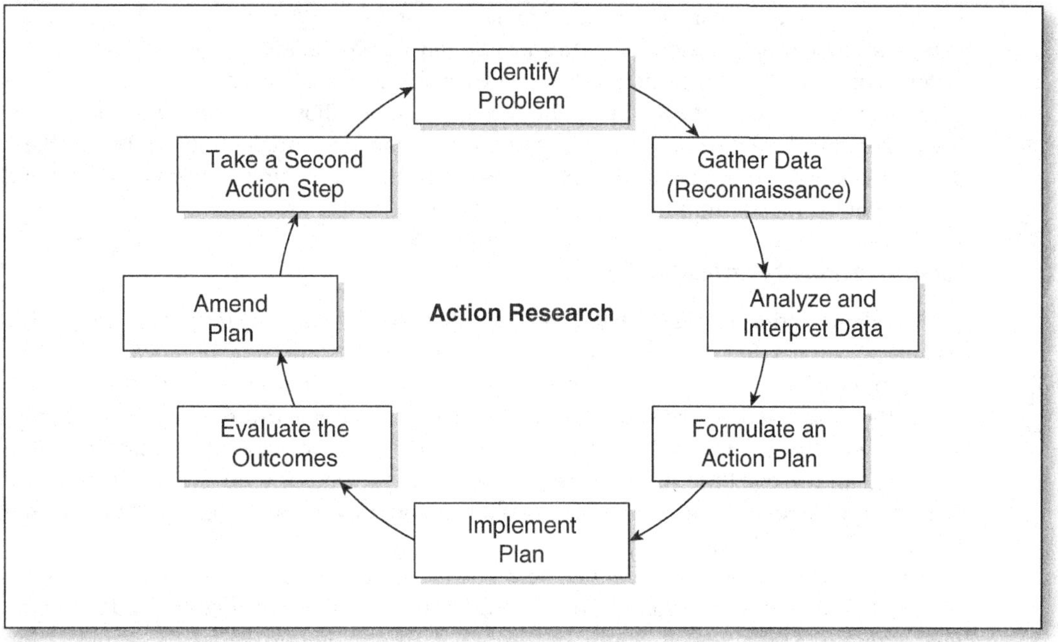

Source: Developed by author.

development of a revised plan to start the next cycle. This cyclic approach is designed to close the gap between research and practice in an increasing number of professions (Rowell, 2006).

Self-Reflection

When considering employing action research, a practitioner-researcher should take time for self-reflection (Mills, 2007). This reflection is to provide the researcher with the opportunity to develop a clear personal delineation of his or her theoretical beliefs regarding practice and how he or she interprets the actions and motivation of individuals. Researchers must be aware of the potential for making biased decisions and cognitive distortions. Personal distortions are more likely when the researcher feels stressed and/or is under pressure (Coghlan & Brannick, 2010). Distortions can be as simple as an overgeneralization or the use of all-or-nothing thinking. Personal values and belief systems are always interwoven in our decisions and in how we interpret reality around us. Being mindful of his or her values and beliefs provides the researcher with the context in which the data are collected and outcomes interpreted.

Identify the Problem (Step 1)

Action research questions in counseling and counseling psychology normally focus on improving practice and clinical outcomes for clients across a larger community. The questions to be answered through action research should imply a solid theoretical basis for the planned action to be taken. Questions should also be developed with the participation of the individuals who are to be involved in the research. The best questions are those that stimulate practitioner-researchers to take a deep look at their practice and how they employ their skills. Excellent action research questions align with the professional goals of the practitioner-researcher and lead him or her to ever improving professional expertise and practice (Riel, 2010).

Identification of Actionable Problem

The identification of researchable issues appropriate for action research requires the practitioner-researcher first to be well prepared and understand new trends and developments in the profession. AR has a complex and large literature of its own, as well as a collection of methods and procedures for "learning the truth" and improving the human condition.[5]

Identifying research questions also involves constantly growing one's personal research skills and knowledge base through reading professional literature for the counseling profession (Akos, 2004). An ongoing learning plan should provide time each week to read and reflect upon journal articles.[6]

One criticism of the counseling profession is that only a minority of counselors have developed the scientific mind-set that can appreciate and value research being done in the field (Bauman, 2004; Rowell, 2006). In this era of accountability, the lack of appreciation for scientifically derived evidence of the effectiveness of counseling programs can put the entire profession at risk (Whiston, 2002).

Good action research questions emerge from a theoretical perspective on change that will move a system toward a better state. By being familiar with trends and directions of the research in the field, the professional counselor can better advocate for the important roles counselors and other mental health workers can play in the betterment of their clients' lives. Being able to discuss new research can also improve a therapeutic community's social and professional life. This need to improve the skills of individual practitioners and the professional life of counseling agencies has led professional organizations to provide inservice courses during annual meetings; it is also why state licensing boards mandate documentation of continuing education for maintenance of a license to practice.[7]

Appropriate and Inappropriate Action Research Problems and Questions

Good action research is best carried out by researchers possessing a solid knowledge base in the field's literature. Grounding in the background of the potential problem or concern is needed to inform action researchers as they develop the idea and clarify their context for the possible AR study.

While being grounded in the literature, the research problem and associated questions cannot be answered simply by conducting a further search of the literature. Questions of fact and/or settled findings from other research into the issue are not appropriate to pursue. The task of a researcher is to identify a new aspect of a problem area to explore when developing an action research study.

An action research problem should not be posed as a testable hypothesis answerable through the analysis of descriptive data, for example, "Can group counseling with several dyads who are in couples therapy reduce incidents of spousal bullying reported by women in the relationships?" Better to ask, "What elements in group counseling work best with couples to reducing bullying behaviors between partners?" Another example of a poor question is "Can the use of infant simulator dolls (e.g., Baby Think it Over®) with nulliparous seventh- and eighth-grade girls reduce the incidence of teenage pregnancy?" Good action research questions cannot be answered with a yes or no. This example could be rewritten as the AR question "What is the optimal approach to use in a pregnancy prevention program of counseling that includes the use of infant simulator dolls with middle school students?"

Practitioner-researchers working in small clinics or in private practice who want access to the professional peer consultation or reviews needed to develop research questions can work cooperatively with their peer practitioners in local professional organizations. State, county, or local societies of professionals can provide this type of support and peer interaction.

All AR problem statements and research questions should be clearly stated and understandable to all who review them. Reviewers will include study participants, who will work with the researcher in finding solutions and working toward improving the system and conditions for the clients being served.

Applications from the Literature

Research Questions from a Participatory Action Research Study

Note: This was a 3-year study of women who emigrated from sub-Saharan African nations to the Fargo, North Dakota, area. Twelve subjects in the first-year effort were used to recruit additional subjects for the subsequent two cycles of the study. The focus of the research was on improving the women's acculturation into American society.

The Statement of the Problem: Although we now know more about acculturation success, biculturation, directional impacts of cultural contacts, and selective acculturation, unfortunately, many new members of society are left to blindly navigate the tortuous processes of adjusting to a new culture, with little organized support from formal and informal agencies. Moreover, new members are hardly involved in seeking solutions to the problem, nor are they encouraged to be proactive in addressing their issues of adjustment. Because acculturation problems manifest at different degrees they are often less obvious except in cases of outright violent confrontations and inter-group schisms. Action research is well suited to the study of underlying tensions, especially in evolving situations.

This project was designed to use action research methods to involve a group of new refugee and immigrant women in the Fargo-Moorhead area of North Dakota and Minnesota to address their acculturation problems by focusing on two critical research questions.

RQ1: What experiences are decelerating successful acculturation, and what can be done about these?

RQ2: What aspirations do the women have for successful acculturation, and what opportunities do they see for achieving these in their respective communities?

Source: Okigbo, C., Reierson, J., & Stowman, S. (2009). Leveraging acculturation through action research: A case study of refugee and immigrant women in the United States. *Action Research, 7*(2), 127–142. doi: 10.1177/1476750309103267

Conduct Reconnaissance and Analyze the Data (Steps 2 and 3)

Lewin's (1948) concept of reconnaissance describes an exploration carried out by the practitioner-researcher to develop a general understanding of the context, theories, values, and beliefs of participants in the research effort. This process can lead to further refinement of the research questions and focus the study on issues of central importance to the participants.

The refinement process involves identifying all potential ancillary research questions. Once they have been identified, these secondary issues are reviewed for possible inclusion in the effort. This is also the step in which initial observations from the field are made and data available from unobtrusive sources reviewed.

Stakeholders

A goal of action research is to democratize the research process while working toward social change and improved conditions for all (Ataöv, Brøgger, & Hildrum, 2010). This process implies the cooperative work of three groups: researchers, participant-researchers, and other stakeholders needed for the success of the effort. Action researchers need to review the community that is home to the group that will participate in the project. Part of that analysis is identifying all potential stakeholders. These stakeholders are individuals that the action being researched may positively and/or negatively impact. These individuals can include co-workers, administrators, other users of the clinic or agency, local union leaders, and the participant's significant others. Care should be taken to ensure that all attitudes and concerns of these individuals are addressed prior to commencing the action research process.

Unobtrusive Data Sources

An important component in the reconnaissance phase in action research is to identify and examine all unobtrusive sources of data ethically open to examination. These can include clinical attendance data, minutes from meetings, funding levels, laws and court appearances, evaluation reports for the organization or group, admission reports, and even divorce reports and filings with family court. One rich source of unobtrusive information that is often overlooked is grant funding request documents. These applications can tell a researcher much about the background of the organization and potential participants in the study.

Applications from the Literature

Example from Part of the Reconnaissance Description in an Action Research Article

Note: This study was focused on reducing the rate of burnout among federal firefighters. It used 65 volunteers for whom complete data were available as the core group of participants. Firefighting is a highly dangerous and stressful job requiring blocks of 72-hour shifts during which firefighters are on call and ready to risk their lives. A segment of a long reconnaissance section is presented here. This section also described a series of one-to-one interviews and the use of psychosocial questionnaires to develop preliminary data.

Reconnaissance: The reconnaissance phase involves deeply exploring issues in the organization. We used the following four techniques to explore the issues in this phase: a review of the literature, observations, interviews, and survey data collection. As we progressed through this phase, we adopted a traditional action research technique whereby we collected information (from the observations, interviews, and surveys) and compared it to current literature in an iterative fashion to develop a model for the experience of burnout in the organization. Collecting data from multiple sources of information allowed us to merge data from different vantage points to provide a more complete view of the context within the department.

Observations: As an initial step in data collection, we spent 90 days conducting observations. The objective of the observations was collecting information about working conditions, social interactions/group dynamics, possible stressors, and other information about what concerns faced the employees of the organization and what they were doing to address those concerns. We spent a total of 200 hours conducting observations in the department. Included in the observations were two 24-hour shift observations and one 12-hour shift (7 a.m. to 7 p.m.) by the first author. A number of themes emerged from the observations. We have classified them into more broad themes based on stressors, burnout symptoms, and consequences of burnout.

A significant stressor was uncertainty related to their jobs. Much of this uncertainty centered on the daily schedule. As one firefighter commented, "We have roll call every morning at 0700 where we find out what we are doing for the day. By 0715, everything has changed." Given that the nature of the firefighting job is inherently uncertain, uncertainties about regularly scheduled items, such as training exercises, were particularly frustrating for the workers.

Another notable stressor came from a perception of politics in the department, particularly as they related to human resources decisions. A number of employees complained about the performance appraisal and promotion systems, suggesting that they were intentionally manipulated to support a "good old boys" system. These political tensions were exacerbated by perceptions that their supervisors were undeservedly promoted, which led to a lack of trust in and support of management that was manifest by a lack of communication between management and employees.

We also observed clear manifestations of burnout. For example, we observed emotional exhaustion among workers; it was common to hear about how employees were "worn out with this job," "emotionally drained from work," or "not provided as much in terms of [emotional] rewards as [the employees] put into the job." Disengagement was observed as a number of workers claimed they were just "doing their time" and "counting the days until retirement."

Finally, we observed some evidence of reduced personal efficacy as employees believed they were not as good at their jobs as they once were, in part because of concerns with training. A potential consequence of burnout was also clear during our observations. Turnover had been historically high in the department, and in the time we conducted observations, two additional employees left. In talking with the employees that departed, both mentioned that they were frustrated with how the department operated, the political environment, the stressful environment, and how their expectations about the job had not been met. Moreover, both left because they believed they had a better chance of being promoted on their new job.

Source: Halbeselben, J. R. B., Osburn, H. K., & Mumford, M. D. (2006). Action research as a burnout intervention: Reducing burnout in the Federal Fire Service. *Journal of Applied Behavioral Science,42*(2), 244–266. doi: 10.1177/0021886305285031

Background Data

Reconnaissance should provide the researcher(s) with information derived from different sources and provide multiple perspectives on the context for the action research. Data collected during the reconnaissance are likely to include qualitative interview and observational material, quantitative information gathered by questionnaires and standardized measures, and unobtrusively derived materials including previous research outcomes. These data, drawn together from different perspectives and collected using different approaches to research, provide a more complete, holistic picture of the research context. The purpose of this organization and review of data from the reconnaissance is to ensure that the research problem and potential action-based intervention is congruent with the context of the possible study.

Reflection is a key skill for practitioner-researchers using action research to bring about change and improve circumstances. This process involves the critical examination of what the researcher is doing and why it is being done (Mertler, 2012). Reflection provides the link between our observations (data) and our judgments. The reflective process requires both reasoning and self-awareness. A necessary element of self-awareness is the recognition of one's own emotions and values and how they may be shading our decisions and interpretations.

Develop a Plan for Action (Step 4)

Following the reconnaissance and preliminary analysis phases, the researcher(s) is ready to develop a plan of action and select a research methodology for evaluating the impact of the action step. The ultimate goal for all action research is to modify the current state of affairs by taking proactive action. This goal statement should be clearly enunciated in the action plan.

Another component of all action plans is a statement of how outcomes will be assessed and what measures will indicate success of the project. An action research project to reduce racism in a work environment may begin to see results within a week following the first sensitivity-group session with participating shop stewards. Other studies may require a longitudinal approach for data collection. The key to all data collection is precision in collecting information and the subsequent organization of those data for analysis. Raw research data should be backed up and stored securely. Data must always be collected using ethical methods that protect both the integrity of the study and the confidentiality of each participant's identity. This can be complex in the case of research with participating individuals over time (longitudinal research).

Raw research data and field notes should also be available for reanalysis and or verification by others in the future. This may necessitate replacing names of participants with code numbers. Code numbers must not be Social Security numbers or workplace badge numbers. Many funding agencies and most universities have published guidelines for the maintenance of raw research data.[8] A typical requirement is that the files should be available for a period of at least 7 years. Naturally, files can be scanned onto digital storage devices and the mass of paperwork carefully disposed.

Applications from the Literature

Action Plan from a School Counseling Collaborative Action Research Study

Note: In this study designed to improve the action research skills of graduate students in school counseling, preservice school counselors were divided into action research teams and were assigned to work cooperatively with the school counselors in one of 15 school districts in Southern California. The focus of their various action plans was on improving the school counseling programs in the school districts that took part.

The Collaborative Research Process: The team's first task was to determine how best to move forward in assisting the site in its efforts to reform the school counseling program. Ultimately the author of the project decided to cross-walk the competencies addressed in the new planning guides with competencies from three sources: (a) the student competencies selected by the site for its guidance center program, (b) the competencies included in the County Standards (San Diego County Office of Education), and (c) the National Standards for School Counseling Programs (Campbell & Dahir, 1997).[9] The research team, in consultation with the head counselor, concluded that making the competencies addressed through the guides explicit and comparing them with other sets of competencies could contribute to the site's planning for the new school-counseling program.

Source: Rowell, L. L. (2005). Collaborative action research and school counselors. *Professional School Counseling, 9*(1), 28–36.

Participants

In many ways, the process of recruiting participants for action research is similar to the approaches used by qualitative researchers. The approach used to select subjects for empirically oriented experimental research tends to be statistically structured to represent a population within a designated **margin of error.** Individuals to be studied through action research are volunteers who have agreed to participate in the research process. The whole action research model is participant centered and concerned with questions of how individuals respond to, and interact with, a new positive action step and/or new activities.

Action research participants are likely to be from an **intact group.** The intact group may be a clinical community; a high school counseling office; an agency- or community-based outreach program; a hospital outpatient service; or a university-based outreach, including service learning projects. In each of these environments, the goal is to identify and involve active participation by individuals.

A major concern when using students of any age in action research is the potential problem of the power relationship between subjects and the researcher. Professors have considerable prestige and power over the lives of graduate students; likewise, school counselors, as professional school employees, have considerable power over students. In clinical settings, the problem may be one of transference manifested as the clinical need for some clients to please their therapist. In these cases of a power imbalance, there is a true need for individuals to recognize and believe they can set their own boundaries and require more information if wanted prior to providing the researcher with informed consent.

Children and those not fully mentally competent are the most vulnerable members of our society and need to have their rights and interests fully protected by parents or guardians (Burns, 2007). This need for careful explanations and obtaining written informed consent must be replicated with each new action cycle with these vulnerable populations.

Applications from the Literature

Sample Selection for Participatory Action Research Effort

Note: Underserved and marginalized populations are often difficult to recruit for a research effort. Action research is a method that such groups find easier to buy into than the traditional quantitative and qualitative methods. In this study of Canadian sex workers, participation by the individuals being studied occurred at all levels of the research effort. They worked with the researcher to focus the study, develop its research questions, and assist in the design of interviews. The authors made use of a snowball sample.

Building Bridges Through Action Research: Initially, all current staff and board members were asked if they would like to be interviewed. Additional interviews were arranged through snowball sampling methods including referrals and word of mouth. All participants in the study were current or former sex workers and key allies in Toronto; each had experience in sex work advocacy, community development, and/or labor organizing, and were past or present members of the organization around which the research was built. The interview sample, therefore, represented a small and targeted case study. This proved to be the most successful research design given the diversity and heterogeneity of the sex industry; achieving a representative sample of sex workers is nearly impossible.

Source: van der Meilen, E. (2011). Action research with sex workers: Dismantling barriers and building bridges. *Action Research, 9*(4), 370–384. doi: 10.1177/1476750311409767

Role of Participants/Researchers

Ideally, participants in action research use their tacit (local) knowledge when helping to design the most effective action to be taken. This local knowledge is also used to assist the researcher(s) in changing and improving what is done (action) and assessing the extent to which it is accomplished. Professional researchers must avoid the trap of seeming to be consultants assisting an organization or group to improve its operation. Rather the relationship should be one that is democratic and in which coercion is avoided. The working relationship between researchers and participants, including the participants' right to opt out of the project at any point, should be clearly stated in the action plan.

Activities

Action research involves action; therefore, the plan should specify the details of the action for the first cycle of the project and how its impact will be assessed. The action plan should describe how and when the actions will be initiated and how long they will continue. This description provides an approximate timeline for the activities and answers such questions as, What will be the focus of group activities or seminars? The structure or nature of new approaches or methods? The design of outreach? Prior to starting any action research activities, all participants should be fully informed as to what will occur and how it will work. They should also know what role they are expected to play in the action's implementation and evaluation.

Applications from the Literature

Excerpt from an Example Action Plan Description

Note: This study, supported by the Mellon Foundation, involved the counselors in two high schools in Hayward, California. The study employed action research to improve education and college planning for immigrant high school students.

Methods and Procedures: An on-the-job action research model of professional development was utilized. Counselors learned and applied the CT equity-centered school change principles as a means of gaining a deeper understanding of the schooling needs of English language learners [ELLs]. . . .

Counselors were invited to participate in several groups that met regularly to engage in collegial dialogue and collaboration. The groups included: (a) an on-site monthly meeting of ESL and "sheltered" subject area teachers across disciplines; (b) a quarterly cross-site subject area meeting of teachers who collaborated in the development of course placement guidelines for mathematics and science classes designated for ELLs; (c) quarterly community dinner forums for the purpose of linking school personnel with each other, with students, and with individuals from community-based organizations around the theme of educating ELLs; and (d) a quarterly meeting of immigrant parents, their students, and school counselors, which was supported by the project resource teacher and bilingual community liaison.

Source: McCall-Perez, Z. (2000). The counselor as advocate for English language learners: An action research approach. *Professional School Counseling, 4*(1), 13–22.

Instrument Development or Selection

Action researchers should always be mindful of the issues of measurement validity and reliability when selecting published measures for data collection (see Chapter 12 for more on this topic). It is necessary to include a description of each published instrument and a statement of the purpose of using it in the study in informed consent agreements. When working with minors and those who may not be mentally competent, the researcher should have evidence of the instrument's developmental appropriateness for all who will be using it.

Most action researchers use questionnaires and interview systems developed specifically for the study. With participatory action research, these questionnaires should have their goal statement developed cooperatively by the researcher and participants. The same process can also suggest a questionnaire format. As nonresearchers may not have the skill or knowledge base to write and publish questions, this task may be reserved for the researcher to perform. This is a good time to employ a **pilot study** group to field-test the questionnaires and interview protocols devised for the study (see Chapter 13 for more on the development of these measures).

Implement the Action Plan (Step 5)

Once approved, the action plan is ready to be initiated by the researcher(s). Care in carrying out each step described in the action plan and in documenting all procedures and processes is needed when the local action research plan is underway. The documentation may include a research journal or diary along with more traditional sources of data, such as observations, interviews, surveys, and published measures. These forms of documentation are needed to provide a trail of evidence that can stand up to any external scrutiny by future IRB committees or funding agencies or other administrative oversight.

As noted previously, the project's record should document all action research activities along with any anomalies and creative modifications that transpired. Much of the same information may appear in other locations, including the notes of the leader of any group counseling sessions, participant-initiated evaluations, and attendance logs and meeting notes from training sessions and group meetings. Action researchers should have a single repository of what happened during all phases and for all steps taken in the action project. Later these notes, along with background information and outcome data, could become part of a presentation before a state or national professional association or be included in a professional publication (see Chapter 17 for more about reporting research).

The implementation of the action research can produce an overwhelming amount of data and documentation. Care is needed to ensure that all components of raw information are carefully catalogued and managed in preparation for integration into a written outcome statement.

Interpret the Outcomes (Step 6)

The action plan may use the information from the reconnaissance and data-gathering phase as a baseline when assessing the project's outcomes and drawing conclusions. In organizing the data into a meaningful whole to draw conclusions and plan for subsequent action steps, action researchers may examine different streams of data first singularly and then together as an integrated whole (see Chapter 15 for a description of mixed methods research).

Component Analyses

Much of the data generated by action research efforts are best described as qualitative. Analysis of these data can also involve the study's participants in the basic qualitative research processes. Participants should assist in the selection of salient issues and have input into the organization of categories for the coding of observational and interview data (Stringer, 2007). This process extends to labeling and testing of the critical themes from the qualitative data.

Applications from the Literature

Two Streams of Findings from an Action Research Study

Note: In an action research study to identify ways counselors can improve at-risk behavior by adolescent girls (ages 15–18 years), the authors established 4 Gestalt-therapy groups for 10 girls each. The groups met weekly for 10 weeks. The authors and their participants used both quantitative and qualitative data sources to address four primary research questions about how well the therapy worked and how efficient it was for professionals working in a school setting.

Evaluation Methods: After their groups ended, students completed surveys at Week 1 and Week 6. They responded to the statement, "I have noticed other changes in myself, related to what I learned in group counseling." . . . Students were asked to list these changes.

The final action research question (i.e., Is group counseling . . . efficient . . . ?) was answered by consulting notes and logs. . . . Records reviewed included eight at-risk girls who had been involved in regularly scheduled, individual counseling. These students shared characteristics and backgrounds similar to the girls involved in groups; all had sought counseling voluntarily. Time invested in individual counseling services for these eight students was compared to time invested in a counseling group of eight students who participated in one of the four counseling groups. . . . Individual counseling sessions were charted for a 10-week period, thus paralleling the duration of groups included in the study.

Source: Zinck, K., & Littrell, J. M. (2000). Action research shows group counseling effective with at-risk adolescent girls. *Professional School Counseling, 4*(1), 50–59.

A study employing quantitative measurements and analyses should involve participants in the process of instrument development and validation. This can take the form of goal setting for the measure and suggesting the types of question items that will fulfill the goals. Goal setting and question determination should be accomplished through a consensus of all involved in the action research. The participants can also have input into the selection of published instruments to be used in the action research. Participant input could include identification of measurement goals and the type of scales that should be acquired for the project. One important issue is the ethical standard for ensuring the confidentiality of published test materials. Participants should not have direct access to the actual instruments they may be answering later. This may require that participants be limited to knowing only about the nature of the instruments available for consideration. The participants can use published reviews (e.g., Buros's *Mental Measurements Yearbook*) as sources of evaluative information. (See Chapter 12 for a discussion of instrument evaluation.)

Integrating and Expanding Interpretations

Findings from action research can be reported as the outcome of each stand-alone component; however, the various findings should be integrated into a conclusion and a set of recommendations for future change and inform the identification of areas where further improvement is indicated.

When the basic data analysis has been completed, the researcher should work with the participants and other stakeholders on building a consensus interpretation of the findings and their implications (Cady & Caster, 2000). A true consensus requires the active participation of the participants in the process, not simple acquiescence.[9] A good starting point for this consensus building is with the positive conclusions about some aspect of the system. Starting with a positive finding tends to smooth the dynamic processes normally encountered in reaching a true agreement. It also helps reduce defensiveness or an emotional backlash if the findings identify systemic problems needing further work.

Drawing Valid Conclusions

When action researchers draw their conclusions, they do not have the type of data that can answer a challenge such as "Prove it." Jean McNiff (2002) made the point that the lexicon of action research does not contain the word *prove*. A preferred approach for action researchers to use in making a case for their findings is to validate the findings and conclusions (McNiff & Whitehead, 2011).

Applications from the Literature

Excerpt of Results Presentation from Action Research Project

Note: This study of 86 undergraduate teacher education students focused on their multicultural understanding of adolescents from income-challenged homes. The study was facilitated by the use of emails between undergraduates and participating middle school students. The undergraduates were mostly Anglo-whites, while only 16% of the adolescents were from European American backgrounds.

Awareness of Biases and Experiential Gaps: A significant outcome of this project was that it allowed students to identify their own biases and false assumptions about their pen pals. At the beginning of the project, the undergraduates had been informed that 83% of the middle school population had been on the free and reduced lunch program.

Another theme that emerged in the project reports was the observation that their pen pals were smart. A discussion of this revealed that because of the poverty level and low test scores of this population, undergraduates assumed that their pen pals were not very bright. When discussing suggested modifications of this project, a group of students . . . noted that they should not be provided the demographics on poverty because "it inevitably makes you stereotype."

The weekly analysis of the undergraduates' letters revealed several examples of what we, as a group, termed middle-class bias. These were instances when students used their own middle-class experience as the sole basis for understanding or interpreting their pen pals' experiences. The following excerpts exemplify this concept: "You have a cow for a pet? What an unusual pet!"; "What is it like to be in such a large family?"; and "What did you do on your birthday? Did you have a party or get any cool stuff?" Comments about "unusual" pets and "large" families were plentiful in the first 3 weeks of the correspondence. Nevertheless, many middle school students stated that they had cows (and bulls), pigs, chickens, and goats as pets [prior to immigrating]. Although hardly unusual among this population, these were animals that none of the undergraduates had ever owned. Similarly, appropriate family size was based on the undergraduates' perspective. Yet it was not uncommon for the middle school students to have families in which there were at least four children. The question on the birthday provides a stark contrast to a statement written by a middle school correspondent: "We didn't do anything for my birthday because, my mom says we are running out of money." ...

The project enabled students to become aware of the gaps in their knowledge base about their correspondents' cultures, lifestyles, and interests. . . . They pondered the U.S.-centric perspective in the question posed to a Jamaican-born correspondent—"How do they celebrate Thanksgiving in Jamaica?"—and a student's initial reaction when asked to think about the validity of the question—that the problem with the question was linked to the lack of either turkeys or Indians in Jamaica.

Source: Schoorman, D. (2002). Increasing critical multicultural understanding via technology: "Teachable moments" in a university school partnership project. *Journal of Teacher Education, 53*(4), 356–369.

If a researcher claims to have improved a system or approach through the use of action research, he or she can expect to be asked to back up that claim with evidence. Initiating permanent changes in how things are done requires that those in leadership positions are convinced to change how they do things or even develop new policies. Skeptical reviewers of research findings may be concerned about the smallness or unique nature of the participants or feel that the link between the action taken and the outcome criteria is too weak and needs further review. Even when the senior leadership of an organization wants to initiate the changes that were indicated through the use of action research, implementation may still be thwarted by midlevel managers who are resistant to change (Marshall, Willson, & de Salas, 2010). This type of skepticism is a normal and healthy aspect of the research process. The same types of concerns are likely to be expressed by the team of **peer reviewers** for journals or professional conferences where the action research effort is being considered for publication.

Reflection is a key component in the process of determining the meaning of what was found and how it relates to research questions. The conclusions of the research should be generated through a collaborative effort of the researchers and the participants. Consensus building and working toward a collective point of view provides a solid base for the recommendations and conclusions.

The process of developing conclusions and recommendations can be enhanced by employing a validation group to assess the interpretations and conclusions the action researchers claim are justified by their findings (McNiff & Whitehead, 2011). This process can involve having others read the data and review the analysis. Once they understand the study, they are then presented with the researcher's insight into why and how the conclusions were reached. Validation occurs when (if) the readers endorse the findings. Such external endorsements provide a demonstration of the validity of the action research's conclusions.

Assessment of the Action's Outcome

The composition of the validation group needed to vouch for the bona fides of the action research conclusions and recommendations has been addressed. McNiff and Whitehead (2011) recommended that the validation group be composed of between 4 and 10 individuals who meet with the researcher and interested participants on a regular basis during the research effort to provide an ongoing or "formative" review of the progress and process of the research. That validation group can be drawn from the researcher's professional colleagues and/or representatives from the administration of the program under study.

Amend the Action Plan (Step 7)

Upon analyzing the outcome report based on information and data from the action research effort, researchers can determine whether or not the original problem has been solved via the intervention. If the problem is resolved, only one more step needs to be taken with the action research project: That final step is to write up outcomes and make them available to the stakeholders and perhaps the wider profession.

Wider dissemination can be easily accomplished by posting the action research report on the statewide web page for professionals in the field maintained by the professional association within the state and/or presenting the findings during a state or national meeting of professionals. High-quality action research projects can also be presented in professional journals such as *Action Research* (http://arj.sagepub.com/) or its blog (http://arj-journal.blogspot.com/).

If the participants, stakeholders, and researchers conclude that the report indicates that more work needs to be done, or that further improvement is possible, then the researchers are justified in planning for another action research cycle. Once again, many issues need to be addressed before an action research effort can be revised and prepared for another round.

The second reconnaissance phase can be abbreviated by using much of the earlier data and literature in structuring the next sequential researchable question. The new question should be linked to the original and add to the original findings or in some way improve the status found after the first action research cycle. Data from the first cycle can serve as the new baseline for the next phase of action research.

Another problem to address when starting a second cycle of research is the informed consent issue. Young people under the age of 18 must have the written consent of their parents and/or legal guardians prior to commencing each research cycle. Unless the original signed consent forms specified a second research cycle, each participant must sign a new informed consent form. Likewise, a second IRB review is needed. Naturally, if an entirely new group of volunteer participants is brought into the study's second cycle, they will need to be developed and encouraged to assist in the formulation of the processes being employed. These individuals also must provide their uncoerced informed consent.

Several political considerations may need to be addressed in the implementation of a second cycle. As in most human endeavors designed to bring about change, people and institutions have more reasons not to change or not do something different than to take positive action. Stakeholders, including administrators of the system or organization being studied, may disagree with the findings of the first action research cycle and believe a second cycle is not justified. Other stakeholders, including colleagues of the participants and researchers, may have significant concerns about the time, energy, and resources being expended on the action research effort and not want another cycle to begin.

Begin a Second Action Research Cycle (Final Step)

The genius of the model for action research developed by Kurt Lewin is that it can turn around and begin anew until the problem is eventually resolved or the system/program cannot be improved upon. When Lewin first proposed action research, he considered it to be a method to resolve a problem and as an approach to have a clear-cut endpoint (Whitehead & McNiff, 2006).

Contemporary organizations may see action research as a process that is finite and appropriate for solving a problem, or they may view it as continuous with the goal of moving the phenomenon or program being studied toward perfection. In many gifted education circles, this continuing to work for improvement is described as moving toward **satori.** The concept of satori is at the heart of Zen Buddhism. It is a Japanese word, now incorporated into English, that can be translated to mean "perfect understanding." Through continuing action research cycles, researchers and participants are striving to make the system or program increasingly more just, efficient, effective, fair, and beneficial for all. Naturally, if an action research effort moves to a second cycle, it may eventually move to a third, fourth, or fifth cycle and so on.

Some problems are seemingly intractable. Examples include closing the achievement gap among students from different ethnic groups or preventing spousal violence. The complexity of such problems implies that many cycles of action-based research are likely to be needed. Others problems in counseling, such as improving parents' engagement with their children, can be easier to achieve and potentially need only a single well-conducted cycle of action research.

SUMMARY

Action research is a method that grew out of Kurt Lewin's theoretical propositions regarding field theory and his development of the model for the study of group dynamics. Lewin's research model engages individuals and brings them into the research process. In action research, participants in the research and researchers work toward solutions together. This democratic approach for conducting research has been embraced by practioners in a number of fields, including those working in education, nursing, evaluation, and the struggle for social justice.

The participatory nature of action research gives strength to the model, as action researchers can draw from local knowledge and methods and from the energy and resources of others. A major problem faced by action researchers involves meeting the ethical canon of informed consent when the nature of the study may change as it occurs. This can be a problem for IRBs and doctoral dissertation committees supervising student action research projects as well.

The original action research model, as developed by Lewin, proposed a 7-step sequence of data collection, reflection, problem development, action planning, implementation, data analysis, and integration of data and drawing of conclusions. These steps are carried out with the cooperation and input of the study's participants. Action researchers can then plan another cycle for their action research, if the results of the first cycle suggest more improvement is necessary or possible.

DISCUSSION QUESTIONS

1. It has been said that "A good case can be made that every competent therapist engages in action research throughout the processes of therapeutic communication with clients." Is this a valid statement? Explain why you agree or disagree with this metaphor.

2. It has also been said that "The basic counseling steps are reflective of the continuing striving for improvement advocated by action researchers and the research process." Is this a valid statement? Explain why you agree or disagree with this metaphor.

3. The first professional researchers who embraced action research were researchers in education and nursing. Clinical psychology and counseling researchers were slower to adopt the action research approach in their investigations. What are some likely reasons for differences among research areas in their readiness to embrace the action research approach?

NOTES

1. The public burning of textbooks written by Jewish scholars and the dismissal of all Jewish professors by the Nazi government in Germany in 1933 saw a quick reaction in the United States. Unfortunately, the rule-bound US State Department used complex and limiting quotas to control who could come to the United States. Its rules would not allow any German scholar to enter this country unless he or she had a means of self-support. This was a difficult criterion to meet, as the Nazis had confiscated all personal wealth and property owned by the would-be émigrés. Private foundations set up The Emergency Committee in Aid of Displaced German Scholars to provide colleges, science centers, and museums with money needed to hire these escaping scholars (Feingold, 1995). A total of 355 of the estimated 6,000 who applied for support could be accommodated.

2. This quotation from Köhler is often mistranslated from the German as "The whole is *greater* than the sum of its parts."

3. Retrieved from http://onkey.livejournal.com/1014692.html

4. The lands known as the Ardoyne were confiscated by English and Scottish aristocrats under a royal warrant in 1613. That warrant was originally approved by Elizabeth I and supported after her death by James I, the monarch after whom the "King James" version of the Bible was named.

5. The Collaborative Action Research Network in cooperation with the Taylor-Francis Group of the United Kingdom began publishing the journal *Educational Action Research.* Ten years later in 2003, a group of scholars who used action research began the journal *Action Research,* published by Sage. Two years later in

2005, an online journal, *International Journal of Action Research,* was begun; it can be found at http://www.hampp-verlag.de/hampp_e-journals_IJAR.htm.

  6. As was noted in Chapter 1, all professionals should give a minimum of 60 to 90 minutes to their professional development each week. A program of reading and reflecting on the studies being presented in professional journals is an excellent way to "stay on top of the game."

  7. Each state sets its own rules for this ongoing education, but most rules are similar to the mandate of the National Board for Certified Counselors, which requires a minimum of 10 approved **continuing education units (CEUs),** or 100 approved clock hours of continuing education, every 5 years.

  8. For example, the Office of the Provost of the University of Pittsburgh has published on the Internet that university's take on the issues of research ethics, including file storage: http://www.provost.pitt.edu/documents/GUIDELINES%20FOR%20ETHICAL%20PRACTICES%20IN%20RESEARCH-FINALrevised2-March%202011.pdf.

  9. Campbell, C. A., & Dahir, C. A. (1997). *Sharing the vision: The national standards for school counseling programs.* Alexandria, VA: American School Counselor Association.

  10. This type of consensus is occasionally described as a Quaker consensus after the approach employed by the Society of Friends to work in harmony and use a consensus model in setting policy and making decisions. This Protestant movement dates from the 17th century and has always believed in religious tolerance and in the development of human potential to its fullest.

SECTION III

Descriptive Statistics and Correlation

"But psychology is a trickier field, in which even outstanding authorities have been known to run in circles, 'describing things which everyone knows in language which no one understands.'"

Raymond Cattell

This pair of chapters describes how research consumers can understand the nature of data collected by researchers and reported in the literature.

Chapter 7 describes the levels of precision used to measure and express variables and appropriate techniques for depicting those data. Additionally, it provides research consumers with examples of how researchers summarize data as a simple statistic.

Chapter 8 provides insight into how two or more measured variables may be codependent. The observation that certain variables have a degree of concordance has been established since the end of the 19th century. These relationships among variables measured on the same individuals are summarized using one of the various methods for correlation. Different correlation methods are appropriate for variables with different levels of precision in their measurement.

Nature of Variables and Data

"USA Today has come out with a new survey. Apparently, three out of four people make up 75% of the population."

David Letterman

OBJECTIVES

By reading and studying this chapter, you should acquire the competency to do the following:

- Explain the nature of a construct and explain why constructs are considered variables.
- Describe the difference between a construct and a property.
- Identify the level of precision (NOIR) for a range of different variables.
- Explain the limitation imposed by the precision category level of a variable and how its central tendency is determined.
- Read and interpret data presentations involving variance and standard deviations.
- Describe appropriate graphic presentations for all levels of scale precision.
- Find z-scores and describe how they apply to areas under the Gaussian normal curve.
- Describe commonly employed standard score transformations.

INTRODUCTION AND MAJOR THEMES

"Before the curse of statistics fell upon mankind, we lived a happy, innocent life, full of merriment and go and informed by fairly good judgment."

Hilaire Belloc

The best therapists are simultaneously aware of many **variables** when working with clients. Some of these variables are psychological constructs, and others are categorical information. All variables do not have the same degree of precision, and care must be exercised when summarizing and reporting data. The different levels of precision of variables imply that a limited range of graphics and arithmetic procedures can be used to describe and summarize them.[1]

CONSTRUCTS

The point was made in Chapter 1 that much of what we understand about the world is the product of what we were told or taught. Another major source of new learning is what we observe others experiencing. This latter source of knowledge about the world includes what the **social learning** theorist Albert Bandura described as **vicarious learning** (Bandura, 1976; Bandura & McDonald, 1963).

Professional counselors are highly trained observers and listeners who learn a great deal about clients through these channels. These observations are mentally clustered into **constructs** held about clients. In the mental health fields, practitioners observe, analyze, and assist clients in modifying aspects of some of these constructs. Constructs are observable clusters of characteristics that may be drawn from an individual's social circumstances, history, beliefs, or ideologies. They are not physical characteristics and lack any physical dimensions. These **psychological constructs** include dimensions such as anger, creativity, jealousy, emotional intelligence, attention-deficit/hyperactivity disorder, love, dependency, enmity, sangfroid, rectitude, and thousands more. While a construct is not a concrete or physical entity, its presence in people varies in degree from person to person. This **variability** implies the noun *variable* is an appropriate description of the degree to which such constructs are expressed by individuals. We employ indirect methods to assess the degree to which an individual exhibits one or more of these constructs (variables). These methods involve formal and informal measurements and observations. They can involve a wide range of techniques, including field-based observation, checklists, inventories, in-office discussions, group process observation, standardized psychometric evaluation tools, and many others.

PROPERTIES AND ATTRIBUTES

In addition to using constructs, counselors can also examine a number of properties that have directly measurable attributes. These properties also vary and thus are variables, and they can be physically seen and directly measured. There is a long list of such properties, including eye color with attributes such as brown, black, green, gray, hazel, blue, etc. Some properties can be scaled to measure various dimensions, including height, serum oxygen levels, weight, annual income, diastolic blood pressure, galvanic skin response, age in months, subcutaneous fat, gender, and hearing acuity. Just because properties are physical entities does not imply they are more accurately measured than psychological constructs. Whenever people employ measurement instruments, there is always some degree of loss of accuracy and precision.

VARIABLES

Not all variables are created equal; they can be expressed at one of four levels of mathematical precision. Variables may be measured as continuous numbers, or they may exist as a series of descriptive names. In the mental health professions, constructs all exhibit a degree of measurable variation. The **precision** of measurement scales used to assess constructs and properties has been organized as a variable with five levels. These are **nominal scales,** two types of **ordinal scales, interval scales,** and **ratio scales.** This sequence of nominal, ordinal, interval, and ratio represents a hierarchy from the least mathematically precise (nominal scales) to the most precise (ratio scales).

Nominal Scales

When the data from a variable exist in categorical form, and those categories cannot be placed into a logical order, then the variable is labeled **nominal.** As the word implies, these categories exist as names only; therefore, the only possible arithmetic operation one can perform with them is counting. For example, clients being counseled as part of their treatment program for an anxiety disorder could include, among many others, those with social phobia, posttraumatic stress disorder, acute stress disorder, trichotillomania, and general anxiety disorder. These mental disorders cannot be sequenced into any meaningful hierarchical scale; they can only be listed. If an arrangement is needed, these mental disorders could be sequenced in alphabetical order or by the nonmathematical reference code number assigned in the American Psychiatric Association's *Diagnostic and Statistical Manual* (2012).

Two Types of Ordinal Scales

Theoretical constructs are not always expressed by measures composed of equal-size units. This restricts the type of arithmetic operations available to the researcher. For example, "faculty rank" is a construct (instructor, assistant, associate, and professor), but it does not qualify for mathematical and statistical operations.

Ordinal Scale Type I

The commissioned corps of officers in the US Army includes the ranks of second lieutenant, first lieutenant, captain, major, lieutenant colonel, colonel, brigadier general, major general, lieutenant general, full general (4 stars), and general of the army.[2] We know these ranks exist in an order, but they are not describable with a mathematical system involving arithmetic operations. To test this, note that if you subtract a first lieutenant from a brigadier general, you don't get a colonel plus change. It is clear that this rank system, like many others (e.g., church hierarchy, NCAA competition level, hospital nurse rank[3]) is an ordered sequence, not a numerical system. For that reason, these types of data are referred to as ordinal data.

CASE IN POINT   7.1

Ordinal scores (positions) from various scales can be compared. Consider the military, where the Army rank of warrant officer is equivalent to the Marine Corps rank master gunner, which is equivalent to the Navy rank of master chief. People holding one of these ranks will have a similar level of responsibility, pay, and authority as their peers in the other branches. Another example is found in academic ranks. In American higher education, the highest academic rank is professor, as it is in British universities. The academic ranks in American universities in descending order are professor, associate professor, assistant professor, instructor, and lecturer. The equivalent academic ranks in the traditional universities of Great Britain are professor, reader, senior lecturer, principal lecturer, and research fellow.

A commonly applied ordinal in educational settings is the level reached in school, or years of education completed. Most graduate students would be hard-pressed to give a meaningful answer to the question "How many years of schooling have you finished?" This is because this variable is an ordinal. Once again, remember our little test: A person with a master of science degree in counseling is not the equivalent of a person with an associate's degree added to another person with a bachelor's degree. The step between a person who completes 3 years of college then drops out and a person who attains a bachelor's degree is a very big step. It is clearly larger than the 1-year step between being a sophomore dropout and being a junior dropout.

Counting college years of education is made difficult by another problem. Does a student who takes 5 years to earn a bachelor's degree have more education than a person who completes the degree in the standard 4 years? Does a doctoral student who takes 6 years to write a dissertation have 5 more years of college than a peer who only took 1 year to write the dissertation?

Ordinal Scale Type II

Professors assign letter grades at the end of every semester or term. Each of these grades is an ordinal datum. We know they are ordinals because they do not have a continuous numerical basis (are not real numbers). The distance between a grade of A and B is not the same in all classrooms, and it is not necessarily the same as the distance between a D and a C in the same professor's classroom. In the pure world of mathematics, letter grades are ordinals, and it is not correct to perform most arithmetic operations with them. Yet we ignore the rules and do what we want with letter grades. We create grade averages and honorific ranks (*cum laude*, meaning with praise; *magna cum laude*, meaning with great praise; *summa cum laude*, meaning with highest praise, *egregia cum laude*, with outstanding praise). We even admit graduate students into our most prestigious programs of advanced study based in part on these averaged ordinal scores.

This violation of the rules of arithmetic also occurs whenever an attitude scale is averaged. For example, when clients evaluate the therapy they received at an outpatient clinic by responding to an opinion-measuring instrument, many clinic administrators feel compelled to average the data. Those data are typically collected as the clients complete their course of treatment and are discharged. The ordinal score from each client's evaluation for each item is added to create a total "opinion score." This total is combined with the total scores provided by other clients of the therapist to determine an average value. As an example, the following frequently appears on questionnaires used for client evaluations of therapist quality:

Overall, how well do you feel your counselor understood your feelings and needs?

5. Always very well attuned to my feelings and needs

4. Usually well attuned to my feelings and needs

3. Not well in touch with my feelings and needs during about half of the sessions

2. Typically not focused on me and my feelings

1. Completely self-absorbed and unaware of my feelings and needs

Clearly, when a number of these items about a therapist are averaged together, he or she would want to have an "average" score that is high, near the value of 5.0. This would indicate that he or she is viewed by clients as being well attuned to their needs. That designation implies a precision level that is someplace between the precision of interval and ordinal scales (Knapp, 1990). This in-between level of precision is designated *ordinal II.*

Another special case is that of a **dichotomy.** There are variables that exist as natural dichotomies (e.g., gender), which cannot be ordered in some form of hierarchy. Thus, such variables are **binary,**[4] making it possible to use them in mathematical analysis. Binary variables can also be artificially created by dividing a ratio or ordinal data set into two parts. One way to do this is to divide the variable at its center point or **median.** Another binary variable could be defined as those who pass the state board's license examination and those who are required to retake it.

Interval Scales

Another class of measurements for variables describes equal interval data without true zero values. These measurement scores are generally described as being **standard scores** or **standardized scores.** They are determined by charting or comparing individual scores against a comparison group. The comparison group is also known as the **norm group** or **normative comparison group.** Such scores can be expressed in a number of formats that share the common property of having scales with equal unit sizes. Having equal-sized units makes it possible to use standard arithmetic and statistical procedures with the measurements. These interval-scaled variables include the Educational Testing Service (ETS)™ scores across the range of tests that corporation publishes, **IQ scores,** scores from developmental inventories and batteries, scores on the Examination for the Professional Practice of Psychology, and scores from the National Board for Certified Counselors' National Counselor Examination.

Ratio Scales

Some variables are measurable using a continuous mathematical scale known as a ratio scale. The ratio scale implies that the units of measurement are "real numbers." This makes the use of fractions and decimals appropriate, as there is a true zero point in the number system. These measures include most physical dimensions, such as the volume of water needed by an outpatient clinic each day, weight of the physical therapist in kilograms, relative humidity of the air in office areas, or range of tones heard by a client expressed in Hz at an intensity of 35 dB. Thus, using a ratio scale, it is possible to determine a patient's body mass index, height in centimeters, oral cavity temperature in degrees Celsius, and beta amyloid peptide count from spinal fluid (Alzheimer's test).

CASE IN POINT   7.2

In a major breakdown of campus communication on November 18, 2011, a dozen nonviolent student protesters at the University of California–Davis were targeted by campus police, who used military-grade pepper spray to force them to disperse. Police-grade pepper spray, like other forms of pepper, can be measured and discussed using a ratio scale of measurement, the Scoville heat unit (SHU).

In 1912 a chemist and pharmacist, Wilbur L. Scoville, employed by Park-Davis Laboratories, devised a measurement scale for the piquancy of peppers and foods containing peppers (Tabasco Inc., 2011). This measure for pepper pungency now has limits defined accurately by modern food chemistry. The pure essence of "hotness or piquancy" is the chemical capsaicin. The oily capsaicin spray interacts with nerve receptors in the mucus linings of the human mouth, eyes, sinuses, lungs and bronchial tubes, nose, ears, and gastrointestinal track as capsacinoid, a chemical that produces a powerful burning sensation.

Photo 7.1   Students and Police at University of California–Davis, November 18, 2011

Wayne Tilcock/The Davis Enterprise

Capsacinoid that is 100% pure has a Scoville scale value of 16 million SHU, 15 times greater than the hottest known natural pepper. The military-grade pepper spray used by some law enforcement officers to incapacitate suspects has an SHU index score of 5.3 million. The pain produced by this military-grade pepper spray can be overwhelming and cause temporary blindness, asthma, and a panic reaction. There is anecdotal evidence that it has caused the death of asthmatics by anaphylactic shock.

NOIR

To better remember these scales, the French word *noir,* meaning the color black, provides the handy acronym **NOIR**. When arranged from least to most precise, the types of measurement scales are the following: Nominal, Ordinal (I & II), Interval, and Ratio. Examples of these four types are seen in Table 7.1

Variables in Research

Practitioner-researchers engage in studies to determine the relationship among variables and find out how some variables influence others. In qualitative research, many of the variables that are of consequence in understanding individuals are revealed by the research itself. In quantitative studies, the researcher manipulates one or more variables to determine the relationship among known variables.

Independent Variables

In quantitative studies, the variable that the researcher analyzes as the likely change agent for one or more other variables is described as the independent variable. The independent variable is considered the engine that brings about changes and/or modifications in an individual's pattern of growth, learning, or behavior.

The independent variable may be an **active independent variable,** meaning that the researcher manipulates the condition or value of the independent variable. For example, independent variables are manipulated when the researcher decides how many hours

Table 7.1   A Collection of Examples of Each of the Four Types of Measures

Nominal	Ordinal	Interval	Ratio
Blood group	Medical pain scales	Fahrenheit scale	Kelvin scale[5]
Handedness	Movie ratings	WAIS III IQ scores	Dollars in the bank
Least liked food	Opinion surveys	ASVAB scores	Vote count
Brand of automobile	Horse race results	Developmental score	Birth weight
Gender	Social class	GRE scores	Chronological age
Breed of dog	Restaurant ratings	Personality profile	Blood pressure
Psychiatric disorder	Pass/Fail cut score	License test score	MMPI subtotals
Myers-Briggs type	Recommendations	Millon BHI scores	Beck anxiety scores
Illegal drug choice	APGAR scores	Serum creatinine	Chronological age

of counseling a client will receive, whether it is to be individual or group counseling, or whether the counseling program will include significant others in the client's life. Active independent variables can be pharmacological or environmental or be based on behavioral rewards.

The variable could also be an **assigned independent variable,** meaning that the practitioner-researcher has no control over how the variable appears for each subject. For example, the subject's gender may be identified as an independent variable, as it is an important factor in many aspects of each individual's persona. However, the practitioner-researcher has no control over which of the participants in a study are male and which are female. There are numerous other assigned independent variables, for example, age, ethnicity, education level, religiosity, number of siblings and/or birth order, number of parents in the home during childhood, immigration status, and many others.

Applications from the Literature

Examples of Independent Variables from the Literature

Example A

Note: In this study, the impact of four independent variables was studied with the dependent variable of forgiveness. Three of the independent variables were based on demographic characteristics of the subjects, and the fourth independent variable was based on scores derived from a compilation of three measures of personality.

Sample: Two hundred and twenty (220) residents in Mafikeng municipal area participated in this study. Of the 220 participants, 88 (40%) were males and 132 (60%) were females. Age of participants ranged from 18–68 years with mean age of 28.8 years (SD = 11.93). Marital status showed 150 (69.1%) were single, 55 (25.3%) are married, and 12 (5.6%) were separated, divorced or widowed.

Design: The study is a cross-sectional study of two hundred and twenty participants. The independent variables were gender, age, religion, education, marital status and education levels (demographic variables) and three personality factors. The dependent variable is willingness to forgive.

Source: Idemudia, E. S., & Mahri, S. (2011). Can gender, religion, education, age and personality predict willingness to forgive? *Gender and Behaviour, 9*(1), 3765–3781.

Example B

Note: In this study, the author examined whether increased exposure to 3,4-methylenedioxymethamphetamine (MDMA; "Ecstasy") causes decreased tissue stores of serotonin and results in behavioral effects when there are massive releases and subsequent depletions of brain serotonin. Such waves of serotonin in the chemistry of the brain of ecstasy users were thought to have a powerful effect on the user's emotional intelligence (EI). Ecstasy use was the independent variable, and psychological affect levels were elements of the dependent variable.

A description and examples of the use of analysis of covariance (ANCOVA) can be found on the student website for this book.

(Continued)

(Continued)

Design: The independent variable (IV) was drug use (non-user, cannabis only user and polydrug user). The dependent variable (DV) was Emotional Intelligence (EI). The basis of any drug-related differences in EI was explored through analysis of covariance.... Drug-related differences in the measures of psychological affect were also explored with drug use as the IV and the measures of psychological affect (anxiety, arousal, depression/hedonic tone) as Dependent Variables. The source of any drug-related differences in the psychological affect measures will be further explored using ANCOVA with the EI and the parenting measures as covariates.

Source: Craig, L., Fisk, J. E., Montgomery, C., Murphy, P. N., & Wareing, M. (2010). Is emotional intelligence impaired in ecstasy-polydrug users? *Journal of Psychopharmacology, 24*(2), 221–231. doi: 10. /0269881108095713

Dependent Variables

In research efforts, the variable that changes in response to the independent variable(s) is known as the dependent variable. Any empirical or qualitative study may have one or more dependent variables. In a qualitative study, the researcher's efforts may be directed toward identifying the possible independent variables of importance in influencing the dependent variable(s). In empirical research efforts, the practitioner-researcher works to determine the extent to which previously identified independent variables (both active and assigned) influence the dependent variable(s).

It is good to keep in mind that an independent variable from one study may be used as the dependent variable in a future study, and vice versa. For example, in a study of charitable contributions, the dependent variable could be the amount of time and or money donated, while the independent variable could be the emotional intelligence level of those participating in the research.

Applications from the Literature

Examples of Dependent Variables from the Literature

Example A

Note: In this research, the dependent variable was the children's level of self-esteem. The principal independent variable was parental alcoholism. The authors introduced other family and home dimensions to learn if they moderate the impact of parental alcoholism.

Family Environment: We developed a measure of family environment based on existing scales, including the Family Environment Scale and the FACES III. Our measure consists of two dimensions: Parental disregard and family stressors. Participants were asked to retrospectively report on perceptions of their family environment. The parental disregard subscale comprised six items (e.g., 'One or both of my parents was not around to take care of me') and the stressors subscale comprised six items (e.g., 'One or both of my parents had trouble keeping a job').

Parental Alcoholism, Family Environment, and Self-esteem: The primary goal of this investigation was to determine if family environment mediates the relationship between the independent variable, parental alcoholism, and the dependent variable self-esteem. Hierarchical regression analysis was performed to test the effects of parental alcoholism on parental disregard, while controlling for participant gender, age, and socio-economic status (SES). The overall model was significant and explained 26% of the variance in parental disregard. Control variables (i.e., participant gender, age, and family SES) were not significantly related to disregard. Perceptions of paternal alcoholism had a moderately large effect, and maternal alcoholism had a small effect on parental disregard.

Source: Rangarajan, S., & Kelly, L. (2006). Family communication, family environment, and the impact of parental alcoholism on offspring self-esteem. *Journal of Social and Personal Relationships, 23*(4), 655–671. doi: 10.1177/0265407506065990

Example B

Note: In this study of over 100 outpatients receiving therapy for serious and persistent mental disorders, the dependent variable involved dimensions of communication ability. The independent variables hypothesized to be related to those dimensions of the dependent variable are listed on the following table.

Independent variable	Dependent variable
Sociodemographic and clinical: visiting psychiatric outpatient services, living in flat vs house, diagnosis of mood disorder or neurosis vs belonging to the heterogeneous group *Health-related:* self rated health, quality of life, self esteem, sense of coherence, mastery	Availability of social integration
Sociodemographic and clinical: age, living alone, living in flat vs house *Health-related:* self rated health, quality of life, sense of coherence, mastery	Availability of attachment
Sociodemographic and clinical: age, years of contact with psychiatric services *Health-related:* quality of life, self-esteem, sense of coherence, mastery	Adequacy of social integration

(Continued)

(Continued)

Independent variable	Dependent variable
Sociodemographic and clinical: age, living in flat vs house *Health-related:* self-rated health, quality of life, self esteem, sense of coherence, mastery	Adequacy of attachment
Sociodemographic and clinical: visiting psychiatric outpatient services, living alone, living with one's children, living in flat vs house, having high school vs college education *Health-related:* self-rated health, quality of life, self-esteem, sense of coherence, mastery	Total ISSI score

Source: Eklund, M., & Hansson, L. (2007). Social network among people with persistent mental illness: Associations with sociodemographic, clinical, and health-related factors. *International Journal of Social Psychiatry, 53*(4), 293–305. doi: 10.1177/0020764006074540

Predictor and Criterion Variables

In studies that are simply relational in design, such as those studying the concordance or correlation among variables, the variable assumed to be the determining issue or factor may be referred to as the **predictor variable.** (This type of research is discussed in Chapter 8.) Likewise, the dependent variable in relationship studies is frequently given the name **criterion variable.**

Applications from the Literature

Examples of Criterion and Predictive Variables

Example A: Predictors

Note: In this study of one graduate program's training clinic, clients who did and did not finish a counseling intervention were studied, and several predictors of completion were identified. The researchers found lower-income clients were "more difficult" individuals with whom to work but that higher-income clients with healthier Global Assessment of Functioning scores were more likely to drop out of counseling as they felt "improved" by the counseling they had completed.

Results: The goal of this study was to establish which among a set of potential predictor variables would be useful in discriminating among the three groups of clients based on the time and manner at which the client-counselor relationship was ended: intake dropouts, therapy dropouts, and completers. Of the 380 client cases examined, 61 (16.1%) were categorized by their counselors as intake dropouts, 218 (57.4%) as therapy dropouts, and 101 (26.6%) as completers. (Percentages do not equal 100% because of rounding.) These results were consistent with those obtained in other training clinics. As expected, completers ($M = 10.26$, $SD = 9.68$) on average attended more counseling sessions than did therapy dropouts ($M = 5.14$, $SD = 4.76$). A number of potential predictor variables were investigated: age, education (seven levels, ranging from eighth grade or less to beyond a master's degree), annual family income (six levels, ranging from under $10,000 to $30,000 and higher), number of children in the client's living unit, number of the client's presenting problems, perceived client difficulty (low, medium, high), Global Assessment of Functioning Scale score, prior treatment (never, more than a year ago, less than a year ago), gender, employment status (four levels: not applicable, currently employed, unemployed less than 6 months, and unemployed more than 6 months), case urgency (crisis, noncrisis), and referral source (self, other).

Source: Lampropoulos, G. K., Schneider, M. K., & Spengler, P. M. (2009). Predictors of early termination in a university counseling training center. *Journal of Counseling and Development, 87*(1), 36–46.

Example B: Criterion Variables

Note: In this study of how counselor training changes a student's understanding of multicultural factors in the counseling relationship, the criterion measures are subtests of the self-report instrument Multicultural Counseling Inventory (MCI).

Results: Criterion variables, MCI Multicultural Knowledge subscale, MCI Multicultural Awareness subscale, and MCI Multicultural Skills subscale (i.e., those not found to have significant program effects), were conducted using student mean scores as the unit of analysis ($N = 516$). Significant differences for student ethnicity were found on the MCI Multicultural Awareness subscale scores. . . .

Tests comparing MCI Multicultural Awareness subscale scores across all ethnic groups revealed that African American students and Hispanic students scored significantly higher than Caucasian students. To control for these effects on MCI Multicultural Awareness subscale scores, . . . dummy variables for six ethnic groups (Caucasian, African American, Asian, Asian American, Latino(a) or Hispanic, and other) were entered, with the Caucasian variable coded zero to function as the constant. Finally, significant gender effects were found on the MCI Multicultural Skills subscale scores. Male participants' scores on the MCI Multicultural Skills subscale criterion variable were significantly higher than female participants' scores.

We examined the models to identify predictors of student multicultural competencies. First, we observed whether the overall prediction of the multicultural criterion was significant. If it was, then we looked for predictor groups, namely, program cultural ambience, instructional strategies, and clinical training that added significantly to the prediction when prior variables were controlled.

Source: Dickson, G. L., & Jepsen, D. A. (2007). Multicultural training experiences as predictors of multicultural competencies: Students' perspectives. *Counselor Education and Supervision, 47*(2), 76–95.

Parametric Versus Nonparametric

The term **parametric** is often applied when describing ratio and interval data. It means that the variables are real numbers that can have the full range of mathematical operations performed on them. The term applied to ordinal and nominal data is nonparametric. The exception to this generalization is **ordinal type II data,** which are not quite interval but are treated as such. While a large number of nonparametric procedures for data analysis can be used with variables of all four levels of precision, the procedures reserved for parametric variables tend to have greater **statistical power**[6] (Cohen, 1988; Siegel & Castellan, 1988).

Level of Precision

When scientific instruments are used to measure a ratio variable, it is very possible that the resulting score or measurement will be highly precise. High precision of measurement can be seen when medicine is measured and distributed in milligrams. Such scientific measurements are normally ratio scales. It is always possible to reduce the level of precision for a variable, but the reverse is not usually possible. Thus, it is possible to convert a ratio scale such as annual family income into an ordinal scale, such as impoverished, working poor, middle income level, upper income level, wealthy, and über wealthy, or even into a binomial, such as top 1% and other 99%. However, an ordinal scale such as movie-rating scores (e.g., 1 to 4 stars) cannot be changed into a ratio scale.

CASE IN POINT 7.3

A good stopwatch can be used to determine the exact amount of time that an individual needs to solve complex cognitive (performance) tasks on measures such as the Wechsler Adult Intelligence Test–IV. These measures of latency of correct response are used to award bonus points for the problem's solution. This is a highly precise method for scoring. If the test's items were only scored as a pass/fail dichotomy, the resulting scale score would be less nuanced.

CENTRAL TENDENCY

A practitioner-researcher can report data collected in a report listing every individual's score on some variable. That exhaustive approach is detailed but difficult to interpret. For that reason, data are customarily described in summary form. Commonly employed summary statistics include the **average.**[7] In science, there are three forms of average collectively called measures of **central tendency.**

Mode

The **mode** is the category that has the greatest number of cases. This statistic is appropriate for variables of all four (NOIR) levels of precision. There is no way to identify a center point among nominal data, and the lack of any type of sequence in the categories prevents the determination of a central category. However, mode can be determined. For example, *At grand rounds it was recently reported that there were more counseling psychologists in attendance than members of any other of the hospital's departments.* This statement presents the mode value or score (counseling psychologists) in a data set (those attending grand rounds) that is measured using nominal data (departments).

The mode can also be found for ratio, interval, and ordinal data. For example, *Surveys have found that most social workers have a master's degree.* Here the modal category (master's degree) of a variable that is ordinal (education level) has been identified for a data set (social workers). A report of a mode for ratio data can take the following form: *An analysis of all group homes in the state indicates that the largest single expense is the salary of the professional employees.* In this case, the mode (largest expense category) is used to summarize ratio data (facility finances).

The center (average) of ordinal data can be calculated for ordinal, interval, and ratio data but not for nominal data. This average of ordinals is referred to as the median and is the case that lies in the middle of an ordered sequence of data. In other words, it is the halfway point in the data, with half the cases above it and half below. Thus, the median is also the 50th **percentile**. It is important to note that ratio and interval data can be lowered in precision and become ordinal data for which a median can be calculated. In the set of numbers 9, 11, 15, 20, 17, 10, 14, the median (Mdn) is equal to 14. If the data set had two values of 14, the Mdn would still be 14. But if the data set were 9, 11, 15, 20, 17, 10, 14, 13, the Mdn would lie between the value of 13 and 14. When the distributions of ratio or interval data are symmetrical and there are no unusual cases, the two statistical values, the mean ($\bar{X}$ or *M*) and the median (Mdn) will approximate the same numerical value.

Then there is the special case of ordinal type II data. These ordinals are summarized as though they were equal-interval data, which they are not. As noted above, the use of opinion scales and **grade point averages (GPAs)** are classic examples of this misapplication of the parametric statistics for central tendency.

Mean ($\bar{X}$ or *M*)

The general public's use of the vernacular word *average* almost always refers to what a measurement specialist would describe as the "**mean** of the data." A statistician would explain the determination of a mean as

$$M \text{ or } \bar{X} = \frac{\sum\limits_{i=1}^{n} X_i}{n}$$

In this equation, the symbol $\bar{X}$ is used to represent the arithmetic average or mean of the data. In many journals, the letter *M* is used as the symbol for the mean because the symbol $\bar{X}$ is difficult to typeset. The uppercase Greek letter sigma Σ instructs us to add all cases from the first individual to the final, or case number *n*. The term X_i represents the score from any individual or case (sometimes called replicate, subject or participant). The lowercase letter *n* represents the number of subjects or participants in the data set. The equation can then be read as, "The mean equals the sum of all cases divided by the number of scores (cases) in the set of data."

The mean can only be calculated for ratio and interval data. It is the arithmetic center point in the data and can be viewed as a balance point or fulcrum for the data. Obviously, it is never possible to determine the mean of most ordinal and nominal data because addition and division are arithmetic operations not available with nominal and ordinal data.

NORMAL DISTRIBUTION

The distribution of scores drawn **randomly** from a large population will assume the shape of the **Gaussian normal curve**. This curve has been applied in millions of research studies in the social sciences as a means of interpreting individual scores and making sense of data that has been collected. The normal curve has even been applied to assist parole officers in interpreting the nature of threats posed by sex offenders they supervise in the community.

Applications from the Literature

Basic Interpretation of Data Matching a Normal Curve

Note: This is an interim report from the Dynamic Supervision Project. The authors developed a dynamic measurement plan to estimate the likelihood that a court-adjudicated parolee originally convicted for a sex offense will become a recidivist. In this study, there were eventually 1,000 offenders originally convicted for sexual offenses involving children or nonconsenting adults. The authors used the term *static risk score* as a one-time measure of the risk of recidivism.

Results: This analysis shows approximately 26 percent of offenders scoring in the low static risk category (9 percent projected recidivism risk over 10 years), 42 percent of offenders scoring in the low-moderate static risk category (13.5 percent projected recidivism risk over 10 years), 22 percent of offenders scoring in the moderate-high static risk category (34.5 percent projected recidivism risk over 10 years) and 10 percent of offenders scoring in the high static risk category (45 percent projected recidivism risk over 10 years). The scores of the 500 stable assessments . . . form a normal curve with about 42 percent of offenders falling into the low stable risk category, about 46 percent . . . falling into the moderate stable risk category and about 12 percent . . . falling into the high stable risk category.

Source: Harris, A., & Hanson, R. K. (2003). The dynamic supervision project: Improving the community supervision of sex offenders. *Corrections Today, 65*(5), 60–64.

The Bell Curve

Graduates preparing to sit for their state's licensing examination have been reported as asking "Is the test graded on a curve?" Few really know what they are asking (for more about the normal curve, see Chapter 9).

Applications from the Literature

Frequently Asked Question About the Licensing Examination of the Association of Social Work Boards (ASWB)

Note: The license examination for professional social workers, like the exams for professional counselors and psychologists, is graded on a pass/fail basis against an absolute standard for performance set by the various states.

Q. Is the exam graded on a "curve" for the whole country or the area you are in?

A. The exam isn't graded on a "curve."

The grading "curve" we are used to from school is a process by which the instructor moves the grading scale up or down, depending on the performance of the group being tested. This does not happen with the ASWB examinations.[8]

Source: Assocation of Social Work Boards. Retrieved from http://www.aswb.org/SWLE/faqs.asp#Curve

Nonetheless, all major licensing examinations use a curve in the scoring process. For students to understand the "curve" that is used in scoring licensing examinations, they must be familiar with the **normal distribution of errors** first defined 330 years ago. In 1686, the second Lucasian Professor of the Natural Philosophy of Mathematics at Cambridge University, Isaac Newton, published a book that changed Western science. It described his new calculus and applied it to understanding gravitation and planetary motion.[9]

In Newton's later life, one of the mathematicians in his orbit was Abraham de Moivre, a Huguenot, who escaped from France when King Louis XIV purged all Protestant intellectuals. This Huguenot émigré was an important mathematician in his own right. de Moivre studied the properties of the binomial distribution and, with the help of the calculus of Newton, was able to mathematically define what is now recognized as the **normal distribution** in 1738 (de Moivre, 1738/1985).[10]

In the early 19th century (1809), Carl Friedrich Gauss applied this mathematical model to the astronomical research dealing with asteroid orbits. It is Gauss whose name is associated with the development of this powerful mathematical tool (Wright, 2008). Today, most graduate students have never heard of either de Moivre or Gauss and refer to the statistical distribution not by its originator but by its shape, the **bell curve.**

The curve depicts a randomly occurring, continuous probability distribution. It can be used to approximate a number of different distributions in nature (Anton, Kolman, & Averbach, 1988). For example, the normal curve can approximate the distribution of the weight of the population of adults, the GRE scores (**raw score** form) of all college seniors applying for admission to graduate school, the length of blades of grass measured in centimeters growing wild in a meadow, or the IQ of the population of clients seeking vocational guidance and employment counseling.

Figure 7.1   Distributed Binomial Scores Overlaid by a Gaussian Normal Curve

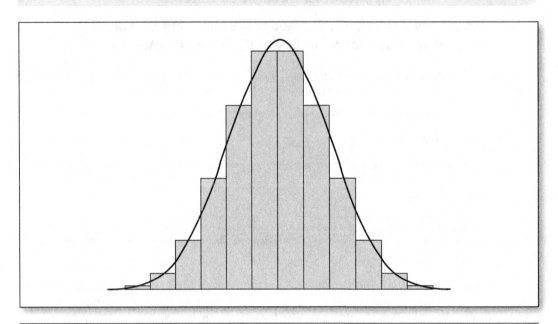

Source: Wright, R. J. (2010). *Multifaceted assessment for early childhood education*, p. 92. Reprinted with permission from Sage.

Central to the use of all standardized measures, including national licensing examinations in the mental health professions, is the assumption that raw scores from the population of tested individuals are distributed as a Gaussian normal curve. When data are plotted from a statistical test, the "goodness of fit" test can be used to determine whether the new distribution is highly similar to the Gaussian normal distribution. (Goodness of fit is described in Chapter 11.) There are several Internet solutions for making this judgment:

From Laura Schultz at Rowan University, http://users.rowan.edu/~schultzl/TI/chi-square.pdf

From Richard Lowry at Vassar College, http://faculty.vassar.edu/lowry/csfit.html

From GraphPad Software, http://www.graphpad.com/quickcalcs/chisquared1.cfm

This calculation can also be done by other statistical software available on many universities' servers. Programs being used today on campuses across the country include, among others, those from ASReml, BMDP, EViews, Maple, Mathematica, Minitab, NMathStats, SAS, SPSS, STATA, and SYSTAT. The technology support office of most universities provides brief inservice courses for individuals wishing to learn to use the local system.

Figure 7.2   An Elaborated Gaussian Normal Distribution

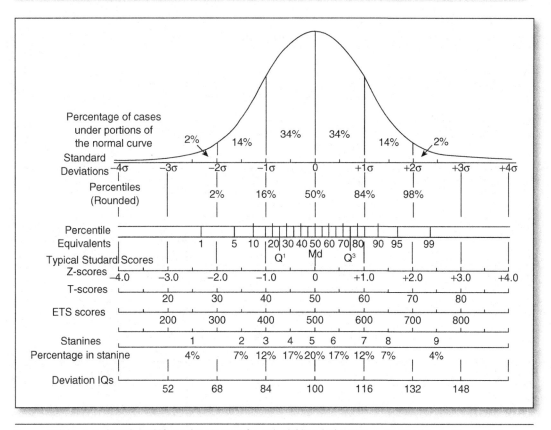

Source: Wright, R. J. (2010). *Multifaceted assessment for early childhood education,* p. 52. Reprinted with permission from Sage.

Skew

There are several ways the normal symmetry of a distribution can be lost. One occurs when there is an excess of extreme scores, that is, too many high or too many low scores. The excess of unusual scores results in a separation of the mean and the median of ratio or interval data being examined. A surplus of unusually high or low scores will cause the mean to be drawn in the direction of the unusual cluster. This excess of scores at either the high or low end creates a **skew** in the data. The median tends to be much less volatile and only exhibits a very small movement when there is an unusual cluster of either high or low scores. Table 7.2 presents GPA data from a counseling study conducted with college freshmen at a small, private university.

In this hypothetical experiment, the participants were 38 freshmen students who had self-referred to the campus counseling center to learn how to improve their study habits

Table 7.2 GPA Data From Experimental and Control Groups

	Experimental Group	Control Group
	2.66	0.16
	2.70	3.20
	2.75	3.21
	1.76	0.75
	3.76	2.78
	2.78	3.78
	3.80	2.80
	2.78	3.80
	1.82	2.82
	2.83	2.80
	2.85	2.85
	2.86	3.86
	2.78	2.80
	2.89	2.80
	2.90	2.90
	3.92	3.92
	1.94	2.94
	2.96	3.96
	2.97	0.07
Number (n) =	19	19
Mean ($\bar{X}$) =	2.83	2.59
Mode =	2.78	2.80
Median (Mdn) =	2.83	2.82
Skew =	0.343	−1.11*
SE-skew = 0.52		

*Significant level of skewness[11]

and achievement in college. These students all achieved less than a GPA of 2.00 during the first semester. In the spring term, half ($n = 19$) were randomly assigned to a small class teaching study skills, test-taking strategies, and critical reading at the college level. The **experimental group** ($n = 19$) all received individual coaching by a counseling intern for 3 hours a week. The coaching covered similar topics as those covered in the classroom (control or comparison group).

The outcome of this study could be measured in terms of the students' GPA for just the second semester (spring term). Data from the study presented in Table 7.2 show a large mean ($\bar{X}$) difference but little difference in the median scores. This indicates a large skewness toward the low side of the distribution within the control group's data. This can be confirmed by visually examining the data from the control group. In that data set, 3 members of the classroom-taught group (control group) ended the spring term with a GPA lower than 1.00 (GPA ≤ 1.00).

This resulting separation of the mean and median of this hypothetical data provides evidence of significant skewness in the data. When the distortion is caused by unusually low scores, the skewness has a negative value, and when there is an excess of unusually high scores, the skewness is referred to as positive skewness. The mean will be greater than the median when the data have a positive skewness. Theoretical distributions depicting these types of skewness are presented in Figure 7.3.

In this age of accountability, practitioners are all too frequently required to justify their interventions and therapeutic choices. In this regard, it is important to note that a few disgruntled clients can introduce **negative skewness** into the data and thereby reduce the mean score for a program of an individual therapist. In the example study described in Table 7.2, there is a very high probability that the scores exhibit a significant level of skewness. The computer-calculated value for the skewness of these data is $Sk = -1.11, p > .01$.

CASE IN POINT   7.4

The nursing, social work, medicine, dentistry, nutrition, and clinical psychology staff of a large urban children's hospital and child guidance clinic went out on strike a few years ago. By the 4th week, both sides were at a serious impasse, and children and their families were suffering. During a press conference called by the public relations office, the press was informed that the clinic staff was being greedy.

The point was made that the average professional earned a salary of over $85,000 per year. When benefits were included in the total package, the average professional staff member received over $125,000 in annual compensation. At a local church, the representatives of the bargaining unit held a press conference a day later. The union reported that the average full-time professional earned just under $58,000 a year. Also, when the benefits were added to the mix, total compensation was only $76,500.

The fact is that both parties reported the same data and both told the truth. The data about pay were badly skewed. Medical staff, board-certified neuropsychologists, and senior nurse administrators were paid at a much higher level than were the larger groups of professionals (counselors, floor nurses, nutritional specialists, social workers, and professional nurse assistants). This excess of high salaries resulted in a positive skew in the salary data. At that time, the vast majority of professional employees were paid lower salaries and had modest benefits.

Figure 7.3   Curves With Negative and Positive Skewness

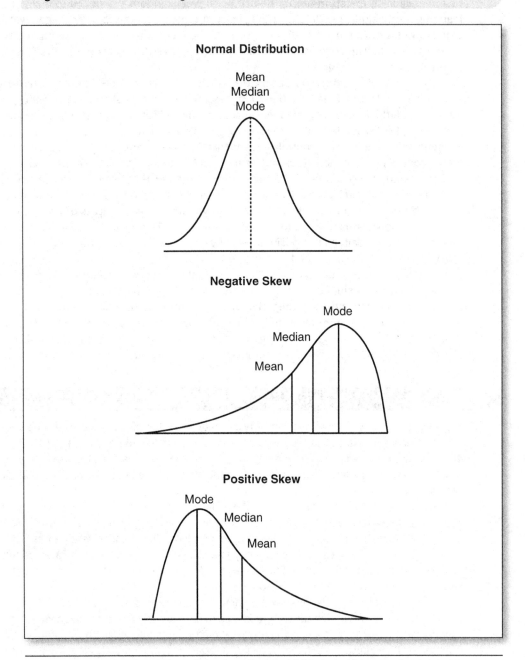

Source: Wright, R. J. (2010). *Multifaceted assessment for early childhood education,* p. 95. Reprinted with permission from Sage.

DATA PRESENTATION

The goal of data presentation is to make it simple for others to visualize and understand the data you wish to describe. The practitioner-researcher has a number of approaches available to employ when presenting his or her data. The precision of the variable being described is one factor to keep in mind when deciding which approach to employ.

Nominal Data

Nominal data are organized in name-only categories and do not exist in any hierarchical sequence. Therefore, the presentation method must not imply a logical sequence or hierarchical ordering of the categories. Three methods for depicting nominal data commonly appear in the scientific literature, official reports, and even in mass media. These are the pie graph, bar graph, and pictograph.

Pie Graphs (Charts)

This form of graphic presentation uses a circle format and therefore implies no beginning or ending point. The lack of a high-to-low value implication makes a pie chart appropriate for nominal data presentations. It is also appropriate for presenting data measured at more precise levels.

Table 7.3   Presenting Descriptive Data

NOIR Classification	Graph Formats	Appropriate Central Tendency Statistics
Ratio	pie graph, bar graph, pictograph, histogram, frequency polygon, continuous curves and ogives	mean median mode
Interval	pie graph, bar graph, pictograph, histogram, frequency polygon, continuous curves and ogives	mean median mode
Ordinal II	pie graph, bar graph, pictograph, histogram, frequency polygon	mean median mode
Ordinal I	pie graph, bar graph, pictograph, histogram, frequency polygon	median mode
Nominal	pie graph, bar graph, pictograph	mode

Nominal data can be presented on a pie graph by first assigning each case (data point) to one of the nominal categories. Next, the number of cases (data points) in each category is converted into a percentage of all the cases in the data set. The final step is the assignment of portions of the "data pie." The pie is divided proportionally according to the percent of the total data set represented by members in each category. This is done by plotting the percent assigned to each nominal category on a circle (pie graph). There are 360° making up any circle, so a nominal category including 25% of the cases would be assigned 25% of the circle (data-pie), and 25% of the 360° of a circle is 90°. Figures 7.4 and 7.5 show some examples of pie graphs.

Pie graphs are widely employed in presenting budget data and other statistical administrative information. The ease of reading and understanding pie charts makes them the graph of choice for many financial officers.

There are a number of free programs for constructing various graphs, including pie graphs. Following are three of these:

National Center for Educational Statistics, http://nces.ed.gov/nceskids/createagraph/default.aspx

National Council of Teachers of Mathematics, http://illuminations.nctm.org/ActivityDetail.aspx?ID=204

MrNussbaum.com, http://mrnussbaum.com/coolgraphing/

In addition to stand-alone software packages for graphing, major statistical packages used extensively by faculty and graduate students in counselor education programs also provide high-quality graphing systems.

ASReml, VSN International, http://www.vsni.co.uk/software/asreml/

BMDP, http://www.statistical-solutions-software.com/products-page/bmdp-statistical-software/

EViews v.7.2, http://www.eviews.com/

IBM SPSS (also see Appendix A), http://www.spss.com/software/statistics/text-analytics-for-surveys/index.htm?tab=1

Maple v.16.0, http://www.maplesoft.com/products/maple/

Microsoft Excel, http://office.microsoft.com/en-us/excel/

Minitab v.16, http://www.minitab.com/en-US/products/minitab/default.aspx

NMath Stats, v.3.5, http://www.centerspace.net/products/nmath-stats/

SAS Institute, http://www.sas.com/ads/google_stats/?gclid=CKfxm-L9iqgCFUta2godcQWECQ

STATA v.12.0, http://www.stata.com/stata12/

SYSTAT v.13, Cranes Software International, http://www.systat.com/

Wolfram Mathematica v.8, http://www.wolfram.com/mathematica/

Figure 7.4   Two Pie Graphs With Nominal Data

(Right) A graph of the types of cases seen by the social workers of a family guidance clinic; (Left) a graph of the types of cases seen by the clinic's professional counselors.

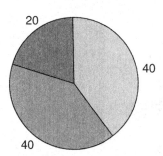

Counselors' Cases as % of Total

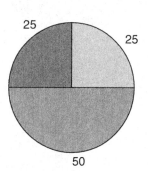

Social Workers' Cases as % of Total

Medium gray = Drug and/or alcohol abuse.

Light gray = Abusive relationships within the family.

Dark gray = Affect disorders.

Source: Developed by author.

Bar Graphs

Like pie graphs, **bar graphs** are appropriate to use when presenting a set of data found at any level of measurement precision, including nominal data. Generally, bar graphs are plotted using two axes meeting at a right angle, the **ordinate** (*y*-axis) and the **abscissa** (*x*-axis). The categories of the nominal variable are then listed along the abscissa, and the number of cases at each nominal category is listed on the ordinate. Bars are drawn to a height (distance from the abscissa) representing the number of cases. This is also described as the **frequency** (*f*). This height can be read against the ordinate to see how many cases occur at any point on the abscissa. Figures 7.6–7.8 show examples of bar graphs.

Bar graphs can also be used to depict variables measured using a more precise scale. Figure 7.7 presents Medicare costs in dollars (ratio scale) from 2001 and projected through until 2017 (time is a ratio scale).

The practitioner-researcher may elect to use a format for the bar graph that is set at a 90° rotation from those above. The same rules apply with this and other formats for bar graphs.

Figure 7.5   Simulated Example of a Pie Graph from Published Data

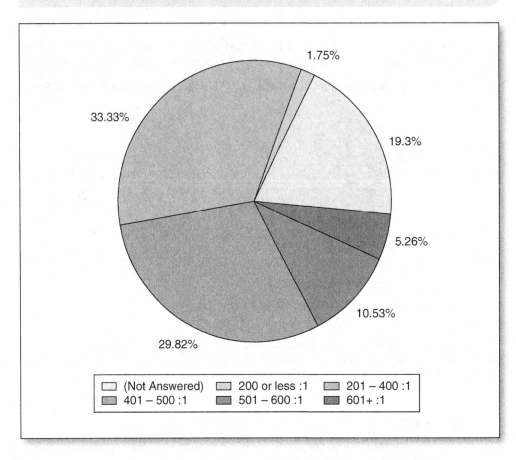

Much Ado About Nothing: Bar graphs can be distorted to reflect the bias of the researcher reporting the data. One of the key ways to do this is to not start the graph at the zero point. By starting the scale at a higher point, a small difference between groups can be magnified to appear much larger than it actually is. Another way to exaggerate findings is to report the log transformation of the original data. Figure 7.9 shows an example of an unexaggerated and exaggerated graph.

Pictographs

Data presentations that would typically be shown as a bar graph or pie graph may also be drawn as a **pictograph**. Pictographs are more dynamic and intriguing for readers than are the more traditional graphical formats. Figure 7.10 is a pictograph. These picture-based graphics involve using line drawings, cartoons, or other artwork to design easy-to-interpret charts. They are used to explain data to children in children's magazines, and they are

Figure 7.6   Bar Graph of Results From an Intervention Program for Released Drug Offenders

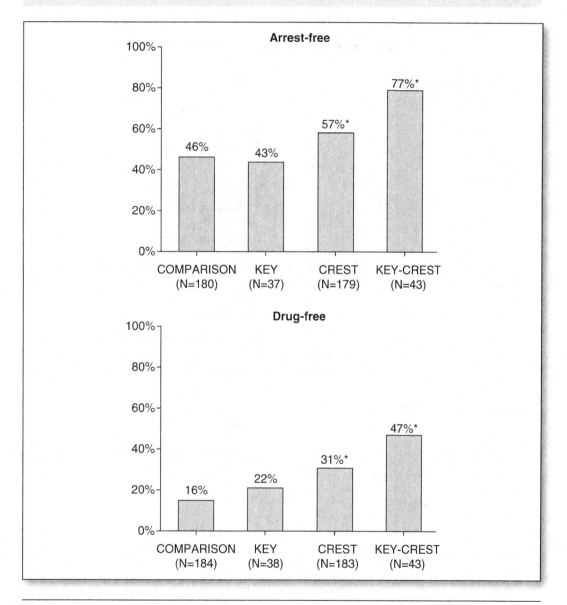

Source: Martin, S. S., Butzin, C. A., Saum, C. A., & Inciardi, J. A. (1999). Three-year outcomes of therapeutic community treatment for drug-involved offenders in Delaware: From prison to work release to aftercare. *The Prison Journal, 79*(3), 294–320. doi: 10.1177/0032885599079003002

Note: This study of three models for providing treatment for addiction to illegal drugs was conducted in Delaware. The KEY program was conducted within the prison environment using a therapeutic community. The CREST program involved the members of the therapeutic community in a work-release program. The KEY-CREST was a combination of both approaches. The asterisks indicate that the difference between this average and that of the comparison group was beyond a chance occurrence.

Figure 7.7 Medicare Costs Projected Through 2021

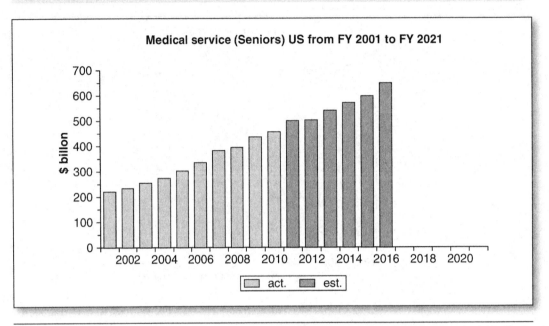

Source: http://www.usgovernmentspending.com/downchart_gs.php?year=2001_2021&view=1&expand=&units=b&fy=fy12&chart=12-fed&bar=1&stack=1&size=l&title=&state=US&color=c&local=s

Figure 7.8 Serum Methadone Levels in Five Patients 1 Week Into a Combined Therapy Treatment Program (Counseling With Methadone)

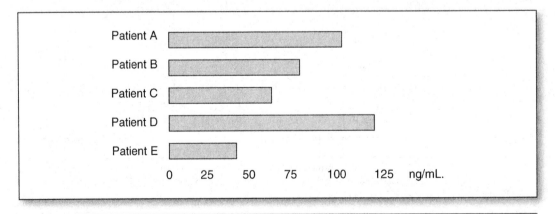

Source: Developed by author.

Figure 7.9   Bar Graph With a Zero Point and Bar Graph Uncorrected Without a Zero Point

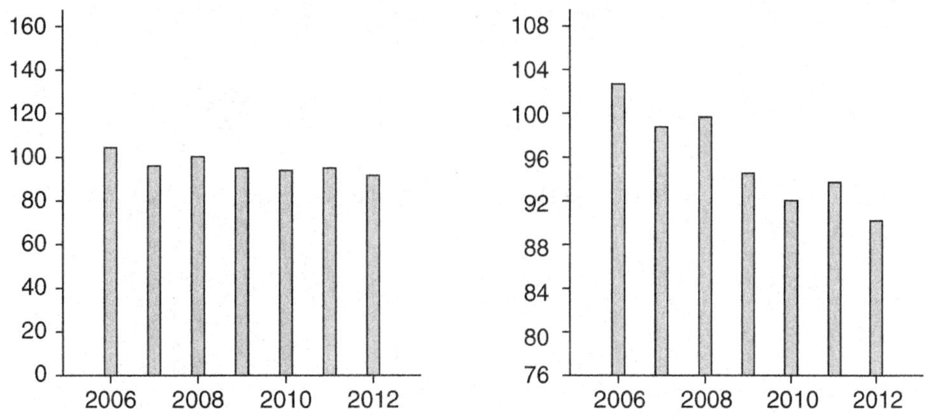

Source: Developed by author.

Note: On the left is a graph showing the 7-year history of staphylococcus infections among clients in a residential drug rehabilitation center for adolescents. The same data are also depicted on the right bar graph. Which graph do you think the center's administrators shared with state child welfare inspectors?

Infections including staphylococcus and HIV are not uncommon among users of illegal drugs. Employees, including therapists, need to pay attention to sanitation when in close physical contact with rehabilitation inpatients (Hughes & Gray, 2009).

employed by mass media designed for adults who are on the go. This format for graphic display of data is inappropriate for presentations that require precise data interpretation.

Ordinal Data Presentation

Ordinal data can also be represented by pictographs, bar graphs, and pie graphs, but these data may be depicted by other formats as well.

Histograms and Frequency Polygons

The alternative formats include **histograms** and **frequency polygons** (line graphs). These graphic display systems are inappropriate for displaying nominal data but ideal for presenting ordinal data. This reflects the fact that they present information in a hierarchical sequence. What histograms and frequency polygons do well is present ordinal and interval data. A histogram appears to be much like a bar graph but for the fact that the columns are all contiguous. Figure 7.11 shows an example of a histogram.

Figure 7.10 Pictograph Showing Shifting Family Size

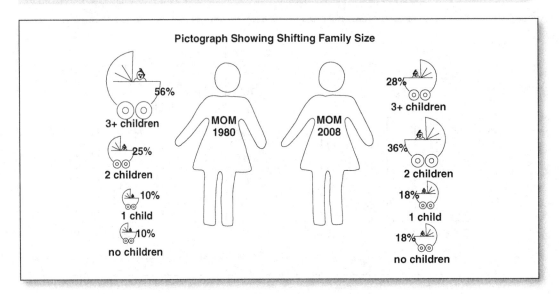

Source: Drawn by author based on data from US Census Bureau.

Figure 7.11 Four Histograms From a Study of Recidivism Among Juvenile Offenders

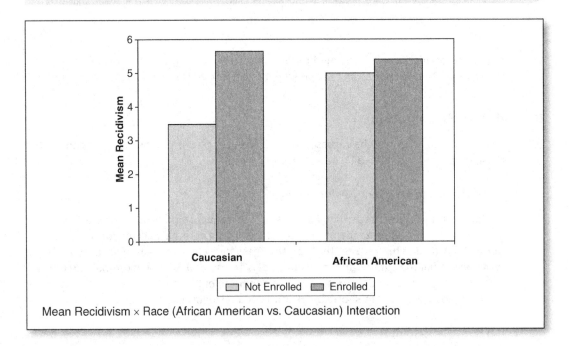

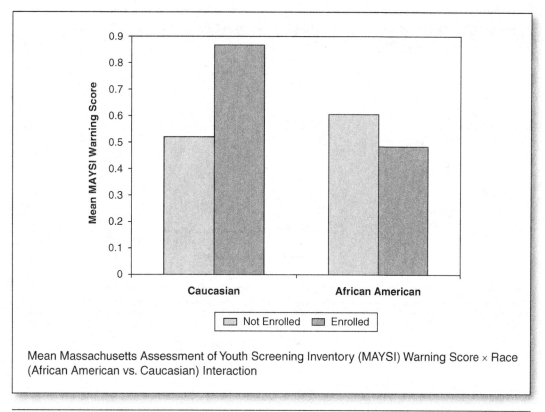

Mean Massachusetts Assessment of Youth Screening Inventory (MAYSI) Warning Score × Race (African American vs. Caucasian) Interaction

Source: Lopez-Williams, A., Stoep, A. V., & Stewart, D. G. (2006). Predictors of mental health service enrollment among juvenile offenders. *Youth Violence and Juvenile Justice, 4*(3), 266–280. doi: 10.1177/1541204006290159

Note: In this study, juvenile detainees between the ages of 13 and 17 years in a correctional facility were assessed using a number of demographic and psychological measures. One research question the authors hoped to resolve was which factors from the youthful detainees' backgrounds were predictive of whether they were enrolled in a counseling-based mental health program at the time of adjudication.

A line graph has no columns but uses point references off the abscissa (horizontal axis), representing frequency of occurrence. The abscissa lists the ordinal groups in sequence described by the line graph. A continuous line is drawn, connecting the points of reference for frequencies of occurrence. The rules for histograms and frequency polygons (line graphs) are similar to those for bar graphs. One difference is that the variable used to group the data must be provided in a logical hierarchical sequence. Figure 7.12 shows an example of a frequency polygon.

Curves and Ogives

When data have equal-size units that are measured as **real numbers,** they can be presented by a smooth, curved line.[12] One form of such a curve, a **continuous distribution**

Figure 7.12 Overlaid Frequency Polygons With Skewed Data of Undergraduate Students' Ideal Number of Sex Partners

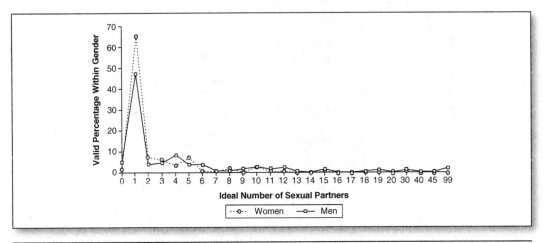

Source: Pedersen, W. C., Miller, L. C., Putcha-Bhagavatula, A. D., & Yang, Y. (2002). Evolved sex differences in the number of partners desired? The long and the short of it. *Psychological Science, 13*(2), 157–161. doi: 10.1111/1467-9280.00428

Note: This depicts the ideal number of sex partners envisioned by 266 undergraduates over the next 30 years of their lives. These data are badly skewed (positive skew), as most students prefer having only one lifelong sex partner.

Figure 7.13 Frequency Polygon Depicting Outcomes From a Solution-Focused Brief Counseling Program

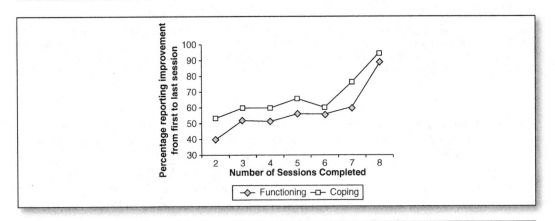

Source: Fischer, R. L. (2004). Assessing client change in individual and family counseling. *Research on Social Work Practice, 14*(2), 102–111. doi: 10. 1177/1049731503257868

Note: This study was conducted over a 2-year period with almost 4,000 subjects and 40 counselors providing a program of solution-focused brief counseling. The maximum number of sessions was eight, and the clients were assessed for their perceived improvement in coping with problems and interpersonal functioning. This frequency polygon indicates that eight may be an ideal number of sessions to provide.

Cartoon 7.1   Fun With Statistics

Cartoon by Merv Magus.

"Chart #1 shows the client satisfaction survey data for our clinic last year, and Chart #2 shows how our program director was able to reinterpret them."

curve, moves from low to high scores along the abscissa (horizontal axis), and the frequency is depicted by the height as measured along the ordinate (vertical axis) of the curve at any point along the abscissa. The other form of the smooth line curve is the **ogive** (pronounced o-jive). This curve is a cumulative statement about the data (see Figure 7.14). Starting with the lowest score on the graph, the frequency of each increasing score is added and plotted as a curve.[13]

Smooth line curves may assume the characteristically symmetric shape of the Gaussian normal curve or any of a number of other shapes, depending on the nature of the scores that are being plotted (see Figure 7.15). The ogive is a variation of the bell curve. By plotting the continuous accumulation of scores along the ogive, the practitioner-researcher can see where any sharp change occurs in the graph's inflection (slope). These points of inflection provide researchers with information about the research participants' average point on one variable when they suddenly have made new insights or when a breakthrough has occurred.

An ogive of this distribution has a slow change in the slope of the curve and starts at a higher level than a truly normal distribution.

Figure 7.14 Ogive and Normal Curve Plotting the Same Data Set

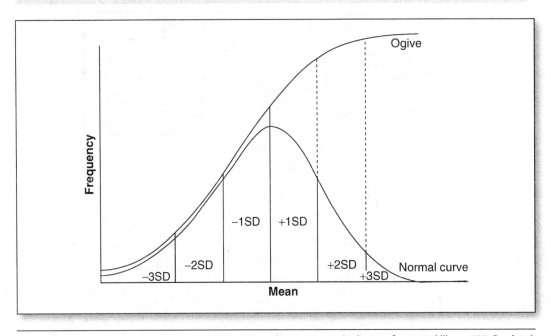

Source: Wright, R. J. (2008). *Educational assessment: Tests and measurements in the age of accountability,* p. 237. Reprinted with permission from Sage.

Figure 7.15 Variations in Smooth Line Graphs

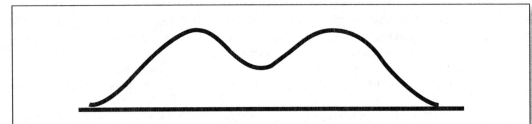

Bimodal curve: Smooth curve depicting the performance of a measure with two different centers of maximum population density. **Bimodal** curves have two modes and may indicate to the researcher that there are two underlying distributions of subjects. This may occur when diverse groups (samples) are combined and measured on a single defining variable. The ogive plotting these data will have two points of inflection, one for each mode.

Source: Developed by author.

Figure 7.16   Bimodal Ogive

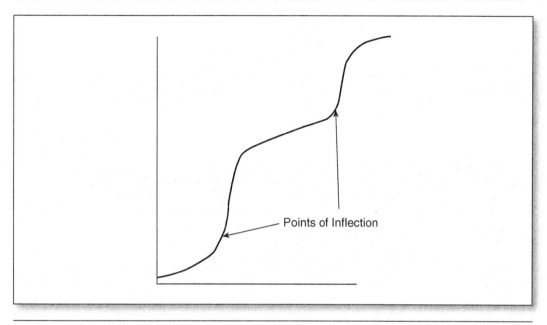

Points of Inflection

Source: Developed by author.

Figure 7.17   Leptokurtic Distribution Leptokurtic Ogive

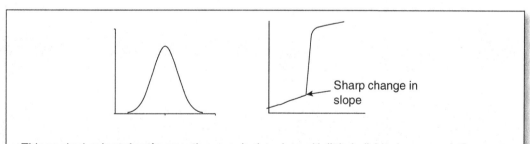

Sharp change in slope

This peaked or **leptokurtic** smooth curve depicts data with little individual score variation reflecting how many scores are near the mean. This may occur when a point is reached in a pharmacology intervention where larger concentrations of the serum medication no longer bring about noticeable improvement for the patient. The ogive for this type of distribution will have one sharp inflection with an abrupt change in slope functions.

Source: Developed by author.

Figure 7.18 Platykurtic Distribution

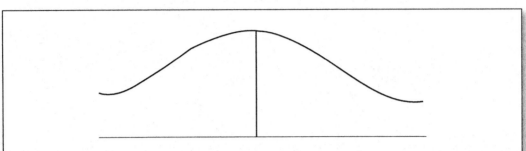

A flat or **platykurtic** smooth curve depicts data with a high degree of variation, with many individuals' scores spread away from the mean. This distribution is sometimes called the **fat tail** distribution. It can occur when there is excess variation in the data. For example, this distribution can occur with data from discourse analysis. When a researcher reads transcripts of interviews searching for and recording the expression of certain empathy versus self-centered concepts, the distribution may be platykurtic, indicating that some participants are very empathetic while others are very self-centered.

Source: Developed by author.

Figure 7.19 Platykurtic Ogive

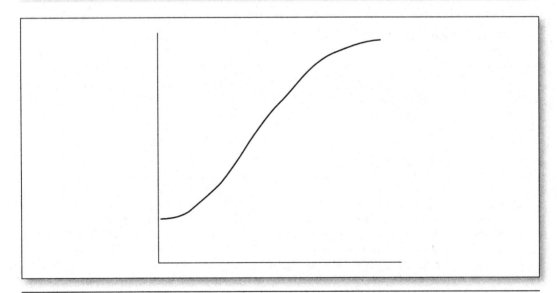

Source: Developed by author.

VARIABILITY AND VARIANCE

Dispersion

For a variable to exist, it must occur in varying amounts in different individuals. Therefore, when scores from all individuals are graphed, there will be a spread of score values. Some will be above the median and some below. In the case of smooth curved data, some individuals will score on either side of the mean and median. The amount of this spread of scores is **dispersion,** and it is described in a number of ways.

Nominal Data

Dispersion for nominal data can only be expressed by counting the categories used to group the data. For example, "During the homecoming parade on campus this year, floats representing all eight social fraternities and seven sororities took part."

Ordinal Data

Ordinal data can be shown as the **range** of scores. This can be expressed as a number representing the distance between the first and last score in the set. "Students of our program had GRE Verbal scores ranging 21 points, from a low of 140 to a high of 161." Or, "The faculty committee included one member from each of four levels of rank, from instructor to full professor."

Ordinal data ranges can be greatly influenced by just one outlying case. In our example above, one graduate student with a 169 on the Verbal section of the GRE would change the range of scores from 21 to 29. To prevent that type of distortion, practitioner-researchers usually report the range of scores between the middle two **quartiles,** or the **interquartile range.** This is the range of scores for the middle 50 % of the cases. The scores must first be arranged from lowest to highest (sequenced hierarchically). Then the 25th percentile can be found as the score below which 25 % of all scores are located. Likewise, the 75th percentile is the case below which there are 75 % of all cases. The score range between these two is the interquartile range.

Finding the Interquartile Range

- First arrange the student-reported hours spent by 19 graduate students completing graduate reading assignments each week in a sequence from low to highest.

  2, 5, 6, 6, 8, 9, 9, 12, 15, 18, 18, 19, 25, 27, 30, 31, 35, 45, 70

- Next find the median and highlight it.

  2, 5, 6, 6, 8, 9, 9, 12, 15, **18**, 18, 19, 25, 27, 30, 31, 35, 45, 70

(Continued)

(Continued)

- Identify the 25th and 75th percentiles and underline the values between them.

  2, 5, 6, 6, **8**, 9, 9, 12, 15, **18**, 18, 19, 25, 27, **30**, 31, 35, 45, 70

- Subtract to find the interquartile range.

  30 − 8 = 22

The interquartile range of time spent by graduate students on assigned reading at home each week is 22 hours.

Ratio and Interval Data

Interquartile range values can be used with interval and ratio data (see the example of GRE scores above), or the degree of score dispersion can be expressed as a statistic. That statistic is named **variance** and can be defined as the average of all squared differences between individual scores and the mean. Thus, to find variance, it is first necessary to find the data's mean (average) and, in turn, subtract the mean from each individual's score $X_i - \bar{X}$. This will produce a series of both positive values from scores greater than the mean, and it will produce equivalent negative values from scores that are less than the mean. The negative and positive values will cancel each other out. In other words, the variation is zero:

$$\sum_{i=1}^{n}\left(X_i - \bar{X}\right) = 0$$

The solution to this conundrum is to make all values positive once they are subtracted from the mean. This is accomplished by multiplying each difference score by itself (squaring it) before adding the squared difference scores together.[14] Negative values when squared become positive. This produces the sum of squared differences from the mean:

$$\sum_{i=1}^{n}\left(X_i - \bar{X}\right)^2 = \text{Total of summed squared deviations}$$

The last step in finding variance is to divide the squared sum of squared differences by the size of the sample, or the n number of cases included in the distribution of scores being described. For technical reasons, we subtract 1 from n when calculating variance for a sample.

$$\frac{\sum_{i=1}^{n}\left(X_i - \bar{X}\right)^2}{n-1} = \text{variance } (s^2, sd^2, \sigma^2)\text{[15]}$$

The symbols used to represent variance are sd^2, s^2, and, in the case of an entire population, the lowercase Greek letter sigma squared (σ^2). In each case, the symbol is a squared value to account for the step taken in calculating the value of variance for the data.[16] There are several free Internet calculators that will find descriptive statistics, including standard deviations (described below). For example, see the following:

http://www.ajdesigner.com/phpstatistics/standard_deviation_population.php

http://www.easycalculation.com/statistics/standard-deviation.php

http://www.mathsisfun.com/data/standard-deviation-calculator.html

http://www.csgnetwork.com/stddeviationcalc.html

In addition, the statistical software maintained on most universities' servers has this capability. Those software packages were listed earlier in this chapter, and an example of IBM-SPSS is given in Appendix A.

The actual values of variance can only be positive or zero. If everyone scores exactly the mean, there is no dispersion, and the value of the variance is zero. All other values for variance must be positive. The problem is that the statistic for variance is not easily interpreted, as it is influenced by the size of the measurement units used to find it. Some variance values may be very high because the variable uses large numbers and reflects considerable individual differences. For example, the level of the enzyme aspartate aminotransferase (AST) is a measure of human liver function. It can be found through standard vein-puncture collection and a serum assay. Table 7.4 presents AST levels for 15 recovering alcoholics enrolled in a 12-step program.

Table 7.4   Serum Levels of Aspartate Aminotransferase

Patient	Age	Serum AST
Ann	26	60
Bill	42	48
Carol	19	52
Doug	55	27
Erin	22	52
Frank	66	130
Grace	53	67

(Continued)

Table 7.4 (Continued)

Patient	Age	Serum AST
Harry	36	70
Ida	62	44
Jim	51	120
Kim	38	96
Liam	25	112
Missy	47	86
Neil	20	32
Oprah	58	9
Range	47	121
Interquartile Range	30	52
Median	42	60
Mean	41.3	67.0
Variance	259.4	1256.6
Standard Deviation	16.1	35.4

Variance and Standard Scores

Researchers have a number of available methods for reporting measurement scores based on the framework of variance and the normal curve.

Standard Deviation

For most measurement applications, variance is presented in the form of **standard deviation.** This statistic is the square root of variance.

$$\sqrt{\frac{\sum_{i=1}^{n}\left(X_i - \bar{X}\right)^2}{n-1}} = \text{Standard deviation}(s, SD, \sigma)$$

The statistic standard deviation is sometimes denoted as s or SD and, in the case of an entire population, as the lowercase Greek letter sigma σ. The utility of the standard deviation statistic is drawn from its relationship to the Gaussian normal curve. This relationship can be seen in Figure 7.2. When data are collected from a **random sample** of a normal population, a distribution of those scores will approximate the normal curve. The approximate proportion of scores that will lie between the mean and 1 standard deviation above the mean ($+1s$) is a constant 34.13%.

The normal distribution is symmetric, so another 34.13% of all the scores in the sample will lie between the mean and 1 standard deviation below the mean ($-1s$). Thus, just over 68% of all scores lie between $-1s$ and $+1s$. By expanding this to almost $\pm 2s$, it is possible to account for 95% of all scores within a normal sample. This represents 47.5% above and 47.5% below the mean.

It is this consistency of the normal distribution that is the foundation of large-scale score reports. The distribution may be of scores that are based on large numbers (e.g., the NBCC Licensing Examination has a possible 160-point range [0–160]), or small numbers (e.g., undergraduate grade point average has a 4-point range [0.0–4.0]), but the relationship of the standard deviation, s, to the distribution will be constant.

z-Scores

Scores from any normal sample can be converted into units of standard deviation. This process makes it possible to compare one set of test scores to the scores from another test or measure. For example, if the undergraduate GPA of an applicant to graduate school is set side by side with the applicant's GRE score, the two seem incompatible. However, both the GPA and GRE can be converted into standard deviation (standard score) format and then compared.

Table 7.5   Mean, Median, and Mode for Each of the Three Groups of Subjects

Sample and Demographic Characteristics for Emerging Adult, Early Adult, and Middle Adult Women			
Variable	Emerging adult women: 18–25 years old	Early adult women: 26–39 years old	Middle adult women: 40–65 years old
n	318	238	245
Average age (years)			
M (SD)	19.47 (1.90)	32.63 (4.06)	51.38 (7.07)
Median	19.00	33.00	52.00
Mode	18.00	36.00	54.00
Ethnic identification: n (%)			
White/European American	256 (80.5)	198 (83.1)	206 (84.1)
Black/African American	22 (6.9)	14 (5.9)	14 (5.7)
Asian American	19 (6.0)	8 (3.3)	8 (3.2)

(Continued)

Table 7.5 (Continued)

Variable	Emerging adult women: 18–25 years old	Early adult women: 26–39 years old	Middle adult women: 40–65 years old
Latina or Hispanic	9 (2.8)	4 (1.7)	6(2.4)
Native American	1 (0.3)	4 (1.7)	2 (0.8)
Multiracial	3 (1.0)	3 (1.3)	2 (0.8)
International	2 (0.6)	3 (1.3)	5 (2.0)
Did not report	3 (0.9)	2 (0.8)	1 (0.4)
Socioeconomic identification: *n* (%)			
Working class	39 (12.3)	30 (12.6)	28 (11.4)
Middle class	252 (79.2)	184 (77.3)	194 (79.2)
Upper class	23 (7.2)	24 (10.1)	19 (7.8)
Did not report	4 (1.3)	0 (0.0)	4 (1.6)
Relationship status: %			
Single	89.6	28.5	17.1
Partnered	2.5	7.1	4.5
Married	1.3	59.7	62.9
Divorced or separated	0.3	3.4	9.8
Widowed	0.0	0.0	3.7
Did not report	6.3	1.2	2.0

Source: Augustus-Horvath, C. L., & Tylka, T. L. (2011). The acceptance model of intuitive eating: A comparison of women in emerging adulthood, early adulthood, and middle adulthood. *Journal of Counseling Psychology, 58*(1), 110–125. doi: 10.1037/a0022129

Note: The authors reported the mean, median, and mode for each of the three groups of subjects in the study. Because age is a ratio variable, they also provided the standard deviation for age within each of the three groups. The variables ethnicity and relationship status were also reported. Because those variables are nominal, only a simple percentage of the total group membership was reported for the different levels. The variable socioeconomic status is an ordinal and sequenced in the presentation, but it too is only reported as a percentage of the membership of the group.

The symbol of this standard score is z. The score z expresses any raw score in terms of its location in the distribution using units of standard deviation. If an individual score and the sample mean are exactly the same, the z-**score** will be 0.0. If the score is equal to 1 standard deviation above the mean, the z-score will be +1.0. To find any z-score, it is necessary to know the original (raw) score, sample mean of the raw scores, and the sample's raw score standard deviation. The z-score can be found as follows:

$$z = \frac{X - \bar{X}}{s}$$

In this equation, the value of X is any individual's score. By subtracting the sample mean and dividing that difference by the standard deviation, the score is changed into a z-score (standard score).

As an example, if an applicant to graduate school has a GPA of 3.25 from a sample of applicants with a mean of $\bar{X} = 2.50$ and a standard deviation of 0.50, that student would have a z-score of +1.50. This indicates that this student has a college grade point average that is equivalent to one and a half standard deviation units above the mean of that year's applicant pool. Here is the calculation:

$$z = \frac{3.25 - 2.50}{0.50}$$
$$z = 1.5$$

Percentiles

Percentiles may represent an ordinal transformation of data. The concept behind percentiles is that each percentile represents 1/100th of the data. The first percentile includes all those data points arranged from the lowest score to the point where 1% of the data are included. The **first quartile** is the 25th percentile, the point that cuts off the lowest 25% of the scores in the data set. The second **quintile** is the point that cuts off the lowest 40% of the scores from the data set. The median is the 50th percentile, and the seventh **decile** is a score that cuts off the lowest 70% of the data.

Percentile equivalents are reported for most standardized tests. These scores are not simply from a basic count of cases in an ordinal sequence but rather are based on comparisons to a data set that was collected previously. The consistency of the normal curve makes it possible to interpolate z-scores into percentiles. For example, the score point in the center of the Gaussian normal curve ($z = 0.0$) is the 50th percentile. That point has half of all scores below and above it. The Gaussian normal curve starts and ends at infinity. Because of that, there can never be a zero percentile point with these transformed scores. Likewise, there can never be a score equal to the 100th percentile.

For example, the NBCC examination has 160 questions each year that are used to determine a license candidate's status. However, the NBCC examination presents each test taker with 200 items. The extra 40 are not identified as experimental but are integrated into the examination and later used to build next year's normal curve against which the next group of license candidates will be compared. A small number of the extra 40 items are used year after year to demonstrate the stability of the examination over time. These items are known as **anchor items.** Not all candidates taking this year's test see the same 40 items. Thus, it is possible for the NBCC examiners to find a distribution of all of next year's 160 items.

The created comparison group is known as the norm group or normative reference group. Thus, a raw score on this year's test is compared to how candidates last year did on the 160 items, and a percentile score can be found. In Table 7.6, z-scores are presented, and areas under the normal curve are given. These can be easily read as percentiles.

Table 7.6 Areas (Percentiles) Under the Normal Curve by z-Score

Table 1 The normal curve

(a) Area under the normal curve

Z	0.00	0.01	0.02	0.03	0.04	0.05	0.06	0.07	0.08	0.09
−3.4	0.0003	0.0003	0.0003	0.0003	0.0003	0.0003	0.0003	0.0003	0.0003	0.0002
−3.3	0.0005	0.0005	0.0005	0.0004	0.0004	0.0004	0.0004	0.0004	0.0004	0.0003
−3.2	0.0007	0.0007	0.0006	0.0006	0.0006	0.0006	0.0006	0.0005	0.0005	0.0005
−3.1	0.0010	0.0009	0.0009	0.0009	0.0008	0.0008	0.0008	0.0008	0.0007	0.0007
−3.0	0.0013	0.0013	0.0013	0.0012	0.0012	0.0011	0.0011	0.0011	0.0010	0.0010
−2.9	0.0019	0.0018	0.0017	0.0017	0.0016	0.0016	0.0015	0.0015	0.0014	0.0014
−2.8	0.0026	0.0025	0.0024	0.0023	0.0023	0.0022	0.0021	0.0021	0.0020	0.0019
−2.7	0.0035	0.0034	0.0033	0.0032	0.0031	0.0030	0.0029	0.0028	0.0027	0.0026
−2.6	0.0047	0.0045	0.0044	0.0043	0.0041	0.0040	0.0039	0.0038	0.0037	0.0036
−2.5	0.0062	0.0060	0.0059	0.0057	0.0055	0.0054	0.0052	0.0051	0.0049	0.0048
−2.4	0.0082	0.0080	0.0078	0.0075	0.0073	0.0071	0.0069	0.0068	0.0066	0.0064
−2.3	0.0107	0.0104	0.0102	0.0099	0.0096	0.0094	0.0091	0.0089	0.0087	0.0084
−2.2	0.0139	0.0136	0.0132	0.0129	0.0124	0.0122	0.0119	0.0116	0.0113	0.0110
−2.1	0.0179	0.0174	0.0170	0.0166	0.0162	0.0158	0.0154	0.0150	0.0146	0.0143
−2.0	0.0228	0.0222	0.0217	0.0212	0.0207	0.0202	0.0197	0.0192	0.0188	0.0183
−1.9	0.0287	0.0281	0.0274	0.0268	0.0262	0.0256	0.0250	0.0244	0.0239	0.0233
−1.8	0.0359	0.0352	0.0344	0.0336	0.0329	0.0322	0.0314	0.0307	0.0301	0.0294
−1.7	0.0446	0.0436	0.0427	0.0418	0.0409	0.0401	0.0392	0.0384	0.0375	0.0367
−1.6	0.0548	0.0537	0.0526	0.0516	0.0505	0.0495	0.0485	0.0475	0.0465	0.0455
−1.5	0.0668	0.0655	0.0643	0.0630	0.0618	0.0606	0.0594	0.0582	0.0571	0.0559
−1.4	0.0808	0.0793	0.0778	0.0764	0.0749	0.0735	0.0722	0.0708	0.0694	0.0681
−1.3	0.0968	0.0951	0.0934	0.0918	0.0901	0.0085	0.0869	0.0853	0.0838	0.0823
−1.2	0.1151	0.1131	0.1112	0.1093	0.1075	0.1056	0.1038	0.1020	0.1003	0.0985
−1.1	0.1357	0.1335	0.1314	0.1292	0.1271	0.1251	0.1230	0.1210	0.1190	0.1170
−1.0	0.1587	0.1562	0.1539	0.1515	0.1492	0.1469	0,1446	0.1423	0.1401	0.1379
−0.9	0.1841	0.1814	0.1788	0.1762	0.1736	0.1711	0.1685	0.1660	0.1635	0.1611
−0.8	0.2119	0.2090	0.2061	0.2033	0.2005	0.1977	0.1949	0.1922	0.1894	0.1867
−0.7	0.2420	0.2389	0.2358	0.2327	0.2296	0.2266	0.2236	0.2206	0.2177	0.2148
−0.6	0.2743	0.2709	0.2676	0.2643	0.2611	0.2578	0.2546	0.2514	0.2483	0.2451
−0.5	0.3085	0.3050	0.3015	0.2981	0.2946	0.2912	0.2877	0.2843	0.2810	0.2776
−0.4	1.3446	0.3409	0.3372	0.3336	0.3300	0.3264	0.3228	0,3192	0.3156	0.3121
−0.3	0.3821	0.3783	0.3745	0.3707	0.3669	0.3632	0,3594	0.3557	0.3520	0.3483
−0.2	0.4207	0.4168	0.4129	0.4090	0.4052	0.4013	0.3974	0.3936	0.3897	0.3859
−0.1	0.4602	0.4562	0.4522	0.4483	0.4443	0.4404	0.4364	0.4325	0.4286	0.4247
−0.0	0.5000	0.4960	0.4920	0.4880	0.4840	0.4801	0.4761	0.4721	0.4681	0.4641

100 STATISTICAL TESTS

Z	0.00	0.01	0.02	0.03	0.04	0.05	0.06	0.07	0.08	0.09
0.0	0.5000	0.5040	0.5080	0.5120	0.5160	0.5199	0.5239	0.5279	0.5319	0.5359
0.1	0.5398	0.5438	0.5478	0.5517	0.5557	0.5596	0.56.36	0.5675	0.5714	0.5753
0.2	0.5793	0.5832	0.5871	0.5910	0.5948	0.5987	0.6026	0.6064	0.6103	0.6141
0.3	0.6179	0.6217	0.6255	0.6293	0.6331	0.6368	0.6406	0.6443	0.6480	0.6517
0.4	0.6554	0.6591	0.662S	0.6664	0.6700	0.6736	0.6772	0.6808	0.6844	0.6879
0.5	0.6915	0.6950	0.6985	0.7019	0.7054	0.7088	0.7123	0.7157	0.7190	0.7224
0.6	0.7257	0.7291	0.7324	0.7357	0.7389	0.7422	0.7454	0.7486	0.7517	0.7549
0.7	0.7580	0.7611	0.7642	0.7673	0.7704	0.7734	0.7764	0.7794	0.7823	0.7852
0.8	0.7881	0.7910	0.7939	0.7967	0.7995	0.8023	0.8051	0.8078	0.8106	0.8133
0.9	0.8159	0.8186	0.8212	0.8238	0.8264	0.8289	0.8315	0.8340	0.8365	0.8389
1.0	0.8413	0.8438	0.8461	0.8485	0.8508	0.8531	0.8554	0.8577	0.8599	0.8621
1.1	0.8643	0.8665	0.8686	0.8708	0.8729	0.8749	0.8770	0.8790	0.8810	0.8830
1.2	0.8849	0.8869	0.8888	0.8907	0.8925	0.8944	0.8962	0.8980	0.8997	0.9015
1.3	0.9032	0.9049	0.9066	0.9082	0.9099	0.9115	0.9131	0.9147	0.9162	0.9177
1.4	0.9192	0.9207	0.9222	0.9236	0.9251	0.9265	0.9278	0.9292	0.9306	0.9319
1.5	0.9332	0.9345	0.9357	0.9370	0.9382	0.9394	0.9406	0.9418	0.9429	0.9441
1.6	0.9452	0.9463	0.9474	0.9484	0.9495	0.9505	0.9515	0.9525	0.9535	0.9545
1.7	0.9554	0.9564	0.9573	0.9582	0.9591	0.9599	0.9608	0.9616	0.9625	0.9633
1.8	0.9641	0.9649	0.9656	0.9664	0.9671	0.9678	0.9686	0,9693	0.9699	0.9706
1.9	0.9713	0.9719	0.9726	0.9732	0.9738	0.9744	0.9750	0.9756	0.9761	0.9767
2.0	0.9772	0.9778	0.9783	0.9788	0.9793	0.9798	0.9803	0.9808	0.9812	0.9817
2.1	0.9821	0.9826	0.9830	0.9834	0.9838	0.9842	0.9846	0.9850	0.9854	0.9857
2.2	0.9861	0.9864	0.9868	0.9871	0.9875	0.9878	0.9881	0.9884	0.9887	0.9890
2.3	0.9893	0.9896	0.9898	0.9901	0.9904	0.9906	0.9909	0.9911	0.9913	0.9916
2.4	0.9918	0.9920	0.9922	0.9925	0.9927	0.9929	0.9931	0.9932	0.9934	0.9936
2.5	0.9938	0.9940	0.9941	0.9943	0.9945	0.9946	0.9948	0.9949	0.9951	0.9952
2.6	0.9953	0.9955	0.9956	0.9957	0 9959	0.9960	0.9961	0.9962	0.9963	0.9964
2.7	0.9965	0.9966	0.9967	0.9968	0.9969	0.9970	0.9971	0.9972	0.9973	0.9974
2.8	0.9974	0.9975	0.9976	0.9977	0.9977	0.9978	1.9979	0.9979	0.9980	0.9981
2.9	0.9981	0.9982	0.9982	0.9983	0.9984	0.9984	0.9985	0.9985	0.9986	0.9986
3.0	0.9987	0.9987	0.9987	0.9988	0.9988	0.9989	0.9989	0.9989	0.9990	0.9990
3.1	0.9990	0.9991	0.9991	0.9991	0.9992	0.9992	0.9992	0.9992	0.9993	0.9993
3.2	0.9993	0.9993	0.9994	0.9994	0.9994	0.9994	0.9994	0.9995	0.9995	0.9995
3.3	0.9995	0.9995	0.9995	0.9996	0.9996	0.9996	0.9996	0.9996	0.9996	0.9997
3.4	0.9997	0.9997	0.9997	0.9997	0.9997	0.9997	0.9997	0.9997	0.9997	0.9998

Source: Kanji, G. K. (1999). *100 statistical tests,* pp. 159–160. Reprinted with permission from Sage.

Note: Researchers do not need to use these tables, as the same information is provided online and by statistical software. The actual table is depicted here to illustrate the concept.

From the information in Table 7.6, it can be seen that an undergraduate student who has a GPA equal to a z-score of 1.50 would be in the 93rd percentile of a normally distributed set of grade point averages.[17] Likewise, a graduate student who has a score on the NBCC Licensing Examination equal to a z-score of –0.7 (the negative sign means below the mean) would be in about the 24th percentile.

Psychologists and counselors are aware of the definition of a cognitively gifted person as having a mental ability score that is 2 or more standard deviations above the mean IQ value of 100. For most tests of cognitive ability, this level equates to an IQ above 129. That IQ score can also be expressed as a z-score. To convert the IQ score to a z-score, the psychologist needs to know that the published mean of IQ tests is 100 and the standard deviation is 15. The math then would be

$$z = \frac{130-100}{15}$$
$$z = 2.0$$

On a table of z-scores, it can be seen that a z-score of 2.0 occurs around the 97.7th percentile. In other words, only a little over 2% of a normal population (1 out of 50) qualifies as being mentally gifted according to this definition.

In 2007, a total of 25,693 students took the 205-question GRE Subject Test in psychology. The mean score was 600, and the standard deviation was 100 (ETS, 2009). Using Table 7.6, it can be seen that a student scoring 450 on this examination is in approximately the 6th percentile with 94% of all graduates scoring better ($z = -1.5$). A score of 660 ($z = +1.6$) would be at about the 72nd percentile, and a score of 780 ($z = +1.8$) would be in the 96th percentile.[18]

Commonly Reported Standard Scores
Based on the Normal Curve

Raw score. A raw score is the total number of actual items on the measure that the test taker answered correctly. To better understand what a raw score indicates, the measure's report should indicate the total number of questions.

Normative percentile. A method of finding any individual's test score percentile is to compare that score to scores of the normative comparison group (i.e., norm group). If a score were at the center point of the norm group, it would be at the 50th percentile, with half of the norm group's scores above and half below. That 50th percentile is also the median of all scores. If a person did better than three quarters of the individuals of the norm group, his or her score would equate to the 75th percentile. Test publishers like ETS report a standard score and the equivalent percentile to the test taker.

Standard scores or scaled scores. There are numerous formats for standard scores (SS), sometimes referred to as **scaled scores**. They all are derived mathematically from a huge normative distribution of scores. Under normal conditions, a large distribution of test scores will follow clear mathematical laws. We know that 34% of all scores will be above and 34% below the mean score (arithmetic average score) by a unit of measurement called a standard deviation. Plus or minus 1 standard deviation includes the 68% of all scores closest to the mean (average). A standard score is based on standard deviation units above (positive values) and below (negative values) the mean. To make interpretation and comparisons easier, these scores are mathematically modified to make them all positive and give them recognizable values. One commonly employed standard score is used to describe an outcome of the GRE. Instead of values above and below the mean, GRE scores are mathematically designed to have a mean of about 150 on the core tests. Each standard deviation is set at a value of about 9. Thus, a quantitative GRE score of 163 is 1.5 standard deviations over the mean. Because 34% of all verbal GRE scores are between the mean (GRE = 150) and 1 standard deviation over the mean (GRE = 159), and the average is also the median (50th percentile), adding the two shows that a GRE of 159 is near the 85th percentile (50 + 34).

Undergraduate college admission tests are also standardized scores. The ACT has a national mean (average) of about 21 and a standard deviation of 5. Thus an ACT score of 11 (2 standard deviations below the mean) is at the 2nd percentile. An ACT score of 18.5 (0.5 standard deviations below the mean) is at the 31st percentile, and a score of 28.5 (1.5 standard deviations above the mean) is at the 93rd percentile.

z-score. This score is a real number that has a practical range of about 6, from about −3 to +3, with a zero value indicating the mean of the data. It is an expression of how far any score is from the mean as measured in standard deviation units.

Stanine. The norm group can be divided into nine parts, with the middle seven parts (stanine 2 to 8) each being 0.5 standard deviation wide (see Figure 7.2). This statistic is a core tool in many vocational placement tests, including those used by the American armed services. Because of the characteristic bell-shaped form of a normal distribution of scores, the central three stanines, 4, 5, and 6, encompass 55% of all cases. Stanines 1, 2, and 3 include the lowest 22.5% of all scores, and the top 22.5% of all scores are in stanines 7, 8, and 9. The top stanine, 9, includes the highest 4% of scores, while the lowest stanine, 1, includes lowest 4% of scores.

Normal curve equivalent (NCE). This is a standard score that has a mean of 50. One standard deviation above the mean (84th percentile) is an NCE score of 71. An NCE score of 29 is 1 standard deviation below the mean, and an NCE score of 10 is the 3rd percentile of the normative distribution of scores.[19]

SUMMARY

Professionals in mental health deal with psychological constructs. Attributes of clients as well as constructs are all variables. Variables can be described by scales, and some scales are more precise than others. The most precise, ratio and interval scales, are described as parametric measures, while most ordinal variables and all nominal variables are nonparametric. Parametric variables are typically presented as continuous line curves. Ordinal variables are generally best depicted using a histogram or frequency polygon. Nominal variables can be presented as pie graphs and bar graphs.

The form of central tendency for data is limited by the precision of the scale used to measure it. Means are reserved for parametric data, the median is used with ordinal data, and the center of nominal data can only be expressed as the mode.

Knowing the mean of parametric data makes it possible for the practitioner-researcher to determine the variance of a data set and its standard deviation. It also is possible to determine whether the symmetry of the normal curve is violated by skewing within the data set. The Gaussian normal curve has many applications, including creating standard scores and finding percentile equivalents to any individual's score on a measure using a parametric scale.

DISCUSSION QUESTIONS

1. In your professional practice, what measures, questionnaires, and other background variables do you plan to collect from prospective clients during intake?

2. On the Internet, search a politically charged topic such as US federal funding for mental health care and examine charts and graphs used to argue various points of view. Bring some of them to class and discuss any errors or distortions you may have found.

3. Develop a list of 10 distributions that are likely to show a high degree of skewness. Try to identify 5 distributions that are likely to show positive skew as well as 5 distributions that are likely to show negative skew.

4. Visit the university's library and read the *Chronicle of Higher Education* issue that lists all university administrator salaries (usually one of the November issues of this weekly paper). Pick a category of administrator and calculate the mean and standard deviation for that position's salary across all universities included in a category of your choice (e.g., *I* for doctoral institutions).

NOTES

1. Students with an interest in these statistical concepts are invited to use the student website for this textbook where there are more computational examples of the various concepts.

2. Congress created the rank "general of the Army" in 1944. It is signified by five stars. Only five senior commanders of the US Army in World War II were ever promoted to this rank.

3. Hospital-based nurses are ranked based on education, experience, and certification tests as nurse technician (NT), certified nurse assistant (CNA), licensed practical nurse (LPN), registered nurse (RN), charge nurse, and supervising nurse.

4. Binary variables can be assigned values of 0 or 1.

5. The Kelvin scale of temperature begins at a point equal to a Celsius scale temperature of −273.15°. At this point, there is no thermal energy (heat) in the phenomenon being measured. This quality of no thermal energy is known as the absolute zero point. At this point, all matter settles into its absolute lowest energy state, and even all subatomic particles stop moving as matter assumes the Bose-Einstein condensate state and produces super fluids as electrons bond (Donley et al., 2001).

6. Statistical power describes the sensitivity of a statistical analysis to detect meaningful differences between groups of subjects on a variable.

7. The word *average* in vernacular English is normally considered as being what a testing expert would call the mean, or arithmetic center, of the set of scores.

8. "Because different test takers receive different sets of questions, . . . ASWB does have to account for differences in the difficulty levels of individual items on different versions of the tests. When a candidate completes an examination, the testing software calculates a raw score—the actual number of questions . . . answered correctly. Because raw scores can be affected by the difficulty of individual items on a particular version ("form") of an examination, these variations are accounted for through an equating process. Equating adjusts the number of items [the test taker needs] to answer correctly up or down depending on the difficulty levels on a particular form (version) of the examination. Through equating, the passing raw score is adjusted for each examination so that fewer correct items are needed to pass a more difficult form of the test (and more correct answers are needed to pass an easier form of the test). Making these statistical adjustments ensures that the overall ability that needs to be demonstrated remains the same from test form to test form. In other words, nobody receives an advantage or disadvantage because of the version of test they receive. This is why ASWB cannot identify an unchanging number of correctly answered items needed to pass the examinations" (from http://www.aswb.org/SWLE/faqs.asp#Curve).

9. Newton was recognized by the government of Charles II as Great Britain's leading scientist and mathematician. Later, in 1705, he was knighted by Queen Anne. Huguenots, including de Moivre, were French Protestants (Calvinists) who were driven out of France in a religious diaspora in the early 18th century. Prior to that forced exile, thousands of Huguenots were massacred by Catholic zealots in the streets of numerous French cities.

10. *Binomial* refers to a probability experiment with only two possible outcomes (e.g., heads vs. tails; yes vs. no; pass vs. fail). A binomial distribution is a chart of those outcomes. As the number of probability experiments increases, the distribution will approximate a bell-shaped curve.

11. The mean for skewness is zero. When the measured level of skewness is equal to or greater than 1.96 times the standard error of skewness above or below zero in the data set, the data can be described as having significant skewness.

12. Real numbers have all the properties required for arithmetic operations. They can be divided and reported as decimals, thus making it possible to interpolate between measurement points. This allows a smooth line curve to be drawn.

13. The term *ogive* was first used by pre-Islamic designers and later by medieval architects to describe the graceful S-shaped arch supports used to hold the massive weight of vaulted stone roofs.

14. When a negative number is squared, it becomes a positive value. I was taught this in eighth grade and have never questioned it since. Likewise, it is not possible to find the square root of a negative number on the number line. The result is an imaginary number, i.

15. The logical divider (n) for the number of cases is replaced by ($n − 1$). This is known as the Bessel correction. It corrects the overestimation in size that occurs when dealing with samples (Warner, 2013). The value n is used when the calculation is based on an entire population (e.g., US Census data), and ($n − 1$) is used with calculations for samples of data. This same principle is seen with sample data where a vector of residuals from original observations will lose a degree of freedom ($n − 1$) when they are recombined to sum to zero. Zero summation around the mean is an axiom of statistics.

16. This is a messy-looking process and can appear to be intimidating to individuals without experience with college mathematics. The good news is that the statistical software used on university campuses today will find this value for any data set entered into the system.

17. Grade inflation on most campuses makes it unlikely to ever find a normal, nonskewed distribution of grade point averages.

18. In the summer of 2011, the scoring system used by the GRE General Test was changed. The GRE Subject Test in psychology (as of 2013) is still unchanged.

19. The least useful of the various standardized test score reporting systems is the **grade equivalent score** (GES). This score is read as a grade level expressed in years of 10 months' length. A GES of 10.6 is February of 10th grade. These scores are ordinals, yet there is a tendency for policy makers to try to find the mean of a set of grade equivalent scores.

The most problematic concern is that most school counselors, and virtually all parents, think that children who are enrolled in the fifth grade and are reported to have a reading GES of 9.1 can read ninth-grade books. This is absolutely wrong. What those data indicate is that the child in fifth grade did as well on the fifth-grade reading test as would the average child in the ninth grade if that ninth grader took the fifth-grade test.

Concordance and Correlation

"Not everything that counts can be counted, and not everything that can be counted, counts."

Albert Einstein

OBJECTIVES

By reading and studying this chapter, you should acquire the competency to do the following:

- Explain the meaning of the term *covariance* and how it is related to *correlation*.
- Describe the shape of scatterplots based on different levels of both positive and negative correlations.
- Discuss and explain the prediction application of correlation coefficients.
- Interpret the coefficient of determination in terms of shared variance.
- Describe similarities and differences between Pearson and Spearman correlation coefficients.
- Explain assumptions that should be met in order to calculate a PPMC and a Spearman rho coefficient.
- Interpret the meaning of the statistics eta and eta-squared.
- Explain the need to use nonparametric correlations with some parametric data.
- Describe the Kendall tau correlation, when it is employed, and how it is interpreted.

INTRODUCTION AND MAJOR THEMES

Descriptive statistics provide information about individual variables. Mutual dependence and its expression as covariance and correlation provide another type of description. The relationship between variables is central to most statistical models and central to making predictive judgments based on current data.

A number of statistical tools are available to express the degree to which two variables share a commonality. With variables measured as continuous numbers (ratio and interval scales), the amount they share in common is expressed as covariance. The mathematical value of covariance is expressed as a **Pearson product moment correlation (PPMC)**. Covariance and its expression in the form of a correlation coefficient are at the heart of most measurement statistics and test development. The squared correlation value provides a convenient method for assessing the utility of correlation coefficients. This squared value, known as the **coefficient of determination (CD)**, can be expressed as a proportion of variance on one variable accounted for (explained) by the other variable.

Charles Spearman provided the correlation (coefficient rho) of choice for use when one or both variables are an ordered rank. Additionally, Maurice Kendall provided a method to correlate the ranked judgments of two independent raters of the same subjects or objects. In addition, there is a universal correlation that presents all possible relationships between two variables, both linear and nonlinear.

Students wishing to learn more about correlational statistics and their calculation are encouraged to visit the student website for this textbook. On that web page, four correlation methods for use with dichotomous data are explained, and examples are given of their use. Also, the advanced methods for correlation—including factor analysis, multiple regression, log linear regression, path analysis, structural equation modeling, and multivariate analysis of variance—are presented.

COVARIANCE

When two tests are given to one group of individuals, a researcher may wish to learn not just the means and standard deviations of each but also the degree of their association or commonality. **Covariance** is a numerical expression of this dynamic relationship between two measures.

In psychology, almost all human characteristics are linked in some way to each other. For example, in the 19th century, early psychologists assumed that all human dimensions were somehow related (Galton, 1883), and they studied the relationship between elements in the human psyche and various properties of the physical self. These earliest studies of individual differences among people plotted scores of individuals on two measures as points on a two-axis graph. This was the same two-axis graph that we all learned about in high school, the **Cartesian graph** (Anton, Kolman, & Averbach, 1988).[1] In social science research, in which data points can disperse widely, the graph is referred to as a **scatterplot**.

SCATTERPLOTS

Scatterplots are commonly used in contemporary research presentations. Scatterplots depict the location of individuals simultaneously on two different measures. The basic graph uses two straight lines drawn at right angles labeled the ordinate (vertical axis) and the abscissa (horizontal axis). The crossing point has the designated value of zero, and the two axes serve as number lines expressing values above and below that zero point. When the Cartesian graph is used to represent two scores or values measured for each member of a group of individuals, the abscissa is normally designated the X variable, and the ordinate is named the Y variable. The two axes provide four different quadrants. The four quadrants are numbered I to IV. When the two measures on individuals are all positive (above zero), the data are plotted in quadrant I. The following graph shows the locations of the four numbered quadrants:

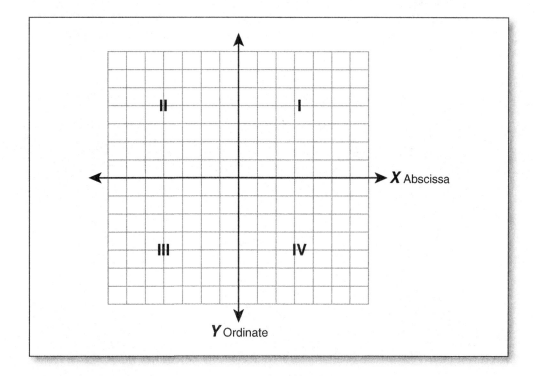

Most correlation data plotted on a Cartesian graph are in quadrant I, so only quadrant I appears on most scatterplots of data used in correlational research. For each subject there are two measures, one on variable X, plotted along the abscissa, and one measured as variable Y, plotted along the ordinate. Each individual's scores are reported next to the individual's identification:

Subject (score on X, score on Y)

These two score values are used to identify a point on the surface of the Cartesian graph that aligns with both scores. A brief tutorial on Cartesian graphing is available at the following site:

http://www.mathsisfun.com/data/cartesian-coordinates.html

An interactive method available for making a Cartesian graph is available here:

http://onlinehelp.smarttech.com/english/windows/help/notebook/10_0_0/
SMInsertingCartesianGraphs.htm

Cartesian graphs and scatterplots can be drawn using Microsoft's Excel software as well as by most statistics software on university servers (see Appendix A). Each axis of a scatterplot provides information about one variable, and the individual points on the plotted graph indicate an individual's score simultaneously on two measures.

From Figure 8.1, it is clear that as a college student spends more time studying and reading, his or her GPA will likely increase. It is also clear that this is not a perfect relationship, because, in some cases, more time spent on reading and studying did not result in a

Figure 8.1 Scatterplot for Hypothetical Undergraduate GPA and Hours per Week Studying

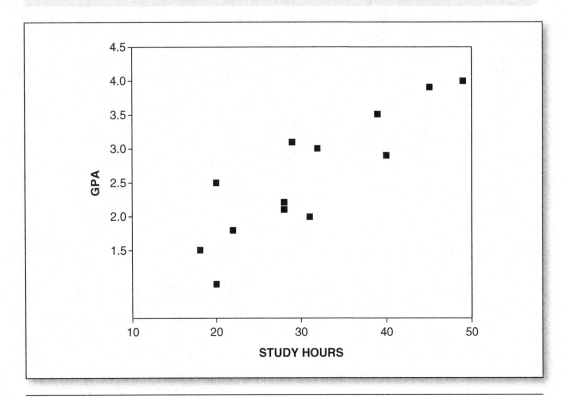

Source: Developed by author.

Note: This scatterplot makes it evident that GPAs over 3.0 tend to occur among undergraduates who spend 30 or more hours a week studying and that honors-level GPAs (over 3.5) occur most frequently among students spending 40 or more hours studying.

one-for-one improvement. Any number of individual factors may enter into this relationship. They could include the student's major, outside employment, child care responsibilities, organizational ability, and many other issues in life.

The scatterplot can indicate to the practitioner-researcher the nature of the relationship between the two variables. In Figure 8.1, the scatterplot shows that increasing amounts of study time goes along with higher GPA levels. It is also possible for a scatterplot to indicate an inverse relationship between two variables, as seen in Figure 8.2.

Figure 8.2   Assessment of "Poor Sleep" Prevalence

Method: To identify children with fragmented sleep patterns, we defined *poor sleep* as sleep that is characterized by either (a) a sleep percentage lower than 90 (i.e., the child spends more than 10% of the sleep period, after sleep onset, in wakefulness) or (b) waking three times or more per night on average (with each night-waking being 5 min. long or longer).

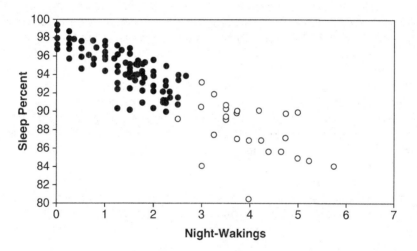

Scatterplot of sleep percentage and number of night-wakings. Open circles denote children identified as "poor sleepers" (sleep percentage lower than 90 or waking three or more times per night).

$$r = -0.89$$

Source: Sadeh, A., Raviv, A., & Gruber, R. (2000). Sleep patterns and disruptions in school age children. *Developmental Psychology, 36*(3), 291–301. doi: 10.1037/0012-1649.36.3.291

Note: Each dot on the graphic represents one child. There are a total of 140 elementary school–age children in the study. Note the pattern in the graph: It implies that as the number of night wakings increases, the percent of available sleep time decreases. This is a negative relationship.

Many times, assessments and measures used in clinical settings have much in common with each other. This tendency is due to the commonality or shared variance of the various measures. We can see this in the tendency for scores from different evaluation tools to be similar for an individual. For example, if one of the subtests of a **personality inventory** is significantly out of alignment with other components of the assessment, that outlying area is viewed as a diagnostic indicator. We expect to see consistency regarding any client. In other words, we generally expect covariance.

Covariance is the statistical expression of the amount of shared commonality. When covariance is numerically high, the two variables tend to move together. Thus, high scores on one measure presage high scores on the other measure. At the dawn of the 20th century, Charles Spearman saw this tendency and postulated the existence of a general (common) factor that runs through most cognitive tasks. In other words, he found that various measures of cognition are all correlated. This hunch led to the empirical work needed to measure mental ability (Spearman, 1904/2000).

Covariance can be either positive or negative. If the value is positive, we know that if one measure is high or elevated, the second will be high as well. Likewise, a low score on one measure is likely to be followed by a low score on a second. A covariance with a negative value is just the opposite. In that case, a high score on one measure is likely associated with a lower score on the second. This can be seen in the well-known relationship between measured levels of manifest anxiety and clerical speed and accuracy. As the anxiety level increases, scores on the test of clerical speed and accuracy, such as the pharmacy test, tend to be lower (Schell & Grasha, 2000).

To actually calculate covariance for two measures with one group of individuals, it is first necessary to find the mean for each measure. These are often represented as $\bar{X}$ and $\bar{Y}$. The individual X and Y scores are subtracted from the appropriate means—$\bar{X}$, and $\bar{Y}$, respectively—and the resulting difference scores are multiplied together for each individual. These multiplication products can then be added and divided by $n - 1$ to find the covariance.[2]

A central step in finding covariance is the multiplication of difference scores. For example, the Personality Assessment Inventory (PAI) reports scores for measures of both "mania" and "anxiety." If both tend to be very high for most individuals, multiplying the two subtraction difference scores together will result in a positive covariance value. In a similar way, if mania and anxiety scores are both low, their cross products (the results of their being multiplied together) will also result in high positive covariance values.[3] However, if the mania scores are generally low and our hypothetical clients have elevated levels of tested anxiety, then the covariance value will be negative. A consistently negative mania score deviation from the mean, multiplied by a positive anxiety score deviation from the mean, will result in a large negative covariance value.

If there is no relationship between the two measurers, the value of the covariance for the sample of clients is zero. This happens when the positive covariance scores of some clients are canceled out by the negative covariance values found for others. Thus, when all of the individual covariance scores for the clients in the sample are added together, the total sum, or total covariance, is zero.

Data for the 12 clients used in Table 8.1 can also be presented as a scatterplot. On the scatterplot, shown in Figure 8.3, the tendency for individuals with higher tested levels of intelligence to be more self-critical is evident.

When measurements are very consistent and there is a one-for-one change in the two variables, the scatterplot will assume a form approaching a straight line (see Figure 8.4a).

Table 8.1   Variance and Covariance Data for Cognitive Tests

	Subject Self-Criticism (T-Score)	WAIS IV, Full-Scale IQ
Alonzo	55	120
Beth	70	136
Craig	45	117
Denise	30	85
Eduardo	85	133
Frederica	65	103
Geoffrey	80	115
Hazel	50	98
Isador	55	124
Juliet	65	121
Kirk	50	107
Louisa	60	110
Mean	59.16	114.08
Variance	231.06	205.35
Standard Deviation	15.20	14.33
Covariance: $Cov_{xy} = 145.28$		

Note: In an ersatz study of cognitive distortion and cognitive capacity, the researcher used 12 subjects who each completed the Self-Criticism Scale of the Cognitive Distortion Test (Briere, 2000) and the Wechsler Adult Intelligence Test, 4th edition (Wechsler, 2008).

Figure 8.3   Scatterplot for 12 Clients on Dimensions of Self-Criticism and WAIS IV IQ

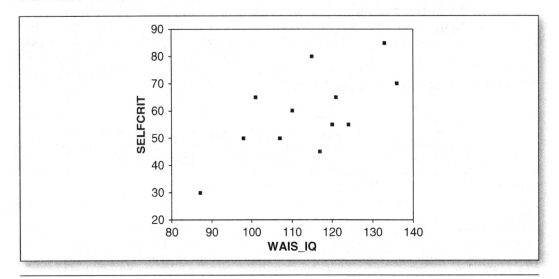

Source: Developed by author.

Note: $r = 0.67$.

Figure 8.4a   Scatterplot Depicting the Relationship of Individual's Height Measured in Inches and in Centimeters

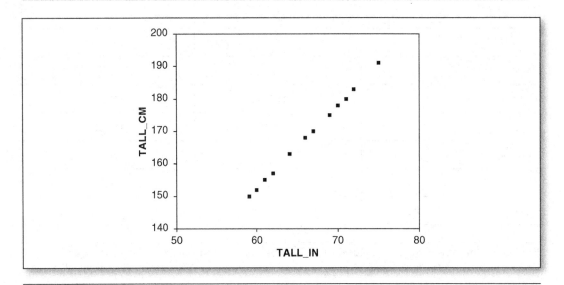

Source: Developed by author.

Note: $r = 0.99$. If both measures are of the same underling dimension, the scatterplot can take the form of a straight line.

If two variables have nothing in common, such as women's shoe sizes and their levels of emotional intelligence, the scatterplot will have no clear shape (see Figure 8.4b).

Figure 8.4b Scatterplot Depicting the Relationship of Women's Shoe Sizes and Their Tested Level of Emotional Intelligence

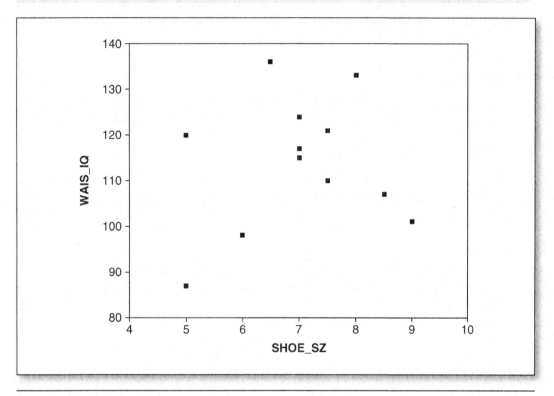

Source: Developed by author.

Note: $r = 0.06$.

CORRELATION COEFFICIENT (PEARSON PRODUCT MOMENT CORRELATION COEFFICIENT [PPMC])

Scatterplots notwithstanding, there are no practical limits as to how large either a positive or negative covariance can become. This makes covariance very difficult to interpret. In 1896, the Goldsmid Professor of Applied Mathematics at the University of London, Karl Pearson, published a paper analyzing some of the voluminous data on **heritability** collected by Sir Francis Galton.[4] Pearson's paper was updated and published again in 1901, at which time he provided a solution for defining the relationship between variables. The paper presented a new statistical tool, the correlation coefficient.

Pearson's new statistic quickly became known as the "Pearson product moment correlation coefficient," or "Pearson's correlation."[5] This correlation coefficient has a minimum value of zero and a maximum value of either plus or minus one (±1.0). The existence of covariance between two variables indicates they share a level of dependency that can be mathematically expressed as a correlation. Zero correlation indicates the variables are completely independent of each other.[6] This requirement leads some researchers to refer to Pearson's correlation as a **zero-order correlation**. Negative covariance is expressed as a negative correlation, and a positive covariance is represented by a positive coefficient. The letter symbolizing a Pearson's correlation is the lower case *r*.

Statistical Assumptions

Pearson's correlation has several underlying requirements. Failure to meet these requirements (assumptions) precludes using Pearson's approach. These requirements are as follows:

1. Both variables are measured as ratio or interval scales (or ordinal type II).

2. Both variables have underlying distributions of scores that follow a normal curve.

3. The scatterplots of the two variables together appear to be linear in shape.

4. The scatterplot is **homoscedastic**.

This last issue of homoscedasticity is a requirement that the relationship between the two variables is about the same at all levels of each of the two variables. If the degree of correlation changes at different levels of the variables, the resulting distribution is heteroscedastic. A good example of a heteroscedastic relationship is that between cognitive ability (IQ) and measured creativity. In Figure 8.5, the scatterplot between IQ and creativity indicates a linear relationship when the measured level of IQ is in the low to average range. Above an IQ of about 120, however, the relationship between the two variables is diminished.

Research Problems With Pearson's Correlation

In addition to these statistical assumptions, there are two other concerns associated with using Pearson's *r* with continuous data (ratio and interval). One of these is the issue of **statistical attenuation**. When only a small segment of the scatterplot depicting the relationship between two variables is isolated for study, the strength of the relationship between them may be masked. A classic example of this is the correlation between the number of students in a classroom and the quality of learning that occurs.

Many undergraduates are taught in lecture halls with in excess of 300 other students. Some students are taught in research seminars with just a handful of other students. Anecdotal experience is that learning is more intense in the seminar setting. Yet, most research, especially with public school education, focuses on a range of only 15 to 35 students per class. The range of the data set is too limited to make a clear statement as to the strength of the correlation between the two variables, measured achievement and class size.

Figure 8.5   Scatterplot of Relationship Between IQ and Creativity

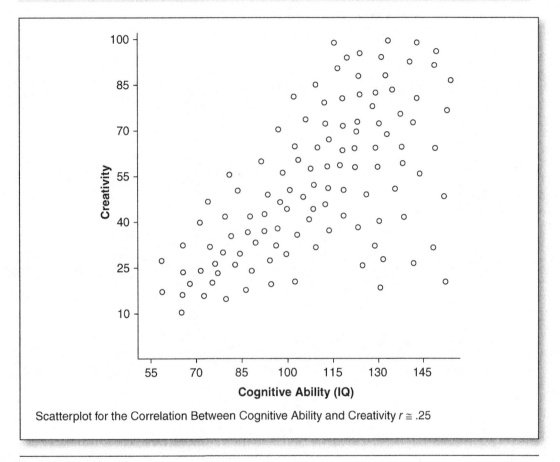

Scatterplot for the Correlation Between Cognitive Ability and Creativity $r \cong .25$

Source: Developed by author.

A second concern for researchers using Pearson's correlation is this statistic's vulnerability to **outliers** in the data. An outlier is any datum point far removed from the main body of the data set. Outliers can happen when data are miscoded or not measured correctly. They also may represent a true anomaly. The easiest correction for this problem is to visually check all scatterplots for the presence of outliers.

Interpreting Correlations

The correlation coefficient can be easily interpreted; however, the correlation coefficient is often misunderstood. It is an expression of the amount of shared variance (covariance) between two measures. It does *not* show a causal relationship. Teaching young

Figure 8.6   Impact of an Outlier in the Calculation of Pearson's *r*

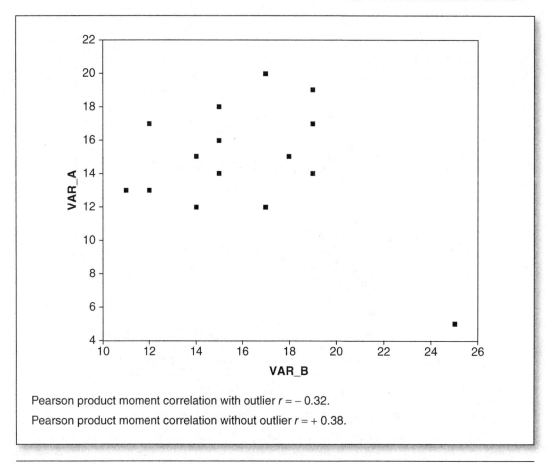

Pearson product moment correlation with outlier *r* = − 0.32.

Pearson product moment correlation without outlier *r* = + 0.38.

Source: Developed by author.

scholars about the error likely to occur when confusing correlation with causation is at least 2,000 years old.[7]

Correlation coefficients only indicate that two measures share a common element. Thus, the fact that there is a correlation (*r* = + 0.50) between the tested levels of IQ with pairs of siblings does not imply that one sibling being bright causes the other sibling to be bright as well. There is clearly some common element connecting these two scores, but the connection is not causal. Common elements behind both may be the stability of their home, the mental ability of their parents, or perhaps the child-rearing practices followed in the home. Likewise, scores on the GRE are correlated with the academic success achieved by graduate students in counseling programs (*r* = + 0.40). However, this does not imply that the success or failure of a graduate student is determined by a test score, only that there is a level of commonality or shared variation between the two variables.

Several online resources have been designed to calculate the Pearson's correlation from raw data on two variables. Following are three of them:

1. Patrick Wessa, Pearson Correlation v. 1.0.3, in Free Statistics Software (v. 1.1.23-r6), Office for Research Development and Education, http://www.wessa.net/corr.wasp

2. Easycalculation.com, http://easycalculation.com/statistics/correlation.php

3. Daniel S. Soper, University of California–Fullerton, http://www.danielsoper.com/ statcalc/calc45.aspx

The full range of correlation methods can be calculated by employing one of the statistical software systems on your university's server. These include, among others, the following:

ASReml, VSN International, http://www.vsni.co.uk/software/asreml

BMDP Statistical Software, http://www.statistical-solutions-software.com/products-page/bmdp-statistical-software/

Excel, Microsoft, 2007, work by Professor A. Colin Cameron, University of California–Davis, http://cameron.econ.ucdavis.edu/excel/ex51correlation.html

EViews, v.7.2, http://www.eviews.com/

IBM SPSS (see Appendix A), http://www.spss.com/software/statistics/text-analytics-for-surveys/index.htm?tab=1

Maple, v.16.0, http://www.maplesoft.com/products/maple/

Minitab, v.16, http://www.minitab.com/en-US/products/minitab/default.aspx

NMath Stats, v.3.5, http://www.centerspace.net/products/nmath-stats/

SAS Institute, http://www.sas.com/ads/google_stats/?gclid=CKfxm-L9iqgCFUta2godcQWECQ

STATA, v.12, http://www.stata.com/stata12/

SYSTAT, v.13, Cranes Software International, http://www.systat.com/

Wolfram Mathematica, v.8, http://www.wolfram.com/mathematica/

Linear Correlation Model

The Pearson's correlation is described as a **linear regression.** The implication is that the coefficient can be summarized as a straight line drawn through the scatterplot of data from the two variables displayed on a two-axis graph (see Figure 8.7 for examples). The proviso is that the line must be drawn in such a way as to be as close as possible to every dot on the scatterplot.

The term **monotonic** is also used to describe two variables that have approximately a straight-line (linear) relationship. This term indicates that the individual scores on two variables, X_i and Y_i, can be ordered in a linear sequence. In high school, we were all taught

Figure 8.7 Five Scatterplots With Regression Lines and Correlation Values

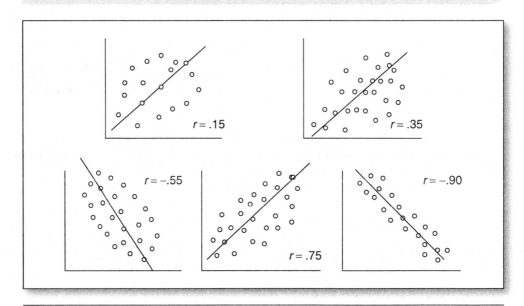

Source: Developed by author.

that a simple algebraic equation can be used to summarize a straight line. The equation from Algebra 1 in high school is also useful with correlations. In terms of linear correlations, the line equation is $Y_i = bX_i + c$. In this case, the individual values of variable Y are equal to the value b multiplied by the individual value for variable X. The value b is known as the line's regression weight and is actually the line's **slope.**

Return to that high school algebra class again, and you will recall that the slope of a line was explained as the "rise over the run." What is going on is that the size of b tells the researcher how much variable X_i increases every time variable Y_i is increased by one unit.

The value c that is added to the equation is a constant. This constant is equal to the point where the regression line (through the scatterplot) crosses the axis of the Y-variable. This y-intercept can be found by extending the line with a ruler and expanding the two-axis graph to include all four Cartesian quadrants.[8]

Calculation Assistance

Once again, many software packages will do the work of calculating correlation coefficients and providing line equations. These include the following:

1. Most hand-held calculators

2. Apps for iPad systems, including http://itunes.apple.com/us/app/regression-calculator/id339270826?mt = 8 and http://itunes.apple.com/us/app/calculator-statistics/

id399554882?mt = 8, and for the Android platform, including http://www
.androidzoom.com/android_applications/education/statistics-calculator-84_nmje
.html and http://www.androidzoom.com/android_applications/tools/topics-in-
statistics_ndnr.html

3. The Web

- Vassar College, http://faculty.vassar.edu/lowry/corr_stats.html
- Chang Bioscience, http://www.changbioscience.com/stat/corr.html
- Mastee Badii, Business Statistics in Health Care Services, Department of Health
  Administration and Policy at George Mason University, tutorial on calculating
  correlations with Excel, http://www.youtube.com/watch?v=LTrgAQraf5Y

4. The statistical software maintained on your university's servers

Cartoon 8.1 Meaning of Mathematical Terms

Cartoon by Merv Magus.

Correlation Matrix

Often psychology and counseling studies include many more than two variables. To show all possible intercorrelations among pairs of variables can require many pages of text. Researchers have developed a matrix format, called a **variance-matrix,** for presenting large numbers of correlation coefficients in one table.

Applications from the Literature

Three Sample Correlation Matrices from Counseling Literature

Note: In this example, the authors numbered the variables listed in the left-hand column and used those numbers along the top row to indicate which variable was presented. The variable sex was correlated by assigning numerical values of zero and 1, thereby creating a binominal (ratio scale) for the participants' gender. Dashed lines were used to replace the six correlations of a variable with itself. Those self-correlations are by definition always $r = + 1.0$. To save space, the authors also elected to include the means and standard deviations for the six variables in the same table. The asterisks relate to the question of how confident the researcher can be about this correlation. That topic is addressed in Chapter 10.

Example A

Correlations, Means, and Standard Deviations Among Study 2 Measures						
Measure	*1*	*2*	*3*	*4*	*5*	*6*
1. Depression	–	–				
2. Anxiety	.68***	–				
3. Self-disclosure of specific event	–.18*	–.03	–			
4. Intensity of specific event	.23**	.15	.27***			
5. Emotional avoidance	.39***	.22**	–14	.44***	–	
6. Sex	.08	.11	.14	.13	.05	–
M	10.16	10.07	3.13	3.72	2.60	0.81
SD	7.78	6.70	1.25	1.11	0.99	0.39

Note: N – 153. Sex was coded as 0 = male and 1 = female.

Source: Kahn, J. H., & Garrison, A. M. (2009). Emotional self-disclosure and emotional avoidance: Relations with symptoms of depression and anxiety. *Journal of Counseling Psychology, 56*(4), 573–584. doi: 10.1037/a0016574

Example B

Note: In this example, the authors provided a list of abbreviations and numbers for the variables in the left-hand column. Across the top, the authors used numbers to represent the variables. The authors elected not to show the nine correlations of 1.0 that occur when a variable is correlated with itself; these unneeded correlations are represented by dashes.

Zero-Order Correlations Among Nine Observed Variables

	2	3	4	5	6	7	8	9
1. Public stigma 1	.68	.66	.22	.24	.28	−.22	−.22	−.13
2. Public stigma 2	−	.76	.27	.27	.27	−.18	−.20	−.12
3. Public stigma 3		−	.21	.19	.25	−.18	−.20	−.16
4. Self-stigma 1			−	.76	.75	−.52	−.54	−.55
5. Self-stigma 2				−	.72	−.45	−.47	−.41
6. Self-stigma 3					−	−.55	−.53	−.53
7. Attitude 1						−	.67	.63
8. Attitude 2							−	.71
9. Attitude 3								

Note: Public stigma 1, 2,3 = the three parcels created from Perceived Devaluation.

Discrimination; self-stigma 1,2,3 = the three parcels created from the Self-Stigma of Seeking Help Scale; attitude 1, 2, 3 = the three created parcels from the Attitudes Toward Seeking Professional Psychological Help Scale.

Source: Vogel, D. L., Shechtman, Z., & Wade, N. G. (2010). The role of public and self-stigma in predicting attitudes toward group counseling. *The Counseling Psychologist, 38*(7), 904–922. doi: 10.1177/0011000010368297

Example C

Note: In this study, the authors provided a table with correlations among six variables. Some of these variables correlate negatively, indicating that higher scores on one are associated with lower scores on the other. The asterisks are an expression of confidence in the importance of the correlation coefficient. This concept is discussed in Chapter 10.

	Therapeutic Alliance	Resistance	Transference Love	Negative Transference	General Adjustment	Pleasantness of Good Events
Therapeutic Alliance						
Resistance	−.52**					

(Continued)

(Continued)

	Therapeutic Alliance	Resistance	Transference Love	Negative Transference	General Adjustment	Pleasantness of Good Events
Transference Love	.32**	−.34**				
Negative Transference	−.36**	−.33"	−.12**			
General Adjustment*	.56**	−.08	−.12*	−.18**		
Pleasantness of Good Events	.31**	−.17**	−.06	−.06	.51**	
Unpleasantness of Bad Events	−.01	.23**	.04	−.08	−.21**	−.02

* = p<.05 ** = p<.01

Source: Nuetzel, E. J., Larsen, R. J., & Prizmic, Z. (2007). The dynamics of empirically derived factors in therapeutic relationship. *Journal of the American Psychoanalytic Association, 55*(4), 1321–1353. doi: 10.1177/000306 510705500411

Correlation and Determination

To understand the dynamic relationship between two variables, research consumers must first calculate the Pearson correlation statistic. Each variable has some amount of variance, and when those two variances follow the same pattern (covariance), the correlation coefficient will approach either positive or negative one (±1.0). When the correlation is near zero, there will be little or no intersection between the two variances. The covariance relationship can be depicted by a **Venn diagram.**

The proportion of variance overlap (i.e., covariance) is a good method to employ when interpreting the usefulness of a correlation statistic. A statistic known as the coefficient of determination (*CD*) provides a numerical value for the area of overlapping variances. It is found by multiplying a Pearson's correlation by itself (r^2), or squaring it.

The overlapping area of variances indicates that dependency exists between the variables. This dependency occurs when one variable changes in value and the other also

Figure 8.8   Venn Diagram Depicting a Correlation as the Intersection of Variances of Two Variables

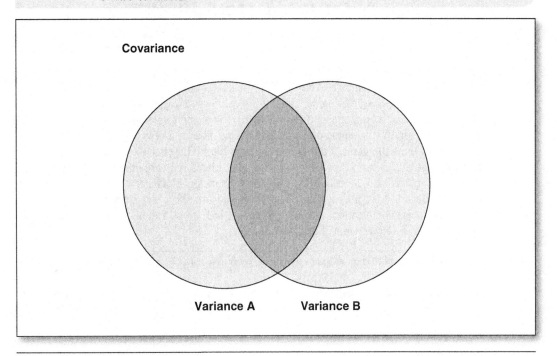

Source: Developed by author.

Note: Covariance is depicted by the shaded area of intersection between two variances.

changes. This can be thought of as an area of explained variation. The coefficient of determination provides the ratio of explained variance to the total variation. Thus, a correlation of $r = +0.5$ indicates to the researcher that 25% ($r^2 = 0.5 \times 0.5 = 0.25$ or 25%) of the variance on one variable is explained by the variance of the other.

For example, the correlation between the resale value of your car and its age is approximately $r = -0.6$. This indicates that about 36% of the variance in used-car prices is explained by vehicle age and the remaining 64% of price variance is related to other factors (e.g., car's make and model, fuel mileage, car body condition, and total miles driven). A large correlation of, say, $r = +0.875$ would indicate that one variable explains about 76% of the variance of the other. Thus, only 24% of the variance of the first variable remains unexplained by the second variable.

Negative values cannot exist for *CD*, as the correlation coefficient is multiplied by itself. Likewise, it is not possible for *CD* to exceed the maximum of +1.0. The limits for the coefficient of determination are zero to one ($0 \leq r^2 \leq 1.0$).

Applications from the Literature

Example of Coefficients of Determination

Note: In this study of 158 students enrolled in a community college, the authors found a Pearson correlation of $r = 0.33$ between the age of students and their grade point averages (GPA). He then explained his results using a cautionary tone.

Results: In this case a coefficient of determination may be more informative than a correlation coefficient. For instance, a correlation coefficient of .33 yields a coefficient of determination of 11%. Thus, 11% of the variance in GPA is predictable by the variance, or dispersion in age. Dispersed scores are characteristic of a heterogeneous group. Only 11% of the total variation between GPA and age is accounted for. The remaining proportion (89%) must be attributed to something besides age. In other words, there are additional variables responsible for determining the characteristics that accompany age and GPA that prevent segregating students only according to age for the purpose of predicting academic success. Additional variables include: financial assistance, dispositional variables, goals and intentions, assertiveness, special attention and class size, instructor characteristics, and crisis intervention. Family background, individual attributes, and pre-college schooling are also accurate predictors of academic success.

Source: Owen, T. R. (2003). Retention implications of a relationship between age and GPA. *College Student Journal, 37*(2), 181–190.

Predicting a Criterion

In Chapter 7, the terms *predictor variable* and *criterion variable* were introduced. They can be understood in terms of the coefficient of determination. When data for two variables are collected in a logical temporal sequence, the variable collected first logically becomes the predictor, and the variable collected second is the criterion variable.

For example, practitioners may want to know which clients are likely to complete a self-referred rehabilitation program for acute drug addiction. In this case, the criterion variable would be a binary (0 or 1) value of completed or not. Several potential predictor variables could be tested, one after another, to determine which correlated best with the criterion variable.

Applications from the Literature

Example Research Question Involving Predictor Variables

Note: A total of 95 upperclassmen enrolled at a Midwestern university participated in this study designed to define which variables were the most predictive of whether graduating seniors go on to further graduate study. They found academic locus of control to be the best single predictor of graduate-level matriculation.

Research Description: Although many undergraduates apply to graduate school, only a fraction will be admitted. A question arises as to what factors relate to the likelihood of pursuing graduate studies. The current research examined this question by surveying students in a 'Careers in Psychology' course. We hypothesized that GPA, a more internal locus of control orientation, and a non-consumer orientation to the educational process would predict the perceived likelihood of pursuing graduate study. Results indicated that academic locus of control orientation was a better predictor of graduate school intentions than GPA or consumer orientation. Results are discussed in terms of the importance of an internal locus of control for graduate school success.

Source: Nordstrom, C. R., & Segrist, D. J. (2009). Predicting the likelihood of going to graduate school: The importance of locus of control. *College Student Journal, 43*(1), 200–206.

Applications from the Literature

Example of Predictor Variable and Coefficient of Determination

Note: This study of 107 middle school–age students in Padova, Italy, examined the relationship between depression and antisocial behavior. The authors found that depressive symptoms predict increases in antisocial behavior but that antisocial behavior does not predict changes in depression. However, level-one depression predicts level-two depression, and level-one antisocial behavior predicts level-two antisocial behavior.

Results: To test for the relationship between depression and antisocial behavior, four models were examined. For the first model that tested for stability in the two constructs, t_1 depression explained 39% of variance in t_2 depression and t_1 antisocial behavior explained 28% of variance in t_2 antisocial behavior. We also calculated the total coefficient of determination that represents a measure of the strength of the relationship between the predicted variable and model. The CD for this model was .92.

Source: Vieno, A., Kiesner, J., Pastore, M., & Santinello, M. (2008). Antisocial behavior and depressive symptoms: Longitudinal and concurrent relations. *Adolescence, 43*(171), 649–660.

Eta (η) and Eta-Squared (η^2)

Researchers frequently include in reports and journal articles the value of eta. This type of correlation expresses the degree of relationship between two variables, including all possible components of that relationship. Eta (η) has a range from zero, indicating that the two variables share no covariance and are totally independent, to a maximum value of $+1.0$. There is no negative value for the **correlation coefficient eta.**

The eta correlation is an indication of all components of commonality between two variables: curved, linear, negative, and positive.[9] If two parametric variables are correlated using Pearson's correlation and then again using eta, the latter coefficient will always be larger. This reflects the all-encompassing nature of the eta correlation. The value of eta-squared (η^2) is a measure of the total variance of one variable that is explained by the second variable.

Table 8.2 presents an array of correlation methods along with a description of when their use is appropriate.

Table 8.2 Symbols and Requirements for Seven Frequently Reported Correlations

Name/Correlation Requirements	Correlation's Symbol	Variable #1 Measurement Type	Variable #2 Measurement Type
Pearson product moment correlation	r	interval or ratio	interval or ratio
Spearman correlation (rho)	r_s	ordinal, ratio, or interval	ordinal, ratio, or interval
Kendall correlation coefficient (tau)	τ	ranked judgments	ranked judgments
Point-biserial correlation*	r_{pb}	dichotomy or binomial	ratio or interval
Phi correlation coefficient*	r_ϕ	two or more nominal categories	two or more nominal categories
Tetrachoric correlation coefficient*	r_{tet}	dichotomy created from ratio or interval data	dichotomy created from ratio or interval data
Eta coefficient of universal correlation	η	data from linear or **curvilinear**, with nominal, ordinal, interval, or ratio measures	data from linear or curvilinear, with nominal, ordinal, interval, or ratio measures

* These are explained and examples of their use are given on the student website for this book.

A point-biserial correlation is a correlation coefficient used to express the correlational relationship between a dichotomy and a set of continuous scores (parametric data).

A phi correlation coefficient is a measure of association for two binary variables and is closely related to the Pearson correlation coefficient.

A tetrachoric correlation coefficient is a rarely used correlation between two artificially dichotomous variables.

CORRELATION FOR ORDINAL I DATA

Ordinal I data are nonparametric and cannot meet the assumptions required for using Pearson's correlation. If one or both variables are ordinal, there are appropriate correlation methods that may be used. These nonparametric correlations do not need to meet the four statistical assumptions listed for Pearson's correlation.

Spearman Correlation

During the early years of the 20th century, Charles E. Spearman was a professor at University College, London. This was during the era of Karl Pearson's prominence as a member of the faculty of London's University College.[10] Working with raw data from cognitive tests, Spearman developed a correlation coefficient that he applied to ordered data. The

Spearman correlation coefficient provides a measure of the **monotonic association** between two variables that are measured as ordinals, intervals, or ratios. It has a minimum value of zero and a maximum value of either plus or minus one (±1.0). When the Spearman coefficient is +1.0, there is no disagreement between the rankings of each individual on two measures. Thus, an individual with the top rank on one variable would also have the top rank on the second variable.

Similarly, if the coefficient is –1.0, the rankings for each individual are in total disagreement; if one rank is high, the rank on the second measure is correspondingly low. Spearman's correlation appears in publications as one of two symbols, the Greek letter *rho* (ρ) or as r_s.

Scatterplots for the Spearman Correlation

The same two-axis format can be used to plot ordinal ranks of individuals on two variables as is used with ratio and interval data. In this case, the points on the graph each indicate two rankings for individuals.

Figure 8.9   Scatterplot for Ranked Data From the Conners Adult ADHD Rating Scale

This theoretical study was conducted using a sample of 20 self-referred students to a university's counseling center. The 20 students were concerned that they might have attention-deficit/hyperactivity disorder (ADHD). As part of their intake, they each completed the Conners Adult ADHD Rating Scale (Conners, Erhardt, & Sparrow, 1999).

The four principal subscales were found, and the students were ranked on each. The following scatterplot depicts the rankings for the students on the variable, Inattention/Memory Problems, and the second variable, Impulsivity/Emotional Lability. The Spearman Correlation coefficient for these data is $r_s = 0.87$.

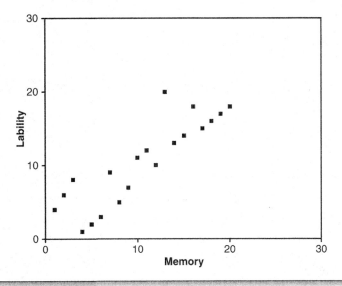

Calculation of Spearman's Rho

Prior to the development of the microchip and software solutions to statistics problems, researchers used paper and pencils and mechanical adding machines to compute correlations. When there were hundreds or even thousands of individuals providing data, the calculation process would require hundreds of hours. In that era, the simplicity of the calculation algorithm developed by Spearman (1904/2000) for his coefficient had great appeal. Calculation of the Pearson's correlation coefficient requires determining variances and doing square root calculations, whereas the r_s statistic requires only simple arithmetic.

Calculation Assistance

The computational formulas for both the Pearson and Spearman coefficients are presented on the student website. All statistical software packages, including IBM-SPSS, also provide for the calculation of these correlations (see Appendix A). As is true of the Pearson correlation, Internet-based providers offer free solutions for calculating Spearman correlations. There are also apps that can be added to hand-held devices to do the calculations. These include, among others, the following:

1. Most hand-held calculators

2. Apps for iPad systems, including these:

   Gear Diary, http://www.geardiary.com/2011/03/31/ipad-app-review-biostatistics/

   Lisisoft, http://appfinder.lisisoft.com/app/biostats-calculator.html

   iMedicalApps, http://www.imedicalapps.com/2011/05/biostats-calculator-evidence-based-medical-research/

   Biostats Calculator, http://biocalc.info/features/non-parametric

3. Apps for the Android system:

   Zoom, http://www.androidzoom.com/android_applications/spearman

4. Internet-based support:

   AToZee Software, http://atozee.co.uk/S151/spearman2.php

   Laerd Statistics, http://statistics.laerd.com/calculators/spearmans-rank-order-correlation-calculator.php

   Leuven Institute for Research on Information Systems (LIRIS), Catholic University of Leuven, Belgium, author Patrick Wessa, http://www.wessa.net/rankcorr.wasp

   Vassar College, http://faculty.vassar.edu/lowry/corr_rank.html

Interpreting r_s

The calculation of a Spearman correlation does not involve variance; therefore, the value of r_s squared has a meaning very different from the concept of a coefficient of determination. The value r_s^2 is a statistic that shows the reduction in the proportion of errors made when predicting the rank-order position of individuals, knowing the rank order on the first variable (Healey, 2010). For example, a Spearman correlation can be found between the rank order of women finishing a 10 kilometer race and the rank order of those runners' body mass index scores. If the value of r_s is 0.75, then the value of r_s^2 is 0.56. The meaning of the latter value is that the errors made in predicting the rank order of race finishers are reduced by 56% when the ranking decision is based on the individual's body mass index.

Unlike Pearson's correlation, the Spearman correlation coefficient is not distorted by outliers in the data set. The statistic rho identifies whether the data from two ranked variables share a monotonic relationship. Ranks are not influenced by the issue of just how low or high an outlying score is. Extraordinarily high scores are simply ranked "first," while an exceptionally low score is simply "last."

Applications from the Literature

Example of Spearman's Coefficient in Data Analysis

Note: The 146 members of the junior and senior classes of a rural Midwestern high school were administered the Kuder Occupational Interest Survey (KOIS) in 1975/1976. This was a regular feature of the high school's counseling program. A follow-up 30 years later was initiated by the authors. Participants were compensated $20 for retaking the KOIS in 2005. Of the original class members, a total of 76 were located and participated in the study. Of these, 36 were men, and 40 were women. Only the table for men is included in this excerpt.

The KOIS has 10 subscales measuring interest in different domains of possible occupations. In the variance-covariance matrix, the 10 domains are numbered from 1 to 10. The Spearman correlations (rho) show the relationship between the 10 subtest scores from 1975 with those from 2005. The correlations on the diagonal (upper left to lower right) show the long-term stability for each of the 10 KOIS domain scores over 30 years. The column and row labeled "S" provides the correlation between the occupations actually held by the subjects and their KOIS scores in 1975 and 2005. The correlations on the diagonal (left to right) are the correlations of the KOIS scale score over time (test and retest after 30 years).

Correlations between 1975 and 2005 Activity Preference Scale Scores and Intra-Individual Stability Coefficients for Men (N = 36)

1975	Activity Preference Scales 2005										
	1	*2*	*3*	*4*	*5*	*6*	*7*	*8*	*9*	*10*	*S*
1	.49***[a]	.08	−.09	−.17	.11	−.12	−.04	.13	.09	−.22	.32

(Continued)

(Continued)

| 1975 | Activity Preference Scales 2005 | | | | | | | | | | |
	1	2	3	4	5	6	7	8	9	10	S
2	.19	.76***[a]	−.18	−.16	−.14	.03	−.49	−.26	−.10	−0.2	−.26
3	−.29	−.23	.39*[a]	.14	.11	−.29	−.07	−.08	−.42*	−0.2	.12
4	−.05	−.31	.34*	.41*[a]	.16	−.24	.10	.01	−.08	−.32	.14
5	.00	−.04	.04	.04	.18[a]	−.09	.01	−.05	−.01	.12	−.13
6	−.03	.02	−.08	−.32	−.20	.56***[a]	−.20	.01	.12	.26	−.41*
7	.25	−.19	−.26	.08	−.23	.45**	.54***[a]	−.03	.05	.19	−.20
8	.08	−.13	−.20	.05	.26	−.16	26	.69***[a]	−.08	−.45**	.08
9	−.09	−.24	−.16	−.04	−.02	.13	.41*	−.11	.53***[a]	−.06	.08
10	−.02	.24	.17	.02	−.13	−.03	−.21	−.28	−.42*	.25[a]	.26
S	.01	−.21	.09	.13	-.07	−.06	.22	.03	−.06	.05	

Note: 1 = Outdoor; 2 = Mechanical; 3 = Computational; 4 = Scientific; 5 = Persuasive; 6 = Artistic; 7 = Literary; 8 = Musical; 9 = Social Service; 10 = Clerical; S = Spearman rho

a. Coefficients indicate stability for like-named scales.

Source: Rottingham, P. J. Coon, K. L., Gaffey, A. R., & Zytowski, D. G. (2007). Thirty-year stability and predictive validity of vocational interests. *Journal of Career Assessment, 15*(1), 5–22. doi: 10.1177/1069072706294517

Correlation statistics are a major tool used for the development and standardization of new measures. When the researcher is developing a new observational scale, the correlation statistic of choice is Spearman's rho. See Chapter 13 for a full discussion of the standardization and development of new measures.

Applications from the Literature

Example of Spearman Correlation Coefficients Used to Document the Usefulness of a New Observational Measuring Scale for Delirium

Note: This study of the effectiveness of a new delirium measurement was completed in a Veteran's Administration hospital. The sample consisted of 22 elderly patients exhibiting delirium but without a history of dementia. The new cognitive test was compared to dementia rankings based on expert opinion. The new measure was composed of several short memory items and required about 10 minutes to individually administer.

Method: The validity of cognitive tests as a measure of delirium severity was determined by comparing scores to quantitative expert ratings by using Spearman correlation coefficients at each of the three time-points. Changes in DSS scores from early to middle, middle to late, and early to late time points were also compared with changes in expert ratings between the corresponding time-points by use of Spearman correlation coefficients.

Inter-rater reliability for DSS scoring and expert rating was determined by means of Spearman correlation coefficients of independent raters' scores of 22 randomly selected videotaped assessments.

Source: Bettin, K. M., Maletta, G. J., Dysken, M. W., & Jilk, K. M. (1998). Measuring delirium severity in older general hospital inpatients without dementia: The Delirium Severity Scale. *The American Journal of Geriatric Psychiatry, 6*(4), 296–307.

KENDALL'S RANK-ORDER CORRELATION COEFFICIENT, TAU (τ)

In 1938, Maurice Kendall published information about a new correlation coefficient he developed designed for ranked ordinal data. His statistic was intended to provide a method of correlating the rankings of two judges of the same products or individuals. The correlation coefficient, tau (τ), can be calculated after a pair of judges has independently ranked objects or individuals. It can also be used for correlation questions that could be answered using Spearman's correlation procedure.

Kendall's tau coefficient has many applications for qualitative research. It may, for example, be used with consensus qualitative research (CQR) efforts as an indicator of the degree to which the various researchers assigning codes agree. The possible range of values for Kendall's tau is from a minimum of minus one to a maximum value of plus one ($-1.0 \leq \tau \leq 1.0$). A high positive value indicates much concordance between the judges; a negative value is evidence that the two judges have very different standards. Finding a negative value for τ indicates a need to retrain the judges as to the criteria they should use.

Applications from the Literature

Two Examples for the Use of Kendall's τ Coefficient in the Behavioral Sciences Literature

Example A

Note: In this study, several tau coefficients were calculated using the interval data of emotional intelligence (EI) scores. These coefficients show the relationship of EI with categorical ordinal data. In this case, with one ordinal ranking score and an interval measure of emotional intelligence, a Spearman correlation would also be an appropriate choice.

(Continued)

(Continued)

Results: Correlation tests showed no significant relationship between EI and age or location of residence. A Kendall's tau correlation test illustrated a negative correlation coefficient (tau = −0.128), linking EI and sex. Therefore, EI levels were significantly higher for females (coded "1") than for males (coded "2"). A significant positive relationship was found for EI with mother's education (tau = 0.205) and father's education (tau = 0.296); therefore the higher the level of mother's and father's education, the higher the reported EI. A Kendall's tau correlation test revealed a positive correlation coefficient (tau = 0.242) between EI and household income. The results imply that as household income increases, so do EI scores.

Source: Harrod, N. R., & Scheer, S. D. (2005). An exploration of adolescent emotional intelligence in relation to demographic characteristics. *Adolescence, 40*(159), 503–512.

Example B

Note: Small samples may violate the need for normally distributed data when using Pearson correlation coefficients. Careful researchers, including the author, tend to use nonparametric correlations instead (e.g., Kendall's τ).

Results: Due to the small No. of 15 subjects for which a normal distribution could not be assumed, nonparametric inferential statistics were used. Kendall's taus were calculated at the client level ($N = 15$) among the 6 variables. The relatively low correlations (all in the 0.30s) between the contextual and interactional ratings indicate that the two constructs are rather distinct. The number of individual and total systemic responses correlates extremely highly with their respective global ratings (tau = 0.84 to 0.92) suggesting a failure of the latter to differentiate the thoroughness and sophistication of therapists' systemic responses. Since the total number of systemic responses was significantly correlated with each of the systemic ratings, global or otherwise (tau = 0.49 to 0.84), and since it is the most statistically stable rating (with the highest interrater reliability, tau = 0.66 at session level, and 0.94 at client level), this variable was used to represent systemic ratings in all analyses.

Source: Krug, W. W. (2000). Rating scale of therapists' systemic responses in an individual treatment context. *Family Process, 39*(2), 207–217.

ADVANCED CORRELATION METHODS

In addition to these basic bivariate correlation approaches, there are correlation methods that involve numerous variables. These are known generally as multivariate methods. Several of these multivariate approaches are described on the student website, which also includes examples from the literature of these methods' use in counseling and other social science research.

The first of these methods is **factor analysis (FA).** A variation of FA, known as **principal component** factor analysis, was used by Charles Spearman in 1904 (2000) to define human intelligence as a single factor or inherited ability. This approach and two others are widely reported in the literature today. One of these is factor analysis with oblique rotations. This approach, first reported by L. L. Thurstone (1927), is used to identify multiple factors hidden within a large collection of individual test items or measures. Thurstone's approach was responsible for theories of multidimensional dimensions for human intelligence and personality. The final method, confirmatory factor analysis, is used to match the structure of one edition of a measurement scale with a newly developed edition.

The second advanced correlation research method is that of multiple correlation or multiple regression. This commonly reported technique provides a correlation coefficient documenting statistical relationship between one variable (criterion) and a group of independent variables (predictors). The approach can be used to establish complex predictive relationships and provide empirical estimates of how an individual will perform on a task or test in the future.

A statistical method aligned with multiple correlation is **log linear regression**. Unlike multiple correlation, which requires parametric (ratio and interval) variables, log linear regression uses only ordinal and nominal variables to make predictive statements. The outcome of log linear regression is expressed as an **odds ratio** of the likelihood of a particular outcome.

A combination of factor analysis and one or both forms of regression are employed to create explanatory models for how variables interact and lead to specific outcomes. These approaches may provide a single "path" to the result (path analysis) or be used to identify latent constructs and build a causal model for outcomes (**structural equation modeling**).

SUMMARY

The chapter opened with the concept of covariance and its measurement. Correlation coefficients have been developed to quantify the amount of covariance shared by two variables. Linear correlation coefficients must be employed with data that are homoscedastic and normal. Curvilinear relations between two variables can also be measured by the universal correlation coefficient eta. The correlation of two variables may be measured with both variables being parametric (Pearson's coefficient) or with one or both being measured as ordinal scales (Spearman's coefficient). Advanced correlation models are also available to researchers to express relationships between several variables and a criterion and to identify causal links among variables leading to an outcome.

DISCUSSION QUESTIONS

1. Most variables in human psychology and sociology are correlated. The strength of those correlations varies, but they tend to be positive. Make a list of pairs of psychological or sociological variables likely to be negatively correlated.

2. Make a pairwise list of sociological or psychological variables likely not to be correlated.

3. What are some reasons for selecting Spearman's rho to determine the correlation between two ratio or interval variables? How does the Spearman rho correlation compare with the Kendall tau correlation?

4. When reporting the outcome of correlational research, which statistic would you emphasize in the discussion section, the Pearson correlation or the coefficient of determination? Why?

NOTES

1. Cartesian coordinated graphs refer to the 17th-century Dutch-French philosopher and mathematician René Descartes (des Cartes). In his studies of analytic geometry, Descartes developed a system of linear coordinated graphing by employing Cartesian coordinates.

2. The logical divider is n, the total number of subjects. That computational approach is followed when the covariance is being calculated for an entire population. The denominator $n - 1$ is the Bessel correction, used to correct for the underestimate that occurs when working with a sample of the population's data.

3. Once again, the rule that negative numbers multiplied together result in a positive value comes into play.

4. At the age of 23, while a graduate student in Germany, Carl Pearson changed his name from Carl to Karl.

5. In the language of mathematical statistics, the first "moment" of any random data set is the mean, while variance is the second moment of the data. In mathematics, when two values are multiplied together, the result is called a *product*. Therefore, *product moment* refers to the process of multiplying differences from the mean scores together.

6. There is a mathematical requirement that a correlation of zero between two parametric variables indicates independence. In statistics-speak, this is described as an **orthogonal** relationship.

7. The Latin legal dictum expresses this error in logic as "*Post hoc ergo propter hoc,*" ("After this, therefore because of this.").

8. The constant can also be found by the use of a simple calculus using a partial differential equation. The differential equation solves for a line equation that minimizes the distance of each point on the graph to the proposed line. This involves squaring each difference score (line to point) and setting weights to minimize the total squared difference. This is occasionally described as a **least squares regression.**

9. The Pearson's correlation is designed to identify linear relationships between variables. This approach to correlating data may not be appropriate when the rate of change for the two variables is not consistent. Inconsistency in the change rates for two variables being plotted results in a curvilinear scatterplot (Cooley & Lohnes, 1971).

10. Charles Spearman was highly critical of the statistical approach followed by Karl Pearson. This began a long feud between the two faculty members that was never healed (Hägglund, 2001). Pearson went on to become a leader of the eugenics movement in England. Spearman developed a model for the human intellect that is central to the major measures of cognitive ability used today.

S E C T I O N   I V

Inferential Statistics and Hypothesis Testing

"It would be so nice if something would make sense for a change."

Alice's Adventures in Wonderland by
Charles Lutwidge Dodgson, aka Lewis Carroll[1]

Applications from the Literature

On Learning Statistics as a Social Science Student

From the Authors' Abstract: . . . students' experiences in a statistics class to investigate what factors contributed to students' anxiety and how instructional strategies helped students learn statistics effectively. The participants were graduate students in the social sciences at a large Midwest university. The findings from the study demonstrate that factors contributing to statistics anxiety include **math phobia,** lack of connection to daily life, pace of instruction, and instructor's attitude. The results also show that using multidimensional instructional methods and instructors being attentive to students' anxiety are helpful strategies to reduce students' anxiety.

Source: Wei, P., & Mei, T. (2005). Students' perceptions on factors of statistics anxiety and instructional strategies. *Journal of Instructional Psychology, 32(3),* 205–214.

The next three chapters present the basic principles of hypothesis testing through the use of statistics and probability. This section presents the use of these principles in their context of use. Because the practice of counselors and other therapists is the central theme of the statistics being described, students can become confident in their ability to understand and interpret research findings. The goal for students should be to understand the logic, application, and interpretation of these methods and approaches. To reach this goal of understanding, students reading this section should avoid "stepping in the minutia" and instead focus on why and when certain methods and procedures are used.

The language of this section uses scientific terminology, including the term *subjects* in place of what are described in qualitative research as participants.

The student website companion to this book provides computational algorithms and computational examples for readers with a need to know more about how the statistical components of quantitative methods operate with empirical data.

Chapter 9   describes the logic behind hypothesis testing based on probability. The issue of controlling error when making scientific decisions about accepting a hypothesis is also elaborated.

Chapter 10   introduces the use of statistics for the hypothesis decision model. The focus is on the statistical models developed by Ronald A. Fisher and William S. Gosset. These include the *t*-test and analysis of variance (ANOVA).

Chapter 11   extends the discussion of statistical decision-making models to ordinal and nominal data.

NOTE

1. C. L. Dodgson was a mathematician specializing in advanced geometry when in 1865 he penned *Alice's Adventures in Wonderland* and, in 1872, *Through the Looking-Glass*. To protect his academic career, he took the nom de plume Lewis Carroll, an inverse of the re-Anglicized Latin translation of his given names, Charles Lutwidge.

Sampling and Sampling Error

"The shrewd guess, the fertile hypothesis, the courageous leap to a tentative conclusion—these are the most valuable coins of the thinker at work."

Jerome Bruner

OBJECTIVES

By reading and studying this chapter, you should acquire the competency to do the following:

- Discuss the use of inductive and deductive logic in planning a research study.
- Compare and contrast the use of statistics and parameters to describe data.
- Frame a population to study through sampling.
- Describe three different approaches commonly employed by researchers for probability sampling.
- Describe three different approaches commonly employed by researchers for nonprobability sampling.
- Explain the concept of standard error as it relates to sampling.
- Interpret confidence intervals reported for sampling means.
- Explain the logic of the null hypothesis.
- Compare and contrast Type I and Type II errors.
- Explain the factors impacting the statistical power of a research study.

INTRODUCTION AND MAJOR THEMES

An appropriate goal for consumers of research in the social sciences is the ability to understand current research for improving each client's condition and mental status. To achieve this goal, practitioners should understand research methods employed to address client-focused issues and concerns. Research approaches employed by counseling researchers may involve a positivistic or scientific framework or a postmodern qualitative framework. The methods used by researchers are based on philosophical tools, including deduction, **abduction,** and **induction** (Peirce, 1877/1998).

While both major paradigms for research in mental health will employ each of these tools, inductive logic and abduction are commonly associated with postmodern research methods, and deductive logic predominates in quantitatively oriented research. This over-simplification of the analytical thinking researchers employ misses the subtle interplay of all three forms of logical arguments. This interplay can be read in most social science research and is especially evident in mixed methods research. (Mixed methods research is described in Chapter 15.)

Deductive logic is a vital step in well-conceived grounded theory research (Miles & Huberman, 1994). Other qualitative approaches to research may employ descriptive statistics and correlation to describe the participants and the interplay of the core constructs and variables that emerge from data. In this case, the statistics may appear in the organization, summarizing, and presentation of data.

Quantitative research methodologies use statistical analysis and probability-based hypothesis testing to assess data from research efforts. Probability-based hypothesis testing is universally employed with studies using **experimental groups, quasi-experimental designs, cross-sectional** and **longitudinal data collection,** and **path analysis.** Inductive logic is essential for all statistical analyses conducted in the process of probability-based hypothesis testing.

Sampling is the first step in the data collection process in quantitative and most qualitative research. Samples from populations can conform to rules of probability by making the selection of cases a random process. **Nonprobability sampling** can be used to select potential participants for qualitative research. Participants in qualitative research are often included because they appear to have the ability to provide very meaningful data. Qualitative research involving more than one rater may use Kendall correlations to determine whether a consensus was reached.

Descriptive statistics from samples usually include means, variances, proportions, and standard deviations. These descriptive statistics are estimates of the population's true **parameters** and involve some degree of error. That potential quantum of error can be mathematically determined and used to define **confidence intervals.** Confidence intervals can be employed to conduct statistical hypothesis testing (Fisher, 1973).

Statistical error is always present when sample data are used to estimate the parameters of whole populations. Thus, when sample data are employed by researchers to answer research questions, there is an inherent possibility of being wrong. The use of the **null hypothesis** provides a logical technique for answering research questions by a process of eliminating what is unlikely to be true. The level of possible error that the researcher will tolerate when deciding to reject the null hypothesis is specified in advance. By tradition, researchers usually set the level of tolerable possible error at 5% or less. This error level is described as **Type I error.**

The amount of error to be tolerated (Type I error) is also a factor in the chance of failing to reject a false null hypothesis. Not being able to recognize when it is appropriate to reject the null hypothesis is known as **Type II error.** There is a tradeoff between the Type I and

Type II error probabilities. Less Type I error is associated with a greater potential for Type II error. A number of other factors also relate to the potential for Type II error.

THE HYPOTHETICO-DEDUCTIVE APPROACH

The modern scientific model has a long tradition and was a central theme in the 17th century for emerging new fields of **natural philosophy** (science).[1] This systematic set of procedures for creating and testing new explanations began during the era of the Enlightenment and continues today. The scientific model is inexorably tied to the philosophy and worldview of Western societies, and it serves as the foundation of the vast majority of scientific literature. It was codified into a system for "doing science" during the first half of the 19th century by August Comte, John Stewart Mill, and William Whewell (Snyder, 2009). Later, their model was elaborated and explained by Charles S. Peirce (1877/1998), who defined the major tools of scientific logic. Those tools identified by Peirce include abduction, induction, and deduction.

Prerequisite for Hypothesis Writing

As was noted in Chapter 1, science does not just happen. To understand science requires a deep and comprehensive knowledge base focused on the phenomenon or condition being studied. Without thorough preparation, the research consumer is likely to not recognize worthless **pseudo-science**. Pseudo-science looks like science, but it does not provide justifiable conclusions. Typically, this form of science employs anecdotal observations as proof of a causal link.

Another common pseudo-science involves the observation of one incident followed by another as sufficient evidence to prove causation. For example, a common pseudo-science conclusion is that marijuana is a **gateway drug** and its use leads to abuse of cocaine and heroin. This conclusion is based on the fact that most hard drug users were first users of marijuana. This is classical pseudo-science because it fails to account for all other possibilities. We can easily see other possible causes leading to hard drug use. For example, almost all hard drug users smoked cigarettes before becoming a user. In fact, we also know that as young children, drug users drank milk. This was long before going on to hard drugs and "clearly the cause of the drug abuse today."

The famous Swiss child psychologist, Jean Piaget, provided the term **transductive** to describe the logic of young children. It is normal for a 4-year-old to link phenomena together that appear together. For example, a child of 4 years may make the assumption that his or her grandparents live at the airport. This insight is a bit of transductive reasoning based on the child's observation that grandparents come from, and then return to, the airport.

This form of pseudo-science is not dissimilar to that of graduate students who do not have a good background in different cultural norms. Such poorly educated students may easily misinterpret culturally appropriate behaviors of their clients as being some type of clinical marker for possible pathology. Likewise, well-intended crusaders against drug use have misinterpreted their data to imply a causal link between marijuana use and opioid abuse.

Deductive Logic

Logical **deduction** starts with a known or assumed truth and defines the possible formal consequences of that assumption. Hypothetical statements can be made based directly on the assumed truth. Thus, the researcher can deduce that certain other cases or conditions will occur based on the precondition set by what is known, and each of these new cases can in turn be assessed on the basis of newly acquired data. For example, a knowledgeable therapist working with children diagnosed with dementia praecox (Niemann-Pick disease type) knows that consumption of fatty (**lipid-dense**) foods can induce incidents of severe confusion and disorientation. Severely confused behavior by a 10-year-old child diagnosed with Niemann-Pick disease could be hypothesized as being related to lipid consumption, and this hypothesis could be confirmed with a simple **serum analysis.**

Deduction also plays a significant role in qualitative research that employs grounded theory. Once a researcher employing qualitative methods reaches the point in data coding at which core higher-order concepts have been identified, deductive logic can be used to identify ways to test the findings with new data (see Chapter 5 for a description of grounded theory).

Abduction

All mental health practitioners use **abductive logic** in their everyday practice. This form of logic allows the therapist to develop a hunch based on the client's demeanor and/or interactions. The clinical hunch is a type of hypothesis suggesting a causal link. What is abduced may or may not be true, and it can only be tested by continued observations and the collection of new data. This form of logic is central for much of qualitative research, and it is also a basic tool for making medical diagnoses (Walecki, Lason, Porebski, & Obtukowicz, 2005). There are literally thousands of possible causes of what we observe, and the abduction process makes it possible to winnow down that range of potential explanations. The goal is always to find the one explanation that is most elegant in its simplicity while explaining the greatest number of cases in the data. This is the essence of **Occam's razor.**[2]

Following fieldwork, qualitative researchers using grounded theory apply abduction with their data. This logical process for analysis is used as the raw qualitative data are coded. Identifying possible categories and linkages requires abductive reasoning.

Inductive Logic

The logic of induction fits easily with qualitative research methods. The qualitative approach for exploring new domains without a clear a priori picture of the important factors within those domains is, by definition, an inductive process. Induction in qualitative research is a key process for interpreting raw data collected by observation and interviews made in the field. Inductive logic makes it possible for the researcher to formulate likely links between observations and identify overarching principles.

Induction differs from abduction, in which the researcher formulates hypothetical links and then tests and reformulates the hypothetical position as needed while working toward an elegantly simple final explanation. Abductive logic leads to a possible "truth" that may or may not work in all occasions, whereas inductive logic provides a core explanation that explains the data and can be applied in other circumstances.

In quantitative research, inductive logic plays a central role in probability-based hypothesis testing. A researcher rarely knows all the possible cases that make up a population. The best guess that a researcher can make about a database is based on what is known or observed about a sample of the population.

For example, we may have observed that all collegiate football players we have ever met are young men. By employing inductive logic, we feel we can safely state, "College-level football players are young men." We have very good reason to believe this to be the case and can feel confident in our conclusion. Unfortunately, our logic did not yield the truth; some college players (a very small minority) are undergraduate women.[3]

Inductive reasoning presents a significant conundrum in science. It is rarely, if ever, possible for a researcher to have exhaustive knowledge of all instances in a population of individual cases. In the preceding example, it should be obvious that we could never visit the locker rooms of all 1,250 college football teams in the United States. This implies that we can only work with a sample of the whole population and, by induction, estimate the true state of the population. It is also evident that there will be a possibility of error when we use induction and make a statement about the true state of affairs for an entire population. It is the task of the researcher to find ways to minimize the possibility of error.

Parameter Is to Population as Statistic Is to Sample

Early in the research process, researchers must answer the question "For whom is the study to have meaning?" Thus, researchers need to decide if their efforts should have meaning for only their local setting or be of use and interest to others working in different settings and/or in different time frames. In the former case, the research effort may be classified as "action research" (see Chapter 6 for a discussion of action research).

If the study is to have applications in settings beyond the base of the researcher, then it is necessary to delineate who the possible users of the study are. This list may include clients who will enter the researcher's program in the years to come and/or clients and therapists of other mental health programs.

Population Frame

Making inferences based on a sample that is meaningful to the larger population requires the researcher to employ care in selecting the sample. The goal is to include individuals in the sample that are representative of all (or nearly all) of the members of the population. The essential elements of a statement of the **population frame** are precision and clarity of language. All readers of a study should know exactly who was included in the group from which a sample was drawn.

The first step in sampling is setting the **frame** for the population to be studied. The population may consist of a defined set of people, events, or items. Counseling researchers most typically study human subjects, and their population frame defines group membership.

Other professions also employ sampling from a defined (framed) population. For example, forensic accountants sample from the population of journal entries taken from the corporate accounts being examined (Golden, Skalak, Clayton, & Pill, 1939/2006). Pathologists study tissue samples from the population of all available tissue of an individual (Jacoby & Youngson, 2005). Industrialists sample from the population of new products coming off their production lines (North, Blackburn, & Curran, 1998).

Population frames may be very large and require an ambitious effort to draw a sample from them (e.g., the population of all licensed psychologists in North America). Population frames can also be far more constrained (e.g., all state licensed male employment counselors in California or all certified elementary school counselors in New Jersey in 2013).

Statistics Versus Parameters

In the language of researchers using empirical designs and methods for their studies, the noun *statistic* refers to data from a sample. The term *parameter* refers to data from an entire population. For example, when a researcher is using the full decennial US Census data, he or she has the national population parameters. If that researcher found the mean and standard deviation for income in a **census tract,** the descriptive data would be statistics about the individuals living in the tract.

Researchers almost always work with samples from populations and report statistical findings. To distinguish between sample statistics and population parameters, two different sets of conventional symbols have been adopted. By this convention, letters of the Greek alphabet are used to indicate population parameters, and letters of the Roman alphabet indicate sample statistics (Ferguson & Takane, 1989). These symbols are provided in Table 9.1.

SAMPLING

Once the population frame has been established, the next task is to decide which model for data sampling will be followed. This selection should be based on the research question that is to be answered by the study. For example, if a county supervisor is considering changing a building's zoning to permit it to be used as a shelter for battered women and wants to know the reaction of the neighborhoods he or she represents, the population frame is likely to be registered voters in the district. The sample should be clearly representative and large enough to provide the politician with an accurate picture.

Table 9.1 Symbols for Sample Statistics and Population Parameters

Description	Name for Parameter	Parameter	Sample Statistic
Mean	Greek letter *mu*	μ	M or $\bar{X}$
Variance	Greek letter *sigma* squared	σ^2	s^2
Standard deviation	Greek letter *sigma*	σ	s or SD

A different approach to that same problem could involve sampling from the opinion setters of the community (i.e., tavern owners, clergy, barbers and stylists, and service club officers). This approach to sampling, known as **purposeful sampling**, is commonly employed in exploratory studies and in qualitative research studies conducted in the field.

Applications from the Literature

Example from a Study Employing Purposeful Sampling

Note: The authors interviewed 10 master therapists and, through qualitative research methods, identified 9 ethical values held by the group, including (a) relational connection, (b) autonomy, (c) beneficence, (d) nonmaleficence, (e) competence, (f) humility, (g) professional growth, (h) openness to complexity and ambiguity, and (i) self-awareness.

Method, Procedure, and Participants: This study utilized data derived from transcripts from a Jennings and Skovholt study in which master therapists were asked questions about their personal characteristics and therapy practices. Well-regarded psychotherapists in a major Midwestern metropolitan area were approached and then asked to nominate three colleagues they considered to be master therapists. Nomination of master therapists was based on the following criteria: (a) This person is considered to be a "master therapist," (b) this person is most frequently thought of when referring a close family member or dear friend to a therapist because the person is considered to be the "best of the best," and (c) one would have full confidence in seeing this therapist for one's own personal therapy. Therefore, this therapist might be considered a "therapist's therapist."

After 212 nominations, the sample of 10 master therapists (7 women and 3 men) receiving the most nominations consisted of 6 doctoral level psychologists, 3 master's level social workers, and 1 psychiatrist. All held at least one license in their respective fields. The master therapists ranged in age from 50 to 72 years ($M = 59.0$ years, $SD = 7.9$ years). Their number of years practicing psychotherapy ranged from 21 to 41 years ($M = 29.5$ years, $SD = 6.6$ years). The theoretical orientations of the master therapists were divided among psychodynamic ($n = 4$), family systems ($n = 2$), existential-humanistic ($n = 2$), and integrative ($n = 2$). All master therapists were European Americans who worked full-time in private practice. Overall, their practices included short- and long-term work, with both managed care and clients who paid out-of-pocket within the fee structure of the community.

Source: Jennings, L., Sovereign, A., Bottorff, N., Mussell, M. P., & Vye, C. (2005). Nine values of master therapists. *Journal of Mental Health Counseling, 27*(1), 32–47.

Probability Sampling

When each individual or case in the framed population has an equal and known opportunity to be selected as part of a sample, the process is described as **probability sampling** (Aiken, 1997). Various probability-sampling approaches have the ability to provide samples that are excellent representations of the framed population from which they are drawn. There are three major forms of probability sampling: **simple random sampling, random cluster sampling,** and **stratified random sampling.**

CASE IN POINT   9.1

Random sampling is an important research tool for a number of federal regulatory agencies. The US Food and Drug Administration has issued instructional guidelines for US Department of Agriculture inspectors tasked with keeping our food supply safe and free from *Salmonella*. The following are two examples from those guidelines:

- For example, a single 10 lb wheel of cheese has arrived for testing. Since cheese is a Category II food, thirty 25 g analytical units must be analyzed. These analytical units should be taken randomly from a wide variety of locations around the wheel.
- For example, fifteen 1 lb bags of pasta have arrived for testing, but 5 of the bags are torn and unusable. In this case, the analyst should only sample from the 10 intact bags. The contents of each intact bag should be mixed to ensure homogeneity before the analytical units are withdrawn. Since the analyst needs one 375 g composite, ten 37.5 g analytical units, from the remaining 10 intact bags, should be used to form the composite. (Andrews, & Hammack, 2003)

Simple Random Sampling

Random sampling requires that there be no bias in how members of the sample are selected. Each element framed as part of the population must have an equal chance of being drawn for membership.[4] This may be accomplished by using a system of generating chance occurrences, such as dice or a number wheel, to select the elements. In 1927, Leonard H. C. Tippet, a student of Karl Pearson, devised and published a table of totally random numbers. This table was the standard of the field until computer-generated random number systems were published starting in the 1950s (Goulden, 2007).

There are at least two free Internet resources that may be used to create a list of random numbers that match the specifications provided by the researcher:

Random.com, http://www.random.org/integers/

GraphPad Software, http://www.graphpad.com/quickcalcs/randomn1.cfm

Systematic Random Sampling

Another approach to sampling may or may not provide a random sample. This approach is referred to as **systematic sampling.** The systematic sampling approach uses methods that begin with a list of all members of the population included in the frame. Then a systematic selection proceeds down that list, selecting every *n*th case for inclusion in the sample. For example, if a practitioner-researcher wanted to test a new antiviolence intervention for adolescents, the sample could be drawn from a facility holding adjudicated youths (the population). The researcher could reduce the population size by working from a list of all male adolescents who were arrested and adjudicated for assault. If the list is not ordered or sequenced, the selection of every eighth name on the list would provide a systematic sample that might closely approximate a random sample. However, if the list used as the basis of the sampling was in order of court-mandated release dates (related to length of the sentence), the systematic sample might include a biasing effect.

Thus, a list may have a systematic bias built into its aggregation. Unless the researcher is assured that all members of the population on the list were placed there in random order, there can be no confidence that the sample is random. Sources of possible sampling bias include using a list that was ordered alphabetically (ethnic group members may have similar family names) or a list of client names sequenced temporally by when they began therapy (a clinic's first patients may be different from the clinic's current clientele).

For example, human resources counselors of a major medical center with over 700 beds and 20 primary nursing stations want to survey the stress level experienced by the 380 registered nurses (RNs) on the full-time staff. To accomplish this, they may employ a systematic survey. The survey may be achieved by interviewing four nurses from each nursing station who are selected based on their seniority. In this example, bias may be an issue, as the most senior nurses may experience burnout more frequently than the younger nurses. Also, some nursing stations may be more stressful than others. For example, those nurses working in the emergency room, critical care unit, and intensive care unit have a very different set of responsibilities than do those working in physical medicine, wound care, or obstetric units.

Applications from the Literature

Example of Research Study Employing Systematic Sampling

Note: In his article, David Hodge explored perceptions of religious discrimination in social work. He hypothesized that the milieu of the collegiate training program socializes new graduates into particular approaches and attitudes in their practices that may be discriminatory against deeply held religious beliefs.

Method: To test these two hypotheses, perceptions were solicited from among graduate student members of two professional organizations: the National Association of Social Workers (NASW) and the North American Association of Christians in Social Work (NACSW). Roughly 30% of graduate students in accredited programs are members of NASW, which raises the issue of selection bias (personal communication with T. Lennon, director of information services, Council on Social Work Education, February 4, 2004). Consequently, perceptions were also solicited from student members of NACSW. To help ensure similarity in the environmental stimulus, only NACSW students enrolled in nonsectarian master's of social work programs were included in the study.

Given the low response rates obtained in earlier studies using mail surveys, the survey was administered by telephone. A state-stratified random sample ($N = 494$) was drawn from the NASW membership with listed telephone numbers ($N = 9,834$), and a systematic sample ($N = 125$) was drawn from the NACSW membership with listed telephone numbers ($N = 451$). Up to eight calls were placed by a professionally trained call-center operator in an attempt to reach each potential respondent. Excluding unreached potential respondents resulted in a response rate of 86% for the NASW sample ($N = 303$) and of 93% for the NACSW sample ($N = 88$).

Source: Hodge, D. R. (2007). Progressing toward inclusion? Exploring the state of religious diversity. *Social Work Research, 31*(1), 55–63.

Stratified Random Sampling

There are two goals for stratified random sampling: One is to ensure the sample is truly representative of the population, and the other is to ensure that input is heard from small but salient minorities within the population.

The first goal is reached by dividing the population in the frame into salient subgroups. Next, the members of the subgroups are sampled using a random sampling model. The groups are based on demography and may involve variables such as gender, socioeconomic status (SES), geography, religion, ethnic group, or a combination of factors. For example, a researcher assessing the strength of "role salience" and "work values" among graduate-level counselor education students may elect to build gender stratifications into the sampling process. This is needed because there are fewer men than women in graduate programs in counseling. Likewise, in fields such as computer engineering where only 1 of every 17 students is a woman, this procedure is even more necessary (Chubin, May, & Babco, 2005).

The second goal for stratified random sampling is to ensure that small minorities have their voices heard. The National Center for Educational Statistics conducts large-scale survey research and releases numerous publications from its data each year. This division of the Office of Educational Research and Improvement has resolved this problem by employing **oversampling**. The process involves identifying a distinct but small minority that may not be large enough in number to be included in a random sample. By randomly oversampling a much larger proportion of the minority group's members, the researcher will have the data needed to make accurate statements about that group. To integrate data from the minority into an overall picture of all subjects, the responses from the oversampled group are weighted to ensure their appropriate level of impact on the total population.

Applications from the Literature

Example of a National Random Sample Drawn by Random Numbers and Stratified by Geography and Population Factors

Note: In this survey research, counselors were concerned with their ability to identify students with substance abuse problems, work effectively with these students, and develop or teach curriculum units on this topic. These findings are not unexpected, given that half of the sample reported not having taken a single course on substance abuse in graduate school and almost half indicated there had been no inservice education on the topic for 3 or more years.

Participants: A national mailing list of 1,910 high school counselors was obtained from the American School Counselor Association for use in this study. From this list, a sample of 500 high school counselors were selected and sent survey materials. The final sample consisted of 289 participants, of which data from their surveys were coded and entered for data analysis. A proportional, stratified random sampling procedure was used to select a geographically representative sample of high school counselors. Specifically, participant sampling was based on the percentage of high school–age children living in each of the nine national divisions identified by the 2000 U.S. Census report. The nine divisions consisted of the following: Pacific, Mountain, West North Central, West South Central, East North Central, East South Central, Middle Atlantic, South Atlantic, and New England. The proportion of high school–age children living in each division was then used to calculate the number of surveys that were mailed to each geographical division. Finally, high school counselors within each of the nine divisions were selected using a random numbers table.

Source: Burrow-Sanchez, C. J., & Lopez, A. L. (2009). Identifying substance abuse issues in high schools: A national survey of high school counselors. *Journal of Counseling and Development, 87*(1), 72–79.

Applications from the Literature

Example of Stratified Random Sampling With Oversampling

Note: The racial/ethnic groups identified in this study follow the published guidelines of the US Department of Education and are the required categories for reporting school statistics to the federal government.

Sampling: The first-stage sampling frame consisted of 1261 primary sampling units (PSUs), consisting of counties, subareas of large counties, or groups of smaller, adjacent counties. The 1261 PSUs were categorized into 16 strata according to their metropolitan statistical area status (i.e., urbanicity) and the percentages of black (*black* refers to black or African American, non-Hispanic students) and Hispanic (*Hispanic* refers to Hispanic or Latino students of any race) students in the PSUs. From the 1261 PSUs, 57 were selected with probability proportional to overall school enrollment size for the PSU. In the second stage of sampling, 203 schools with any of grades 9–12 were selected with probability proportional to school enrollment size. The third stage of sampling consisted of randomly selecting, in each chosen school and in each of grades 9–12, 1 or 2 classrooms from either a required subject (e.g., English or social studies) or a required period (e.g., homeroom or second period). All students in selected classes were eligible to participate. Schools, classes, and students that refused to participate were not replaced. To enable a separate analysis of data for black and Hispanic students, 3 strategies were used to oversample these students: (1) larger sampling rates were used to select PSUs that are in high-black and high-Hispanic strata, (2) a modified measure of size was used that increased the probability of selecting schools with a disproportionately high minority enrollment, and (3) 2 classes per grade, rather than 1, were selected in schools with a high minority enrollment.

A weight based on student sex, race/ethnicity, and grade level was applied to each record to adjust for school and student nonresponse and oversampling of black and Hispanic students. The overall weights were scaled so that the weighted count of students equals the total sample size and the weighted proportions of students in each grade match the national population proportions.

Source: Eaton, D. K., Kann, L., Kinchen, S., Ross, J., Hawkins, J., Harris, W. A....Wechsler, H. (2006). Youth risk behavior surveillance-United States, 2005. *Journal of School Health, 76*(7), 353–372.

Random Cluster Sampling

Frequently it may not be feasible to collect data needed for a random sample from a population. This may be a problem of logistics and staff support or one of access. One solution is to examine the population for the existence of naturally occurring clusters. Once such clusters have been identified, it is possible to randomly identify clusters that will be included in the study. For example, if a researcher is interested in learning the extent to which homeless adolescent girls living with a displaced homemaker have experienced violence or assault during the past year, clinical interviews may be the best method for data collection.

In a large urban setting, this hypothetical researcher learns that there are 24 homeless shelters that accept displaced homemakers and their minor children. The shelters each report that they house between 20 and 34 women for a total of about 600 women with children. More than half (58%) of the minor children are girls, and each homeless family has an average of 2.5 children. It is clear to the researcher that she does not have the resources to make a random selection and then interview an appropriate sample ($N = 100$) of teenage girls. The best decision is therefore to **randomly select** five of the shelters and interview all the teenage girls at those shelters.

Applications from the Literature

Research Example of a Random Cluster Sampling Study

Note: The authors report a clearer impact on the variability of descriptive statistics from the sample, such as means, than on the variability of correlation coefficients. This tendency for sampling design effects to be greater for measures of central tendency than for measures of covariation among variables has been noted in other research.

Sampling: The second stage (secondary sampling units) consisted of a probability selection of an average of 17 block groups or enumeration districts from each primary sampling unit. Within each of these, a listing area of 45 or more households was selected; 20 households in each of these areas were included in the sample. These households were given a short screening interview to allow oversampling of certain groups (e.g., African Americans, cohabiting couples). Members of these groups in the cluster were selected with certainty, and others were selected at a lower rate. In the final stage, an adult from each household was randomly chosen as the eligible respondent.

Source: Johnson, D. J., & Elliott, L. A. (1998). Sampling design effects: Do they affect the analyses of data from the National Survey of Families and Households? *Journal of Marriage and the Family, 60*(4), 993–1001.

Quality of Probability Samples

If a researcher wished to know the average length of the marriages of client couples attending couples therapy, he or she could examine all data files, collect the needed information, and use it to calculate the answer. If 500 couples attended therapy sessions over the past few years, the researcher likely will take a sample of the data and find the answer. If the researcher randomly selected a sample of just three couples and found the length of their marriages, the resulting statistic would be suspect. The sample size of three couples would be inadequate for one to have much confidence in the findings. Tables for sample sizes have been devised to provide guidance for researchers using probability sampling.

CASE IN POINT   9.2

The 1948 US presidential election provides a good example of what can occur with a non-probability sample. That election year, the Republican challenger, Thomas Dewey, was assumed to be able to easily defeat the Democratic incumbent, Harry S. Truman. The major polling companies all agreed: Gallop gave Dewey a victory margin of 49.5% to 44.5%, and the Roper organization predicted a Dewey victory by 52% to 37%. The polls were conducted with an appropriate-size sample and reported confidence interval sizes that were typical.[5]

The error that was made was carrying out the polling over the telephone. This biased the data by introducing a nonrandom factor. While many homes in middle-class, urban neighborhoods had many telephones, fewer rural and farm communities had widespread telephone service. Likewise, many poor families could not afford telephone service in 1948.

Statistical models have been developed to guide researchers in deciding how many subjects are needed to build a valid sample. The size of the sample is not the only issue that has an impact on the quality of a sample and the ability of the researcher to infer from sample data to the whole population. Another issue to consider is whether the sample represents a true frame that includes all members of the population being studied. The researcher must understand the universe of cases, elements, or individuals that are to be studied before beginning any sampling.

A second concern in the evaluation of the quality of a sample is the level of coopera-

Photo 9.1   President Truman's "Loss"

Associated Press photo by Byron Rollins.

tion from all identified subjects. And a final concern is whether true and unbiased answers are provided during the data collection phase of the study. This last issue is impacted by designing a high-quality data collection tool or measure.

Table 9.2 Appropriate Sample Size for Different Size Populations

N	S	N	S	N	S
10	10	220	140	1200	291
15	14	230	144	1300	297
20	19	240	148	1400	302
25	24	250	152	1500	306
30	28	260	155	1600	310
35	32	270	159	1700	313
40	36	280	162	1800	317
45	40	290	165	1900	320
50	44	300	169	2000	322
55	48	320	175	2200	327
60	52	340	181	2400	331
65	56	360	186	2600	335
70	59	380	191	2800	338
75	63	400	196	3000	341
80	66	420	201	3500	346
85	70	440	205	4000	351
90	73	460	210	4500	354
95	76	480	214	5000	357
100	80	500	217	6000	361
110	86	550	226	7000	364
120	92	600	234	8000	367
130	97	650	242	9000	368
140	103	700	248	10000	370
150	108	750	254	15000	375
160	113	800	260	20000	377

N	S	N	S	N	S
170	118	850	265	30000	379
180	123	900	269	40000	380
190	127	950	274	50000	381
200	132	1000	278	75000	382
210	136	1100	285	100000	384

Source: http://www.fns.usda.gov/fdd/processing/info/SalesVerificationTable.doc; from Krejcie, R. V., & Morgan, D. W. (1970). Determining sample size for research activities. *Journal of Educational & Psychological Measurement, 30,* 607–610.

Key: N = population size

S = minimum size for sample (Krejcie & Morgan, 1970, p. 608).

Cartoon 9.1

An Inconvenient Sample

"I know like nothing, I'm like totally out of politics, but I really want to answer your survey questions about the candidates."

Cartoon by Merv Magus.

Nonprobability Samples

The mathematics of probability and the random selection process are the foundations of probability sampling (Aiken, 1997). These methods make it possible to understand how likely it is that the sample is a good representation of the population. However, nonprobability sampling is employed in the preponderance of published research in the counseling journals.

While **nonprobability samples** do not involve random selection and elegant mathematical models, they still may provide an excellent approximation of a population's parameters. A nonprobability sample is either a **sample of convenience** (accidental sample) or a purposeful or **quota sample**. These two techniques are commonly employed in qualitative research and in marketing research. While nonprobability sampling violates the premises of statistical analysis, advanced statistical testing is frequently carried out with nonprobability samples.

Applications from the Literature

Sample Descriptions Used in Research With Older Adults

Note: The authors compared the performance of older adults (65–100 years) on select psychological measures for a random sample of community-dwelling adults and two samples of convenience. Differences were observed on fewer than half of the variables.

Random Sample: The sampling plan was designed to achieve a 2% sample (1200 participants) of seniors in the Capital Regional District (CRD). A roster of over 56,000 names of persons 65 years of age and older living in the CRD was obtained from the British Columbia Department of Vital Statistics. The list is based on enrolment in the universal Medical Services Plan of British Columbia and maps onto census figures for the population age 65 and over for the area (16+ %). The population roster, therefore, probably approaches 100% of the seniors in the area. A series of random draws was made from this roster, and individuals were contacted by letter and then by telephone until the 2% target sample was achieved. They were asked to participate in a general survey of the lives of seniors and how they cope with daily problems. A total of 1632 eligible individuals (i.e., community-dwelling adults) were contacted. Of these, 1278 (87.3%) agreed to be interviewed and 354 (12.7%) refused to participate. The random sample consisted of 510 men and 768 women ranging in age from 65 to 100 years ($M = 75.13$).

Convenience samples: Three structured samples of convenience were recruited. Two of the samples consisted of older adults age 65 years and over drawn from the same general population (community-dwelling residents of the CRD) as the random sample. Participants were recruited by two different advertisements placed in local newspapers. Participants in the *memory sample* responded to a request for volunteers to participate in a study examining "memory functioning in later life." The memory sample consisted of 61 adults (23 men and 38 women) ranging in age from 65 to 92 years ($M = 75.51$). Participants in the *relationships sample* responded to a request for volunteers to participate in a study examining "patterns of family and social relationships in later life." The relationships sample consisted of 54 adults (17 men and 37 women) ranging in age from 65 to 100 years ($M = 74.68$). Finally, a *young adult sample* was recruited. These volunteers were students enrolled in the introductory psychology course at the University of Victoria. This sample consisted of 40 adults (19 men and 21 women) ranging in age from 19 to 28 years ($M = 22.17$).

Source: Huktsch, D. F., MacDonald, S. W. S., Hunter, M. A., Maitland, S. B., & Dixon, R. A. (2002). Sampling and generalizability in developmental research: Comparison of random and convenience samples of older adults. *International Journal of Behavioral Development, 28*(4), 345–359. doi: 10.1080/01650250143000247

Samples of Convenience

It has often been quipped by professors of psychology that the discipline of psychology knows more about undergraduate students and white rats than any other organisms on the planet. We know so much about undergraduates because it is common for college students to participate as experimental subjects in faculty-sponsored research to earn a grade in their class. Clearly, this available sample is convenient for the researcher to use. Researchers using their college students as data sources are not truly studying a random sample of any population, except perhaps college students in psychology classes, but these students are a convenient sample for university-based researchers.

There are many other examples of samples employed in research that cannot be extrapolated to other venues. These include clinical populations in therapy at a clinic, graduate students in a counseling psychology program, or undergraduates seeking counseling at the university's mental health facility.

In a similar way, much of the clinical research published by practitioner-researchers is based on data collected from the therapists' clients. Even a number of well-known psychometric instruments are standardized on samples of convenience.

Applications from the Literature

Example of a Sample of Convenience

Note: To control for the small number of minority-group adolescents available, the samples of participants (paid volunteers) included only Anglo ($N = 52$, 60%) and Hispanic ($N = 35$, 40%) youth in tests for group differences. Anglo and Hispanic youth did not differ in reported incidence of sexual or physical abuse or in suicide attempts.

METHOD, Participants: This was a convenience sample. All study participants were engaged into the project through one of two runaway shelters in Albuquerque, New Mexico. To be eligible for the program, the adolescent had to have a primary alcohol problem (e.g., alcohol dependence

(Continued)

(Continued)

and marijuana abuse but not vice versa) and be between the ages of 12 and 17. Moreover, his or her family needed to reside within 60 miles of the research site, and the adolescent's parents must have agreed to the possibility of family therapy. Youth who were wards of the state and without an identified family to return to (including foster or other family member) were not eligible for the program given the family therapy requirements.

Source: Slesnick, N., & Prestopnik, J. L. (2009). Comparison of family therapy outcome with alcohol-abusing, runaway adolescents. *Journal of Marital and Family Therapy, 35*(3) 2009. 255–277. doi: 10.1111/j.1752-0606.2009.00121.x

Purposeful Sampling

This sampling technique provides a selection of participants that are part of a sample that matches certain purposes held by the researcher. This opens the sampling process to many potential biasing effects.

Perhaps the most commonly employed purposeful sampling design for research involves screening certain cases out of the population for analysis. In qualitative research, a common practice is to select certain members of the community identified as having important information. Once identified, these informants are used to provide a rich source of insight into the culture and practices of the population.

Clinical research commonly uses screening measures. School counselors screen kindergarteners for possible learning problems. Once identified, those children receive more follow-up. The screening process means that the sample identified as being at risk for learning problems is different from the whole population of kindergarteners. Universities have been known to screen which faculty will be interviewed by accrediting teams during a campus visit. Researchers focused on the role of the father in American families may screen all members of the population being studied to identify a sample of single fathers with sole caregiving responsibility for two or more preadolescent children. Once again, this group is not an accurate representation of all American fathers.

Quota Sampling

Researchers with a predetermined structure for the sample they will collect frequently employ quota sampling. Quotas are normally expressed in terms of percentages of participants to be included in each of several categories of the sample being taken. For example, a marketing agent attending a conference for professional counselors may ask each visitor to his or her booth to complete a questionnaire about the product being purveyed. The marketing agent knows in advance that 30% of the sample of possible customers should be faculty teaching in graduate programs, 20% should be counselors affiliated with large clinical settings (e.g., Department of Veterans Affairs facilities), and 50% should be counselors in private practice. With this in mind, questionnaires are collected from counselors in one group only until that group's quota is filled, at which time the focus will be on filling the remaining categories of the sample. This approach is clearly not a stratified random sample. In this case, there is no effort to randomly fill the strata (groups). Anyone who rambles past the booth could become a member of the sample, until all of the groups' quotas are reached.

Applications from the Literature

Example of the Use of Quota Sampling in Research

Note: For the 324 women in this study, age was directly related to sports participation and exposure to sports. Additionally, older women were found to have been less happy with their body shape than younger women. Both sports media exposure and sports participation were related to more positive body image and attitudes.

Method: Because the study's goal was to examine the way women of all ages respond to sports media and report feelings of body dissatisfaction, a quota system was used. Researchers in three areas—the Northeast, the Deep South, and the Southwest—determined their area's representation with regard to age, race, and gender. A matrix was created for each region that identified the percentage of respondents needed in each category, such as Black women between 35 and 50 or Hispanic women between 18 and 29, to represent the population of each region. An overall *N* of 660 males and females was the target; therefore, each researcher computed percentages needed for each demographic group based on an *N* of 220 per region. Finally, researchers went into the field, provided with instruments with a coversheet attached that described the gender, approximate age, and race of the participant they were to recruit for the study.

Source: Bissell, K. L. (2004). What do these messages really mean? Sports media exposure, sports participation, and body image distortion in women between the ages of 18 and 75. *Journalism and Mass Communication Quarterly, 81*(1), 108–123. doi: 10.1177/107769900408100108

Volunteer Samples

By asking individuals to volunteer to participate in a study, another source of potential bias is introduced. Research has shown that **volunteer samples** tend to be more liberal, be female, be younger, have higher IQ scores, have higher SES, be more unconventional, be more arousal seeking, and have more education than the general American population (Gall, Borg, & Gall, 1996).

Using volunteers in research also means using online surveys and surveys mailed to possible participants. For this reason, researchers should follow up with a sample of the nonrespondents to surveys to determine if that group is in some way different from those who responded to the request for information or who volunteered to participate.

SAMPLING ERROR

By having a method to quantify the amount of **sampling error** that exists in statistics based on samples from a population, the researcher can make intelligent statements about the meaning of the findings. These statistics are constantly reported by political pollsters in the form of "with a **margin of error** of plus or minus 4 points, we can report that . . . ."

Standard Error of Samples

Statistics are based on data obtained from a sample. The idea of sampling is to estimate the true dimensions (parameters) of the population. Random samples provide the best, least biased estimate of the population's parameters (Kendall & Stuart, 1967).

Standard Error of the Mean ($SE_{\bar{X}}$)

The sample mean ($\bar{X}$) is an estimate of the population's mean (μ). If the researcher draws another random sample from the same population and calculates a second mean, the two sample means should be similar. They may even be the same, but more typically, there is a small difference between them. If our hypothetical researcher had far too much time and repeated this process over and over, the resulting collection of sample means would be likely to vary slightly but cluster near a central value. That central value could be thought of as the mean of the means ($\bar{\bar{X}}$), and it is an even better estimate of the population parameter (μ).

If our researcher (the one with extra time to spend) collected many means from independent samples from a population, it would be possible to find the standard deviation of this collection of sample means. A distribution of means from many samples follows the normal "bell" curve with two exceptions: (1) The shape of the curve for sample means tends to have less variance than what is found in population data, and (2) if a distribution of sample means drawn from a population is based on skewed data, the distribution of means will have much less skewness (von Hippel, 2005).

Figure 9.1   Theoretical Distribution of Means with $\bar{X}$ Normal Curve Comparison

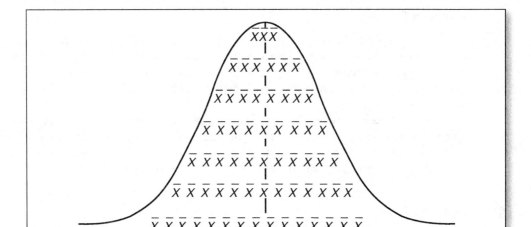

Source: Developed by author.

When we plot the means from samples of subjects, many of the extreme scores found under the bell curve's **asymptotes** (fringe areas of the normal curve) disappear. The result is less variation than is found in the original raw data from the entire population. The standard deviation of sample means is called the standard error of the mean ($SE_{\bar{x}}$).[6] An assumption about the distribution of sample means is that each sample is relatively large ($n \geq 30$). The need for 30 or more subjects per sample is part of the **law of large numbers,** which states that the larger the sample is, the closer its mean will approximate the population mean. A second, related assumption about the calculation of standard error statistics is that the population is at least 10 times larger than the sample.

Computation of Standard Error of the Mean

It is difficult to picture a practitioner-researcher ever having the time to sample and resample from a population in an effort to find the standard error of the mean. Fortunately, the standard error of the mean can be estimated based on sample statistics. Once again, this statistic will be more accurate if it is based on a reasonably large sample.

Computation of Standard Error of the Mean From Sample Data

This simple expression can be read to say that the best estimate of the standard error of the mean ($SE_{\bar{x}}$) equals the sample's standard deviation (s) divided by the square root of the number of subjects in the sample:

$$SE_{\bar{x}} = \frac{s}{\sqrt{n}}$$

For example, say a hypothetical sample of 36 inner-city preschool-age children, diagnosed with significant developmental delay and being at risk for cognitive impairment, were found to have a mean serum lead [$Pb(PO_4)_2$] level of 82 ug/dL and a standard deviation of 22 ug/dL. In this case, the standard error equals the standard deviation of 22 divided by 6 (square root of 36). Thus, in this study, the standard error from the serum analyses of blood lead levels from 36 developmentally delayed young inner-city children is 3.67 micrograms of lead phosphate per deciliter ($SE_{\bar{x}} = 3.67$ ug/dL).

Interpreting Standard Error

In addition to finding the standard error of the mean, it is also possible to find the standard error of most other descriptive statistics. The interpretation of standard error statistics is similar to that of other standard scores. Each standard error statistic indicates how much a sample statistic fluctuates or varies around the parameter. If the standard error statistic is small, the researcher can have confidence that the sample statistic (e.g., sample mean) is a close approximation of the population's true parameter (e.g., population mean). In the narrative portion of a journal article, the size of the standard error for a statistic is typically provided along with the statistic.

Applications from the Literature

Example of Reporting Standard Error of the Mean

Note: In this study, the authors reported means and the size of standard errors as [+ or −] some value. The abbreviation *f/v* stands for "fruit and or vegetable."

Results: Of the top ten food choices of fruits and vegetables reported in the survey, iceberg lettuce, the most recorded f/v, had the lowest lutein/zeaxanthin content of less than 1 mg/100g. Cooked spinach, the ninth most recorded f/v, had the highest mean lutein/zeaxanthin content (lutein/zeaxanthin content > 7mg/100g). Orange fruit lutein/zeaxanthin consumption amongst college age Caucasians (616.9 [+ or −] 66.7mcg/100g) was twice that of college age African-Americans (364.2 [+ or −] 66.6mcg/100g) and higher than all other groups. Likewise, there was a difference in the amount of mean lutein/zeaxanthin content obtained from orange juice between males and females (879.2 [+ or −] 126.5mcg/100g vs. 595.7 [+ or −] 49.7mcg/100g).

Source: Osaseri, U. E., Kwok, S. Y., Kwok, W., & Tam, C. F. (2008). College students' dietary practices affect Lutein/Zeaxanthin intake: A two-generation, ethnic and gender study. *College Student Journal, 42*(3), 715–729.

Confidence Limits

If a researcher decides to report the mean of a sample's data set and also reports the standard error of measurement, it is then possible to present the confidence limits around the mean. Confidence limits are a statistical statement of the width of a band above and below the sample statistic where the true parameter is likely to be found. It is important to note that these confidence limits may not be wide enough for the researcher to be comfortable in stating that the true parameter lies within the range of possible scores between the upper and lower confidence limits.

In many studies, the researcher chooses to report confidence limits larger than 1 standard error above and below the statistic. In the case of standard error statistics, such as the standard error of the mean, the value of $\pm 1.0\,SE_{\bar{x}}$ is normally increased. The usual increase in the standard error selected is almost 2 times the standard error (in the case of sample statistics, the multiplier is 1.96 or $\pm 1.96\,SE_{\bar{x}}$). This number is chosen because it provides a statistical marker that includes 95% of all cases that could occur on a random basis. This can be charted on a graphic display, as shown in Figure 9.2.

When these graphic presentations are not provided, experienced readers of research of mental health science journals will normally just mentally double the standard error

Figure 9.2 Graphic Depiction of Confidence Interval Limits Around Means

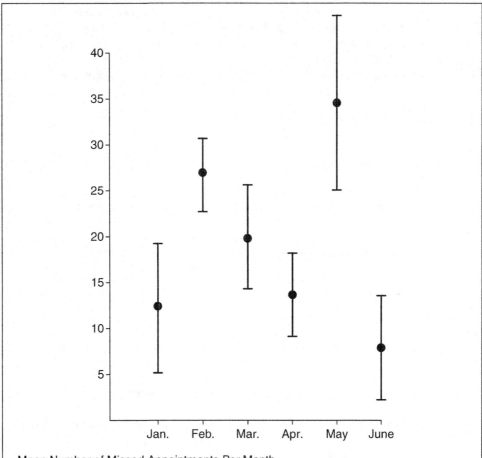

Mean Number of Missed Appointments Per Month

This graph depicts theoretical data from a clinic. It presents the number of appointments cancelled or otherwise missed by clients over a 6-month period. The mean "missed appointments for each month" is indicated with a dot. The bars depict a ±1.96 standard error around each month's mean.

Source: Developed by author.

statistics provided by the author to estimate the confidence limits. For example, if a graduate program in counseling reported that the mean Miller Analogy Test (MAT) score for its students was $\bar{X} = 440$ with a standard error of 15, a reader would know that about 95% of the program's students had MAT scores of 440 ± 30, or between 410 and 470.

CASE IN POINT   9.3

ETS has published guidelines for how it wants colleges and universities to report the GRE scores in promotional material and in information for public consumption. Instead of using the mean and standard error statistics for such publications, ETS suggests something a bit less complex be employed, namely, the interquartile range. This means the scores corresponding with the 25th and 75th percentiles of the distribution of GRE scores. This band enclosing the middle half of all students is believed to be easier to interpret. Also, this range is not as influenced by outliers in the data as are statistics such as confidence intervals, which are based on calculating a mean and standard deviation.

Calculation Assistance

Confidence limits can be calculated at several websites or by using Microsoft's Excel software. Example websites that offer this functionality include the following:

Confidence intervals and sample sizes, Creative Research Systems, http://www.surveysystem.com/sscalc.htm

Confidence intervals using Excel, Alan Ouyang, http://www.bloggpro.com/automatically-calculate-confidence-intervals-in-excel/

Confidence intervals, McCallum and Layton, http://www.mccallum-layton.co.uk/stats/ConfidenceIntervalCalcProportions.aspx

Applications from the Literature

Example of the Reporting of Confidence Levels Using a Graph

Note: In this study, the authors used experimentally naive male Sprague-Dawley rats bred at the university. The experimental animals were approximately 100 days old (adolescence) at the time of the study and were motivated by being deprived of solid food until they lost 15% of their original body weight. In one study (left-hand graphic), they were given a 1% solution of sugar-water, and in the second (right-hand graphic), they were given a 5% solution of sugar-water. Some experimental animals were only given a sugar-water reinforcer throughout the study, while a random split of subject animals received sugar-water for 5 of the 10 trials and then solid food (pellets) for the last 5 trials.

The dependent variable was the activity level exhibited by the subject animals. The mean activity levels are plotted on the graph for each of the 10 trials. The last five trials for the experimental group switched to solid food pellets had the size of the standard error of the mean shown along with the plot of the means for those five trials. The standard error bars depict the distance, both above and below the sample mean, where the mean for the total population of adolescent white rats could lie.

Results and Discussion: The figure below [Figure 9.3] presents the rates of responding, in responses per min, in successive 5-min intervals of the session that were observed in Experiment 1. Each graph presents the results for each pair of conditions in the first and second halves of the session. Each function represents the mean for all subjects responding during the final sessions of the condition in which sucrose reinforcers were delivered in both the first and second halves of the session (closed squares) or in which food pellets were delivered in the second half of the session (open squares). The error bars represent the standard error of the mean for all subjects responding during that particular 5-min interval.

Figure 9.3   Response Rates of White Rats With Confidence Intervals

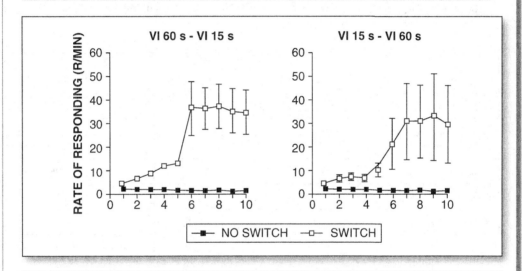

Source: Weatherly, J. N., Rue, H. C., Davis, C. S., & Melville, C. L. (2000). Delivering different reinforcers in each half of the session: Effect of reinforcement rate. *Psychological Record, 50*(3), 543-556.

The standard error may be calculated and reported for many other statistics as well. In the following excerpt from a journal article, David Ayers (2002) analyzed the mission statements of 102 community colleges in the southern part of the United States. From his analysis, he identified seven themes in the mission statements. He reported the proportion of community colleges with each of the seven identified themes. Along with the proportion statistics, he also provided standard error values for each of the reported proportions, and he used those statistics to provide 95 % confidence bands for each proportion.

These data can be read as reporting that 0.7843 (or 78.43%) of the community colleges have a mission statement expressing an emphasis on accessibility. Also, the parameter for the proportion of all community colleges having a mission statement that speaks to accessibility falls between 71% and 86%. This is found by starting with the sample's proportion of 78.43%, then adding and subtracting approximately 2 times the standard error of the proportion's standard error statistic of 0.04 or 4%.

Applications from the Literature

Example from a Display of Standard Errors of Proportions

Table 9.3   Frequencies, Proportions, and 95% Confidence Levels of Mission Statements Reflecting Salient Themes

Salient Theme	Frequency Error	Proportion	Standard	Low	High
Access	82	.7843	.040	.71	.86
Workforce and Economic Development	79	.7745	.040	.69	.85
Comprehensiveness	79	.7745	.040	.69	.85
Quality and Excellence	73	.7156	.040	.62	.80
Responsiveness	71	.6960	.046	.61	.79
Service Area	56	.5490	.049	.45	.65
Diversity	51	.5000	.049	.40	.60

Source: Ayers, D. (2002). Mission priorities of community colleges in the Southern United States. *Community College Review,* *30*(3), 11–30.

Note: n = 102.

HOW DIFFERENT IS DIFFERENT?

Any sample drawn from a population will involve an unknown amount of sampling error. We can use sampling statistics (e.g., mean and standard deviation) as estimates of parameters of the population. By using standard error statistics, we know just how likely our sample statistics are to correctly define the population's parameters.

This can be turned around and used as an empirical tool in studies involving counseling effectiveness. For example, most universities provide a required first-semester course for newly admitted freshmen judged to be at risk for academic difficulties. A random sample of 60 (3 course sections) from the 120 at-risk students could be provided individual counseling and instructional support. After the semester, the mean first-term grade point average (GPA) of the untreated portion of 60 freshmen could be determined. Likewise, the mean of the treated sample could also be found, and the standard error could be calculated for each group. If the confidence intervals around the two means encompass each other, the researcher could conclude that the treatment's affect on the sample was nothing more than what could have occurred by chance.

Applications from the Literature

Use of Confidence Limits to Test Whether a Group Differs from a Known Value

Note: The researchers studied the relationships of fathers (caregivers) in the United States with boys and with girls. Likewise, American women caregivers were also evaluated for their interactions with children of both genders. These subjects were then compared with adults from 22 other cultural groups around the world. The prime focus was on the role of fathers. Below is a small sample from Wade Mackey's findings.

Results: The actual value of the percentage of all-children in Men-only groups was 20.5%. This value of 20.5% was within .25% of the predicted value (20.25%) and was within the confidence limits of the predicted value: 17.20%–23.30%.

Source: Mackey, W. C. (1995). U.S. fathering behaviors within a cross-cultural context: An evaluation by an alternate benchmark. *Journal of Comparative Family Studies. 26*(3), 443–458.

HYPOTHESIS TESTING

Using confidence limits to evaluate the degree that groups differ is the essence of the empirical process of hypothesis testing. In conducting empirical research, the first logical step is to define the research problem. The next step in the scientific process is to state an informed estimation of relationships and or causal links that underlie the research problem. This second step takes the form of a hypothesis statement. This may be in the form of a question (e.g., "Can a program of individual counseling and instructional support improve the GPA of at-risk first-term freshmen?").

The hypothesis is written using language such that it is amenable to being answered with observed or measured data. For example, one might start by stating: "A formal program of counseling and instructional support can improve the freshman year GPA for first-semester students at risk for academic difficulty." However, as appealing as this hypothesis may be, it is not yet in an appropriate form to be answered with empirical data.

The Null Hypothesis

All sampling statistics contain some amount of sampling error. This fact of life for researchers is the reason great caution is taken when using empirical research methods. Researchers *can never prove a hypothesis is true*. This is because of the ever-present possibility of statistical error being the real reason for any finding from an analysis of the data.

The solution to this research conundrum is the use of what is described as the "null hypothesis." The agricultural scientist and statistician Ronald A. Fisher first described the use of the null hypothesis in his research (Fisher, 1925/1990). Instead of proving that our hypothetical explanation is true, we can prove the negative equivalent of our hypothesis cannot be supported by our findings.[7] In Fisher's system, the null hypothesis that the group that received the treatment differs from a similar group that did not receive the treatment becomes a testable statement.

In a hypothetical experiment, an unnamed university randomly divided 120 at-risk freshmen into two groups. One of these groups was provided with intensive individual counseling and academic coaching, while the other was provided nothing out of the ordinary. The null hypothesis would be "that at the conclusion of the term, there would be no difference between the two groups." This is written in equation form as follows:

$$H_0 : \bar{X}_1 = \bar{X}_2$$

This symbolic expression may be read as "The null hypothesis (H_0) is that the mean of the treated sample ($\bar{X}_1$) is equal to the mean of the untreated group ($\bar{X}_2$)."

The zero value (the null) is implied by the same expression. The null hypothesis could be rewritten to reveal the zero:

$$H_0 : \bar{X}_1 - \bar{X}_2 = 0$$

This reads, "The null hypothesis is that the treated sample's mean minus the untreated sample's mean equals zero."

If the sample data do not support the null hypothesis ($H_0 : \bar{X}_1 \neq \bar{X}_2$), then one of two possible alternatives may exist: Either (1) the sample of treated students had a better GPA than did the untreated sample ($H_1 : \bar{X}_1 > \bar{X}_2$), or (2) the untreated sample did better ($H_2 : \bar{X}_1 < \bar{X}_2$). The second statement is that the untreated sample mean grade point average is greater than the mean grade point average of the treated sample of freshmen. This latter finding would be unexpected, but it is always possible. For that reason, social science researchers almost always assume that their research may have a paradoxical outcome and include two potential alternatives when planning research projects.

Single-Sample Case, the z-Test

It is possible to employ a null hypothesis when there is only one sample and a known population parameter. In this form of research question, the researcher determines whether a sample's statistics are unbiased estimates of the population's parameters. The research question may also be based on a theoretical population parameter or one that is drawn from the literature describing the whole population.

Theoretical parameters include neutral points on opinion surveys. For example, on an opinion survey with weighted positive and negative statements, there is usually a neutral point. This is often worded "neither agree nor disagree." A population parameter could be the mean net worth of families living in a US Census block. The test sample may be all single-parent households in the same Census block. The null hypothesis is that there is no difference between the sample (single-parent homes) and the whole population of the Census block. That would appear as $H_0 : \overline{X} = \mu$. This will also have two logical alternatives: $H_1 : \overline{X} > \mu$ and $H_2 : \overline{X} < \mu$.

Level of Significance

After establishing the null hypothesis but before collecting data, the researcher must make an a priori decision as to just how different the means from the two samples need to be for the null hypothesis to be rejected. The researcher needs to determine the point at which "different enough" is reached.

The decision about when to reject (or, more accurately, fail to accept) the null hypothesis is based on probability. The areas under the normal curve are used to determine the probability of being in error when rejecting the null hypothesis. For example, a researcher may decide that a difference between the treated sample's mean (college freshmen at risk for failure) and the untreated sample's mean must be at or beyond 1 standard error of each other.

To reject the null hypothesis and support one of the alternatives, the treated sample's mean must fall either above or below a standard error of the untreated sample's mean. For example, if the treated group has a mean GPA of 2.95 and a standard error of 0.25, while the untreated group has a mean GPA of 2.4 and a standard error of 0.17, we can set up confidence bands:

$$\text{treated group: } 2.70 \le \overline{X}_1 \le 3.20$$

$$\text{untreated group: } 2.23 \le X_2 \le 2.57$$

There is no overlap between the simultaneous confidence intervals surrounding each mean. Thus, the null hypothesis could be rejected. It is important not to overinterpret the failure to reject a null hypothesis. This decision does not "prove" the null hypothesis was true. Only one conclusion can be drawn when a null hypothesis is not rejected. That conclusion is that the sample data did not provide enough evidence to make the rejection of the null hypothesis logically possible.

CASE IN POINT 9.4

In many ways, the testing of the null hypothesis is much like a court trial. If not enough evidence is presented to the jury at a trial, the jury decides to acquit. The jury's verdict to acquit is not the same as a statement that the accused person is innocent but only that the jury did not see enough evidence to convict the individual beyond a reasonable doubt. The standard of "beyond a reasonable doubt" is similar to the level of confidence a researcher requires to reject the null hypothesis. Just as a verdict to acquit is not a statement of innocence, a decision to not reject the null does not imply acceptance of the null hypothesis as the truth.

Sampling error is the problem that researchers strive to avoid. Standard error is distributed following the rules of the normal curve. Thus, 1 standard error indicates that the likelihood we were correct in rejecting the null hypothesis is 68% and the possibility we made a mistake is 32%.

The 5% and the 1% Solutions

The type of error in the example means the researcher could have made the wrong choice in rejecting the null hypothesis about a third of the time (32%). In scientific practice, this is viewed as far too great a chance of being wrong. In our example, this error could result in the university using valuable resources (counselor time and instructional time) on

Figure 9.4 Probability Limit to Reject the Null Hypothesis at 1 Standard Error

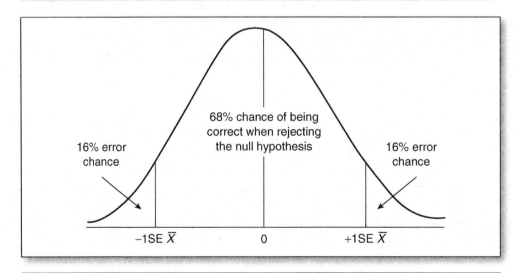

Source: Developed by author.

a project that is not effective. For the past 100 years, researchers have settled on tolerating a no more than a 5% probability of being wrong in rejecting the null hypothesis. On occasion, the probability of being in error in rejecting the null hypothesis is set even lower, at 2% (0.02) level or even 1% (0.01). As the researcher makes it ever more unlikely he or she will make an error in rejecting the null hypothesis, it becomes increasing more possible that our cautious researcher will miss a true finding and not reject a null hypothesis that should be rejected.

Alpha and Beta

Researchers have designated two types of research error related to the null hypothesis. One is the probability of making an error of commission and rejecting a null that was really "true." The probability of making that mistake, known as a Type I error, is designated as the Greek letter **alpha** (α). The probability of rejecting a false null hypothesis, known as Type II error, is symbolized by the Greek letter **beta** (β). Type II error can be thought of as an error of omission. Generally, Type I error is thought to be more of a problem than Type II error. This is because Type II error leads to a decision not to change or modify activities or programs, whereas a Type I error can lead the researcher to publish a false finding and possibly do harm to others.[8]

The probability of making a Type I error is the mathematical complement of the amount of confidence a researcher can have in the decision to reject the null hypothesis.[9] Thus, if there is a 5% probability of making a Type I error (α), the researcher can have 95% confidence in the decision to make the choice to reject the null hypothesis ($1.0 - \alpha$ = Confidence).

This probability of being wrong when rejecting the null hypothesis is symbolized by the lowercase Roman letter p. For a researcher to reject the null hypothesis, he or she must have data that says there is no more than 1 chance in 20 (or 5 in 100) of being wrong in rejecting the null hypothesis ($p < 0.05$) or an "alpha level of 0.05."

Type II error probability is controlled by a number of factors, including the size of the sample of subjects or objects, the alpha level, the accuracy and sensitivity of the measurement instruments or observation tools, the size of the effect causing the two samples to have differing means, and the amount of variance in the data. The probability, beta, of making a Type II error is the complement of power ($1.0 - \beta$ = Power). Table 9.4 shows the relationships among these factors of experimental error and the null hypothesis decision-making process.

Table 9.4   Type I and Type II Errors

Set an alpha level and then take a chance.	Null hypothesis is true in reality.	Null hypothesis is not true in reality.
Reject the null hypothesis	☹ ERROR—Type I: probability = alpha	☺ Correct decision: Confidence = 1 − alpha
Fail to reject the null hypothesis	☺ Correct decision: power = 1 − beta	☹ ERROR—Type II: probability = beta

The researcher will never know for sure if the null hypothesis was true or not and so will never be sure whether he or she has made a correct decision or an error. The research process is designed to provide the practitioner-researcher with knowledge of the probability of being wrong so the researcher can reasonably either reject or fail to reject the null hypothesis. It is up to the researcher to make the final call.

Applications from the Literature

Null Hypothesis Discussion in a Research Article

Note: In this study, Kazuo Mori used two samples of 27 pre-kindergartners to assess the level of amusement experienced by 4-year-old children in response to two different versions of the book *Little Black Sambo*. One version was a translation of the original (Iwanami version), and one version did not have racial overtones (Chibikuro Sampo version). A third book for preschoolers was used as a placebo. Because the null hypothesis could not be rejected, the author explained that her finding did not "prove" the null hypothesis was correct.

Null Hypothesis: The results seemed to prove statistically the equivalence of the two versions. However, it is not true. There exists a methodological difficulty in proving the equality of two groups of data. Ordinary statistical tests are valid only for proving differences among the obtained data. The logic behind statistical tests is that if no differences are assumed (the null hypothesis) and if the probability of achieving a difference in the observed data under the null hypothesis is smaller than a predetermined value (i.e., the probability of Type I error; $\alpha = .05$), the null hypothesis should be denied; therefore, differences exist. Consequently, the purpose of statistical tests is to detect significant differences, but not to prove equality.

It seems possible to use ordinary statistical tests to prove the null hypothesis. For example, if the difference between two-sample means is not statistically significant, it seems to have proved that there is no difference. However, the correct conclusion from "not-achieving-statistical-significance" is just a failure to reject the null hypothesis. Such failure does not warrant a conclusion that the null hypothesis is proved. Accordingly, the null hypothesis in the present study that the revised version was equivalent to the Iwanami version in terms of amusingness was not proved just by negating the presence of significant differences between the two versions.

Source: Mori, K. (2005). A comparison of amusingness for Japanese children and senior citizens of the story of *Little Black Sambo* in the traditional version and a nonracist version. *Social Behavior and Personality, 33*(5), 455–466.

"Play It Again, Sam"

Empirical research with behavioral science variables might involve a series of related hypotheses. These multiple hypotheses require several tests for their null hypotheses. For example, in a hypothetical study of a counseling intervention with clients experiencing PTSD, the practitioner-researcher may employ a clinical instrument to measure the effectiveness of a cognitive-behavioral therapeutic intervention. If the dependent variable is measured using the Beck Depression Inventory (2nd edition), there will be two possible null hypotheses, one for the BDI-2 Somatic subtest and one for the BDI-2 Affective subtest

(Beck, Steer, & Brown, 1996). The difficulty is that the possibility of making a Type I error is additive when multiple hypotheses are tested. If each null hypothesis is tested at the 0.05 level ($\alpha = 0.05$), the chance of making a Type I error doubles to $\alpha = 0.10$. Thus, there will be 1 chance in 10 that one of the two hypotheses will be rejected when it should not have been.

Thus, as the number of possible null hypotheses increases, so does the additive possibility of a Type I error. Had the researcher used 15 personality measures from Cattell's well-known scales of personality, the 16PF questionnaire, the possibility for a Type I error being included among the 15 tests of the null hypotheses would be evaluated at the $\alpha = 0.75$ level. In other words, there would be a 75% chance that a Type I error would occur with the tests of 15 null hypotheses.

A solution for this problem of multiple null hypotheses and the additive nature of Type I error was developed in 1935 by Carlo Bonferroni. The essence of what is known as the **Bonferroni inequality** is the need to make the alpha level for each test of a null hypothesis more stringent (numerically smaller). The task is to reduce the alpha levels until their summation is equal to the desired level (e.g., $\alpha = 0.05$). In the example above, with two null hypotheses being tested at $\alpha = 0.05$, each would need to be lowered to $\alpha = 0.025$. The sum of the two alpha levels would then equal the goal $\alpha = 0.05$ level. In the example with 15 null hypotheses, the Bonferroni inequality would require the researcher to reduce the alpha levels for the analyses to $\alpha = 0.0034$.

Applications from the Literature

Example of the Application of the Bonferroni Inequality in Research

Note: This study of future mate preference includes 1,496 college freshmen (642 men and 854 women) enrolled in 4 elite and flagship universities. They were taking an introductory class in psychology that had a research participation requirement. Independent-samples *t*-tests are discussed in Chapter 10.

Results: [Men] in the [University of Texas] sample, more than men in the other samples, valued a potential wife's cooking and housekeeping skills, financial prospects, and chastity. Additionally, men in the Texas sample reported greater preference than did men in at least two other samples for a wife who embodied refinement and neatness, social status, a similar religious background, and ambition and industriousness. The differentiation of the Texas sample from the other samples is not specific to the mate preferences reported by men. Women in the Texas sample, more than women in the other samples, valued refinement and neatness, good financial prospects, chastity, desire for home and children, social status, and similar religious and political backgrounds in a potential husband. . . . Independent means *t*-tests for sex differences in the 18 preferences, for each sample separately, and then for the four samples combined [were conducted]. The Bonferroni procedure was used to correct for increased Type I error rate. By the Bonferroni procedure, statistical significance was reduced from .05 to .003.

Source: Buss, D. M., Shackelford, T. K., Kirkpatrick, L. A., & Larson, R. J. (2001). A half century of mate preferences: The cultural evolution of values. *Journal of Marriage and Family, 63*(2), 491–503.

Tradeoffs and Sample Sizes

In setting a level for alpha, the researcher makes a statement about the relative concern he or she has regarding Type I and Type II errors. By choosing to employ a very stringent standard for the possibility of a Type I error (e.g., $\alpha = 0.001$ or even $\alpha = 0.0001$), the researcher greatly increases the probability of a Type II error. Every researcher using empirical research methods must make this tradeoff.

One way to reduce the likelihood of a Type II error is to increase the sample size for the study before starting to collect data. As the size of the sample increases, the standard error of the data's statistics is reduced. Lower sampling error increases power and thereby reduces the probability (β) of a Type II error.

A current trend in empirical research with mental health variables is to set the alpha level at $\alpha = 0.05$ and the probability of a Type II error 4 times higher, at $\beta = 0.20$. This provides a power level of 0.80 (the complement of β). The effect size with mental health–related variables tends to be small. This implies that the number of subjects needed in the sample will be fairly large in terms of most research published in counseling journals ($n_1 + n_2 \cong 600$; StatSoft, 2011).[10] When the variables under study are critical to the health and safety of subjects, the amount of error (alpha and beta) will be held to higher standards, and sample size will be even more important.[11]

Power Analysis

Researchers studying variables related to mental health have known that power was a concern for their research methods since the time of Ronald Fisher. During the 1990s, conducting a **power analysis** became an issue that researchers must address. The following appears in the most recent edition of the *Publication Manual of the American Psychological Association* (2010b).

> Take seriously the statistical power considerations associated with tests of hypotheses. Such considerations relate to the likelihood of correctly rejecting the tested hypotheses, given a particular alpha level, effect size, and sample size. In that regard, routinely provide evidence that the study has sufficient power to detect effects of substantive interest. (p. 30)

Power analyses are conducted prior to starting the research study. These a priori analyses can be used to estimate the sample size needed to achieve a desired power level. The commonly accepted level for power in behavioral science research is based on a Type II error level of $\beta = 0.80$. The effect size may be learned from previous experience with a pilot study or from a review of the literature. The probability of making a Type I error is typically set at $\alpha = 0.05$ or 0.01. These variables can be used to estimate the needed sample size.

Calculation of Power and Sample Size: Heinrich Heine at the University of Düsseldorf (Germany) has published a freeware program that does power analysis (Balkin & Sheperis, 2011). This program, called G*Power 3, is available for both the Apple and Microsoft operating systems at http://www.psycho.uni-duesseldorf.de/abteilungen/aap/gpower3/. Another software option for calculating statistical power is available from NCSS; information about PASS 11 is offered at http://www.ncss.com/pass.html.

Applications from the Literature

Example of Interplay of Type I and Type II Error in Research

Note: These data were collected by defense lawyers working for the Delaware Department of Public Instruction. They were defending the state against a civil rights suit by the Delaware Coalition to Save our Children. The suit involved policies related to special education placements.

Four of Delaware's 16 school districts randomly selected 60 elementary-level students to be part of the evidence base for the state. The goal of having 240 students participate in the study was missed, because 10 students did not have complete data.

Data Analysis: The alpha level was set at the traditional .05 due to the nature of this inquiry. The analysis was exploratory because we were concerned with identifying potentially differential effects for African-American and Caucasian students. As such, control of Type I error was not as large a concern as control of Type II error. The magnitude of effects, not just their statistical significance, was of interest. Therefore, effect sizes were also calculated where applicable.

Source: Hosp, J. L., & Reschly, D. J. (2002). Predictors of restrictiveness of placement for African-American and Caucasian students. *Exceptional Children, 68*(2), 225–238.

SUMMARY

Central to the scientific model for creating new knowledge is the logic of **hypothetico-deductive reasoning.** Deductive logic is needed for both qualitative and quantitative approaches to research in the mental health professions, but it is most generally linked to the development of research questions for empirical (quantitative) study. Inductive logic is needed in quantitative research whenever sample statistics are employed. It is through induction that it is possible to extrapolate findings based on sample data to an entire population.

In describing populations, the researcher reports parameters for descriptive characteristics found in analyzing the data. These parameters are represented by Greek letters, while statistics collected describing samples from the population are represented by Roman letters.

There are two primary types of samples. Probability samples are designed to align closely with the whole population. A random process is used to identify the elements, cases, or individuals to be included. The other approach is nonprobability sampling. Nonprobability samples may or may not provide a good representation of the entire population.

This form of sampling includes samples of convenience; convenience samples are commonly employed by clinic-based and most college- and university-based practitioner-researchers. This reflects the fact that few practitioners have the opportunity to randomly select to whom therapy will be provided. Another nonprobability sampling method is the use of purposeful samples, a commonly employed approach in postmodern research. Key informers from a population are identified for study and used to provide critical information not otherwise available to the researcher. Yet another approach is quota sampling, a method commonly employed in marketing research.

All samples provide approximations of a population's parameters with some degree of error. The amount of error can be reduced by using larger random samples, but there will always be some error in sample statistics. The amount of error can be estimated and reported along with the statistic. The standard error can be converted into a set of confidence limits, providing a bracket of scores that are highly likely to encompass the location of the true parameter. Typically, these confidence limits represent the 95 or 99 percentile points within which the researcher can assume the true parameter of the population is actually located. The probability of being wrong in that assumption is described as alpha, and it is complementary to the confidence level selected by the researcher (i.e., $\alpha = .05$, $p < .05$, and confidence $= 95\%$; $\alpha = .01$, $p < .01$, and confidence $= 99\%$). Alpha level, or the possibility of erroneously rejecting the null hypothesis when it is in fact true, is known as Type I error.

In the empirical tradition, hypothesis testing involves developing a null hypothesis that, when shown to have a very low probability of being true, can be rejected. Because Type I error is additive, when several null hypotheses are tested a correction for the alpha level, an adjustment known as the Bonferroni inequality is employed.

Type I error is divided into the two directions under the normal curve. One direction represents the chance that the parameter falls above the upper confidence level, and the other half is reserved for the possibility that the true population parameter falls below the lower confidence limit.

A mistake can also be made (Type II error) by not rejecting a false null hypothesis. This likelihood is described as the beta level or β. Researchers normally work to keep this level low, in the $\beta = .80$ or $\beta = .70$ range. Power, the complement of beta, is controlled by several factors, including sample size and treatment effectiveness.

DISCUSSION QUESTIONS

1. How can stratified random sampling make sample data more sensitive? Can the same thing be accomplished by employing quota sampling? Explain your position.

2. How can you reconcile the need for random sampling with the ethical mandate to provide informed consent with an opt-out choice for potential participants?

3. Describe a study in which the researcher would be more (or equally) concerned with avoiding a Type II error than with avoiding a possible Type I error.

4. For a mental health professional working alone, what is a realistic sample size for a research study involving an innovative treatment? How did you reach that decision?

NOTES

1. For example, Isaac Newton's most revered work, *Philosophiæ Naturalis Principia Mathematica,* published in 1687, first presented the concept of calculus and explained the gravitational principles governing our solar system. This Latin title translates as "Mathematical Principles of Natural Philosophy."

2. Occam's razor is a principle in science dating from the 14th century in England, where it was espoused by a friar and teacher, William of Ockham, who was excommunicated for his trouble. Isaac Newtown expressed the principle in 1687: *We are to admit no more causes of natural things than such as are both true and sufficient to explain their appearances.* This same need to find elegant simplicity in explanations for the natural world has been used by agnostics to argue that supernatural beings are not provable and are superfluous to scientific explanations.

3. Katie Hnida was the first woman to score in an NCAA Division 1-A college football game. She accomplished this as placekicker for the University of New Mexico on August 30, 2003.

4. The chance that each element in the population is a member of the sample changes each time one individual or element is selected for inclusion in the sample. If a researcher selected a sample of 20 from a population of 100, the first to be selected had 1 chance in 100 of being selected. However, the second individual selected had 1 chance in 99 of being selected. One solution (rarely employed) is to sample with replacement.

5. In 1936, the *Literary Digest,* published by Funk and Wagnalls, published a poll of its readers predicting that challenger Alf Landon would beat President Roosevelt. Roosevelt was reelected, and the election turned out to be the worst defeat a Republican presidential candidate had ever experienced. The *Digest* lost all credibility and soon ceased publication.

6. The *standard* in standard error refers to the normal curve and the interpretability of the statistic in terms of the normal curve. The *error* describes how sample statistics only approximate population parameters.

7. This is where generations of students have reached their frustration limit. The concept is truly convoluted and nonintuitive. Think of the null hypothesis process as one of elimination. In many old detective movies, the sleuth identifies the true miscreant by first eliminating all other possible suspects. By eliminating alternative possibilities, it becomes possible to infer the answer to the research question.

The term *null* is not common in American vernacular, but it is commonly employed in the United Kingdom and other English-speaking countries to mean "zero." The null hypothesis could be thought of as the "zero hypothesis." The use of the traditional British term, *null hypothesis,* reflects the language preference of the original social scientists, almost all of whom were British, who first developed and used statistics in hypothesis testing. Examples include Sir Francis Galton, Karl Pearson, Egon Pearson, Sir Cyril Burt, William Gosset, Sir Ronald A. Fisher, and Sir Maurice Kendall.

8. There is a greater potential for research journals to report false positives than to report false negatives. This reflects a preference journal publishers have for printing positive findings. A study that leads to not rejecting the null hypothesis is much more difficult to have published. If hundreds of studies are concluded each day, and there is a 5% chance of a false positive (Type I error), then these findings have a good chance of becoming part of the scientific literature (Storey, 2002). One place where positive and negative findings are published on an equal footing is in the dissertations and these written by graduate school students. The faculty sponsoring committee has the task of assuring that the final product is accurate and complete.

9. The mathematical complement of any decimal is another decimal that, when added to the original, will sum to +1.0.

10. This does not imply that other power-related factors do not make a difference. It only means that if other factors are held constant, the roles of alpha and sample size are central issues in Type II error likelihood.

11. An example of a question informing a critical decision is "Is it necessary for a woman to undergo a mastectomy based on available test data?" Such a decision must be made with great confidence and a very low likelihood of a Type I error. In that example, the null hypothesis could be "There is no indication of a significant cancer in the breast tissue." If they rejected the null hypothesis, the surgeon and patient would schedule surgery.

Scientific Method and Hypothesis Testing

"Statistics is the grammar of science."

Karl Pearson

OBJECTIVES

By reading and studying this chapter, you should acquire the competency to do the following:

- Explain the relationship between confidence intervals and William Gosset's Student's *t*-test.
- Compare and contrast single-and-independent sample *t*-tests.
- Use the *t*-test to evaluate the significance of Pearson correlation coefficients.
- Explain analysis of variance in terms of the partitioning of the sum of squares.
- Read and interpret *F* ratios.
- Describe the assumptions governing the use of analysis of variance.
- Describe post hoc comparisons in analysis of variance.
- Set up experimental studies using factorial analysis of variance.
- Describe interactions and multiple comparisons with analysis of variance.
- Describe study designs employing analysis of variance with repeated measures.

INTRODUCTION AND MAJOR THEMES

This chapter presents five related empirical approaches used for hypothesis testing. Each of these statistical methods is probability based; therefore, the practitioner-researcher has a chance of being wrong when deciding to accept or reject the null hypothesis. These five approaches are *t*-tests, one-way analysis of variance, factorial analysis of variance, analysis of covariance, and repeated-measure analysis of variance.

The family of tests known as the "Student's *t*-test" has made it possible to use small samples to determine whether one group differs from a population, whether pretest results are different from posttest results, or whether two groups differ from each other. The core element of these procedures is a series of modifications in the normal curve to match different size samples. The *t*-test is effective and practical, but it is limited to evaluating either two groups at a time or one group twice.

Analysis of variance (ANOVA) is a method for testing multiple groups at the same time. It is built around a simple fraction. The fraction's numerator is the portion of variance that is a result of the treatment (independent variable). The denominator is the portion of variance caused by individual differences within the treatment groups. The central step in ANOVA is the partitioning of the total variance. The ratio of variance related to the treatment or (independent variable) to the variance related to individual subjects within their treatment groups is referred to as the *F* ratio. Sir Ronald Fisher charted probabilities of various *F* ratios, providing a method for testing the null hypothesis related to the impact of the independent variable. Factorial ANOVA includes more than one independent variable and tests for potential interactions among independent variables (e.g., aptitude-treatment interactions).

MAKING INFERENCES ABOUT DIFFERENCES

One-Sample Case

It is possible to test a null hypothesis based on the difference between a sample statistic and the population parameter. For example, it is possible to test whether the graduates of one university's counseling program have different scores on the licensing examination compared with the population of all counseling program graduates. In the case of mean scores, the null hypothesis for such a study is that the population's mean is the same as the sample's ($H_0 : \bar{X} = \mu$). The alternative hypotheses are that the sample mean is greater than that of the population ($\bar{X} > \mu$) or that the sample mean is less than that of the population ($\bar{X} < \mu$). For example, a graduate department could check the National Counselor Examination scores for recent graduates and test the null hypothesis that the average score of graduates from that program is not different from the national average score.

A Tale (or Tails) of Two Hypotheses

To find the **critical value**, the researcher could use the table of probabilities under the normal curve. That table allows the researcher to convert an obtained *z*-score into a statement of the probability about committing a Type I error. If a researcher obtains a *z*-score of -1.65, that score falls at the .05 level of probability. Also, that value of *z* is found under the negative side or "tail" of the bell curve.

The null hypothesis, ($H_0 : \bar{X} = \mu$) is one that provides two logical alternatives ($\bar{X} > \mu$; $\bar{X} < \mu$). For that reason, two tails (positive *z*-score and negative *z*-score) must be considered. To meet the need for two alternatives to the null hypothesis, the *z*-score should be set at the 2.5 percentile level and at the 97.5 percentile level at ($z = \pm 1.96$). Thus, the alpha level of .05 (95% confidence) is broken in half, 2.5% for the possibility of a negative value for the z-score and 2.5% (97.5 percentile) for the possibility of a positive z-score.

This is the principle of the **two-tailed hypothesis.** If the probability of making a Type I error was set at only 1% ($p < .01$) or ($\alpha = .01$), we could have 99% confidence that we will make the correct decision if we reject the null hypothesis. To reach the 99% level of confidence requires a z-score equal to or exceeding $\pm$ 2.58.

Research conducted with mental health related variables and human subjects implies the need for the two-tailed null hypothesis test. In the behavioral sciences, there is always the possibility for an unanticipated or paradoxical finding to occur.

Applications from the Literature

Example of the Use of Single-Sample *t*-Test in Research

Note: In a study of the state of school counseling, a random sample of 600 members of the American School Counselor Association (ASCA; 5% of the 12,000 ASCA membership) were identified and mailed a survey by the authors. After 3 mailings, 241 or 40% of the surveys were returned. A final sample of 207 counselors who met all the demographic requirements for the study was used to provide the data for the hypothesis test.

Results: The mean counselor-student ratio of the participants was 1 counselor per 465 students ($SD = 312$). A one-sample *t*-test indicated this ratio significantly exceeded ($t = 9.87, p < .0001$) ASCA (1999a)[1] recommendations of 1 counselor per 250 students. Elementary school counselor participants had the highest mean counselor-student ratio of 1 counselor per 594 students ($SD = 393$). Middle school counselors had a mean ratio of 1 counselor per 387 students ($SD = 206$), while high school counselors had the lowest counselor-student mean ratio of 1 counselor per 338 students ($SD = 122$).

Source: Astramovich, R. L., & Holden, J. M. (2002). Attitudes of American School Counselor Association members toward utilizing paraprofessionals in school counseling. *Professional School Counseling, 5*(3), 203–210.

One-Tail Research

The z-score required to reject the null hypothesis is a less restrictive value than is needed with the two-tailed testing procedure. A **one-tailed null hypothesis** has only one alternative, because all possibility of a z-score in the opposite direction has been removed. The one-tail null hypothesis is either $H_0 : \bar{X} \leq \mu$ or $H_0 : \bar{X} \geq \mu$. Having stated one of these null hypotheses, the researcher formulates the alternative hypothesis as either $H_1 : \bar{X} > \mu$ or $H_1 : \bar{X} < \mu$, respectively.

The advantage for the researcher of using a one-tailed hypothesis testing procedure is that the z-score needed to reject the null hypothesis is not as large. At $\alpha = .05$, the minimum value needed for the z-score to enable the null hypothesis to be rejected is 1.65, and at $\alpha = .01$, the minimum required z-score is 2.33 (see Table 10.1). In terms of statistical power, these z-scores allow the researcher to require about a third fewer subjects in the sample to provide a beta level equal to what is required for a two-tail test. In other words, employing a one-tail hypothesis-testing approach has a real and very practical advantage.

It has been argued that the one-tailed approach to hypothesis testing is used too frequently without appropriate justification (Lombardi & Hurlbert, 2009). In their review of journal articles employing a one-tailed hypothesis test, Celia Lombardi and Stuart Hurlbert concluded that none of the sampled articles could justify the use of a one-tailed hypothesis-testing procedure. Likewise Graeme Ruxton and Markus Neuhäuser (2010) argued that researchers employing one-tailed hypothesis-testing procedures must build a strong justification for their decision.[2] It is not easy to build a case for the idea that there could *never* be a paradoxical or reversed finding.

Table 10.1   Distribution of Probability on a *z* Table (Normal Curve) Emphasizing One-Tail Hypothesis Testing

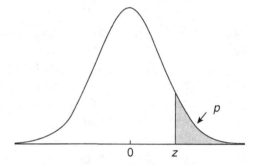

z	Second decimal place of *z*									
	.00	.01	.02	.03	.04	.05	.06	.07	.08	.09
0.0	.5000	.4960	.4920	.4880	.4840	.4801	.4761	.4721	.4681	.4641
0.1	.4602	.4562	.4522	.4483	.4443	.4404	.4364	.4325	.4286	.4247
0.2	.4207	.4168	.4129	.4090	.4052	.4013	.3974	.3936	.3897	.3859
0.3	.3821	.3783	.3745	.3707	.3669	.3632	.3594	.3557	.3520	.3483
0.4	.3446	.3409	.3372	.3336	.3300	.3264	.3228	.3192	.3156	.3121
0.5	.3085	.3050	.3015	.2981	.2946	.2912	.2877	.2843	.2810	.2776
0.6	.2743	.2709	.2676	.2643	.2611	.2578	.2546	.2514	.2483	.2451
0.7	.2420	.2389	.2358	.2327	.2297	.2266	.2236	.2206	.2177	.2148
0.8	.2119	.2090	.2061	.2033	.2005	.1977	.1949	.1922	.1894	.1867
0.9	.1841	.1814	.1788	.1762	.1736	.1711	.1685	.1660	.1635	.1611
1.0	.1587	.1562	.1539	.1515	.1492	.1469	.1446	.1423	.1401	.1379
1.1	.1357	.3335	.1314	.1292	.1271	.1251	.1230	.1210	.1190	.1170

(Continued)

Table 10.1 (Continued)

z	Second decimal place of z									
	.00	.01	.02	.03	.04	.05	.06	.07	.08	.09
1.2	.1151	.1131	.1112	.1093	.1075	.1056	.1038	.1020	.1003	.0985
1.3	.0968	.0951	.0934	.0918	.0901	.0885	.0869	.0853	.0838	.0823
1.4	.0808	.0793	.0778	.0764	.0749	.0735	.0721	.0708	.0694	.0681
1.5	.0668	.0655	.0643	.0630	.0618	.0606	.0594	.0582	.0571	.0559
1.6	.0548	.0537	.0526	.0516	.0505	.0495	.0485	.0475	.0465	.0455
1.7	.0446	.0436	.0427	.0418	.0409	.0401	.0392	.0384	.0375	.0367
1.8	.0359	.0351	.0344	.0336	.0329	.0322	.0314	.0307	.0301	.0294
1.9	.0287	.0281	.0274	.0268	.0262	.0256	.0250	.0244	.0239	.0233
2.0	.0228	.0222	.0217	.0212	.0207	.0202	.0197	.0192	.0188	.0183
2.1	.0179	.0174	.0170	.0166	.0162	.0158	.0154	.0150	.0146	.0143
2.2	.0139	.0136	.0132	.0129	.0125	.0122	.0119	.0116	.0113	.0110
2.3	.0107	.0104	.0102	.0099	.0096	.0094	.0091	.0089	.0087	.0084
2.4	.0082	.0080	.0078	.0075	.0073	.0071	.0069	.0068	.0066	.0064
2.5	.0062	.0060	.0059	.0057	.0055	.0054	.0052	.0051	.0049	.0048
2.6	.0047	.0045	.0044	.0043	.0041	.0040	.0039	.0038	.0037	.0036
2.7	.0035	.0034	.0033	.0032	.0031	.0030	.0029	.0028	.0027	.0026
2.8	.0026	.0025	.0024	.0023	.0023	.0022	.0021	.0021	.0020	.0019
2.9	.0019	.0018	.0018	.0017	.0016	.0016	.0015	.0015	.0014	.0014
3.0	.0013	.0013	.0013	.0012	.0012	.0011	.0011	.0011	.0010	.0010

Adapted with rounding from Table II of R. A. Fisher and F. Yates, *Statistical Tables for Biological, Agricultural, and Medical Research*, 6th Edition, Longman Group, Ltd., London, 1974, (Previously published by Oliver & Boyd, Ltd., Edinburgh). Used with permission of the authors and publishers.

Source: Adapted from Walpole, R., & Myers, R. H. (1989). *Probability and statistics for engineers and scientists* (4th ed.). Published by Collier Macmillan. Copyright © Macmillan Publishers, Ltd.

In most cases, there are online solutions for finding the areas under the normal curve for *z*-scores. Among these computational helpers are the following:

World Class Manufacturing, http://world-class-manufacturing.com/Sigma/score.php

John Walker, University of Kent at Canterbury, England, http://www.fourmilab.ch/rpkp/experiments/analysis/zCalc.html

Richard Lowry, Vassar College, http://faculty.vassar.edu/lowry/tabs.html#z

Additionally the statistical software on your university's server can provide this calculation. (See Appendix A for an example from IBM-SPSS.)

Applications from the Literature

Examples of Two- and One-Tailed Approaches to Hypothesis Testing

Example A: Two-Tailed Example

Note: The focus of this study was an investigation of the influence of spanking on children from African American and European American families. One assumption tested was the role that spanking has on stress and childhood mental health. National longitudinal data were used to provide the basic measurement. The sample from the national database included 1,139 European American and 713 African American children and adolescents.

Results: In these models, maternal depressive symptoms appeared to be the only covariate that was related to African American children's depressive symptoms. Maternal depressive symptoms were also related to higher levels of depressive symptoms for European American youth. The size of the association between mother and child depressive symptoms was larger ($t = 2.23$, two-tailed test) for European Americans compared to African Americans. Further, among European American children and adolescents, age was positively related to depressive symptoms, whereas being male, amount of household income, and maternal education were negatively associated with depressive symptoms.

Source: Christie-Mizell, C. A., Pryor, E. M., & Grossman, E. R. B. (2008). Child depressive symptoms, spanking, and emotional support: Differences between African American and European American youth. *Family Relations, 57*(3), 335–350. doi: 10.1111/j.1741-3729.2008.00504.x

Example B: One-Tailed Example

Note: This study was conducted with Anglo American and Mexican American families that included two adolescent children. The differential impact of parenting was measured by a number of questionnaires and surveys answered by both parents and siblings in their families. During the following 4 weeks, telephone interviews with the parents were conducted twice a week asking what activities had happened during the day. The interviews were conducted in the parent's choice of English or Spanish.

Results: Evidence consistent with our hypothesis of more gender-typed differential treatment of siblings in Mexican-oriented than in Anglo-oriented families is reflected in a Culture Group by Sibling Gender interaction (i.e., larger differences in the treatment of sisters vs. brothers in the Mexican-oriented group); given our directional hypothesis, we report effects at $p < .10$ or higher. Evidence of larger differences between mothers and fathers in Mexican-oriented families is reflected in a Culture Group by Parent interaction.

Source: McHale, S. M., Updegraff, K. A., Shanahan, L., Crouter, A. C., & Killoren S. E. (2005). Siblings' differential treatment in Mexican American families. *Journal of Marriage and Family, 67*(5), 1259–1274. doi: 10.1111/j.1741 -3737.2005.00215.x

t-Tests

Small samples have an increased likelihood of sampling error. For that reason, most of the individuals developing statistical methods for testing hypotheses focused on large samples and large databases. Yet there existed then and now a method for testing the null hypothesis with a small sample of data.

Mental health variables are evaluated in many studies involving small samples of clients. When the practitioner-researcher wishes to evaluate a treatment, program, or condition, the *t*-test is commonly used to analyze the outcome. The variable of interest in these studies becomes the independent variable. In such studies, the outcome or scores that make up the data comprise the dependent variable.

CASE IN POINT   10.1

Background of the Student's *t*-test and Its Use

In the 1750s, Arthur Guinness began a brewery in Dublin, Ireland. That brewery was wildly successful. In the 19th century, the brewery set up a laboratory and began to hire scientifically trained specialists to oversee the production of its products. In 1899, a young Oxford-educated chemist, William S. Gosset, became an employee of Guinness. He devised methods to test small samples to determine the quality of large shipments of raw materials arriving at the Guinness facility. He was able to support his method for assessing small samples by devising a statistical test. The Guinness Company was concerned with sharing trade secrets with competitors and did not want employees to publish anything. After pleading his case to Edward Cecil Guinness, William Gosset was granted special permission to publish if he used a nom de plume. In 1908, Gosset elected to publish his statistical tables and computational system as the "Student" (Mankiewicz, 2001).

Single-Sample Student's *t*-Test

Through a series of statistical analyses conducted in London with Karl Pearson, Gosset was able to redefine the normal curve of probability to accommodate samples that are small in size. To apply his table to different-size samples, he introduced the concept of **degrees of freedom (*df*)**. The table is unique for each degree of freedom between 1 and infinity. Degrees of freedom are the number of cases in a sample that are free to vary. When a statistic is calculated, a degree of freedom is lost.[3] Thus, for single-sample hypotheses, the number of degrees of freedom is simply 1 less than the number of subjects in the sample ($df = n - 1$).

According to the Gosset *t* table (Table 10.2), a class of graduate students with 26 students would need a critical value of *t* to be larger than the value required for a significant *z*-value (noted above on the normal curve). With 26 students, the number of degrees of freedom is 25 ($df = n - 1$, or $df = 26 - 1$). At 25 degrees of freedom, the required level for rejecting a two-tailed null hypothesis at $\alpha = .05$ (2.5% on both sides) is 2.056.

Computation of the Single-Sample *t* Ratio

The test procedure for obtaining a *t*-score is similar to finding the *z*-score for a single-sample case. To compute the *t*-score, one first finds the difference between the sample's mean and the mean of the population, as when conducting a *z*-test. Then one divides that difference by the standard error of the mean, that is, the sample's standard deviation divided by the square root of the sample's size.

$$ t = \frac{\bar{X} - \mu}{\frac{s}{\sqrt{n}}} $$

Once this calculation is completed, the next step is to find the critical value on Gosset's *t* table for the appropriate alpha level.

The computational functionality exists online and in an iPad app:

GO2STAT, Statistics Visualizer for iPad, http://itunes.apple.com/ca/app/statistics-visualizer/id371888586?mt=8

Online single-sample *t*-test calculator, SYSTAT Software, http://studentsttest.com/

Photo 10.1   Guinness Chemist and Statistician William Sealy Gosset (aka Student) in 1908

Wikimedia Commons.

Table 10.2   Gosset's Table of the Probability Values for *t*

df	\multicolumn{5}{c}{p (one-tailed probabilities)}				
	.10	.05	.025	.01	.005
1	3.078	6.314	12.706	31.821	63.657
2	1.886	2.920	4.303	6.965	9.925
3	1.638	2.353	3.182	4.541	5.841
4	1.533	2.132	2.776	3.747	4.604
5	1.476	2.015	2.571	3.365	4.032
6	1.440	1.943	2.447	3.143	3.707
7	1.415	1.895	2.365	2.998	3.499
8	1.397	1.860	2.306	2.896	3.355
9	1.383	1.833	2.262	2.821	3.250

(Continued)

Table 10.2 (Continued)

df	p (one-tailed probabilities)				
	.10	.05	.025	.01	.005
10	1.372	1.812	2.228	2.764	3.169
11	1.363	1.796	2.201	2.718	3.106
12	1.356	1.782	2.179	2.681	3.055
13	1.350	1.771	2.160	2.650	3.012
14	1 345	1.761	2.145	2.624	2.977
15	1.341	1.753	2.131	2.602	2.947
16	1.337	1.746	2.120	2.583	2.921
17	1.333	1.740	2.110	2.567	2.898
18	1.330	1.734	2.101	2.552	2.878
19	1.328	1.729	2.093	2.539	2.861
20	1.325	1.725	2.086	2.528	2.845
21	1.323	1.721	2.080	2.518	2.831
22	1.321	1.717	2.074	2.508	2.819
23	1.319	1.714	2.069	2.500	2.807
24	1.318	1.711	2.064	2.492	2.797
25	1.316	1.708	2.060	2.485	2.787
26	1.315	1.706	2.056	2.479	2.779
27	1.314	1.703	2.052	2.473	2.771
28	1.313	1.701	2.048	2.467	2.763
29	1.311	1.699	2.045	2.462	2.756
30	1.310	1.697	2.042	2.457	2.750
40	1.303	1.684	2.021	2.423	2.704
60	1.296	1.671	2.000	2.390	2.660
120	1.289	1.658	1.980	2.358	2.617
∞	1.282	1.645	1.960	2.326	2.576

Adapted from Table III of R. A. Fisher and F. Yates. *Statistical Tables for Biological, Agricultural, and Medical Research*, 6th Edition, Longman Group, Ltd., London, 1974. (Previously published by Oliver & Boyd, Ltd., Edinburgh). Used with permission of the authors and publishers.

Source: Kachigan, S. K. (1991). *Multivariate statistical analysis: A conceptual approach* (2nd ed.). New York, NY: Radius Press, p. 290.[4]

Note: With this table, the two-tail alpha levels for the .05 level are in the column labeled .025, and the alpha level of .01 is found in the column labeled .005. Also, note that at an infinite number of degrees of freedom (a mathematical impossibility), the critical values for the *t*-test are identical with those of a *z* table reflecting the normal curve of probability.

Format for Reporting a *t*-Test

A commonly used format employed by researchers to report findings based on a *t*-test provides the reader with the following: (1) *t*-test ratio, (2) degrees of freedom, and (3) probability of making a Type I error in rejecting the null hypothesis. This takes the following standard format (hypothetical outcome): ($t = 5.55$, $df = 20$, $p < .01$). In this example, the *t* ratio is 5.55, there are 21 subjects ($df = 20$), and the probability of a Type I error is less than .01 (confidence level = 99%).

"*t* for Two," the Two-Sample Student's *t*-Test

The widest application of Gosset's statistical model and tables is with two samples. Within this approach, there are two variations of the two-sample *t*-test. One is the case for conducting pretesting and posttesting on a single group of subjects.[5] This is referred to as either a correlated-samples *t*-test or as a repeated-measures *t*-test. Correlated samples refer to research conducted with carefully matched subjects. One of each matched pair is then randomly assigned to be in one group and the other in the second group. Another version of correlated samples occurs when two related subjects are assigned to the separate groups. For example, a study of smoking habits with fathers and their teenage sons could have all the fathers in one group and the boys in the other.

Correlated-Samples or Repeated-Measures *t*-Test

In this case, the *t*-test computation is very similar to the test for a single sample. The *t* ratio is calculated with the average difference score in the numerator and the standard error of the difference in the denominator. The null hypothesis is almost always two-tailed, $H_0 : \bar{X}_1 = \bar{X}_2$, with two alternatives, $\bar{X}_1 < \bar{X}_2$ and $\bar{X}_1 > \bar{X}_2$. The small samples normally analyzed using this *t*-test model imply that the probability of a Type II error may be greater than with other empirical approaches employing large samples of subjects. (See the computational examples on the student website for this book.)

Online Calculation Assistance for Two-Sample *t*-Tests

The following websites offer online calculation assistance for two-sample *t*-tests:

GraphPad Software, http://www.graphpad.com/quickcalcs/ttest1.cfm

SYSTAT Software, http://studentsttest.com/

Department of Astronomy and Physics, College of Saint Benedict and St. John's University, http://www.physics.csbsju.edu/stats/t-test_bulk_form.html

Change Bioscience, http://www.changbioscience.com/stat/ttest.html

Rejecting the Null Hypothesis Using a Correlated-Samples t-Test: The final step in the process of using a repeated-measures or correlated-samples *t*-test is to compare the calculated *t* ratio with Gosset's critical value. That value can be found in Table 10.2 and

Cartoon 10.1

What Type of Test Was That?

"No, I said we need a *t*-test, not a tea test."

Cartoon by Merv Magus.

in the printouts from statistical software. The degrees of freedom (*df*) for a correlated-samples or repeated-measures *t*-test are equal to the total number of subjects minus 1 for loss due to the mean that was calculated, $\bar{d}$ (mean difference between pre- and post-tests). Thus, if there were 10 subjects who were given a pretest prior to a treatment or intervention and a posttest following the program, there would be 9 degrees of freedom (*df* = 10 − 1). On Table 10.2, it can be seen that to reject the null hypothesis (H_0:) with 95% confidence (α = .05), a *t* ratio equal to or greater than 2.262 is needed. To reject the null hypothesis with 99% confidence in the decision (α = .01) requires a *t* ratio equal to or greater than 3.250. See the example in the boxed material: "Sample of a Correlated *t*-Test in the Literature."

Applications from the Literature

Sample of a Correlated *t*-Test in the Literature

Note: In this study, the researchers tested three groups of adult subjects with insomnia for the effectiveness of three treatments: relaxation therapy, sleep hygiene, and binaural beats (sound) therapy. Each intervention was tested against a baseline of sleeplessness. The correlated *t*-test was employed because the same subjects were tested (baseline) and then tested again after the intervention.

Results: We have shown that the treatment phase as a whole has a significant effect, but we were also interested in analyzing the independent effect of each treatment type compared to baseline. Thus, we compared each treatment type in stage 2 (first treatment intervention) with the baseline, using a correlated *t*-test. Results are: $t = 10.26$ ($df = 9$, $p < .001$) for sleep hygiene, $t = 6.28$ ($df = 9$, $p < .001$) for binaural beats and $t = 5.89$ ($df = 9$, $p < .001$) for muscle relaxation.

Source: Bogdan, V. A., Balázsi, R., Lupu, V., & Bogdan, V. (2009). Treating primary insomnia: A comprehensive study of self-help methods and progressive muscle relaxation. *Journal of Cognitive and Behavioral Psychotherapies, 9*(1), 67–82.

Two Independent Samples *t*-Test

The *t*-test for independent samples may be the best choice when a practitioner-researcher wishes to evaluate the effectiveness of an intervention. The approach involves creating two groups of subjects from a pool of potential subjects by randomly assigning individuals to each of two groups. One group is provided with the new or experimental treatment (experimental group), and the other group is not provided with the treatment (**control group**). The control group may be provided with a diversionary experience or some **placebo** treatment. (For a more detailed discussion of experimental design, see Chapter 14.)

Many times it is not ethical to withhold a treatment from a group of subjects. This dilemma is common in higher education research in which a group of students cannot ethically or practically be ignored while an equivalent group is provided a special condition. A variation of the two-sample independent *t*-test is used to analyze data from this type of research. The first group receiving the new approach is still an experimental group, and the second group (**comparison group**) is provided with a competing treatment or program. For example, the experimental condition or treatment may involve a new technology-supported instructional model, while the standard lecture/seminar format for instruction may be the comparison condition or treatment.

In both cases, the null hypothesis is that the two groups (experimental and control) are not significantly different from each other ($H_0 : \bar{X}_E = \bar{X}_C$), and the two possible alternatives are $\bar{X}_E > \bar{X}_C$ and $\bar{X}_E < \bar{X}_C$.

CASE IN POINT   10.2

In 2004, promotion exams for firefighters in Akron, Ohio, were taken by qualified employees of the fire department. After 23 minority firefighters did not reach passing levels on the examination, they brought suit against the City of Akron, claiming the promotion test was discriminatory and biased against them.

(Continued)

(Continued)

In most American courts, it is a standard policy to use a four-fifths rule to make a judgment in such questions of possible discrimination. Under that rule, if $\frac{4}{5}$ (80%) or more of the protected class are treated equally as compared with the nonminority group, the complaint can be dismissed. In the Akron case, the lawyer for the minority firefighters brought a statistician to court who used a single-sample t-test to prove with scientific accuracy ($\alpha = .05$) that the minority firefighters were discriminated against via the promotion test. That jury trial was decided in favor of the complainants. The final state appeal resulted in the 23 minority firefighters being awarded $1,891,000 (*Howe v. City of Akron,* 789 F. Supp. 2d 786 [N.D. Ohio 2010]).

Computation of the Two Independent Samples t-Test: The conceptual computation model is similar to those for other members of the t-test family of statistical analyses. The numerator is the difference between the means of the two groups (experimental and control or experimental and comparison). A computational model for the independent-samples t-test is found on the student website for this book. As was noted earlier in this chapter, there are a number of online solutions for doing the actual arithmetic of calculating the t-test ratio.

Decision to Reject H_0: The last step in the process of using a two-sample t-test is to decide whether the t ratio is large enough to reach the needed critical value. The researcher must first determine the number of degrees of freedom that were in the study. In the two independent sample t-test, two means are calculated from the data, $\bar{X}_1$ and $\bar{X}_2$. Thus, the total degrees of freedom equals 2 less than the total number of subjects used in the study ($df = [n_1 + n_2] - 2$). If each group had 12 subjects, the total df would be 22. In Table 10.2, the critical value for the $\alpha = .05$ level is 2.074. To reject the null hypothesis with 95% confidence in the decision requires a t ratio equal to or greater than 2.074. To reject the null hypothesis with 99% confidence in the decision at the $\alpha = .01$ level requires a t ratio equal to or greater than 2.819. Notice that as the required alpha level needed to reject the null hypothesis becomes lower (less chance for a Type I error), the required critical value for the t ratio increases.

Assumptions for Using t-Tests: To use a t-test, the researcher must meet four assumptions. By meeting these assumptions, the researcher improves the power of the study and reduces the possibility that any difference between the two groups was the result of a factor unrelated to the treatment being studied or evaluated.

1. The dependent variable being analyzed is composed of parametric data. Ratio and interval data are needed to calculate the mean, standard deviation, and standard error of the data.

2. The data are normally distributed and approximate a bell-shaped curve. The Gosset t-test has been shown to be statistically **robust** to moderate violations of this assumption (Box, 1953).[6]

3. The two samples were randomly chosen from the same population.

4. Both samples have the same or very similar variances. This assumption is also known as the assumption of homogeneity of variance.

Applications from the Literature

Sample of Both Repeated-Measure *t*-Test and Independent-Sample *t*-Test

Note: In this study, there were 180 incarcerated youth with an age range of 13–18 years. Some were in lockdown facilities for serious offenders, and others were in facilities that treat adolescents who have been abused and/or neglected. The pretest was a modified (for low reading levels) version of the Monitoring the Future Questionnaire. The article by Morehouse and Tobler reported on a number of related studies. In most cases, the follow-up data were collected using the same questionnaire following a program of intensive individual and group counseling. The pretest-posttest designs employed in the study were evaluated using a repeated-measures *t*-test.

Design 1: Panel Intervention Youth vs. Cross-Sectional Comparison Youth. The 132 panel intervention youth showed a highly significant reduction in alcohol and other drugs (AOD) use from pre-test to post-test as measured by the quantity-frequency index (t [df, 262] = 4.25, $p < .001$) and the number-of-drugs index (t [df, 262] = 4.99, $p < .001$). The two-group *t*-test for independent samples revealed no significant difference between the pre-test comparison youth and the post-test comparison youth on the quantity-frequency index (t [df, 453] = 0.43, $p < .67$) or the number-of-drugs index (t [df, 454] = 1.19, $p < .06$).

Youth who received 5–30 hours of intervention ($n = 101$) were compared with those who received 1–4 hours (the low-dosage group, $n = 31$), using a two-group independent *t*-test. The difference between groups in terms of reduction in AOD use was highly significant for the quantity-frequency index (t [df,.130] = 3.32, $p < .001$), as well as significant for the number-of-drugs index (t [df,.130] = 2.14, $p < .035$).

Source: Morehouse, E., & Tobler, N. S. (2000). Preventing and reducing substance use among institutionalized adolescents. *Adolescence, 35*(137), 1–28.

Applications from the Literature

Example of the Use of Independent-Samples *t*-Tests

Note: This study was part of a larger research effort to explore personal histories of women who have survived abuse and violence. It is a cross-sectional study covering the life span of women from 18 to 72 years. Women were drawn from all walks of life, including women incarcerated in the Kansas state women's prison.

Results: An independent-samples *t*-test was conducted to determine if there was any statistically significant difference in Intimate Partner Violence (IPV) score for race/ethnicity defined as White

(Continued)

(Continued)

and Non-White. While the difference in means was not significant for physical abuse or for economic abuse, there was a statistically significant difference for Whites and Non-Whites in the category of psychological abuse. The test was significant, $[t (df, 276) = 2.91, p < .004]$. White people reported experiencing higher frequencies of psychological abuse in an abusive relationship (Mean = 3.22, SD = 1.06) than Non-White people (Mean = 2.83, SD = 1.16).

There was a statistically significant difference for both physical and psychological abuse for those who were incarcerated versus those who were not currently incarcerated. The independent samples t-test was significant for physical abuse, $[t (df, 283) = 3.25, p < .001]$ and psychological abuse, $[t (df, 283) = 2.43, p < .016]$. For physical abuse, the means were higher for those who were incarcerated (Mean = 2.67, SD = 1.00) than for those who were not incarcerated (Mean = 2.26, SD = 1.10). Likewise, for psychological abuse, the means were higher for those who were incarcerated (Mean = 3.25, SD = 1.00) than for those who were not incarcerated (Mean = 2.93, SD = 1.10).

Source: Pyles, L. (2006). Economic well-being and intimate partner violence: New findings about the informal economy. *Journal of Sociology and Social Psychology, 33*(3), 101–126.

t-Test and Correlation Coefficients

The family of t tables developed by William S, Gosset also have an application in the testing of Pearson product moment correlation (PPMC) coefficients. The null hypothesis with Pearson's coefficients is that there is no correlation beyond what could occur by sampling error. The goal of hypothesis testing is to determine if the coefficients are significantly different from zero. As the value of a correlation coefficient could be positive (above zero) or negative (below zero), this is a two-tailed null hypothesis test. The null hypothesis can be expressed as $H_0: r = 0$. The two-tail alternative hypotheses are $r > 0$ and $r < 0$. The computation of the t ratio for the PPMC is tested against a critical value from Gosset's table using degrees of freedom equal to the total number of subjects minus two ($df = n - 2$). The loss of 2 accounts for the two variables being correlated.

$$t = r\sqrt{\frac{n-2}{1-r^2}}$$

Applications from the Literature

Example from a Published Article Testing a Correlation Coefficient

Note: This study focused on 20 law schools affiliated with private universities across 13 states. The 20 schools all had admission standards that accepted students with low scores on the LSAT standardized test. The author studied the correlation between African American enrollment numbers and the school's mean LSAT scores.

Results: Statistical analysis of the changes in the 25th percentile LSAT scores and the number of African-American students enrolled indicates a negative relationship ($r = -0.58$), meaning that as the 25th percentile scores increase, the number of African-American students enrolled decreases. This correlation is significant at the $\alpha = .01$ level, meaning that the probability that this happened by chance was just 1%, or one chance out of 100.

Source: Nussbaumer, J. (2006). The disturbing correlation between ABA accreditation and declining African-American law school enrollment. *St. John's Law Review, 80*(3), 991–1003.

> "The analysis of variance is not a mathematical theorem, but rather a convenient method of arranging the arithmetic."

> Ronald A. Fisher

ANALYSIS OF VARIANCE FOR ONE INDEPENDENT AND ONE DEPENDENT VARIABLE (ONE-WAY ANOVA)

ANOVA Model

Practitioner-researchers often wish to make comparisons among several treatment conditions. For example if five different counseling strategies (four treatment groups and a control group) are being evaluated to identify the most effective approach, multiple *t*-tests could be used. One obvious problem is that the number of pairwise comparisons increases exponentially. In this case, the number of independent-sample *t*-tests needed is 10. Using so many *t*-tests dramatically increases the likelihood of making a Type I error.

Fisher's Solution

Ronald A. Fisher devised an approach to solving this problem. His method was first published in 1921 in the *Journal of Agricultural Science* (Fisher, 1921). His solution was to begin with the best estimate of the population's mean, the **grand mean** of all the group means ($\overline{\overline{X}}$). This is found by adding all group means and dividing that total by the number of group means. The number of groups is often labeled *k*. The variance around this grand mean can be found and considered to be the total variance for all subjects on that variable. Fisher then created a fraction by dividing total variance into two component parts, **variance between groups,** the numerator, and **variance within groups,** the denominator. This fraction is then read as a ratio of between variance to within variance:

$$F = \frac{Between\ groups\ variance}{Within\ groups\ variance}$$

Photo 10.2 Sir Ronald A. Fisher

The calculation of variances is modified to account for the number of groups and subjects and called **between-groups mean square (BGMS)** and **within-groups mean square (WGMS)**. Thus, the F ratio is defined as $\dfrac{BGMS}{WGMS}$.

Table of F Ratio Probabilities

Fisher found that the F ratio from ANOVA does not distribute as a normal curve but is a positively skewed distribution with a minimum approaching zero and a maximum of infinity. The F ratio distributions change when the number of subjects and number of treatment groups change. Fisher devised distribution tables for thousands of combinations of subjects and treatment conditions. These tables of probability for different ratios are known as F tables. Today the F ratio and related probability for testing null hypotheses (critical values) are provided on the printouts of statistical software. (See Appendix A for an example from IBM-SPSS. The student website has a sample Fisher's table of F ratios.)

Ratios of F and t

The distribution of F ratios is a simple transformation of the distribution of t ratio probabilities. At a consistent number of degrees of freedom (df), $F = t^2$ or $t = \sqrt{F}$.

ANOVA Null Hypothesis Test

In analysis of variance, an independent variable with two or more levels is used to establish groups (e.g., experimental treatment versus control groups). This independent variable is also known as a **main effect.** The dependent variable is the quantity or scores on an outcome measure.

The term *analysis of variance* reflects what the actual arithmetic is designed to do. The null hypothesis for an ANOVA-analyzed data set is that there is no difference between the groups in terms of group means, or $H_0 = \bar{X}_1 = \bar{X}_2 = \bar{X}_3 = ... = \bar{X}_k$. This null hypothesis expresses the idea that all the group means are the same from the first to the last or (kth) group. Analysis of variance can replace the independent-samples t-test and assess differences between two groups or test for differences among three or more groups.

There are several possibilities when a null hypothesis for three groups is rejected:

- $\bar{X}_1 \neq \bar{X}_2 \neq \bar{X}_3$. In this case, all three group means are significantly different.

- $\bar{X}_1 \neq \bar{X}_2 = \bar{X}_3$. In this case, the mean for group 1 is significantly different from the means for groups 2 and 3. The means for groups 2 and 3 are not significantly different.

- $\bar{X}_1 = \bar{X}_2 \neq \bar{X}_3$. In this case, the mean for group 3 is significantly different from the means for groups 1 and 2. The means for groups 1 and 2 are not significantly different.

Naturally, the number of these alternatives increases dramatically as more group means are included in the null hypothesis. For example, if there were four groups, there would be 7 possible alternatives.

Reporting the ANOVA Decision

The F ratio, once calculated, can be used to test the null hypothesis of the ANOVA. The calculation of the ratio's numerator involves finding the sum of squared differences associated with the different group means. This is known as the **between-groups sum of squares (BGSS)**. When the BGSS is divided by its appropriate degree of freedom, it becomes the between-groups mean square (BGMS). Likewise **within-groups sum of squares (WGSS)** can be calculated and divided by the appropriate degree of freedom and provide the within-groups mean square (WGMS). (See the student website for the basic algebra of these computations.)

An outline for the ANOVA model is seen in Table 10.3. For example, if there were 3 treatment groups, the appropriate df for the numerator becomes 2 (k groups − 1 or 3 − 1). Then if each group had 8 subjects, the df for the denominator would be 21 ($n − k$ or 24 − 3). For the hypothetical study, the ratio would appear as $F_{(2, 21)}$. The minimum value (critical value) for rejecting the null hypothesis at $\alpha = .05$ is 3.47, and at $\alpha = .01$ it is 5.78. (These values can be found in the F table on the student website.) In many published studies, the author has elected to report a probability level for rejecting the null hypothesis as a p-value. This takes the form of $p < .05$ or $p < .01$. To save space, this may appear under the table and be associated with the F ratio by an asterisk.[7]

ANOVA results can also be reported without a table. To save space, authors may report the result of an analysis of variance in the narrative portion of the results section of the article. The format for reporting in narrative form is to show the F ratio with its degrees of freedom (numerator, denominator) and the probability of having made a Type I error. That probability is shown as $p < .05$ or $p < .01$. These probabilities are read, respectively, as

Table 10.3   Theoretical Model One-Way Analysis of Variance Summary Table

	Sum of Squares	Degrees of Freedom (df)	Mean Square	F Ratio
Between Groups	BGSS	$k - 1$	$\dfrac{BGSS}{df}$	$\dfrac{BGMS}{WGMS}$*
Within Groups	WGSS	$n - k$	$\dfrac{WGSS}{df}$	
Total	Total Sum of Squares	$n - 1$		

* $p < .05$.

Source: Developed by author.

"point-oh-five" or "point-oh-one." They indicate that the obtained F ratio is greater than chance variation and has led to rejecting the null hypothesis with little risk of making a Type I error. In the case where the null hypothesis cannot be rejected, the p-value is typically replaced by the letters $n.s.$, indicating there was no significant difference and the null hypothesis could not be rejected.

Table 10.4 Sample of a One-Way ANOVA Table From an Online Journal

Summary of ANOVA for Roommate Satisfaction Among Roommate Dyads Based on Racial Composition				
SOURCE	df	ss	MS	F
Between groups	3	988.19	329.40	4.50*
Within groups	146	10679.72	73.15	
Total	149	11667.91		

Note: $N = 150$.

$*p < .01$.

Source: Phelps, R. E., Altschul, D. B., Wisenbaker, J. M., Day, J. F., Cooper, D., & Potter, C. G. (1998). Roommate satisfaction and ethnic identity in mixed-race dyads based on racial composition. *Journal of College Student Development, 39*(2) 194–203.

Note: Rosemary Phelps and her colleagues used the Roommate Relationship Inventory, Ethnicity Questionnaire, and Multigroup Ethnic Identity Measure in African American–white ($N = 54$), Asian American–white ($N = 37$), Hispanic American–white ($N = 11$), and white ($N = 48$) randomly assigned roommate dyads at a large, public, predominantly white, southeastern university. The table reports an ANOVA comparing the four groups of dyads in terms of satisfaction with their roommate. In this case, the F ratio indicates that the null hypothesis of no dyad differences across the different combinations can be rejected at the 0.01 level.

Applications from the Literature

Sample of One-Way ANOVA Reported in Narrative Form

Note: In this study, there were 88 doctoral students ($df = 87$), and there were two levels to the between-groups variable (published or unpublished) providing just 1 degree of freedom. The research question involved a dependent variable measuring "self-efficacy as a researcher (RSES)," and the independent variable (main effect) was the two groups of graduate students, one with a track record of publications and one group that had never been published.

Results: In fact, the scholarly publication experience variable explained 15.4% of the variance in the research self-efficacy scores for these data. Therefore, the doctoral students who had published a scholarly work scored at a significantly higher level on the RSES than did the students with no scholarly publications, $F_{(1, 87)} = 15.84, p < 001$.

Source: Lambie, G. W., & Vaccaro, N. (2011). Doctoral counselor education students' levels of research self-efficacy, perceptions of the research-training environment, and interest in research. *Counselor Education and Supervision, 50*(4), 243–258.

Another strategy for reporting ANOVA outcomes involves using a table missing many of the traditional components. These truncated tables may be combined with a table of group means and standard deviations.

Applications from the Literature

Several One-Way ANOVAs Depicted on One Table

Note: In this example, the author provided the number of subjects, mean, and total standard deviation for a series of seven dependent variables. The independent variable for each of the seven analyses was marital status (Never Married, Married, and Separated/Divorced). On this table, she reported the F ratios and degrees of freedom. The table was kept short by not providing the sum of squares or mean square values. The reader can see which of the null hypotheses were rejected by the asterisks and associated p-value. The p-value is the possibility of being wrong when rejecting the null hypothesis.

The dependent variable for each of the seven ANOVAs was the maternal report of the child's behavior.

Table 10.5 One-Way ANOVAs for Maternal Marital Status and Maternal Reports of Behavioral Problems, 1992 Data

Variable	n	mean	SD	F	df
Behavior Problems					
Total	355			2.98	2,352
Never Married	127	108.00	15.01		
Married	108	111.00	14.14		
Separated/Divorced	120	106.18	15.27		
Number of Children					
Total	376			3.60*	2,373
Never Married	135	2.70	1.34		
Married	116	3.17	1.66		
Separated/Divorced	125	2.94	1.10		
Neighborhood Conditions					
Total	373			8.46**	2,370
Never Married	133	2.65	1.17		
Married	116	3.26	1.18		
Separated/Divorced	124	3.02	1.15		

(Continued)

Table 10.5 (Continued)

Variable	n	mean	SD	F	df
Safety					
Total	317			3.05*	2,314
Never Married	120	2.90	.96		
Married	99	3.17	.88		
Separated/Divorced	98	3.15	.90		
Income					
Total	305			53.14**	2,302
Never Married	118	13,419	12,982		
Married	87	31,963	17,976		
Separated/Divorced	100	14,448	9,693		
Home Inventory					
Total	362			19.35**	2,259
Never Married	129	850.86	13.28		
Married	113	965.43	13.34		
Separated/Divorced	120	886.23	12.99		
Relationships with Fathers					
Total	318			10.56**	2,315
Never Married	119	−.77	2.87		
Married	103	.36	2.33		
Separated/Divorced	99	−1.30	2.60		

* $p < .05$. ** $p < .01$.

Source: McKinney, R. (2002). Ecological factors and their relationship to maternal reports of behavioral problems in African American adolescents. *Child Study Journal, 32*(1), 53–73.

Interpreting the Outcome

The significance of differences between groups is established by the ANOVA process. However, the ANOVA process does not answer two important questions:

1. How useful is the independent variable in bringing about group differences? In other words, what is the strength of association (correlation) between the categorical independent variable (groups) and the dependent variable (measured scores)?

2. Are the differences among three or more groups significant? To answer this question means finding which group's mean is significantly different from the means of the other groups.

Eta-Squared: The first question is answered by creating a correlational statistic that estimates the effectiveness of the treatment or condition used to form the groups in the study. With ANOVA, this can take the form of a simple statistical ratio of between-groups sum of squares (*BGSS*) to the total sum of squares (*Total SS*) within the study. The total sum of squares is simply *BGSS* + *WGSS*. The ratio of *BGSS* to *Total SS* is a new statistic, **eta-squared** (η^2).

$$\eta^2 = \frac{BGSS}{Total\ SS}$$

The eta-squared statistic can be expressed as a percentage and read as the percent of total variance in the dependent variable that is explained by the treatment or grouping variable.

Applications from the Literature

Reporting Eta-Squared

Note: This paper by Stephenson Beck and his colleagues involves a convenient sample of 111 women and 95 men enrolled in undergraduate public speaking classes. Data were collected using a questionnaire during a class meeting. The gender of the students was the main effect, resulting in 1 degree of freedom for the between-groups sum of squares. In this study, the eta-square of .14 can be read as indicating 14% of the variance in undergraduate teasing is a function of gender. The authors also made a common error in reporting their findings. It is not logically possible to find that the probability of making a Type I error is zero. It is always greater than zero.

Results: Significant results were found for the role of the participant ($F_{[1,\ 204]}$ = 33.04, $p < .00$, eta squared = 0.14). Participants indicated that they engaged in teasing episodes more frequently as the instigator (Mean = 3.26) than as the target (Mean = 2.95). In general, college students reported instigating teasing slightly more than once or twice a week and being the target of teasing slightly less frequently.

Source: Beck, S., Clabaugh, S. E., Clark, A., Kosovski, M. C., Daar, R., Hefner, V. . . . Suri, R. (2007). Teasing among college men and women. *Communication Studies, 58*(2), 157–172.

Multiple Comparisons: Even when the null hypothesis is rejected for a basic ANOVA with three or more groups, the researcher is still not finished. The next step is to delineate which groups differ significantly from each other.[8]

Once again, it was Ronald A. Fisher who solved this problem. He did so with the development of a variation of multiple *t*-tests that he named the least significant difference test

(Fisher's LSD; Fisher, 1925/1990). The LSD statistic is usually calculated post hoc following the rejection of the null hypothesis from an ANOVA. Researchers occasionally use the term **protected Fisher LSD test**. This term emphasizes that the test is used only after finding a significant F ratio with ANOVA. For each pairwise comparison, a t ratio is calculated with the numerator being the difference between the means of the two groups. The denominator is a standard error found by combining all subjects across all groups. The decision to reject the various null hypotheses is made using a table of t ratios. Because the LSD procedure does not account for the additive nature of Type I error, it thereby tends to increase the potential for a false finding (Hayter, 1986). This increment in the potential for error is generally known as the problem of **familywise Type I error (FWE)**. Subsequently, other procedures for multiple comparisons have been developed with a greater capacity for reducing FWE (Westfall, Kropf, & Finos, 2004). The tendency to overestimate the number of significant differences is why Fisher's LSD is described by some authors as a liberal method for conducting multiple comparisons. Fisher's method may find too many significant differences.

Other methods for conducting multiple comparisons, after finding a significant F ratio through ANOVA, include the following:

- Tukey's honestly significant different (HSD) procedure is for use when all of the groups from the ANOVA are equal. The Tukey-Kramer test is a variation of the HSD used when the groups are not balanced and have different numbers of subjects.
- The Bonferroni procedure is highly conservative and involves adjusting the alpha level needed for the individual pairwise comparisons. It does require equal-sized samples for each group. The Bonferroni-Holm correction procedure has the advantage of not requiring the comparison group pairs to have equal-sized samples.
- Ryan or Ryan-Einot-Gabriel-Welsch F (REGWF) is a conservative post hoc test that is best used when the various groups all have the same number of subjects (Cramer & Howitt, 2004).
- The Scheffé test is a highly conservative but low-power post hoc technique for both unequal and equal-sized groups.
- The Sidak-Holm comparison is a post hoc technique that does not require equal group sizes and is slightly more conservative than the LSD procedure.
- The Student-Newman-Keuls (SNK) procedure is another approach for multiple comparison testing that does not control for the FWE issue with the alpha level. SNK requires equal-size groups of subjects.
- Duncan's multiple range procedure also requires that the group sizes all be equal, and it does not control for the FWE problem.
- Dunnett's t-test is a procedure for making multiple comparisons of the mean of the control group with each of the other sample means. This is often used in biomedical research, which frequently uses true control groups receiving placebo treatments.

To understand the results of multiple-comparison tests, practitioner-researchers only need to return to the cell means and see which of the significantly different means was the greater and which was smaller.

Applications from the Literature

Two Different Multiple-Comparison Tests

Example A

Note: Many physically abused women blame themselves and try to cover up the injuries they receive when their significant others batter and abuse them. Michael Rice and Kathie Records used 4 groups of 10 adult women each in this study. These groups included women who were abused or battered and pregnant, pregnant but not abused, not pregnant but abused, and not abused and not pregnant (control group). Three clinical groups were compared with the control group using ANOVA. Dunnett's method is the appropriate choice for research with a true control group and a significant F ratio from an ANOVA.

Results: Analysis using Dunnett's t indicated that the cardiac response rates of the nonabused nonpregnant control group were significantly different from the other groups at several points in time. The control group of nonabused nonpregnant women was significantly different from the nonabused pregnant women at the 10-min recumbent baseline (*Mean* difference = 31.4, *SE* = 8.77, $p < .05$), 1-min standing (*Mean* difference = 27, *SE* = 8.29, $p < .05$), and 5-min standing (*Mean* difference = 22.7, *SE* = 6.83, $p < .05$) times. The cardiac response rates of the control group did not significantly differ from the abused nonpregnant group at any of the times.

Source: Rice, M. J., & Records, K. (2006). Cardiac response rate variability in physically abused women of childbearing age. *Biological Research in Nursing, 7*(3), 204–213. doi:10.1177/1099800405283567

Example B

Note: In this research study, 254 self-identified gay men were divided into three groups for analysis. These groups of men were diagnosed as having AIDS, as being without AIDS but HIV positive, or as being HIV negative. A 5-dimension scale of body dissatisfaction, the Multidimensional Body-Self Relations Questionnaire, provided 5 of the 6 dependent variables. The 6th dependent variable was a measure of depression. Two of the body image dimensions and the depression levels (CES-D) were significantly different for the groups. Several protected LSDs[9] were employed to test all significant findings.

Results: Demographic variables were assessed to determine if there were any systematic differences between the three groups. Results from a one-way analysis of variance (ANOVA) on the total score from the CES-D revealed a significant main effect for HIV/AIDS status, $F_{(2, 251)} = 4.4, p < .05$. Fisher's protected least significant difference (LSD) post hoc tests were then performed to determine which groups differed from each other. Results indicated that the AIDS group (*Mean* = 22.6, *SD* = 12.7) reported higher levels of depressed mood than the HIV negative group (*Mean* = 16.1, *SD* = 11.5), neither of which differed from the HIV positive group (*Mean* = 18.2, *SD* = 13.3).

Source: Blashill, A. J., & Vander Wal, J. S. (2011). Components of body image in gay men with HIV/AIDS. *American Journal of Men's Health, 5*(1), 6–10. doi:10.1177/1557988309356942

Assumptions of ANOVA

Four mathematical assumptions (requirements) must be met when conducting an analysis of variance:

1. **Parametric data.** This assumption requires the dependent variable to be measured as either an interval or a ratio variable.

2. **Independence.** Subjects are randomly assigned to the various treatment groups within the study. The independence of the data can be verified by using the **Durbin-Watson test.**

3. **Normality.** This assumption requires the distribution of scores for the dependent variable to approximate a normal curve within each group being analyzed. This assumption is tested occasionally by using a goodness-of-fit test (e.g., Anderson-Darling A2, Kolmogorov-Smirnov D). Normality is less of a concern if the total number of subjects is greater than 50.

4. **Homogeneity of variance.** The standard deviations for the dependent variable within each group should be approximately equal. The ANOVA model is fairly robust to violations of this assumption, and unless the ratio of the largest standard deviation to the smallest is greater than 2, this assumption is usually ignored.[10] The robustness of the F-test in analysis of variance is even greater if all the sample sizes (within groups) are the same. This equality of sample sizes is known as a balanced design.

Failure to meet the assumptions of ANOVA does not mean the null hypothesis cannot be tested. The practitioner-researcher can use a nonparametric ANOVA. Nonparametric ANOVAs are explained in Chapter 11.

ANALYSIS OF VARIANCE WITH TWO OR MORE INDEPENDENT VARIABLES

Hypothesis Testing With Two Independent Variables

The practioner-researcher can often identify two or more independent variables that are of simultaneous concern and that may interact to impact the dependent variable (outcome). This interaction possibility can be tested by using analysis of variance. When there is more than one independent variable, the research design is referred to as **factorial ANOVA.**

As an example, if there are two independent factors or variables (e.g., gender of the client and three levels of group therapy intensity), the analysis of variance would be a **two-way factorial ANOVA.** In statistical shorthand, this would appear as a 2 × 3 ANOVA. The numerals indicate that there were two independent variables, one with 2 levels (gender) and one with 3 levels (group intensity). These two independent variables are both described as **factors** or

Table 10.6 Cells for a 2 × 3 Analysis of Variance

	Group intensity 1	Group intensity 2	Group intensity 3
Male clients ♂	$n♂G1$	$n♂G2$	$n♂G3$
Female clients ♀	$n♀G1$	$n♀G2$	$n♀G3$

Note: Depicted in this table are 6 cells, each with a sample of 11 subjects. The cells are defined by gender of the subject and the therapy group to which they were assigned.

as main effects. This study would have a total of six groups of subjects, often referred to as **cells.** Within each cell are a number of subjects designated n.

The main effect, or factor, for gender is tested as H_0: $\bar{X}_{\sigma} = \bar{X}_{\varphi}$, while the null hypothesis for second main effect, or factor, tests the three group types. That null hypothesis may be expressed as $H_0 : \bar{X}_{G1} = \bar{X}_{G2} = \bar{X}_{G3}$. Thus, all males, irrespective of which counseling group they were in, and all females, irrespective of their group, are used to answer the main effects research question about gender. Likewise, the main effect null hypothesis for three counseling groups includes all clients (males and females).

Before testing two independent variables with factorial analysis of variance, the researcher should have background evidence for a belief that there is an interaction between the independent variables.[11] The null hypothesis testing for a significant interaction is $H_0 : \bar{X}_{\sigma G1} = \bar{X}_{\sigma G2} = \bar{X}_{\sigma G3} = \bar{X}_{\varphi G1} = \bar{X}_{\varphi G2} = \bar{X}_{\varphi G3}$.

The two-factor ANOVA provides three hypothesis tests, one for each of the two independent variables (main effects) and one for the interaction. The actual computation is an extension of the system used for analysis of variance with one independent variable. (See the student website for details on these calculations.)

Each of the research questions (main effect) is answered as though it were the only research question. Thus the sum of squares for factor A is found by summing over factor B as if that factor was not there. Likewise, the main effect for B is found by summing over factor A. The most important of the three research questions is that of the interaction effect (A × B). This is a test of whether the main effects of both A and B have a dependent relationship. Thus, the group means for the different levels of factor A vary according to the levels of factor B. The interaction can be significant whether or not a main effect is significant. Likewise, either or both main effects may be significant if the interaction is not significant.

Table 10.7   Fully Elaborated Two-Factor Analysis of Variance Summary Table (3 × 4 ANOVA)

Source of Variance	Sum of Squares	df	Mean Squares	F Ratio	Probability of Type I Error
Main Effect A	SSA	2	MSA	$MSA/MSError$	$p < .05$
Main Effect B	SSB	3	MSB	$MSB/MSError$	$p < .05$
Interaction A × B	SS(A × B)	6	MSAB	$MSAB/MSError$	$p < .01$
Error	SSError	108	MSError		
Total	Sum Total	119			

Note: The one-way analysis of variance term within-subjects sum of squares is replaced by a more generic expression, error. This term is used because some factorial ANOVA models use a different denominator in the F ratio calculations. (See the student website for more on this issue of models for ANOVA.)

Applications from the Literature

Example of a Two-Way ANOVA

Two-Way Factorial ANOVA for the Controllable Source

Source of Variance	SS	df	MS	F
Main Effects				
Self-esteem	8.273	2	4.137	4.340[*]
Performance	19.526	1	19.526	20.202[**]
Interaction	60.253	2	30.127	31.606[**]
Error	148.697	156	0.953	
Total	238.903	161		

* $p < .05$; ** $p < .01$.

Source: Chandler, T. A., Lee, M. S., & Pengilly, J. W. (1997). Self-esteem and causal attributions. *Genetic, Social & General Psychology Monographs, 123*(4), 479–492.

Note: In this study of undergraduate students, the authors organized two independent variables. One measurement was based on identifying three groups of subjects with different levels of **self-esteem**, and the second independent variable was two performance feedback formats (levels) expected by the subjects. There were 6 cells of data, rendering a 3 × 2 ANOVA model. Both main effects and the interaction were significant, and the three null hypotheses could be rejected.

Interpreting and Explaining Significant Interactions

In two-way factorial ANOVA, the primary research question is whether the interaction is significant. When the interaction's null hypothesis is rejected, the researcher is obligated to provide an explanation of the finding. There are two components of the explanation, tests for **simple effects** and graphs of the interaction.

Tests for Simple Effects

Following the rejection of the interaction null hypothesis, the researcher can dissect the study and analyze the separate components. In most cases, this is a two-step process. Step 1 is to break the cell structure down and employ a series of **one-way ANOVAs** to identify where the significant difference occurs. In the example of the hypothetical 2 × 3 (gender by group intensity type) two-way ANOVA described earlier, the researcher could break the interaction into two one-way ANOVAS, one testing the three groups of males and the other testing the three groups of females:

$$H_0(\male): \bar{X}_{G1} = \bar{X}_{G2} = \bar{X}_{G3}$$

$$H_0(\female): \bar{X}_{G1} = \bar{X}_{G2} = \bar{X}_{G3}$$

Alternatively, the division could have been by group instead of by sex, with three null hypotheses looking at possible differences in outcomes (dependent variable) between males and females:

$$H_0(G1): \bar{X}_{\male} = \bar{X}_{\female}$$

$$H_0(G2): \bar{X}_{\male} = \bar{X}_{\female}$$

$$H_0(G3): \bar{X}_{\male} = \bar{X}_{\female}$$

By cutting along the levels of factor B (group intensity type), the researcher ends up with a series of pairwise comparisons that can be made using series of three t-tests (with Bonferroni corrections).

In the first case, where the two genders are divided for further analysis, two ANOVAs are needed to test the null hypotheses (males and females). It may be possible in one or both cases to reject the null hypothesis that there was no difference among the three levels of group intensity. When a difference is identified by these simple-effects ANOVAs, the next step is to employ a multiple-comparison procedure (e.g., Fisher's LSD) to identify which data cells are significantly different from other data cells.

Graphing Interactions

Another method used to depict and explain a significant interaction in two-way ANOVA is the use of graphic presentations. The graphs are set up with the dependent variable on the ordinate and one independent variable on the abscissa. Usually, the dependent variable on the abscissa has a larger number of levels. The second independent variable is plotted on the graph as a series of lines connecting cell means. The points on the plot are the cell means.

An illustrative example of the graphing of a significant interaction in a 2 × 2 ANOVA is found in the following study.

Applications from the Literature

Two Examples of Simple Effects Test Results
Following a Two-Way Analysis of Variance

Example A

Note: In a study of 70 young adult men, a measure of hypermasculinity was used to identify two groups, hypermasculine and not-hypermasculine. A second independent variable involved three levels of threat posed by feedback comments of a female partner (actor) in an experimental task. The dependent variables included measures of emotion (anger) and blame expressed by the men. The significant interaction between the two independent variables was analyzed by a simple effects procedure.

(Continued)

(Continued)

Results: Univariate F tests were conducted to follow up the significant simple effects testing the moderate condition. Low and high hypermasculine men were found to report significantly different levels of anger, $F_{(1, 63)} = 5.62$, $p < .05$, and blame, $F_{(1, 63)} = 4.35$, $p < .05$. High macho men's ratings of anger in the moderate threat condition were higher while their ratings of blame were lower than those of the low macho men.

Source: Downs, K., & Gold, S. R. (1997). Distress and anger in the hypermasculine man. *Violence and Victims, 12*(1), 19–35.

Example B

Note: In a cognition laboratory, 33 undergraduate students were fitted with electroencephalogram (EEG) recorders and shown film clips of animals suffering and dying. The students were randomly divided into two groups. One group was instructed to suppress any internal reaction to the films and avoid displaying any emotions. The second group, the control group, was instructed to watch the film clips and was given no instruction about their feelings. Next, each subject was asked to perform a simple task (Stroop task), and while he or she worked, the EEG was recorded. The results from the Stroop test, as measured by reaction time and EEG tracings, provided the dependent variables for the research.

In this study, the letter M is used to represent the mean or $\bar{X}$, d is the difference between the control group mean and the comparison group's mean, and ERN is the recorded wave form of error-related negative emotions during electroencephalographic activity.

Results: The analysis revealed a main effect for response, $F_{(1, 31)} = 13.66$, $p_{rep} = .99$, $d = 1.33$, with errors generating larger negative deflections ($M = -2.19$, $SD = 1.51$) than correct responses ($M = -1.02$, $SD = 1.45$), a pattern typical of the ERN. This effect was qualified by an interaction between condition and response, $F_{(1, 31)} = 3.89$, $p_{rep} = .88$, $d = 0.71$. A simple-effects test showed that subjects in the control group had large ERNs, $F_{(1, 31)} = 17.67$, $p_{rep} = .99$, $d = 1.51$, with larger negative deflections on error trials ($M = -2.42$, $SD = 1.48$) than on correct trials ($M = -0.85$, $SD = 1.06$). Subjects in the emotion-suppression group showed much smaller ERNs, $F_{(1, 31)} = 1.36$, n.s., and their ERNs did not differ between error trials ($M = -1.69$, $SD = 1.52$) and correct trials ($M = -1.23$, $SD = 1.44$).

Source: Inzlicht, M., & Gutsell, J. N. (2007). Running on empty: Neural signals for self-control failure. *Psychological Science, 18*(11), 933–937. doi 10.1111/j1467-9280.2007.02004x

Graphs follow a significant interaction in which the interaction's null hypothesis was rejected. Lines on graphs of significant interactions depict the levels of one independent variable. The abscissa is used to depict the second independent variable. The ordinate provides the dependent variable's information.

However, if the interaction for the null hypothesis from a 2 × 2 ANOVA cannot be rejected, the graph of the "noninteraction" would show two parallel or nearly parallel lines. Interactions with intersecting lines are described as being **disordinal interactions.** Graphed lines that do not intersect but clearly are not parallel may also indicate that the interaction was significant. When graphed lines for a significant interaction are not parallel but do not intersect on the graph, they are described as representing an **ordinal interaction.**

Applications from the Literature

Example of a Graphic Display for a 2 × 2 ANOVA

Note: In this study of 271 students in the 8th and 9th grades in Singapore, the dependent variable was based on scores from a survey of suicidal ideation included in a larger survey (Student Ideation Questionnaire–Junior High School Version, SIQ–JH). Students were administered the SIQ–JH in their classrooms. The independent variable, parent marital status, was established by using a short demographic survey with the sample of adolescents. The result was a 2 × 2 ANOVA design with 4 cells.

These were then plotted as a linear coordinate graph with the adolescents' gender plotted on the graph with two lines. Parental marital status was plotted as two points on the abscissa. The dependent variable, suicidal ideation, was scaled on the ordinate with possible scores ranging from 10 to 35. The four cell means were used to set the points that were connected by the lines representing the two genders.

	Two Married Parents	Single-Parent Household
Adolescent Boys	$\bar{X} = 13.39$	$\bar{X} = 29.50$
Adolescent Girls	$\bar{X} = 20.45$	$\bar{X} = 21.40$

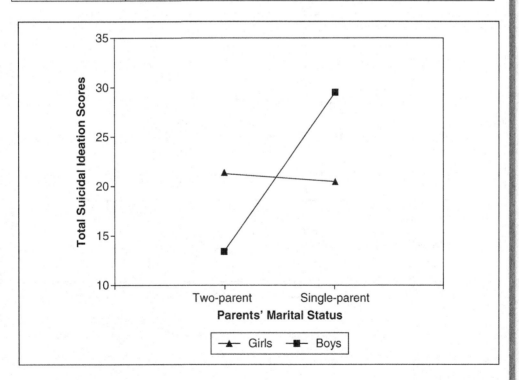

On this graph the two lines (Boys and Girls) cross each other. This is an indication of an interaction.

Source: Ang, R. P., & Ooi. Y. P. (2004). Impact of gender and parents' marital status on adolescents' suicidal ideation. *International Journal of Social Psychiatry, 50*(4), 351–360. doi:10.1177/0020764004050335

Computational Assistance

Since the marriage of computers and statistical software in the 1960s, very few researchers use the manual computational methods devised by Ronald Fisher. Today, two-way factorial ANOVA can be calculated by scores of different statistical software packages. Many of these are free and briefly described at the following URL: http://statpages.org/javasta2.html#Excel. Most users of MicrosoftWindows can do one- and two-way analysis of variance using Excel (http://courses.statistics.com/software/Excel/XL2way.htm) The large, multipurpose statistical packages are available on university systems and even for sale in campus bookstores.

Applications from the Literature

Two-Way Interactions: (1) Not Significant, (2) Significant Ordinal Interaction, and (3) Significant Disordinal Interaction

Note: In this review article, David Berliner and Leonard Cahen made the point that researchers in the behavioral sciences should look for the interaction between treatments used in experimental research and the critical traits of subjects that define the effective range of any treatment. They labeled this concept the "trait-treatment-interaction." Graphs were used to describe the various forms of interaction that may occur in such studies.

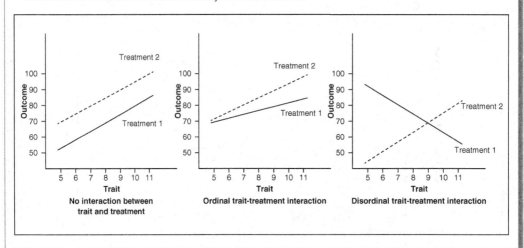

Source: Berliner, D. C., & Cahen, L. S. (1973). Trait-treatment interaction and learning. *Review of Educational Research, 1*(1), 58–94. doi:10.3102/0091732X001001058

Multiway ANOVA

In the complex world of psychological research, many ANOVA studies are reported in the literature that have more than two main effects and an interaction. See the student website for an example of a three-way ANOVA.

ANALYSIS OF COVARIANCE (ANCOVA)

Covariates

In most research studies involving mental health variables and human subjects, there is a possibility that changes in the dependent variable are influenced by **extraneous factors** (variables) in the environment and/or within the subjects. Subject-related extraneous variables include, among others, education level, cognitive ability, libidinal strength, empathy, years in the United States, hours per week spent on the Internet, number of tweets per week, aggression, anxiety, shyness, physical health, and wealth. Environmental extraneous factors include the time available, language/accent of the researcher, bias/discrimination, ongoing background activities/noise, researcher's gender/visage, and outdoor weather or room climate.

CASE IN POINT   10.3

There is a well-documented comorbidity between posttraumatic stress disorder (PTSD) and nicotine addiction. PTSD is a proven precursor to heavy smoking behavior. Serum levels of nicotine metabolites are positively correlated to the severity of PTSD symptoms. In this situation, initial therapeutic contact and early intervention for PTSD may need to be carried out in an environment where the client has the opportunity to smoke (Rasmusson, Picciotto, & Krishnan-Sarin, 2006).

The implication for researchers is to use intensity of smoking as a covariate factor in studies of treatment effectiveness for PTSD. Two dimensions can be measured to assess this covariate factor, the Minnesota Nicotine Withdraw Scale and a measure of the felt need to smoke such as the Urge to Smoke Scale (West & Ussher, 2010). Such studies should also use ethnicity/race as a fixed factor (independent variable) in research, because there is biochemical evidence that different groups of individuals metabolize nicotine at very different rates (Derby et al., 2008).

Even with random selection of subjects from the population and random assignment to the study's groups, there is always the possibility of an unlucky occurrence in the selection process that introduces an extraneous variable into the study. An approach to controlling extraneous variables is to consider them as **covariates.** The term *covariate* implies that the extraneous variable is correlated with the dependent variable. In a hypothetical study of the efficacy of several therapeutic interventions, the cognitive ability of the subjects could easily have an impact on the dependent variable (e.g., self-esteem). Thus, cognitive ability would be what Schuyler Huck and Howard Sandler (1979) described as a **rival hypothesis** or alternative explanation for any group differences.

Making Adjustments

Analysis of covariance (ANCOVA) is a method for purging the impact of an extraneous variable from the relationship between the independent variable(s) and the dependent variable (Wildt & Ahtola, 1978). The computational process involves removing the portion of the dependent variable's variance that is correlated with the outcome variable. That process leaves the part of the variance that is uncorrelated with the extraneous variable (covariate) behind for analysis and hypothesis testing. The result is that each individual's score is "adjusted" by removing the covariate from it.

When the cell means are calculated, they are referred to as **adjusted means.** Because the ANCOVA method takes an equal portion of variance from each cell in the design, there is an assumption that the correlation (regression) of the covariate and dependent variable are consistent for all groups and conditions in the study (Winer, 1971).

Applications from the Literature

Example of the Use of ANCOVA

Note: A total of 177 self-referred adults seeking counseling help from a university-based clinic were divided for treatment into two groups. The two levels of the independent variable were (1) the clients received both individual counseling therapy and psychoactive medications from a staff psychiatrist and (2) the patients received only counseling therapy. The dependent variables were measures of therapy outcome, the Global Assessment of Functioning Scale (GAF) and the Clinical Global Impressions Scale (CGI). These measures were used both before the treatment program (pretest) and again after the conclusion of the therapy. The pretest data were used as covariates in the analysis (ANCOVA). This equalized the groups prior to the initiation of the therapies.

Main Analysis: In order to examine whether medication use during therapy affected patient improvement, an analysis of covariance (ANCOVA) was conducted with each of the indices of therapist-rated patient improvement (i.e., GAF, CGI) controlling for initial severity. The first ANCOVA tested whether medication use affected patients' Axis V GAF ratings at termination (while controlling for the intake GAF rating). In this ANCOVA, the patients' GAF rating at termination was entered as the dependent variable, whether patients' use of medications during course of therapy was the independent variable, and the patients' GAF rating at intake was entered as the covariate. Results indicated the null hypothesis could not be rejected, $F_{(1,171)} = .51, p > .05$.

Source: Brown, J. S., Stellrecht, N. E., & Williams, F. M. (2005). A comparison of therapy alone versus therapy and medication in a community clinic. *Journal of Cognitive Psychotherapy, 19*(4), 309–316.

Assumptions of ANCOVA

The four assumptions of analysis of variance—a dependent variable measured with parametric data, independence and randomly assigned subjects, normality for the data in each cell, and homogeneity of all data in each cell—all need to be in place. In addition, a fifth assumption is required for ANCOVA. That assumption is that correlations (regression slopes) between the covariate and the dependent variable be consistent for each data cell. This is the assumption of **homogeneity of regression.** Research has documented that this fifth assumption of ANCOVA is an absolute necessity (Hollingsworth, 1980). (A discussion of ANCOVA and its assumptions is available on the student website).

REPEATED-MEASURES ANALYSIS OF VARIANCE

Research studies can be designed that repeat a measure (dependent variable) with the same subjects. This is useful in pretest-posttest designs and many other research efforts that take place with repeated testing over a period of time. Another variation of the **within-subjects design** appears in studies that have several very highly correlated dependent variables. In this case, the multiple dependent variables are analyzed as if they were a **repeated measure** of a single variable.

Most repeated-measures research is carried out with one repeated measure and two or more fixed-factor independent variables. In a hypothetical hypnotherapy study to reduce a phobia, with subject testing at three or more intervals over time, the practitioner-researcher is likely to compare the outcome with that of another group not receiving hypnotherapy for the phobia. The researcher may also wish to determine whether the approach works better for men or women. Thus, the repeated measure is the number of hypnotherapy sessions (3 levels), and the other independent variables are control vs. treatment (2 levels) and the gender of the clients (2 levels). Thus, this would be a $2 \times 2 \times 3$ ANOVA with a repeated measure on the third factor. The repeated factor is traditionally listed last in the sequence. Occasionally, journal articles are published using the terminology **split-plot** factorial ANOVA, or mixed-model ANOVA, to describe a repeated measure in the study.[12]

Advantages of Repeated-Measures ANOVA

Researchers employing repeated measures on the same subjects reduce the possibility that individual differences interfere with the relationship between the independent and dependent variables. This provides the study with more power than is available in the between-groups ANOVA designs. The approach is also less costly, as it requires fewer subjects to reach a reasonable level of statistical power. (More is available on the student website about repeated-measures ANOVA and its application and assumptions.)

Computational Tasks

Repeated-measures ANOVA programs are not yet available as apps for hand-held systems. However, computational solutions are available on the computer servers of most college campuses and are sold in university bookstores.

SUMMARY

Researchers making inferences based on samples must be concerned with sampling error. A solution is to express any statistic within a likely range that best approximates the population's parameter. This range, known as a confidence interval, can be employed to assess differences between different samples.

Scientific hypothesis testing is based on the null hypothesis process. The goal of the researcher is to have data that make it possible to reject the null hypothesis and thereby imply the correctness of a logical alternative. As there is always an amount of error in sample data, researchers must decide in advance how much can be tolerated. This is set a priori as the alpha level. It protects against Type I error. An adjustment (Bonferroni) is needed for the alpha level when multiple hypotheses are tested with one set of data, reflecting the fact that the alpha error possibility is additive. The possibility of failing to reject a null that is wrong is also controlled; this is the beta level or the chance of making a Type II error. One central factor in Type II error is the size of the sample that was used. Another is the alpha level selected.

Hypothesis testing methods were developed at the turn of the 20th century by British behavioral and agricultural scientists. These tests include z-tests and t-tests for single samples and t-tests for both independent and correlated samples. The null hypothesis for each of these test procedures implies a zero value for any observed differences between groups. In all these cases, the test procedure involves calculating a ratio between differences and standard error. Another application of the t-test method has been identified for use with Pearson's correlations.

Analysis of variance was developed by Ronald Fisher to provide a method of testing for possible significant differences across two, three, or more treatment groups or conditions. The primary tool used to test the null hypotheses is the table of F ratios devised by Fisher to find the probability of a chance occurrence of a ratio of variances. A series of mathematical assumptions should be met when employing Fisher's ANOVA.

In the analysis of variance, it is possible to include more than one independent variable. These **factorial** designs can include random variables, assigned variables, or a combination of both. When an extraneous variable is identified, its impact on the dependent variable can be statistically purged, and the F ratio can be found between the adjusted group means for the experimental groups on the dependent variable. This analysis of covariance method requires homogeneity of regression across all data cells of the study.

The power and efficiency of a research study can be improved by repeated-measures ANOVA. By measuring subjects several times (e.g., pretest-posttest), the researcher reduces error variance brought about by independent samples of subjects.

DISCUSSION QUESTIONS

1. Explain why the interaction effect of a two-way factorial ANOVA is of more interest to researchers than are the two main effects.

2. Why are repeated-measures designs for ANOVA considered more efficient than is factorial ANOVA?

3. ANCOVA is described as being more statistically powerful than a basic ANOVA. Explain why this is the case.

NOTES

1.   ASCA (American School Counselor Association). (1999[a]). *American School Counselor Association 1999–2000 membership directory and resource guide.* Gainesville, FL: Naylor.

2.   Skeptical professors frequently tell their students to check any findings reported using a one-tailed hypothesis against an appropriate table and see if the null hypothesis would have been rejected if the researcher had used a two-tailed hypothesis-testing procedure. This skepticism reflects the fact that the human spirit, ingenuity, and motivation can produce totally unexpected results and should use a statistical model that is open to all possibilities.

3.   If all students in a seminar were to count their pocket change and add up the amount of change carried by everyone, it would be possible to find the mean amount of pocket change. By subtracting each student's contribution to that total, one student's change amount, the last person to subtract from the total, would be determined by all the other student contributions and the known mean. Literally, we could tell that student what they had by knowing what all the others had with them and knowing the total that was used to find the mean. That student lost his or her degree of freedom.

4.   The original work by Gosset appeared in a 1908 paper titled "The Probable Error of a Mean" under the pseudonym Student. That original work can be seen at the following archival site from York University in Great Britain: http://www.york.ac.uk/depts/maths/histstat/student.pdf. Following this publication, it appeared in numerous tables of statistical probability, including Ronald A. Fisher and Frank Yates's classic work, *Statistical Tables for Biological, Agricultural and Medical Research* (3rd ed.), London, UK: Oliver & Boyd. The original table for Student's *t*-test now appears in virtually every statistics methods book published.

5.   The pretest, posttest design is one of the most commonly employed methods for assessing the value of therapeutic interventions with clients.

6.   George E. P. Box is the son-in-law of Sir Ronald A. Fisher, the originator of analysis of variance.

7.   Many researchers who do not fully understand the hypothesis-testing system will mistakenly report a probability of $p < .000$. This is not logically possible as there is always a chance for Type I error, be it ever so slight. They arrive at this decision when the software doing the arithmetic for them only reports to 1 chance in 1,000 and not below. The correct notation is $p < .001$.

8.   In ANOVA with only two groups, no further testing is needed after finding a significant F ratio.

9.   *Fisher's protected LSD* is an expression indicating that the ANOVA was significant prior to conducting the post hoc Fisher's tests. The term *protected* is not employed if the ANOVA was not significant but the post hoc comparisons were carried out anyway.

10.   The easiest way to statistically test for homogeneity of variance is to use the F max test. The numerator of this ratio is the group variance that is larger than any of the others. The denominator is the smallest variance found for one of the groups. The critical value on the F table is found by using the number of subjects less 1 for both groups as the degrees of freedom. In this case, the researcher is hoping the F ratio is not significant, thereby assuring that the groups have homogenous variances.

11.   Factorial ANOVA is a research tool useful for the analysis of aptitude-by-treatment interactions.

12.   The somewhat archaic term *split-plot* reflects the fact that many of the early developments in the mathematics of ANOVA models were brought about by statisticians working in schools of agricultural sciences. This included Ronald A. Fisher. When these statisticians referred to a split plot, they were describing the division of a farm field into plots.

Inferences Using Categorical and Nominal Information

"The chi-square statistic, I believe, is the great contribution to statistical methods by which the unsurpassed energy of Prof. Pearson's work will be remembered."

Ronald A. Fisher

OBJECTIVES

By reading and studying this chapter, you should acquire the competency to do the following:

- Explain the similarities and differences between parametric and nonparametric statistical procedures in hypothesis testing.
- Explain the use of single-sample chi-square in hypothesis testing.
- Employ simple chi-square to test a hypothesis related to categorical memberships.
- Describe and explain two statistical hypothesis tests for single-sample ordinal data.
- Explain the use of contingency tables in chi-square testing.
- Explain the advantage of the Wilcoxon-Mann-Whitney over Gosset's *t*-test.
- Describe the Kruskal-Wallace analysis of variance for ordinal data.

INTRODUCTION AND MAJOR THEMES

Statistical tests developed for hypothesis testing and described in Chapters 9 and 10 all share one major assumption, namely, the population from which the samples were drawn is normally distributed. A second assumption of equal sample variances is also a requirement in both the various analysis-of-variance models and the Student's *t*-test. In the real world of conducting research, these assumptions about the dependent variables frequently cannot be met. There is also a requirement that the dependent variable be measured as either interval or ratio data. This assumption cannot be met when the dependent variable is composed of rank (ordinal) data or even as nominal characteristics of the subjects.

Another class of statistics has been developed for use in hypothesis testing that does not require these statistical assumptions of the dependent variable. These are described as **nonparametric statistics** and are generally **distribution-free.** There are a number of such statistical tests designed for various types of studies and data. Several of the most commonly applied of these approaches are discussed in this chapter. Many more are described and explained on the student website.

NONPARAMETRIC HYPOTHESIS TESTING

When using nonparametric statistical procedures for hypothesis testing, one follows a similar logical sequence of steps as when using parametric procedures such as analysis of variance. In both systems, a null hypothesis is written based on the researcher's well-informed understanding of the phenomenon being studied. A decision about the required level of alpha and which statistical procedure to use must be made. After data collection and the ensuing nonparametric statistical analysis, one decides whether to reject or fail to reject the null hypothesis. If there are more than two groups in the study and the null hypothesis is rejected, a form of multiple comparisons is needed to explain the significant findings.

Because the dependent variable is composed of nonparametric data (ordinal and nominal), there is less mathematical precision in the whole hypothesis-testing procedure. This is evident as a slight loss in statistical power and an enhanced possibility of making a Type II error. The likelihood of a Type I error, which is set by the researcher, is well controlled.

Applications from the Literature

Explanation for Choice of Nonparametric Methods

Note: In this study, the authors used a nonparametric ANOVA (Kruskal-Wallis) with the Wilcoxon-Mann-Whitney test as the multiple comparison method. Wilcoxon- Mann-Whitney tests are a hypothesis-testing system for ordinal data that is similar to the parametric Gosset's *t*-test.

Analysis: To compute *p*, we use the Kruskal-Wallis test to compare groups of more than two experiments and the Wilcoxon-Mann-Whitney test to compare pairs of experiments. These tests are the non-parametric counterparts of the more popular ANOVA (analysis of variance) and Student's *t*-test for independent samples, respectively. The choice of non-parametric statistics is motivated by the fact that our data do not meet the requirements for their more powerful parametric counterparts (e.g., normal distribution).

Source: Colombetti, M., & Dorigo, M. (1994). Training agents to perform sequential behavior. *Adaptive Behavior, 2*(3), 247–275. doi: 10.1177/105971239400200302

TESTS FOR SINGLE SAMPLES

Chi-Square (χ^2) for Single Samples

In Chapter 10, methods for testing a null hypothesis with a single sample of subjects based on parametric data were described. Those methods, the single-sample z-test and t-test procedures, tested whether a sample's mean was similar to or differed from a population's mean. When the dependent variable is assessed as a nominal classification or an ordinal rank, however, the z-test and Student's t-test are not appropriate.

The solution to the problem of hypothesis testing with nonparametric statistical methods was pioneered by Karl Pearson (father of the product moment correlation). In 1900, he published research about plant genetics and introduced a new distribution of probability for the likelihood that observations of categorical membership will differ from theoretical expectations (Pearson, 1900). The distribution of these probabilities was published in table format and given the name **chi-square** (χ^2).[1]

Photo 11.1   Professor Karl Pearson

MacTutor History of Mathematics Archive.

The chi-square for a single sample can also be described as a **goodness-of-fit** test. This term is used whenever the single-sample chi-square is employed to determine whether a data set matches a certain model. In this regard, the test of the assumption of normality in t-tests and ANOVA is carried out with a goodness-of-fit test to determine whether a sample's distribution approximates the normal curve.

With this application of chi-square, the null hypothesis is that the dependent variable follows the normal curve and does not depart from its pattern. Thus, the researcher hopes to find that the null hypothesis cannot be rejected. If the null hypothesis is rejected, the researcher then knows that the data do not meet the assumption of normality. Other nonparametric statistical approaches can be used to still complete the research and answer the original research question. Three of these nonparametric approaches are described in this chapter, and a number of others are described and explained on the student website.

The goodness-of-fit chi-square can also be used with ogive-format curves. This process is a common tool used in test construction with procedures known as item response theory (IRT).

The underlying distribution of chi-square probabilities used to test a null hypothesis is continuous, while the nominal or ordinal data being tested are categorical. This creates a discontinuity, resulting in many errors when the number of cases in the data being tested is small or when the chi-square model itself is small (e.g., when $df = 1$). The correction for this problem is known as **Yates's correction for continuity** (Siegel & Castellan, 1988). Yates's correction is one that reduces the numerator in the chi-square ratio as a correction for the small sample being tested.[2]

Chi-square is an important statistical tool in its own right, but it also serves as the test statistic for a large range of other nonparametric approaches. Furthermore, it is versatile enough to be employed as the hypothesis test statistic in many observational (qualitative) research studies. In qualitative studies, the researcher may organize data observations into categories whose differences may then be analyzed using chi-square. Its simplicity of calculation has also made the chi-square statistic a favorite for practitioner-researchers conducting action research projects.

Applications from the Literature

Use of Chi-Square in a Qualitative Research Study

Note: In this study, graduate students of clinical programs reflected on the change they experienced as a result of completing course(s) in multicultural counseling. The study included 102 women and 22 men. The research used a critical incidents technique to gather information from graduate students about the changes they experienced in association with their participation in multicultural counseling courses. Trainees were also asked what course elements were linked to their personal changes.

Qualitative Analysis: A content analysis was performed for the first two questions, regarding (a) what changes occur to participants in a multicultural counseling course and (b) to what, specifically, participants attribute change. To enhance the credibility and trustworthiness of the study, a White female coinvestigator with experience in qualitative methods was involved in initial category development. The primary researcher (the first author) was potentially biased, given her extensive experience (13 years) with multicultural training and having heard many firsthand reports of personal changes from trainees.

Results: The frequencies of participant responses for each theme of personal change were categorized by the two demographic groups (i.e., White, and racial or ethnic minority). Chi-square tests were performed for differences in frequencies of response between White and racial or ethnic minority student groups for each theme of personal change. There were no significant differences between the White and racial or ethnic minority groups' response frequencies for each type of personal change reported. Similarly, chi-square tests were performed for differences in frequencies of response between White and racial or ethnic minority student groups for each theme of the attributes of personal change. Again, no significant differences were found between White and racial or ethnic minority students regarding response frequencies for the attributes of personal change reported.

Source: Sammons C. C., & Speight, S. L. (2008). A qualitative investigation of graduate-student changes associated with multicultural counseling courses. *The Counseling Psychologist, 36*(6), 814–838. doi: 10.1177/0011000008316036

Null Hypothesis

The null hypothesis of one-sample research with nominal data is that the subjects have been categorized according to a predicted pattern. For example, the researcher may feel that the counseling department's graduate students tend to vote for and support the Democratic Party more frequently than is true of the general population of all voters in the county in which the university is located. The null hypothesis is that the expected pattern of voting choices for graduate students of the counseling department is the same as that of all voters in the county. Thus, the null hypothesis can be expressed as "The expected numbers (countywide) equal the observed numbers of voting graduate students" (H_0: $O = E$).

Example Problem

The total voting pattern for our hypothetical University County in 2012 was 40% Democratic, 55% Republican, and 5% other parties. There are 60 graduate students in our counseling program; thus, to support the null hypothesis, we would expect 40% of 60 graduate students to vote Democratic (expected = 24), 55% of the 60 to vote Republican (expected = 33), and 5% of the 60 graduate students to vote for another party (expected = 3). When given an anonymous questionnaire, the 60 counseling students replied showing that 80% had voted Democratic (observed = 48), 10% had voted Republican (observed = 6), and 10% had voted for the Green Party (other; observed = 6).

Calculating Chi-Square

The computational algorithm that is appropriate to use with this one-sample case is

$$\chi^2 = \sum_{i=1}^{k} \frac{(O - E)^2}{E}$$

The central part of this equation is the subtraction of the expected value from the observed value for each category (cell) in the study's design. The symbol k is used to represent the number of cells. This value is squared and divided by the expected value. This is repeated for each categorical group (cell) and then the results are added together to find the chi-square.

In our example, there are three cells (categories); thus, $k = 3$.

$$\chi^2 = \frac{(48 - 24)^2}{24} + \frac{(6 - 33)^2}{33} + \frac{(6 - 3)^2}{6}$$
$$= 24 + 22 + 1.5$$
$$= 47.5$$

Notice that squaring each numerator means that all chi-square values will be positive. There is no mathematical possibility for a negative chi-square. Thus, all hypothesis tests are one tailed.

In single-sample chi-square analyses, the degrees of freedom (df) is one less than the number of cells or categories ($k - 1$). In this case, there are 3 cells (Democrats, Republicans, and others) indicating that $df = 2$. Using Table 11.1, we find that the χ^2 needed for $\alpha = 0.05$ is 5.99 and for $\alpha = 0.01$ is 9.21. The computed χ^2 exceeds the critical value of chi-square on the table.[3] Thus, we can reject the null hypothesis and report that graduate students in counseling do not vote with the same preferences as voters in the rest of the county. As a follow-up to the single-sample chi-square test, it is possible to do pairwise chi-square comparisons such as a chi-square to see if the students lean more toward the Democratic Party than does the county's general population.

Cartoon 11.1

Serious Research Tool

"My chi-square analysis at a=0.05 shows that Dora got significantly more candy than Chris or I did."

Cartoon by Marv Magus.

Applications from the Literature

A Single-Sample Null Hypothesis Test Using χ^2

Note: In this study of 243 children receiving special education services, the author used a team of judges to evaluate each of the learning objectives listed on the official Individual Educational Plans (IEPs). Her goal was to measure the extent to which each long-term and short-term objective on the IEP was supported by assessment data presented to the IEP team that had developed the plan. In this example, five null hypotheses were tested, each by using one-sample chi-square analysis. There were four contingencies (cells) for each null hypothesis tested. The four contingencies were the four logical possibilities showing whether the long-term educational goals for each child agreed or disagreed with the outcome of the individual psychoeducational diagnostic assessments. The author found low levels of correspondence between the IEP and the data from the child's assessments. In the section shown here, only two of the five chi-square tests are significant at $p < .05$ or less.

(Continued)

(Continued)

Analysis: The final assignment of 1's and 0's were set into a two element binary pattern compar-ing the psychological assessment (PA) with the long-term goals (LTG). Each of the "categories" is a different chi-square analysis for various components of the psychological assessment, e.g., Learning Patterns. The data were analyzed through the procedure of five different contingency tables each analyzing a single sample of scores from children with disabilities. The test statistic was chi-square (χ^2).

Contingency table analysis and chi-square (χ^2) results examining the relationship between the Psychoeducational Assessments (PA) and the Long-Term Goals (LTG) for the ld, ed, and emr populations

Category	Number[a]	PA/LTG No/No	PA/LTG No/Yes	PA/LTG Yes/No	PA/LTG Yes/Yes	Chi-square
Affective	238(5)	111	31	51	45	15.40*
Cognitive	238(5)	144	6	80	8	1.80**
Achievement	238(5)	21	47	26	144	6.50***
Learning patterns	238(5)	103	11	97	27	5.64****
Other	240(3)	143	21	32	44	51.21****

[a]Numbers in parentheses indicate missing cases.

*$p < .0001$.

**$p < .2$.

***$p < .01$.

****$p < .02$.

Source: Schenck, S. J. (1980). The diagnostic/instructional link in individualized educational programs. *Journal of Special Education, 14*(3), 337–345. doi: 10.1177/002246698001400307

Table 11.1   Chi-Square Table

df	.10	.05	.01	.001
1	2.71	3.84	6.64	10.83
2	4.60	5.99	9.21	13.82
3	6.25	7.81	11.34	16.27
4	7.78	9.49	13.28	18.47
5	9.24	11.07	15.09	20.52

df	.10	.05	.01	.001
6	10.64	12.59	16.81	22.46
7	12.02	14.07	18.48	24.32
8	13.36	15.51	20.09	26.12
9	14.68	16.92	21.67	27.88
10	15.99	18.31	23.21	29.59
11	17.28	19.68	24.72	31.26
12	18.55	21.03	26.22	32.91
13	19.81	22.36	27.69	34.53
14	21.06	23.68	29.14	36.12
15	22.31	25.00	30.58	37.70
16	23.54	26.30	32.00	39.25
17	24.77	27.59	33.41	40.79
18	25.99	28.87	34.80	42.31
19	27.20	30.14	36.19	43.82
20	28.41	31.41	37.57	45.32
21	29.62	32.67	38.93	46.80
22	30.81	33.92	40.29	48.27
23	32.01	35.17	41.64	49.73
24	33.20	36.42	42.98	51.18
25	34.38	37.65	44.31	52.62
26	35.56	38.88	45.64	54.05
27	36.74	40.11	46.96	55.48
28	37.92	41.34	48.28	56.89
29	39.09	42.56	49.59	58.30
30	40.26	43.77	50.89	59.70
40	51.80	55.76	63.69	73.40
50	63.17	67.50	76.15	86.66
60	74.40	79.08	88.38	99.61
70	85.53	90.53	100.42	112.32

Source: Abridged from Fisher and Yates (1974).

Warner, R. M. (2008). *Applied statistics: From bivariate through multivariate techniques.* Thousand Oaks, CA: Sage, p. 988.

Note: On this table, provided by Rebecca Warner, the value of chi-square needed for various *df* are provided for four levels of alpha.

Chi-Square Contingency Tables

Pearson's chi-square may also be employed to assess null hypotheses involving two or more independent classifications (nominal variables) and to test null hypotheses based on those classifications.

Chi-Square (χ^2) for Two or More Independent Variables

The chi-square statistic (χ^2) is the appropriate research tool for analysis whenever data consists of a number of cases observed in a series of independent nominal or categorical groups. Nominal data such as gender, ethnicity, therapeutic regimen, political affiliation, and even eye color can be used as an independent variable. Other independent variables for analysis by a chi-square can be ordinal data such as socioeconomic status, final placement in a contest, or ranked position within a profession.

Null Hypothesis for χ^2 With Two or More Independent Variables

The basic null hypothesis for research involving chi-square with two or more variables is that the observed distribution of cases by level (cell membership) is the same for all levels of the independent variables. Chi-square is used to determine the probability that the observed frequencies within the cells follow a random pattern or reflect a sampling error.

Applications from the Literature

Using Chi-Square in Hypothesis Testing

Note: The acronym MDMA stands for the chemical name of the street drug "meth," or 3,4-methylenedyoxymethamphetamine. In this study of factors linked to meth use, the author's Research Question I was "What is the relationship between alcohol and illicit substance use, on the one hand, and differing diagnostic criteria of young adult MDMA users, on the other?" Hypotheses 1 and 2 were "Gay, lesbian, and bisexual young adult users of MDMA are more likely to be dependent users of MDMA than are heterosexual young adult users of MDMA," and "Young adult male users are more likely to be dependent MDMA users than are young adult female users."

Results: Sociodemographic characteristics of respondents are presented in Table I according to classification of MDMA usage. There was no significant difference among recreational, abusing, and dependent young adult MDMA users in age, {[Chi-Square] $(14, N = 268) = 11.80, p = .62$}; gender, {[Chi-Square] $(2, N = 268) = 1.38, p = .50$}; racial background, {[Chi-Square] $(10, N = 268) = 7.21, p = .71$}; employment status, {[Chi-Square] $(6, N = 268) = 3.33, p = .76$}; or sexual orientation, {[Chi-Square] $(4, N = 268) = 2.01, p = .73$}. Therefore Hypotheses 1 and 2 of Research Question I were not supported. Of the 268 respondents, 84 (31.3 %) reported having been homeless at least once in their life, whereas 31 (11.6%) participants identified themselves as homeless in the previous 6 months. Nearly 3 out of every 10 respondents had dropped out of high school before the age of 18. MDMA dependence was significantly higher in individuals who either reported having dropped out of high school, {[Chi-Square] $(2, N = 268) = 5.86, p = .048$}, or acknowledged recent homelessness, {[Chi-Square] $(10, N = 268) = 18.44, p = .049$}.

Source: Dew, B. J., Elifson, K. W., & Sterk, C. E. (2006). Treatment implications for young adult users of MDMA. *Journal of Addictions and Offender Counseling, 26*(2), 84–98. doi: 10.1002/j.2161-1874.2006.tb00010.x

Computational Example of Chi-Square Contingency Table

The first step in the process is to establish a contingency table in the form of a matrix presenting all the levels of the independent variables. In the contingency table, there can never be a cell that does not have one or more cases from the observed data (there can be no zero cells). For instance, a practitioner-researcher interested in a gender equity question regarding faculty professional advancement at a small college could employ a chi-square analysis. In that process, the first step would be to establish a table for the two variables. In this hypothetical study, one independent variable (gender) has two levels, and the second independent variable has four levels (faculty ranks). The contingency table presents the observed data in a 2 × 4 table (see Table 11.2). Data for such a table could be found in the faculty listing in the back of any college bulletin and on the university's website. Also, most academic department webpages list all faculty and provide their academic rank.

Table 11.2   Example of a 2 × 4 Chi-Square Contingency Table

	Instructor	Assistant Professor	Associate Professor	Professor	Marginal Totals
Male Faculty	A	B	C	D	$A + B + C + D$ Marginal Total for Males
Female Faculty	E	F	G	H	$E + F + G + H$ Marginal Total for Females
Marginal Totals for Faculty Ranks	$A + E$ Total Instructors	$B + F$ Total Assistant Professors	$C + G$ Total Associate Professors	$D + H$ Total Professors	$A + B + C + D + E + F + G + H$ Total Faculty

Once the cells are populated with the number of observed cases falling into each of the two categories (gender by rank), the next step is to calculate what would be expected if the cells followed a random pattern. This is found as a series of simple proportions. For example, we observe that 50 of the 90 full-time faculty of the college are males. For that reason, we expect that $\frac{50}{90}$ or 56% of the total in each rank of the faculty will be men. Thus, the expected number of faculty in cell A (male instructors) should be 56% of the total of $A + E$. Likewise, the total number of female faculty is 40, so we can expect that 44% of each category of faculty rank should be the women of the faculty.

Using the observed number of faculty in each of the cells in Table 11.2, we can find the expected population in each. For example,

$$A \text{ (male instructors)} =$$

$$\frac{50}{90} \text{ multiplied by } A + E \text{ (all instructors)} =$$

$$\frac{50}{90} \times 24 = 13.33$$

Likewise, the expected number of female professors is found as $\frac{40}{90}$ of the total 29 professors on the faculty, or $H = \frac{40}{90} \times 29 = 12.89$. This ratio approach can be employed to complete the contingency table, as shown in Table 11.3.

Table 11.3   Example Data From a Hypothetical Gender Equity Study

	Instructor	Assistant Professor	Associate Professor	Professor	Marginal Totals
Male Faculty	$O = 9$ $E = 13.33$	$O = 8$ $E = 10$	$O = 12$ $E = 10.56$	$O = 21$ $E = 16.11$	50 total males
Female Faculty	$O = 15$ $E = 10.67$	$O = 10$ $E = 8$	$O = 7$ $E = 8.44$	$O = 8$ $E = 12.89$	40 total females
Marginal Totals for Faculty Ranks	24 total instructors	18 total assistant professors	19 total associate professors	29 total professors	90 total faculty

To find the chi-square statistic, it is necessary to employ Karl Pearson's formula once again: $\chi^2 = \sum_{i=1}^{k} \frac{(O-E)^2}{E}$. This equation will have eight cells of $\frac{(O-E)^2}{E}$ to calculate and add together. Thus, $\chi^2 = \frac{(9-13.33)^2}{13.33} + \frac{(8-10)^2}{10} + \frac{(12-10.56)^2}{10.56} + \frac{(21-16.11)^2}{16.11} + \frac{(15-10.67)^2}{10.67} + \frac{(10-8)^2}{8} + \frac{(7-8.44)^2}{8.44} + \frac{(8-16.11)^2}{16.11}$

After all that arithmetic, we can report $\chi^2 = 13.1$. To test the null hypothesis, it is necessary to know how many degrees of freedom are associated with the contingency table. In chi-square studies with a contingency table, the degrees of freedom are found as the number of rows minus one times the number of columns minus one [$df = (r - 1)(c - 1)$]. In this hypothetical example, there are 2 rows (gender) and 4 columns (faculty rank). Thus, the total is $df = 3$. Using Table 11.3, we can reject the null hypothesis of gender equality for the promotion of the college's faculty at the $\alpha = .01$ level.

Applications from the Literature

Example of Chi-Square Contingency Table in a Counseling Journal

Note: In this international study, there were two independent variables (nation: Russia and United States) and three medical conditions (AIDS, hearing impairment, and spinal cord injury). Thus, the principal chi-square analyses involved 2 × 3 contingency tables. One table was needed for each of the four dependent variables (ability focus, disability focus, negative emotions, and stigma). These categories were the product of open coding of an open-ended questionnaire completed by undergraduate students in two countries.

The sample of subjects was freshmen students from a midsize Russian university (N = 60) and a midsize southern university in the United States (N = 55). Each group answered a series of open-ended items about their stereotypes regarding individuals with disabilities. The two groups were tested for differences in their coding nodes with chi-square analyses. Data are reported in Table 11.4.

Results: To examine where differences might exist between the two samples, further chi-square analyses were conducted. . . . The results of separate chi-square analyses on each superordinate category indicated a significant difference for two superordinate categories: Ability Focus, $\chi^2 = 22.06$, $p < .05$, for which the highest percentage of responses was located in the Hearing Impairment category (United States = 60% and Russia = 48%), and Negative Emotions, $\chi^2 = 9.09$, $p < .05$, for which the highest percentage of responses was in the AIDS categories (United States = 45% and Russia = 56.6%). The following two comparisons between the superordinate categories of the Russian and U.S. samples were not significant: Disability Focus, $\chi^2 (df, 2) = 4.28$, $p < .05$, and Stigma, $\chi^2 (df, 2) = 4.24$, $p < .05$).

Source: Martz, E., Strohmer, D., Fitzgerald, D., Daniel, S., & Arm, J. (2009). Disability prototypes in the United States and the Russian Federation: An international comparison. *Rehabilitation Counseling Bulletin, 53*(1), 16–26. doi: 10.1177/0034355208329357

Table 11.4   Comparison of Frequencies of Superordinate Prototypes by Disability Between Russian and US Samples

	AIDS		HI		SCI		Row Total
Responses Reported	*n*	*%*	*n*	*%*	*n*	*%*	*n*
Ability focus (RU)*	117	44.0	128	48.0	21	8.0	266
Ability focus (US)*	44	24.0	111	60.0	30	16.0	185
Disability focus (RU)	230	27.0	274	32.0	356	41.0	860
Disability focus (US)	205	30.0	187	27.0	295	43.0	687
Negative emotions (RU)*	142	56.5	70	28.0	39	15.5	251

(Continued)

Table 11.4 (Continued)

Responses Reported	AIDS		HI		SCI		Row Total
	n	%	n	%	n	%	n
Negative emotions (US)*	28	45.0	14	23.0	20	32.0	62
Stigma (RU)	31	58.0	4	7.0	19	35.0	54
Stigma (US)	24	73.0	4	12.0	5	15.0	33

AIDS = acquired immunodeficiency syndrome; HI = hearing impairment; SCI = spinal cord injury; RU = Russian sample; US = US sample.

Percentages were calculated by frequency of disability category and row total. Note that two superordinate categories (positive emotions and random responses) were eliminated because of zero cells (which violates the assumptions of the chi-square test of significance).

Beyond the Use of Two-Dimensional Contingency Tables

Researchers may need to conduct a nonparametric analysis of data when more than two ordinal variables are used to group and organize the participants. For example, the study described above of faculty rank and faculty gender could be expanded to include a much larger academic unit, such as a state university. In this case, the researcher is likely to layer the data for analysis. The logical third layer after the dimensions of rank and gender is the colleges and/or schools within the university. Thus, a two-way (rank by gender) contingency analysis with chi-square could be conducted for the members of each component of the university. For example, a separate analysis would be conducted with data from the law school, college of arts and letters, school of education, college of medicine, school of engineering and science, school of business and finance, college of agriculture, school of health and recreation, and others.[4]

The same model for analysis could be used to test employment status equity on other dimensions, including ethnicity or race, political affiliations, or, at some denominational colleges, the religious backgrounds of faculty and staff.

Applications from the Literature

Two Layers of a Multilayer Employment Equity of Social Work Educators Across the Colleges and Universities of Canada

Note: Other dimensions of equity for social work faculty studied by the authors included salary, ethnic group, academic background, and sexual orientation.

Results: Gender of 184 faculty members, approximately two thirds (117) were women and one third (67) were men, including full professors, associate professors, assistant professors, lecturers, instructors, and other full-time teaching faculty members. No faculty members were identified as "other" in the gender category. Some of the lecturers and instructors held tenure-track positions but were in the rank of lecturers and instructors until they completed their doctoral degrees. Due to the small sample size, the data on rank [were] aggregated and analyzed using only two categories: those who are usually in tenured positions (i.e., full professors and associate professors) and those who hold un-tenured positions (assistant professors and other full-time teaching faculty including full-time lecturers and instructors). The analyses revealed strong evidence for an unequal rank distribution of men and women: 43.6% (51) of female faculty were categorized as full or associate professors, as opposed to 77.6% (52) of male faculty ([Chi-Square] = 20.012, df = 1, $p < .0001$). The Internet search revealed that 48.6% (17) of 35 deans and directors of schools are women. The questionnaire data revealed no statistical difference in gender distribution of faculty members in administrative leadership positions. However, when the field directors were excluded from these senior faculty positions, men were more likely to be in senior administrative positions (29.9% of men) than women (14.5% of women; [Chi-Square] = 6.225, df = 1, $p = .013$). In other words, only 1 in 7 women were in senior leadership positions when field directors were excluded from the analysis, as opposed to close to 1 in 3 male faculty members.

Source: Sakamoto, I., Anastas, J. W., McPhail, B. A., & Colarossi, L. G. (2008). Status of women in social work education. *Journal of Social Work Education, 44*(1), 37–62.

Data Management and Calculation Assistance

There are a large number of statistical software solutions for computing chi-square. The major statistical software programs supported on university servers all have solutions for chi-square problems. The Excel program on most Windows operating systems can also be used to calculate chi-square, http://www.gifted.uconn.edu/siegle/research/ChiSquare/chiexcel.htm. In addition, the following is a partial list of websites that will find the chi-square value from raw data:

David Eck, Jim Ryan, and the Mathbeans Project funded by the National Science Foundation, http://math.hws.edu/javamath/ryan/ChiSquare.html

GraphPad Software, http://www.graphpad.com/quickcalcs/chisquared1.cfm

JavaScript-Source freeware, http://www.quantpsy.org/chisq/chisq.htm

In addition, there are computational apps for the Apple iPad:

http://itunes.apple.com/us/app/chisquare/id301179602?mt=8

http://itunes.apple.com/us/app/statistics-visualizer/id371888586?mt=8

And there are chi-square computational apps for the Android system:

http://www.appbrain.com/app/chi-square-calculator/com.businesscompassllc
.chisquare/

http://www.androidzoom.com/android_applications/productivity/chisquare-calcula
tor_bnjm.html

http://www.androlib.com/android.application.com-businesscompassllc-chisquare-
xDDq.aspx

CASE IN POINT 11.1

An elegant, nonparametric method for hypothesis testing with small samples was the product of an informal social gathering. Ronald Fisher reported in his 1935 text the story of enjoying tea served al fresco at Cambridge with several university colleagues and their wives. During this afternoon tea, Dr. Muriel Bristol-Roach made the astonishing statement that she could tell whether the tea was added to milk already in the cup or whether the tea was in the cup before the milk was added. She insisted she could taste the difference. The gathering expressed their skepticism, as there was no known chemical process that could support such a proposition. It was Fisher who proposed an empirical experiment with eight cups of tea and milk. Dr. Bristol-Roach was not able to see how Fisher mixed the tea for her to sample. The cups were presented in an array with [four with tea first and four with milk first], and she gave her opinion of the sequence followed in making each mix. As it happened, she was correct for all eight assessments. The impressed statistician quickly determined the exact probability (based on the binomial theorem) of her performance to be $\frac{70}{256}$ or, $p = 0.273$.

This little experiment provided the core idea behind the principle of randomness central to Fisher's exact test (Salsburg, 2001). See the student website for more about Fisher's exact test and its application to small samples.

Wilcoxon-Mann-Whitney Test (WMW)

In 1945, Frank Wilcoxon published an article that was to change the field of non-parametric statistics. Wilcoxon's ideas provided a statistically powerful, distribution-free alternative to Gosset's t-test. That paper presented Wilcoxon's rank sum test. The statisticians Henry Mann and Donald R. Whitney later modified this test to allow the two independent samples being tested to have different numbers of subjects and published it as the Mann-Whitney U-test in 1947. Following that publication, the Mann-Whitney U-test was the name used to describe this versatile statistical procedure. Beginning in the 1990s the name Wilcoxon was gradually added to the moniker of the test, and today we describe the statistical procedure as the Wilcoxon-Mann-Whitney (WMW) test.

Applications from the Literature

Explaining the Reason for Employing the Wilcoxon-Mann-Whitney Statistical Procedure

Note: The study worked with 88 adults; 44 were diagnosed with ADHD, and 44 matched non-ADHD controls. All participants were not taking psychoactive drugs, had no sensory impairment, and had valid driver's licenses. The driving tests were all conducted in the university's driving-simulation laboratory and involved a real auto cab, controls, and dashboard. The computer simulations of driving were interactive, providing visual, auditory, and sensory input to the "driver" linked to the simulator's controls.

Results: Distributions of naturalistic and simulator performance scores did not meet normality assumptions. For example, rate-of-event measures (e.g., rate of crashes or rate of speeding tickets per year) were positively skewed because of a relatively low base rate of occurrences. For these measures, non-parametric Wilcoxon-Mann-Whitney tests were used to examine differences in the distributions of ADHD and comparison group performance scores. The test statistic U measures the degree of separation or shift between the two samples by comparing ranked scores.

Source: Knouse, L. E., Bagwell, C. L., Barkley, R. A., & Murphy, K. R. (2005). Accuracy of self-evaluation in adults with ADHD: Evidence from a driving study. *Journal of Attention Disorders, 8*(4), 221–234. doi: 10.1177/1087054705280159

Application of the WMW

The Wilcoxon-Mann-Whitney statistic can be used with ordinal data as well as parametric data. It is an alternative to Student's t-test and makes no assumption about the nature of the underlying distribution of data from which the samples were drawn. Unlike many other distribution-free statistical procedures, the WMW does not increase the likelihood of Type II error. The WMW is as statistically powerful as Student's t-test. The primary test statistic is the WMW U statistic, which is normally converted into a z-score for analysis.

The versatility of the WMW lends itself to a number of applications in counseling and other mental health research efforts. It can be an especially effective research tool in studies involving equity. For example, if a human relations department specialist felt that annual employee evaluations of a hospital had a pattern indicating possible bias (ethnic, gender, age, etc.), the WMW could provide a method to evaluate the suspected problem.

WMW Null Hypothesis Test

The WMW assesses the probability that two independent groups of data (X and Y) have the same distribution; thus, H_0: $p[X = Y] = \frac{1}{2}$. This is a two-tailed hypothesis with one of the alternatives being that group X is **stochastically** dominate over group Y and the second alternative being that group Y is stochastically dominate over group X.

Data Management and Computational Assistance

A more elaborate description of the calculation of the WMW tests, including computational examples, is available on the student website. Major statistical packages supported by university servers provide computational solutions to either the Mann-Whitney or the Wilcoxon-Mann-Whitney tests for independent samples. Microsoft's Excel can also be used to calculate the Wilcoxon-Mann-Whitney statistic; see http://blog.excelmasterseries .com/2010/09/mann-whitney-u-test-done-in-excel.html.

There are also online computational methods for computing the WMW statistic, including the following:

Richard Lowry (Vassar College), http://faculty.vassar.edu/lowry/utest.html

Patrick Wessa (Catholic University of Leuven, Belgium), http://www.wessa.net/rwasp_ Reddy-Moores%20Wilcoxon%20Mann-Witney%20Test.wasp

EasyCalculation.com, http://easycalculation.com/statistics/mann-whitney-u-test.php

In addition, there are apps for users of Apple iPad systems, including these:

Biostats Calculator 1.3.1, http://www.filecluster.com/iPad/Biostats-Calculator-137705 .html

iMedicalApps, http://www.imedicalapps.com/2011/05/biostats-calculator-evidence-based-medical-research/

Users of the Android system also can add an app to calculate the WMW test:

iMedicalApps, http://www.imedicalapps.com/2011/05/biostats-calculator-evidence-based-medical-research/

Applications from the Literature

Report of Results from Research Using Wilcoxon-Mann-Whitney *U*-Tests

Note: Patients receiving physical medicine service from a medical center typically are provided with several weeks of various therapies, including counseling or clinical psychology. One major class of patients includes those recovering from cerebral vesicular accidents (CVAs or strokes). In this study, the focus was on neuropharmacology as a treatment. The sample included 58 adult stroke victims who were all over the age of 40 at the time of the CVA. Two groups ($n = 34$ and $n = 24$) were provided different classes of therapeutic drugs. Measurement of the dependent variables "ability to perform activities of daily living" (ADL) and sensory-motor functioning was conducted after 30 days of treatment.

Abstract: Patients were subsequently divided into two groups based on the drugs received either immediately before the onset of neurological symptoms or during subsequent hospitalization. Patients receiving phenytoin, benzodiazepines (troazollam, choldiazepoxide, or alprazolam), neuroleptics (chlorpromazine, prochorperazine, or haloperidol), or other antihypertensive drugs (colidine or prazosin) constituted the "detrimental drug" group ($n = 24$). Patients receiving other medications formed the "neutral drug" group ($n = 34$). The two groups of patients were similar with respect to stroke risk factors, prognostic factors, and initial functional deficits. Compared to patients in the "neutral drug" group, patients in the "detrimental drug" group had poorer sensorimotor function (Mann-Whitney $U = 157$, $z = -2.04$; $p = .04$) and were less independent in activities of daily living (Mann-Whitney $U = 139$, $z = -2.37$; $p = .02$) 30 days after the stroke. "Detrimental drug" group patients also had overall slower 30-day recoveries (Mann-Whitney $U = 154$. $z = -.89$; $p = .004$).

Source: Goldstein, L. B., Matcher, D. B., Morgenlander, J. C., & Davis, J. N. (1990). Influence of drugs on the recovery of sensorimotor function after stroke. *Neurorehabilitation and Neural Repair 4*(3), 137–144. doi: 10.1177/ 136140969000400303

ANALYSIS WITH THREE OR MORE LEVELS OF AN INDEPENDENT VARIABLE

Kruskal-Wallis One-Way ANOVA

In 1952, two professors at the University of Chicago, William Kruskal, a mathematical statistician, and Allen Wallis, a professor of econometrics, published an extension of the Wilcoxon-Mann-Whitney U-test. The new Kruskal-Wallis H-test is an analysis method for testing a null hypothesis with ranked data for the dependent variable and with three or more levels of one independent variable. The primary statistic, H, is normally analyzed as a chi-square.

Null Hypothesis for the Kruskal-Wallis One-Way ANOVA

The null hypothesis for research employing **Kruskal-Wallis one-way ANOVA** focuses on the data medians for the various levels of the independent variable. Thus, the null hypothesis is the equality of the medians for the (k) levels of the independent variable. The alternative is that the medians are significantly different.

Computational Assistance

All major software packages supported on the servers of universities provide computational assistance with calculating and testing the H statistic. In addition, the Kruskal-Wallis one-way ANOVA can be calculated with the assistance of Microsoft Excel:

Excel, Microsoft, http://blog.excelmasterseries.com/2010/09/kruskal-wallis-test-done-in-excel.html.

There are also online solutions available for the Kruskal-Wallis one-way ANOVA:

Richard Lowry, Vassar College, http://faculty.vassar.edu/lowry/kw3.html

Chinese University of Hong Kong, http://department.obg.cuhk.edu.hk/ResearchSupport/KruskalWallis.ASP

An iPad app for the Kruskal-Wallis ANOVA is available through the iTunes store:

TC-Stats, Taft College, https://itunes.apple.com/us/app/tc-stats/id493316048?mt=8

And apps for the Android platform are available from the following:

Rawapps, http://www.rawapps.com/189364/prostats/

eXpertise2Go, http://expertise2go.com/e2gStats/

Applications from the Literature

The Use of the Kruskal-Wallis One-Way Analysis of Variance

Note: Professionals in the helping professions are likely to experience role strain and the stress that is associated with it. Nurse researchers have made role strain a research focus since the 1980s.

The authors tested four independent samples of nurses working with psychiatric patients. Each sample was drawn from nurses with different amounts of clinical experience. The nurses

Self-Rated Competence in PMHNP Role Dimensions by Years of Practice					
	Group Mean Competence Rankings Across Years of Practice Categories				
Variable (PMHNP Role Dimensions)	0-2 years (n = 27)	3-5 years (n = 16)	6-10 years (n = 26)	11+ years (n = 61)	KW p Values ($\alpha = p \leq .05$)
Conducting psychiatric evaluations	28.3[a]	48.5[b]*	74.1[c]*	78.1	.000
Differentiating psychiatric from neurological/medical diagnoses	34.3[a]	56.5[b]	73.2	74.5[c]	.000
Developing treatment plans	28.6[a]	57.3[b]	63.1	81.2[c]	.000
Applying therapy modalities	33.0[a]	46.7	61.9[b]	81.7[c]	.000

were tested with seven measures related to role strain. Each of these measures provided data to assess a separate null hypothesis, for a total of seven dependent variables measuring role strain.

Variable (PWlHNP Role Dimensions)	Group Mean Competence Rankings Across Years of Practice Categories				
	0-2 years (n = 27)	3-5 years (n = 16)	6-10 years (n = 26)	11+ years (n = 61)	KW p Values ($\alpha = p \le .05$)
Managing medications	29.9[a]	57.4[b]	74.5	74.9[c]	.000
Managing multiple tasks	34.8[a]	55.5[b]	75.8	72.6	.000
Intuitive decision making	24.3[a]	55.3[b]	69.7	80.9[c]	.000

Note: PMHNP = psychiatric mental health nurse practitioner; KW = Kruskal-Wallis. *A change in superscript indicates a significant & change in group mean competence rankings as detected by Mac u-Whitney procedures.

Also note that the authors chose to reject the null hypotheses at ($\alpha < .05$). The computational results provided a level of Type I error probability of .000. This is a bit misleading. The logic of science implies that there is always some amount of error possibility when rejecting the null hypothesis. A better report would have presented the probability level as $p < .001$.

Source: Alber, L., Augustus, L., Hahn, S., Penkert, J., Sauer, R., & DeSocio, J. (2009). Applying Benner's model to psychiatric mental health nurse practitioner self-ratings of role competence. *Journal of the American Psychiatric Nurses Association, 15*(2), 126–137. doi: 10.1177/1078390309333181

SUMMARY

It is not always practicable to use parametric statistical analysis methods. This reflects the fact that dependent variables may be expressed as categorical membership or as ordinal ranks. Even ratio- and interval-level dependent variables may violate statistical assumptions required for *t*-tests and ANOVA.

The use of nonparametric statistical procedures is similar to the use of parametric methods in that both analytical procedures start with the development of an appropriate null hypothesis and a decision as to the confidence level required to reject the null hypothesis. The advantage of most parametric statistical tests is that they have lower likelihoods of making a Type II error than their nonparametric counterparts. The exception to this principle is the signed-ranks tests developed by Frank Wilcoxon and the Wilcoxon-Mann-Whitney *U*-test. These measures are as statistically powerful as Student's *t*-test and do not increase the chance of a Type II error.

A one-way ANOVA for three or more groups using ordinal dependent data can be performed using the Kruskal-Wallis procedure. This procedure is an extension of the two-independent-group

Wilcoxon-Mann-Whitney procedure that can test hypotheses involving more than two independent groups. When the null hypothesis from a Kruskal-Wallis ANOVA is not accepted, Wilcoxon-Mann-Whitney tests can be used to provide a method for multiple comparisons.

DISCUSSION QUESTIONS

1. Chi-square has been demonstrated to be a good research tool for testing gender equity questions. Use your new knowledge and one of the computational assistance software approaches to test an equity issue in an institution or environment in which you have an interest. For example examine the faculty listing on the web page of an academic department or college. Create a null hypothesis and use a chi-square contingency table to test the observed data. Then report your findings to the class.

2. Discuss what types (precision levels) of data can be analyzed using chi-square.

3. In what ways is the Wilcoxon-Mann-Whitney U-test similar to the t-test?

4. Outline a research study, including research questions and a null hypothesis, to evaluate the efficacy of psychotherapy by using an appropriate nonparametric statistical procedure.

NOTES

1.   The name *chi-square* uses the 22nd letter in the Greek alphabet, *chi* (χ). It is pronounced like the letters *ky* as in the word *sky*, not *hy* as in *shy*. The distribution of chi-square was popularized by Pearson's hypothesis-testing method; however, it was first developed by a forgotten professor of earth sciences and a geodesist, Frederick Robert Helmert, in 1875, 25 years prior to Pearson's publication.

2.   Yates's correction for small numbers of subjects or for chi-square problems where the $df = 1$ is Yates's chi-square $= \chi_Y^2 = \sum \dfrac{\left(|O - E| - 0.5\right)^2}{E}$.

3.   Chi-square is both the name of the test statistic developed by Karl Pearson and the name of a very useful method to test the null hypothesis using nominal and ordinal forms of data.

4.   One often overlooked academic group in such equity studies is the administration from the office of the president on down through the various vice presidents and provosts, deans, and directors.

SECTION V

Measurement and Psychological Assessments

"I didn't fail the test, I just found 100 ways to do it wrong."

Benjamin Franklin

Psychological testing is a big industry involving thousands of published and unpublished "research instruments." Third-party payment plans now typically require that therapeutic treatment plans be based on scientifically derived data, and this is one driver of testing. In addition, employment and school counselors have used educational, personality, and occupational preference tests as part of the services provided by their programs since the origin of their professions.

The wide use of psychological measurements notwithstanding, there continues to be great misunderstanding of them by the professionals who use them (McIntire & Miller, 2007).

Chapter 12   examines the issues related to using psychological measurements in a clinical setting. Today's insurance regulations and governmental policies limit the therapeutic hours available to work with clients. One way to improve the efficiency of counseling is through the use of psychological assessments. Psychological measures can help clients frame their problematic areas. This chapter presents the ethical concerns involved in the use of these measures, how to interpret the scores and profiles they provide, and how to identify and select appropriate measurement tools. Additionally, the chapter describes how to evaluate the usefulness and quality of psychological measurements.

Chapter 13   builds upon Chapter 12 and describes how clinicians can construct valid and reliable questionnaires, interviews, and checklists for use in their professional practice. Such locally developed instruments can be employed to help understand each client's progress. They also can provide the information about clients the practitioner needs to make data-informed decisions about treatment effectiveness. The second major theme of the chapter relates to collecting data from a sample of individuals, such as a clinic's staff or clients.

CHAPTER 12

Understanding and Evaluating Tests and Scores

"I often say that when you can measure what you are speaking about, and express it in numbers, you know something about it; but when you cannot measure it, when you cannot express it in numbers, your knowledge is of a meager and unsatisfactory kind."

Lord Kelvin

OBJECTIVES

By reading and studying this chapter, you should acquire the competency to do the following:

- Describe the qualifications required for practitioners using assessments and clinical measures in their practice.
- Explain three theoretical bases for the format of tests of personality.
- Describe and compare two methods of finding measurement reliability.
- Define and elaborate on the meaning of the statistic "standard error of measurement."
- Describe approaches used to find the reliability of criterion-referenced tests and performance assessments.
- Explain the relationship between validity and reliability.
- Contrast criterion and predictive validity.
- Discuss the validity requirement for measurement appropriateness.
- Evaluate the quality of published tests and measurements.
- Explain the concepts of standardized tests and standards-based testing.
- Interpret statistical symbols for test and measurement data.
- Understand the relationship of reliability to standard error.
- Explain the impact of the norm group on the validity of scores from a published test or measurement.
- Describe the meaning and several potential causes of the "score gap."
- Establish the appropriate conditions for assessing children who are English-language learners.
- Identify and locate independent quality reviews of tests and measurements.

INTRODUCTION AND MAJOR THEMES

Published assessments and measures are used by practitioners in the mental health fields to better understand and assist their clients. Employment counselors routinely use published measures to select people for hiring, and admission counselors use them to decide whom to select for specialized programs and higher education. Measures are also employed by clinical practitioners to assist clients in exploring their personal talents and aptitudes. Furthermore, assessments are involved in placement and custody decisions and as part of entitlement benefit decisions. Standardized measures are part of most diagnostic workups and provide guidance to multidisciplinary teams assisting clients.

Central to using such assessments is the need to understand how to interpret outcomes to clients and how to evaluate and compare instruments. The American Counseling Association (2003) addressed the issue of the proper use of assessments. Its recommendation was that the education of professional counselors require all new practitioners to understand concepts of reliability, **standard error of measurement,** and validity.

Assessments and other measures come with different levels of complexity for test administrators. For that reason, is there a need for standards addressing who may ethically use which type of assessment?

Training of Test Administrators

Scoring and interpreting various psychological assessments require that the practitioner administering the assessment be well trained for the task. Most assessment publishers require test users to have one of three levels of qualification. This three-level classification was a part of the first ethical statement published by the American Psychological Association in 1950 (Turner, DeMers, Fox, & Reed, 2001). Even though this 1950 policy has been long since superseded by other statements on qualifications and ethics by that organization, the original three-level model persists in the policies of test publishers and in the psychological literature.

Level A. This level of qualification requires only that the individual administrating the assessment have an ethical need to use these measures. No specialized education in testing and assessment is required at this level. This level of qualification includes most research assistants. The types of measures appropriate at this level include admission assessments and other standardized measures given de rigueur in the hospital clinic, school, and counseling center.

Level B. To be qualified to use B-level measurements and assessments, the user must have earned a master's degree in counseling, education, or psychology and have advanced training in measurement, including studies in measurement statistics, reliability, and validity. Those with advanced education in child development and childhood assessment may also qualify at level B without a master's degree, as can members of professional organizations requiring their members to be well qualified in test administration and interpretation. These organizations include, among others, the American Counseling Association, the International Reading Association, and the American Speech-Language-Hearing Association. Level B includes most group-administered tests of intelligence, measures of occupational preferences, attention-deficit disorder scales, and preschool developmental assessments.

Level C. To be qualified to use C-level measures, the individual must be highly educated and have had advanced training in psychological measurement. Typically, these people hold a doctorate in counseling, developmental psychology, or educational or school psychology or a have a PhD in other clinical fields in psychology. They hold advanced licensure from a state agency and are members of professional associations such as the American Psychological Association, American Counseling Association, or the National Association of School Psychologists. These professional associations require adherence to an ethical canon related to the education and training of those using C-level tests. These measures include most individually administered tests of personality or intelligence.

A large test publication firm, Pearson Assessment, has added an additional qualification level (level M) for medical personnel who employ clinical assessments in areas such as psychiatry and neurology.

There are two major classifications of assessments and tests. One type is focused on educational achievement and outcomes from the teaching-learning process. The other includes numerous varieties of psychological assessments, inventories, and tests. Psychological assessments provide a method for the practitioner to assess a client's traits, mutable attributes, preferences, prejudices, personal characteristics, personality, and cognitive dimensions (abilities and skills).

This chapter is divided into four segments. The first addresses issues of the ethical use of psychological assessments and measures. The second section addresses the core issues related to the statistical qualities of psychological measures. Next, this chapter provides a model for the evaluation and selection of a measurement for use in a clinical setting. The fourth component examines emerging formats used in psychological measurements.

ETHICS AND PSYCHOLOGICAL TESTING

Professional associations hold themselves to be keepers of the best traditions and practices of their fields and assume that the general public will have confidence in their work and respect for their members. To ensure this continuing regard of the public, the various professional associations publish guidelines for the ethical behavior and practice of their members. In the field of psychological assessment, the primary associations with an interest in the issues have published a single document on ethics. This document is the combined effort of the American Counseling Association (ACA), the American Educational Research Association (AERA), the American Psychological Association (APA), the American Speech-Language-Hearing Association (ASHA), the National Association of School Psychologists (NASP), the National Association of Test Directors (NATD), and the National Council on Measurement in Education (NCME).

The following are four principles drawn from that document (Joint Committee on Testing Practices, 2005):

1. The first of these principles for the ethical practice of testing involves communication with those taking the test. The purpose of the test and the areas to be measured should be fully understood by the test taker prior to the time of the test. The use of scores from the test should be explained and the test takers should be told how long their results will be kept on file.

2. The second area involves confidentiality. It is necessary for the test administrator to put into place procedures that ensure that the scores from individuals are never disclosed to people not having professional need for those data. In the case of minors, or those not competent, the parents or guardians are included in the group who should have access to the test score data.

   At another level, confidentiality involves the assessment or test itself. It is critically important that test materials be stored in a secure location and never released for review by interested others.

3. The third point is that the interpretation of the test scores should be carried out in a way consistent with the guidelines provided by the test developer and publisher. This also implies that the professional interpreting the scores should be trained in the use of the measure and knowledgeable of the assessment scores that the measure provides. Clients should be informed of their scores and the interpretation of the scores in a developmentally appropriate way, using understandable language. Clinicians who discuss score reports and profiles with clients should avoid psychological jargon and provide clear descriptions to the participants. This includes the process used by the various agencies in setting cut scores and defining the interpretation of findings. If there is a scoring error it should be corrected immediately and that correction carried through on all records.

4. Finally, a single score or profile on a test should never be used to determine the placement of an individual. Interpretations should always be made in conjunction with other sources of information.

An additional final principle involves instrument development and selection. A test or assessment should never be used for a purpose for which it was not designed and has not been standardized. The test or assessment's publisher should provide a manual documenting that the measure is reliable and valid for the tasks it is designed to accomplish. In addition, the manual accompanying the assessment or test should provide users with detailed directions. Also, the measure should provide evidence that there is no consistent gender bias or ethnic or racial group bias represented in the scores.

MEASUREMENT SCORES FROM PSYCHOLOGICAL TESTS

Personality Tests

These instruments measure the way humans behave in family and social settings and the thought processes behind those behaviors (Spies, Plake, & Murphy, 2005). A number of clinical assessment measures employ an interpretative scoring method. These include many **projective assessments,** including the Thematic Apperception Test (TAT) (Murray, 1943). The TAT was designed to tap into the client's deepest and most repressed psychological needs, motivations, and personality. It is scored as a series of themes produced in the oral responses of the client to less than fully defined stimulus photo plates.

The famous Rorschach inkblot test has been used since the 1920s and continues to provide a nebulous stimulus for clients to use as a basis for bringing their own definition to the 10 Rorschach plates (Rorschach, 1921/2007). Oral responses by clients being tested are recorded and transcribed, and one of two systems is commonly used to quantify the meaning behind the oral responses. The two widely used scoring models are those by Zygmut A. Piotrowski (1987) and John E. Exner Jr. (2005).

Statistically Based Scoring

Most modern personality measures are based on structured questionnaires that have been refined through factor analysis. Scores from these psychological tests tend to be in the form of statistical summaries. Likewise, measures of cognition, vocational preference, and sexuality are provided in statistical form. In statistical scoring, individuals' scores are defined by how they compare with the scores and score profiles of other individuals. Central to most of these are the normative groups used as the standard of comparison for individual clients taking the measure.

Normative Reference Groups

Published measures almost always rely on a comparison group known as the normative comparison group or, more simply, norm group to define the meaning of individual scores. Statistical data collected from norm groups are used to describe how any individual does compared to members of that group. These comparison scores may take several forms such as raw scores, percentiles, standard scores, stanines, and normal curve equivalent (NCE) scores.

Commonly Reported Scores

- **Raw score.** The total number of actual items on the measure that the client answered correctly or in an indicated direction. To better understand what a raw score indicates, the test report should indicate a statement of how many questions there were in total.
- **Percentile.** A part out of 100 of equal size; a 100th part of any group or set of data or objects. If raw scores are used, they must first be arranged in an ordinal sequence from lowest to the highest. A percentile includes 1/100th of all cases. The 1st percentile includes the lowest 100th part of the scores, while the 99th percentile consists of the best 100th part of the raw scores from the test. Because this type of percentile begins as an ordinal sequence, it is an ordinal Type I number and considered to be nonparametric.
- Another method of finding a test score's percentile is by comparing that particular score to the scores of the norm group. This method uses the norm group to set the standard of comparison for individuals who take the test. If a person's score is at the center point of the norm group, it would be at the 50th percentile, with half of the norm group's scores above and half below. That 50th percentile also has the name *median*. If a client's score was higher than three quarters of the norm group, her score would equal to the 75th percentile. When percentiles are found based on a normative distribution, then each individual percentile is a parametric score.

(Continued)

(Continued)

- **Standard scores or scaled scores.** There are numerous formats for standard scores (SS), sometimes referred to as *scaled scores*. They all are derived mathematically from a huge distribution of scores. Under normal conditions, a huge distribution of test scores will follow the mathematical laws of the normal curve (see Chapter 7 for a review). We know that 34% of all scores will be above and 34% will be below the mean score (arithmetic average score) by a unit of measurement called a standard deviation. Therefore, plus or minus 1 standard deviation includes the 68% of all scores closest to the mean (average).

  A standard score is based on standard deviation units above (positive values) and below (negative values) the mean. To make interpretation and comparisons easier, these scores are mathematically modified to make them all positive and give them recognizable values. One commonly reported standard score is the client's cognitive ability as measured by a test of IQ. Instead of values above and below the mean, IQ scores are mathematically designed to have a mean of 100. Each standard deviation is set at a value of 15. Thus, an IQ of 115 is 1 standard deviation over the mean of 100, and an IQ of 85 is 1 standard deviation below the mean of 100. Because 34% of all IQ scores are between the mean (IQ = 100 = 50th percentile) and 1 standard deviation over the mean (IQ = 115), adding the 34 percentile points to the 50th percentile shows that an IQ of 115 is at the 85th percentile.

- **Stanine.** The norm group can be divided into nine parts, with the middle seven parts (stanine 2 to 8) each being one half of a standard deviation wide. Because of the characteristic bell-shaped form of a normal distribution of scores, the central three stanines (4, 5, 6) encompass 55% of all cases. Stanines 1, 2, and 3 include the lowest 22.5% of all scores, and the top 22.5% of all scores are in stanines 7, 8, and 9. The top stanine, 9, includes the highest 4% of scores, while the lowest stanine, 1, includes the lowest 4% of scores.

- **Normal curve equivalent (NCE).** This is a standard score that has a mean of 50. One standard deviation above the mean (84th percentile) is an NCE score of 71. An NCE score of 29 is 1 standard deviation below the mean, and an NCE score of 10 is at the 3rd percentile of the normative distribution of scores.

Technical Manual

When a new assessment is marketed, the publisher should provide a **technical manual** describing the norm group used to provide the point of comparison for interpreting each client's outcome. The norm group should be a good representation of all individuals in America today. Also, it should be large enough that when divided by age or gender for comparison, the subgroups still provide a representative sample of individuals making up the norm by gender and/or age group. These norm groups should reflect all races, both genders, various SES levels, and different geographic regions.

Another consideration when evaluating a test is the era of the cohort of individuals included in the comparison sample (Kolen, 2006). Many measures base normative scores on old comparison groups. This happens when the test is not revised for 10, 20, or more years. Norm-group standardizations usually occur starting 1–2 years before the publication of new editions of the measure. Individuals today are very different from those of the 1980s and 1990s, so score comparisons with an old cohort are less valid than are comparisons to a contemporary sample.

The technical manual should also provide proof that there are no biasing effects in the normative group. The **Rasch IRT technique** can be applied to the task of analyzing test items for bias. This analysis is known as testing for **differential item functioning (DIF)**. Using the Rasch model, it is possible to determine whether an item functions differently for different groups (e.g., gender, ethnicity, SES). Bias can be easily seen by examining the **item characteristic curves** (ICCs) of various groups of students.

An ICC is an ogive that shows on a graph the relationship of item performance and the underlying ability of the clients taking the assessment. On these ogives, the abscissa presents the various levels of known examinee ability. These are expressed in standardized units above and below the mean, which is designated zero. The ordinate depicts the cumulative number of examinees who chose the right answer on the item. An ogive differs from the Gaussian normal curve in that it shows the cumulative number of examinees passing the item (see Chapter 7 for a review). The ICC curve can be compared among ethnic groups or between genders to find out whether they match or are significantly different. This is an application of goodness-of-fit (Chapter 10) statistics. All items across all groups should have ogives that align with one another.

The technical manual should also present information as to the reliability and validity of the psychological measure. Of the two dimensions of measurement quality, the primary issue is with reliability, because no measure can ever be valid if it is not first reliable.

RELIABILITY OF PSYCHOLOGICAL MEASUREMENT SCORES

> *"Every careful measurement in science is always given with the probable error. . . . Every observer admits that he is likely wrong, and knows about how much wrong he is likely to be."*
>
> Bertrand Russell

A test or assessment with a low level of reliability can be thought of as a random number generator. Reliability is a simple mathematical statement of the dependability, stability, and consistency of the outcome scores from a measure. When a test provides scores that have a high level of reliability, a client is likely to earn the same score on that measure each time the client is reevaluated. Any change in scores from one testing to the next may be seen as an indication the client has changed, not that the measurement is unstable. When reliability is low, on the other hand, scores from a second administration of an assessment or test have no or very little relationship to the scores from the initial administration of the test. Only by employing a highly reliable assessment can client change be monitored.

Low levels of reliability may reflect any number of interfering factors, including those related to the test taker's health, comfort, and motivation; the testing environment; and the clinician's frame of mind and assessment administration skill. Reliability is also linked to factors directly related to the test or assessment and its items.

Stability as a Measure of Reliability

The central issue in the value of any assessment procedure or psychological measurement is stability. The stability of a measure can be demonstrated and assessed using a number of systems. These include test-retest, alternate form, and alternate form over time tests of reliability.

Test-Retest Reliability

One way to demonstrate reliability is to administer a test or assessment to a sample of individuals, then administer the instrument again after a period of time. The Pearson correlation between the two administrations of the assessment provides a measure of test **stability, or test-retest reliability.** The seeming simplicity of this approach is misleading. How much time elapses between test sessions is a significant confounding factor in the stability of the test. Naturally, the closer together the two test sessions are in time, the more likely the two scores will be similar to one another.

Table 12.1   Reliability Coefficients and Related Statistics

A. Correlation	Mathematical expression of covariance between two variables that can provide an expression of the stability of test scores over time.
Pearson coefficient r	Minimum is zero, and the maximum is ± 1.00. This can be employed as a measure of stability over time (test-retest reliability).
Spearman coefficient ρ	Greek letter *rho*, maximum ± 1.00, minimum of zero. This can be employed as a measure of stability.
Standard error of measurement *SEM*	A measure of how far true score potential spreads around an obtained score. This value is inversely linked to score reliability.
B. Internal Reliability	Forms of correlation that include an expression of the internal consistency of a test's items
Cronbach's α	Coefficient alpha. This measure of internal consistency has a minimum of zero and maximum of +1.00.
Kuder-Richardson KR-20	This measure of internal consistency has a minimum of zero and maximum of +1.00.
Coefficient kappa κ	This reliability measure for criterion-type measurements has a minimum of zero and maximum of +1.00.
Split-half reliability $r_{1/2}$	Maximum ± 1.00, minimum of zero. This can be employed as a measure of stability.
Spearman-Brown r_{SB}	This measure of internal consistency has a minimum of zero and maximum of +1.00.

There is no exact time interval that is the standard for test publishers to use in establishing test-retest reliability. A 2-week interval is commonly employed in this process, but it is not required by any regulation.[1]

CASE IN POINT   12.1

The Federal Aviation Administration (FAA) requires that all people holding a valid pilot's license be retested on a regular basis. For the private pilot who only flies for pleasure, the retest involves a physical examination by a flight surgeon, a flight test, and an oral examination administered by an FAA examiner every 2 years. Commercial and airliner pilots are tested more frequently and more intensely. The effectiveness of retesting depends on the reliability of the test procedure. The more time between test administrations, the more impressive the test-retest reliability.

In a similar way, most states require counselors and psychologists to engage in continuing professional development and undergo biannual relicensing. To date, none of the states requires a retesting program, but in the future they may.

Alternate-Form Reliability

When a test and retest are administered close together in time, the experience of having taken the test before can interfere with the score on the second test (see Chapter 14 for a discussion of this issue of interference). This can be problematic with projective measures. For this reason, many publishers provide alternative forms of the assessment or test. Alternative forms make it possible to evaluate a client initially with one version and retest with the alternate form. The correlation between the two versions is referred to as **alternate-form reliability.**

When an extended time interval elapses between the administration of the first and second assessments, it becomes possible to demonstrate **alternate forms over time reliability.** When an instrument has this reliability, the practitioner can use it to assess the progress clients make as a function of a therapeutic intervention.

Internal Consistency

When two alternate forms of a measurement are administered to the same sample of individuals in one extended testing session, the correlation between the two scores also provides an alternate-form reliability coefficient. However, the extended time period needed for this testing, and the inevitable fatigue that would result, makes this approach to finding alternate-form reliability less practicable than other methods.

As a practical matter, coefficients of internal reliability are positive and fall in a range between a low of .00 and a theoretical maximum of 1.00.

Split-Half Reliability

Reliability similar to alternate-form reliability can be determined through a less intensive approach to testing. Split-half reliability is a measure of reliability calculated as the internal consistency of the test. Finding split-half reliability simply involves dividing the measurement into two equivalent parts, for example, using all the odd-numbered items as though they represented one measurement and all the even-numbered items as the second measurement. Scores from the two halves could then be correlated to find reliability. This coefficient is one of several estimates known as internal consistency reliability.[2]

Spearman-Brown

A problem with **split-half reliability coefficients** is that the reliability of any measure is related to a number of factors, including the number of items or questions. As a general rule, measures with more items are more reliable. By dividing the test into two parts, the clinician-researcher has reduced the reliability of the assessment. In 1910, two psychometricians working independently, without knowledge of each other's efforts, found the same solution to this problem of reliability loss. Charles Spearman and the lesser-known William Brown both submitted their findings for publication to the *British Journal of Psychology*. The editors elected to publish both papers back-to-back in the same issue, thus providing a name for the new reliability statistic, the Spearman-Brown prophesy formula (W. Brown, 1910; Spearman, 1910).

The Spearman-Brown prophesy formula (r_{SB}) can also be used to estimate the change that would happen if the test were lengthened or shortened by any number of items (Feldt & Brennan, 1989). The Spearman-Brown coefficient lies along a scale from a minimum value of .00 and a maximum value of 1.00 (see the student website for more computational detail about the r_{SB} reliability statistic).

Applications from the Literature

Example of Reliability Coefficients Reported in the Development of a Psychological Test

Note: This pilot study (study 1) of a widely used research instrument, the Attitudes Toward Women Scale (AWS) involved a sample of 43 female college students, their mothers, and their grandmothers (total = 129). It assessed reliability for the full 55-item version and for abbreviated versions of 25 and 15 items. Study 2 included 511 male (n = 255) and female (n = 356) college students enrolled in an undergraduate psychology class. The two tests were administered in class 3 weeks apart. The items of the AWS do not have "right" and "wrong" answers. For that reason, the KR-20 reliability coefficient could not be calculated.

Internal and Test-Retest Reliabilities of the 55-, 25-, and 15-item Attitudes Toward Women Scales			
	Cronbach alpha	*Spearman-Brown split half*	*Test-retest*
Study 1			
55-item (*N* = 103)	.92	.93	
25-item (*N* = 118)		86	_____
15-item (*N* = 122)	.85	M	_____

Results and Discussion: Cronbach alpha and Spearman-Brown reliabilities for the 55-item, 25-item, and 15-item scales are presented in the next table for study 1. The table also presents the reliability coefficients for the split-half reliability of the 15-item scale.

	Cronbach alpha	Spearman-Brown split half	Test-retest
Study 2			
Total Sample (N = 511)			
15-item pretest	.81	.83	.86
15-item posttest	.84	.87	

Source: Daugherty, C. G., & Dambrot, F. H. (1986). Reliability of the Attitudes Toward Women Scale. *Educational and Psychological Measurement, 46*(2), 449–453. doi: 10.1177/001316448604600221

Kuder-Richardson

In 1937, two psychologists, G. Frederick Kuder and W. Richardson, presented a new solution to the problem of finding reliability through the study of a test's internal consistency (Kuder & Richardson, 1937). The 20th equation they developed proved to be an appropriate approach. Their formula, abbreviated as KR-20, can be calculated without cutting the test into two equivalent parts. This approach assumes that each item is scored as a dichotomy (i.e., right or wrong). For that reason, it is frequently used to demonstrate the reliability of achievement and cognitive ability tests that use a multiple-choice format. The KR-20 coefficient is also scaled from .00 to a maximum of 1.00.

Applications from the Literature

Description of the Use of the Kuder-Richardson Coefficient

Note: The purpose of this research was to examine the relationship between cultural mistrust and psychological health. The participants for this study were 125 African American students, 83 of whom were women and 42 men, from a large, predominantly white, Midwestern university. The excerpt is background information about the paranoia measure used in the main body of the research carried out by Bell and Tracey.

Instruments: Millon Clinical Multiaxial Inventory Paranoia Scale (MCMI-PA). The MCMI-PA was included as an indicator of global distrust of others and is a 35-item scale from the Millon Clinical Multiaxial Inventory (MCMI). The MCMI is a self-report test of the continuum model of

(Continued)

(Continued)

psychopathology. Respondents answer true (T) or false (F) to the statements. Millon reported a 5-week test-retest reliability estimate of .77 on a sample of inpatients and outpatients, and a Kuder-Richardson Formula 20 (KR-20) coefficient of .82 for a similar sample for the paranoia scale. Coefficient alpha for the present sample was .66.

Source: Bell, T. J., & Tracey, T. J. G. (2006). The relation of cultural mistrust and psychological health. *Journal of Multicultural Counseling and Development, 34*(1), 2–14. DOI: 10.1002/j.2161-1912.2006.tb00022.x

Cronbach's α

When a measure of internal consistency is needed for a measurement that includes items not scored as a dichotomy, an appropriate reliability coefficient assessing internal consistency is the coefficient alpha, α. For this reason, Cronbach's α is widely reported for psychological assessments. The α coefficient can be thought of as an extension of the Kuder-Richardson KR-20 method. The coefficient α also is equivalent to all split-half reliability coefficients that could be created from the test, but it goes further. Cronbach's α coefficient includes the ability to calculate reliability estimates when the test is divided into many parts (Cronbach, 1951; Cronbach & Meehl, 1955).

Standard Error of Measurement

The approaches for assessing the stability and reliability of a measure are based on samples of subjects and only estimate what would happen with a whole population. (This principle was discussed in more depth in Chapter 9.) In **classical measurement theory,** when all of the other factors that can influence test scores are somehow magically removed, any difference between the scores on the test and retest for individuals can be thought of as being caused by measurement error (Gulliksen, 1950). If a hypothetical subject could tolerate being retested hundreds of times, the summation of all measurement errors from that exhaustive exercise would approach the value of zero. This is because sometimes the measurement error would add points to the test's score and other times it would shave points off the observed test score.

True score = Observed score $\pm$ Measurement error

In other words, the error of measurement is random and distributes as a normal curve around the theoretical true scores for individuals. The standard deviation of these measurement errors is the statistic known as the standard error of measurement (SE_m).

There is little likelihood of ever determining a test's standard error of measurement by this empirical approach. However, there is a way to estimate the value of the standard error of measurement as a function of the test's reliability. In the following equation, SE_m represents the standard error of measurement, and s represents the standard deviation of the set of scores:

$$SE_m = s\sqrt{1 - Reliability}$$

As an example, the Stanford-Binet Intelligence Scale, 5th edition, has a standard deviation of 15 and a reliability of .98. Therefore, the standard error of measurement is found as

$$SE_m = 15\sqrt{1 - 0.98}$$
$$SE_m = 15 \times 0.14$$
$$SE_m = 2.1$$

The implication here is that a client who is tested and found to have an IQ of 127 has a true IQ score that (at a 95% level of confidence) lies between 123 and 131. This range is equal to plus or minus 2 standard errors of measurement around the observed IQ score. This principle is similar to that of finding confidence intervals around mean (average) scores discussed in Chapter 9.

The Stanford-Binet is America's oldest measurement system still in continuous use. Since its first edition in 1911, its reliability in measuring the IQs of middle-class, white-Anglo individuals has been highly respected. Yet, even this "old nugget" is not without measurement error. The point is that all measurements have a degree of error that is part of the scores they provide. Many tests may be seen by individuals taking them as being **high-stakes assessments.** This includes license examinations, admissions tests, and job placement tests. Few test scores on a psychological measurement can be described as truly life or death, but an exception is described in Case in Point12.2.

CASE IN POINT 12.2

Tests of intellectual functioning are now a matter of life and death. In 2002, the US Supreme Court in a landmark case, *Atkins v. Virginia*, 536 U.S. 304, ruled that it is a violation of the constitution to execute an individual who has a significant intellectual disability. This ruling was based on the Eighth Amendment to the US Constitution, which prohibits the imposition of "cruel and unusual punishment."

This ruling has two implications for forensic psychologists assigned to assess the intelligence level of a convicted individual. First, each generation of IQ tests has more stringent standards based on the improving capabilities of the normative samples in America. This increment is occurring as a result of increasing levels of education, better nutrition, and other factors (Flynn, 1987). Thus, the normative bar is set higher today than it was a generation ago. The implication is that a lower IQ score will result if a recently normed measure is used (e.g., WAIS-IV and SB-5) for conducting the forensic assessment. Knowing this fact, and working to avoid commuting a death sentence, some states require that to be declared mentally deficient and ineligible for being put to death, the mental deficiency must have been documented before the age of 18 years. That IQ assessment is likely to have been made using an older edition of the IQ test with what is assumed to be lower standards for scoring above the minimum of two standard deviations below the mean. If the cognitive assessment is conducted on the adult convict using a modern IQ test that was recently normed, he or she would likely have a lower mental ability score.

(Continued)

(Continued)

The second issue for forensic psychologists is the statistical issue of standard error of measurement. Most states use the standard of having an IQ less than 70 as defining a significant mental deficiency (Death Penalty Information Center, 2012). The standard error of measurement of both the WAIS-IV and SB-5 is about 2. This means that if the examining clinician finds a full-scale IQ of 71, he or she could, with 95% confidence, report the score as falling between 68 and 75. Such a finding could open the door for mitigating circumstances being found in the sentencing phase of the trial and possibly saving the life of the convicted prisoner.

Reliability of Performance Tests

Written essays and performance test items present other difficulties in terms of traditional concepts of reliability. The problem is all the more complex when the assessment score is based on a subjective evaluation of the client's performance. Reliability of an evaluation is enhanced when two or more clinicians are used to make independent assessments and provide scores or assign codes. Whenever two or more raters are used to subjectively evaluate a performance, another form of reliability becomes possible, **interrater reliability.** Because subjective evaluations frequently provide ordinal data, their reliability can be determined by employing Spearman's rho coefficient. Spearman's reliability coefficient provides a measure of the commonality of ratings provided by two raters. The reliability coefficient, when assessed as a Spearman coefficient rho (ρ), has a maximum value of +1.00 and a minimum value of −1.00. This latter case is highly unlikely unless one rater has no idea about the behavior or activity being evaluated. (See Chapter 8 for a discussion of Spearman's coefficient.)

Applications from the Literature

Use of Interrater Reliability Measures With Qualitative Data

Note: Graduate departments in most universities are responsible for selecting their students. This study focused on finding a reliable method to read and rate the admission statements written by applicants for a Midwestern university's graduate program in social work. The study included the written personal statements provided by the 119 applicants for the 64 available full- and part-time admission slots.

Discussion: Further, the results of this study appear to show that the inter-rater reliability of the personal statement scoring instrument is not particularly high. This raises the question as to whether the scoring of the personal statement is sufficiently reliable to rate applicants consistently given the small number of raters. The findings on inter-rater reliability also suggest, however, that individual subjectivity is reduced through the use of multiple raters, as demonstrated by the larger positive correlation between any two pairs of raters as compared to a pair of individual raters. . . . Further tests for inter-rater reliability could be supplemented by test-retest reliability measurement, to see if scores vary depending on time of scoring. These cautions and limitations might suggest that the impact of this measure should be lessened in determining admission until a more reliable measure is developed, and that at least two, and ideally more than two, raters should be used in the rating process.

Source: GlenMaye, L., & Oaks, M. (2002). Assessing suitability of MSW applicants through objective scoring of personal statements. *Journal of Social Work Education, 38*(1), 67–82.

Criterion-Referenced Tests

Mandated state-licensing tests, including those required for certification as a professional counselor or psychologist, result in pass-fail outcomes. These measures are considered to be examples of **criterion-referenced tests,** as they require a predetermined raw score (criterion score). That predetermined score, sometimes called a **cut score,** indicates at what level of performance the test taker may be classified as having mastered the field. Criterion-referenced measures depend on an absolute standard of quality rather than a relative standard set by the performance of others in a normative comparison group (R. Glaser, 1963).

Such a criterion-based licensing test usually has a more constricted range of raw scores than do most **achievement tests,** which are scored using a normative comparison group. This is because the criterion for passing is frequently set very high by the state-licensing agency.

Coefficient Kappa

This high standard for passing means that raw score data from criterion-based, dichotomously scored tests tend to be skewed toward the high side (negative skew). Such skewing reduces the variance among scores and therefore requires a different model for determining reliability. One of the various solutions to this problem is based on the **threshold loss** model (Cohen, 1960). *Loss* refers to the chance agreement between two assessments. Coefficient kappa (κ) is the proportion of agreement after the random chance for agreement is removed and is calculated as follows:

$$\kappa = \frac{\text{Proportion agreement} - \text{Proportion agreement by chance}}{1.00 - \text{Proportion agreement by chance}}$$

The calculation of this coefficient requires that the criterion test be administered twice to a group of subjects. The coefficient has a maximum level of 1.00 (perfect agreement or concordance among ratings on the tests) and a minimum of .00 (no agreement).

VALIDITY

"The most serious mistakes are not being made as a result of wrong answers. The truly dangerous thing is asking the wrong question."

Peter Drucker

Validity and Reliability

The reliability of a psychological measurement is a statement about the consistency and stability of scores derived from the instrument. Unfortunately, the scores from any measurement instrument may be consistent but wrong.

Validity is a statement of both the appropriateness of the measure and its components and of the veracity of the test scores and their interpretations. Thus, all tests must be judged not just as methods to quantify differences between individuals but also as measuring devices with a role to play in the social context of the client's life.

Cartoon 12.1   Well, he is reliable.

Cartoon by Merv Magus.

His reilability is excellent, but the validity cretainly needs much more improvement.

A test or assessment may be a reliable measure of anxiety but not be valid for some clients. For example, clients with limited language skills would not be accurately measured by a scale like the Manifest Anxiety Scale (Reynolds, Richmond, & Lowe, 2003). Reliability only provides information on the likelihood that similar scores will occur on retesting, not on whether the measure is of the correct dimension.

Likewise, a reliable test of cognitive ability may be used in the selection process for hospital employees who will work to maintain the building's grounds. As there is no body of evidence supporting a link between cognitive ability and being a groundskeeper, such a test would be inappropriate and clearly not be a valid employment-screening device.

The two undergirding concepts in the framework of validity are (1) the fidelity of the test or assessment to the stated goal(s) for the measurement and (2) the appropriateness of the interpretations and applications for which the scores are used.

Criterion Validity

One method to demonstrate fidelity and document the validity of a measure is to employ correlation to find the degree of agreement of a psychological test score and another, known criterion. The criterion could either be another well-accepted measure of the underling dimension being assessed (**criterion validity**) or a direct observational assessment of the dimension **predictive validity** (Cronbach & Meehl, 1955).

Concurrent Validity

The core concept of **concurrent validity** is that the validity of a measure can be established by referencing scores from another measure or standard. This form of validity is expressed as a correlation. A high degree of correlation demonstrates that the measure has a degree of fidelity with the accepted measures of the domain.

One limitation to the usefulness of this form of criterion validity is the difficulty in identifying an appropriate criterion (Kane, 2006). Nebulous psychological dimensions such as creativity, emotional intelligence, and parenting skill are examples of variables that are very difficult to operationally define. For that reason, many authors of psychological assessments use an array of other related measures to document a new instrument's validity. This process of using multiple measures is central to establishing **construct validity.**

Applications from the Literature

Example of Concurrent Validity in Developing a Psychological Assessment

Note: This validity study assessed the concurrent validity of a recent edition of the Cognitive Ability Scale using a sample of toddlers between the ages of 26 and 46 months. This research was followed 3 years later when the children were entering kindergarten and again 3 years after that when they were in the third grade.

Evidence for the Preschool Form's concurrent criterion-related validity is presented in the manual in terms of the relationship of the Cognitive Ability Scale, 2nd ed. (CAS-2) and the Bayley Scales of Infant Development–Second Edition (BSID-2), the Wechsler Preschool and Primary Scale of Intelligence–Revised (WPPSI-R), and the Pictorial Test of Intelligence–Second Edition (PTI-2). Correlations are high for both the CAS-2 and the General Cognitive Quotient (GCQ) ($r = .67$ to .82) and the Nonvocal Cognitive Quotient (NCQ) ($r = .80$ to .87).

Source: Swanson, J. R., Bradley-Johnson, S., Johnson, C. M., & O'Dell, A. R. (2009). The Cognitive Abilities Scale–second edition preschool form: Studies of concurrent criterion-related, construct, and predictive validity. *Journal of Psychoeducational Assessment, 27*(1), 46–56. doi: 10.1177/0734282908322454

Predictive Validity

The second form of concurrent validity, predictive validity, involves the correlation between a measure and an observed or measured outcome. This can be thought of as a specialized variation of concurrent validity (Sax, 1997). For example, the correlation between the GRE Advanced Test in Psychology and performance during the first year in a graduate program in counseling is in the $r = 0.56$ range (Chemyshenko & Ones, 1999; House & Johnson, 2002). These correlations are expressions of predictive validity. Predictive validity implies that GRE scores from the test taken as an undergraduate can be used to make predictive statements about how well graduate students will do as they complete a year of advanced studies (GPA), how well graduate faculty will rate them as students, and how well they will do as clinical interns in the health sciences (Greenburg, Durning, Cohen, Cruess, & Jackson, 2007). Establishing this form of validity involves determining the correlation or regression between the criterion (graduate school success) and the predictor (GRE Advanced Test in Psychology).

Limits: The stability (reliability) of the measures determines the upper mathematical limit that criterion validity can reach. This relationship is expressed as follows:

$$\text{Maximum predictive validity} = \sqrt{\text{Predictor's reliability} \times \text{Criterion's reliability}}$$

Thus, if the criterion has a reliability quotient of $r = .85$ and the predictor a reliability quotient of $r = .90$, the maximum predictive validity would be $r = \sqrt{0.765}$ or $.875$.[3]

One method for devising a reliable criterion is to identify individuals or cases that exhibit the behavior or dimension and those that do not. A criterion variable could be patients on a psychiatric service who comply with the physician's orders and those who do not. Or the criterion could be master's degree students who continue their education and earn a doctorate and those who do not.

Time can also be a limiting issue. The predictive validity of many measures is reduced over the time between when the predictor is measured and when the criterion is assessed. This reflects the deterioration that occurs in the reliability of measures over time intervals.[4]

Construct Validity

An important conceptualization of validity needed in the development of new psychological assessments is known as construct validity. This validation approach was first elaborated by Lee Cronbach and Paul Meehl in 1955. By their definition, construct validity is a validity assessment used for measures of an attribute or quality that is not operationally defined. It is used when no available criterion exists that could be used as a metric of the variable in a criterion validation study.

The process of construct validation links the theory behind the psychological construct with how it is being measured. The goal for this approach to validity is to document that an assessment has fidelity with the theoretical conceptualization of the variable being measured.

This process must start with a clearly stated theoretical framework for the variable to be assessed. The first step in delineating the theoretical foundation is an exhaustive literature search. This search focuses on those elements to be considered as part of the construct that is to be measured and that will describe the possible measurement properties of those elements. The literature review also provides parameters for the construct by identifying those related characteristics not to be included in a comprehensive description of the construct.

Variables not part of the construct being measured may interfere with the measurement process and invalidate the measure (Linn & Miller, 2005). For example, the measurement of the construct "empathy" by a written test may require the ability of subjects to read well. Reading is not part of empathy, but it would be considered a **construct-irrelevant element** appearing as a component of the measure.[5] The identification and removal of that construct-irrelevant element would be needed to ensure good construct validity for the measure of empathy.

Construct validity includes assumptions about content representativeness and the agreement of the measures with its theoretical structure; thus, it is an inclusive form of validity (Messick, 1989). The various identified dimensions within a new construct being evaluated for validity should each have several indicators or measures theoretically linked to the construct's framework. The intercorrelations among the various indicators and their measures provide an indication of the validity of the construct. There are two subsets to construct validity, **discriminant validity** and **convergent validity**. It is best if different indicators for discriminant and convergent validity are derived from different modalities for data collection (e.g., questionnaire, interview, observation).

Discriminant Validity

This form of validity is shown when the elements of a new construct's measurement have very low correlation with other constructs not theorized to be part of the new construct. For example, the theoretical construct of an "artistic nature" may or may not be a covariate of verbal creativity or of cognitive ability. In this case, the researcher would hope these traits do not correlate with the measures of the new construct.

Convergent Validity

This form of construct validity is seen when the correlations among elements of the new construct do correlate. For example in the ersatz construct "artistic nature," measures of "fashion knowledge" and "color acuity" may be thought to be theoretical components. Measures of these dimensions should be highly correlated with each other but relatively uncorrelated with cognitive ability and verbal creativity.

For the validity of the construct to be high, the correlations among the indicators through different methods for measurement should be high (D. T. Campbell & Fiske, 1959). The approach of employing both discriminant and convergent validity is known as the **multitrait multimethod method (MTMM).**

The outcome of the MTMM process of establishing construct validity can be further verified through the use of **confirmatory factor analysis (CFA;** Ferketich, Figueredo, & Knapp, 1991). In CFA, the **factor structure** should align the trait measures along the factors proposed in the construct's theory. (Factor analysis is explained on the student website.)

Content Validity

The form of validity most commonly associated with achievement tests, admission tests, and licensing examinations is **content validity.** Content validity is explained as the fidelity of the curriculum or attributes being tested with the various test items. Content validity also implies that the measured behaviors lie within the desired domain central to the appropriate performance area. Thus, the measure should assess the essential processes needed for what is being learned or included in the domain of behaviors. As an example, an evaluation of how well a graduate student learned clinical interviewing skills should go beyond simple textbook-based assessment. Instead, to have content validity, an assessment of clinical abilities should focus on practicum experiences and laboratory simulations. To be a valid measure of the clinical skills included in the assessment, the measured performance of those skills must be representative of the domain of skills within the field. Content validity can be described as a judgmental form of validity as it relates to complex behaviors such as clinical skills. However, a different approach to content validity is possible when the content validity of a measurement of achievement in a domain of knowledge is evaluated.

Before any measure of achievement content is designed, there must first be a blueprint that maps out the domain of knowledge to be assessed. The technical name for such a blueprint is **table of specifications.** Care should be taken to assure that each included item of measurement is aligned with the specifications of the content domain. A potential pitfall is in trying to measure low-consensus parts of the field for which items are not easy to develop. In low-consensus areas, content validity is much more complex to establish and is frequently bypassed in favor of a different form of validation (B. J. Miller, Sundre, Setzer, & Zeng, 2007). In counseling, high-consensus domains include quantitative methods, including statistics. Lower consensus is found in controversial areas like the mind-body dualism debate or debates over behaviorism and behavioral approaches versus client-centered approaches to therapy.

Appropriateness and Validity

The second undergirding factor in measurement validity is appropriateness. This refers to the uses to which tests are put. If a reliable and well-designed test is used to make a **high-stakes decision,** the results can have a number of possible unintended outcomes and side effects.

With the use of any assessment technique, the clinician makes tradeoffs. These measurement tradeoffs often reflect the clinician's emphasis on one altruistic goal or value over competing values.

Professional societies and state agencies typically hold a number of values that can impact the use of a test or the application of the scores derived from a test. A partial list of these altruistic values includes equal opportunity, assisting those with the most need, encouraging effort, fostering diversity, rewarding achievement and accomplishments, promoting public health and safety, respecting personal privacy, and supporting the common good. It is important to note that such values are not exclusive of each other and several can be served at the same time. However, conflict can arise between some values. It is the purpose of social policy to define which of the competing values should be served first.

The appropriateness of any test, and the validity of that test's use, should be the central concern of both those administering assessments as well as those being assessed and measured. For example, when a school's psychologist assesses a child from a racial or ethnic minority, the testing should be done to optimize the child's educational development. Such an assessment may lead to providing the student with learning support. That outcome is evidence that one of our society's values is being served, namely, to provide focused assistance to students who are academically at risk. Yet another value may be violated (equality) if this child increases an overrepresentation of minority children receiving learning support. In cases such as this one, it is the test user (school psychologist) in consultation with the child's parents who must decide which goal to serve.

A similar problem can occur with the selection of graduate students to receive fellowship support. The same values conflict noted above, between the goal of increasing diversity and the goal of enrolling students from prestigious programs who score well on selection instruments such as the GRE, may arise. As a solution to this potentially vexing dilemma, it is possible to consider alternative selection methods. The admissions and selection committee may elect to interview all applicants, review faculty recommendations, and examine work samples before making an award.

CASE IN POINT   12.3

The development and application of policy related to the use of measurements can provide unexpected results. The city of New London, Connecticut, developed an employment policy to test all applicants for law enforcement positions for their mental ability. The city's policy was that all police officers would have intelligence in the "normal range." Thus, those with measured IQ scores that were "too high" were screened out. This was to avoid the costly process of training new officers who would become bored and quit the job.

In 1996, an applicant was administered the Wonderlic Cognitive Ability Test and was measured as having an IQ of 125. He was rejected by the city's police department as being "excessively intelligent." The applicant, Robert Jordan, launched a suit in US federal court, and in 1999 Judge Peter C. Dorsey rejected his case and ruled in favor of the city's policy. Judge Dorsey based his ruling on the fact that all bright applicants, without regard to ethnicity or gender, were rejected. A news story about this situation can be read at http://www.nytimes.com/1999/09/09/nyregion/metro-news-briefs-connecticut-judge-rules-that-police-can-bar-high-iq-scores.html

Appropriateness as a dimension of validity implies there is an obligation for test publishers to clearly discuss all potential side effects and the full spectrum of ramifications that can result from the use of any test or assessment. This includes an obligation to test subsamples representing various minority groups (Joint Committee on Testing Practices, 2005). In part, appropriateness is met by a thorough analysis of the other aspects of the test's validity. However, the social policy implications need to be addressed specifically. Beyond this, the test user is obliged to evaluate all the potential consequences and consider all alternatives available before making an important evaluation based on measurement outcomes.

CASE IN POINT   12.4

In March 2005, a faculty committee with policy responsibility for admissions within the University of California system voted against continuing the use of Preliminary SAT (PSAT) scores in the selection of National Merit Scholarship award winners on the campuses of the university. The argument presented was one of validity and appropriateness. The faculty position was that the PSAT was never designed as a merit scholarship test. Also, they argued that as a result of the use of the PSAT, a disproportionately large proportion of white-Anglo and Asian students were awarded scholarships (Arenson, 2005). This directly relates to the issue of the social context and societal impact of the PSAT.

Testing Minority Group Members

There are many potential pitfalls in the assessment of individuals from racial and ethnic minorities. One lies in the normative standardization sample used by the test developer. It is difficult to build a norm group with adequate numbers to represent the diversity that exists within our society. Socioeconomic levels, living arrangements, geographic location, ethnicity, and mental ability levels all should be represented in a normative sample. Large-scale test developers and publishers strive to have a sample of tens of thousands that accurately represents the population of the United States. Other measures use a more refined and smaller sample. For example, the WAIS-IV used a normative sample of 2,200 adults between the age of 16 and 90 years who were stratified by gender, age, ethnicity, education level, and geographic region. With this approach of dividing the normative sample into many small groups, the potential for an anomalous normative subgroup is increased. (See Chapter 9 for a discussion of representative sampling.)

The question of appropriateness is also involved with assessments and tests with English-language learners. The expectation that any assessment protocol in English can be easily translated into another language is a fallacy. Likewise, it is a fallacy to assume that individuals who have lived in another language environment can be ready to think and answer assessment questions in English after a few months of immersion in an English-speaking environment. It takes about 3 years of immersion in an English-speaking environment for the native speakers of other languages to develop an English-language conversational ability, and an additional 4 years of immersion are needed to develop the cognitive framework in English to do academic work in an abstract and highly decontextualized context (Dong, 2007; Roseberry-McKibbin & Brice, 2005).[6] Recognizing this problem, many publishers have revised and standardized their assessments in other languages. Even this does not ensure the individual's ability to answer questions in the native language. There is a period in the process of learning a second language when the second-language learner is not fluent in either language. **Semilingualism** occurs when the student is not ready to speak conversational English and has lost some fluency in the original native language ability.

Cohort

Another pitfall in designing a normative reference group is using an inappropriate age cohort. The norm group used for a published test is typically developed and tested a year or so prior to the final publication of the new test or assessment. New editions of important measures are frequently published decades apart. In 100 years, there have only been five editions of the Stanford-Binet Intelligence Scales. Thus, it is possible that individuals being assessed today will have their scores based on a norm group who were tested 10 or 20 years ago. Different age cohorts have different cultures and skills and may not be an appropriate comparison group for a contemporary cohort. Our society is not static, and each age cohort experiences a different world.

CASE IN POINT   12.5

Face validity appears occasionally in the literature. This is not truly a matter of validity but rather one of inductive reasoning. The notion that a test or assessment should somehow appear to be an important and interesting task is the central theme of face validity. This is simply a public relations matter (i.e., if it looks like a duck and quacks like a duck, then it probably is a duck). The idea is that individuals will be more motivated if the measurement instrument appears to be well designed and in some way important.

COMPUTERS AND PSYCHOLOGICAL TESTS

A new ethical concern and a new opportunity are emerging through the use of online testing programs. Much of the work in assessing clients in the counseling profession is being eliminated by computer-based testing and online testing. Recognizing this sea change, the American Psychological Association formed a task force to examine the issues (Naglieri et al., 2004).

That committee found over 750,000 online Internet sites offering psychological tests in 2003. By the spring of 2012, that number had grown to over 2,000,000. A survey in 2003 by the Pew Foundation reported that almost a quarter of the American population had used the Internet to look for information about a mental health issue such as depression (Lenhart, Fallows, & Horrigan, 2003). By 2012, about 80% of American adults were online, and 80% of that group used the Internet to look up health-related questions including about mental health (Pew Internet & American Life Project, 2012).

Advantages of Online Psychological Testing

Online testing brings significant advantages to the practitioner-researcher. One is cost. An online test can be developed, revised, standardized, and distributed throughout the world at a fraction of the cost of traditional paper-and-pencil tests.

A second major advantage is the speed of online testing systems. Clients can be measured at a computer terminal in the practitioner's office, and within seconds of the client's completing the instrument, the system scores, assesses, and develops a case report for the client and another one for the clinician. This rapid communication makes online psychological testing increasingly popular.

The online approach to psychological testing also makes it possible for those with limited transportation availability or those with a significant mobility disability to be tested in a convenient location, such as a local clinic. It also facilitates psychological testing at offshore military posts and in rural areas where there are few university-based test centers.

Types of Online Psychological Testing

The first broad category of online psychological tests includes surveys and opinion questionnaires designed to assist in personal development and growth. These may or may not have a sound scientific foundation and may or may not have a meaningful normative basis for scoring and interpreting outcomes (Naglieri et al., 2004).

The second of the groupings of online measures includes traditional assessment tests used in psychodiagnostic evaluations. Until recently, these even included measures such as the MMPI-2 and the Beck Inventories.[7] Because copyright owners have been aggressive in the protection of their intellectual property, a bevy of vendors have developed clone assessments that look and are scored like the major diagnostic instruments. The individual using the cloned assessment must be cautious; the quality of such online psychological measures is always suspect.

The final type of online psychological assessments includes measures of cognitive ability and intelligence. These are also products of online entrepreneurs and as such vary greatly in quality. These systems normally use a simple linear program presenting a number of "cognitive ability" items. Once the total raw score is identified and a "norm-based IQ" reported, these programs will ask the online respondent to pay for a diagnostic write-up based on what was revealed by the "IQ test." Here are four of the many such tests:

http://www.free-iqtest.net/

http://giqtest.com/

http://www.intelligencetest.com/

http://www.iqtest.com/prep.html

Computer-Adaptive Testing (CAT)

Most large-scale assessments of academic achievement and aptitude are moving to online systems. The days of the paper-and-pencil achievement test are clearly numbered. State license examinations for professional counselors and psychologists are now given online, as are graduate and professional school admission tests.

Online measurement programs use computer-adaptive testing models that require detailed information about the difficulty of each individual achievement test or admissions test item (Hambleton, 2004). Computer-adaptive testing not only provides online assessments for graduate and professional school admission but is also used in 17 states to administer mandated high-stakes assessments in the public schools. This approach to testing is highly efficient and reduces the lag time for getting feedback into the hands of school counselors and school psychologists. It also reduces the length of time needed for test administration.

Computer-adaptive testing (CAT) employs software that first estimates the ability and background knowledge of each test taker. This estimation is made using a core group of standard items. Once the ability estimation has been made, it is used to guide and individualize the selection of test items from the large item bank. Test items are then presented to the examinees in an interactive format. Each time the individual answers a question, the computer determines his or her ability level and presents another question written at the optimum difficulty level. Once the software has decided that a particular learning standard has been measured for the examinee, it moves on to select test items from another learning standard. On a standard paper-and-pencil test, every individual must answer every question, whereas with computer-adaptive testing, items that the computer determines are superfluous are skipped. This provides for optimal efficiency and minimizes the amount of time each test taker must spend being tested. Thus, in a room full of business school applicants taking an online test like the GMAT, it can be assumed that beyond the opening questions, everyone is seeing a different test.

EVALUATION AND SELECTION OF A PSYCHOLOGICAL TEST

A primary skill for counselors is to be able to evaluate the quality of any published psychological test by reading its test manual and accessing independent test reviews. There are hundreds of published tests for use in clinical practice, and many of them are rubbish. Other published tests may be well designed but are still inappropriate for a particular therapist to use.

The first step in selecting the optimal published test for a given clinical setting involves identifying the goals for testing. It is an axiom of measurement that the test must match the purpose defined by the client and therapist. Once measurement goals have been delineated, it is then appropriate to review all possible measures that meet the identified goals for testing.

Information Sources

The largest collection of tests is maintained by the ETS®. That collection extends back over 100 years and includes over 25,000 published tests. Online test descriptions can be reviewed on the ETS webpage http://ericae.net/testcol.htm#ETSTF.

Since 1938, independent reviews and evaluations of tests have been available from the Buros Institute of Mental Measurements on the campus of the University of Nebraska, Lincoln. Currently, a total of over 3,500 tests are described and reviewed in this collection. Another Buros' publication, Tests in Print, went into its eighth edition in 2011. This publication provides a method to see the various available measurements focused on a topic of interest. It then directs users to volumes of the Mental Measurements Yearbooks where that instrument was reviewed.

Test reviewers for the Buros Institute are independent measurement specialists who are not paid for their services. These reviews and descriptions can be found on the Buros Webpage, http://buros.unl.edu/buros/jsp/search.jsp. In 2013, the fee for this service was $15 per test review. Reviews and test descriptions are available online through the research database of many university library systems. The most widely used library access source is through the EBSCO system

In addition to the Mental Measurements Yearbook, the Buros Center also publishes a Spanish language version of tests in print. This publication offers information pertaining to both original tests and measures published in the Spanish language and also Spanish language versions of tests originally written, and standardized in English.

The review protocol followed by the Mental Measurements Yearbook has changed little over the 75 plus years of the Buros publications. Major publishers of tests in English speaking countries around the world are contacted by the editors of the MMY on a regular basis regarding possible new editions of older measures or new publications. Publishers also can initiate the process by contacting the Buros Institute. There is no mandate for publishers to have their new measures evaluated in the review process, but it can be seen as part of the Standards of the Joint Committee on Testing Practices (2005).

The test reviews cover the range of published measures used in psychology and education. Of the measures reviewed, 57% are psychological assessments. The greatest proportion are measures of personality.[1]

---

[1] The editors of the Mental Measurements Yearbook have reported a table listing the types of assessments that have been reviewed in the recent Yearbooks in, Carlson, J., F., & Geisinger, K. F. (2012). Test reviewing at the Buros Center for Testing. *International Journal of Testing, 12*(12), 122-135. doi: 10.1080/15395058.2012.661003

The review process is well controlled with two independent reviewers working from a published set of guidelines for their evaluations. At the time of this publication the 19th Mental Measurement Yearbook was in final development. Its development drew reviewers from a database of 900 professors and measurement experts. The professional editors of the Buros Center serve as fact checkers to assure the quality of each review that is submitted.

The published guidelines include the following 5 points:

(1.) **Description**: The review begins with a statement of the purpose and intended population of study for the measurement. An example of this is seen in the following ersatz review for the *Schantz-Williams Artistic Temperament Assessment, 2nd ed.*
Schantz-Williams Artistic Temperament Assessment 2nnd ed.
Purpose: "Designed to assess extent to which an individual has an artistic temperament."
Population Ages: 8.0 to 89.0 years
Publication Year: 2012
Acronym: SWATA-2
Administration: Individually or in small groups (n < 9)
Price Data 2012: $4.95 per test form and $110.00 for complete kit including 20 test forms, *Technical Manual,* and *Administration and Scoring Directions*

(2.) **Development**: This part of the review lists and explains the underlying assumptions and theoretical perspective guiding the development of the instrument. The reviewer also describes the test's items and their appropriateness and quality.

(3.) **Technical**: In the Buros' system there are three major divisions of statistical information provided to readers of reviews: reliability, validity, and standardization.
Reliability: This includes the types and magnitudes of the reliability data provided by the author(s) of the measure. This includes both consistency and also measures of reliability over time.
Validity: This section addresses both the appropriate use of the test and describes evidence for the test as a measure of the intended construct. If the test or measure was designed as a predictive (selection) instrument the reviewer should discuss the quality of data documenting that the measure is a successful approach to making accurate predictions.
Standardization: In this section the reviewer describes the authors' sampling method by describing the model employed to provide population representation. It also discusses the quality and diversity of the normative reference group used in standardizing the instrument or measure.

(4.) **Commentary**: Here the reviewer describes and elaborates on the overall strength and weakness of the measure and its theoretical basis.

(5.) **Summary**: This is normally a concise paragraph summarizing and providing the reviewers' conclusions and recommendations about the measurement.

SUMMARY

Clinical practitioners in the mental health fields use published assessments and measures to understand and assist their clients. Standardized measures are part of most diagnostic work-ups and provide guidance to multidisciplinary teams assisting clients. Thousands of psychological assessments have been published and reviewed by the Buros Institute of Mental Measurements.

To be of any value, an assessment or other measure must be reliable. This quality may be represented by the stability or consistency of the measurement instrument. Useful and ethical instruments must also be valid and provide an accurate measure of a construct or psychological domain. Validity can be described for an instrument in terms of its fidelity to the theoretical framework of the dimension or concept being assessed. Valid measures must also be appropriate for both the task and subjects and match the approved social policies that are impacted by use of the measure with individuals.

DISCUSSION QUESTIONS

1. Review the curriculum of your graduate studies. Under the guidelines for the use of test measurements, what "level" of assessment or test are you now qualified to ethically employ with a client?

2. What factors could reduce the reliability of an otherwise well-constructed assessment? How could they be controlled?

3. The National Board for Certified Counselors certification examination has posted several sample questions on its webpage http://www.nbcc.org/NCE/Sample/. Review these items and discuss them in terms of content and construct validity.

4. In the hope of selling individualized cognitive profiles, several entrepreneurs offer free online tests of mental ability, four of which were listed previously in this chapter. Select one such test, review its items, and delineate the factors of cognition that it assesses.

NOTES

1. An example of this issue is seen when the Educational Testing Service sends SAT score reports that are 5 or more years old to colleges. ETS posts a caution on the score transcript, stating that the score may have diminished utility for college admission.

2. It must be noted that this method assumes that only a one-dimensional test is being divided into equivalent halves. If the test battery was built of a number of distinctly different components, it would be necessary to determine the internal consistency of each of those areas (subtests) independently.

3. This indicates that the optimal criterion validity would be greater than the validity of the criterion. This is very unlikely to ever happen in the real world of data. The maximum validity as defined in this example is a theoretical, not a realistic, limit.

4. Some dimensions of attitude and evaluation stay consistent over time. For example, measures of occupational preference have been demonstrated to be consistent over a quarter of a century (Lawler, 1993). Student evaluations of their undergraduate professors represent another stable quantity. Those professors whom undergraduates view as being outstanding will be revered decades from now. Unfortunately, the reverse is also true.

5. Another way to describe these construct-irrelevant elements is as *statistical covariates.*

6. To achieve a level of fluency in English that permits the use of context-reduced academic language known as cognitive academic language proficiency (CALP) requires 7 years, 4 more than the 3 years needed to reach a basic conversational level in English.

7. The copyright holders for these instruments have defended their measures, and these are now available to practitioners to use in their offices using both in-office computer-administered (CD) or online-administered formats.

CHAPTER 13

Instrument Development and Survey Research

"Here's an interesting survey. Most people surveyed said they don't believe celebrities should get special treatment. Apparently they didn't survey any celebrities."

Jay Leno

OBJECTIVES

By reading and studying this chapter, you should acquire the competency to do the following:

- Describe the steps in designing a questionnaire-format clinical instrument.

- Plan a clinical instrument for the identification of a client's concerns using Likert-type questionnaire items.

- Explain how a practitioner would go about writing high-quality questionnaire items designed to collect demographic data from clients.

- Explain the similarities and differences between two hierarchical questionnaire-item types.

- Explain how quality interview protocols can be developed and how they may be used in a clinical setting.

- Construct a high-quality semantic differential questionnaire designed to assess a client's self-evaluation of his or her status.

- Describe methods for establishing the validity and reliability of questionnaire and interview data.

- Explain the difference between a population and a sample.

- Describe factors that govern the required size of a sample of subjects.
- Plan and develop a high-quality rating scale that could be used to evaluate a graduate intern during a placement experience.
- Plan and develop a high-quality checklist for use with new client intake.

INTRODUCTION AND MAJOR THEMES

The need for clinicians to be efficient and time effective in their work with clients is increasingly driven by the requirements of health insurance companies and other third-party payers (Puterbaugh, 2004). One effective method for collecting useful client information in support of therapeutic work is through self-reported questionnaire data and/or structured interviews carried out by well-prepared clinical assistants.

Literally thousands of psychological questionnaires and interview protocols have been developed and are available to the practitioner. Only a small segment of these are offered by publishers of psychological tests and assessments. The vast majority can be found on the Internet, in research articles from the professional literature, and in appendices of doctoral dissertations and master's degree theses.

There is a way that clinicians can apply the skills to develop, use, and interpret data from questionnaires. Those skills are needed to conduct local action research projects and ethical and valid program evaluations. The ability to carry out both types of projects is part of the training mandates for new counselors from the American Counseling Association (ACA) and the Association for Assessment in Counseling and Education (AACE, 2010) in association with the American Mental Health Counselors Association (AMHCA, 2010) and the Council for Accreditation of Counseling and Related Educational Programs (CACREP, 2009).

STEPS IN DESIGNING CLINICAL INSTRUMENTS

Questionnaires are an ordinary part of the lives of all Americans. Our opinions are forever being sought out on questionnaires by merchants, politicians, and service providers. We frequently find questionnaires about our personal behaviors and opinions in magazines targeting specific segments of the readership (teens, young adult women, men, even expectant parents). These pseudo-scientific instruments in magazines are supposedly able to reveal our latent attitudes, desires, ambitions, and sexual attractiveness and a host of other dimensions. Newspapers have learned to incorporate results of survey questionnaires into the papers' narratives using what have become known as "infographics" (Utt & Pasternak, 2000). Several large newspapers, including the *New York Times* and *USA Today,* have hired well-known polling companies to develop statistical background information for their articles.

Politicians also use pseudo-scientific questionnaires to "poll" their constituents while advertising the politician. These questionnaires are not designed to gain information but to drive home the politician's point of view and to provide a place to ask for a political contribution.

Sample Items From a Pseudo-Scientific Political Opinion Questionnaire Administered in a Congressional District With a Conservative Representative in November 2010

- Do you think things in this country are generally going in the wrong direction, or do you feel things are starting to improve?

  1. ___Completely Wrong Direction

  2. ___Mostly Wrong Direction

  3. ___Starting to Improve

  4. ___Unsure

- Are you against President Obama's plan to relocate suspected terrorists from Guantanamo Bay prison into the United States?

  1. ___Opposed

  2. ___Unopposed

  3. ___No Opinion

- How concerned are you that as other countries like China buy up hundreds of billions of dollars of our national debt they will have more of a say in directing our nation's future economic policies?

  1. ___Very Concerned

  2. ___Moderately Concerned

  3. ___Somewhat Concerned

  4. ___Unconcerned

  5. ___No Opinion

- Should House Republicans fight to curb spending and oppose the Democrats' wasteful pork projects, like the $30 million for salt marsh harvest mice in Nancy Pelosi's hometown of San Francisco?

  1. ___Yes

  2. ___No

  3. ___No Opinion

Goals and Objectives for Clinical Questionnaires

Just because questionnaires are employed frequently does not mean that they provide meaningful data. There are several steps in the process of developing a high-quality psychological questionnaire with sound measurement characteristics.

All too often, graduate students in the behavioral sciences begin developing questionnaire items before they have established a clear goal or set specific objectives for their questionnaire. One result of this willy-nilly approach is that the new instrument asks an inordinate number of irrelevant questions. All individuals, including young researchers, have a measure of curiosity that can result in asking questions that are off the mark. Each item on a questionnaire must be there for a reason, and that reason can't be "I thought it would be interesting to know," or "I was just curious." Items must be tied directly to the objectives for the instrument.

Objectives should be developed from a deep understanding of the field and needs of clients. This understanding may also reflect the researcher's experiences as a practitioner as well as a careful review of the literature. Once a draft of the objectives has been developed, the items should be vetted by other professionals (Patten, 2001).

The development of a questionnaire requires that several questionnaire items be written for each of the goal's primary objectives. Editing after field testing or (pilot testing) and factor analysis (see student website) will reduce the number of questions to the minimum needed to provide answers for each objective.

Questionnaire Formats

Psychological questionnaires can be designed using two primary formats, semantic scales and hierarchical scales.

Likert Scales

The dominant format for questionnaires is a semantic scale of measurement known as the Likert scale. The technique was named for a social scientist, Rensis Likert, who while completing his doctorate at Columbia University devised a new approach to questionnaire construction. In his dissertation in 1932, Likert presented his new method of adapting an ordinal scale to provide a method for subjects to provide a measure of their attitudes and feelings.

Two of Likert's (1932) Original Questionnaire Items

In the interest of permanent peace, we should be willing to arbitrate absolutely all differences with other nations that we cannot readily settle by diplomacy.

___SA   ___Ap   ___Undecided   ___Ds   ___SD

(Continued)

(Continued)

The United States, whether a member or not, should cooperate fully in the humanitarian and economic programs of the League of Nations.

___SA ___Ap   ___Undecided   ___Ds   ___SD

Note: SA = Strongly approve

Ap = Approve

Ds = Disapprove

SD = Strongly disapprove

Design of Likert Scales: As with all measurement devices, the Likert scale starts with justifiable goals and well-thought-out objectives. After the practitioner-researcher has defined what opinion or attitude will be measured, the next step is to write several simple, declarative sentences about that topic of interest. These sentences should contain only one central idea; the researcher should avoid writing **double-barreled questions**. Double-barreled items ask about more than one issue at a time yet only provide for a single answer. An example is the stimulus sentence "I am very satisfied with my therapist and the clinic." This statement is best broken into two stimuli sentences: "I have an excellent therapist," and "I am very satisfied with this clinic."

Always avoid jargon or other words and phrases that could hold multiple meanings or be beyond the understanding of those responding to the questionnaire. For example, a declarative sentence such as "I experience paracusia or other manifestations of auditory hallucinations," would not be acceptable because it contains vocabulary the client is not likely to understand. Better to use the stimulus sentence "I sometimes hear voices in my head."

Applications from the Literature

Example Stimulus Sentences from a Factor on a Personality Test

Item	Factor Loading*
I see myself as a good leader.	84
I would prefer to be the leader.	76
I am a born leader.	72
People always seem to recognize my authority.	68

Item	Factor Loading*
I am assertive.	64
I have a natural talent for influencing people.	63
I like having authority over people.	62
I have a strong will to power.	52
I am going to be a great person.	46
If I ruled the world it would be a much better place.	42
I am an extraordinary person.	42

Source: Ackerman, R. A., Witt, E. A., Donnellan, M. B., Trzesniewski, K. H., Robins, R. W., & Kast, D. A. (2011). What does the Narcissistic Personality Inventory really measure? *Assessment, 18*(1), 67–87. doi: 10.1177/1073191110382845

Note: These are 10 scaled items using a 5-point Likert format questionnaire. The full Narcissistic Personality Inventory is composed of 40 Likert-type items. Factor analysis identified three independent factors on this measure from a study involving a large-scale sample of college students. The first, Leadership/Authority, is shown here. The other two factors, not shown, are Grandiose/Exhibitionism and Entitlement/Exploitativeness.

* Factor loading is the correlation between a measured variable and each identified factor or latent variable. See student website for information on factor analysis.

Response Choices: Likert scales use a fixed series of answer choices arranged in an ordinal sequence to measure the strength of the respondent's attitudes or opinions or the frequency of behaviors. The answer choices follow each declarative statement in the instrument. Answer options with Likert-type scales normally provide five or seven options in an ordinal sequence for respondents to express the strength of their agreement or disagreement with the stimulus sentence. When Likert-type scale questions have seven answer options, there is a slight improvement in reliability over the use of five answer options. When the number of options is increased beyond seven, the reliability of the question actually decreases (J. Dawes, 2008). The problem with a seven-option scale is in selection of descriptors that clearly express qualitatively different levels of an attitude, behavior, or attribute. For example, consider the following seven-option Likert-format item:

All newly licensed professional counselors should have had solid graduate-level academic preparation in behavioral research and statistics.

    ___A) Agree
    ___B) Moderate agreement
    ___C) Slight agreement
    ___D) Neither agree nor disagree
    ___E) Slight disagreement

___F) Moderate disagreement
___G) Disagree

In this example, the problem is in selecting adjectives that represent clearly different levels on an ordinal scale (i.e., *moderate* vs. *slight*). The researcher must be able to provide in the directions a clear explanation of the distinction between the adjectives used. Another problem with this format is that the zero-value answer "neither agree nor disagree" is in the center of the ordinal group. To avoid having values below zero (negative numbers), the format sometimes is changed to this:

___A) Agree
___B) Moderate agreement
___C) Slight agreement
___D) Slight disagreement
___E) Moderate disagreement
___F) Disagree
___N) Neither agree nor disagree

By creating an ordinal scale, the clinical researcher assumes that the intensity of feelings or attitudes is linear and that the underling psychological dimension is accessible to those answering the questionnaire. A related problem with all self-reported data is the veracity of the answers given by respondents, especially given the tendency for individuals to want to look good to others. For example, respondents who have personality disorders may not be able to provide truthful responses. These include both Cluster A personality disorders (e.g., paranoia) and Cluster B disorders (e.g., narcissism) (Ziegler, MacCann, & Roberts, 2012). It is also possible for a client to fake a bad score on personality tests as a controlling method and/or as a way of maintaining a therapeutic relationship.

The ease of administration and scoring are reasons why Likert-type measurements are widely employed in psychological assessments. The clinical diagnosis of difficulties such as attention-deficit/hyperactive disorder ADHD is usually made by practioners employing a Likert scale such as the Conners' Adult ADHD Rating Scales (Conners et al., 1997, 1999). That instrument was developed through factor analysis using an initially large pool of possible Likert-type items and then distilled into a 66-item measurement. (See the student website for more on factor analysis.)

Likert-type scales are commonly employed to assess self-perceptions and attitudes on a number of different dimensions (Mcleod, 2008). As originally conceived, the Likert scale was used so that respondents would express opinions on either side of a neutral point (e.g., *neither agree nor disagree* or *no opinion*). Without the neutral point, the scale takes the form of a measure of intensity or frequency. Following are five examples:

Scaled to Measure Agreement
Good counselors explain to their clients how best to solve their problems.

_____Absolutely agree

_____Agree

____Undecided

____Disagree

____Strenuously disagree

Scaled to Measure Frequency (with operational explanations)
Do you hear voices in your head?

____Constantly, several times a day

____Frequently, about once a day

____Occasionally, about 4 or 5 times a week

____Very infrequently, 1 or 2 times a month

____Never

Scaled to Measure Likelihood
Other people show me respect.

____100% of the time

____Most of the time

____Half of the time

____Rarely happens

____Never

Scaled to Measure Importance
Therapists establish boundaries with clients.

____Critically important

____Important

____Moderately important but not central

____A low priority

____Irrelevant

Scaled to Measure Judgment
What do you feel would be the impact on morale if a merit pay program is started for all therapists employed in your clinic or counseling center?

___A) Powerful positive impact
___B) Minor positive impact
___C) No impact either way
___D) Minor negative impact
___E) Powerful negative impact

When a Likert-type scale has an even number of options, there is no neutral position. It is likely that the question's author wants to force a response in one direction or the other. For example, this is a six-option item assessing teaching:

The professor for this course seems very well prepared in research methods.

____A)   Agree
____B)   Moderate agreement
____C)   Slight agreement
____D)   Slight disagreement
____E)   Moderate disagreement
____F)   Disagree

Research questionnaires designed to elicit political opinions are typically constructed using a Likert-type scale with an even number of choices, forcing the respondent to have an opinion. This can be seen on the online Likert-scaled assessment The Political Compass Test at http://www.politicalcompass.org/test/.

Likert Scale Quality: Practitioner-researchers creating a Likert scale should take steps to ensure the quality of their new measurement instrument. One of these steps is to work with a group of 8 to 12 individuals who do not have a vested interest in the researcher's project. These individuals should assess the individual items and write what they would answer for each and why. The goal of this step is to ensure that individuals interpret the questions in similar ways and that those interpretations are shared by the researcher. It also demonstrates that the questionnaire's items are aligned with the researcher's original goals and, thus, the content validity of the new Likert scale.

A second step in this process is to **pilot test** the instrument in the field with an independent sample of individuals not part of the planned study (e.g., clients in a colleague's practice). This step can be used to verify the factors of the questionnaire and make final improvements to wording problems or problems with the directions. This field test also indicates the length of time required to administer and score the questionnaire.

Special Populations: On assessments of children, the answer options are normally reduced to just three or are presented as pictures using visual analogies instead of declarative sentences. The child's answers on the scale of responses can be represented by smiley faces. The problem with having only three options is the significant loss of reliability that occurs with fewer than five options (Murphy & Likert, 1938).

As with children, adults with mental defects or significant disorders can be assessed using measurements employing Likert-format questions. One of these, the CERAD Behavior Rating Scale for Dementia, second edition, by James Mack and Marian Patterson (2001), has the primary caregiver for the disabled individual provide the answers.[1] The scale asks about the frequency of certain behaviors associated with dementia.

Likert Scale Statistics: There are two basic rules for the construction of semantic questionnaires including Likert-type scales. One is the assumption of unidimensionality, meaning that the scale measures only one factor (latent or obvious). Thus, if a measure is designed

Figure 13.1   Example of a Discrete Visual Analogy Format Likert Scale

Note: There are four measurement items shown here. The therapist presents these plates to a kindergartener or young child one at a time and asks if the activity is one the child would enjoy. The child answers by pointing to the face that shows how he or she feels about the activity. These answers may provide an opening for the skilled therapist's communication with the young client.

Source: Wright, R. J. (2010). *Multifaceted assessment for early childhood education*. Thousand Oaks, CA: Sage, p. 104.

to quantify a variable such as "workplace climate," very likely several dimensions of this variable will be part of the scale. These may include staff age and experience, number of employee days absent per month, and level of staff involvement in the decision-making process. Several other variables are probably measured by these items as well, but clearly workplace climate is not a unidimensional measure.

The second is the assumption of homogeneity of variance across all items. This assumption implies that each of the items on a scale has a similar dispersion of high and low scores when responded to by a large number of people ($N > 30$). Items meeting this assumption are described as being **tau equivalent.** The rationale for this assumption is the assurance that each item in a measure makes an equal contribution to the final score compared to the other items.

Clinical practitioners presenting the outcome from a series of questionnaires composed of Likert-type items should remember that data from individual Likert questions are ordinal. When the researcher reports data for one item with a sample of respondents, the central tendency should be reported as a median value on the scale.[2] Likert-type item data may also be presented as a graph, using either a pie chart or histogram. It is clear from a review of the behavioral science literature that this ordinal data rule is frequently violated.[3]

Questions about the quality of data collected using Likert-type questions is addressed by documentation of the content validity of the questionnaire's items. This should be well established before the questionnaire is used by developing appropriate goals and objectives for the measurement and constructing items matching those objectives (Cox & Cox, 2008).

Cronbach's Alpha: The reliability (consistency) of a one-dimensional scale made up of Likert-type items can be found using Cronbach's alpha procedure. When a researcher has identified several separate unidimensional scales within a measure, they should be reported as subscales. It is still possible to estimate the reliability of an entire instrument made up of various subscales by using a stratified-alpha reliability coefficient (Kamata, Turhan, & Darandari, 2003).

Test-Retest Reliability: Using the instrument twice, with the administrations separated by a period of time, is another method to demonstrate reliability. This is done by first calculating the medians of each Likert item on the pretest survey and again on the posttest survey. Next, the scores from the two administrations of the instrument are correlated. This correlation provides a measure of reliability (stability).

Semantic Differential Scale

Another format for developing and writing questions for psychological instruments was developed by Charles E. Osgood at the University of Illinois. He gave this connotative approach to psychological measurement the name **semantic differential scale (SD).** The SD is an economic and highly flexible technique for eliciting data on the opinions and attitudes of clients (Heise, 1970). A search by the online Questia™ search engine identified 960 published social science research articles employing the semantic differential scale.

Semantic Differential Scale Structure: Individuals answer an opinion question (stimulus statement) using a linear array of points between two polar opposing adjectives (R. M. Dawes, 1977). The traditional format for the SD scale uses a 7-point vernier between the two bipolar adjectives. This format would take the following form:

- *How do you describe your sibling relationships?*

    Bad   ___ ___ ___ ___ ___ ___ ___   Excellent

    −3 −2 −1 0 +1 +2 +3

Indifferent	___ ___ ___ ___ ___ ___ ___	Supportive
	−3 −2 −1 0 +1 +2 +3	
Jealous	___ ___ ___ ___ ___ ___ ___	Unresentful
	−3 −2 −1 0 +1 +2 +3	
Estranged	___ ___ ___ ___ ___ ___ ___	Close
	−3 −2 −1 0 +1 +2 +3	
Power Based	___ ___ ___ ___ ___ ___ ___	Balanced & Mutual
	−3 −2 −1 0 +1 +2 +3	

When an SD scale has no fixed numerical markers, it is described as a **continuous scale.** An advantage of the continuous format is that it removes the zero point and forces the respondent to have a position. The following is an example of a semantic differential question with a continuous scale using five related items on the same affective dimension:

Indicate your opinion below by marking (X) on the lines between the two extreme adjectives.

- *How do you describe your father?*

Spineless	_____	Powerful
Unnecessarily punitive	_____	Gentle & Caring
Demoralizing	_____	Encouraging
Cold	_____	Loving
Violent	_____	Tranquil & at Peace

This type of semantic differential can be assessed by using a ruler. The opinion of the individual on the items can be read as the distance in centimeters away from the negative adjective. Once measured, the average distance in centimeters can be mathematically determined and used as a statistical expression of the strength and direction of a respondent's attitude.

Continuous-type semantic differential scales of measurement can also be designed to facilitate easier interpretation by placing tick marks along the line used to express the level of opinion. Here's an example:

Indicate your opinion below by marking (X) on the lines between the two extreme adjectives.

- *The counseling center is considering a new rule to forbid both clients and staff from bringing a firearm or other weapon on the center's property. Please indicate your attitude toward this newly proposed policy for the center.*

At Risk	l____l____l____l____l____l____l____l____l	Secure & Safe
Disappointed	l____l____l____l____l____l____l____l____l	Overjoyed
Hostile	l____l____l____l____l____l____l____l____l	Pleased

Frightened   l____l____l____l____l____l____l____l____l   Comfortable

Defeated   l____l____l____l____l____l____l____l____l   Confident

Statistics for Semantic Differential Scales: The number of bipolar adjective pairs used to assess a psychological dimension or issue is related to the overall reliability of a combined score from the adjective pairings. The minimum number of bipolar adjective pairs needed to design a stable and reliable scale has been empirically shown to be five (Osgood, Suci, & Tannenbaum, 1957).

Factor-analytic research into the use of semantic differential scales has shown that they usually are influenced by three latent **orthogonal**[4] **factors** underlying the attitudes and opinions of respondents. These **latent factors** are good vs. bad, fast vs. slow, and powerful vs. powerless (Heise, 1970; see Figure 13.2). These three factors are generally referred to in a shortened form as evaluation, potency, and activity or **EPA.** In the development of an SD scale, the researcher can achieve a relatively stable SD scale by including bipolar adjective pairs related to each of these three themes (Heise).

Because each individual adjective pair on a semantic differential scale is an ordinal, theoretically, they should not be analyzed with parametric statistics. In practice, this rule is more violated than followed. Most researchers sum and average (calculate means and medians) the scores obtained from the bipolar adjective pairs. These statistics of central tendency are then used in further statistical analysis.

Figure 13.2   Representation of the EPA Model

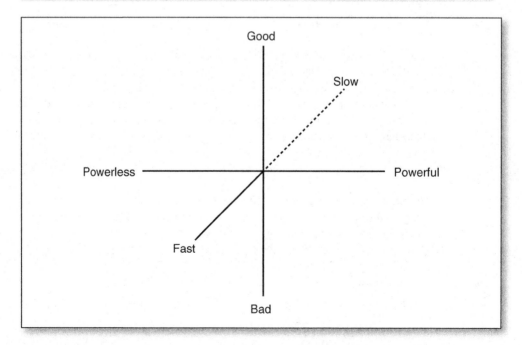

Thurstone's Hierarchical Scale

The oldest of the various ways to construct a measure to assess a single dimension of psychological affect, attitude, or opinion is the **Thurstone scale** (Thurstone, 1927). (See the student website for two other hierarchical scaling methods.) This method starts with a clearly stated measurement goal. Once an appropriate goal for the instrument has been identified, the clinical researcher must develop about 100 possible questionnaire items expressing every possible level of feeling about the issue under study. These are winnowed to about 10 items sequenced by the strength of opinion being expressed.

For example, if a college counseling staff were asked to develop an instrument to measure undergraduate student reactions to a new zero-tolerance underage alcohol and drug policy, a series of stimulus stems must be developed covering the broad spectrum of possible feelings on the topic. This new instrument would arrange items by the amount of harshness versus positiveness expressed toward the issue, in this case, a new drug and alcohol policy. Such a range for the stimulus stems for the items may be from "I would immediately transfer to another more tolerant university," to the more positive "It would make my parents happy," to the highly positive "I will get more done without inebriated classmates."

Photo 13.1   L. L. Thurstone

www.indiana.edu

The score of each undergraduate subject would be found by summing the harshness-to-positiveness score for each of the 10 items. This method, known as the **equal-appearing interval technique,** provides a scale that has parametric properties and can be analyzed using parametric statistics. A second advantage of an **equal-appearing interval scale** is that it has great stability and reliability.

Applications from the Literature

Example of Thurstone's Method in Developing a New Psychological Assessment

Note: This study involved developing a Thurstone scale to measure one's tendency to violent behavior. The 12 items are arranged from low levels of violence to the maximum level.

Crime and Violence Scale:

Subscale: General Conflict Tactic Subscale

(Continued)

(Continued)

1. Discussed it calmly and settled the disagreement?
2. Left the room or area rather than argue?
3. Insulted, swore, or cursed at someone?
4. Threatened to hit or throw something at another person?
5. Actually threw something at someone?
6. Pushed, grabbed, or shoved someone?
7. Slapped another person?
8. Kicked, bit, or hit someone?
9. Hit or tried to hit anyone with something (an object)?
10. Beat up someone?
11. Threatened anyone with knife or gun?
12. Actually used a knife or gun on someone?

Source: Conrad, K. J., Riley, B. B., Conrad, K. M., Chan, Y., & Dennis, M. L. (2010). Validation of the crime and violence scale (CVS) against the Rasch measurement model including differences by gender, race, and age. *Evaluation Review, 34*(2), 83–115. doi: 10.1177/0193841X10362162

RATING SCALES AND CLINICAL CHECKLISTS

Practitioner-researchers skilled in the construction of valid and reliable rating scales and checklists have the ability to provide a valuable therapeutic tool for use with clients. Rating scales and checklists are widely used in both inpatient and outpatient clinical settings by professional staff and by therapists. When a clinician begins a treatment program with a new client, the two should work together to identify ways of measuring progress toward the client's goals. Buros Mental Measurements has published reviews of over 300 rating scales and another 70 psychological checklists. These are only the tip of a vast iceberg of psychological instruments, most of which are not commercially published. Investigation of most psychological dimensions using an Internet search engine will reveal many more unpublished research rating scales and checklists. The vast resources available notwithstanding, most client-developed objectives for therapy may not be measurable using a published psychological assessment.

Applications

Checklists and rating scales are used to measure many complex, nonclinical adult behaviors, including Olympic sports (figure skating, diving, and dressage), advanced flying skills of instrument pilots, and the developing interview skills of intern counselors. In counseling centers, checklists and rating scales are used to measure dimensions of personal change difficult to assess by other means. These measuring devices can be designed to assess client socialization, executive function, attention problems, various dimensions of emotional development, and many other domains of the psyche.

Construction

There are three primary rules of building a useful rating scale or checklist: keep it focused, keep it clear, and keep it simple. To ensure the instrument has the correct focus, the practitioner-researcher should begin with a clear goal for the data to be collected. Thus, prior to the instrument's construction, the clinical researcher must decide on the primary objectives to be served and type of data to be obtained by the new measurement.

Once the objectives for the measurement are understood, the next step is to conduct a detailed analysis of the behavior to be assessed. Equipped with this information, the practitioner-researcher is ready to develop individual items. Items should be written to match the component parts of the behavior being assessed. Next, the clinician should decide on a logical sequence for the items to appear on the new instrument. Finally, the actual items are written.

Formats for Construction of Checklists and Rating Scales

The format for checklists tends be tallies, simple counts, or a record of dichotomous (binary) outcomes (*yes* vs. *no*). Checklists play a role in both the diagnostic phase and in the process of monitoring and charting client change. Many times they are integrated with a rating scale to provide a complete perspective on the client.

The ordered nature of a rating scale implies that the items measure the degree something is happening or the relative value of a client's behavior or work products. Rating scales are employed in all walks of life, not just in the behavioral sciences. They are seen on the tables of restaurants to measure customer satisfaction level, as a way to judge the strength and direction of one's politics (http://www .politicalcompass.org/test/), and even to show the relative strength of Wi-Fi signal reception by a hand-held device.

Rating scales often provide clinicians with a number-line format for recording their observations and judgments. This number line may represent a judgment by the clinician or be the self-reported perception of the client. The rating scale may be in the form of a frequency of occurrence scale, a behavioral intensity scale, or an estimate of the severity of symptoms or problem.

Cartoon 13.1   Survey by Bottle

— Survey by Bottle —

"It's a questionnaire from some graduate student studying island cultures."

Cartoon by Merv Magus.

Scales Design

The development of a reliable rating scale for a psychological dimension requires the rating scale have about 10 items focused on aspects of the targeted issue. These items are developed by exploring the literature and then brainstorming a long list of possible characteristics linked with the psychological dimension. The list of characteristics can be drawn from the literature of the behavioral sciences and/or from the clinical experiences of the scale's designer.

Next, the characteristics are translated into declarative statements. Pilot testing and/or focus groups can be used to reduce the size of the instrument by removing redundant and ineffective items. Once a large group of subjects has completed the rating scale, the data can be factor analyzed to further verify the instrument's structure. An example of this type of psychological rating scale is presented in Table 13.1.

In Table 13.1, there are 12 self-perception ratings related to social anxiety and shyness. Some of these have a positive **valance** (1, 2, 4, 6, 7, 8, 10) and the others a negative valance. By including items that switch directional emphasis (valance) the rating scale presents a rating task involving a greater level of cognitive complexity and thereby prevents the respondent from developing a mind-set (Wright & Richardson, 1977).

Table 13.1 Hypothetical Measure of Adult Shyness and Social Anxiety

Which best describes your social comfort level?	Always	Sometimes	Rarely	Never
1. My home is always filled with neighbors and friends.				
2. I am a social magnet.				
3. I never seem to be invited to parties.				
4. Others seek my friendship.				
5. I feel faint when I am asked to speak to a group.				
6. My opinion is sought out by others.				
7. Everyone wants to sit near me at meetings and at church.				
8. Someday I would like to run for political office.				
9. When in front of a group I am so rattled I cannot read my remarks.				
10. I have been described as "the life of the party."				
11. I plan quiet vacations alone or with my immediate family.				
12. I avoid reunions and other gatherings where there are many people.				

Applications from the Literature

Development of a New Self-Report Depression Scale

Note: The National Institute of Mental Health developed this short questionnaire for screening individuals for clinical depression. The sample included a random selection of members from randomly selected households in two counties, Kansas City, Missouri, and Washington County, Maryland. A total of 2,846 individuals over the age of 18 years were interviewed, and the original total of a possible 300 items was reduced to 20.

Development of the Scale: The CES-D items were selected from a pool of items from previously validated depression scales. The major elements of depressive symptomatology were identified from the literature and factor analytic studies. These components include: depressed mood, feelings of guilt and worthlessness, feelings of helplessness and hopelessness, psychomotor retardation, loss of appetite, and sleep disturbance. Only a few items were selected to represent each component. Four items were worded in the positive direction to break tendencies toward response set as well as to assess positive affect (or its absence).

INSTRUCTIONS FOR QUESTIONS: Below is a list of the ways you might have felt or behaved. Please tell me how often you have felt this way during the past. week. HAND CARD A.

Rarely or None of the Time (Less than 1 Day)

Some or a Little of the Time (1-2 Days)

Occasionally or a Moderate Amount of Time (3-4 Days)

Most or All of the Time (5-7 Days)

During the past week:

1. I was bothered by things that usually don't bother me.

2. I did not feel like eating; my appetite was poor.

3. I felt that I could not shake off the blues even with help from my family or friends.

4. I felt that I was just as good as other people.

5. I had trouble keeping my mind on what I was doing.

6. I felt depressed.

7. I felt that everything I did was an effort.

8. I felt hopeful about the future.

9   I thought my life had been a failure.

10. I felt fearful.

11. My sleep was restless.

12. I was happy.

13. I talked less than usual.

(Continued)

(Continued)

14. I felt lonely.

15. People were unfriendly.

16. I enjoyed life.

17. I had crying spells.

18. I felt sad.

19. I felt that people dislike me.

20. I could not get "going."

Source: Radloff, L. S. (1977). The CES-D scale: A self report depression scale for research in the general population. *Applied Psychological Measurement, 1*(3), 385–401. doi: 10.1177/014662167700100306

Rating scales can be modified to make it possible for young children to rate conditions that are beyond their ability to verbally express. One of the most commonly employed of these is the Wong Children's Pain Scale (Wong, Hockenberry-Eaton, Wilson, Winkelstein, & Schwartz, 2001). This measurement scale is seen in the offices of pediatric clinicians and hospitals everywhere.

Figure 13.3   Children's Pain Scale

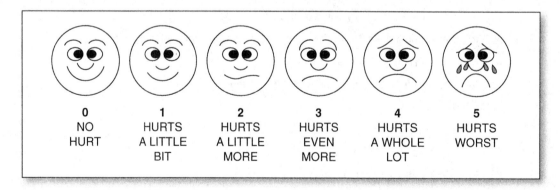

| 0 | 1 | 2 | 3 | 4 | 5 |
| NO HURT | HURTS A LITTLE BIT | HURTS A LITTLE MORE | HURTS EVEN MORE | HURTS A WHOLE LOT | HURTS WORST |

Source: Wright, R. J. (2010). *Multifaceted assessment for early childhood education.* Thousand Oaks, CA: Sage.

Checklists

Rating scales are designed to be evaluative. Generally, they provide users of the instrument with several levels of behavior to select between. Checklists, on the other hand, are not complex and typically are answered with dichotomous, *yes* versus *no* choices or as simple counts of a behavior's occurrence.

There are many good reasons for a clinician to develop checklists for use in his or her practice. One central use for checklists is in the identification and differential diagnosis of client's problems. For example, a number of published checklists are used for the identification of ADHD and other neuropsychological problems among children and adults (T. E. Brown, 2001; Conners et al., 1999; Glutting, Sheslow, & Adams, 1979/2003; Ryser & McConnell, 2002). Checklists developed by a practitioner can provide more highly focused and reliable information about his or her clients than is produced by most commercial instruments. Practitioner-developed checklists can also be used with a client to chart the improvement that is occurring during a therapeutic intervention.

Another reason for a checklist is to provide a framework for sequencing or evaluating the completion of a series of ordered tasks or behaviors (Scriven, 2005). Even surgeons have begun to use checklists to reduce the rate of surgical errors.[5] Finally, checklists can provide a structure for observations of client activities in various settings.

Checklists serve as a memory aid in times of high stress. The safety of staff and clients can depend on well-thought-out checklists designed to detail emergency procedures. As an example, every counseling center or clinic needs to delineate procedures to follow in the event of an armed intruder. Those procedures should be sequenced and printed on a checklist that is available to each staff member and reviewed with all employees on a regular basis.

Figure 13.4 Possible Armed Intruder Checklist: Entering a Clinical Setting

If a potentially armed intruder is seen on the facility's grounds or in the building, take the following steps:

1. Obtain as much information as possible from the individual reporting the intruder.

2. Call 911 requesting immediate police assistance and designating which entrance they should use.

3. Contact the security director for the facility.

4. Have a designated person greet the police at the preferred entrance (possibly the security chief).

5. Make a public announcement on the public address system, by computer messaging, and in an abbreviated form on the staff Twitter accounts.

   a. Alert! Alert! Alert! An armed intruder is reported in the facility. (Repeat this brief announcement three times.)
   b. Police are in route and will be here soon.
   c. Stay calm and listen to our directions.

(Continued)

Figure 13.4 (Continued)

> d. Institute lockdown immediately in the nearest secure room or office. Do not be in an open area, lounge, or station.
> e. Stay in place; do not use stairs or elevators. Stay in a locked room until given the all-clear.
>
> Repeat this message every three minutes.
>
> 6. Immediately contact all scheduled clients and explain that the clinic is closed during an ongoing emergency. DO NOT ELABORATE.
>
> 7. Contact all late-shift employees and volunteers and tell them to stay away until they are contacted.
>
> 8. Designate one contact person for the press.
>
> 9. Answer all incoming phone calls with "We cannot talk. We are in an emergency situation." Then hang up the telephone.
>
> 10. After the emergency is over, make an all-clear announcement and remind all individuals not to talk to the press.
>
> 11. Coordinate with the police in all matters, including what to tell the media.
>
> 12. Set up a place for the facility's designated spokesperson to meet with the media.

Note: This type of a checklist should be reviewed by both campus security and the local police authorities. It should be one part of a comprehensive emergency plan for the institution. Other parts of the emergency plan for a clinical location could include plans related to weather (e.g., tornados, flash floods) and other forms of disaster (e.g., wildfires).

Checklist Design

The development of a checklist starts with the identification of the behavior or activity being evaluated or remembered. That behavior or activity should be subjected to a task analysis designed to list all steps and parts that should be completed. In addition to making a list of needed components, the developer of the checklist must decide on the correct sequence that must be followed for a client to have optimal results. It is always best if several knowledgeable people review the final list before it is field-tested.

Practitioners should keep a few things in mind when developing a checklist:

- The items should reflect easily observable behaviors.
- The item sequence should match the natural order that will likely be followed.
- The wording should be unambiguous and clear.
- The items should provide a place to mark (X) when they have been accomplished.
- Each item should be written with consistent language and voice.
- Each item should provide only one issue to be evaluated.
- Each item should appear in only one location on the checklist.

Applications from the Literature

Use of Checklists and Questionnaires in Mental Health Research

Note: Mothers who brought their children to a rural mental health military base service unit for psychiatric assessment were screened by clinic staff for study eligibility. Children had to be between ages 6 and 17, nonpsychotic, without an intellectual disability, not viewed as being at risk of child abuse, and not needing hospitalization. Mothers were included if they were the primary custodial parent, lived with the child, and were not viewed as needing immediate psychiatric intervention. Over 200 volunteered to participate. The interviews and questionnaires these women answered required about 3 hours. The mothers were given $50 for their time, and their children received $20 gift vouchers from a local mall.

Measures: Caregiver Strain Questionnaire (CGSQ). This 21-item scale [was] developed by Brannan and colleagues for the Fort Bragg evaluation of children's mental health services. Bickman measured objective and subjective parental burdens experienced in caring for their emotionally distressed children over the preceding six months. Originally called the Burden of Care Questionnaire, it consists of 11 items measuring objective strain and 10 items measuring subjective strain, each answered on a five-point Likert scale, with higher scores indicating more strain. Reliability is high (Cronbach alpha =.93). In our study the overall alpha was .92, with .91 for objective strain and .83 for subjective strain....

...Child Behavior Checklist (CBCL), a 113-item checklist format measure assessing emotional and behavioral problems of children ages four through 16, asks parents to rate the extent of each problem in the past six months on a scale from 0 to 2, with higher scores indicating greater problem severity. In addition to computing an overall score for total items, we examined scores for the 31 items composing internalizing behaviors (for example, depressed, anxious) and the 33 items tapping externalizing behaviors (for example, aggressive, delinquent). Reliabilities are generally over .90, with evidence of convergent validity with other scales and an ability to discriminate between clinical and nonclinical groups. Alpha in this study was .94 for the total scale, .84 for the 31 items on the internalizing subscale, and .91 for the 33 items on the externalizing subscale.

Source: Sales, E., Greeno, C., Shear, M. K., & Anderson, C. (2004). Maternal caregiving strain as a mediator in the relationship between child and mother mental health problems. *Social Work Research, 28*(4), 211–223.

Checklists as Frequency Records

Clinicians can design checklists to provide a record of the frequency of a behavior. Checklists can be as prosaic as a list of what the therapist wishes to discuss during a case conference or during chart rounds. An immense range of behaviors can be assessed using this approach. Topics for assessment can include pro-social–antisocial behaviors, eating habits, organizational ability, alcohol consumption, smoking behaviors, cleanliness habits, compliance with directions, activity level, and many others. The use of a frequency record several times during a treatment program can provide a record of behavioral change.

CASE IN POINT 13.1

Hospitalized patients in the psychiatric unit who are aggressive and act out need to be monitored and have their treatment regimen modified as needed. In preparation for a case conference, the clinician may develop and use a checklist to tabulate the occurrence of the patient's inappropriate behaviors. This hypothetical document can be employed again later to assess the success of modifications in the treatment protocol. That checklist could take the following form:

Patient's ID No. _____ Week of: ___/___/____ to___/___/____

Frequency of Occurrence of Behavior	Monday	Tuesday	Wednesday	Thursday	Friday
Refuses to participate in group discourse	XXX	X		XX	XX
Ignores others in day room	XXXXX	XX	X	X	XXXXX
Takes others' property	XX	X		X	XXX
Refuses compliance requests by PNA	XXX	XX		XXX	XXXX
Refuses to follow directions	XXX	X		XX	XX
Other concerns					

Note: In a review of the patient's pattern of behaviors, it is evident that the activity level increases just before and after weekends. This may indicate that there are visitors during the weekend programs that increase the patient's volatility.

Factual and Demographic Questions

When meeting a new client, many practitioners collect factual and demographic information about the client. These factual characteristics can normally be documented with just one item. Questions of fact or demography should provide the respondent with exhaustive and mutually exclusive categories, or they should ask for a specific number or date (Patten, 2001). For example, the following items are asking demographic questions and only need to be asked once:

- Your birth date ___/___/____
- Gender ___(male) ___(female)
- Marital status:
  a. ___Married living together
  b. ___Unmarried in a committed relationship
  c. ___Separated
  d. ___Widowed

e.   ___ Divorced

f.   ___Single

- Number of children living at home _____ (Boys) _____(Girls)
- Employment status

    a.   ___Employed full-time
    b.   ___Employed part-time
    c.   ___Unemployed and actively looking for work
    d.   ___Unemployed
    e.   ___Retired

A number of demographic dimensions are difficult to express in mutually exclusive and exhaustive categories. One of these is the issue of race. All humans share a common set of genes (100% commonality), and all differences between groups and individuals are expressed as minor alterations of the sequencing of genetic material onto the chromosomal structures within individual humans (National Academy of Sciences, 2009). The American psychologist and theorist Robert Sternberg has discounted the whole issue of race by describing it as a social construct, not a biological dimension worthy of research outside of a socialization context (Sternberg, Grigorenko, & Kidd, 2005). Yet, race persists as an important part of American culture.

Central to our racial classifications is skin color. A problem with this system is that not all people of what we define as members of a racial group have the same color of pigment in their skin; even children in the same family can vary greatly in their coloration. Other phenotypic variations within a color group can wash out completely. A third or more of African Americans in the United States today share the DNA of the white owners of their ancestors (Willing, 2006). The US Department of Education (2007) uses the following demographic scale to classify individuals:

- Hispanic/Latino of any race
- American Indian or Alaska Native
- Asian
- Black or African American
- Native Hawaiian or Other Pacific Islander
- White
- Two or more races

This classification system entangles two dimensions, race and ethnicity. Americans are increasingly multiracial in background, and these categories provide less and less useful information.

Online Surveys

Survey research is still dominated by paper-and-pencil questionnaires. However, it is increasingly being conducted online (Van Horn, Green, & Martinussen, 2009). The future inevitably will see fewer paper-and-pencil surveys and more survey questionnaires designed, administered, and analyzed through the Internet. The obvious problem with this approach to data collection is the uneven distribution of computer equipment and computer skills among the general public. In 2012, about 80% of all American homes were online (Pew Internet & American Life Project, 2012). Fewer homes of ethnic minorities have home computer systems than do homes of whites, who have on average higher SES. Additionally, an age gap exists, with younger members of our society being more computer literate and having greater access to online systems than do the elderly. Thus, online surveys may be measuring from a population frame that is not aligned with the population of the greater community.

Substantive research in the social sciences involving the use of survey questionnaires can now be developed, administered, and analyzed over the Internet. Internet-based survey research can be employed by practitioner-researchers who have an immediate need for data and do not have the lead time necessary to conduct survey research through the mail. Funding agencies and their grant applications frequently provide very short timelines for applications to be completed and submitted. An online needs assessment can provide one of the critical components of an application for federal or state funding of a clinic or social service program.

Elected representatives of professional associations also use online surveys to assess the membership's attitudes toward the organization's policies and goals. When these surveys are sent, organizations rarely send prenotification of their intent to employ an online survey. Research has found no significant difference between return rates for surveys that have had prenotifications and return rates without prenotifications (Hart, Brennan, Sym, & Larson, 2009). Likewise, modifying the email subject line has little impact on the rate of participation in online surveys. Even a blank subject line has been shown to work about as well as identifying the email as being from a researcher or a university (Porter & Whitcomb, 2005).

One goal of survey researchers is to have a large and representative sample of respondents. Survey strategies used to improve rates of completion and return have included offering individuals who complete the survey entries to a lottery for a prize. However, this approach has not been shown to work (Heerwegh, 2006).

Applications from the Literature

Online Research from Across a Large Geographic Area

Note: The authors use the term ***telemental*** to describe providing therapy through the use of video-telephone links. Online research makes it possible to include a national sample in a study without spending a large amount.

Hypothesis: Clinicians who have no telemental health training and who have been in the mental health field longer will use telemental health less frequently than those who have had training and who have spent less time in the field.

Method: The current study used two groups: participants in the online survey and participants from in-person interviews. The participant profile for the online survey was as follows: the majority was female (74%); 33% were between 45 and 54 years of age; 22% were between the ages of 25 and 34 and 35 to 44, respectively. Participants resided in different provinces and territories, including Nova Scotia (4.9%), New Brunswick (11.6%), Quebec (8.5%), Ontario (14.6%), Manitoba (13.4%), Alberta (12.2%), British Columbia (22%), and the Yukon (1.2%). Respondents' professional designations included social workers (38%), nurses (12%), psychologists (11%), administrators/program managers (9%), students (8%), community health workers (5%), and psychiatrists (4%).

Source: Simms, D. C., Gibson, K., O'Donnell, S. (2011). To use or not to use: Clinicians' perceptions of telemental health. *Canadian Psychology, 52*(1), 41–51.

Formatting issues should be considered when using online questionnaires. Many online questionnaires provide open boxes in which respondents can provide more elaborated answers to a question. The size of the box provided is a limiting factor in how much a respondent writes (Fuchs, 2009). The researcher should base the selection of an online survey system on what is expected from the survey. To know what to expect, researchers should employ a focus group using a paper-and-pencil draft of the survey. This experience will provide the practitioner-researcher with the background to make an appropriate selection of online survey system.

A number of commercial providers provide survey development, website hosting, and data analysis services. These systems are good ways to conduct a single survey of a defined sample. Following are websites of three of the many providers of these services:

SurveyMonkey, http://www.surveymonkey.com/

WorldAPP's Key Survey, http://www.keysurvey.com/

Stat Pac, http://www.statpac.com/demo.htm

Practitioner-researchers may also buy commercial software to compose and administer online surveys on an ongoing basis. Owning such software makes it possible to receive a constant flow of updated information from a community of stakeholders. Once a practitioner-researcher has his or her database established, it is then possible to query members of the service community on an ongoing basis.

Snap Surveys, http://www.snapsurveys.com/

Checkbox Survey Solutions, http://www.checkbox.com/

Raosoft, http://www.raosoft.com/

STRUCTURED INTERVIEWS

In Chapter 4, the use of open-ended questions during interviews was described in terms of qualitative research. Another interview method, the structured interview, provides a structure and can provide quantitative data that requires little clinical interpretation. There are 40 published structured psychological interview protocols reviewed in the *Mental Measurements Yearbook* (http://buros.unl.edu/buros/jsp/search.jsp).

Assistants and interns can use structured interviews to screen self-referred new clients to a busy counseling center. The interview can facilitate an efficient treatment decision for a new client. All individuals who employ a structured interview should be well trained in the use of the instrument. That training should be renewed on a regular basis to prevent interviewer drift. *Drift* describes the tendency for people to modify their behaviors as they repeat an activity. Such modifications must be avoided when staff interviewers use a structured interview instrument.

Development of a structured interview starts with a set of goals and specific objectives. These goal statements guide the writing of a series of questions to be asked of interviewees. Format issues also need to be addressed. For example, space might or might not be provided for taking **marginal notes** on the interview form. Marginal notes make it possible to document descriptive behavioral observations not covered by the protocol. In addition, structured interviews should provide detailed and explicit directions for those who will administer the interview to others.

SAMPLING

When interviews or questionnaires are employed by a practitioner for research or program evaluation, the question "Whom will be asked to provide the data?" must be addressed. If the new instrument is part of a research effort, the practitioner-researcher must also decide if the new measure will be used by others in different venues.

Populations and Samples

Most medical and clinical facilities ask the entire population of patients to respond to a questionnaire as part of the discharge procedure. When data are collected from all people treated in the facility, those individuals define the population for that study. On the other hand, if only 15% of the licensed counselors of a state are asked to complete a survey, then those counselors are a sample of the state's population of counselors. Samples are used to estimate what is true for the whole population. (See Chapter 9 for more on populations and samples from them.)

A population can be defined by using any number of physical, political, or geographic boundaries. These boundaries are referred to as the population frame.

When the task of a researcher is to determine a community's opinion, the population could be defined as all adults residing in the community, or as all people including children over the age of 5 years living in the community, or all adults over the age of 18 who are likely to vote. Any one of these populations may be too large for the exhaustive surveying of all of its members. The logistics and expense of large-scale data collection normally preclude this possibility. For that reason, most practitioner-researchers collect survey data from a sample of the community. Naturally, the best sample is one that is an accurate

Applications from the Literature

Sample Description from a Counseling Education Research

Note: This study needed the cooperation of departmental administrators of CACREP-accredited programs offering doctoral-level programs. The authors secured cooperation from less than half of those programs. It is not clear whether the entire population of doctoral student completers and dropouts were appropriately represented in the final sample from the 17 cooperating graduate departments.

Research Goal: The purpose of the present study was to fill the gap in the current research on this topic by obtaining the voices of the students, studying students at the programmatic level, and targeting counselor education doctoral students who had not been a target population in previous research. More specifically, this study describes, from the students' perspectives, the factors that influence counselor education doctoral students' decisions to persist in or leave their programs.

Participants: Thirty-three current and former (defined as graduates and students who left programs) students from 17 of the 41 CACREP-accredited doctoral programs that were accredited at the time of our data collection participated in this study. Students in CACREP-accredited programs were selected because of the consistency in program parameters that accreditation affords. The majority of the sample consisted of Caucasian women ($n = 28$), U.S. citizens ($n = 29$), full-time students ($n = 26$), and students in the early stages of doctoral study.

Source: Hoskins, C. M., & Goldberg, A. D. (2005). Doctoral student persistence in counselor education programs: Student-program match. *Counselor Education and Supervision, 44*(3), 175–189.

representation of the entire community. Researchers can employ a number of approaches to select an appropriate sample.

Probability Sampling

With probability sampling, each person in the population has a known, nonzero chance of being included in the sample. This eliminates any possible selection bias, thereby enabling the researcher to analyze the collected data using parametric statistics and interpret outcomes based on standard statistical distributions (Kalton, 1983). The forms of probability sampling include simple random sampling, systematic random sampling, stratified random sampling, and random cluster sampling.

Nonprobability Sampling

Much survey research is conducted following a nonprobability model. These approaches do not permit others to generalize from the reported findings of researchers. Types of nonprobability samples include samples of convenience, purposeful samples, quota samples, and volunteer samples. Each of these nonprobability-sampling systems is described in

Chapter 9. Nonprobability sampling with interviews and open-ended questions are frequently used in mixed methods research (Chapter 15) to provide depth to the data collected during a structured experimental study.

Sample Size

All samples are imperfect representations of the population and include an amount of sampling error (see Chapter 12 for a discussion of standard error of measurement). The larger the size of a randomly selected sample, the lower the amount of sampling error. Several factors enter into the choice of a sample size. These include

- the population size;
- the acceptable error margin (score plus or minus some amount of error);
- the confidence the researcher wishes to achieve in the outcome; and
- the distribution of subjects.

Table 13.2   Number of Subjects Needed to Make Up an Appropriate Sample[6]

Population Size	95% Confidence		99% Confidence	
	(+/−5)	*(+/−3)*	*(+/−5)*	*(+/−3)*
100	80	92	87	95
250	152	203	182	220
500	217	341	296	394
1,000	278	516	400	649
1,500	306	624	461	828
2,000	322	696	500	961
3,000	341	787	545	1,144
5,000	357	880	588	1,350
10,000	370	964	624	1,561
100,000	383	1,056	661	1,815
1,000,000	384	1,066	665	1,846

Source: Developed by author.

The size of the population is a consideration in determining sample size. The relationships between the population size and other parameters of the sample are not linear. As the population increases, the required sample size does not increase in proportion (see Table 13.2). Thus, a national sample can be surveyed using as few as a thousand or so randomly selected respondents from the population.

The error margin is the size limit of the possible difference between what would be found for the whole population and the sample findings. Therefore, an error margin of (±4) indicates that the sample's finding is within plus or minus 4 points of the true outcome for the whole population.

The confidence level is the probability that the outcome for the whole population would fall within the limits selected as the error margin. Thus, a 95% confidence level indicates that the researcher knows that the outcome from the sample has a 95% chance of being within the error margin of the true population value. Reversing that, the researcher knows that there is only a 5% chance that the true finding from the whole population would fall outside the error margin selected by the researcher.

From Table 13.2, it is clear that a survey of the 1,000 professional employees of a medical center at the 95% confidence level, having a plus or minus margin of error of 3 points (±3), would require a sample size of 516. If one accepted a larger amount of error (±5), the appropriate sample size would need to be only 278. As another example, to sample a population of 500 outpatients with 95% confidence and a margin of error of (±5), a sample of 217 patients would be required.

Oversampling

The method of simple random sampling is appropriate for determining the big picture of a total population. What may be lost is the minority voice. In a hypothetical medical center employing 1,000 workers, there may be 25 Asian American workers, 125 African American workers, 100 Hispanic workers, and 750 white workers. As determined above, a sample of 278 would be needed to represent the whole facility (±5 for error) at the 95% confidence level. However, it may happen that none of the Asian American workers would be randomly selected to be part of the sample. The other minorities may likewise be over- or undersampled according to the vagaries of the random sampling process.

Therefore, to include all voices, it would be necessary to sample all stratifications at the same 95% confidence level with an error level of (±5). Thus, 24 of the 25 Asian employees, 94 of the 125 African American employees, 80 of the 100 Hispanic employees, and 254 of the 750 white employees would be in an oversampled data set. The large subsamples are the result of sampling each group as though it were a separate population. This approach makes it possible to draw conclusions about each of the ethnic groups within the medical center. Thus, a total stratified sample of 452 workers would be needed to represent the population of 1,000. To balance the influence of the oversampled components of the sample, a series of weights are applied to their contribution to the final statistical summary of the population.

SUMMARY

The construction of a psychological questionnaire begins with the establishment of a measurement goal and the specification of objectives. The primary format for questionnaires includes semantic approaches to measurement (Likert Scales and semantic differential scales) and hierarchical scales (e.g., Thurstone). Likert-type questionnaire items are ordinal measurements. Semantic differential item totals provide an approximation of an interval scale of measurement. Hierarchical scales using equal interval–appearing adjectives also provide a parametric level of measurement for survey data.

Rating scales can also be designed with interval-appearing levels describing the subject being rated. The process of building a rating scale normally includes an analysis of the problem or environment to determine which dimensions need to be included in the new rating scale. Checklists may involve simple dichotomous responses such as yes-no or a basic count of occurrences.

Demographic questions ask individuals about their status, health, ethnicity, age, gender, and other matters of fact. These questions can be written with categories for respondents to use in responding.

Much of research based on survey data is now using data collected via online systems. Online survey systems are also sold for institutional use and maintained on an academic department's computer or on a clinic's server. Owning the software makes it possible to be in ongoing contact with a database of members of the community being served.

Before a questionnaire or other scale is ready to be applied in different venues or have data from it generalized into other locations, it must be tested on a large sample of individuals. This involves establishing membership in the target population; once the population has been framed, a sample can be selected from it. To be generalized to other locations, the sampling should be based on a scientific probability sampling procedure (i.e., simple random sampling, systematic sampling, stratified random sampling, or cluster sampling).

DISCUSSION QUESTIONS

1. What steps should a professor of clinical research take to optimize the reliability of a questionnaire used to assess graduate students' sense of self-efficacy as researchers?

2. How can the validity of a rating scale used to assess a client's acquisition of basic interpersonal skills be demonstrated?

3. Design a 10-question Likert-type scale or a 5-item semantic differential scale that can quantify the opinion of other class members on a topic of common interest (e.g., the university's bookstore, computer support services from the campus-based IT staff, student parking access, the university's food service options, etc.). Share your questionnaire with your classmates and discuss its strengths and weaknesses.

4. Create a checklist for a college senior to follow when getting ready to attend graduate or professional school as a full-time graduate student in residence. List all steps in sequence that must be followed for an optimally smooth transition into advanced education.

5. Frame the population for and design a cluster sampling system (probability sample) for the undergraduates of this university with the goal of assessing student perceptions of the campus's counseling office. As an alternative, do the same activity based on the campus of another institution with which you are familiar.

NOTES

1. The acronym CERAD represents the Consortium to Establish a Registry for Alzheimer's Disease at Duke University Medical Center.

2. The range of nonparametric statistical tests may be applied to answer research questions based on questionnaire data from a Likert-type scale. (See Chapter 11 for a discussion of nonparametric statistics.)

3. Reliability of measures using Likert-type items is improved when several questions ask about the same dimension. One can then add individual ordinal answers together and use the totals as Type II ordinal data. These data can be used in parametric statistical approaches for hypothesis testing and correlational research. Many psychometricians disagree with this premise (Jamieson, 2004). Some of those maintaining a traditional approach to research with Likert scales have referred to the practice of using parametric statistics as an "ordinal sin."

4. Uncorrelated or independent and latent factors explain almost all of the within-subjects variance on a semantic differential scale.

5. See Connolly, C. (2009, January 15). Surgery checklist lowers death rate. *The Washington Post.* http://www.washingtonpost.com/wp-dyn/content/story/2009/01/14/ST2009011402914.html.

6. To calculate other required sample sizes, see http://www.surveysystem.com/sscalc.htm.

SECTION VI

Organizing and Applying Research Skills

"Quality means doing it right when no one is looking."

Henry Ford

This section provides ways to design high-quality research in the social sciences and to apply those methods in mixed combinations and in the evaluation of programs and systems. It concludes with information and insight into how to write research proposals and research reports.

Chapter 14   In this chapter, the validity of entire approaches used in conducting a research study is examined. This discussion of research design focuses mostly on descriptive, correlational, and experimental research methods. The special issues of trustworthiness of interpretative (qualitative) designs are also integrated in this presentation. (These qualitative designs are more fully addressed in Chapters 4 and 5.)

Chapter 15   This chapter describes the great debate over research philosophies and methods that occurred in the last half of the 20th century and its partial resolution in the form of mixed methods research. The pragmatic solution for many research problems is a blend or mix of both qualitative and quantitative research.

Chapter 16   This chapter is concerned with applying all the concepts of qualitative methods, quantitative methods, measurement design and data description, and mixed methods research to conduct evaluation research. Evaluations present outcomes from formative and summative elements that assess what happened in a project or program, and they provide answers to pragmatic questions of effectiveness and cost.

Chapter 17 The last component of Section VI provides guidance in developing and writing a proposal for research. In addition to writing methods and sources of research ideas, this chapter provides guidance in writing a full research report or article for publication.

CHAPTER 14

Organizing Valid Research

"Research is formalized curiosity. It is poking and prying with a purpose."

Zora Neale Hurston

OBJECTIVES

By reading and studying this chapter, you should acquire the competency to do the following:

- Explain the terms *experimental* and *control groups*.
- Compare population validity with ecological validity.
- List and explain the major threats to internal validity in social science research.
- Explain the differences among pre-experiments, quasi-experiments, and true experiments.
- Describe experimental designs for research in terms of organization and threats to internal validity they may or may not control.
- Explain representativeness and its relationship to population and ecological external validity.

INTRODUCTION AND MAJOR THEMES

As a researcher focused on agriculture, Ronald Fisher had complete control of all potential factors that could impact the experimental conditions he organized. This level of experimental control is a luxury never afforded to those who do research in the behavioral sciences. The need for valid answers to problems of the human condition led practitioner-researchers to develop a number of approaches for systematically improving research validity and for reducing the potential of extraneous factors to influence outcomes (D. T. Campbell & Stanley, 1963).

In previous chapters, statistical methods were elaborated describing how quantitatively oriented behavioral researchers can establish, and then empirically test, research hypotheses. However, the finding that the null hypothesis can be rejected does not provide proof of a causal link between the independent and dependent variables. Only when appropriate statistics are employed within the context of a valid research design is cause-and-effect "scientifically established."

There are two primary concerns when determining the quality of any research design. One is the external generalizability of the study's findings. The second is the operational integrity of the link between independent and dependent variables. The latter issue is described as **internal validity** and the former as external validity (Shadish, Cook, & Campbell, 2002).

Within external validity, one major focus is on the research environment: This is known as the **ecological validity** of the study. Ecological validity is an expression of how close the experimental setting, equipment, and tasks are to the real lives of the subjects involved. A second major factor in external validity is described as **population validity** (Bracht & Glass, 1968). Population validity is determined by the representativeness of the sample of subjects used and the potential for specific characteristics of the sample of subjects to interact with the experimental condition or treatment.[1]

INTERNAL VALIDITY

Internal validity addresses the question of whether there is a bona fide cause-and-effect link between the independent variable and the dependent variable. It is sometimes referred to as **causal validity.** For example, if a clinician is working with a population of young people in a residential treatment center for severe eating disorders (anorexia nervosa, both restrictive and binge/purge types), he or she may initiate research into the effectiveness of a family therapy intervention. Once the population is defined and a sample randomly selected, it can be divided into two parts, an experimental group and a control (or comparison) group. This research effort might involve providing several treatments, including a program of family therapy along with nutritional counseling and antidepressant medications, to the experimental or **treatment group.** In this hypothetical effort, the other half of the sample would be provided with nutritional counseling and antidepressant medications only. This latter group, not receiving family therapy, composes the hypothetical control group. The quality of this possible research effort will, in part, be a function of the amount of experimental control the researcher has. For example, if patients and their families are asked to volunteer to participate in family therapy, the two groups may be very different when the study begins (volunteers vs. nonvolunteers). This restriction on the researcher prevents a truly random approach for assigning individuals to the two groups and introduces many alternative explanations for an outcome difference between the two groups.

In this hypothetical study of treatment options for eating disorders, the potential alternate explanations for outcome differences between groups may supersede the researcher's goal of determining whether family counseling is effective. These experimental validity problems have led leading theorists in psychology, including Wolfgang Köhler, to grouse that "psychology is a very unsatisfactory science" (Crick, 1995, p. 71).

Applications from the Literature

Description of a Control Group

Note: In this study, the researchers compared stroke patients (CVA) in an inpatient rehabilitation program with a nonrandom sample of 80 volunteers who served as the control group. The researchers had no control over the experimental group (i.e., they had no control over who was a stroke patient) and had to use a grab bag of volunteers as the control group.

Compare this research design to the next one by Rusted and colleagues in which subjects were randomly assigned to participate in the experimental group (art therapy) or the occupational therapy program (control or comparison group). Clearly, the second study has many fewer problems with what have been called "rival hypotheses" for the findings (Huck & Sandler, 1979).

Methods, Control Group: Participants in the control group consisted of 80 volunteers gathered from various sources in the community (hospital employees and their friends/family, church groups, and civic organizations). Potential participants were excluded if they reported a history of neurological illness or injury (e.g., stroke, seizures, traumatic brain injury) or severe psychiatric illness. All control participants were living independently in the community in their own residences. These control participants were derived from a larger sample of community volunteers in a validation study.

Source: Vickery, C. D., Sepehri, A., & Evans, C. C. (2008). Self-esteem in an acute stroke rehabilitation sample: A control group comparison. *Clinical Rehabilitation, 22*(2), 179–187. doi: 10.1177/0269215507080142

Organizing Both an Experimental and a Control Group

Art therapy and activity groups took place in parallel in each centre, on the same day at the same time each week. Each group comprised an art therapist (AT) or occupational therapist (OT), an assistant, and up to six clients. All therapists and assistants attended induction meetings where the research protocol was outlined. Handbooks outlining the research protocol were prepared and distributed. Following standard practice, art therapists were given a minimum of fortnightly supervision sessions with the senior AT. Similar supervisory sessions with the Research Psychologist were offered to the OTs but were not taken up. All assistants worked under the guidance of the therapists and attended regular supervision sessions with the psychologist.

For the art therapy groups, a group-interactive, psychodynamic approach was employed. A variety of art materials were presented for use within the sessions. For the activity groups, a selection of recreational activities was made from a range currently in use in different centres in the locality. OTs were instructed not to use any formal occupational therapeutic methods or any form of art and craft work in the activity groups. Participants were randomly assigned to art therapy (experimental) or activity (control) groups with a maximum of six per group. Random allocation was based on participants' ID numbers being drawn by chance. Groups met for one hour per week over 40 weeks.

Source: Rusted, J., Sheppard, L., & Waller, D. (2006). A multi-centre control group trial on the use of art therapy for older people with dementia. *Group Analysis, 39*(4), 517–536. doi: 10.1177/0533316406071447

Threats to Internal Validity

The potential problems involving internal validity in experimental studies were first listed and explained by Donald Campbell (1957). His list was then organized around various research designs employed in the social sciences (D. T. Campbell & Stanley, 1963). Possible problems can be organized into three principal clusters: time-related factors, measurement-related factors, and issues of research structure.

Each of the potential problems in internal validity is linked to the length of time the research requires to complete. Most studies of counseling programs are **longitudinal** in nature and run throughout the course of a client's treatment. Even brief, solution-focused counseling programs can last 6 or more weeks (Sklare, 2005).

CASE IN POINT   14.1

In 1921, Lewis M. Terman of Stanford University began a seminal study of gifted children in California by following 1,528 youngsters who tested well on an IQ test. The study extended for the rest of the children's lives (Shurkin, 1992). The population Terman identified had a mean age of 11 and a mean IQ score of 150. At the start of the study, parents and teachers were asked to complete long questionnaires (28 pages) about the identified gifted children. Each child was given a medical examination and an anthropomorphic assessment. Three hours of achievement testing and an individually administered IQ test were also added to each child's database. During the study, follow-up interviews and testing were carried out every 11 or 12 years after the initial child-hood testing. During later adulthood, follow-up studies were conducted on a 4- or 5-year cycle.

This huge effort outlived its originator and followed surviving members of the population into the 21st century, when a few centenarians were still being studied in their old age by researchers from Harvard and Stanford universities.

This type of study is described as longitudinal research. Such studies provide critical information about human development and aging. The logical problem with such studies is possible attrition over their course. For example, World War II would have occurred when the population was about 30 years old, and a number of the male cohort from the original database may have been lost to combat. Also, because these academically gifted individuals lived through the Great Depression, their educational aspirations may have been modified in ways that do not apply to current youth. Many other stress factors from that era may have contributed to the unusually high suicide rate experienced by Terman's population (8%). Another problem with the study is with its population validity due to an obvious bias in the study's selection process. In Terman's sample, there were no children of Chinese, Mexican American, or Italian heritage. Additionally, there were only 30 African American children and 90 children of Japanese heritage in the study's gifted population.

Time-Related Factors in Validity

The potential for a loss of internal validity in a research effort as a function of time can be divided into three areas of concern.

- **Maturation.** As time passes, individuals age and mature. This simple fact of life can produce differential outcomes at different ages/stages in human development. The issue of maturation can have a powerful effect when the effectiveness of counseling teenage adolescents is being researched. The developmental era of puberty and adolescence is one of rapid cognitive, physical, and conceptual development, as well as one of social-emotional change. Development and improved social understanding may occur whether the young person meets with a counselor or not. Throughout every lifetime, there are identifiable points in time when each human is optimally sensitive and ready for cognitive reorganization and acceptance of a new level of understanding. For example, during the ages most associated with college attendance, youth begin to wrestle with tasks of adult identity formation and learn new, more subtle approaches for interpersonal interaction.

There is a natural tendency for practitioner-researchers who are assessing a counseling program to draw conclusions from apparent score changes from pre- to posttests.

Before-and-after comparisons present a special statistical problem related to reliability. The subtraction of pretest scores from the posttest scores for individuals provides what are known as **subtraction residuals.** These residuals have very low reliability and are, for the most part, composed of measurement error (Salthouse, 2001). For that reason, they are neither reliable nor valid for use as a dependent variable.[2]

- **History.** Internal validity threats linked to history concern the possibility that there may be a significant occurrence between when the pretest and the posttest data are collected. The research findings can be compromised by unexpected disruptions and events. Life-changing events for one individual pose a random error. When the occurrence has an impact on most or all of a study's subjects, the findings may be compromised.

Sometimes internal validity is threatened by world-changing events. For example, therapists and practitioner-researchers are likely to have had their work disrupted for days or even weeks as a result of the terror of September 11, 2001. You will always know exactly where you were, and what you were doing, when you realized that the United States was being attacked on 9/11. This example demonstrates the potentially powerful disruptive effect of historical events.

Major disruptions do not just occur on a national stage. Local events (e.g., hospital or clinical renovation and reconstruction, the calling of a code blue, or a violent disturbance in or near the clinic) may also profoundly impact counseling programs.

Applications from the Literature

Brief Case Study Describing the Impact of History on Therapeutic Intervention

Note: In this brief case study, the authors employed a survey to determine if there was a significant disruption in psychodrama, sociometry, and group psychotherapy as a function of the terrorist attacks of September 11, 2001.

(Continued)

(Continued)

Introduction: To find out psychodramatists' opinions about issues facing the profession that might have been affected by the terrorist acts of 09/11/2001, a survey was mailed to 200 individuals selected at random from the Directory of the American Board of Examiners in Psychodrama, Sociometry and Group Psychotherapy. Of the 78 respondents, 45 (58%) indicated that they felt the terrorist acts changed the profession "some-to-extensively." Client issues, populations of clients served, approaches to psychotherapy, and training in psychodrama were major areas of perceived change. While 78 respondents may not represent the entire profession, it was hoped that the opinions conveyed could guide discussions as the healing professions attempt to cope with the after-effects of acts of terrorism.

Source: Kranz, P. L., Lund, N. L., & Steele, R. A. (2003). Survey of psychodramatists' opinions: Professional issues post 9/11. *Journal of Instructional Psychology, 30*(2), 173–175.

- **Mortality or mobility.** Individuals and families move into and out of communities every day. This simple fact can play a major role in the outcome of a clinical treatment. The loss of even a single client can change the dynamic of a counseling group. Likewise, the late addition of individuals to a group can also have a profound impact on its functioning. This phenomenon is amplified for clinical settings experiencing extraordinarily high rates of turnover. For example, a study of treatments for tobacco/nicotine addiction among an adolescent population normally uses a pretest to establish use levels and a posttest to gauge the program's effectiveness. There is a high likelihood that dropouts from the treatment program will be the heaviest smokers, and their loss will modify the overall mean scores on measures of cigarette smoking at the end of the treatment.

Research efforts with pretests tend to take a longer time to run from pretest to posttest than do studies with only posttests. For this reason, such studies may be more subject to problems of mortality.

Differential mortality can also be artificially created in an effort to control an outcome from a research study. An example is seen in Case in Point 14.2.

CASE IN POINT   14.2

A colleague described how as a post–master's doctoral student she was one of seven graduate students in her department classified as a teaching associate (TA). These TAs independently taught two sections of undergraduate psychology. The professor in charge of the classes also taught one class. As new instructors, the TAs' syllabi were short and to the point. However, the lead professor had an enormous syllabus for his class with 20 pages of readings, reports to prepare, and projects to complete. When the classes met for the first time, there was a rush of students to drop the class being taught by the lead professor, and many of these fleeing students were subsequently added to the sections taught by TAs. The TAs' classes became larger and even overcrowded, while the professor's was reduced to a small seminar-size group. After the drop-add period passed, he cancelled his first syllabus in favor of a more student-friendly version.

The result of his gamesmanship was that the professor ended up with a small class of motivated students while the TAs ended up with overcrowded classes of less motivated undergraduates.

Applications from the Literature

Empirical Demonstration of the Mortality Effect in Research

Note: This longitudinal study followed two groups of 6th-grade children through their adolescent years to the 12th grade. Each year, they were assessed for the use of illegal and illicit drugs. The annual assessment asked which of nine substances they had used during the past year (including LSD, tobacco, alcohol, marijuana, inhalants, and cocaine) and how often they had used the substances. Year-by-year comparisons were conducted.

Discussion: The first hypothesis predicted that dropouts would demonstrate significantly higher baseline mean use of licit and illicit substances when ANOVA was used. This hypothesis was confirmed; dropouts consistently reported higher mean use than stayers for each of the four substances assessed: tobacco, alcohol, marijuana, and hard drugs.

Source: Tebes, J. K., Snow, D. L., & Arthur, M. W. (1992). Panel attrition and external validity in the short-term follow-up study of adolescent substance use. *Evaluation Review, 16*(2), 151–170. doi: 10.1177/0193841X9201600203

Measurement-Related Factors in Validity

Each of the next three factors is linked to the sequence and type of measurements the researcher uses. All individuals responding to a survey may not perceive measurements as having the same amount of importance. Also, administrators have much more faith in the value of measures of all types than do clinicians. Thus, the selection or development of a measure is an important consideration in any empirical study (Guskey, 2007). Once measurement tools are selected, the problem becomes one of how and when they are employed in the study.

- **Instrumentation.** This term is used as shorthand to represent changes occurring with the measuring technique and instruments over time. Subtle changes may occur with interviewers, observers, and raters. Such changes are known as **rater drift** and are viewed as a normal process reflecting the experience people gain over time while they are collecting data. Changes may also occur with test materials when they are reused. Any items handled by people being tested (e.g., Rorschach ink blot plates or psychodramatic materials) will deteriorate with time and use. Even the practice that subjects get in the use of computerized testing software can change the outcome during online data collection.

Applications from the Literature

Researcher's Discussion of Internal Validity

Note: This discussion by Michael Harwell provides insight into problems associated with using several raters as data collectors in his review of the validity of research into the evaluation of written essays.

(Continued)

(Continued)

Internal Validity: A careful monitoring of rating behavior and an appropriate change of pace if there is evidence that rater fatigue is affecting the quality of the ratings can stave off the effects of instrumentation. Changing the interval between ratings or the number of participants or products being rated over a fixed time may also help. Of course, rating skills also may improve during the course of a study.

This phenomenon is similar to carryover effects in repeated measures designs. Carryover effects can be constant across raters or peculiar to individual raters and generally involve an improvement of skills through a particular kind of carryover effect, a practice effect. Unsystematic practice effects, by which some raters improve more than others, implies the assumption of consistency of raters' ability is no longer tenable. Although this condition by itself does not ensure invalid ratings, it increases the likelihood that the validity of the ratings may be compromised.

Source: Harwell, M. (1999). Evaluating the validity of educational rating data. *Educational and Psychological Measurement, 59*(1), 25–37. doi: 10.1177/0013164499591002

- **Testing.** If a pretest is used to evaluate a clinical program's effectiveness, its presence may alert clients to issues in the treatment program deemed to be important. There is also a normal tendency for most scores on any measure to improve slightly on a second testing. When a test or measure (pretest) causes direct or indirect changes in subsequent measurement or posttest, that pretest is referred to as being a **reactive measure.** The closer together in time two sequential measures occur, the greater is the potential for the first to be a reactive measure and interfere with the other. This effect has been demonstrated in a number of personality and intellectual areas with individuals, and it may even impact studies of cognition (Roediger & Karpicke, 2006). For example, school psychologists are required (by state and federal regulations) to reevaluate children on a regular cycle after a decision has been made to provide special educational services. If the initial evaluation included the Wechsler Intelligence Scale for Children, 4th edition, the evaluating professionals will use a different measure for the reevaluation (e.g., Stanford-Binet, 5th edition). By changing evaluation tools, they reduce the possibility that the pretest will be a reactive measure.

- **Regression toward the mean.** What Sir Francis Galton (1886) originally referred to as **regression toward mediocrity** is known today as **regression toward the mean.** This statistical principle provides a mathematical model explaining why unusually high scores on any measure tend to move lower, toward the mean, on retesting.[3] Likewise, exceptionally low scores tend to improve on retesting to values slightly closer to the mean. In an evaluation of the impact of a counseling intervention, an initially low score on a measure of a dependent variable such as "self-esteem" may improve later when the sample is retested, but this improvement may reflect a measure of change related to regression toward the mean.

The **placebo effect** is well known in biomedical research. This effect may also be a form of regression to the mean. Patients used for research trials are frequently at their low point with their medical condition. Following treatment and reevaluation, there may be some small improvement. When the small improvement occurs, even after only a symbolic treatment (placebo), the change is described as a placebo effect but may actually represent statistical regression toward the mean from the extremely low starting point.

Applications from the Literature

Discussion of the Role of Placebo Effects in Psychotherapy

Note: Stewart Justman makes the unsettling point that unlike biologically based therapies such as psychiatry, one-to-one psychotherapy does not need to be concerned with placebo effects because much of the therapeutic process can be interpreted as a placebo. This controversial finding does not represent the consensus of the scientific literature on therapeutic efficaciousness.[5]

Placebo Effect: The point is confirmed, for good or ill, by case histories of patients led to insights about themselves that are believable and encouraging but possibly false. "To be effective, interpretations, the primary means of transmitting the therapist's conceptual framework, need not be correct, only plausible." . . . Unlike a medical doctor carrying out a sham procedure, the psychotherapist on this showing need not disbelieve in proffered interpretations that may be quite untrue but nevertheless make enough sense to the patient for that person to invest in them. And if the healer who is not just an actor but believes in his or her words and deeds makes an especially effective conduit for the placebo effect, then the therapist committed to a "plausible" interpretation is such a conduit.

"With many patients the placebo may be as effective as psychotherapy because the placebo condition contains the necessary, and possibly the sufficient, ingredient for much of the beneficial effect of all forms of psychotherapy. This is a helping person who listens to the patient's complaints and offers a procedure to relieve them, thereby inspiring the patient's hopes and combating demoralization." It is presumably because of this inspirational effect that various modes of psychotherapy seem to work equally well even though founded on different presuppositions.[4]

Source: Justman, S. (2011). From medicine to psychotherapy: The placebo effect. *History of the Human Sciences, 24*(1), 95–107. doi: 10. 1177/0952695110386655

Applications from the Literature

Comparative Influence of a True Placebo and Regression to the Mean

Note: Neil Hawkins and David Scott use a placebo in the treatment program for adjunct epilepsy. The role of a placebo effect and the effect of regression to the mean were compared for their relative influence. The dependent variable was the documented cost-effectiveness estimates of various treatments.

(Continued)

(Continued)

Introduction: Natural variation may lead to a placebo effect within clinical trials due to regression to the mean. Regression to the mean occurs because patients with acutely severe disease are recruited into trials, leading to the preferential selection of patients who are currently experiencing a temporary worsening, or the nadir, in their condition. These patients are likely to show improvement when disease severity is next measured, regardless of any treatment benefit, as they tend toward their individual mean state. The extent to which this regression to the mean effect is seen in general practice will depend on the criteria used to select patients for treatment. If these are similar to those used in the trial, the effects of regression to the mean are likely to be similar. However, if patients with milder disease are treated in clinical practice, the effects of regression to the mean will be reduced.

Source: Hawkins, N., & Scott, D. A. (2010). Cost-effectiveness analysis: Discount the placebo at your peril. *Medical Decision Making, 30*(5), 536–543. doi: 10.1177/0272989X10362106

Research Structure

Human nature can play havoc with the design of behavioral science research (Suter, 2012). Subject selection is the primary challenge to the internal validity of all research efforts. Another potential source of experimental invalidity is the nature of human emotional responses to experimental treatments and the novelty of participating in a study.

- **Selection.** The issue of selection (random vs. nonrandom) is directly linked to comparisons that may be made when assessing effectiveness of programs, therapists, and treatment regimens. The lack of randomization in the selection of participants and the assignment of people to groups presents a potential source of systematic bias. This selection bias may also be introduced in the form of self-selection (volunteerism) on the part of subjects.

Applications from the Literature

Self-Selection as a Source of Internal Invalidity

Note: In this study by Lisa Fredman and her colleagues, research into the strain on caregivers was reviewed and discussed in terms of the validity of sampling and how subjects are selected for inclusion in caregiver research.

Introduction: Selection bias may result from self-selection in who becomes a caregiver, especially the primary caregiver. Taking on the caregiver role may be influenced by gender, familial relationship to the care recipient, marital status, geographic proximity, availability, and psychological and physical health factors. These factors are often confounders of the association between caregiving and outcomes of interest. For example, among siblings, unmarried daughters are most likely to become a caregiver to an elderly parent. Unmarried women report more depressive symptoms than do those who are married which may be one reason for high rates of depression among daughter caregivers. Likewise, self-selection of healthier elderly persons as caregivers may lead to comparing healthier, more resilient elderly caregivers to sicker noncaregiver peers, which may be one reason why few studies observed associations between caregiving and physical health decline. Caregivers who volunteer for research studies or who use support groups may be less likely to be representative of caregivers in general. These types of self-selection may influence recruitment into caregiver samples, as well as study results.

Source: Fredman, L., Tennstedt, S., Smyth, K. A., Kasper, J. D., Miller, B., Fritsch, T. . . . Harris, E. L. (2004). Pragmatic and internal validity issues in sampling in caregiver studies: A comparison of population-based, and ancillary studies. *Journal of Aging and Health, 16*(2), 175–203. doi 10.1177/0898264303262639

- **Interpersonal.** The nature of human beings poses significant problems for researchers. Within this category are two related problems of **envy** and the **spread of effect.** When some individuals are selected (experimental group) to take part in a "special counseling program," it is natural for those not included (control group) to feel envious. This may result in subtle aggression against the program and its participants by those who were "left out." To keep the peace, peer counselors not providing the special program are likely to share major elements of the program with others. This makes any comparison between the two groups of individuals meaningless. Additionally, nonselected individuals may show an unusual level of competitiveness. Some members of the "control group" will show their envy and resentment by working to ensure that they produce a better outcome than is produced by individuals in the new counseling program under study. Conversely, it is also possible for others to see being in the control group as confirmation that they are not respected, and they may become increasingly disengaged; for example, undergraduates not selected for the experimental group may disengage from the university and its support programs.

There is no way to design an empirical study that is totally free of the interpersonal factors of human feelings and the resulting behavior (Trochim, 2006). The best way to minimize these threats is to keep the groups compartmentalized and unaware of each other. The other obvious answer is to switch to a naturalistic approach and employ an ethnographic method to study the impact of a counseling program through observation or participant observation. (See Section II for a discussion of qualitative designs for research.)

- **Novelty.** Most instructors are familiar with the feature-length movie *Dead Poets Society,* starring Robin Williams as an iconoclastic teacher (Haft, Witt, Thomas, & Weir, 1989). To break the mind-set of a classroom of blasé preparatory school students, the teacher (played by Robin Williams) did several absurd stunts such as standing on his desk to teach. Naturally, such behaviors caught the attention of the otherwise uninspired students. While the teacher's tactics were interesting and novel, the logical question is "What is his next act?"

Bored individuals can be excited and interested by a novel approach or technique, but when the luster has worn off, so will motivation and interest in the program. Researchers must be mindful of this tendency for the novelty of a new program to bring about temporary change. For example, being invited to participate in a group by a member of the university's counseling staff may be a novel experience that will stir interest, but after a few sessions, when the novelty wears off, the counselor may find he or she needs to introduce new dimensions and activities for the group. Adolescents and young adults often need ever more stimulation to remain engaged (Thomas, 2009).

Controlling Threats to Internal Validity

The design of experimental research requires the practitioner-researcher to organize a plan for how subjects will be deployed into the various groups and how and when data will be collected.

Symbols for Designs

An article by Bradshaw and Roseborough (described later in this chapter) introduced symbols developed by Donald Campbell as a form of shorthand for describing research designs. Campbell's system centers on the independent variable and how subjects are assigned to groups. The major divisions of the independent variable are treatment groups, comparison groups, and/or control groups. In experimental studies with less potential for problems of internal validity, control group subjects should exhibit **proximal similarity** to those in the treatment and/or comparison groups (D. T. Campbell & Russo, 1999). Thus, differences between the control group and other groups can be interpreted as an indication of treatment efficacy. Comparison groups are often employed in behavioral research in lieu of control groups. Many times it is either unethical or impractical to select a group of subjects and then not provide the experimental treatment. Professional societies endorse a policy that each client has a "right to service" on an equal basis with other clients. An experimental program under study by a practitioner-researcher may be providing beneficial effects. In such a case, clients assigned to the no-treatment control may feel their rights to equal access to services have been violated.

Applications from the Literature

Ethical Problem in Using a Control Group

Note: In this study of HIV/AIDS prevention, the thorny issue of the ethics of using a control group was resolved by providing the control group with a prevention program at a later time. The original sample were adjudicated as being delinquent and assigned to a residential facility. Their time in detention was set, and they were offered the opportunity to participate in an HIV/AIDS prevention program. Many volunteered, and a treatment and control group were established. By the end of the treatment phase, all were back at home (in the community) with their families.

Method: The adolescents were asked to participate on a voluntary basis, and those that agreed had to sign a consent form. Ninety-eight percent of the adolescents approached by the research team (both the treatment group and the control group) agreed to participate. Sixty-one adolescents underwent an intensive HIV/AIDS-prevention intervention program, and 78 adolescents served as a control group. Of these adolescents, 128 (92 percent) were reassessed at the post-intervention assessment phase (100 percent of the treatment group and 86 percent of the control group) and 122 (88 percent) were reassessed at the follow-up assessment phase nine to 12 months later (92 percent of the treatment group and 85 percent of the control group). Thus, the retention rate in this study was very high. It should be noted that the majority of the participants in both groups (more than 75 percent) were back in the community by the time of the follow-up assessment phase.

The participants in the control group who completed the follow-up data assessment phase (66 respondents) received only personal counseling about HIV/AIDS after the completion of all data collection (that is, delayed-intervention control group). A valid control group should include adolescents who receive no HIV/AIDS prevention counseling at all, but such an approach raises ethical problems, particularly in light of the high risk of infection in this population (Cook & Campbell, 1979). The delayed intervention approach was used in this study to provide the adolescents with basic knowledge about the disease and means to prevent it. Although a delayed intervention approach has its limitations, it is used frequently.

Source: Slonim-Nevo, V. (2001). The effect of HIV/AIDS prevention intervention for Israeli adolescents in residential centers: Results at 12-month follow-up. *Social Work Research, 25*(2), 71–87.

An experiment may include several comparison groups. Membership in one or another comparison group can be based on random assignment from a population. More commonly in research in the behavioral sciences, membership in the comparison groups is based on the subjects' membership in an intact group. Thus, the groups may be composed of very different individuals. For example, a large university may have graduate departments preparing graduate students in clinical psychology, social work, and various other professional counseling options. If the office of institutional research studied the instructional effectiveness of each program's faculty in terms of first-year student achievement, there is a clear potential for alternative explanations for the findings. Yet, there is no clear way to randomly assign students to one or another of the available majors.

Experimental research starts with a randomly drawn sample from the population, which is then subdivided to populate the various experimental and control groups of the study. In Campbell's notation system, the letter R is used to indicate that subjects were randomly assigned to the experimental groups. This R then appears on the left side of the study's diagram.

Some authors use a system of lines to depict when nonrandom, intact groups are used in research. If the study did not randomly assign subjects, the letter R is left out, and a dashed line may be drawn between the various comparison groups. The letter O indicates an observation (e.g., test score) was made of the participants. This could be either the pretest or posttest in an experimental study. The letter X is used to symbolize the presence of

Photo 14.1 Donald T. Campbell

LeHigh University Digital Library.

a treatment or intervention. In the case of a control group not provided with a treatment, the position normally occupied by an X is left blank. Authors occasionally use the letter E to symbolize the experimental group and the letter Y to indicate comparison groups.

The graphic presentation is read from left to right. The temporal sequence and time passage is depicted by distance from the left side of the graph.

True, Quasi-, and Pre-Experiments

Donald Campbell and Julian Stanley (1963) made a distinction between different formats for experimental research. Experiments that use groups for control and treatment conditions that randomly assign subjects to groups are **true experiments.** Organizing this type of research is complex and not practical for many settings, yet true experiments offer the best control for potential problems of internal validity. Since the administration of President George W. Bush, federal support only goes to social science researchers proposing to use a true experiment in their study (RMC Research, 2005).

Many times, it is either unethical or impractical to design research that includes random assignment of subjects. Controlled designs for research that do not randomly assign subjects to groups are described as **quasi-experiments** (Cook & Campbell, 1979). Research efforts lacking both random assignment and control groups are described as **pre-experiments.** Pre-experiments are often employed in action research and in program evaluation.

This section of the chapter presents designs for empirical research. Their names, graphs and hypothesis-testing methods, as well as the internal validity problems they address, are listed in Table 14.1 and described in the text.

Basic Case Study

When the case study is used as a stand-alone empirical tool for hypothesis testing, many problems of internal validity may arise.[6] Brief, one-shot surveys of personal opinions are

Table 14.1 Table of Commonly Used Behavioral Science Designs for Research

Design's Name	Design's Graphic Format	Internal Validity Problem Addressed
Basic case study Pre-experiment	X 0	None of the internal validity problems addressed
One-group pretest-posttest Pre-experiment	0 X 0	Mortality (possible) Selection

Design's Name	Design's Graphic Format	Internal Validity Problem Addressed
Static-groups comparison Quasi-experiment	X 0 ——— 0	History Instrumentation Regression Testing
Pretest-posttest control groups True experiment	R 0 X 0 R 0 0	History Instrumentation Maturation Mortality (possible) Regression Selection Testing
Nonequivalent pretest-posttest Comparison groups Quasi-experiment	0 X 0 ——— 0 0	History Instrumentation Maturation Mortality Regression Testing
Posttest-only control group True experiment	R X 0 R 0	History Instrumentation Maturation Mortality Regression Selection Testing
Solomon four-groups True experiment	R 0 X 0 R 0 0 R X 0 R 0	History Instrumentation Maturation Mortality Regression Selection Testing
Separate-sample pretest-posttest True experiment	R 0 (X) ——— R X 0	Interpersonal Regression Selection Testing

very commonly used in many areas of social, political, and behavioral science and in marketing research. The approach is occasionally described as a **descriptive study,** because its purpose is to describe the current status of a group.

A basic case study may ask a sample of individuals in a population to provide their opinions about a topic of interest to the researcher. For example, end-of-term student evaluations of a professor's teaching may be measured. The null hypothesis is that the median opinion is neutral. Unfortunately, this design for data collection presents problems of valid interpretation. The null hypothesis of a neutral opinion can be tested using a Wilcoxon-Mann-Whitney test of the mean Likert evaluation score and the theoretical neutral score (i.e., 3 on a 5-point Likert-type evaluation scale, *neither agree nor disagree*).

One-Group Pretest-Posttest

The addition of a pretest to the basic case study provides a small increase in control over internal threats to validity, but it retains many potential flaws. This quasi-experimental research design is not uncommon in action research, and it is also used to evaluate the success of therapeutic interventions (Bangert & Baumberger, 2005).

One problem with this design is that the pretest may sensitize subjects in the study to the treatment or intervention taking place. As discussed earlier in this chapter, the major error often committed in the analysis of data from a study with a pretest is the use of subtraction. An appropriate approach for statistically testing the null hypothesis of no change between the pretest and posttest is by using a correlated-samples *t*-test or a Wilcoxon signed ranks test.

Static-Group(s) Comparison

The null hypothesis for this type of quasi-experimental study is that there is no difference between two or more nonrandom groups of subjects. This research method is very commonly employed in the behavioral sciences, especially in educational and psychological research. An archaic name that is sometimes applied to this approach is **causal-comparative.**

Many times, research groups are a natural creation of circumstance. For example, research comparing the academic productivity of the faculty of different universities would need to use intact groups. It is not possible to randomly assign new PhD graduates to start their careers in different academic departments. Thus, it is necessary to employ preexisting groups, or what D. T. Campbell (1957) called **static groups.** These groups are also referred to as *samples of convenience.*

As no randomization is possible in a study with intact groups, the practitioner-researcher cannot know if the groups were equivalent at the start. To improve the validity of the findings from static-group comparisons, researchers may match subjects in the two groups along various dimensions known to correlate with the dependent variable. In the case of a hypothetical study of scholarship and research productivity, the practitioner-researcher could elect to match the groups of faculty at various universities for dimensions such as teaching load, institutional type,[7] and size of the academic department in which the faculty are employed.

Outcome data from a static-group comparison may be analyzed using Fisher's ANOVA, ANCOVA, an independent-sample t-test, or the Wilcoxon-Mann-Whitney test. If there was extensive matching, the appropriate statistics for testing the null hypothesis include the correlated-sample t-test and the Wilcoxon signed ranks test.

Applications from the Literature

Example of the Use of Matching to Improve the Validity of a Static-Group Comparison

Note: The authors recognized the validity problem of using intact, naturally occurring groups in this study of the impact of being confined by order of the courts for residential drug treatment versus not being placed in a residential program. Christopher Krebs and his colleagues elected to match members in the two groups for age, race, gender, and history of previous arrests for drug use.

Method: The sample used in our study is large ($N = 129,577$), and the data include a variety of important measures such as individual criminal history, probation officer contacts, urinalysis, and supervision type. The data represent all Florida drug-involved offenders admitted to probation. As the data include probationer cases from across Florida, the generalizability of the findings is greater than that based on a single program in one location.

Propensity score modeling provides a comprehensive approach to estimating treatment effects with observational data. For example, using propensity score adjustments is one of the more common approaches to dealing with the bias in observational studies created by nonrandom assignment to treatment. Although propensity scores can be used in several ways, this study uses propensity scores to create post hoc treatment comparison matches among drug-involved probationers.

Source: Krebs, C. P., Strom, K. J., Koeste, W. H., & Lattimore, P. K. (2009). The impact of residential and nonresidential drug treatment on recidivism among drug-involved probationers: A survival analysis. *Crime and Delinquency, 55*(3), 442–471. doi: 10.1177/0011128707307174

Pretest-Posttest Control Group

This true experimental design for research controls most of the potential problems of internal validity. This design can be expanded to compare a number of treatment conditions with the control group. The greatest potential problem with the pretest-posttest control group research design is having only a few subjects in the two groups. Small samples can have low statistical power and are open to Type II error.

Another issue is the potential for the pretest to become confounded with the treatment. This problem of external validity can be significant. For example, if a professor of behavioral research has all students take a "knowledge of statistics test" (KOST) on the first day of class, some students may use that measure as a learning experience and work to learn certain algorithms they saw on the KOST. The items of the KOST may also cause some students to focus on certain issues in the course's curriculum. These and other factors may produce an outcome effect on the posttest independent of the treatment (the class in research).

The statistical approach for treating the null hypothesis is to first use Fisher's ANOVA to ensure the scores on the pretests are equivalent across the groups. Next, if there was a significant difference between the pretested groups, ANCOVA should then be used to correct for those pretest differences while analyzing differences among posttest data.

Applications from the Literature

Pretest-Posttest Study With Randomization

Note: This is part of a pretest-posttest study of the effectiveness of a nonviolent crisis intervention (NCI) training program with the staff of a residential institution for dementia patients. The random assignment of subjects to groups made this a true experiment; however, several issues mortality and history did interfere with data collection and played a role in the outcome. The design is as follows:

```
R  O  X  O
R  O     O
```

Design: This was a randomized controlled trial comparing premeasures and postmeasures of staff receiving the intervention or randomized to the wait list. In addition, focus groups of subjects in the intervention group were carried out, and an experienced investigator recorded discussion and developed themes related to the participants' perceptions of the workshop and skills learned.

Forty staff members at the nursing home were randomized to either receive the 7½-hour training program (an adaptation of the NCI curriculum) or be placed on the wait list. Measures were given before training and six weeks after the training was complete. Twenty-eight staff members completed follow-up measures, of which 15 received the training. Twelve staff members did not complete the follow-up measures due to illness, scheduling conflicts, and a bus strike during the postmeasure time period. Staff included all professional and nonprofessional employees.

The training program consisted of a single 7½-hour workshop conducted for staff participants in groups of 10 to 12. The content included a component of the NCI curriculum, specifically those release techniques and containment holds deemed reasonable and prudent for the geriatric population living in the typical long-term care facility.

Source: Schindel-Martin, L., Morden, P., Cetinski, G., Lasky, N., McDowell, C., & Roberts, J. (2003). Teaching staff to respond effectively to cognitively impaired residents who display self-protective behaviors. *American Journal of Alzheimer's Disease and Other Disorders, 18*(5), 273–281. doi: 10.1177/153331750301800510

Nonequivalent Pretest-Posttest Control Group

When randomization is not practical or ethical, one logical alternative is the quasi-experimental **nonequivalent pretest-posttest comparison** design for research. As with the true experiment, this design may be expanded by adding a number of other groups for comparison with the control group. By adding pretests, this approach can be seen as an extension of the static-group comparison. The method can provide good control over many of the potential problems of internal validity. One key to improved validity is the selection process used for defining the groups to be compared. The use of matching is one way to ensure group equivalence, or what Donald Campbell described as "proximal similarity," prior to the introduction of the treatment (D. T. Campbell & Russo, 1999). A potential external validity problem with this approach is the possible influence the pretest can have on the outcome.

The statistical analysis for the null hypothesis of mean posttest score equality can be documented by Fisher's analysis of variance (or a nonparametric analysis of variance described on the student website) with the posttest data. If there is a possible inequality between the groups on the pretest, the appropriate statistical test procedure is analysis of covariance. In that case, the pretest is used as the covariate and the adjusted posttest data as the dependent variable.

Posttest-Only Control Group

This approach to designing research relies on random assignment of subjects to groups. This bypasses the potential problem of pretest sanitization and eliminates issues of regression, testing, and instrumentation. Random assignment also trumps the possibility of a selection problem or time-linked factors, including history, maturation, and mortality.

The statistical analysis of the null hypothesis can involve t-tests or Wilcoxon-Mann-Whitney tests. If there are three or more groups, either Fisher's ANOVA or one of the nonparametric ANOVA models would be appropriate.

Solomon Four-Groups

In 1949, Richard Solomon published an article describing an approach to designing research that accounts for the potential influence of pretests. His design provides a check on pretest interference in the relationship between the treatment and outcome. His method combines a pretest-posttest design with a posttest-only control group design into one experimental model. Of these four randomly assigned groups, two are pretested, and two have no pretest. Two of the four groups are provided the treatment, and two groups are not. The following table shows all the pretests and posttests with subscripts used to identify the observations or measurements.

Treatment group 1	R	O_1	X	O_2
Control group 1	R	O_3		O_4
Treatment group 2	R		X	O_5
Control group 2	R			O_6

The pretests are O_1 and O_3, while O_2, O_4, O_5, and O_6 are posttests. Step 1 in the study determines whether there is a pretest effect. This effect can be assessed with a t-test for the null hypothesis, H_0: $O_2 = O_5$. If there is a significant effect for pretest interference, the study should employ analysis of covariance to reduce the pretest's impact. Another approach to analysis that avoids the problem of pretest interference simply tests the null hypothesis, H_0: $O_5 = O_6$.

It is also possible to analyze all the data with a two-way analysis of variance. One factor is the treatment factor, or H_0: $O_2 + O_5 = O_4 + O_6$. The second main effect is whether there was a pretest or not, or H_0: $O_2 + O_4 = O_5 + O_6$.

The large number of null hypotheses tests and statistical analyses that a Solomon four-groups design requires implies that the assumption of statistical independence may not be satisfied. There may be too much data analysis using a limited amount of data. A correction for this exists in the form of the Bonferroni inequality described in Chapter 9.

Applications from the Literature

Example of the Use of a Solomon Four-Groups Design

Note: All participants were obligated by their department to participate in a research study as subjects during the semester. The undergraduate women who participated in this research had the option to participate in an alternative research study with content that was not as disturbing. All subjects were "volunteer" undergraduate women majoring in psychology. Volunteering introduces a potential problem of population validity.

The problem of providing appropriate control groups for the study was resolved by the researchers' decision to use different, non–woman focused, film clips of violent behavior. Therefore the treatment groups watched film clips of violence against women from the popular media and TV, and the control groups watched an equivalent set of film clips about violence against men.

Design: A Solomon Four-Group design was used. This design allows for the response after the experimental treatment to be assessed, in comparison to the pretreatment response as well as in comparison to a control group receiving an alternative treatment. It also allows for any sensitizing effect because of the pretreatment measure to be detected.

Material: The stimulus material consisted of two videos, each showing three different excerpts. The excerpts consisted of violent episodes appearing in commercial films that were either on the video circuit or on television. Each excerpt lasted approximately 3 min, the entire video sequence lasted under 10 min. In the experimental conditions (Groups 1 & 3), the three excerpts displayed violence against women; however, in the control conditions (Groups 2 & 4) the excerpts showed violence against men.

Results: . . . A Solomon Four-Group design is best evaluated using an ANCOVA comparing the post-test scores of Groups 1 and 2, with their pretest scores used as covariates. The results of the ANCOVA indicated there was a significant difference between the disempowerment scores of the group who viewed the female-victim clips in comparison to those who viewed the male-victim clips ($F_{1,32} = 4.35$, $p < .05$). The means of the two groups, adjusted for the covariate were: female-victim group, $M = 31.73$; male victim group, $M = 28.16$. This indicates the experimental group experienced heightened feelings of disempowerment after watching the clips showing violence against women in comparison to the control group who watched the male-victim clips.

Source: Reid, P., & Finchilescu, G. (1995). The disempowering effects of media violence against women on college women. Psychology of *Women Quarterly*, *19*(2), 397–411. doi: 10.1111/j.1471-6402

Separate-Sample Pretest-Posttest

The separate-sample pretest-posttest design resolves the problem of pretest interference and can be used when all subjects must be given the same treatment or intervention. The control group is only hypothetical, because the pretest of one randomly assigned group is compared with the posttest from a second randomly assigned group.

Potential problems of internal validity are related to the pretest-posttest time interval and to a possible change in the skill of data collectors. The latter validity problem is more likely to occur if the data are collected through one-on-one interviews or assessments. The statistical analysis of the null hypothesis can involve t-tests or Wilcoxon-Mann-Whitney tests or both parametric and nonparametric ANOVA.

Retrospective Pretest

An alternative method for collecting pretest and posttest data is the Campbell and Stanley concept of retrospective pretests. The method has appeared as an approach to evaluation in recent program effectiveness studies (Adler-Baeder, Kerpelman, Schramm, Higginbotham, & Paulk, 2007; S. J. Bailey & Deen, 2002; Lynch & Fleming, 2005). This method involves first providing the treatment or intervention, then giving a posttest. Next the subjects are asked to complete a pretest that asks them to remember their level of learning or problem status prior to the treatment.

Symbolically, the design is represented as $X\ O_{post}\ O_{pre}$.

While removing the possible problem of pretest interference, it does introduce a number of other hazards, including the possibility that subjects wish to appear to have been successful in the experimental program (Lamb, 2005). It is also dependent on personal recall, which is easy to fake. This approach provides a solution to logistical problems that occur when providing pretests and posttests.

EXTERNAL VALIDITY

> *"Like all sciences and all valuations, the psychology of women has hitherto been considered only from the point of view of men."*
>
> Karen Horney

Population Validity

This factor directly addresses whether the findings of a study should be generalized to other venues. The core issue is whether the subjects are an idiosyncratic local group or a representative sample of the larger population. (See Chapter 9 for a discussion of samples.)

Research exhibiting ecological validity has what Egon Brunswik (1956) described as **representativeness.** This construct has two principal dimensions. One holds that the sample studied must represent all members of the target population who were not part of the research, and the second is the ecology of the study.

Ecological Validity

The concept of ecological validity is a crossover point between the positivist paradigm and quantitative methods of scientific psychology on the one hand and the phenomenological paradigm of qualitative research on the other. Ecological validity is concerned with the linkage between what occurs in a controlled research setting or university laboratory and what actually occurs in the field (Cole, Hood, & McDermott, 1997). Qualitative research normally involves data collection in the field and can therefore claim ecological validity. Research using quantitative experimental designs is not as easily shown to provide ecological validity.

Research exhibiting ecological validity must have a dimension of representativeness (Brunswik, 1956). The experiment must represent conditions beyond the experimental confines that are equivalent to the conditions for the population that is the target for generalization. For example, a study of the efficaciousness of different amounts of training being provided to would-be forensic psychologists could begin with a representative sample from the population of licensed clinicians wishing to qualify as expert witnesses. This hypothetical study could then have the subjects (therapists licensed as clinical counselors or psychologists) assigned to programs with varying amounts of time spent in a **moot courtroom** simulation, including critiques by trial lawyers. In this case, the level of ecological validity is relatively high because the moot courtroom has the **gestalt** of an actual courtroom. In this case, the improved ecological validity is likely to also improve the external validity of the study.

Richard Snow (1974) made the point that human participants in an experimental study are not a tabula rasa, as experimental researchers often assume. He argued that greater behavioral stability occurs in natural settings as opposed to controlled environments. Snow also averred that treating all human factors in an experiment as something needing control is a self-defeating game. His position was that standard empirical models do not account for the many dimensions to which subjects respond in an intervention under study. Snow provided several methods for improving the representativeness of research in the social sciences, including the following:

- Carefully observe what subjects are actually doing during the experiment.
- Whenever appropriate, conduct research in the field.
- Audit and carefully note the environment and social context in which the research occurs. Major disruptions or background problems need to be enumerated and described. Even something as prosaic as a thunderstorm ongoing at the time of the study can have an impact on outcomes.
- Use a control group in situations where subjects are free to interact in their own customary manner within the experimental situation.

Threats to Population Validity

The complexity of organizing empirical research studies with human subjects all too often leads to the use of small but accessible samples (e.g., undergraduates who have participation requirements). Such samples may have certain idiosyncratic and limiting characteristics in common such as age range, political point of view, ethnicity, and education level (Smart, 1966).

This possible external validity problem is one of representativeness related to potential interactions of subjects and experimental conditions. Internal validity problems of selection differ from this external validity issue in two dimensions: (1) the nature of the experimentally accessible population versus the target population and (2) interactions between **personological variables** of the accessible population and the treatment (Bracht & Glass, 1968).

Experimentally Accessible Population Versus the Target Population: Drawing a sample to populate the groups of a study involves first identifying the population for which the study should be meaningful. Random selection of an adequate-size sample from the identified (framed) population makes it possible to randomly assign subjects from the sample to groups.

Most practitioner-researchers can only work with the population that is accessible to them, thus limiting the generalizability of the study's findings. For example, if a marriage counseling center compares two approaches to therapy, the practitioner-researcher could publish a report detailing the findings from the comparison. However, a claim that the findings are true for other clinical settings cannot be made. One solution to this conundrum is to carefully define the sample and the population from which it was drawn. Only when readers of the research have detailed information about the clinic and its programs and client population can they make an informed decision about the applicability of findings to their own practices.

Interactions Between Personological Variables and the Treatment: Characteristics of the sample may interact with one or more treatment conditions, thereby making the findings of research less meaningful for others who read the study. For example, clients with low levels of cognitive and verbal ability may not respond as well to an intervention using person-centered counseling as would a sample of more verbally skilled clients. One solution to this problem is to include problematic issues, such as verbal ability, as a second factor in the study or statistically correct it with ANCOVA.

Threats to Ecological Validity

The best evaluators of the ecological validity of any research effort are the clients and therapists for whom the study was intended. This issue is also a central theme in establishing the trustworthiness of a qualitative study's findings. To make generalizability possible, the study's design must avoid potential ecological validity hazards. This includes providing potential users with all information needed to make a decision about the worth of the study. Decisions by others to generalize a study's findings are made in the context of the environmental circumstances of the readers. Potential ecological pitfalls in experimental research were categorized by Glen Bracht and Gene Glass in 1968.[8]

Describing the Independent Variable

> Generalization and replication of the experimental results presuppose a complete knowledge of all aspects of the treatment and experimental setting, (Bracht & Glass, 1968, p. 438)

Research designed to inform other practitioners must provide a careful and exact description of each independent variable. This element of the ecological validity (describing the independent variable) should be addressed in the methods and/or procedures section of each article or research presentation. This segment provides a carefully detailed list of activities, equipment, sequence of events, and timeline involved in the implementation of the independent variable. If it is correctly written, any reader can gain the background necessary to replicate every detail of the research.

Measurement of the Dependent Variable

> Generalization of results depends on the identification of the dependent variables and the selection of instruments to measure these variables. (Bracht & Glass, 1968, p. 439)

Defining the dependent variables is central to research with new constructs and in the development of new measurements. Construct validity requires the researcher to assure readers that variables being described are accurate representations of the construct. If the measure is purported to assess self-concept, it should be just that and not a measure of another dimension such as self-delusion. This is related to the issue of construct validity discussed in Chapter 12.

A rapid expansion of the number of psychological constructs, dimensions, and new measures occurred in the 1950s and 1960s. This rapid expansion of the field had the potential to dilute the public's perception of the profession. In 1955, Lee Cronbach[9] and Paul Meehl published a statement on measurement validity addressing the specific problem of construct validity and the generalizability of research findings. They provided a set of six criteria needed to assure the public that the measurement or dependent variable has good criterion validity. The following principles are part of the **nomological net (NN):**

1. The construct is given clear expression.

2. The NN may include numerical evidence, theoretical evidence, and observable properties.

3. The construct must have observable manifestations and be more than a theory.

4. Continuous elaboration of the construct's NN links it with other variables and constructs.

5. The construct and its NN may not stand independent of all other constructs but must occupy a needed niche within the larger domain.

6. The application of the construct makes theoretical sense in all venues where it is applied. Cronbach and Meehl pointed out that in physics, the concept of heat operates at room temperature and can also precisely describe the surface heat of the sun.

Applications from the Literature

Critical Review of Research Without a Clearly Defined Set of Variables

Note: In their review of psychological research literature, France and Finney pointed out that external validity has not been demonstrated for a number of common hypothetical constructs used by both researchers and therapists in the behavioral sciences.

Authors' Discussion: Even though the differential relationships found between the awareness, importance, ego-extension, and reliance factors and the external criteria support their distinction, strong external validity evidence is still lacking. In other words, these relationships do not provide evidence that the awareness items are really measuring the latent factor of awareness, that the importance items are really measuring importance, and so on.

Source: France, M., & Finney, S. J. (2009). What matters in the measurement of mattering? A construct validity study. *Measurement and Evaluation in Counseling and Development, 42*(2), 104–120, doi: 10.1177/0748175609336863

Multiple-Treatment Interference

When two or more treatments are administered consecutively to the same persons within the same or different studies, it is difficult, and sometimes impossible, to ascertain the cause of the experimental results or to generalize the results to settings in which only one treatment is present. (Bracht & Glass, 1968, p. 438)

A series of multiple treatments is frequently used in mental health settings. This presents a validity concern described as *reactive arrangements.* For example, the cause of change may never be known for a client who was provided intense behavioral counseling while being on a regimen of psychoactive drugs and also regularly participating in group counseling. The assumption is that one treatment carries over and alters the effectiveness of the next treatment.

Additionally, if treatments are presented in a particular order or sequence, then the sequence becomes another factor that must be considered in teasing out which treatments are independently effective. This problem is described as a *sequencing problem* (Barlow & Hayes, 1979).

Applications from the Literature

Potential Problem of Multiple-Treatment Interference

Note: Research with an AB design refers to studies where a baseline is found for a targeted behavior, designated A, followed by an intervention and a remeasure of the target behavior, designated B. This is similar to the design introduced by Donald Campbell (1957) for an observation such as a pretest or posttest using the letter O. Campbell's symbol for a treatment or intervention is X. Thus, a pretest-posttest research study could be represented by the shorthand OXO.

Method: The study used a single-system AB multiple baseline design across 22 participants to evaluate change in clinical outcomes. The AB design included a (A) baseline phase, and (B) cognitive-behavioral intervention phase. A pretest/posttest design (OXO) was used to evaluate the attainment of treatment goals and self-concept.

Applications to Practice: First, the increased attention received by clients in the study could have influenced the outcomes. The lack of a baseline-only comparison makes it impossible to rule out this factor. Because the intervention package utilized multiple interventions, it is also not known what specific factors might have influenced change. Second, there is the potential of multiple treatment interference in that all clients had ongoing contact with a psychiatrist and case manager. The case management model was a low intensity model with quarterly contact that focused on monitoring and referral as needed. The contact with the psychiatrist was limited to brief quarterly visits that were primarily medication checks, and it is unlikely that these visits confound the design to any significant degree.

Source: Bradshaw, W., & Roseborough, D. (2004). Evaluating the effectiveness of cognitive-behavioral treatment of residual symptoms and impairment in schizophrenia. *Research in Social Work Practice, 14*(2), 112–120. doi: 10.1177/1049731503257872

Hawthorne Effect

> A subject's behavior may be influenced partly by his perception of the experiment and how he should respond to the experimental stimuli. His awareness of participating in an experiment may precipitate behavior which would not occur in a setting which is not perceived as experimental. (Bracht & Glass, 1968, p. 439)

In 1933, Elton Mayo published a book describing his research on management and human factors in industrial settings (1933/2003). One of the findings he reported was that worker behavior can be modified just by the workers knowing they are part of an experiment. Mayo's research was conducted at the Hawthorne Works, a factory owned by Western Electric in suburban Chicago. Three experimental studies were conducted to determine the optimal level of lighting in the factory. A preliminary conclusion from Mayo's work was that having researchers observe workers and make modifications (lighting levels) in the work environment brought about improved productivity. The ethereal nature of the behavioral changes found in the Hawthorne factory was apparent on two later reevaluations of the impact of lighting levels. In these later studies, employee productivity had returned to the original pre-experimental levels. The assumption was that the presence of researchers making observations could no longer inspire worker behaviors.

The Hawthorne effect has also been described as the **observer effect**. It has an implication for field research and other forms of qualitative research designs in which the presence of an observer can change the behavior being observed (Monahan & Fisher, 2010).

Photo 14.2 Hawthorne Works Circa 1933

Write On New Jersey.

Novelty and Disruption Effects

> The experimental results may be due partly to the enthusiasm or disruption generated by the newness of the treatment. The effect of some new program in a setting where change is common may be quite different from the effect in a setting where very few changes have been experienced. (Bracht & Glass, 1968, p. 439)

This form of reactivity occurs in environments where there has been great stability before a significant change is introduced. For example, some prisons have begun programs in which inmates train young dogs from animal shelters to become assistance dogs. In this type of program, there is a very large change in prisoner attitude and behavior. The novelty factor is likely involved in the measured changes in behavior for the incarcerated dog trainers. The problem with the novelty effect is that it may not continue in the long run.

The opposite effect may also occur. Occasionally, a new treatment approach may not work because it is unique and seen by the target clients as threatening the status quo. In such cases, patience is needed to determine whether the new approach can possibly work.

Experimenter Effect

> The behavior of the subjects may be unintentionally influenced by certain characteristics or behaviors of the experimenter. The expectations of the experimenter may indirectly bias the administration of the treatment and the observation of the subjects' behavior. (Bracht & Glass, 1968, p. 439)

In qualitative research, the possibility of experimenter (observer) bias is always present and is something developing researchers are taught to recognize and account for in their research. In quantitative research, too, the experimenter can unwittingly bias the outcome in many ways.

For example, a stilted or biased review of the previous literature may lead a researcher to construct a false research premise. Recruiting the sample may lead to an unconscious filtering of participants and the biasing of results. Bias may also be introduced during the implementation of the study or during the collection of data, and bias may occur during the analysis of data. These problems can be controlled by establishing research designs that incorporate **research blinds.**

Research blinds as part of the study's design can control a number of threats to validity. Research blinds are required by most funding agencies, as is the use of a **control group blind.** This is better known as a **single-blind study.** In it, subjects do not know if they are in the treatment or control group. This approach reduces the threat of a placebo effect. More control occurs with a **double-blind study** in which the researcher collecting the data also does not know which subjects were in which groups. This second level of control removes the possibility of researcher bias in the scoring process. The third level is a **triple-blind study** in which even the person entering data for statistical analysis and hypothesis testing does not know which groups were treated and which were control groups.

As humans develop, we become ever more adept at reading the subtle cues given by others (Gosselin, 1995). A major component in qualifying a therapist to use interpretative instruments, (e.g., the Thematic Apperception Test) is teaching him or her to avoid accidentally giving hints to those being evaluated. Likewise, much of the learning process for becoming proficient using advanced cognitive measures (e.g., WAIS-IV) involves learning not to provide inadvertent cues. Just a small eyebrow movement or the pursing of one's lips can tell the client he or she needs to expand or change an answer.

When a researcher anticipates a particular outcome—and particularly when further funding is riding on the outcome—he or she may find it difficult not to inadvertently introduce research bias. Cases of out-and-out data faking are rare but not unheard of in behavioral science research (Aldhous, 2011). More likely, an unconscious biasing of the study occurs.

For example, psychologists and other researchers studying paranormal phenomena, including extra sensory perception, dowsing, facilitative communication, psychokinesis, and other associated dimensions, have been accused of reporting findings more reflective of wishful thinking than empirical evidence (Abbot et al., 2001; Hansen, 2001; Hines 2002; Walach & Schmidt, 1997).

CASE IN POINT   14.3

Experimenter effect was identified by Robert Rosenthal and his colleague, Kermit Fode, in 1963. The effect, named the **Rosenthal effect,** involved an experiment with a research seminar on infrahuman learning.[10] The seminar included a laboratory where white rats were trained to run through complex mazes to reach a food reward. The 12 psychology students in the seminar were presented with two groups of laboratory rats for their learning experiments. Rosenthal's students were told the rats were from two different strains, one bred to be "maze-bright" and the other to be "maze-dull." Later, when the data were tabulated, the maze-bright rats had learned to solve the maze significantly faster than had the maze-dull rats. However, the rats were all from the same breeding stock and were not different.

Two years later, Rosenthal and Lenore Jacobson (1966) conducted an experimental verification using children of the South San Francisco School District. Rosenthal's team administered a nonverbal IQ test, Flanagan's Test of General Ability (TOGA; 1960 edition), to the children and explained to the teachers that the TOGA measured the likelihood a child would bloom and make significant cognitive gains. Students in 18 elementary classrooms were evaluated. Rosenthal randomly assigned 20% of the children in each class to be labeled "late bloomers." Teachers were given the names of those children and told their TOGA scores "indicated that they would show unusual intellectual gains during the academic year" (p. 115). On retesting at the end of the school year, there was a significant improvement in scores for the hypothetical "late bloomers." The effect was most pronounced with first and second graders.

Since then, the Rosenthal effect has been used in schools, prisons, and therapy groups and by leadership consultants and motivational speakers.

Pretest Sensitization

When a pretest has been administered, the experimental results may partly be a result of the sensitization to the content of the treatment. The results of the experiment might not apply to a second group of persons who were not pretested. (Bracht & Glass, 1968, p. 439)

Posttest Sensitization

Treatment effects may be latent or incomplete and appear only when a post-experimental test is administered. (Bracht & Glass, 1968, p. 439)

Applications from the Literature

Description of Pretest Sensitization in Psychological Research

Note: By analyzing the outcome scores from a study with a pretest and another without a pretest, Kim and Willson identified a pretest sensitization effect for four previously published studies.

Description: Pretest sensitization refers to "the potential or actuality of a pretreatment assessment's effect on subjects in an experiment." Pretests may change the scores at posttest not only for the same or similar scales but also for dissimilar scales in which the constructs may be completely different. Whatever the usage of the pretest in research, the presence of pretests can alter the nature of interventions and cause problems in measuring the treatment effect per se.

Pretest effects are explained by some researchers as a motivational factor or a direct teaching function. In general, pretests may enhance arousal or increased attention to the coming events such as treatment and posttest. Pretests may alert the subjects to the relevant topics and direct the subjects' attention selectively to what the researchers intended to look at. This arousal to the

(Continued)

(Continued)

intervention or posttest, regardless of whether it is general or specific, performs differently under various conditions of research.... The pretest effects on cognitive outcomes are on average greater than those on measurements of affect. Moreover, it was noted that pretest effects vary with the characteristics of subjects (e.g., age and ability level) as well as the characteristics of testing (e.g., duration between pretest and posttest). Hence, these study characteristics are typically included for consideration in pretest studies. In accordance with ... [a previous] ... meta-analysis, the current study takes types of measures, duration between pretest and posttest, similarity of pretest and posttest, and subjects' mean age into account in the procedures advocated.

Source: Kim, E. S., & Willson, V. L. (2010). Evaluating pretest effects in pre-post studies. *Educational and Psychological Measurement, 70*(6), 744–759. doi: 10.1177/0013164410366687

This threat to generalizability is seen when treatment effectiveness is apparent only when a posttest is used. This is not the same as a simple motivational issue, with subjects working hard to score well on a test. Posttest sensitization involves how the individual's cognitive processes, first engaged by the treatment, become modified by taking a posttest. Posttest sensitization is an aspect of information processing that involves the reorganization of a cognitive framework during the posttest assessment (Cortese, 2007).

Interaction of History and Treatment Effects

The results may be unique because of "extraneous" events occurring at the time of the experiment. (Bracht & Glass, 1968, p. 439)

Problems arise in research when variables are modified in a nonrandom way by background events and circumstances. The internal validity issue of history as a time-bound factor differs from this concept of an interaction of history and the treatment. This interaction may be better thought of as an issue of "current events." It describes how background ecology and human interactions can have a nonrandom effect on the measurement of outcomes. The history issue with internal validity takes place over time, whereas this interaction can appear suddenly at the time of data collection. A practitioner-researcher may make the mistake of collecting data or having a "meaningful dialogue" with a client on the day when the first significant snowstorm of the season begins or during a violent thunderstorm. That researcher will quickly realize the effect defined as thunderstorm anxiety or storm phobia (specific phobia, storm type [APA, 2012]).

Other days when the collection of meaningful data is made impossible by distractions include election day, religious holidays and/or holy days, graduation days for self or children, weddings, or the days prior to a personal vacation. Small disturbances to ongoing activities can occur frequently in clinical settings; these include among others fire drills, tests of emergency communication systems, and labor disputes and strikes. The antics of a clinic's custodian on a riding lawnmower outside the office window have also been shown to interfere with data collection (Page, 1975). Even the disruptive impact of one client in a group acting out during a researcher's observation can distort the group's data (Peckham, Glass, & Hopkins, 1969).

Interaction of Time of Measurement and Treatment Effects

> Measurement of the dependent variable at two different times may produce very different results. A treatment effect which is observed immediately after the administration of the treatment may not be observed at some later time, and vice versa. (Bracht & Glass, 1968, p. 439)

The problem of generalizing from one research project to other populations and settings is complicated by the time frame when the treatment and outcome measurements occurred. Findings may be very appropriate for one cohort in time but not for others. A related issue is that effective treatments for one age cohort may not succeed with clients of another age cohort. These effects are well known by advertisers and political operatives, who target their advertisements to specific individuals.

Historians face a similar issue that has been labeled **presentism.** Scholars of history strive not to let the interpretations, moral reasoning, and beliefs of the present era cloud their understanding and assessment of previous eras (Howell & Prevenier, 2001).

For clinicians, the conditions and constraints under which treatments may be effective change with time. For example, the use of psychoanalysis as a clinical therapy method was highly popular from the 1920s through the 1960s. The fad-like interest of the public in the psychoanalytical method influenced many aspects of our culture, including fiction, conversational jargon, and the media (e.g., films and television drama). This golden age for psychoanalysis in America lost its hold on popular culture with the development of neobehavioral and humanistic approaches to therapy (Stepansky, 2009).

Validity problems associated with different age cohorts are more noticeable with younger populations. Adolescents and young adults in 2013 are very different from the cohort of young people in 2000. This new generation is more wired into social media and has a culture and vocabulary of its own making. Yet many psychological assessments have not resampled recently to establish a modern normative basis for score interpretation.

Cartoon 14.1   "Semantic Drift in the Classroom"

© ZITS © 2007 Zits Partnership, Dist. By King Features

The problem of age cohort groups occurs in therapeutic service delivery. For example, vocational and career counselors all too often work from employment models and assumptions that are no longer current. The changing culture of new cohorts also applies to counselors working in schools or in family practices. Therapists must be aware of and understand the culture of young people today. However, therapists must avoid the trap of stretching the boundaries set by clients by trying to affect airs and attempting to fit into youth culture. Such posturing will quickly be detected, and the therapist will be labeled a phony with subsequent loss of credibility.

SUMMARY

When evaluating experimental research, one must consider two critical dimensions. One is the internal validity of the research effort, and the other is its external validity. The latter is usually discussed in terms of population validity and ecological validity.

All empirical research involves certain tradeoffs. Internal validity, the assurance that the independent variable is the agent causing the observed change in the dependent variable, is functionally linked to the amount of control the researcher employs. For example, highly controlled research methods (e.g., a Solomon four-group design) are likely to provide a high degree of internal validity. A static-group comparison, on the other hand, may have less internal validity, because data for static (intact) group comparisons can be collected in a field setting where less research control is possible. However, data collected in a field setting are likely to provide a greater degree of generalizability to other real-world situations than data collected in a clinical setting.

While control groups are excellent components of research in the behavioral sciences, they may be highly unethical or impracticable to use. Withholding treatment from some patients to satisfy the need for a control group raises an ethical problem. This thorny dilemma is sometimes resolved by employing a separate-sample pretest/posttest research design. Another solution is the creation of a placebo condition for the control group that simulates the experimental condition without providing the treatment.

DISCUSSION QUESTIONS

1. Early in the chapter, a hypothetical study of the effectiveness of family counseling in therapy programs for young people with anorexia nervosa was described. What are the primary threats to the internal validity of this study?

2. The principle of informed consent is a cornerstone of modern research ethics. Which of the possible external validity problems could be impacted when a practitioner-researcher informs subjects that they are part of an experiment?

3. How can research blinds address both internal and external validity problems?

4. In research involving pretests, will randomly assigning subjects to groups resolve possible internal validity threats linked to mortality? Why or why not?

5. Excerpts from 15 articles are used to illustrate points in this chapter. Use the library or Internet to obtain one of these articles and read it. Make a list of all potential internal validity threats you can identify and describe how those possible problems could be reduced by modifying the study's procedures.

NOTES

1. In Chapter 12, the concept of validity and reliability of tests and other psychological measurements was introduced. This chapter addresses the validity of entire approaches to doing research, not just the tests that were used to collect data.

2. One appropriate statistic to use in comparing pre- and posttest scores is regression residuals. This basic statistical process requires knowledge of linear correlation (Kremelberg, 2010). A second method to solve this problem of analysis with pretests and posttests is to use ANCOVA.

3. Regression toward the mean occurs for subsamples that have extreme scores. The process is related to the amount of error variance in the scores of the pretest and posttest. Highly correlated measures for the pretest and posttests, with low levels of standard error, experience less regression toward the mean; while, tests with low levels of pre- to posttest correlation will experience a greater amount of regression to the mean.

4. Quoted studies in this excerpt from Justman's article are Frank, J., & Frank, J. (1991). *Persuasion and healing: A comparative study of psychotherapy* (3rd ed.). Baltimore, MD: Johns Hopkins University Press, pp. 48 cf & 292; Jopling, D. (2008). *Talking cures and placebo effects*. Oxford, UK: Oxford University Press, pp. 44–48, 261–262.

5. Seligman, M. E. P. (1995). The effectiveness of psychotherapy: The *Consumer Reports* study. *American Psychologist, 50,* 965–974. Available at http://horan.asu.edu/cpy702readings/seligman/seligman.html

6. Case studies are an appropriate and common research method in qualitative research. The case study method is elaborated in Section II of this book. The one-shot case study is a method for organizing a research effort that uses a post hoc measure to study the status of a group.

7. The Carnegie Foundation for the Advancement of Teaching has developed and published a taxonomy of types of colleges and universities in the United States: http://classifications.carnegiefoundation.org/.

8. The language of the 1960s predates the third feminist movement (1980–present). Scholarly books and articles of the 1950s and 1960s typically used only male pronouns unless a specific woman was mentioned (Freedman, 2003). Before the 1950s, professional journals included the first name of female authors but only the initials for the given names of male authors. Back then, the issue of the credibility of scientific findings presented by female scholars was not always assumed.

9. Lee Cronbach was a member of Lewis M. Terman's sample of gifted children in the longitudinal study begun at Stanford University in 1922.

10. Rosenthal's class at Harvard was "experimental psychology."

Mixed Methods Research

"There is something fascinating about science. One gets such wholesale returns of conjecture out of such a trifling investment of fact."

Mark Twain

OBJECTIVES

By reading and studying this chapter, you should acquire the competency to do the following:

- Explain how the philosophical debate between positivism and postpositivism led to the development of mixed methods research.
- Describe the advantages of and inherent problems with using mixed methods research designs for research.
- Discuss transformative research and how mixed methods research can be used to improve society and institutions.
- Describe and compare exploratory, explanatory, and embedded mixed models for research in the social and behavioral sciences.
- Describe the four major elements of mixed methods research that should be examined in evaluating the quality of a mixed method research study.

INTRODUCTION AND MAJOR THEMES

The theoretical basis for how a practitioner-researcher actually does his or her researching is ingrained during graduate school and usually reflects the worldview of faculty mentors. American researchers in the social sciences once accepted the models and theoretical basis from the physical and biological sciences. That dominant approach was highly structured and convergent and required the logic of inductive reasoning. This was described as the positivist movement because those professing it were following Auguste Comte's (1865/1988) belief that every rationally justifiable assertion can be mathematically proven or scientifically verified. Stewart Piper (2006) characterized positivism as a worldview in which "society is viewed as composed of physical phenomena that can be understood and explained and whose actions can be predicted" (p. 187).

By the middle of the 20th century, a new school of thought in the social sciences began to be heard. This group, which would become known as postpositivists, emphasized the use of deductive logic and rejected the concept that all knowledge is based on unchallengeable truths only verifiable by direct measurement. Karl Raimund Popper (1935/2002), an economist and philosopher, proposed that what we know is composed of conjectures and that reality as we know it is constructed.[1] Thomas Kuhn (1996) espoused this shift in worldview for researchers (paradigm shift), and it quickly became a central theme of the postpositivist movement. This movement views our social reality as a convenient social construct and a projection of our consciousness (Piper, 2006). Gaining insight into these personal constructs requires an interpretative form of research.

By the 1960s, there was a lively debate between the two groups of faculty and other scholars regarding the appropriate worldview for guiding research. The debate soon became ugly, and partisans for each paradigm became entrenched and uncompromising. The result was what has been described as the 25-year paradigm war (Oakley, 1999).

Photo 15.1 David Hume

Wikimedia Commons.

One outcome of that brouhaha has been an increasing acceptance of a more pragmatic approach to research that combines research methods and skills from both paradigms. This multi-methodology strategy, or mixed methods research, is seen as a way for a researcher to develop a holistic view of the phenomenon being studied. By being open to both major paradigms and proficient with two methodologies, the practitioner-researcher can gain a clearer picture of phenomena studied and draw more valid conclusions from research.

GREAT PARADIGM WAR

The notion of a war between philosophers and theorists may be counterintuitive or even seem whimsical. But the polite academic debate about the appropriate worldview for a social scientist boiled over into pitched battles in academic departments and training centers everywhere. The casualties included faculty who were denied tenure, articles that were rejected for publication in the elite journals, and graduate students rejected for admission or advancement based on their philosophical position.

Casus Belli

The scientific model based on the logic of philosophical positivism dominated theory development and empirical research in the social and behavioral sciences during the first 60 years of the 20th century. The 1960s saw more critical voices argue that the dominate worldview (positivism) needed amendment (Bryman, 2004; Cicourel 1964). The goal was more than to just revamp and revise obvious problems with positivistic theories and quantitative research methods (Alise & Teddlie, 2010). The new philosophical movement recognized the importance of each individual's interpretation of the world of experiences and the sensory inputs he or she receives. One term applied to postpositive theory is *constructionism*. Constructionist research methods were interpretative in nature and qualitative in design (see Chapters 4 and 5).

In part, those following an interpretative model reflected the interests of underrepresented groups who rarely were considered as research stakeholders. A goal for these scholars was to bring cultural capital to these constituencies, including feminists, homosexuals, the impoverished, and nonwhite minorities (Teddlie & Tashakkori, 2009).

Declaration of Hostilities

By 1980, an all-out war raged between those supporting the quantitative/empirical and interpretative/qualitative approaches to the behavioral sciences (Gage, 1989). In 1971, Alvin Gouldner (1971/1980) had written, "It is no exaggeration to say that we theorize today within the sound of guns" (p. vii). At stake was the respect of the profession, publication space in professional journals, research funding, faculty positions and tenure, funding for graduate students, and even the curricula being taught. At that time, many held an inherently fallacious assumption that acceptance of a paradigm implies not just a framework for the researcher but also that all other paradigms incompatible with it are inherently wrong.

The arguments focused on the very nature of knowledge and reality. Qualitative researchers (postpositivists) held a relativistic position that what we know of "reality" is constructed by each individual. This is antithetical to quantitative/empirical (positivist) beliefs and all the core assumptions of measurement and empirical hypothesis testing.

Applications from the Literature

Overview of the Nature of the Paradigm Wars

False Dichotomies: The war between proponents of the quantitative and qualitative camps has been bitter and relentless over the last several decades. Unfortunately, much of the qualitative-quantitative debate has involved the practice of polemics, which has tended to obfuscate rather than to clarify, to stereotype rather than to enlighten, and to divide rather than to unite.... Out of these disputes, misleading clichés have emerged that have taken a life of their own. The intricacies and subtleties of research have been reduced to simplistic but obdurate reifications.

The impasse reached has only exacerbated the situation, leading both sets of purists to entrench further their epistemological stances. In the meantime, paradigm superiority has been treated as an end in itself, with proponents of both camps being fixated about what is "good" or "right" about one ideology and what is "bad" or "wrong" about the other. In effect, rather than being a conflict about philosophy, it has been treated as a conflict about morals. It is no wonder that scholars have concluded that "epistemological purity doesn't get research done."

This deep division among researchers has prompted many students to ask "Why can't we all just get along?" At the very least, researchers should strive for peaceful coexistence. This can be accomplished by researchers on both sides of the fence toning down their rhetoric and refraining from using pejorative and inflammatory language when referring to the other paradigm, because such negative discourse does irreparable harm to the social and behavioral science field.

Source: Onwuegbuzie, A. J. (2002). Why can't we all get along? Towards a framework for unifying research paradigms. *Education, 122*(3), 518–531.

Armistice (*jus post bellum*)

Nathaniel Gage (1989) described a tumultuous meeting in the spring of 1980. This meeting was held in Bloomington, Indiana, and attended by about 200 philosophers and behavioral scientists representing the two worldviews. This group debated each other and argued in defense of their preferred paradigms for the social and behavioral sciences. By the end of the meeting, its leader, Egon Guba, was able to have participants begin to talk to each other. Gage concluded that the paradigm wars dragged on for the remainder of the 1980s and came to a "sanguinary climax" around 1989.

Today, the two camps have become more integrated in their approach to science. The result is a pragmatic process for research in which theorists and researchers use constructs of the "new paradigm" by following both the "scientific" approach and qualitative research methods (Bryman, 2004). This pragmatic blending of the two worldviews is best seen in designs of **mixed methods research.**

CASE IN POINT   15.1

In 1971, a senior colleague was a recent graduate of an undergraduate psychology program (BA). That spring, he was interviewed as an applicant for the graduate program in educational psychology at a "research I" university. The large departmental faculty had been fully engaged in the paradigm war for several years and had recently elected to divide itself into two separate departments. The two new faculties were in the process of dividing up the common property (graduate assistantships, office space, support staff, and even copy machines) when he was interviewed. Representatives from these two groups both took part in his admission interview. My colleague reported that he felt like a child during a divorce in which the two parents each hope to get primary custody.

It became obvious that the interview was to determine which faculty group would provide his fellowship support. Their questioning was focused on his philosophy and views of theory development and research, not on his academic potential and motivation.

By 2000, there had been a significant decline in the number of students in the two departments, and many of the original participants had retired or moved on to other institutions. The university then quietly recombined the two faculty groups into a single department.

ARGUMENTS REGARDING MIXED METHODS RESEARCH

One outcome of the great paradigm war and its many battles has been the emergence of a new approach to research that blends qualitative and quantitative methodologies. This new approach, mixed methods research, is not without critics. Most critical reviews argue that it lacks ideological purity and has no clear philosophical basis (Giddings, 2006; Howe, 2004; Pawson & Tilly, 1997). Others are concerned that it is a way of co-opting postpositivism and the constructivists. Lynne Giddings took this concern further and metaphorically described mixed methods research as "positivism in drag." She argued that the mixed methods approach is cover for continuing the methodological hegemony of quantitative/empirical approaches to research.

Critics notwithstanding, there are several clear indications of the end of the paradigm wars. David Morgan (2007) argued that there has been too much concern about paradigms. He believed that too many theorists, including Thomas Kuhn (1996), had overemphasized the role of paradigms by conceptualizing the research process as being a top-down system. Morgan argued for the need for research to be guided by pragmatism, not dogma.

The mixed method approach provides that pragmatic framework for researchers.

The National Science Foundation has begun accepting the use of mixed methods research and now provides grant funding to support researchers planning to use a mixed method design. In July 2005, the NSF held a national workshop to promote the use of

Cartoon 15.1

"Great news, a paradigm shift is occurring."

Cartoon by Merv Magus.

mixed methods in science and science education research.[2] This meeting built on the recommendations of David Berliner (2002) that research needs to use a variety of methods best suited to answer the research question.

Rationale

The researcher who approaches subjects through just one line of research has only a narrow view. A one-dimensional approach does not provide a truly holistic understanding of the role of the environment and individuals functioning within it. A broader, more holistic understanding can be achieved through mixed methods research. The integration of different research approaches into one study can occur at any point in the process. The great advantage of mixed methods is that it facilitates seeing many sides of the issue being studied and provides a richer, more complete answer to research questions than any one method alone.

Mixed methods provide a way to augment the numerical presentations of the traditional empirical research design. Written ethnographic descriptions and case study examples can add to the interpretability and generalizability of quantitative findings. Likewise, quantitative studies can be humanized and gain greater external validity by the integration of qualitative methodologies.

Employing mixed methods provides a **complementary pairing** in which one methodological approach can compensate for a weakness of another (Greene, Caracelli, & Graham, 1989). For example, a practitioner-researcher may be interested in defining and describing what highly effective therapists do when working with clients. This study may involve many structured observations, client interview checklists, and questionnaires for both clients and their therapists. This large amount of data can be statistically reduced with factor analysis and empirical hypothesis tests. (Factor analysis is described on the student website.) These techniques, when well applied, can isolate what appears to be the core of being an effective therapist. A presentation of these findings would be improved by the addition of open interviews with several archetypical examples of highly effective and less effective practitioners. The use of empirical data analysis can provide a way of identifying the ideal informants for the qualitative interview process. This use of mixed methods research is described as providing an **enhanced design** (Greene et al.). The final report would then present a data-based assessment of what is needed for a practitioner to be effective and would describe effective and less effective practitioners.

Mixed methods research may also be transformative in nature. In **transformative mixed methods research,** the practitioner-researcher incorporates the theoretical base from an area of social justice (Creswell & Plano Clark, 2010). This superordinate worldview then informs each step in the research process, including problem identification, literature review and rationale setting, data collection, and data analysis and interpretation. The theoretical base is drawn from social justice theories for areas including disabilities critical theory (McColl, James, Boyce, & Shortt, 2006), critical theory of feminism (Sevenhuijsen, 1998), critical theory of aging and ageism (Laws, 1995), and critical theory for race and ethnicity (Delgado & Stefancic, 2001).

Applications from the Literature

Two Examples of Transformative Mixed Methods Research

Note: The authors of this study used small-group interviews with minority female school students from low-SES backgrounds. They employed both quantitative measures and statistical procedures and conducted deep interviews with the participants. The focus of the study, as seen by the research questions, was to develop an understanding of how minority girls approach the study of science. This study answered the following research questions:

Example A

Quantitative Research Questions

1. Did the students in the sample score differently on the scales of the attitudes toward science survey?

2. What attitudes-toward-science profiles emerge from the scores on the attitudes toward science survey?

Qualitative Research Questions

1. What are the urban, low-SES, African American girls' attitudes toward science and science learning?

2. What aspects of their experiences and understandings contribute to differences in attitudes?

Mixed Methods Question

1. How can the understandings that emerge from the qualitative data be used to provide a deeper understanding of the attitudes-toward-science profiles?

Abstract: The purpose of this study was to increase the science education community's understanding of the experiences and needs of girls who cross the traditional categorical boundaries of gender, race and socioeconomic status in a manner that has left their needs and experience largely invisible. A first of several in a series, this study sought to explore how African American girls from low SES communities position themselves in science learning. We followed a mixed method sequential explanatory strategy, in which two data collection phases, qualitative following the quantitative, were employed to investigate 89 African American girls' personal orientations towards science learning. By using quantitative data from the Modified Attitudes toward Science Inventory to organize students into attitude profiles and then sequentially integrating the profile scores with year-long interview data, we found that the girls' orientations towards science were best described in terms of definitions of science, importance of science, experiences with science, and success in science. Therefore, our mixed method analysis provided four personality orientations that linked success in school and experiences with science to confidence and importance of science and definitions of science to value/desire. In our efforts to decrease the achievement gap, we concluded there should be more emphasis on conceptual understanding and problem-solving skills, while still being cognizant of the danger of losing the connection between science and society which so often plagues achievement focused efforts. Our continued efforts with this group of girls will center on these instructional techniques with the goal of addressing the needs of all science learners.

Source: Buck, G., Cook, K., Quigley, C., Eastwood, J., & Lucas, Y. (2009). Profiles of urban, low SES, African-American girls' attitudes toward science: A sequential explanatory mixed-methods study. *Journal of Mixed Methods Research, 3*, 386–410.

Example B

Note: This study was part of a series of research efforts by the author to gain insight into the sexual victimization of women. The core data set included transcripts from 100 interviews with women who had been sexually assaulted or coerced to have unwanted sexual relations with and by a man. The design involved a collaborative effort by two authors working in parallel to improve the reliability of the study's findings.

Conclusions: Qualitative analysis of our data has resulted in numerous "a-ha" types of insights that would not have been possible had we relied solely on quantitative data analysis (e.g., identification of incapacitated rape and sexual precedence, heterogeneity in the way that sexual assaults arise) and also helped us to understand puzzling quantitative observations (e.g., the mismatch between Sexual Experiences Survey reports and descriptions of incidents). These insights, in turn, led to testable, quantitative hypotheses that supported our qualitative findings, lending rigor and convergence to the process. We never could have anticipated what these insights would be and that is what is both scary and exhilarating about qualitative data analysis, particularly for a scientist who has relied on quantitative data analysis and a priori hypothesis testing. The lengthy process of reading, coding, rereading, interpreting, discussing, and synthesizing among two or more coders is undeniably a major investment of time. However, we believe that it is time well spent if the goal is deeper understanding of data. Not only did the use of multiple coders and reliability checks prevent the analysis from being biased by a single person's perspective, but also working collaboratively was a great advantage in that it fostered deeper and more creative thinking than working alone. It is *the process* of doing qualitative analysis—immersive, iterative—that is critical in developing ideas and making intellectual leaps.

Source: Testa, M., Livingston, J. A., & Van Zile-Tamsen, C. (2011). Advancing the study of violence against women using mixed methods: Integrating qualitative methods into a qualitative research program. *Violence Against Women, 17*(2), 236–250. doi: 10.1177/1077801210397744

Another important advantage of mixed methods research was described by Jennifer Greene and her colleagues as providing **triangulation** of the findings leading to convergence (Greene et al., 1989). The concept of using multiple measures and research approaches is not new, having been proposed by D. T. Campbell and Fiske in 1959. In that article, Campbell and Fiske proposed using several different measures and different methods to study a single phenomenon. Triangulation implies three points, one for each research method being employed and one for the phenomenon of research interest (Creswell, 2008).

Applications from the Literature

Mixed Methods Research Triangulating to Answer a Complex Question

Note: This cross-cultural study of 490 middle-aged parents with at least one "young" adult child (age range 18–35 years) involved data collection using questionnaire items and an open-ended interview. The answers to questionnaire items were used in a logistical regression analysis. (Logistical regression is described on the student website.) That statistical test provided a model indicating what factors in the lives of parents improve the odds they are happy and satisfied in their parental role. This statistical analysis, the central analytic step in the study, was enhanced by an analysis of the open-ended interview data. These two approaches triangulated on an answer to the basic research question, *What makes a parent happy in the role?*

Findings: Analyses combined a logistic regression analysis and a thematic analysis of open questions asking: "What is it about being a parent that makes you happy today?" and "What is it about being a parent that makes you unhappy today?" After the collection of survey data, one individual carefully read the interview transcripts of verbatim data and analyzed these data using the methods of "constant comparison." This method involves scrutinizing transcripts for similar themes and then examining in detail within themes. Several broad categorical themes for each question surfaced, which were then coded. These codes were rechecked by a second researcher to gain confidence that interpretations were supported by the results and were internally consistent. This final level of coding facilitated an analysis of frequencies, which could then be run separately for ethnic group and other important respondent characteristics (e.g., level of happiness, gender, immigration history). In this way, we could ascertain consistent areas of structured agreement, as well as perspectives that did not fit modal patterns (e.g., negative case analysis or "exceptions to the rule"). This technique is consistent with other qualitative data analyses adopting a mixed methods approach.

Source: Mitchell, B. A. (2010). Happiness in midlife parental roles: A contextual mixed methods analysis. *Family Relations, 59*(3), 326–339. doi: 10.1111/j.1741-3729.2010.00605.x

Triangulation provides a measure of assurance as to the external validity of the research findings. The concept of triangulation was first introduced in the 1960s (Webb, Campbell, Schwartz, & Sechrest, 1966). Using triangulation in mixed methods research increases the confidence of the researcher that rival, but plausible, explanations for a social phenomenon under study can be dismissed.

The participation of two or more practitioner-researchers in the mixed method effort also reduces the potential for single experimenter bias (Denzin, 1978; Greene & McClintoc, 1985; Sieber, 1978). Research partnerships are often a feature of mixed methods research, as the level of competence and understanding of methodologies varies among individual researchers. By wedding two research skill sets, the mixed methods research team becomes capable of more complex research designs.

Triangulation as a research strategy normally involves two parallel streams. In one, the researcher conducts qualitative interviews or does field observations. Concurrently with the ongoing qualitative data collection, empirical data are also being collected and analyzed. In the final step, findings from the two separate streams are integrated into a single outcome statement and conclusion.

Applications from the Literature
Description of Tradeoffs and Compromises in Completing a Complex Series of Mixed Model Evaluation Studies

Note: This study was funded by the US Department of Justice to evaluate a community-based intervention program providing support and care for sexual assault survivors. Both qualitative and quantitative data were collected as part of this series of evaluation studies. The project had the acronym SANE for Sexual Assault Nurse Examiner and provides critical guidance for any therapist working with assault victims.

Conclusion: We began this project well-versed in the mixed methods literature, and we had a methodologically diverse research team with staff trained in both quantitative and qualitative methods—and our experiences were still quite challenging, but perhaps that's the nature of innovation. The epistemological issues were surprisingly sticky as we had assumed, perhaps naively, that the pragmatist approach of giving primacy to the research questions would somehow avoid entanglements. But precisely because we had histories with post-positivist and constructivist approaches, we had no choice but to try to reconcile these conflicts.

In an unorthodox solution, we divided into subgroups consistent with the notion that different components of a project can indeed be guided by different paradigms, and then rejoined in the end for the kind of dialectical debates.... In other words, we had to draw from multiple theories of mixed methods research to find our way through. The closure we experienced at the end was more exhaustion than epiphany because it is a little difficult to reflect critically when the meter's running.

We hope our candid reflections on our struggles will spark more dialogue about how to bring theory and practice into closer alignment in mixed methods research. Our goal was to explain how and why a SANE program contributed to increased prosecution rates, and to that end we believe we succeeded. The resulting model could not have been produced with only one type of data or one stakeholder perspective. For instance, without the qualitative data from the survivors themselves, we may have erroneously concluded from the quantitative data that SANE programs should directly encourage victims to report and prosecute their assaults. Our findings seriously question the utility of such recommendations. The SANE program's de-emphasis on legal matters and focus on patient health was paramount, and in the end, this practice philosophy did contribute to increased victim participation in the criminal justice system. We did not fully understand that fact until we interviewed the SANE nurses; this was the only component of the study in which we were working more fluidly with multiple data sources.

Source: Campbell, R., Patterson, D., & Bybeel, D. (2011). Using mixed methods to evaluate a community intervention for sexual assault survivors: A methodological tale. *Violence Against Women, 17*(3), 376–388. doi: 10. 1177/10778 01211398622

Prevalence

Research into the uses for mixed methods research has shown that about 15 % of social and behavioral science articles published in prestigious journals include mixed methods research designs (Bryman, 2004). Of the 230 mixed methods research studies reviewed by

Alan Bryman, the most common strategy involved collecting data by use of a survey, questionnaire, or interview. These approaches accounted for over 82% of all published mixed methods studies. About two thirds of that group employed a combination of structured survey or questionnaire along with open interviews.

Barriers to Mixed Methods Research

Mixed methods research may not be the appropriate choice for all researchers. Use of mixed methods requires that the practitioner-researcher have expertise in two different approaches and the ability to appreciate two different worldviews. This precludes most methodological purists and strident veterans of the paradigm wars.

To be ready and qualified for conducting mixed methods research, the practitioner-researcher should understand qualitative data collection procedures, including field observations, ethnographic and open-ended questions, and the identification and interviewing of key informants from the population. Additionally, the researcher should be competent at coding and with identifying central themes in qualitative data.

Likewise, researchers employing mixed methods should have competency with instrument development and validation, descriptive statistics, correlation, and probability models for hypothesis testing and inferential analysis (Creswell & Plano Clark, 2010).

One logical method for achieving a mix of research approaches is to recruit a small research team with expertise in both quantitative and qualitative approaches. The downside of using a team approach is that the process becomes more expensive and takes longer to complete than using just one method (Creswell & Plano Clark, 2010). Unless the team has a common vision of the goals for the study, there is a possibility that questions of interpretation and meaning can become muddled. A bit of creativity and cooperation is needed to find ways to use empirical hypothesis tests with qualitative data, and qualitative researchers have been known to discredit the role that statistical inference can play.

Working with a small mixed methods research team requires team coordination and cooperation. This means planning as a team and engaging in ongoing communication. A critical question is how the data are interpreted and reported. The team must decide what priority should be given to both sources of data when the study's conclusions are written.

Mixed Methods Research Designs

Mixed methods research focuses on collecting, analyzing, and synthesizing a mixture of both qualitative and quantitative methods in a study. Mixed methods research studies may include several related research efforts that are reported together and synthesized into a central statement of conclusions. At its heart, the mixed method approach to research includes both quantitative and quantitative data, thereby providing a more complete and valid set of findings than either method could provide alone (Greene et al., 1989).

CASE IN POINT 15.2

We are all familiar with the television reporting that goes on during a national election. Months before an important election, the networks with news shows and major print publications commission scientific polls of the electorate. The results are parsed and analyzed over and over until the next poll is available. This parsing is often county by county and precinct by precinct. This is clearly an empirical sampling exercise built on the foundation of quantitative theory.

One problem with polling is that it is a blunt instrument for measuring something as ethereal as a voting preference (Carroll, 2010). This process is improved when election reporters are embedded by their networks and/or print media into the election campaign. Embedding provides a qualitative dimension to the election coverage. The reports filed from the campaign trail provide news consumers with a richer understanding of the candidates and the electioneering process.

The polling intensifies as voting occurs. Specialized polling, usually involving cluster sampling, is conducted at voting sites that have been shown to be a good match for the total population of voters, providing yet another quantitative perspective on the election. These so-called exit interviews consist of a simple checklist that asks a few demographic questions and for whom the voter cast a ballot. Once again, this is a quantitative step. Election reporters also conduct "person in the street" interviews with people exiting the polling place who are willing (volunteers) to be interviewed. These short interviews also provide viewers/readers with insight as to why the voters voted as they did.

There is another round of data analysis once the results are in. Voting data from the participating electorate are decollated by age, gender, religion, education, sexual preference, and geography. This huge collection of raw data becomes the grist of election reporters' analytic processes. Data synthesis and analysis occur as the election night ends and continue for the next few days. The analysis is much like the conclusions and discussion section of a research report using mixed research methods.

Steps in Designing Mixed Methods Research

Nancy Leech and Anthony Onwuegbuzie (2010) provided stages for the development and use of mixed methods research. Each stage is further divided into a number of smaller steps.

Research Formulation Stage

During this first stage, the practitioner-researcher establishes a goal for the research and provides objectives to guide the study. The goal and objectives are based on a thoughtful analysis of the literature and the development of a literature-based rationale for the study. This review should include both qualitative and quantitative studies and describe the context of the reviewed research as well as its findings.

Mixed methods research goals for conducting the study are likely to include universal goals such as adding to the existing literature and expanding the knowledge base, better understanding a salient phenomenon and/or developing new ideas about it, and examining the past and defining ways to predict future activities and outcomes. Specific goals can be linked to testing new approaches or methods as part of more universal goals (Onwuegbuzie & Leech, 2006).

Next, research questions are linked to the goals by a series of research objectives. In mixed methods research, the research objectives play a vital role, because they drive the choice of research approach, sample, instrumentation, and measurements and how the analysis of data will be conducted (Onwuegbuzie & Leech, 2006). These objectives also provide the researcher with parameters, helping the researcher stay focused on what is vital and identify what may be tangential and out-of-bounds for a particular study.

A final component of research formulation is the development and clear statement of a rationale for using mixed methods research. This rationale may include a statement of how the mixed method approach will improve the practitioner-researcher's ability to develop meaningful interpretations of the outcome data. The qualitative component of the research can pinpoint the appropriate sample for quantitative evaluation and assist in focusing the research questions. Onwuegbuzie and Leech (2006) have suggested that one rationale for employing a mixed method design is to monitor the fidelity of the treatment and the instrumentation for proper use and interpretation.

Certain phraseologies imply a quantitative focus for research questions. These quantitative question stems include the following:

1. What causal link can be identified between . . . ?

2. Is there a predictive relationship between . . . ?

3. What is the impact of . . . ?

4. Which approach is most effective . . . ?

5. Is there an influence on . . . ?

6. What are the causes of . . . ?

Research questions for the qualitative components of mixed methods research may include phrases such as these:

1. How do participants interpret . . .?

2. What would be learned by an exploration of . . . ?

3. Participants will be identified . . .?

4. What frames the belief system of . . .?

5. What is the description of . . .?

6. What are the long-term (longitudinal) influences on . . . ?

Applications from the Literature

Example of Research Objectives from a Mixed Model Research Report

Note: The researcher began the study in consultation with the professionals in a care center in Romania using the research resources of a British university. In Romania, many children without parents resided in residential training schools and were transitioned into employment and independent living as they approached adulthood. The end of the communist era changed that, and the population had the choice of remaining in state-run care for an extra few years before leaving. The sample included 34 young adults leaving a residential care program. The design included both open-ended questions from interviews and the responses of clients to structured questionnaires.

Research Design and Methodology: The exploratory process also included actions at the "host" site of the research [including] consultations with academics and practitioners and visits to after-care projects, which highlighted the importance to include professionals' views on the subject too, in order to get a more comprehensive picture.

As a result of the exploratory phase, the following research objectives were defined:

- To explore young people's experiences and how they make sense of leaving care and after care;
- To identify care leavers' needs for support in transition from care to independent living and adulthood;
- To draw lessons for leaving care practice and policy from the experiences of both young people, as service users, and professionals as service providers.

The findings of the exploratory phase led the researcher to decide to focus primarily on service development, as services were highly needed and at an early stage, but the further progress of the research changed the focus to an in-depth understanding of care leavers and their experiences which was identified as the main data source which should inform service development.

Source: Dima, G., & Skehill, C. (2008). Reflective analysis of a mixed-methods approach to study the experiences of young people leaving care in Romania. *Cognition, Brain, Behavior: An Interdisciplinary Journal, 12*(4), 369–388.

Null Hypotheses for Mixed Methods: Null hypotheses and probability-based statistical analysis can play an important part in mixed methods research. (The rules for this logic and procedures for this approach were detailed in Chapters 9 and 10.) Qualitative research normally derives principles and makes conclusions from the interpretation of data. That interpretation can inform the researcher as to what approach to employ in hypothesis testing and in the formation of null hypotheses.

Planning Stage

The mixed methods research taxonomy developed by Leech and Onwuegbuzie (2010) describes the second step in this research model as planning for the study. This includes the selection of the optimal research design and a method for framing a population and sampling.

Explanatory Designs: Mixed methods research normally emphasizes one form of data interpretation and analysis (quantitative or qualitative) over the other. When this is done, the primary research method is usually first to be implemented. The lower-priority approach is then used to explain and enhance the findings. When the priority approach is quantitative and the secondary focus is on explaining and clarifying a study's empirical evidence by using qualitative methods, the research is described as an explanatory mixed method study (Creswell, 2008).

Applications from the Literature

Example of Hypotheses from an Explanatory, Mixed Methods Research Study

Note: This is a study of the impact of service learning on 59 undergraduate students who were fulfilling a requirement of a class in educational psychology. The authors employed an explanatory mixed method research design. Service learning involved unpaid pre-internship experiences working in community agencies. Assessments of outcomes and attitudes were made 3 times during the semester. The quantitative research hypotheses were tested by a repeated measure analysis of variance.

Overview: An explanatory mixed-methods design is described in two sections, one for the quantitative analysis and one for the qualitative analysis. Finally, the two sets of findings are synthesized through a single discussion.

Design: Specifically, quantitative methods are used to test the following four hypotheses:

Hypothesis 1. Service-learners will improve their scores on writing assignments, examinations, and course grades from the beginning to the end of the semester.

Hypothesis 2. Service-learners will improve their civic action, interpersonal and problem-solving skills, political awareness, leadership skills, social justice attitudes, diversity attitudes, course values, and academic and field interests.

Hypothesis 3. Service-learners will decrease apprehension levels and increase lifestyle commitments to service.

Hypothesis 4. School teachers will evaluate tutors more favorably than mentors and social-recreational leaders compared to after-school teachers.

Qualitative methods are used to detect major themes of service-learning guided by two major research questions: "What" and "how" is the "value added" by participating in service-learning?

Source: Simons, L., & Cleary, B. (2005). Student and community perceptions of the "value added" for service-learners. *Journal of Experiential Education, 28*(2), 164–188.

The development of a new or modified measurement device can be a logical by-product of mixed methods research. For example, if a practitioner-researcher is interested in measuring a previously unmeasured psychological construct, he or she can use quantitative data to identify factors and structures within questionnaire items. These can be verified and explained by employing a qualitative assessment method, such as interviewing participants using open-ended questions.

Applications from the Literature

Example of Instrument Development Employing an Explanatory Mixed Method Design

Note: After conducting a literature search and an analysis of measures of other dimensions of adolescent self-esteem, the author devised a questionnaire to measure her area of research concern. The study started with a quantitative assessment of the questionnaire. This was based on her first three research questions. The development of the instrument can be described as a mixed method based on the use of open-ended questions to answer research question 4.

The Present Study: To explore the construct of linguistic self-esteem, I piloted a novel researcher developed questionnaire called the Language Efficacy and Acceptance Dimension Scale (LEADS) as a potential tool for measuring this construct. . . . Two commonly used standardized measures of language proficiency in English and Spanish were administered in order to explore the relationship between this new construct and language proficiency. Given the documented findings that both language proficiency and self-esteem are important predictors of academic competence, it will be important to determine if linguistic self-esteem is distinguishable from language proficiency, providing evidence indicating that language may be conceptualized as a part of self-esteem.

To further explore the validity of the construct of linguistic self-esteem and the validity of the tool designed to measure this construct, I conducted interviews with students about the LEADS items. These data were analyzed to explore linguistic self-esteem as a potentially useful construct in understanding the linguistic, psychological, and scholastic experiences of these bilingual students. Hence, this study uses both quantitative and qualitative finding to explore the contribution of language to the assessment of bilingual self-esteem as well as to understand the experience of Spanish-English bilinguals in the United States.

Research Questions: The following questions guided the exploration of the construct of linguistic self-esteem, testing the validity of the Language Efficacy and Acceptance Dimension Scale (LEADS) as a potential tool for measuring this construct:

Research Question 1: Is the LEADS a valid measure of the predicted construct: Do LEADS items load on the same factor (i.e., the predicted construct of linguistic self-esteem)?

Research Question 2: Is linguistic self-esteem a construct that is separable from language proficiency?

Research Question 3: Is the concept of linguistic self-esteem related to or redundant with dimensions of the self measured with existing instruments?

Research Question 4: How do students talk about this proposed concept?

Source: Neugebauer, S. R. (2011). A new measure to assess linguistic self-esteem in adolescent Latino bilinguals. *Hispanic Journal of Behavioral Sciences, 33*(4), 425–446. doi: 10.1177/0739986311423354

Exploratory Designs

Creswell (2008) described mixed method exploratory designs as being sequentially organized, with qualitative research being the first approach to data collection. That phase is then followed by quantitative analytical methods to explore leads and theories identified by the qualitative component. Another name applied to this approach is Type IV exploratory investigation (Tashakkori & Teddlie, 1998).

The first step in an exploratory design is the identification of general issues or problems. This is followed by formulating open-ended questions to guide the qualitative component of the research. The qualitative process can assist the researcher in formulating quantitative questions that should be answered and provide a theory for explaining the phenomenon under study. By employing quantitative methods, the researcher can test the hypothetical model suggested by the qualitative part of the study.

Applications from the Literature

Exploratory Study Using Mixed Methods Research

Note: This exploratory study was conducted on the campus of an elite New England private university. The sample consisted of minority undergraduate women and explored how they coped with the stress of undergraduate life. The author focused on the multiple and intersecting race- and class-linked stress factors in their lives. She also identified the coping strategies these college women used to manage distress. The study is based on data from 80 volunteering students between 18 and 25 years of age.

Data Analysis: Written descriptions of stressors were coded and analyzed. Coding, gleaning, and rich interpretation of the written text defines thematic analysis. Guided by the literature that identified academics, finances, and relationship distress among Black college students, stressors were examined and coded for these and other themes. Five primary themes cut across the data in an organized pattern. Sub-themes were recognized and analyzed for patterns that clustered unique aspects. Patterns were further investigated and a decision was made to collapse certain text into subthemes based on similarities and differences between texts. . . .

Qualitative Results: Five categories of stress themes were identified: (1) relationship troubles, (2) academic pressure, (3) inadequate resources, (4) family obligations, and (5) microaggressions.

Quantitative Analysis: An ANOVA examined respondents' immigrant history status and the four types of coping on the Africultural Coping Systems Inventory, ACSI, (collective, spiritual, cognitive emotional, and ritual).

Source: Robinson-Wood, T. L. (2009). Love, school, and money: Stress and cultural coping among ethnically diverse black college women; A mixed analysis. *Western Journal of Black Studies, 33*(2), 77–86.

Embedded Design for Mixed Methods

This variation of mixed methods research tends to be used when a major focus of the study is on process. Embedded designs, sometimes described as nested designs, usually provide for the collection of qualitative data while an experimental treatment is ongoing. In embedded research, qualitatively analyzed case studies or field research based on grounded theory are collected in parallel and concurrently with the ongoing quantitative study. These qualitative data are collected to broaden the researcher's understanding of the workings, operation, and impact of the treatment condition. Embedded designs use quantitative methods to answer the question, What happened? At the same time, qualitative methods are answering the question, How did the outcome occur?

The introduction of qualitative data collection can provide formative information to the researcher about how the research treatment is being provided and how participants are receiving it. This approach is a common design for use in program evaluation studies (see Chapter 16 for more on evaluation research).

Embedded mixed model research can be used with the two major forms of quantitative research. For one, it may become part of a correlation/predictive research study. As is noted in Chapter 8 and on the student website, much contemporary research in counseling and other social sciences involves the use of multiple correlation, logistic regression, and path analysis. These powerful statistical tools can provide a method of seeing the relationship of numerous variables as they moderate each other and impact a phenomenon of interest. The embedding of qualitative methods into a correlational/predictive research study can provide a basis for interpretation of the correlational relationships. Qualitative methods can provide an explanation for why the variables can predict or determine the odds of a phenomenon's occurrence.

The introduction of qualitative methodology into correlational/predictive research provides a method for identification of **moderator variables** (Castro, Kellison, Boyd, & Kopak, 2010). Moderator variables interact with a correlational relationship and define the conditions that change the regression relationship between predictor and criterion variables. For example, socioeconomic status may moderate the predictive relationship between graduate school success and GRE scores. Verbal or narrative data from participants and/or observations of activities and behaviors can provide qualitative themes or **mediator variables.** For example, a therapeutic intervention may work better with women than it does with men. In that case, the moderator variable would be client gender. In statistical analysis, the linear regression for subjects from different levels on the moderator variable will have very different regression coefficients.

Mediators are identified dimensions or conditions that explain the relationship between variables. When a structural equation is written to explain a phenomenon, a mediator may become an **endogenous variable** (see the student website for more about this). For example, the measured level of racial identity may mediate the effectiveness of a counseling intervention for incarcerated youth.

While correlation can indicate the amount of shared variance between a predictor and criterion, it does not inform researchers as to why or how that relationship exists. The salient themes (mediators) identified by the qualitative research process can be organized into ordinal levels or into interval data and used in multivariate research.

Applications from the Literature

Mixed Model Embedded Regression Research

Note: In this large-scale research effort, all participants were randomly selected from college enrollment data and individually interviewed. A series of questionnaires was also completed by participants. Participants were paid a $10 honorarium for their effort. The focus of the study was on causes of depression among a college-age population. A number of variables were analyzed using stepwise multiple regression (see student website), and a number of potential moderators and mediators were tested and new regression equations developed and compared to assess the effect of the moderators.

Abstract: Based on a sample of 649 students from 3 New England colleges, this study examined the long-term effects of childhood corporal punishment on symptoms of depression and considered factors that may moderate or mediate the association. Similar to national studies, approximately 40% of the sample reported experiencing some level of corporal punishment when they were 13 years old. Findings indicated that level of corporal punishment is positively related to depressive symptoms, independent of any history of abuse and the frequency of other forms of punishment. Although parental monitoring and perceived norms regarding corporal punishment had no direct or moderating effects, level of parental anger during corporal punishment was the strongest predictor of depression. The association between "angry corporal punishment" and symptoms of depression in young adulthood is partially mediated by mastery and self-esteem.

Source: Turner, H. A., & Muller, P. A. (2004). Long-term effects of child corporal punishment on depressive symptoms in young adults. *Journal of Family Issues, 25*(6), 761–782. doi: 10.1177/0192513X03258313

Embedded mixed model designs can also be employed in experimental studies, including quasi-experimental research efforts. Embedding implies that a secondary database, derived from qualitative methods, is included in the analysis of information collected by using quantitative methods. Most frequently, design priority is given to the experimental component, and qualitative research techniques are embedded within the study. The qualitative component may be employed during the treatment process, or it may be used prior to the treatment to establish a baseline condition for the participants or provide guidance to the researcher in organizing the treatment. The use of a priori qualitative research methods may also inform the researcher's construction of a quantitative measure for assessing outcomes (Creswell, 2007). By following up on an experimental study with a qualitative component, the practitioner-researcher also will have a deeper understanding of the phenomenon or treatment under study.

Applications from the Literature

Example of an Embedded Mixed Methods Research Design

Note: In the United States, as in this clinical setting from England, many undergraduate women self-refer to university health centers and campus-based women's clinics with complaints of heavy menstrual bleeding (menorrhagia). The "aid" that this study tested involved an interactive clinical guidance tree. With this health counseling intervention, college women could learn of options, outcomes, and possible problems with various therapeutic options.

Abstract: This paper seeks to provide a case example of the use of mixed methods in the analysis of a complex intervention (a computerized interactive decision aid) to test whether their use affords insights into potential moderators of the intervention (i.e., patient factors that were associated with the impact of the intervention).

Methods: We conducted a pragmatic randomized controlled trial ($n = 149$) of a decision aid in women ... with menorrhagia. Alongside the trial, a qualitative study was conducted with interviews with a sample of women who had received the intervention ($n = 18$). Hypotheses generated by the qualitative study were used to inform subsequent quantitative subgroup analyses.

Results: The results from both studies showed that the decision aid was broadly beneficial. The qualitative study found that women with less formal education reported greater levels of benefit from the intervention. However, quantitative analyses of formal education as a moderator of treatment effect found that the intervention provided the greatest benefit in women with greater formal education.

Source: Protheroea, J., Bowera, P., & Chew-Grahamb, C. (2007). The use of mixed methodology in evaluating complex interventions: Identifying patient factors that moderate the effects of a decision aid. *Family Practice, 24*(6), 594–600.

MATCHING DATA ANALYSIS TO MIXED METHODS RESEARCH DESIGNS

The bottom line for all mixed methods research is to completely answer the original research questions (Onwuegbuzie & Leech, 2006). In mixed methods research where qualitative research techniques are employed to help frame the quantitative part of the study (e.g., embedded designs), the identified emergent themes from the qualitative component can be used to devise an ordinal scale for assessment. This process can lead to developing a Likert- or intensity-type questionnaire based on the emergent themes. In the quantitative portion of the study, data from those questionnaire items can be subjected to factor analysis designed to determine the latent structure of the new questionnaire. The scores from the new questionnaire may also be used to create subgroups of the population for statistical comparison using other quantitative measurements (Castro et al., 2010).

Comparisons using probability-based hypothesis testing (e.g., ANOVA or chi-square) may also be based on demographic characteristics. Thus, more complex hypothesis tests employing two- or three-way ANOVA or regression approaches may also be used to answer the original research questions.

Sampling for Mixed Methods Research

Sampling for behavioral and social science research can be divided into two major approaches. These categories also correspond to the two dominant research paradigms used with social science research. One approach includes probability sampling and its various approaches. (Probability sampling is described in Chapter 9.) Probability-based sampling strategies are central to statistical hypothesis testing and quantitative research.

The second major division of sampling techniques includes various forms of nonprobability sampling. Many of these methods are employed extensively in conducting qualitative forms of research (Kemper, Stringfield, & Teddlie, 2003).

The goal for exploratory mixed model research is to generalize the qualitative research findings from an intensively studied small sample to a larger group (Creswell & Plano Clark, 2010). This second step or phase in exploratory mixed method study requires a larger probability-based sample, which is analyzed using descriptive and correlational statistics. This stage is also likely to include statistical hypothesis testing and/or the application of measurement validation statistics. In mixed methods studies, both forms of sampling are likely to be used together to answer research questions. Thus, in exploratory mixed model research, the first phase (qualitative component) of the research provides a framework for descriptive statistical presentations and hypothesis testing in the second phase.

The first phase in the sampling process can focus on informers selected for having key or critical insight into and knowledge of the phenomenon, community, or system being studied. This qualitative component can involve fieldwork or **content analysis** from interviews, open-ended questionnaire responses, expository writing, or other forms of narrative. The sampling and data collection approach should provide the researcher with emergent theories about the processes and relations within the larger community, setting, or population.

In the case of sampling for explanatory mixed methods research, the statistical descriptions and inferential analyses use samples established by either probability sampling or by the use of a sample of convenience. The application of qualitative research normally involves interviewing a sample of the subjects used in the first phase of the research. These samples within samples can be identified in several ways (Kemper et al., 2003). If the quantitative study identified a subgroup within the first phase of research as being in some way anomalous, that subgroup or subsample may be targeted for further qualitative study.

The practitioner-researcher may also elect to focus the qualitative portion of the study on apparent archetypes identified through the use of quantitative analysis. Pragmatic reasons also can determine the participants who are followed in the qualitative section of the study. One method researchers have used is to include a final question on a structured questionnaire asking respondents if they would agree to be interviewed later by a member of the research team. This makes the qualitative research in the second stage possible, but it also introduces an element of volunteerism to the study.

Other pragmatic limitations can include the time available to the practitioner-researchers and the participants. The availability of participants may also be limited by the problem of meeting institutional consent. For example, counseling and school psychology research conducted in school settings presents special problems. Classroom teachers do not appreciate the loss of instructional time that occurs when students are excused from class to be part of a focus group or interviewed individually. Parents may present another roadblock by not wanting their child to fall behind in schoolwork by missing class time. They may also be highly suspicious of the researcher's and school's motivation for wanting to "shrink" their child.

Similar problems can occur with patients in rehabilitation programs and those in residential treatment facilities. In these locations, the researcher's need for access to the desired participants is very likely to have low priority for the staff of the clinical facility. An additional problem is that outpatients with little money or free time may not be able to afford the transportation, child care, and lost wages involved with returning to the clinic several times for research follow-ups. This type of logistics problem can bias the demographic distribution of subjects available for follow-up.

Certain undergraduate students can also be difficult to schedule for follow-up interviews and group sessions as part of a qualitative research effort. For example, students pledging a social society (fraternity/sorority) will have little free time available until after pledge week. Football players and other student athletes have rigorous training and game schedules that are mandatory and enforced by the coaching staff. Likewise, students with a heavy load of laboratory-based science classes (e.g., engineering and premedical majors) also are difficult to schedule. A similar problem exists when scheduling nonresident undergraduates. These students (commuting students) frequently have many responsibilities away from campus. Commuters are likely to hold jobs and/or have complex family and caretaking responsibilities beyond the university.

Applications from the Literature

Example of Sampling for the Qualitative Portion of an Explanatory Mixed Methods Research

Note: In this mixed method study of the subjective well-being of early adolescent students by a university-based team of school psychologists, the authors used a middle school population (seventh and eighth graders). Written informed parental consent and student assent was requested for all 1,000 potential student participants. The researchers obtained permission from 401 or 40% of the population. These students were used for the initial regression analysis (quantitative component). Research limitations made it possible for the team to follow up with a sample of only 50 students in the qualitative segment of the study. For this second sample, a second round of informed consent/assent was needed.

Participants: Qualitative data were collected from a subset of the 401 student participants via focus groups conducted in the spring of 2007. A purposeful sampling approach was utilized to identify participants for focus groups equally representative of students in general and gifted education; students were recruited to participate regardless of their initial level of SWB [adolescents' subjective well-being] or perceived teacher support. A total of 50 students in the seventh and eighth grade participated in the eight focus groups analyzed in the current study. The majority of participants were female (62%), in the seventh grade (56%), and Caucasian (50%); other participants identified their ethnicity as Hispanic/Latino (16%), multiracial (14%), Asian (10%), and African American (8%). Approximately 18% of participants reported receiving free or reduced-cost lunch.

Procedures: The research team secured separate written parental consent and student assent for student participation because of the introduction of methods (i.e., focus groups) not included in the original request for participation. . . . Focus groups were composed of students with similar educational experiences (i.e., gifted or advanced/general education) and grouped by gender. Each focus

(Continued)

(Continued)

group was held during the school day and lasted 20 to 60 minutes. The groups comprised of boys tended to be shorter in duration because they (a) contained fewer participants and (b) yielded more concise responses; girls frequently provided a personal story or experience to illustrate their points. Consistent with the findings from the regression analysis completed within the quantitative portion of the study, a focus group protocol was developed from the Child and Adolescent Social Support Scale using the instrumental and emotional support questions as the framework for the development of open-ended questions. Specifically, participants were asked to describe how teachers show that they care about them, show that they treat kids fairly, make them feel comfortable asking questions, and make sure that they learn something well. Participants were then asked to answer the same four questions, but based on teacher behaviors that did not convey support (e.g., "What do teachers do to make you feel like they don't care about you?"). A single moderator led all focus groups to ensure a standardized questioning procedure. The moderator monitored the group to allow all participants an equal chance to participate. A field-note taker recorded each sentiment conveyed by participants. Each focus group was recorded, transcribed, coded, and analyzed.

Source: Suldo, S. M., Friedrich, A. A., White, T., Farmer, J., Minch, D., & Michalowski, J. (2009). Teacher support and adolescents' subjective well-being: A mixed-methods investigation. *School Psychology Review, 38*(1), 67–85.

Sampling for embedded mixed model research also involves two levels of sampling. While qualitative research may be embedded into a primarily quantitative study for many reasons, embedding is most commonly done to focus on process. In such studies, the qualitative component may be seen as occurring in parallel with the quantitatively assessed experimental study. This is a commonly employed technique for conducting evaluation research (see Chapter 16).

The quantitative core of the research could be a pretest-posttest study or one of the more advanced of the experimental approaches described in Chapter 14. In an evaluation, the initial sample may be thought of as a nonrandom or convenient sample. In a causal comparative study, the sample is more likely to be randomly selected and probability based using a quasi-experimental design or possibly a true control group design. The introduction of qualitative methods in these studies is usually done to monitor the treatment's presentation and the participant's ongoing (**formative**) pattern and depth of interaction with the experimental process.

This qualitative part of the study may involve using one of several time or event sampling approaches to make field observations. It may also involve semistructured or open-ended interview questions. The participants for this component may be a randomly selected subsample or a carefully selected group of key informers. For example, in a study of the impact of a new approach to teaching positive parenting practices and skills to a group of pregnant teenagers, the researcher may embed a researcher as a qualitative monitor of the group sessions with the girls and group facilitator. The practitioner-researcher may identify one or two participants from each group for an extended interview. These interview transcripts can be used to add to the qualitative component of the embedded mixed method data.

The embedded qualitative component can also take the form of a case study of a selected portion of the participants. The case study may involve just one or two people, or it may involve a larger number of people working together within a larger structure being studied. For example, in the study of the quality of care provided in state-funded child guidance centers, the researcher may employ a pretest-posttest design with all clients to study the efficacy of the centers. Budget constraints could limit the researcher's plans to gain a deeper, qualitative understanding of the operation of the state-operated clinics. However, the use of case study research with one or two of the centers could provide this information and augment the quantified **summative** component of the study.

Writing and Reporting Mixed Methods Research

The American Psychological Association (2010b) describes a standard format for research articles and presentations in the social and behavioral sciences (see Chapter 17). That format provides for five or six major narrative component parts plus an abstract, references, and acknowledgments. In 2007, the new *Journal of Mixed Methods Research* (JMMR) recommended maintaining the same central narrative segments for its publication (Creswell & Tashakkori, 2007).

Introduction Section

The JMMR suggests a different emphasis and organization within the narrative sections of a mixed model research article or presentation. The introduction section of mixed model research articles should present a literature review that frames the research problem and leads to three varieties of research questions: quantitative, qualitative, and mixed model questions.

Related Research

The second section should provide an overview of theoretical perspectives on the topic being studied, from universal principles (macro perspectives) to specific applications and problems (micro issues). This may also be the location for a review of the related methodological literature review that focuses on research approaches and their theoretical perspectives.

Method

The third section describes, justifies, and explains the methodology for the study. This description explains how the mixed methods research design can answer the research questions developed and presented in the report's first section. In this third section, the use of mixed methods research should be justified through examples and prototypes from the professional literature.

One recommended approach for describing a mixed model research design is to use a research map or flowchart. That graphic should depict the activities and operations in the study and be organized sequentially along a timeline or by themes (Creswell, 2012). This map is much like a schematic diagram or blueprint of the study, making it easier for readers and participants to see what occurs and the sequence of research activities.

Humans learn in different ways and think and process information using words, images, graphics, and other sensory input. If a written narrative is used exclusively to convey the research, many individuals attempting to interpret the methods section may get lost in the words and miss the author's point (Wheeldon, 2010). The use of maps improves the explanation of the research methods by providing information in a graphical format.

Figure 15.1a Mixed Methods Research Map for Sequential Study

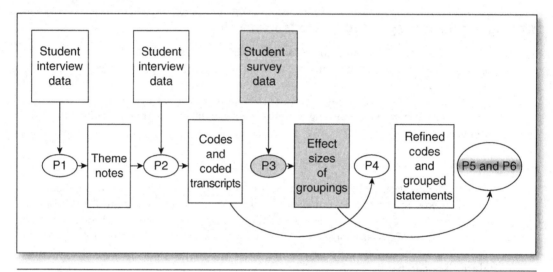

Source: Wesely, P. M. (2010). Language learning motivation in early adolescents: Using mixed methods research to explore contradiction. *Journal of Mixed Methods Research, 4*(4), 295–312. doi: 10.1177/1558689810375816

Note: In this study using middle school students, Pamela Wesely elected to use an exploratory mixed methods research design to study students' motivation as it relates to dropping out of a language emersion program.

The approaches for sampling should be explained in detail in the methods section. Sampling processes must be designed to provide data that can be rigorously collected and managed for both streams of the study. The author should provide an explanation as to how the design used for the study will demonstrate and document its validity and trustworthiness.

Results

The two streams of the mixed model research should be analyzed and presented in the results section. This can be accomplished by sequentially answering each of the research questions with analyses of data from the study. The quantitative questions are answered by analyzing data following the statistical procedures of correlation and parametric and nonparametric statistical hypothesis testing.

Figure 15.1b   Thematic Structure in a Mixed Methods Research Article

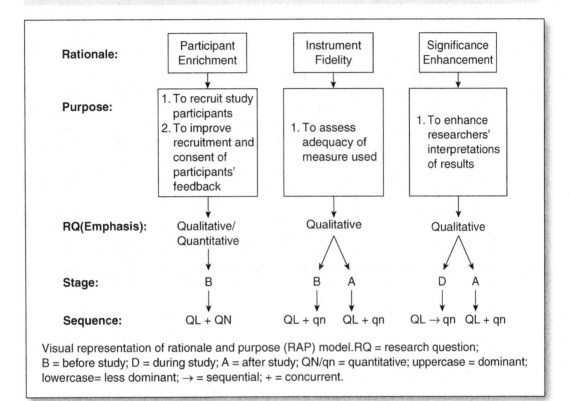

Visual representation of rationale and purpose (RAP) model. RQ = research question; B = before study; D = during study; A = after study; QN/qn = quantitative; uppercase = dominant; lowercase= less dominant; → = sequential; + = concurrent.

Source: Onwuegbuzie, A. J., Witcher, A. E., Collins, K. M. T., Filer, J. D., & Moore, C. W. (2007). Students' perceptions of characteristics of effective college teachers: A validity study of a teaching evaluation form using mixed-methods analysis. *American Educational Research Journal, 44*(1), 113–160. doi: 10.3102/0002831206298169

Note: The authors' exploratory mixed method study of college teaching with a population of over 900 graduate and undergraduate students at a state university used a Likert scale instrument measuring teaching effectiveness, a set of demographic questions, and a narrative evaluation of what makes any teacher effective. The qualitative assessment identified four emergent themes of effective college teaching, three of which were further analyzed using quantitative methods.

The qualitative research questions are addressed after the author(s) first describe the role played in the data collection by the researcher(s). This statement of role provides a framework for an analysis of how data interpretation may be impacted by the perspectives of the researchers. In mixed methods research, the researcher is obligated to assure that inferences made in the qualitative component of the study are useful, credible, transparent, and trustworthy (Bryman, 2004; Guba & Lincoln, 1989).

Creswell and Tashakkori (2007) also proposed that theses and dissertations follow a six-section format similar to the format encouraged for contributors to the *Journal of*

Mixed Methods Research. This format includes six sections of narrative: (1) introduction, (2) literature overview, (3) methodology overview with quantitative methods and qualitative methods, (4) results from the qualitative stream, (5) results from the quantitative stream, and (6) integration of results and discussion of the findings.

EVALUATION OF MIXED METHODS RESEARCH

Each time a person reads a research study or attends a research presentation, he or she is engaged in a process of mentally evaluating the usefulness and quality of the study. An individual should consider five primary elements when evaluating a mixed method study (O'Cathain, Murphy, & Nicholl, 2008).

Evaluation of the Overall Design

To evaluate the overall design of the study, a reader should consider if the study had adequate resources, was provided with enough access to subjects, and had a well-prepared research team with competence in both qualitative and quantitative methods. Was the review of related literature deep, and did the author present a literature analysis documenting the full scientific perspective on the issue being studied? Were the research goal and central objectives clearly framed by the literature review?

Evaluation of the Qualitative Component

The qualitative approach should be evaluated for its appropriateness. Of the many qualitative methods, was the one selected for this mixed method study the most appropriate? Also, did the author explain the sampling method for the qualitative method, and was a timeline for data collection and analysis provided? How well were the qualitative procedures described? How did the author document the trustworthiness and credibility of the qualitative data?

Evaluation of the Quantitative Component

The rules for conducting and reporting reliable and valid findings based on quantitative methods have been well elaborated and routinized over the past century and a half. There are several simple indicators to examine. Did the researcher employ the appropriate analytical method, and were all statistical assumptions examined and reported? Was there an adequate number of subjects, and how representative were the sample selected and subgroupings? What problems of internal and external validity does the research design imply?

Evaluation of the Mixed Method Design

A first question about the central method is whether the use of a mixed method design was clearly indicated for this study. Also, was the design feasible within the limitations of the author(s)? Was the design well described, including the form of mixed model employed?

Were the two streams of research well integrated, and did they add to the full understanding of the phenomenon being studied? Were all the research questions answered?

Evaluation of the Integration of Mixed Methods

A mixed method study should integrate the findings into a meaningful explanation. Did the authors discuss how the ideas of each person on the team were integrated into the final analyses of data? Did the researchers share information during the study? Does the discussion reflect a well-integrated study or a collection of diverse strands and ideas? Was the final conclusion a clear holistic statement of the findings from the research?

SUMMARY

Mixed methods research is a highly pragmatic approach to conducting meaningful and valid research in the social and behavioral sciences. Once a logical compromise in the great paradigm wars of a previous generation, it is now widely employed by graduate students in their doctoral dissertations and is seen as the principal research method in about 15% of the professional journal articles in the social sciences. Mixed methods provide improved research validity by triangulating several streams of research to meet a research objective and answer research questions. Studies can be organized with qualitative methods embedded within a quantitative design or by testing research themes following a qualitative exploration of study data. Thus, mixed methods research can explain phenomena by providing a deeper explanation of qualitative outcome data. Mixed methods research can also improve the human condition by focusing on issues with the potential to transform institutions and society.

DISCUSSION QUESTIONS

1. It has been said that logical thinkers find it easier to move from a purely quantitative paradigm to a qualitative paradigm for research, and not the reverse. Explain why this is or is not true.

2. When there is a dramatic happening involving people, the morning television network "news" shows use mixed methods research to provide a picture of what actually happened. This typically starts with a factual recitation from observations. This video-supported narration is normally followed by the television "reporter" using a semistructured or open interview technique with survivors or others affected by the occurrence. Watch and take notes of a morning newscast and describe an example of the application of mixed methods research to produce a news story.

3. Read research segments in the boxed material sections. Select one of them, retrieve it from the university's library or an online database, and read it carefully. Then draw a map to explain the flow of the mixed method study.

4. Evaluate the quality of the research reported in the article in question 3. What are its strengths and weaknesses? You may need to review Chapters 5 and 14 when making this evaluation.

NOTES

1. Karl R. Popper was a Viennese professor who was almost caught up in the Holocaust following the Anschluss as Nazi Germany took control of Austria in 1938. He escaped and moved first to New Zealand and then to England, where he became a professor at University College in London. He was made Knight Bachelor by Queen Elizabeth II in 1965.

2. Not all departments of the federal government follow the same rules for awarding subventions and grants for research projects. The Departments of Education and Health and Human Services still follow the rules of the Education Reform Act signed into law by President George W. Bush in 2002. That act requires the use of scientific evidence described as being developed by "randomized clinical trials" or true experiments with randomly assigned control and treatment groups (see Chapter 12 for more on true experiments).

Approaches for Evaluation

"One of the great mistakes is to judge policies and programs by their intentions rather than their results."

Milton Friedman

INTRODUCTION AND MAJOR THEMES

Evaluation is an integral part of the life story of everyone working in an agency, school, clinic, or university. Evaluation is a central theme in the effort to document accountability for the resources used by these agencies and institutions. The American public enthusiastically supports verifying the quality of publicly funded programs and entities. This press for accountability has increased over the years as the cost of programs and amount of funding they receive have increased. One result of this public concern is that both the number and importance of assessments in, and of, our institutions are growing.

All elements of health care and related caregiving professions, including therapeutic counseling and clinical psychology, receive careful scrutiny and periodically require proof of their effectiveness and worth. This requirement for documentation is a fact of life in this era of accountability. Revisions in professional standards enunciated by professional societies are a clear indication of this fact. Professional associations have modified their standards for the education and certification of new professionals and are moving to ensure that all practitioners are literate in evaluation methods and possess research skills.

The evaluation of programs and activities provided by mental health professionals can become politically charged and lead to denials of funding, rejection of support, and community hostility. Thus, most evaluations are conducted in a political environment where the evaluator must carefully negotiate the expectations and goals of the evaluation with the project's stakeholders. These negotiations should include issues of control, budget, data sources and data availability, and dissemination of findings from the evaluation.

PROFESSIONAL MANDATES

Requirements for evaluation in counseling have two levels. At one level, new counselors must have a knowledge base in the evaluation of their professional practices. At the second level is the mandate for counselor education programs to employ a prescriptive model for the evaluation of their graduate counselor education activities and resources.

Evaluation skills, along with a knowledge base in research methods, measurement, and basic statistics, are part of the mandated educational standards for all future counselors and are part of all professional requirements for those working in the various specialized disciplines of counseling and clinical psychology. These professional requirements are presented in Chapter 1 of this text. CACREP (2009) goes a step further and provides a model for all graduate counselor education programs to follow to earn and maintain accreditation.

CASE IN POINT 16.1

This age of accountability and data-based evaluation can humble even the most prestigious of our medical and educational institutions. The Joint Commission on Accreditation released its 2010 report on the quality of care provided in the 3,000 accredited hospitals and medical centers in the United States. Its evaluations are process based and focus on compliance with the standards of care established by the Joint Commission and the American Hospital Association. Only 405 of these evaluations identified hospitals that diligently followed appropriate protocols for treating patients. Some of the most well-known and prestigious medical centers and hospitals did not make the cut and fell into the mediocre range, including all hospitals in Chicago, New York City, and Houston along with internationally known stalwarts such as the Cleveland Clinic, Massachusetts General, Duke University Medical

Center, University of San Francisco Medical Center, Ronald Reagan UCLA Medical Center, Mayo Clinic, and Johns Hopkins University Medical Center (Sack, 2011). The Joint Commission has placed over 200 hospitals on notice that they are in jeopardy of losing accreditation if they do not improve, and the US Department of Health and Human Services may stop funding hospitals found not to be in compliance.

This process of accreditation based on evaluation is now being expanded to include behavioral and rehabilitation service providers. The Joint Commission has developed a new set of standards for compliance by agencies providing these services. These are available at http://www.jointcommission.org/accreditation/behavioral_health_care.aspx.

The American School Counselor Association (ASCA; 2012) has made a clear statement in the *National Model: A Framework for School Counseling Programs* that school counselors should be equipped and able to serve in the role of researcher/evaluator. In addition, the ASCA calls for school counselors to have the knowledge and skills to perform regular **program audits**.

Applications from the Literature

From the Executive Summary of the ASCA National Model

Use of Data

A comprehensive school counseling program is data driven. The use of data to effect change within the school system is integral to ensuring every student receives the benefits of the school counseling program. School counselors must show that each activity implemented as part of the program was developed from a careful analysis of students' needs, achievement and/or related data.

Action Plans: For every desired competency and result, there must be a plan outlining how the desired result will be achieved. Each plan contains:

1. competencies addressed

2. description of the activity

3. data driving the decision to address the competency

4. timeline in which the activity is to be completed

5. who is responsible for delivery

6. means of evaluating student success

7. expected results for students

Source: http://www.ascanationalmodel.org/

School Counseling Program Audit

The American School Counselor Association developed and published a worksheet useful for auditing the extent to which a school counseling program is meeting the specifications and mandates of the *ASCA National Model: A Framework for School Counseling Programs*. That audit form is found at http://www.ascanationalmodel.org/files/Program%20 audit.pdf. This 11-page checklist can guide a school's counseling program and help it align its programs and activities with the national standard.

Program Approval Mandate for College Counselor Education From the Council for Accreditation of Counseling and Related Educational Programs (CACREP, 2009)

Section VI

Evaluations in the Program

A. Program mission, objectives and student learning outcomes are developed and revised when necessary through self-study on a regular schedule. This evaluation process is based on input from program faculty, current and former students, and personnel in cooperating agencies.

B. The program faculty conducts a developmental, systematic assessment of each student's progress throughout the program, including consideration of the student's academic performance, professional development, and personal development.

C. Faculty establish a comprehensive, integrated plan of program evaluation, indicating how the mission, objectives, and student learning outcomes are met. Program evaluations must be ongoing, with formal evaluation occurring as follows:

   1. an annual evaluation that documents how, where, and the extent to which program objectives are addressed in course syllabi;

   2. a review by program faculty of programs, curricular offerings, and characteristics of program applicants;

   3. at least once every three years, program faculty conduct and document findings of formal follow-up studies of program graduates to assess graduate perceptions and evaluations of major aspects of the program;

   4. at least once every three years, program faculty conduct and document findings of formal follow-up studies of clinical site supervisors and program graduate employers to assess their perceptions and evaluations of major aspects of the program; and

   5. at least once every three years, program faculty document use of findings from VI. C.1, 2, 3, and 4 above in program modifications.

D. An official report that documents outcomes of the comprehensive program evaluation shall be prepared and distributed on a systematic basis (at least once every three years) to students currently in the program, program faculty, institutional administrators, and personnel in cooperating agencies (e.g., employers, site supervisors).

E. Students have regular and systematic opportunities to formally evaluate faculty and the students' curricular experiences.

F. Provide annual results of student course evaluations to faculty.

G. Present written faculty evaluation procedures to program faculty at the beginning of each evaluation period and whenever changes are made in the procedures

MODERN ERA OF EVALUATION AND ACCOUNTABILITY

Not only is knowledge of programmatic evaluation and evaluation methods part of the new requirements for all new professionals, it is also an important tool in the skill set of successful leaders in both academic and clinical settings. Federal and state agencies as well as private foundations all require applications for external funding to include a model for the evaluation of the project to be funded. Oversight boards for community mental health agencies and clinics also require documentation of the effectiveness of the programs being offered.

The call for evaluation and outcome assessments also comes from insurance providers, including Medicare and Medicaid (Nordal, 2012). The need for documentation of clinical effectiveness is recognized by Medicare and Medicaid through financial incentives provided to psychologists and counselors who participate in the Physician Quality Reporting System (PQRS). In 2015, therapists who are eligible for payment for services will be compensated at a lower rate if they do not participate in PQRS.

Universities must conduct a total self-study evaluation on a 5- or 10-year cycle to maintain institutional accreditation. As noted above, counselor education programs have triennial requirements for program evaluation by CACREP. Even public schools are required by state education departments to conduct 5-year evaluations of all programs and develop strategic plans for continued improvement. The American School Counselor Association's *National Framework* (ASCA, 2012) requires that all school programs conduct an "annual audit" using an evaluation checklist.

As Milton Friedman noted, it is not just good intentions that count but tangible results that must be demonstrated in this new era of accountability. An important advantage of carefully conducted evaluations is that they provide programs and agencies with data-based answers to even the most complex questions that may be asked by the general public, the media, or state legislators.

The public focus on accountability is not going away anytime soon. The accountability concept is deeply ingrained in the political psyche of Americans and has been a theme in both local and national elections.

Background on Evaluation as a Research Model

In the United States of the 1930s, the nation experienced a horrific depression, and the focus of Franklin D. Roosevelt's administration was on emergency measures that would put people back to work and help the economy recover. Little attention was paid then, or during the wars of the 1940s and early 1950s, to the effectiveness of all the programs and projects initiated by the federal government (Manchester, 1984). The goal of the era was just to "do something" and prevent a total disaster.

The next large infusion of federal funding into programs touching the lives of people came during the administration of Lyndon Johnson with his Great Society programs of the 1960s. The Department of Health and Human Services was initially created and made a cabinet-level office during Eisenhower's administration, but it was expanded and given increased funding and authority under Johnson's leadership. The department originally included the Office for Education and was known as the Department of Health, Education, and Welfare (US Department of Health and Human Services, 2010).

This new department received large blocks of money, including a budgeted $1 billion in 1965 for the first Elementary and Secondary Education Act (Pub. L. 89-10, 1965). Along with those funds, the government also established a mandated model for providing a systematic evaluation of all funded projects and programs. These guidelines, known as the Education General Administrative Regulations (EDGAR), are still followed and must be included when designing an evaluation for proposed funding. EDGAR also provides the model to follow in accounting and evaluating a funded program or project once it has been completed. These guidelines are published as an appendix to the *Federal Register* each year. The 2011 edition covers over 2,000 pages in 4 volumes and is available online at http://www.ed.gov/print/policy/fund/reg/edgarReg/edgar.html.

Applications from the Literature

Sample Evaluation Requirement from a State's Block Grant Application Process

Note: In 2012, the state of Alaska awarded six of these 2-year grants. Each winning agency was provided funds to add new counselors and related staff and was also required to hire a professional evaluator. The evaluation is mandated to be data driven with measurable outcomes.

Project Evaluation Requirements: The Division of Behavioral Health expects implementation of the 5-steps of the Strategic Prevention Framework to have fidelity to the process; thereby leading to increased prevention capacity and infrastructure at the regional and community level. As a result of this process, communities will develop a data-driven approach to alcohol use/abuse prevention, using evidence-based and culturally appropriate interventions, including environmental strategies. Strategies will be delivered in the most efficient manner possible while affecting measurable outcomes. Ongoing monitoring and evaluation are, therefore, necessary to determine if these outcomes are being achieved. Evaluation efforts are integral to the success of the SPF grantees, providing documentation of population-level change resulting from the selected strategies. As stated in the Evaluation section on pages 8 [sic], there is a requirement for each grantee to hire an evaluator for the purpose of developing both a local evaluation and assisting with the state and national evaluation components.

Evaluation will include both a local project evaluation to document the successful outcomes associated with your selected strategies and resulting community-level population change, as well as participation in the SAMHSA national cross-site evaluation. Remember an evaluation plan will be developed following the selection of your project strategies.

Local Project Evaluation: Once you have completed Steps 1–2 and begin the Step 3 process of selecting strategies to impact your community's conditions, you will also begin the development of a project evaluation, with clear and measurable outcomes. The evaluation plan will serve as a blueprint by which the applicant will evaluate the progress of the proposed strategies. All strategies must identify how they will be measured.

For the purposes of this RFP all applicants will focus on the following long-term outcome:

- *All Alaskan communities, families and individuals are free from the harmful effects of alcohol use, dependency and addiction.*

Your project evaluation plan should address each of the following questions:

1. *How much did you do?*

This will measure "outputs" or the **quantity of services** being offered or the number of people served.

   o How many people [do] you propose to serve or impact? How often will this service or intervention occur?
   o How will you collect this information?

2. *How well did you provide your prevention strategies / interventions?*

This will measure the **quality of prevention efforts.**

   o How will you collect feedback from your participants or how will you assess your efficiency and capacity?
   o How will you use that information to improve your efforts?

3. *Will anyone be better off because they participate[d] in your prevention efforts?*

Identify between two to four measurable **short-term outcomes** you hope to achieve through your prevention efforts. A short-term outcome should be a change in: attitudes/perceptions, knowledge, skills, behavior, or external conditions as a result of your prevention work. Your short-term outcomes should contribute to the identified State-level Population Indicators for Alaska.

Source: State of Alaska, Department of Health and Human Services, Request for Funding Proposal (RFP) for Fiscal Year 2012–2014. Retrieved from http://notes3.state.ak.us/pn/pubnotic.nsf/0/28b23bca6927db8389257868006a97b7/$FILE/RFP+-+FY12+SPF+SIG.pdf

Professionalism and Evaluation

The need for programs and systems to be "held to account" spurred the development of the field of program evaluation. Twenty years after Lyndon Johnson signed the first Elementary and Secondary Education Act into law, a new professional society, the American Evaluation Association (AEA), was formed. This association of 4,000 professional evaluators publishes several journals and holds annual meetings where new developments in the science of program evaluation are presented. The AEA (2005) has defined an evaluation as the activities required for "assessing the strengths and weaknesses of programs, policies, personnel, products, and organizations."

Evaluation is at the top of higher-order thinking skills possessed by humans (Bloom et al., 1956). This mental ability uses the capacity to do basic thinking, to analyze what has been learned, and to synthesize the analytic results of these mental processes into concepts. Evaluation is beyond these skills and processes and makes it possible for humans to differentiate between and within concepts. In a similar way, evaluation research methods use all other research techniques and skills in the task of evaluating a program, activity, or project.

Evaluation Constraints

Practitioner-researchers charged with the responsibility to be program evaluators may find several constraints placed on their efforts. The evaluation's primary goal is usually to provide valid and meaningful evidence about the program. Evaluation data may be used to determine if the program should continue, be expanded, modified, or terminated. For individuals working within a project, the evaluation process is likely to be viewed as a high-stakes process. This view of the evaluation increases the stress level felt by everyone involved and may contribute to the evaluation experiencing both covert and overt constraints.

The most frequent constraining factors on evaluators include the hidden agendas of stakeholders, budget limitations, time limits, data and sampling difficulties, and the political climate of the evaluation (Bamberger, Rugh, & Mabry, 2012).

Cartoon 16.1 High-Stakes Evaluation

"Before I pull this handle I need to have you fill out this survey about how I have treated you."

Hidden Agendas

"First get your facts; then you can distort them at your leisure."

Mark Twain

The high-stakes nature of evaluations can result in pressure being brought to bear on the practitioner with responsibility for the evaluation. Managers of projects and programs being evaluated can have private agendas. For example, one of the high school's counselors may be asked to serve as an evaluator of the Title I program in the middle school. If the middle school principal is looking for a way to discredit the project's lead teacher, or even downsize the program, the practitioner-evaluator (high school counselor) may face a number of problems, including access to positive or affirming data, access to unbiased parents of children served by the program, or access to conduct direct observations. Likewise, if the program's lead teacher is applying for a new administrative position with the school system, he or she may present as much positive material as possible while cloaking unfavorable data.

Required self-studies are another form of program evaluation and may face similar problems of manipulation. For example, the regular evaluation of a high school's counseling program is often required to qualify to receive state block grant funding. This self-study process is similar to the triennial evaluation mandated for university-based counselor education programs by CACREP. Whenever the evaluator has a vested interest in the outcome of the effort, the task of conducting an ethical study with high integrity can be a challenge. One solution is to recruit outsiders (e.g., counselors from other schools) to conduct the evaluation.

Community counseling agencies receiving public funding are reviewed on a regular basis by the state or municipal funding agency. As these centers are usually funded under statewide block grants from the federal government, they are required to adhere to the federal evaluation mandates. This evaluation requirement is established by US Department of Health and Human Services, Substance Abuse and Mental Services Administration, and NationalCross-Site Evaluation. (For more information about this agency, see http://www.samhsa.gov/.)

When a fully licensed practitioner is self-employed or is a partner in a small practice, he or she is well advised to find other local practitioners and form a consortium or join a local chapter of a statewide professional organization. These local chapters are a place for sharing ideas and receiving ongoing inservice education. They can also provide a sounding board and provide unbiased guidance concerning issues that arise in single practice.

Budget Limitations

As a general rule of thumb, evaluations are budgeted at about 10% to 20% of both the **direct costs** and **indirect costs** of a project. Direct costs are the actual funds (cash) spent on a project, including all salaries and mandated benefits (e.g., Social Security), equipment rental, photocopying and other communication costs, and the host of other operational expenses involved with providing a human service. Indirect costs include all fringe benefits and other fixed expenses linked to the new project. Successful grant applications typically have all direct costs reimbursed by the funding agency.[1]

Time Constraints

Evaluation is a labor-intensive and time-consuming endeavor. The primary need is for the evaluator to be provided with the time to carry out the evaluation plan, complete needed analyses, write the required reports, and make the required presentations of the findings. All too often, these tasks are added to an already full schedule of responsibilities. Time should be released from other responsibilities if a practitioner is assigned to serve as an evaluator.

Another solution to the time problem is to employ outside evaluation experts on a per diem or contract basis. Independent consultants are normally compensated at a rate of between $500 and $750 per day (as of 2013) plus travel and living expenses. A number of universities have consulting faculty available to work on short-term projects with outside clinics and agencies.

Sampling and Data Constraints

The initiation of an evaluation can destabilize the ongoing politics and social milieu of an agency, department, or other workplace. This loss of stability and associated anxiety about what the future holds for those involved may impact data collection. Efforts of an evaluator to collect unbiased and cogent information and data can be sabotaged by several issues and problems that the presence of the evaluator triggers. In settings where there has been animosity or mistrust between administrators and their employees, evaluators may be viewed as an intrusive extension of management. The assumption that an evaluation report may be used to justify a reduction in force (RIF) may result in individuals with important data becoming defensive and exhibiting passive-aggressive behavior toward evaluators and the evaluation process (Bamberger et al., 2012). This passive-aggressive behavior may take the form of "lost documents," documents and records being delivered late or misfiled, or documents that are difficult to identify. Absenteeism may increase on days when it becomes known that evaluators will be present. It is also possible that observations are set up and provide a staged showcase instead of a valid look at the activities of the project.

By working to achieve total transparency and maintaining a balanced perspective, evaluators can assuage many of these concerns. The goal for evaluators must be both to meet the needs of the project's stakeholders and at the same time find ways to engage important individuals in the evaluation processes. Cooperative participation is enhanced when the evaluator maintains a highly professional attitude and is forthright about the process. Cooperation is also improved when the evaluator is open to input from all informants as well as the stakeholders and no final statement is written until everyone has had his or her say.

CASE IN POINT   16.2

Great Evaluation Hoax of World War II

In 1941, the Nazi government of Germany established a walled ghetto for Jews in Theresienstadt in what is today the Czech Republic. In 1943, the Nazi government began a program to improve its international image. It selected the Theresienstadt ghetto as a showcase for how well Jews were treated. It became known by the ironic sobriquet "the Paradise Ghetto." The Danish monarch, King Christian X, was concerned about the welfare of the hundreds of Danish Jews transported to live in the Theresienstadt ghetto. Denmark was a neutral country during the war but was occupied by German forces to "protect it from a British Invasion."

Theresienstadt's claim to fame is the Verschönerung, or beautification program, by which the Nazis cleaned up the ghetto, provided food parcels and clothing to the ghetto's inhabitants, and even opened small shops in preparation for a visit on June 23, 1944, by two Swiss delegates of the International Red Cross and two representatives of the government of Denmark. These delegates, like most of the world at the time, had heard stories of atrocities happening to Jews in the Nazi camps. The evaluation tour was micromanaged and well staged, and the town's population of 30,000, fearing retribution, all played their roles. The result was a positive report to the International Red Cross and Denmark's King Christian X about the conditions for individuals sequestered in Theresienstadt. In a few months, the war turned and began going well for the Allies. German leaders, no longer worried about public relations, sent thousands of Theresienstadt inhabitants to the death camp at Auschwitz. More about this great hoax can be found at http://www.jewishgen.org/forgottenCamps/Witnesses/TheresEng.html.

Evaluations may also be stymied if the evaluators are unfamiliar with the culture and language of the individuals in the program or group being studied. In the United States, there are thousands of population clusters of individuals who have elected to live together with people sharing similar ethnic heritages. These communities frequently perpetuate the traditional culture and language. Some of these communities are well known, like the "China Towns" of large metropolitan centers. Others are not so evident, like the 250-year-old Pennsylvania Dutch communities that still run their own schools, follow 18th-century customs, and speak an old dialect of Swiss-German. In parts of Florida and California, a child may live in a Cuban- or Mexican-style community.

Evaluators collecting data, observing programs, or assessing outcomes in these communities should have a true knowledge of the group's culture and facility with its language. This may be difficult to achieve without bringing people from the culture into the evaluation as colleagues and coevaluators.

CASE IN POINT 16.3

Importance of Knowing the Culture

The greatest Broadway smash hit in 1957 was Meredith Wilson's *The Music Man.* One song from Act I of that production, "Rock Island," was set in a passenger car on a railroad train. The car was filled with traveling salesmen worried about a charlatan, the ersatz Professor Harold Hill, who was giving their profession a bad name in the small towns where he worked his marching-band scam on the locals. One of the major themes of "Rock Island" is the refrain "But he doesn't know the territory!"

This humorous observation that one needs to understand the language and culture of the setting where work is to be done was reiterated in 2011 by the American Evaluation Association in its policy statement about the need for evaluators to have cultural competence before attempting to evaluate individuals and systems in settings alien to them.

Applications from the Literature

AEA Statement on Cultural Competence in Evaluation

Cultural competence is a stance taken toward culture, not a discrete status or simple mastery of particular knowledge and skills. A culturally competent evaluator is prepared to engage with diverse segments of communities to include cultural and contextual dimensions important to the evaluation. Culturally competent evaluators respect the cultures represented in the evaluation. Several core concepts are foundational to the pursuit of cultural competence (American Evaluation Association, 2011).

- First, culture is central to economic, political, and social systems as well as individual identity. Thus, all evaluation reflects culturally influenced norms, values, and ways of knowing—making cultural competence integral to ethical, high-quality evaluation.
- Second, given the diversity of cultures within the United States, cultural competence is fluid. An evaluator who is well prepared to work with a particular community is not necessarily competent in another.
- Third, cultural competence in evaluation requires that evaluators maintain a high degree of self-awareness and self-examination to better understand how their own backgrounds and other life experiences serve as assets or limitations in the conduct of an evaluation.
- Fourth, culture has implications for all phases of evaluation—including staffing, development, and implementation of evaluation efforts as well as communicating and using evaluation results.

Political Context of Evaluations

On a national scale, it is not uncommon for evaluation data to be deliberately skewed to reinforce a political belief and related policies. The process is sometimes called **push surveying**. A push poll or survey is a way of delivering a political message in the guise of a scientific evaluation or probability-based statistical survey. This and other related evaluation tools and methods are described by professionals in the field as **pseudo-evaluation** methods.

Political interference in an evaluation can take the form of pressure applied to the evaluator by the primary stakeholder. Pressure can be subtle: Perhaps the evaluator is reminded that the primary stakeholder will be awarding several more contracts for evaluations in the future. Evaluators in private practice may be tempted to place a finger on the scale to distort the data to meet the stakeholder's wishes. Large evaluation consulting groups and university-based evaluators are less likely to respond to these pressures. Using a number of formative evaluation reports with the stakeholder advisory group can promote transparency and make it easier to resist political pressures.

Another problem is that some projects develop a life of their own and can never be totally discontinued, negative evaluation recommendations notwithstanding. Some projects become administrators' favorite "pets." The evaluation team may soon feel a push to find something good to say about such a project. Over the years, school counselors have seen numerous interventions and programs designed to modify student behavior come and go. Sadly, these innovations rarely have any impact but are included in the program because they are the pet project of someone in authority.

A real possibility exists of an overall positive bias in the evaluation literature. That positive bias is a simple reflection of the political pressure on evaluators. For example, a family physician, John J. Cannell, was surprised to read that all 55 county school districts in West Virginia (where he practiced medicine) were above average on nationally normed achievement tests. With a little research, he found that all 50 states, and most of the nation's urban and rural school districts, also reported being "above average" on these tests. This doctor named this illogical observation the "Lake Woebegon effect." Humorist Garrison Keillor wrote, "The little town that time forgot. Where all the men are good looking, all the women are strong and all the children are above average," to describe his mythical hometown, Lake Woebegon, Minnesota (Wright, 2008). Neither the national press nor the US Congress was amused at the possibility that the public had been misled for years by the test publishers and our school systems.

CASE IN POINT   16.4

Political expediency has trumped careful evaluations of programs on a number of occasions. Two examples include abstinence pledges, coordinated outside the schools, and DARE programs, often directed by professional school counselors with middle schoolers.

A number of community-based groups have set up a system of "virginity pledges." These pledges are signed by teens while in a group setting with their program's counselor and are accompanied with the award of a symbol of purity for the adolescent to wear (e.g., a silver wedding ring inscribed with the word *purity*). Millions of teens have made the pledge since the movement started in 1993. Careful evaluation research used a control group model to assess the summative outcome of the program. The evaluators followed virgin adolescent pledge takers in a 5-year longitudinal review. The experimental group was the pledge signers; the control group was a matched group of nonsigners. After 5 years, there was no difference between the two groups in sexual behaviors; frequency of sexually transmitted disease; participation in vaginal, anal, and oral sex; and age of first sexual experience. Of the pledging group, 82% reported that they had never signed a pledge. The pledge group was less likely to use birth control methods (Rosenbaum, 2009).

The Drug Abuse Resistance Education (DARE) program began in the 1980s in Southern California as a cooperative effort between law enforcement and the public schools. It grew in popularity and was approved for federal funding during the administration of President Clinton. By the year 2000, over 36 million students were taught with the DARE curriculum each year. The lead professionals in this effort were school counselors. Since the 1980s, there have been over 100 evaluations of the effectiveness of the DARE program. None of the well-controlled evaluations have demonstrated a positive effect for DARE (Ogilvie, 2011). The US Department of Education will no longer permit Elementary and Secondary Education Act (ESEA) funds to be used to support DARE programs in the schools. Yet the programs continue with state and local funding. This reflects their great popularity with parent groups and police departments (Patton, 2012). Parents would rather schools do something, even if it does not work, than do nothing about the problem of drug and alcohol abuse. Police departments like the program, as it provides officers with access to the schools and provides good public relations for their departments. Thus, local politics has trumped the evaluation findings, and DARE lives on.

Evaluation Tools and Methods

Numerous methods for doing an evaluation have been identified over the years. To carry out evaluation activities, the evaluator must select the most appropriate strategy for collecting and analyzing data regarding the program being studied. Strategies range from those that are purely phenomenological to those that are highly rational and linear. The latter are drawn from the empirical sciences (Fetterman, 1988). The linear model for evaluation stresses educational outcomes or products and studies the amount of change that occurred over the duration of the program. A qualitative approach to evaluation, on the other hand, examines the ongoing ecology of the project and employs many interpretative steps using qualitative data sources.

Evaluators and Their Skills

Each evaluation must be individually designed to fit the program being reviewed. One central skill needed for this process is the ability to cooperatively set meaningful evaluation goals with stakeholders.

Designing an evaluation requires evaluators to be well versed in many research and assessment areas. Skills needed to design and carry out meaningful evaluations include the knowledge base of educational measurement used to design and assess instruments for the study and the ability to select appropriate published evaluation measures. The evaluator must also be able to draw from the research literature to establish data collection methods and from descriptive and inferential statistics for data management and analysis. Finally, high-quality systematic evaluations also draw from the techniques of qualitative research methods such as ethnography, case study, observation, hermeneutics, and connoisseurship (Patton, 2002).

Open and structured interviews are also a common element of the evaluation process; therefore, evaluators should have superior people skills and the capacity to draw participants into the process. Finally, evaluators must be able to write accurate and crisp reports describing what was done and how successful the project may have been. This type of writing minimizes jargon and is accessible to all stakeholders and participants in the project.

Evaluation Standards

Evaluation methodologies range from the appropriate to the inane. In 1981, a set of standards for evaluating the quality of evaluations was first developed and published (Stufflebeam, 1981). These standards for evaluation were updated again in 1994 and in 2011 by the Joint Committee on Standards for Educational Evaluation and the American National Standards Institute (Yarbrough, Shulha, Hopson, & Caruthers, 2011). These standards are presented in four broad areas:

- **Utility.** Describes the evaluator's credibility and capability to carry out all aspects of the evaluation and related analyses, including carefully identifying and engaging appropriate stakeholders, writing clear and precise interim and final reports, and designing and using appropriate survey instruments for data collection. Utility can be expressed as the extent to which stakeholders find the evaluation process and products of value in meeting their needs (Yarbrough et al., 2011).

o Obviously, a significant portion of an evaluation's utility is a function of the credibility of the evaluator. When stakeholders view the evaluator as being trustworthy, principled, and fair, they are inclined to view the evaluator and the evaluation as being credible. Participants and stakeholders are likely to participate meaningfully in the evaluation process and endorse the evaluation's findings and recommendations when the evaluator is seen as credible.

o The evaluation's utility is enhanced when the appropriate stakeholders are engaged in the evaluation. This implies the evaluator has deliberated with the stakeholders to identify the program's values and intentions. Ongoing communication between the evaluator and the stakeholders is part of this engagement process.

o The purpose of the evaluation should be clear to all and open to revision based on the needs of the stakeholders. The identification of all purposes, both overt and hidden, is part of this process. The purposes, once fully known, guide the design of the evaluation and inform the processes to be used. Along with identifying all the purposes of the evaluation, the evaluator should identify the cultural values guiding the evaluation and its final application.

o An evaluation may be technically sound and provide valid judgments and recommendations but be otherwise useless to the stakeholders. To be useful, the evaluation's stakeholders must understand all the processes used, be able to interpret the findings in their context, and find the judgments significant and of value.

o For an evaluation to have utility for stakeholders, it must be delivered in an ongoing and timely manner. One of the initial steps in conducting an evaluation is to specify when all interim and final reports will be submitted. Additionally, the dissemination of findings must be well understood in advance by all involved parties. Evaluators should work with stakeholders to ensure that all findings and recommendations will be appropriately and ethically employed after they are delivered.

- **Feasibility.** Addresses questions of a practical nature such as cost, time commitments for essential personnel, and the local politics steering the evaluation of the program being evaluated.

o The central feature of this standard is the management model employed in conducting the evaluation. Quality evaluation management makes optimal use of resources and is creative in identifying and capitalizing on diverse resources for the project.

o Part of quality management is a careful plan that details responsibilities, time frames, and schedules for all activities.

o Planning is an ongoing and iterative process that is always open to change when the circumstances require (Yarbrough et al., 2011).

o The procedures designated in the planning process do not interfere with the normal operation of the program and are agreed to by the stakeholders. Likewise, the procedures are concordant with all union contracts, meet all legal obligations, fit within the cultural context of the program, and provide an efficient and cost-effective method to evaluate whether the goals are being met.

• **Propriety.** Concerns human relations among those who are party to the evaluation, including subject rights and anonymity, data confidentiality, integrity of all outcome statements regarding individuals, and related responsibilities for evaluation management.

o This standard is one of the ethical principles followed during the evaluation. All subjects have protected rights, and in the United States and in many other countries, they are afforded constitutional protections. These must be respected throughout the project, from the design stage to final report and the dissemination of the outcomes and recommendations.
o In addition to respecting human rights, the evaluation must always meet the ethical standards of the profession.
o Evaluators should be open to contrary interpretations of data and mindful of the context within which outcome findings are interpreted.
o Evaluators should work with stakeholders to address problems of social justice and power through the evaluation process.
o Evaluators must ensure that complete and credible information is provided to stakeholders throughout the evaluation process.
o Evaluators have a responsibility to identify and be open about any potential and actual conflicts of interest that could compromise the evaluation. All such conflicts must be resolved prior to the planning phase of the evaluation.
o The evaluator should account for all expended resources and employ sound accounting principles with all funds.

• **Accuracy.** Involves the quality of all formative and summative data, the accuracy and trustworthiness of all analysis and statistical presentations in the report, and the scientific justifiability of all conclusions and recommendations. The evaluation should eliminate or minimize all inconsistencies, distortions, and possible misconceptions.

o At all levels of the evaluation process, the procedures should provide consistently reliable and trustworthy information. This information should be complete and not edited to make a point or support a point of view.
o Contrary perspectives, misinterpretations, and fuzzy logic can all distort the findings. Evaluators have an obligation to prevent such problems.
o Evaluators should clarify how different stakeholders use and define evaluation conclusions differently. These differences must be addressed by the cooperative development of a framework for understanding that is appropriate for the context and culture in which the findings will be used.
o The validity of all measures employed and the validity of all conclusions based on quantitative data must be assured. Likewise, the trustworthiness of all qualitative data and conclusions based on it must be established.

o The context and program being evaluated should be fully and completely described. Beyond simple written descriptions, the evaluator may use digital audio and video recordings, artifacts such as brochures and meeting minutes, and news accounts of the program.

o Evaluations will generate a copious amount of data. It is the responsibility of the evaluator to organize those data and protect the integrity and security of all information.

o Data management and analysis require a degree of sophistication that may require an evaluator to contract with other individuals who have the expertise needed to employ the most appropriate method of analysis.

More is available on standards for evaluations from http://www.ericdigests.org/ 1996-1/the.htm.

"When the cook tastes the soup, that's formative assessment; when the customer tastes the soup, that's summative assessment."

Robert E. Stake

Stakeholders

When a decision has been made that an evaluation is needed, the designated evaluator's initial task is to identify all stakeholders for the project. Any individual can be a stakeholder if he or she is impacted by the project or program being evaluated. These individuals may include members of the governing board, administrators, other salaried professionals in the organization, hourly staff employees, and participants or clients being served by the activity. Identifying and including stakeholders in the evaluation improves the evaluation's transparency and the level of acceptance and cooperation that the evaluators will experience.

Evaluators must be mindful of the private agendas that some stakeholders may bring to the process of evaluating the program. As each stakeholder or group of stakeholders becomes involved with the process, it is important to determine what, if any, special interest they may represent. The evaluator has the job of understanding and keeping all hidden agendas in check.

The number of stakeholders can quickly swell to an unmanageable size. In that case, the evaluator should identify representatives from the various stakeholder groups who can serve on an advisory committee. The committee should facilitate two-way communication with all potential stakeholders.

It is also necessary to identify concerns stakeholders may have with the program evaluation process (Fleischman & Williams, 1996). For the most part, agency and clinic employees view themselves as being overworked, underpaid, and burdened with great responsibility while being given no real authority. It is easy for these individuals to become skeptical of an evaluation process and view it as just another waste of their time.

To avoid resistance, the evaluator should work with the advisory committee of stakeholders to write an evaluation management plan that includes the formative and summative questions to be answered during the evaluation.

Applications from the Literature

Problem Statement and Methodology from an International Evaluation Study Using an Action Research Approach

Note: In this study, 79 patients on intake to the psychiatry unit were studied as part of an evaluation. The formative evaluation employed interviews with the patients' caregivers or guardians. These data were shared with the professional staff during regular monthly meetings. During these feedback meetings, ideas were explored regarding possible new directions to take and new methods to follow. These monthly meetings were central to the action research core of the evaluation of the clinical programs provided by the inpatient psychiatry unit.

The last sentence in the following description provides the evaluation question guiding this study.

Methodology: Adult mental health services across Australia are providing assessment, treatment and rehabilitation for people with a range of psychiatric disorders via a network of providers that includes inpatient psychiatric units, community programs and a private sector including general practitioners and psychiatrists.

Within many services in New South Wales, it is a commonly stated belief that despite community based crisis and treatment teams, greater numbers of inpatient beds are still required, and demands for crisis admission appear to exceed availability in many areas. When the majority of staff believes that inpatient care is the only option for a large number of patients, proposing alternatives may seem unrealistic.

In theory, such alternatives require early detection and effective intervention before the crisis has escalated. In practice, staff may believe that they have already exhausted all of these options and that admission is inevitable. There have been no reports that have examined this disparity between theory of effective early intervention and staff beliefs that they are already practicing this without result. It is, therefore, of some interest to question whether community treatment alternatives are being used effectively and to understand the organizational changes required if community treatment has any potential to further impact on demands for inpatient beds.

Source: Tobin, M., Dakos, T., & Urbanc, A. (1997). Using action research to facilitate organizational change in mental health service delivery. *Australian and New Zealand Journal of Psychiatry, 31*(5), 739–743.

Evaluation Goals and Questions

Well-controlled and carefully planned evaluations are normally carried out to meet a requirement from an oversight organization, such as a state or federal funding source or an accrediting body. The basic evaluation problem in such cases can be straightforward and based on published standards and/or criteria.

Evaluations may also be conducted to meet an organization's desire to learn how it can be more effective and better meet the needs of its clients. In this type of evaluation, the stakeholders play a major role in defining the direction of the study. Once the stakeholder advisory committee has been formed, it should be given the responsibility of working with the evaluator to identify the goals for the evaluation. The step immediately following goal setting involves developing evaluation objectives aligned with each of the goals. The advisory committee of stakeholders has the task of reviewing and approving objectives for the program's goals and selecting an evaluation model to achieve the goals.

These goals are usually stated clearly in the funding application. For accreditation evaluations, the goals of the program are part of the organization's mission statement. These goals then become the basis for setting evaluation objectives and devising evaluation questions to address each.

Formative and Summative Evaluation Components

In the process of making judgments and recommendations about a project or program, evaluators employ two principal assessment strategies to answer the evaluation's questions. Some of these evaluation questions are answered before the project or program starts, and others are answered during the operation of the project or program. These start-up and ongoing evaluation questions can be part of the formative dimension of the evaluation. **Formative assessments** involve ongoing observations, reviews, measures, and data collection used to inform project managers and provide them with guidance in setting the course of the program. Formative assessments provide information needed to make midcourse corrections and continually improve the process and products of the program. Formative components of an evaluation can include both qualitative research methods and quantitative techniques for measuring what is happening.

Applications from the Literature

Excerpt from an Evaluation of Online Undergraduate Classes

Note: In this study, 191 undergraduates enrolled in one of 7 online undergraduate classes were used to evaluate the online learning process. The authors used the online format of the course to collect formative and summative questionnaire-based data about the students' backgrounds and perceptions of the online class experience.

Instrumentation: The summative evaluation included 23 closed-ended format questions. The first seven questions were identical to the demographic questions included on the formative tool. The additional 16 closed-ended questions solicited students' perceptions of their course experience. Seven of those items were similar to items asked on the formative survey. Again, factors such as interactions, accessibility, and design of instruction were included, as well as items designed to assess overall satisfaction with the course.

   Data Collection: Using the formative instrument, data were first collected at the beginning of the semester. The instrument was placed on the course Website and students were directed to complete it. Then, at the end of the term, students were given access to the summative instrument and instructed to complete it. Students completed the instruments at their own worksite and at their convenience.

Source: Stewart, B. L., Waight, C. L., Norwood, M. M., & Ezell, S. D. (2004). Formative and summative evaluation of online courses. *Quarterly Review of Distance Education, 5*(2), 101–109.

Summative evaluation describes the final assessment of outcomes from the project. These assessments provide a statement about the effectiveness of the project or program once it is completed. This type of assessment of outcomes can be used to guide future efforts and provide a rationale for the continuation of the project. The summative component of an evaluation is usually numeric and may employ both descriptive and inferential statistics.

Context, Input, Process, and Product

The primary approach to systematic evaluations used today is the context, input, process, and product (CIPP) evaluation model of Daniel L. Stufflebeam (2003). Stufflebeam expanded the initial model for evaluations in 2007 to add product evaluation review dimensions for the assessment of impact, effectiveness, sustainability, and transportability. The CIPP model provides valid and reliable methods for assessing the extent to which goals and objectives held by a program's stakeholders have been met. The model also provides a structure for the systematic collection and analysis of formative and summative data, thoughtful analyses of products and processes, and the writing of a cogent and accurate report. Systematic evaluations using the CIPP approach are mandated by most grant funding agencies, including the US Departments of Education and Health and Human Services, and most private philanthropies.

Photo 16.1   Daniel L. Stufflebeam

Ohio State University.

- **Context.** Context evaluation assesses needs, assets, and problems within a defined environment. This can include a review of all background data available in the system and interviews with the program's leadership and other stakeholders. The context also includes a review of the original program's goals.
- **Input.** Input evaluation assesses competing strategies and the work plans and budgets of the selected approach. The political viability and feasibility of the initial evaluation plan is part of this evaluation. The proposed evaluation strategy should be assessed and compared to possible alternative approaches.
- **Process.** Process evaluations monitor, document, and assess program activities. This includes presenting regular formative evaluation reports to appropriate stakeholders based on observations, digitally recorded documentation of activities, accounting statements, progress reports, interviews, and other assessments of the program's outcomes to date.
- **Product.** The 2007 revision of the CIPP approach provided four new elements of this area of evaluation review.
  - ○ **Impact.** This evaluation is focused on the program's reach to all target populations. It also examines the impact the program has inadvertently had on nontargeted populations.

- o **Effectiveness.** Overall effectiveness is assessed as the significance and quality of the outcomes. It includes documentation of all positive and negative findings.
- o **Sustainability.** This is the extent to which a program's contributions are being integrated into the institution and the likelihood they can be sustained over time.
- o **Transportability.** This is an optional component of an evaluation. It documents the likelihood the project could be adapted and applied in another setting.

During the year, the person designated as the evaluator of a program (e.g., a counseling clinic) should keep lines of communication open. To facilitate scheduling and transportation problems, these meetings may be conducted as virtual meetings in an online venue and via email. An interim formative report should be prepared about halfway during the evaluation's cycle. This report provides stakeholders with a tentative analysis of how goals are being met. This formative report from the evaluation is likely to result in tweaking ongoing activities.

Management Plan

Once goals are set and each objective for the evaluation identified, it is then possible to devise an evaluation management plan. The feasibility standard is addressed by developing a comprehensive and practical but frugal evaluation plan to assess the effectiveness of the program or project being evaluated.

A specific data collection strategy needs to be devised for assessing each objective. This process starts by listing all evaluation tasks that will be designed and completed for the evaluation. Many ongoing evaluation tasks and activities are formative in nature and collected as the project goes along. The data collection strategy should also provide a plan for making summative evaluation statements.

The two most critical questions to be asked when designing a management plan include timing and responsibility. The question of time relates to when each part of the evaluation should be conducted, while the question of responsibility is answered by knowing who has the task of doing the various data collection procedures. This is best expressed graphically as a two-axis **Gantt chart.** This chart is essentially a timeline of what will occur and when it will happen. The abscissa of this chart is a timeline extending throughout the life cycle of the project. The ordinate of the Gantt chart presents a list of tasks required for the program's evaluation (Clark, Polakov, & Trabold, 2010). Bars on the chart provide a visual reference for the timing and sequence of evaluation activities. If several people are responsible for collecting data for the evaluation, the name of the person tasked with each component can be imposed on the Gantt chart's timelines. The management plan should also specify data collection procedures to be used for the evaluation of the various dimensions of the program. This information can be added to the structure of the Gantt chart.

Management plans should address the organization and storage of all evaluation data and artifacts collected throughout the evaluation process. Evaluating a clinical program

Table 16.1 Sample Gantt Chart for Planning the Evaluation of Two Goals for a School Counseling Program

Task	Timeline / Assignment	Evaluation Indicator of Success
Goal: Provide Career Guidance		
1. Expand general library holdings in career education	(Counselor A) **********	1. Count of new career software and new career focused books for young readers
2. Provide career choice tests during career education classes	(All Counselors) **********	2. Total number of tests administered and follow-up counseling sessions
3. Workshops on interviewing and job applications	(Counselor C) ***********	3. Number of workshops, and total hours of student attendance
4. Contact regional employers for possible beginner jobs	(Counselor C) ***********	4. Number of contacts made, number of job openings identified
5. Job placement for non-college bound students	(All Counselors) **********	5. Year to year change in % of graduates employed 20 or more hours per week
Goal: Reduce Bullying Behaviors		
1. Follow-up on anonymous postings on counselor web page	(All Counselors) ******************************	1. Reduction in number of referrals for harassing and bullying behavior
2. Victim group counseling sessions	(All Counselors) ********** **********	2. Survey of students for outcome of counseling program
3. Parent support group for the families of bullying victims	(Counselor B) ***** ***** *****	3. Parent attendance count and survey of parental perception of session effectiveness
4. Behavioral counseling with bullies	(Counselor B) ******************************	4. Reduction in rate of recidivism for counseled bullies
When task should be completed	S—O—N—D—J—F—M—A—M—J—J	

Source: Wright, R. J. (2012). *Introduction to school counseling.* Thousand Oaks, CA: Sage.

that provides social or psychological services raises special problems related to the nature of evaluation data. Data collection must occur in legal and ethical ways that safeguard the rights and welfare of all involved. Once again, informed consent is needed for many types of measurement used in counseling and other therapeutic areas. The careful collection and storage of raw data is an important part of the propriety standard. Procedures should be established and specified to maintain the confidential nature of the evaluation's data. This plan should specify who has access to the evaluation data and what security measures are to be taken.

Once the objectives for the evaluation have been specified and evaluation personnel are in place, it is time to select research methodologies to collect and analyze data. All research methodologies described throughout this textbook can be useful for data collection and analysis.

COLLECTION OF EVALUATION DATA

An ongoing process in conducting a systematic evaluation of a clinical program or other project is data collection. The data collection process begins even before the study has established an advisory committee of stakeholders and a set of evaluation goals. The process starts with framing the project or activity to be evaluated and identifying potential baseline data. Baseline data provide a point of comparison for the findings from the evaluation. It may be the number of individuals sharing a problem, measures of the degree or intensity of the problem being addressed, measures of personal satisfaction or wellness by clients and individuals to be served by the project, and indicators of personal affect by the clients or participants in the project or activity.

An evaluation with its formative and summative dimensions is likely to be conducted over a period of time and is likely to include observational data, interview data, meeting notes, general wellness assessments, neurological and/or psychiatric data, counseling records, demographic information, curricula used to present the program to individuals and groups, and any other demonstration of products generated under the project. Formative data collection may also require the development of questionnaires or interviews designed to meet a specific need and measure a specific topic or dimension within the project or activity.

Careful selection of published assessment instruments and their appropriate and ethical use may provide a critical source of summative evaluation data. The key to using any published measure is having a solid background in using the instrument and being scrupulous in following the published directions for both administration and scoring of the measure. (See Chapters 12 and 13 for information on assessing the quality of a measure.)

Qualitative Evaluation Methods

Evaluations can be conducted using a qualitative research approach. An evaluator's qualitative research questions tend to be broader than those associated with quantitative approaches to evaluation. The qualitative evaluation question identifies the topic being analyzed and focuses the subject's attention on the time frame and activity that are being investigated (Vaterlaus & Higgenbotham, 2011). For example, if an employment counseling service was evaluated, a qualitative evaluation question could be "How do unemployed college graduates feel about their job networking skills after a seminar on developing and using networks to find employment?" This approach to evaluation makes it possible to collect evaluation data still being formed by the clients receiving service.

Most qualitative research methodologies can be time-consuming and labor-intensive. For that reason, qualitative evaluations generally employ semistructured interviews and/or questionnaires as a primary data-gathering method. Open-ended questions can be used to engage clients in the evaluation process prior to introducing more structure into the process. These questions may take the following form: "Please describe your experiences as a participant in the series of seminars dealing with personal anger management." With informed consent, the interviewing process can be digitally recorded to provide the basis for subsequent analysis by the evaluation team members.

Applications from the Literature

Goals and Evaluation Questions from a Qualitative Evaluation

Note: Two individuals from the Marriage and Family Therapy Program of Purdue University used a focus group of graduate students to provide a qualitative evaluation of the program. The evaluation was successful, and recommendations from the evaluation were used to improve the graduate program.

Participatory Qualitative Evaluation: We recently conducted a focus group in our own training program. We wanted to get a sense of both Master's- and Doctoral-level students' experiences of our program, and find out what they thought about several current practices and proposed changes. These students were at various stages in their training. Through the focus group results, faculty learned what students thought and used this information to reflect on, and in some cases change, program policies. For example, we streamlined our clinic procedures and eliminated redundant procedures regarding paperwork and on-call scheduling. The students who participated told us that they enjoyed the group process and the opportunity to discuss various aspects of the program. The group leader presented the results at a student-faculty meeting, which allayed students' fears that their input would not be used. In addition, the participants requested and received written feedback from the faculty about their concerns.

Below is a list of questions we used to guide the focus group.

1. Think of a metaphor (object, story, song, movie, television show) that symbolizes your overall impression of this program. Write it down or draw it and describe what it means.

2. If you became the director of this program, what would you change or not change?

3. What would you say the goals of our training program are? Are we meeting these goals?

4. If a student interviewing for the program asked you to describe what the relationships between the faculty and students are like, what would you say?

5. If we had an opening for another faculty member and you were in charge of writing the "want-ad" for the perfect MFT professor, what would you write?

6. Describe any ethical or professional concerns you have about the MFT program.

7. What gender and cultural issues stand out for you in this program? How do they affect you?

8. In what ways could program faculty change this program to reduce student stress without compromising training goals and objectives?

9. Imagine yourself at your doctoral graduation. As you look back, what will be your fondest memory? What will be your biggest disappointment?

10. If you were leading this group, what is one question you would have wanted me to ask? What is your answer to that question?

11. What do you hope comes of this process and evaluation?

When leading a focus group, the leader should begin by explaining the group's purpose and the reasons why people were asked to participate. In our evaluation, the purpose was to improve the MFT graduate program, increase student input and satisfaction with the program, and plan immediate and long-term changes. The leader should inform participants of how their feedback will be presented to and used by faculty in future decisions about the program.

Source: Deacon, S. A., & Piercy, F. P. (2000). Qualitative evaluation of family therapy programs: A participatory approach. *Journal of Marital and Family Therapy, 26*(1), 39–45.

Quantitative Evaluation Methods

Stakeholders with administrative responsibility tend to prefer evaluation designs that emphasize the use of quantitative methodologies. These users of evaluation reports have a clear bias toward statistics. Narratives and case study material central to qualitative evaluations tend to be seen as mere journalism, while a statistical table with significance levels for rejecting null hypotheses seems to be "real" science and therefore credible (Patton, 2012). Federal funding agencies' requirements for evaluators to provide scientific evidence of program effectiveness adds to the pressure to emphasize quantitative methodologies.

Applications from the Literature

Excerpt of Results from Quantitative Programmatic Evaluation

Note: The well-funded program, designed in Hong Kong and brought to the United States and known as Positive Adolescent Training through Holistic Social Programs (P.A.T.H.S.), was evaluated after being implemented in 207 American secondary schools with 33,700 students during the 2006–2007 school year. This evaluation emphasized both descriptive and numerical findings. Subsequent studies were later published evaluating P.A.T.H.S. with qualitative analyses based on focus group research.

(Continued)

(Continued)

Results: Reliability analyses with the schools as the unit of analysis showed that Form A was internally consistent: 10 items related to the program (alpha = .98, mean inter-item correlation = .84), 10 items related to the instructor (alpha = .99, mean inter-item correlation = .93), 16 items related to the benefits (alpha = .99, mean inter-item correlation = .93), and 39 items based on whole Form A (alpha = .99, mean inter-item correlation = .78).

Quantitative findings based on the closed-end questions are presented here and several observations that can be highlighted. First, roughly three-quarters of the respondents perceived the program in a positive manner. For example, roughly 81% of the students indicated that they participated actively during class; roughly 78% felt that the classroom atmosphere was pleasant.

Second, over four-fifths of the respondents gave a positive evaluation of the instructor. For example, about 88% of the respondents indicated that the instructor was ready to provide help when needed, and they encouraged the students to participate.

Third, roughly four-fifths of the respondents perceived that the program promoted their development, including social competence (82%), emotional competence (81%), and overall development (83%).

Fourth, while roughly three-quarters of the participants would recommend the program to their friends with similar needs, only a simple majority (66.13%) would join similar programs in the future.

Finally, roughly 85% of the respondents indicated that they were satisfied with the program. Regarding the degree of program adherence estimated by the workers, the mean level of adherence was 87.10%, with a range from 38.25% to 100%.

Source: Shek, D. T. L., & Sun, R. C. F. (2008). Evaluation of project P.A.T.H.S. *Adolescence, 43*(172), 807–822.

Many times, evaluations are based on data that already exist in a large-scale database. There are many sources of such data collections, including the National Center for Educational Statistics, the Department of Health and Human Services Database Archive, and the data sets maintained by all 50 states. Evaluations based on these databases cannot follow the normal format for designing and conducting a program or accreditation evaluation, as they must be after-the-fact efforts. These ex post facto evaluations are quantitative and summative in nature. The fact that the data are available without cost makes these evaluation studies very popular with graduate students writing their dissertations.

Mixed Methods in Evaluation

When evaluators and stakeholders are less concerned with competing epistemologies, they may decide to follow a pragmatic approach for designing the evaluation. (See Chapter 15 for more on mixed methods research.) The combination of multiple approaches in an evaluation is known as mixed methods evaluation (MME). Evaluators using MME are free to create various evaluation questions and activities that are unconstrained by a standard of ideological purity. This provides the flexibility to design sensitive and nuanced evaluations. MME, by combining both qualitative and quantitative components, strengthens the evaluation and makes findings and recommendations harder to challenge. Its strength comes from the triangulation of findings from different evaluation formats into a single outcome, which has been described as "knowledge generating" (Patton, 2012).

These mixed methods evaluations employ focus groups and open-ended interview questions along with numeric data collected from summative assessments, closed-format questionnaires, and structured interviews. In this way, they provide a complete picture of the program and its activities. MME generates more data and gives evaluators more material to work with while answering a larger range of evaluation questions. Because of these advantages, MME is the most common form of evaluation used to conduct programmatic evaluations and self-studies.

Because MME provides different types of evaluation data, the evaluator must weigh the various findings and integrate these different streams of information. This makes it possible for the evaluator to write conclusion statements and organize recommendations based on the synthesis (McConney, Rudd, & Ayres, 2002). For projects that run for weeks or months, the evaluation will also be able to identify trends and project into the near future if the project is to be continued.

Evaluative Action Research

Evaluation using action research has a slightly different focus than do other approaches for evaluation. (See Chapter 6 for more on action research.) The reason for using action research is to provide information for the continuous improvement and development of the program being evaluated. Evaluative action research is less centered on the evaluator and more concerned with those who are actually part of the project being evaluated. This results in a wider group of stakeholders, including various individuals with unique perspectives on the project. By participating in action research, this wider group can feel ownership and contribute to the ongoing improvement of the project.

In an action research–focused evaluation, all individuals are encouraged to reflect on what they are doing and why they are doing it that way. Members of the evaluation team facilitate those reflective moments and work with participating individuals in interpreting what new ideas and understandings are being revealed. From this process come the ideas for the action step when a modification is made and evaluated.

Evaluative action research makes it possible for individuals delivering a program's services to review their strategies and refine them over time. This form of research needs to create and maintain a careful record of the ideas that were developed and approaches that were tried (Lienert, 2002). These records facilitate sharing with the wider organization, or even the profession, ideas about what works and what approaches and ideas did not pan out.

REPORTING

Report Writing

The evaluator prepares written and oral presentations of all outcomes and recommendations following the careful analyses and syntheses of the evaluation's data. Perhaps the most complex task in the evaluation process is the synthesis of data into a series of conclusions and recommendations.

This synthesis process is possible for evaluations that were clearly focused on the project and not lost in a sea of peripheral concerns and idiosyncratic interests of one or more of the stakeholders. Collecting a mass of detail about tangential issues does not get to the core elements of the project and results in a confusing and often contradictory set of findings and unconvincing recommendations.

A straightforward list of summative evaluation data can be misleading if not placed in a context of what happened throughout the project. For that reason, writing the final report requires both sensitivity to the ongoing processes involved and a clear focus on the program or project's impact.

At its core, the final report reflects the considered judgment of its author, the evaluator. However, stakeholders and individuals who were part of the program or project and were included in its activities should have input. In the development of the final report, the author should review the various formative assessments that preceded the summative phase. These interim statements can document a possible progression and spot monotonic trends as the project matured.

The utility standard requires the final report to provide a clear description of the program or project. Written reports provide the rationale for the evaluation and describe its context, setting, participants, and evaluators. This presentation gives readers a concise description of all activities that were part of the effort. It also presents any unusual findings and modifications needed to the management model as the project occurred. It should provide an accurate statement of the findings and provide clear and unbiased interpretation of all data.

As various types of information are collected to answer specific questions based on goals and objectives for the program, the final report should also address each goal and objective by presenting all relevant evidence collected and analyzed for each objective. A conclusion statement should be made regarding each of the objectives. Conclusions may include kudos and target problem areas. The final project report should list all successes and challenges and point ahead to possibly using the project in other settings or venues in the future.

Dissemination

The final step in an evaluation is the publication of the final report and the wider dissemination of the results and recommendations. All too often, the final report from a systematic evaluation of academic or clinical programs ends up filed in an archive with the funding agency and forgotten. The best result that can occur from the final evaluation report is for its analysis and recommendations to be incorporated into plans for the coming institutional budget cycle. Another sterling outcome for an evaluation report and recommendations is to see the program introduced (transported) to other venues in different institutions.

Prior to dissemination, the evaluator should discuss the process for publicly releasing the final report. This discussion should include both the administrators who are central stakeholders and other stakeholders who participated in the evaluation process. It is important to keep in mind that the report is owned by the agency or individuals that contracted and paid for the evaluation process. It is a good strategy to focus one of these discussions on ways to carry out the recommendations and ideas from the evaluation (Erford, McKechnie, & Moore-Thomas, 2004).

The final evaluation report can be used as a basis for publishing a brochure about the agency or counseling program. Most office computers provide software that can be used to publish a simple bifold public relations statement. Cut and paste some photos or logos and use a color printer, and the brochure can become an effective advertisement for the activities of the agency, department, or program.

In an edited form, the final report can be uploaded onto the agency's office website, or sections of it can appear in a blog about the services being provided by the program or department. Another option is to write a column for a community newspaper. Local community newspapers are frequently platforms for local advertising, and editors are often desperate for interesting content for their publication. An article about the successes and activities of the local agency or counseling program would be a good fit to the needs of many community newspaper editors.

Other venues for dissemination include the **rubber chicken circuit.** This odd sobriquet describes the numerous lunch and dinner meetings that stakeholders can attend as a "guest speaker." Payment for providing one of these community service presentations is usually a free lunch or dinner. During these events, the visiting dignitary (stakeholder) is expected to make a speech. This presents the individual with the opportunity to make a pitch for support for different projects and for resources needed. Service clubs and community booster clubs have regular meetings and are always on the lookout for someone who can speak for 15 or 20 minutes on a topic of community interest. Local newspapers normally list these clubs and their meeting locations. The organization's program chair is the contact person for speakers.

Finally, the evaluator or administrator of the program can prepare an abbreviated summary document and submit it for consideration as a presentation before a regional or even national meeting of a professional association. Regional meetings of professional associations are normally more open to welcoming new researchers and evaluators as presenters. The annual meetings of most are listed in higher education publications such as the *Chronicle of Higher Education* (http://chronicle.com/section/Events/77/). Careful planning when the original budget for the program being proposed was developed can provide funding lines for travel and related support for attending meetings and making a presentation based on evaluation data.

SUMMARY

Evaluation is a complex form of research that assesses the worth or value of a program, project, or activity. Evaluation differs from other forms of research by happening in a real-world context where political considerations play a significant role. Evaluations involve many stakeholders and require the careful management of people and resources. Evaluation has come into its own as a major profession since funding for educational, health-related, and social service agencies was massively increased starting in the 1960s.

The fact that humans respond to being evaluated with anxiety increases the likelihood that constraints and barriers may be presented whenever an evaluation is begun. These constraints, if not deftly handled by the evaluator, can compromise the integrity and value of the evaluation.

Standards for judging the quality of any evaluation have been published and include concerns with the evaluation's utility, feasibility, propriety, and accuracy. The actual evaluation model endorsed by agencies that fund research, social programs, human service projects, and other programmatic efforts to improve the human condition is known as the CIPP model. This includes the evaluation's context, inputs, processes, and products developed.

Evaluation researchers can select from the full range of research methods to establish the approach that will be most efficient in answering the evaluation (research) questions posed by the project's stakeholders. While the design may emphasize qualitative or quantitative methods, it is more common for the evaluator to employ a mixed method evaluation design. Occasionally, evaluators and stakeholders will decide to make the evaluation an ongoing developmental effort. In that case, the evaluation design of choice may be an action research evaluation.

DISCUSSION QUESTIONS

1. In 2012, an online approach to cognitive behavioral therapy was being tested as a method for treating an anxiety disorder. The therapy is delivered through a cell phone app (Carey, 2012). This approach for service delivery will soon be applied to a number of anxiety disorders and used to modify behaviors such as alcohol abuse. If your clinical practice wished to use this method with some clients experiencing anxiety disorders, how could its effectiveness be evaluated? Describe the hypothetical clinical setting, stakeholders, and formative and summative evaluation questions, and provide an appropriate research approach for each question.

2. Plan a visit to your university's library and ask to read one of the recent grant applications made by the office of government relations on behalf of the institution. Pay special attention to the evaluation model spelled out in that document. Describe the steps the university is taking to evaluate what it is doing with these outside funds.

3. Identify an agency or organization that you would like to help receive funding for a needed project. This may be conducted as a theoretical exercise and not involve meeting with potential stakeholders. Next, develop a one-page plan for a project or program for that organization, including a statement of one or two goals. Finally, use the Internet to identify granting agencies and philanthropies that fund that type of project. Read the agencies' requirements for evaluation and make a brief report to the class about your findings.

NOTE

1. There are also in-kind costs. These are donated by sources not charged to the grant by the service provider. These are the value of pro bono services, volunteer time, buildings and offices dedicated without fee to the project, and similar things of value contributed to make the project work.

CHAPTER 17

Writing Research Proposals and Reports

"No passion in the world is equal to the passion to alter someone else's draft."

H. G. Wells

OBJECTIVES

By reading and studying this chapter, you should acquire the competency to do the following:

- Explain the role of a research problem statement in a research proposal.
- Describe various sources of ideas for the development of a research proposal.
- Compare the research proposal formats of qualitative and quantitative research proposals.
- Contrast the language used in writing qualitative and quantitative research proposals.
- Discuss the differences among research proposals, research presentations, and articles.

INTRODUCTION AND MAJOR THEMES

The focus of this chapter is on the steps followed when a practitioner-researcher develops a research proposal. Various writing skills and methods for developing those skills are also presented. The format prescribed by the American Psychological Association for writing research proposals and articles is emphasized throughout the chapter. This includes both mechanical issues such as citing and presenting references and organizational issues such as outlining and selecting pronouns.

The first part of the chapter explores the difficult task of identifying a research problem and writing research questions and hypotheses to guide the study. It also examines similarities and differences between qualitative and quantitative research proposals.

DEVELOPING A RESEARCH PROPOSAL

Most graduate programs require that students demonstrate their research skills by organizing a proposal for research on a topic or issue of interest. This proposal may or may not become the student's eventual master's degree thesis or doctoral dissertation topic, but it serves as a demonstration of the skills needed for such undertakings.

Writing at this level requires a new mind-set for many students. The planning, organization, and writing of a long, integrated research proposal are very different from writing the five-paragraph essays or term papers required of many undergraduate students. This type of writing introduces the need to organize one's thinking on a chapter-by-chapter basis.

Authoring a research proposal requires concentration and large blocks of time. It cannot be done in a rush or over a weekend. Finding and reading scores of related journal articles, outlining what the articles can contribute to the literature review, and sequencing them into an argument can take many weeks and occasional flashes of insight. The analytical thinking required for this task cannot be stopped and easily restarted an hour or two later. Some part-time graduate students have attempted to integrate proposal writing into their regular workday between seeing clients. These students find that nothing gets accomplished. As soon as they finally get back on track, they are called away and will need to recapture the moment of insight all over again.

With much practice, new authors will find their **"voice"** and become ever more fluid in presenting their thoughts in writing. Consider the many books and articles you have read, and the differences in authorial voice will become evident. Some writers' narratives are convoluted and hard to follow, while others are so technical as to be virtually unreadable. Obviously, the most appreciated writers are those who can be both precise and clear to readers. This implies a need to be aware of who the audience for the writing is and these readers' interest and knowledge levels. Some developing authors catch a serious case of **lexiphanicism** complicated by an abundance of malapropisms. Quality writing is scientifically correct but logical and easy to follow and written in language accessible to readers.

Defining a Research Problem

Writing a research proposal requires a dose of both insight and imagination (Gall, Borg, & Gall, 1996). Imagination must rest on a firm basis of knowledge in the field of interest and a mind open to new conceptualizations. Researcher imagination is not the exclusive province of qualitative scholars but is also a central skill for those employing empirical methods in quantitative studies.

The purpose of research is to apply imagination and careful methodologies to develop comprehensive explanations for the elements of our lives. Imagination makes it possible to consider alternate explanations, see alternative applications for experimental approaches, break the linear chain of causal relationships, and anticipate endogenous factors within systems.

As with imagination, insight is most likely to occur through cognitive processes that are well grounded in the literature of the field. The researcher must have a deep perception and understanding of what is being studied. This implies the capacity to see latent elements within data that are linked with outcomes and findings.

In developing a proposal, new researchers may be advised to concentrate on a segment of the profession in which they have a true interest. This type of writing is labor-intensive, and without an interest in the topic being developed, the researcher may easily become bored and disaffected by the task. In developing a research proposal as a class requirement, students have an opportunity to test the waters and determine whether a particular topic has the potential to maintain the student's motivation throughout a research project or whether it is a fallow concept and will not be intensely interesting.

Keep It Simple

New researchers tend to bite off too much with their first formal research problem statement. The research problem statement guides the research effort and provides the researcher with practicable limits. If the topic is too broad, the project may become a never-ending series of tasks and analyses. For example, the idea to study changes in clients' self-esteem through therapeutic intervention is interesting but far too broad. The answer to this question could easily fill a major textbook. A scan of the Questia® computer database on this topic identified 3,993 articles and 2,083 textbooks—all addressing this one topic.

In narrowing the focus of the research proposal, the researcher should read literature summaries and decide on an appropriate aspect of the topic to explore in more depth through a thorough reading of the literature. This may lead to a new, more refined research problem statement such as "What is the effectiveness of Ellis's rational emotive behavior therapy as a method to improve the self-esteem of children with one or more undocumented immigrant parents?"

In the proposal development process, students should discuss their nascent ideas for research problems with student colleagues and various faculty members who may be especially knowledgeable on the topic. Working within the graduate department's guidelines, students may contact faculty and other scholars from other institutions. This may be necessary if the review of recent literature identifies individuals affiliated with other institutions as important resources. When reaching out to others, the student should have read extensively and have specific questions to ask the outside authority.

Avoid Trivia

As the researcher reduces the scope of a research question and focuses on a manageable problem for study, it is important to maintain the interest and value of the problem for the practice and/or profession. It is all too easy to get mired in minutiae and lose the big picture. Trivial research problems only document the obvious and add nothing to the general understanding of humanity. For example, a trivial research problem could be "Does adolescent [acne vulgaris or common] facial acne lower self-esteem?"

Research Problems From the Literature

In Chapter 3, the process of reviewing the literature was described. One advantage of reading the current research is that it provides ideas about still unanswered questions and unsolved problems. Literature in the social sciences holds the sequential record of the development of the disciplines and points to new issues to be addressed through further research. In the conclusions of published research studies, authors normally provide ideas that need to be pursued in the future.

Applications from the Literature

Two Examples of "Needed Future Research Efforts" from Published Journal Articles

Example A

Note: The authors encourage others to study the interaction of work, affect, and the effectiveness of group therapy for psychological disturbances.

Discussion: However, because there have been few studies of the effects of affective experience, affective expression, and work in the group treatment of patients with complicated grief, the results should be regarded as tentative and in need of further replication. In addition, the findings may be limited to the specific nature of the therapies, patients, and measures of the present study. Thus, generalization should be exercised with caution. Nevertheless, . . . similar findings concerning a direct relationship between the experience of positive feelings and favorable outcome in cognitive-behavioral group therapy for patients with binge-eating disorder . . . [have been reported]. In light of their findings and ours, we believe that further investigation into the role that affect and work play in the group treatment of patients experiencing complicated grief as well as other disorders is definitely warranted.

Source: Piper, W. E., Ogrodniczuk, J. S., Joyce, A. S., McCallum, M., & Rosie, J. S. (2002). Relationships among affect, work, and outcome in group therapy for patients with complicated grief. *American Journal of Psychotherapy, 56*(3), 347–361.

Example B

Note: Counselor education programs are required to be gatekeepers for the profession, removing graduate students who may be inappropriate candidates for graduate degrees and professional licensure. The authors surveyed CACREP institutions to identify programs with formal procedures for making such identifications and how they provide remediation or transition out of the program.

Recommendations for Further Research: This study should be replicated comparing CACREP and non-CACREP programs to determine if similar results will be obtained regarding indicators and clusters of student impairment. Because CACREP programs are required to have polices in place to address student impairment, and non-CACREP programs do not, there are possibly differences of opinions between counselor educators in these two types of programs regarding impairment.

Further research comparing responses of counselor educators in the university with those of on-site clinical supervisors should be undertaken. On-site clinical supervisors work closely with counseling students who participate in field-based training, and it would be beneficial to explore whether their opinions regarding indicators of impairment differ from counselor educators' opinions.

Additional research should be conducted to determine if there are relationships between cluster membership found in this study and the gender, the ethnicity and/or the age of the impaired students.

Source: Li, C., Lampe, R., Trusty, J. G., & Lin, Y. (2009). Cluster analysis of impaired counseling students: A survey of master's level CACREP accredited programs. *Journal of Professional Counseling, Practice, Theory, & Research, 37*(1), 38–50.

Extending and Elaborating Research of Others

Ideas for research problems may involve extending research recently completed or currently underway. Graduate students in large programs at research universities often work with a research scholar at their own school to pursue answers to questions linked to ongoing large-scale projects. In a sense, these graduate students apprentice to senior scholars as they develop their own research skills and begin a research program of their own. In the United States, 282 universities are listed in one of the 3 doctoral research classifications of the Carnegie Commission.

Federal agencies also have established well-conceived research programs that students can use as the source of ideas. These projects publish huge longitudinal databases in accessible online forms that are remarkable in depth and range. They are so large that it is possible to study questions concerning small minority groups and the intersections among demographic dimensions. Thus, it is possible to develop a research idea, collect and analyze all needed data, and write a dissertation without leaving home.

Applications from the Literature

Annotated List of Mental Health National Databases

Note: In addition to this list of available free research data sources, other databases are also provided online by the US Census, the National Center for Educational Statistics (NCES), and most state departments of health and education. Similar databases are available online to scholars in most industrial democracies around the world.

Database: Substance Abuse and Mental Health Data Archive

Sponsor: Substance Abuse and Mental Health Services Administration

What's in it: Data from surveys and studies including SAMHSA's National Survey on Drug Use and Health and the National Institute on Drug Abuse's Monitoring the Future study.

Database: Clinical Trials Network (CTN)

Sponsor: National Institute on Drug Abuse

What's in it: Data on about 3,000 participants from 13 clinical trials of substance abuse treatments.

Database: Add Health (National Longitudinal Study of Adolescent Health)

Sponsor: NICHD and 17 other agencies

What's in it: Four waves of health, behavior and social contexts data on about 21,000 people first surveyed in 1994 who are being followed into adulthood. It also includes some parent and biomarker data.

Database: The NICHD Study of Early Child Care and Youth Development

Sponsor: NICHD

(Continued)

(Continued)

What's in it: Longitudinal data on more than 1,000 children and their families, designed to address the relationship between child care and children's development. Beginning in 1991, researchers have followed the same children from birth to adolescence, using an extensive array of variables and measures.

Database: CHILDES and TalkBank databases

Sponsor: National Science Foundation and the National Institutes of Health

What's in it: These related databases capture spoken language from about 150 studies in audio and video formats. CHILDES includes conversations between children and their caretakers and playmates; TalkBank covers adult communication, including that of people with aphasia, language problems that arise from brain damage.

Database: National Institute of Mental Health (NIMH) Human Genetics Initiative

Sponsor: NIMH

What's in it: Phenotype data, genotype data and biomaterials (such as DNA samples and cell line cultures) on more than 4,000 people with bipolar disorder, schizophrenia, Alzheimer's disease, autism and depression, 4,000 controls and 12,000 of their relatives.

Database: Neuromorpho

Sponsor: NIH

What's in it: The world's largest centralized, curated repository of digital reconstructions of neurons, representing a wide variety of species, brain regions and cell types. It contains colorful two-dimensional images as well as a virtual reality display that allows you to manipulate, zoom or rotate the images.

Source: DeAngelis, T. (2008, September). *Information gold mines: Large-scale data bases are free, accessible and provide great research fodder.* Washington, DC: American Psychological Association. Retrieved from http://www.apa.org/gradpsych/2008/09/research-databases.aspx

Doctoral dissertations and research-based master's degree theses usually provide a section of conclusions and recommendations describing future research needed in the area of the author's study. Currently enrolled graduate students can visit libraries of universities offering doctoral degrees in counseling and related fields and read dissertations of former graduated students. Dissertations are also available online through the academic library databases and systems known as ProQuest (University Microfilms International). That system publishes over 70,000 new graduate works a year and provides a database that began in 1938.

Writing, Citing, and Plagiarism

The goal of every author should be to write in order to be understood by readers. It is an obligation of the author to give readers the full context within which the research idea and the study were developed (American Psychological Association, 2010a). Thus, all work done by others that influenced the study must be carefully cited and referenced. All information or data that are not common knowledge must also be cited and referenced. For example, it is common knowledge that B. F. Skinner was a behaviorally focused researcher, but the fact that B. F. Skinner did not like intrusive commercials in the media should be cited and referenced. That citation could look like the following:

- During his era, the psychologist B. F. Skinner was no fan of product commercials as they were broadcast on the radio and television (Skinner, 1976/2005).
- The proper reference for the citation in the reference section would look like the following:
- Skinner, B. F. (2005). *Walden two* (Rev. ed.). Indianapolis, IN: Hackett. (Originally published 1976)

Occasionally, beginning practitioner-researchers try to avoid plagiarizing by using many direct quotes. However, the use of numerous direct quotes can be tedious for readers. Practitioner-researchers should develop the ability to paraphrase the ideas of others who influence the author's writing.[1]

Direct quotes should be cited with their page numbers for easy acquisition by the readers. That citation may take the form of *(Abbott & Costello, 1951, p. 18)*. Or, if there is more than one page, it may appear as *(Howard, Fine, & Howard, 1949, pp. 207–210)*. That rule applies to both short quotes that appear in the narrative or long quoted sections (40 or more words) that are indented without quotation marks (freestanding block quote). If the quoted source is an electronic publication that has no page numbers, count the number of paragraphs from the top of the document to where the quote is located and provide the paragraph number abbreviated as *(para. 13)*.

Cartoon 17.1

You Told Me to Reference Everything

Cartoon by Merv Magus.

"We are concerned with the quote you used that starts on page 4 and ends on page 23."

In all scholarship, practitioner-researchers should exercise great care to avoid any form of plagiarism. Such behavior, committed intentionally or committed by accident, is considered academic fraud. There is no "statute of limitations" on academic fraud, and the indiscretion of a student can destroy a professional career later in life. (See Cases in Point 17.1a and 17.1b.)

CASE IN POINT   17.1a

On March 1, 2011, German chancellor Angela Merkel lost her minister for defense, the Baron Karl-Theodor zu Guttenberg, to an academic scandal that occurred in 2006 at the Bayreuth University. Graduate students researching the background of the baron found that his 476-page doctoral dissertation had passages lifted without attribution from other published sources. Prior to that revelation and subsequent revocation of his graduate degree by the university, Herr Baron Guttenberg had been on the fast track to become German chancellor himself in a few years.

When this academic fraud became known, hundreds of thousands protested in the streets of Berlin holding signs that read *"Nicht mehr spielen Arzt"* (No more playing doctor). The German newspapers and news channels were filled with this academic scandal for weeks leading up to his resignation from the Bundestag in March of 2011. Even the police began an investigation into a possible violation of strict German copyright laws (Kimmelman, 2011).

CASE IN POINT   17.1b

In 1982, the assistant secretary for education for Pennsylvania, Dr. Ronald H. Lewis, was nominated by then Governor Kean to become New Jersey's new commissioner for education. Two days after the nomination was published, an investigative reporter for the Newark, New Jersey, *Star-Ledger* presented his findings about Dr. Lewis. The 121-page dissertation Mr. Lewis had submitted to Farleigh Dickinson University in 1973 contained 66 pages of material copied from other sources without giving any acknowledgement. Needless to say, he did not get the new position. Later he took an administrative position with the Atlanta, Georgia, school system, but he lost this in 1989 when members of the school board learned of his plagiarism at Farleigh Dickenson University 16 years earlier (Smothers, 1989).

WRITER'S MIND-SET

"Asking a writer what he thinks about criticism is like asking a lamppost what it feels about dogs."

John Osborne

Very few are "born writers" with natural skills always available to present thoughts in clear and engaging prose. For most, writing is a skill that must be learned and carefully developed. One way to improve this vital skill is through constant practice. Most developing writers are so excited to get their ideas down on paper, they often do not recognize errors they are making. This tendency to blitzkrieg one's writing can lead to great disappointment. Never race to finish a draft before the idea fades; instead, go with the flow of ideas and follow an outline.

Outlines make writing a long narrative like a research proposal manageable. This is especially true of writing a review of the literature. The writer's outline may be a simple sequential listing of topics to be presented and articles that address the sequence of issues.

Writers must learn that a first draft is just that, a first attempt that needs to be developed and refined. Each editing and rewrite improves the narrative, and after three or so drafts, most proposals will reach a level of polish needed to clearly transmit the author's vision.

The first editing should be done by the author. This is easy to do poorly. Individuals often do not see the syntactical and logical errors in their writing when sight-reading their drafts. One way to improve self-editing is to slowly read every word of the draft aloud or to another interested person. Following rewriting, the second draft should be read by a colleague, such as a fellow graduate student or academic adviser. This developmental phase may be painful, but criticism can facilitate major improvement. To be a good writer requires that the author learn to suppress the tendency to be defensive and overly sensitive to criticism. As British playwright John Osborne noted in his quip about the lamppost, this level of detachment is not always easy to achieve.

Sample Format for a Research Proposal

Cover Page

Title of the Research Proposal

A research proposal in partial fulfillment of the requirements for the class

Psy. 666, Research Methods in Counseling Psychology

Student's Name (without previous degrees)

An abstract of about 200 words explaining the proposed research, including the research problem, research questions or hypotheses, the participants, sampling method, research design, and how the study will potentially add to the literature of the discipline.

Subsequent Pages

Introduction

In this section, the proposal's author explains the broad nature of the research problem and provides a context for doing the research. In describing the research problem, the author should draw from previous literature and build a case for why the study is needed. Descriptions of the problem also demonstrate how systems, programs, and individuals could be impacted by having a better

(Continued)

(Continued)

understanding of what is to be studied. The best proposals show the researcher's enthusiasm for this topic and pique readers' interest.

This opening section provides the researcher with the place to state his or her case for pursuing the topic and the opportunity to offer a framework for how and what is being studied.

Review of the Literature

The second section may be one of the longest components of the proposal. This is where the researcher provides readers with a clear statement of what is known about the research problem and related issues.[2] While being focused on present conditions related to the research problem, the literature review may also provide historical context and theoretical background.

The organization of this section is dictated by the nature of the study. If the research is to compare two or more competing approaches, the review may be structured like a debate in which research supporting each approach is presented and contrasted. If the research problem is to test an extension of a well-known theoretical model, the review may begin with the theory and its supporting evidence in different contexts. Next, the proposal would show how the theory may also apply in the new context being proposed by the researcher.

Some studies are measurement bound, and the proposal's author may focus the review on previous steps taken to develop the instrument and validate a new construct. Proposals for qualitative studies will include a philosophical framework for the study and detailed explanations of the methods used.

One goal for the author is to make clear to readers why a particular study is needed and how it is justified. The gaps in our present knowledge should become evident.

Research Questions and Hypotheses

If the review of literature is well conceived and structured, the hypotheses and/or research questions should be self-evident. These statements will become the focus of the study and therefore are central to the proposal. Some authors prefer to use the less formal approach of posing research questions to guide the project. Research questions prevent the research effort from becoming too grandiose and out of control by limiting the study to a particular issue.

Many faculty committees prefer to see formal hypothesis statements. These formal statements can be readily changed into null hypotheses for statistical analysis.

Hypotheses and null hypotheses, needed for most quantitative types of research, can be derived from the original research problem and its related research questions. Hypothesis statements take a position that can be verified or refuted by data, while research questions are more open-ended and exploratory in nature. Below are five research questions, each with an alternative hypothesis that could be derived from that question.

Research Problem 1: Too much bullying is going on in our middle school.

Research Question 1: Is there a relationship between the counselor-to-student ratio in middle schools and the number of disciplinary referrals for bullying behaviors?

Hypothesis 1: There will be a reduction in discipline referrals for bullying when the school counselor-to-student ratio is decreased significantly.

Research Problem 2: Serious tobacco use–related diseases have driven up the cost of health care in this state.

Research Question 2: What factors will reduce tobacco use by adults in this community?

Hypothesis 2: Increasing the state tax on all forms of tobacco by 50% will significantly reduce tobacco use in the community.

Research Problem 3: Over the past 5 years, the incidence of domestic violence reported to law enforcement has increased by a third.

Research Question 3: What demographic factors are related to the amount of domestic violence in this community?

Hypothesis 3: Job loss during the recession is highly correlated with the reported level of domestic violence.

Research Problem 4: Many war veterans are returning home with disabling injuries that require them to use a mobility-assisting device such as a wheelchair, thus curtailing their employability.

Research Question 4: What support programs will improve the employability of individuals with disabilities that require the use of a mobility-assisting device such as a wheelchair?

Hypothesis 4: A prompt and efficient network of accessible public transportation will improve the employability of mobility-impaired American war veterans.

Research Problem 5: Anxiety-related disorders are a major reason for referrals to this clinic.

Research Question 5: Client anxiety levels fluctuate depending on the client's level of affect.

Hypothesis 5: Following states of high agitation and affect, clients will experience a reduced level of measurable anxiety through client-centered therapy.

Methods

The methods section of the proposal documents an appropriate way to answer the research questions/hypotheses. This part of the proposal has several important components, including the subjects (or participants), the instruments, the study's design and timeline, and the procedures followed.

Subjects or Participants: Readers need information about who will take part in the study. They should be informed in this section about the number of individuals to be studied and their demographic characteristics. If this section is well written, it would be possible for a reader to replicate the sample of individuals who will be studied.

Instruments: Measuring tools that may be used in the proposed study should be described and their usefulness for the research explained. These measurements may include scales and checklists

(Continued)

(Continued)

that the researcher will develop. In that case, the various methods for documenting the measurement appropriateness of the new instruments, including focus group studies, pilot group studies, and factor analytic studies, should be fully described.

If the proposal's author plans to employ published measures, they must also be described and justified. Information to assist in that task is available from two online resources, the ETS tests-in-print webpage (http://ericae.net/testcol.htm#ETSTF) and the website of the Buros Institute of Mental Measurements (http://buros.unl.edu/buros/jsp/search.jsp). These descriptions in the proposal should be provided on a construct or variable-by-variable basis and present evidence of reliability, validity (including developmental validity), and normative group appropriateness for this proposed study.

Design and Timeline: Many possible designs may be employed by the researcher. A selection from the quantitative approaches detailed in Chapter 14 or the qualitative approaches discussed in Chapters 4 and 5 may stand alone or be combined in a mixed methods design (Chapter 15). In addition to determining the most appropriate design for research, the proposal's author should develop a tentative timeline for the project. This timeline may change once the pragmatic concerns of both the researcher and others involved in the project are fully identified. Yet it is important at the proposal phase to begin thinking through the nature of commitment that a research program can require.

Procedure: In this section, the proposal's author delineates every step he or she will take. This includes identifying a source of participants and describing how they will be selected or recruited, how they will be provided with the necessary information to give informed consent, and how and when the IRB will be engaged. It describes how subjects will be assigned to groups and how the data will be collected. The use of appropriate research blinds should also be explained in this section. Any treatment or experimental conditions should be described. In proposals for qualitative studies, the approach the researcher plans to employ for coding and organizing data and observations should be elaborated and justified.

Limitations

The last narrative part of a research proposal is a statement as to possible limitations of the proposed study and potential problems that may occur during its completion. This includes a review of possible issues related to internal and external validity of the proposed study. It is also a place for authors of qualitative research proposals to describe potential biasing effects that they may inadvertently introduce into the data collection and analyses.

Extended Review of the Literature

The literature itself can serve as the research data in a form of research known as a **meta-analysis.** These analyses statistically combine relevant previous research on a topic and produce a highly reliable statement of these studies' combined outcomes. Several statistical approaches for weighting and summarizing the findings of research use different methods, samples, and outcomes. The nonparametric statistic, chi-square, often serves as a hypothesis-testing tool for the combined data. Readers must evaluate meta-analyses carefully, as it is possible for author bias to influence which research is included.

Applications from the Literature

Example of Meta-Analysis Research

Note: In a meta-analysis of 66 articles focused on African American subjects, the authors found a positive association between perceived racism and psychological distress. They also found a moderation effect for psychological outcomes, with anxiety, depression, and other psychiatric symptoms having a significantly stronger association than quality-of-life indicators.

Introduction: Perceived racism or racial discrimination and its psychological correlates have garnered much attention over the past two decades. Supported by conceptual models of racism-related stress and psychometrically sound instrumentation . . . [other researchers have found] . . . that perceptions of racism are inversely associated with psychological well-being and positively associated with psychological distress. In their review of the literature on community samples . . . [different researchers] . . . concluded that discrimination and racism are "generally associated with poor health status" and that the "association was the strongest in the case of mental health" compared to physical health. This conclusion has been supported by subsequent narrative reviews across sample types. For example, . . . [in a review of] . . . 138 studies examining the association between perceived racism and health published from 2000 to 2004, . . . [plus an additional] . . . 115 empirical studies published from 2005 to 2007 . . . [for a total of] . . . 253 studies reflected an international perspective and included European, Asian, African, and Middle Eastern countries, as well as Australia. On the basis of the reviews, the authors also concluded that perceptions of racism tend to be negatively associated with both mental and physical health. This conclusion was echoed in a review of the literature with only U.S. samples. However, it should be noted that the findings in these reviews are not conclusive and also are not specific to Black Americans.

Source: Pieterse, A. L., Todd, N. R., Neville, H. A., & Carter, R. T. (2012). Perceived racism and mental health among black American adults: A meta-analytic review. *Journal of Counseling Psychology, 59*(1), 1–9. doi: 10.1037/a0026208

WRITING RESEARCH ARTICLES AND PRESENTATIONS

Research in the human services is probably only complete when its findings are published (Burnard, 2004). There is a well-accepted approach for the organization of research presentations and articles when they appear in mental health–focused journals. This approach is required in journals published by the American Counseling Association (ACA), the American Psychological Association (APA), and the National Association of School Psychologists (NASP) and is also followed by the vast majority of science journals in the health, medical, biological, and physical sciences (American Psychological Association, 2010b).[3]

This APA format is also followed by authors of the many thousands of research papers presented during the meetings of learned societies and professional associations in the mental health professions and published online. Generally, graduate departments in counseling and other therapeutic branches of psychology require all written student research presentations and proposals to follow these APA guidelines.

Within the APA guidelines, the approaches used in proposing and presenting qualitative and quantitative research differ in several subtle ways.

Qualitative Research Format for Both Proposals and Presentations

The great variety of qualitative research methods makes it impossible to provide a single template for such articles and presentations. As was noted in Chapter 5, perhaps the most complex writing tasks in the initial development of a qualitative research proposal and later writing of the article or presentation involve describing the participants and the method being employed.

In the description of the method, it is necessary for the author to justify and explain in great detail how the researcher went about collecting and analyzing research evidence. This includes a discussion of the philosophical framework for the approach selected and the basic research assumptions subsumed within that approach.

Explaining and describing the coding steps in a proposal before the study has begun can be daunting, and revisions in the plan may be necessary once the research process is underway. For that reason, many faculty research supervision committees provide leeway for students as they develop their graduate research proposals. Student researchers may be required to meet with their committee as the coding process begins and again during the process to receive guidance.

Also in the methods section, researchers are expected to explain how their personal background and experiences may influence their work. The careful elaboration and discussion of potential bias is essential for committee reviews as well as for eventual readers of possible findings.

Participants

Unlike the selection process in empirical research, the selection of participants in qualitative research studies is usually purposeful and not random. Thus, researchers are required to explain and justify which participants are studied. This need is magnified by the small samples of participants normally used in qualitative research studies. In a similar way, the researcher should also address the question of sampling sufficiency. A related requirement is proving to the reader that data saturation was reached in the study (Strauss & Corbin, 1998).

Language

In most qualitative research presentations, the interpretative role of the researcher is shown by the use of first-person pronouns and descriptions of the actual activities, concerns, feelings, and possible mind-sets of both participants and researchers. Thick descriptions, replete with numerous verbatim quotations and anecdotal observations, make up much of the data presentation in qualitative studies (Fetterman 1989). Qualitative research reports are normally written using a central theme or core and present an introduction and a detailed description of the participants, researcher's methods, and evidence supporting the central finding (core) of the study.

Applications from the Literature

Language in Qualitative Research: First-Person Pronouns and Direct Quotations

Note: In this study, the author examines the various aspects of help seeking, and the social and institutional responses to such efforts, through the narratives of 19 women in a domestic violence shelter.

Conceptual Framework: It is from this framework that I examine the success and failure of help seeking from the perspectives of battering survivors living in a domestic violence shelter. Through qualitative, semistructured interviews, women in this study described a myriad of help seeking, including calling the police, obtaining orders of protection, asking friends and family for support, utilizing victim and social services, and seeking medical attention. Although some successful and empowering experiences were reported, most efforts were fraught with failure and disappointment. With respect to their standpoints, I argue that women's resistance to intimate partner abuse and success at utilizing avenues of help seeking are shaped by structural inequalities predicated on patriarchy, poverty, and racism or ethnic bias.

Findings: Responses by friends and relatives varied greatly with some women reporting that they had received much assistance, whereas others reported being abandoned by those close to them. Unfortunately, the latter appeared to be the most common. As Michelle recalled, "My mom calls me and says, 'Well what did you do? What did you do to deserve that?'" After such reactions by family members, feelings of guilt and self blame emerged. As Terri explained, "My older sister goes, 'I don't understand you not leaving him before.' It makes you feel bad when your sister says that. You kind of question who you are and what you're about . . . what really happened. It makes you want to say, 'It was really my responsibility. How did I cause him to do that to me?'"

Although some women had little or no support from their families or friends, others were too ashamed to tell their relatives about the abuse. Anna Marie, an undocumented immigrant, was particularly concerned about her parents' reaction: "Now that I went through all this abuse, I'll try to do the best I can to go forward and not go back to Mexico defeated. They don't know what happened between my husband and me. I don't want to tell them anything."

Source: Moe, A. M. (2007). Silenced voices and structured survival: Battered women's help seeking. *Violence Against Women, 13*(7), 676–699. doi: 10.1177/1077801207302041

Quantitative Format for Proposals and Presentations

Language

In most quantitative research proposals and presentations, the author uses an approach to writing that reinforces the objectivity of the researcher. This includes avoiding first-person pronouns and describing the role of the researcher in the third person. Therefore, neither *I* nor *we* collected these data; rather, the *author(s)* collected these data. Speculation is also avoided until after all data are collected and subjected to statistical analyses. Even the individuals being studied are described using the scientific terminology of *subjects, replicates,* or *respondents.*

Quantitatively focused researchers avoid inflammatory language and never express total (100 %) confidence in their conclusions. Most quantitative studies end with a call for further confirmation through replication. This tentative framing of conclusions identifies areas in need of further study and provides students and young researchers with a source of fresh research ideas.

Scientific Neutrality

A researcher employing quantitative research methods focuses on maintaining a neutral stance toward possible outcomes. As was noted in Chapter 14, scholars work to avoid unintentional researcher bias by building blinds and developing control groups. This same neutrality is also present in the language of quantitative research proposals and in the specification of two-tailed hypotheses.

Applications from the Literature

Use of the Descriptive Term *Respondents* in Research

Note: This study is unusual in being a large-scale application of online survey research methods. It also examines the impact of abortion decisions on the biological fathers as well as on the pregnant women involved.

Sample: Surveys were completed by 374 women and 198 men. U.S. citizens comprised 81% of the female sample and 78% of the male sample. Citizens from England (6.5% male and 4% female surveys), Canada (4.5% male and 6.4% female surveys), and Australia (2.5% male and 2.7% female surveys) contributed the next largest number of surveys. Respondents also identified the following as country of citizenship: France, Ireland, Norway, Romania, Czechoslovakia, Germany, Sweden, New Zealand, South Africa, Kenya, Mexico, Nicaragua, Brazil, Nepal, and South Korea.

Source: Coyle, C. T., Coleman, P. K., & Rue, V. M. (2010). Inadequate preabortion counseling and decision conflict as predictors of subsequent relationship difficulties and psychological stress in men and women. *Traumatology, 10*(1), 16–30. doi: 10.1177/1534765609347550

Applications from the Literature

Use of the Third Person by an Author to Identify Her Role

Note: The author outlines a survey study of 305 counselors examining the relationship between school counseling program implementation and school counselor leadership practices.

Assumptions and Limitations: This study was designed to provide further understanding about school counselor leadership practices and their relationship to the implementation of school counseling programs. However, certain assumptions and limitations applied to this investigation. For this study, the researcher assumed the ASCA National Model for School Counseling Programs was the most current training framework for school counselors. It has been supported by the largest professional organization to represent school counseling.

Source: Mason, E. (2010). Leadership practices of school counselors and counseling program implementation. *National Association of Secondary School Principals Bulletin, 94*(4), 274–285. doi: 10.1177/0192636510395012

APA Format for Research Reports

The American Psychological Association has provided a format for articles being submitted for publication in journals it sponsors. This nine-part format has been widely adopted by other journal publishers.

1. **Title page.** This page provides a brief title that reveals the main issues being considered and the name (without degrees or titles) of the author(s) and his or her institutional affiliation. The title page also provides the first use of the **running head** for the paper.

2. **Abstract page.** This double-spaced page provides a précis of the study. It is written in a highly readable format using about 200 words. It describes the purpose of the study, variables and participants studied, the research approach, and the primary result or finding. It also provides a short list of keywords that will be used to create Internet links.

3. **Introduction.** This section provides a rationale for having done this study. Issues that led to the effort to learn more are presented in a logical sequence. In this part of the research article, the author may describe what led him or her to realize a need to employ research tools to resolve a concern. The motivation may have been an anomaly noticed during therapy or a paradoxical response of a client to an intervention. It may also have been an issue discovered during an audit or system evaluation of a program. The study may also have been conducted to resolve conflicting observational findings from other practitioners.

4. **Review of the literature and research hypotheses.** In terms of word count, this is the longest part of the narrative portion of a research article. It provides the background for the study and a framework indicating where this study fits within the literature of the field. In critical theory research, it may also discuss policy and historical trends and societal forces.

   In the review of the literature, the practitioner-researcher provides a careful synthesis of related scientific literature from the field being studied. This review should have been developed by combining results from multiple searches of all associated topics, dissertations, online journals, and recent texts in the field.

Empirical research articles should provide readers with a synthesis of previous research that is evenhanded and unbiased. This "scientific" review should demonstrate all likely explanations for the problem or issue under study. The ability to organize the arguments being presented and analyze them is a necessary skill for all authors to develop. These analyses should be synthesized and presented as a coherent statement leading to the research questions and hypothesis statements.[4]

The literature review section also is where the author presents and explains all constructs used in the study. This involves defining the constructs and describing the method used to measure them.

This research synthesis leads to the research questions, which are a logical outcome of the background and research synthesis. These statements typically appear in the final paragraph or two of the review of the literature section. The research questions or hypotheses that guided the research efforts present readers with the parameters the author used in the study.

Not all authors present working hypotheses for their research. Each hypothesis is a statement of what the practitioner-researcher expected to occur, and in empirical research, it is statistically tested in its null form. In quantitative research, the hypotheses must have been committed to and written prior to making or collecting any data. Many dissertation committees require formal hypothesis and null hypothesis statements of graduate students. These technical hypothesis statements will appear in the proposal and be repeated in the final dissertation or in subsequent publications by the student. These written hypotheses provide the graduate student-researcher with guidance as to the scope and focus of the study and ensure the study is grounded in the literature of the field.

Many qualitative studies are exploratory or descriptive in nature and not amenable to a crisp hypothesis statement. Likewise, a number of multivariate studies using empirical data cannot be organized around a hypothesis.[5]

Case study research and other qualitative research efforts are in themselves hypothesis generators and do not have an a priori hypothesis. Qualitative research does start with a research question, as do case studies and descriptive studies.

5. **Method.** The method section of a research paper provides detailed answers to questions readers will have about the study and how it was conducted. This section addresses three main areas: (1) who was involved, (participants or subjects); (2) materials and measures used; and (3) what was involved in the effort.

   a. **Participants or subjects.** In this section, the individuals who were the focus of the research effort are carefully and completely described. Individuals can be laboratory animals, children, adults, families, tribes, communities, etc. Four questions to be answered in this section are these: What was the total population? Who was selected to participate? How was that selection made? What are the demographic characteristics of all who were engaged?

Sample Subject Descriptions

1. Eight patients from the inpatient rehabilitation unit of a public hospital were included in the study. They all were members of the same therapeutic group and met 3 times a week during 2-hour therapy sessions. They included 5 Anglo-Whites, 2 African Americans and 1 Hispanic. Three were women and 5 men. They ranged in age from 19 years to 32 years of age with an average of 26.33 years. All 8 were disabled by their addiction and were receiving Medicare assistance. All had been adjudicated and found guilty of possession and abuse of illegal substances.

2. Twenty adolescent girls from a single-gender, urban, parochial high school ranging in age from 14 to 16 years were selected from a population of 440 girls attending that school. They were all from middle-class homes, and all but 4 were Anglo-White. The minority students included an Asian American and three African American girls. A total of 48 girls were originally nominated by the head of the school (principal) to participate in this study, and 29 of the girls and their parents agreed to participate. One girl was lost to serious illness (infectious mononucleosis), and another 8 dropped out of the program during its initial phase.

3. Twelve patients of a rehabilitation hospital with back/neck injuries were included in this study. All but 1 were male, and the median age of the group was 22.5 years (range 16.5 to 34.1). All had suffered a traumatic injury between the C-5 and T-2 vertebrae and were wheelchair bound. The injuries were stabilized, and each patient was in either the first or second week of a scheduled 10-week-long program for rehabilitation. All were covered by private insurance programs, and all volunteered to participate in the experimental group-counseling program.

4. A group of 24 volunteering residents from a southwest Florida independent living center with a median age of 83.5 years was included in this study. This group included 5 men and 19 women. They were all screened for any sign of dementia prior to the study and found to be functioning without evidence of significant cognitive loss. Of the 19 women, 12 were widows and living alone at the center. All of the men and 7 of the women were living at the residence with their spouse. The mean length of their marriages was 54 years. Twenty of the sample were Anglo-Whites, two were of Southwest Asian descent, and two were Cuban Americans.

5. The study was populated with volunteers from a sophomore-level undergraduate class in experimental psychology at a medium-size Midwestern state university. The 50 students enrolled for this study were required to participate in this research effort or in one of the others sponsored by members of the department. The group was generally middle-class and included 6 Hispanics, 3 Asian Americans, 4 African Americans, and 39 Anglo-Whites. The students were from rural and suburban communities within the state and had an average age of 21.2 years.

b. **Materials and measures.** Anything that is brought to the research must be fully and completely described and its use explained in detail. This description includes any modification or alteration of the measurement or equipment beyond its standard use.

Equipment includes, among other things, electronic monitoring devices, recording systems, software-presented treatment conditions, games, and simulations. Measurements include published instruments and unpublished simple checklists, surveys, unstandardized tests, open-ended questionnaires, field observations, and so forth. If a published instrument such as a test or questionnaire was employed, the researcher must report its measurement quality indicators (e.g., standard error, reliability quotients, validity, and differential item functioning). Also, the researcher should show why his or her choice of measurement was appropriate and valid for the research purpose.

Applications from the Literature

Example of Instrumentation in a Neuropsychological Study of ADHD

Note: About 15% of all youngsters treated with stimulant drugs do not respond well to the pharmacological approach to therapy, and many parents object to the administration of psychoactive drugs to their children. This study was designed to open a new area for research into ways to improve the lives of children with ADHD without using stimulant drugs. In this study, 19 children with a mean age of 9 years who were diagnosed as having ADHD (DSM-IV standards) were studied by using an approved autonomic nervous system biofeedback modality (ANSBM) device.

Instruments: In order to feed back information about the ongoing heart rate variability (HRV) to the central nervous system (CNS), the subject's ECG was ... an input to the system. A non-standard one lead derivation (two electrodes on the right arm and one on the left) provided the physiological signal.... The signal after amplification by a low frequency amplifier with optical insulation ... reached an A/D (analog to digital) converter (Keithley DAS-800) board in a PC. Changes in colors of a picture in the television screen followed the HRV of the subject at a frequency lower than 15c/s.... The subject's self controlled stimulus was provided by pink noise sound and by color stimulation.... In a softly dimmed room the subject sat in a semi-supine position on a comfortable couch, in front of a large TV screen (28 in.), with earphones on.

Source: Eisenberg, J., Ben-Daniel, N., Mei-Tal, G., & Wertman, E. (2004). An autonomic nervous system biofeedback modality for the treatment of attention deficit hyperactivity disorder: An open pilot study. *The Israel Journal of Psychiatry and Related Sciences, 41*(1), 45–53.

In writing the article or dissertation the author must match the measurement instruments with the variables and constructs introduced in the introductory section of the paper. As the author provides validity, reliability, and normative data, he or she will add citations and references to this section from the published test manual and other articles and reviews reporting its use.

c. **Activities.** Finally, a discussion of the "procedures" employed is also included in the methods section of the paper. This delineates what actually occurred, when it occurred, and how both the participants and researchers were engaged in the activities of the study. This should detail not only what occurred but also what modifications were made to the standard procedure or approach outlined in the proposal.

6. **Results.** This is the technical section of a research paper. It provides descriptions of participants, summaries of data derived from measures taken during the study, and statistical analyses carried out to understand what was found. This section does not draw conclusions or speculate about the meaning of what was found. This section typically presents tables and other graphics along with statistical summaries.

7. **Conclusions and discussion.** This section provides the author's interpretation of what was found in the research effort. It is not technical and often draws on the literature from previous studies to place the findings in perspective. It also is a place where the author provides ideas and directions for possible future research efforts. Finally, it describes any possible problems of internal and external validity and cautions the reader about possible biasing effects on the outcome from internal and external factors.

8. **References.** This part of the research paper is a complete list of all articles, research presentations, books, dissertations, and online sources of information that were referred to in writing the paper. It is not a bibliography of all background reading the author completed but only a precise list of those items the author referenced in the paper. This section follows the standard format described in the 6th edition of the *Publication Manual of the American Psychological Association* (2010b).

9. **Extra items.** The author may elect to provide extra notices at either the opening or ending of the paper. The author may provide a statement of who supported the study with funding or materials. Often the author will express appreciation for help received from other peers and colleagues. The author may also acknowledge individuals who contributed materials, time, expertise, and/or equipment to support the research effort.

SUMMARY

Research proposal writing is a time-honored way to help graduate students organize and practice their nascent skills as practitioner-researchers. The process of writing a research proposal is labor-intensive and requires long blocks of time for uninterrupted concentration. It requires time to think through a potential problem area and refine a focus on it and then more time to conduct extensive literature searches on the topic. Even when a large amount of cogent research has been brought together, more time is required to reflect on the material and identify common themes and points of debate. These issues should be presented in the proposal as a way to frame the study being proposed.

In this process, it is important for the proposal's author to narrow his or her research goal to a manageable research problem that is not grandiose or too broad to actually be completed. The author must also avoid trivial issues that will be apparent to readers.

In developing the proposal for research, and later when writing up the research as an article or dissertation, the author must be very cautious about using the thoughts of other people. In academic life, plagiarism is an unforgivable sin that has a very long shelf life. Such errors (by commission or omission) have destroyed successful careers long after the student has graduated.

An important mind-set for authors to develop is humility, as shown in the ability to accept criticism without a defensive, affect-laden response. Critical reviews should be sought out and considered carefully. Each new draft of a writing effort improves the writing over the original.

The usage of language in qualitative and quantitative research does differ a bit, and the method section of qualitative and quantitative research proposals will emphasize different issues. Yet the basic need for a well-conceived research proposal and an approach that is appropriate to the research task is central to all good research in the social sciences.

DISCUSSION QUESTIONS

1. Visit a university library in person or online and read two or three dissertation conclusion sections. Make a list of the future research ideas that the authors present in the discussion or conclusions section or chapter.

2. Identify several journals in your area of graduate specialization. Visit their publication websites and read their guidance for authors submitting articles for consideration for publication. Write a summary of those publication requirements and share your findings with your classmates.

3. Offer your editorial assistance to an undergraduate student in the social sciences as a volunteer reader/editor of his or her term paper for a course or area you know well.

4. Visit the office of the dean or assistant who keeps the collection of research proposals submitted by graduate students for their master's degree theses or doctoral dissertations. Read one and develop a flowchart showing how the former student used the previous literature to build a case for his or her research questions.

NOTES

1. The exception to this general rule is in the presentation of evidence and in developing thick descriptions in qualitative research studies.

2. The exception to this approach of reviewing previous research before collecting data is "grounded theory," in which the researcher attempts not to be influenced by what happened in the past.

3. While most journals in the mental health and medical professions follow the publication format and guidelines of the American Psychological Association, a number of other approaches and formats are employed in related professional publications. For example, the American Anthropological Association uses the *Chicago Manual of Style,* the American Sociological Association publishes its own style guide, some divisions of the National Council of Teachers of English use the Modern Language Association's *MLA Handbook for Writers of Research Papers.*

4. Naturally, critical theory research will identify and argue for a point of view in the literature review.

5. The widely used factor analysis statistical techniques are often applied to the task of organizing data and providing a structure for later hypothesis writing. Likewise, the use of path analysis and the development of structural equations and models are empirical methods that can lead to new ways to explain phenomena without starting with a hypothesis. These methods and other approaches to multivariate analysis are elaborated on the student website.

Appendix A

Computer-Based Data Management

COMPUTERS AND STATISTICAL SOFTWARE

In Chapter 10, there is a photograph of Sir Ronald Fisher at work doing statistical analysis using a mechanical adding machine. He could spend many hours doing the statistical tests that today's graduate students complete with less than a second of computer time. The modern computer revolution began during World War II, and by 1948 the first true computer, the Electronic Numerical Integrator And Calculator (ENIAC), was online at the University of Pennsylvania. That system, with its 15,000 vacuum tubes and miles of copper wire and cables, was not as powerful as an iPad or tablet computer today.

Photo A.1 ENIAC, The World's First Electronic Computer

U.S. Army.

Software for organizing and analyzing data began to appear in the 1960s. The Biomedical Data Processing (BMD) was the first commercially distributed statistical software. It appeared on university mainframes in 1965, followed by the Statistical Package for the Social Sciences (SPSS) in 1968. Computers of that era were huge, slow devices that inputted data through batch processing (i.e., 80-column-wide data punch cards).

Statistical software has made it possible for social science researchers to manage large and complex databases and use highly advanced statistical analysis methods. Researchers using most forms of social science research need to collect and manage data. Those using quantitative methods frequently have thousands of data points to organize and interpret. Qualitative researchers may use software to summarize and describe participants' answers to demographic questions and questionnaire items.

The availability of software does not mean that the researcher or the consumer of research has no need to learn research and statistical methods. The software can do the "heavy lifting" of calculating, but the researcher must know when to use a particular statistical method. Researchers need both basic knowledge, such as about the precision of the measurements, as well as understanding of technical issues such as statistical assumptions. Users of research need to understand the processes, logic, and procedures of the data analysis and statistical testing employed by the researcher. An old adage in statistics goes, "Statistics are like sewers, what comes out is a reflection of what you put in." An unethical or poorly trained researcher could probably use powerful statistics software with his or her data to prove just about anything.

Today there are numerous programs for data management, organization, and analysis. Most universities host several on their servers for student and faculty use. Some also sell or rent their statistical software to students and faculty for home use. This makes it convenient for students and faculty to work with their data at home or on campus. Software packages include Addinsoft XLSTAT (rental, Windows only), Minitab 15 and 16 (rental or perpetual, Windows only), JMP 10 (rental, Mac only), Systat 13 (rental, Windows only), Statistica 10 (rental, Windows only), and IBM SPSS 20. For individuals thinking about a rental agreement, the most expensive of these packages is IBM SPSS (rental, Mac and Windows). The BMD-P statistical software system is only available for institutional use.

There are a number of open-source and free software packages for data management and analysis. One of these was written to be a free system with many of the same features of IBM SPSS. That system, PSPP, can be downloaded for free at http://savannah.gnu.org/projects/pspp/. Other free software packages for data management and statistical analysis include the following:

ADaMSoft, http://adamsoft.caspur.it/English/ADaMSoft6.html

Dataplot, http://www.itl.nist.gov/div898/software/dataplot/

US Centers for Disease Control and Prevention, Epi Info 7, http://wwwn.cdc.gov/epiinfo/

CHOICE OF IBM SPSS

Of the many options available for the management of data and data analysis, this book has focused on IBM SPSS. This choice reflects the availability of the system on virtually all university servers and the fact that it can be used away from campus on home computers using either Mac or Windows operating systems. Additionally, it can produce powerful graphics as well as organize data and crunch numbers. IBM SPSS is also available for business applications, including for users of Red Hat Ent Linux (RHEL) Dsktp wWrkstn, and Red Hat Entrprs Linux (RHEL) Dsktp.

PLANNING FOR DATA COLLECTION

Long before any numbers are crunched, researchers begin processing their data by organizing a data codebook. Data codebooks are the firewall that prevents confusion and chaos when entering data into a computer and when interpreting computer output.

As an example, in a hypothetical college counseling study, the researcher is interested in using the 16 bipolar subtests scores from the fifth edition of Raymond Cattell and colleagues' (2002) *16PF*.[1] In this hypothetical study, the researcher also collects students' first-semester undergraduate GPA, gender, age in months, and commuter versus resident status. In this example, the researcher samples 200 undergraduates who will serve as participating subjects for the study. This combination of subjects and variables will produce a database containing 20 variables and 4,000 discrete pieces of data.

The process of constructing a codebook begins with a simple list of all variables that will be part of the analysis. Each variable should be given a short but clearly recognizable name. In the example using undergraduates, the 16PF scores include the following:

1. Warmth (reserved vs. warm; factor A)

2. Reasoning (concrete vs. abstract; factor B)

3. Emotional Stability (reactive vs. emotionally stable; Factor C)

4. Dominance (deferential vs. dominant; factor E)

5. Liveliness (serious vs. lively; factor F)

6. Rule-Consciousness (expedient vs. rule-conscious; factor G)

7. Social Boldness (shy vs. socially bold; factor H)

8. Sensitivity (utilitarian vs. sensitive; factor I)

9. Vigilance (trusting vs. vigilant; factor L)

10. Abstractedness (grounded vs. abstracted; factor M)

11. Privateness (forthright vs. private; factor N)

12. Apprehension (self-assured vs. apprehensive; factor O)

13. Openness to Change (traditional vs. open to change; factor Q1)

14. Self-Reliance (group-oriented vs. self-reliant; factor Q2)

15. Perfectionism (tolerates disorder vs. perfectionistic; factor Q3)

16. Tension (relaxed vs. tense; factor Q4)

Researchers need to be able to interpret which variable is measuring which characteristic. Left to its own devices, the SPSS software will assign a number as the label for each variable. To avoid confusion, it is always wise to provide an easily understood name for each variable. The variable names and their descriptions should appear in the codebook. The names of the variables may appear very truncated, because IBM SPSS v. 20.0 permits variables to have names no more than eight characters long.

In addition to identifying the variables in the codebook, it is also necessary to indicate the possible values for each variable. Thus, gender may be coded 1 and 2, but the codebook should also explain which number is the code for which gender. Variables such as GPA are presented as ordinal II continuous numbers ranging from 0.00 to 4.00. The bipolar subtests of the 16PF questionnaire are scored on a 10-point standardized score scale (1 = low and 10 = high).[2]

Because data will be input on a case-by-case basis, each subject needs to be identifiable. This is easily done by creating a variable named IDNo or SubjNo or ID#. A list of actual participants and the assigned identifier should be maintained where it can be used later to identify participants. If the study is totally anonymous, serial numbers on the questionnaire or test form should be used instead of the participants' names to provide identification. This ability to go back and see the original data is needed whenever an anomaly, such as an outlier in the data, is identified by the IBM SPSS data plot.

In addition to containing names for each variable in the study, the codebook also needs to include category and level identifiers.

Table A.1   Sample Codebook for Hypothetical Study Using the *16PF* Questionnaire

Variable's Name	Meaning or Interpretation	Levels or Codes
ID Number	Participant Identification Number	1–200
FactorA	Warmth	1–10
FactorB	Reasoning	1–10
FactorC	Emotional Stability	1–10
FactorD	Dominance	1–10
FactorF	Liveliness	1–10
FactorG	Rule-Consciousness	1–10
FactorH	Social Boldness	1–10
FactorI	Sensitivity	1–10
FactorL	Vigilance	1–10
FactorM	Abstractedness	1–10

Variable's Name	Meaning or Interpretation	Levels or Codes
FactorN	Privateness	1–10
FactorO	Apprehension	1–10
FactorQ1	Openness to Change	1–10
FactorQ2	Self-Reliance	1–10
FactorQ3	Perfectionism	1–10
FactorQ4	Tension	1–10
Age	Animate Existence	Number of months since birth
GPA	Freshman Grade Point Average	0.00–4.00
Gender	Student Gender	Men = 1 Women = 2
Reside	Living on Campus or Not	Campus Resident = 1 Commuting to Campus = 2

VARIABLE IDENTIFICATION AND ENTRY

After starting the IBM SPSS software, begin the process of entering and identifying variables by pressing the Variable View button on the bottom of the Data Editor page. A window will open, providing a place for the variable's name. Step 1 is to identify the name of the variable. Variable names can be drawn from the list in the codebook. The variables of the 16PF subtests may be named by their identifying factor number (FactorA to FactorQ4). The researcher may elect to use an abbreviation for the actual factor name if the full name does not fit (e.g., Warm, EmotStab, and OpenChng). Gender is another variable in this hypothetical study, as are GPA and age, that will fit within the allowed eight letters or numbers. The variable Place of Residence could be abbreviated as Reside (see Table A.1 for an example list of variables).

Variable names should start with a letter and may include symbols (e.g., $, #, @), upper- and lowercase letters, and numbers, but they may not have a blank position. The period and the underscore can also be used within variable names. For example, A._$@#1 is a valid variable name (IBM SPSS, 2011).[3] Variable names should not end with either an underscore or with a period. Likewise, certain names are excluded by the program, including ALL, AND, BY, EQ, GE, GT, LE, LT, NE, NOT, OR, TO, and WITH. Once the page of variables is set, it is easy to return to it and repair any errors made during the process of variable identification.

As the name of the variable is entered, a toolbar describing variable type and characteristics will open, providing a way to describe the nature of data used to measure the variable. The toolbar provides screens for identifying the following characteristics about each variable: (1) type of measurement, (2) maximum data width, (3) decimal position, (4) label, (5) values, (6) missing cases, (7) columns, (8) align, and (9) measure. Of these, only the first five are central to the management of a database.

The first screen provides a list of possible data types for the variable (e.g., numeric) and a place to input the maximum width or number of characters used to express the score on the variable. At this point, SPSS will need to know where the variable's decimal point is positioned. Data should have a decimal point entered consistently during data entry, and SPSS will use the same decimal point in its descriptive output.

The Variable View toolbar will also ask about the values that the variable may assume, and if they are categories, it will ask for a brief written label for each. As an example, the variable Gender may have two values, one each for women and men. Their labels and values may be Women = 2 and Men = 1. The level of measurement (i.e., nominal, ordinal, continuous) is also identified on a screen from this toolbar.

After the variables have been entered and their characteristics established, they will appear as column headers across the Data Editor page used to display the full data set for the study.

Figure A.1   IBM SPSS 20 (2011) Variable View Screen

	Name	Type	Width	Decimals	Label	Values
1	IDNumber	Numeric	8	0	Identifier	None
2	GPS	Numeric	4	2	Fresmen Grad...	{.92, .92}...
3	Gender	Numeric	6	0	Student Gender	None
4	FactorA	Numeric	8	0	Warmth	None
5	FactorB	Numeric	8	0	Reasoning	None
6	FactorC	Numeric	8	0	Emotional Stabi...	None
7	FactorD	Numeric	8	0	Dominance	None
8	FactorF	Numeric	8	0	Liveliness	None

Note: In a hypothetical study, data from 16 subtests of the 16PF questionnaire on personality and 3 other demographic questions were input to the database. A small segment of the full Variable View spreadsheet is depicted in Figure A.1. In this case, the variable Gender was entered as a numeric variable. It could have also been coded as *F* and *M* for female and male, respectively. If letters were used, the Gender variable would have been assigned the Type label of String Variable. In the world of IBM SPSS, there are two types of data in databases. One is "numeric," and the other is "string" data. Numeric data can be used in mathematical calculations, while string data are used as grouping variables that are not mathematical. String data may be alphabetical. The software makes it possible to move from one type to the other for analysis. This may be done by assigning ordinal ranks to a string's levels.

Variables can use up to eight characters for their identification. The actual number needed is shown in the column "Width." The column "Label" provides a place for a longer description of the variable than the eight-character name allows. The "Value" column provides an interpretation of the meaning of the numeric and string variables. The default None indicates that a numerical variable can be read as a number and no special interpretation is needed.

Data Entry

Working from raw data and with a codebook for organization, the researcher can enter data into IBM SPSS through the software's Data Editor screen. To reach that point, simply turn on the SPSS program and press the button labeled Type In Data.[4]

The IBM SPSS system provides a spreadsheet format for entering and depicting data. Rows on the spreadsheet each show data from one individual, while the unshaded columns represent the variables being studied. Each cell presents one piece of data on one variable for one subject. Data can be entered in any order, including going down a column of a variable or across a row for an individual subject's data. Data are entered by clicking on the cell to be filled and typing in that space. When entering data from numeric variables, integer values that exceed the defined width specified for the variable can be entered, but the Data Editor will display either scientific notation or a portion of the value followed by an ellipsis (. . .), indicating the value is wider than the variable's previously defined width. It is always possible to return to the Variable View screen and change the defined width for the variable.

The Data Editor provides the flexibility to add or change the values of data in the cells. By double-clicking on a filled cell, the researcher can directly edit the cell's entry by using the keyboard. It is also possible to use cut-and-paste methods to move a cell's entry to one or more cells on the spreadsheet.

Learning About the Data

Descriptive statistics can be calculated and displayed from the Data Editor. Across the top bar of the Data Editor spreadsheet there are 10 buttons, the 6th of which, Analyze, opens a drop down window offering 10 classes of statistical options for examining and analyzing the data.

The first option provides frequencies for the values in each variable. This option also provides the opportunity to graph those frequencies. A good way to double check the data set and search for outliers is to conduct a search for outliers.

Figure A.3 is an example of the output for a database of grade point averages from 25 undergraduate men ($n = 13$) and women ($n = 12$).

Figure A.4 is the IBM SPSS output providing descriptive statistics for the 25 undergraduate grade point averages.

Another option for users of IBM SPSS is to find the Pearson correlation coefficients between two variables in the database. This is found on the same drop-down screen under the Analyze button as simply Bivariate Correlation.

In the correlation output shown in Figure A.5, the coefficient expressing the correlation between GPA and warmth is almost $r = 0.30$ (0.299). The null hypothesis that there is no significant relationship between the two variables cannot be rejected ($p = 0.147$).

In addition to correlation calculations, SPSS can also create scatterplots depicting the data. To do this, click the 8th button on the top row, Graphs, and then the Chart Builder

Figure A.2 IBM SPSS 20 (2011) Data Editor Screen

	IDNumber	GPA	Gender	FactorA
1	1	.97	1	1
2	2	1.11	2	6
3	1	2.91	1	2
4	2	2.27	2	4
5	1	3.04	1	9
6	2	2.84	2	5
7	1	2.41	1	3
8	2	3.06	2	5
9	1	2.31	1	4
10	2	1.83	2	8
11	1	2.77	1	7
12	2	2.90	2	7
13	1	2.49	1	8
14	2	3.95	2	6
15	1	2.84	1	9
16	2	.92	2	5
17	1	2.38	1	6
18	2	2.00	2	2
19	1	2.98	1	7
20	2	3.51	2	5
21	1	1.78	1	4
22	2	2.70	1	8
23	1	2.17	2	3
24	2	2.68	2	7
25	1	2.22	1	10

Note: This screen depicts part of the hypothetical study in which data are being entered from a codebook by using the computer's keyboard. Data from just 25 cases of the sample of 200 freshmen and for only 3 of the 20 variables are shown.

Figure A.3   IBM SPSS Frequency Output Table

Freshmen Grade Point

		Frequency	Percent	Valid Percent	Cumulative Percent
Valid	.92	1	4.0	4.0	4.0
	.97	1	4.0	4.0	8.0
	1.11	1	4.0	4.0	12.0
	1.78	1	4.0	4.0	16.0
	1.83	1	4.0	4.0	20.0
	2.00	1	4.0	4.0	24.0
	2.17	1	4.0	4.0	28.0
	2.22	1	4.0	4.0	32.0
	2.27	1	4.0	4.0	36.0
	2.31	1	4.0	4.0	40.0
	2.38	1	4.0	4.0	44.0
	2.41	1	4.0	4.0	48.0
	2.49	1	4.0	4.0	52.0
	2.68	1	4.0	4.0	56.0
	2.70	1	4.0	4.0	60.0
	2.77	1	4.0	4.0	64.0
	2.84	2	8.0	8.0	72.0
	2.90	1	4.0	4.0	76.0
	2.91	1	4.0	4.0	80.0
	2.98	1	4.0	4.0	84.0
	3.04	1	4.0	4.0	88.0
	3.06	1	4.0	4.0	92.0
	3.51	1	4.0	4.0	96.0
	3.95	1	4.0	4.0	100.0
	Total	25	100.0	100.0	

Figure A.4   Output From IBM SPSS: Descriptive Statistics

Freshmen Grade Point

N	Valid	25
	Missing	0
Mean		2.4416
Median		2.4900
Std. Deviation		.73210

Figure A.5   Output From IBM SPSS: Pearson Correlation Between GPA and 16PF Warmth

Correlations

		Freshmen Grade Point	Warmth
Freshmen Grade Point	Pearson Correlation	1	.299
	Sig. (2-tailed)		.147
	N	25	25
Warmth	Pearson Correlation	.299	1
	Sig. (2tailed)	.147	
	N	25	25

button. The variables can be identified, and by clicking on Scatter Plot, the type of graphic shown in Figure A.6 is generated.

From the Analyze button and its drop-down menu of options, a range of parametric and nonparametric statistical methods are available. As a final example, Figure A.7 shows the result of a *t*-test for the null hypothesis test stating, "There is not a significant difference between the measured level of first semester GPA between freshman men and women." This is found by using the drop-down window under Analyze and selecting Comparison of Means.

Figure A.6   Output From IBM SPSS: Scatter Plot

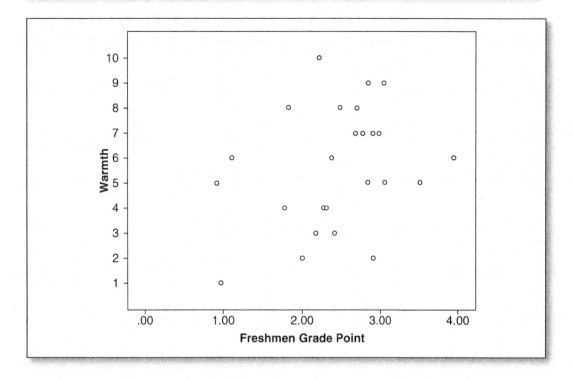

Figure A.7   Two Tail *t*-Test for the Equality of Means

	Number	Mean	Standard Deviation	df	t	Significance level
Men	13	2.45	0.57	23	0.03	0.97
Women	12	2.44	0.90			

NOTES

1. Cattell, R. B., Cattell, A. K., & Cattell, H. E. P. (2002). *16PF* (5th ed.). San Antonio, TX: Pearson Assessments.

2. These are a type of standard scores called Sten scores. They have a mean of 5.5 and a standard deviation of 2.0.

3. IBM SPSS. (2011). *IBM SPSS 20 statistics core systems users guide.* Retrieved from ftp://public.dhe .ibm.com/software/analytics/spss/documentation/statistics/20.0/en/client/Manuals/IBM_SPSS_Statistics_ Core_System_Users_Guide.pdf

4. Data can be entered through the keyboard or through databases that already exist. Details on how to enter data into the IBM SPSS data editor can be found in the systems manual in endnote 3 or in a good SPSS guidebook such as James Cunningham and James Aldrich's (2012) *Using SPSS: An Interactive Hands-on Approach* from Sage (Thousand Oaks, CA).

Appendix B

American Psychological Association's Ethical Principles of Psychologists and Code of Conduct

Standard 8: Research and Publication

To read the full set of ethical standards and principles developed by the APA, see http://www.apa.org/ethics/code/index.aspx.

8.01 INSTITUTIONAL APPROVAL

When institutional approval is required, psychologists provide accurate information about their research proposals and obtain approval prior to conducting the research. They conduct the research in accordance with the approved research protocol.

8.02 INFORMED CONSENT TO RESEARCH

(a) When obtaining informed consent as required in Standard 3.10, Informed Consent, psychologists inform participants about (1) the purpose of the research, expected duration and procedures; (2) their right to decline to participate and to withdraw from the research once participation has begun; (3) the foreseeable consequences of declining or withdrawing; (4) reasonably foreseeable factors that may be expected to influence their willingness to participate such as potential risks, discomfort or adverse effects; (5) any prospective research benefits; (6) limits of confidentiality; (7) incentives for participation; and (8) whom to contact for questions about the research and research participants' rights. They provide opportunity for the prospective participants to ask questions and receive answers. (See also Standards 8.03, Informed Consent for Recording Voices and Images in Research; 8.05, Dispensing with Informed Consent for Research; and 8.07, Deception in Research.)

(b) Psychologists conducting intervention research involving the use of experimental treatments clarify to participants at the outset of the research (1) the experimental nature of the treatment; (2) the services that will or will not be available to the control group(s) if appropriate; (3) the means by which assignment to treatment and control groups will be made; (4) available treatment alternatives if an individual does not wish to participate in the research or wishes to withdraw once a study has begun; and (5) compensation for or monetary costs of participating including, if appropriate, whether reimbursement from the participant or a third-party payor will be sought. (See also Standard 8.02a, Informed Consent to Research.)

8.03 INFORMED CONSENT FOR RECORDING VOICES AND IMAGES IN RESEARCH

Psychologists obtain informed consent from research participants prior to recording their voices or images for data collection unless (1) the research consists solely of naturalistic observations in public places, and it is not anticipated that the recording will be used in a manner that could cause personal identification or harm, or (2) the research design includes deception, and consent for the use of the recording is obtained during debriefing. (See also Standard 8.07, Deception in Research.)

8.04 CLIENT/PATIENT, STUDENT, AND SUBORDINATE RESEARCH PARTICIPANTS

(a) When psychologists conduct research with clients/patients, students, or subordinates as participants, psychologists take steps to protect the prospective participants from adverse consequences of declining or withdrawing from participation.

(b) When research participation is a course requirement or an opportunity for extra credit, the prospective participant is given the choice of equitable alternative activities.

8.05 DISPENSING WITH INFORMED CONSENT FOR RESEARCH

Psychologists may dispense with informed consent only (1) where research would not reasonably be assumed to create distress or harm and involves (a) the study of normal educational practices, curricula, or classroom management methods conducted in educational settings; (b) only anonymous questionnaires, naturalistic observations or archival research for which disclosure of responses would not place participants at risk of criminal or civil liability or damage their financial standing, employability or reputation, and confidentiality is protected; or (c) the study of factors related to job or organization effectiveness conducted in organizational settings for which there is no risk to participants' employability, and confidentiality is protected or (2) where otherwise permitted by law or federal or institutional regulations.

8.06 OFFERING INDUCEMENTS FOR RESEARCH PARTICIPATION

(a) Psychologists make reasonable efforts to avoid offering excessive or inappropriate financial or other inducements for research participation when such inducements are likely to coerce participation.

(b) When offering professional services as an inducement for research participation, psychologists clarify the nature of the services, as well as the risks, obligations and limitations. (See also Standard 6.05, Barter with Clients/Patients.)

8.07 DECEPTION IN RESEARCH

(a) Psychologists do not conduct a study involving deception unless they have determined that the use of deceptive techniques is justified by the study's significant prospective scientific, educational or applied value and that effective nondeceptive alternative procedures are not feasible.

(b) Psychologists do not deceive prospective participants about research that is reasonably expected to cause physical pain or severe emotional distress.

(c) Psychologists explain any deception that is an integral feature of the design and conduct of an experiment to participants as early as is feasible, preferably at the conclusion of their participation, but no later than at the conclusion of the data collection, and permit participants to withdraw their data. (See also Standard 8.08, Debriefing.)

8.08 DEBRIEFING

(a) Psychologists provide a prompt opportunity for participants to obtain appropriate information about the nature, results, and conclusions of the research, and they take reasonable steps to correct any misconceptions that participants may have of which the psychologists are aware.

(b) If scientific or humane values justify delaying or withholding this information, psychologists take reasonable measures to reduce the risk of harm.

(c) When psychologists become aware that research procedures have harmed a participant, they take reasonable steps to minimize the harm.

8.09 HUMANE CARE AND USE OF ANIMALS IN RESEARCH

(a) Psychologists acquire, care for, use, and dispose of animals in compliance with current federal, state and local laws and regulations, and with professional standards.

(b) Psychologists trained in research methods and experienced in the care of laboratory animals supervise all procedures involving animals and are responsible for ensuring appropriate consideration of their comfort, health and humane treatment.

(c) Psychologists ensure that all individuals under their supervision who are using animals have received instruction in research methods and in the care, maintenance and handling of the species being used, to the extent appropriate to their role. (See also Standard 2.05, Delegation of Work to Others.)

(d) Psychologists make reasonable efforts to minimize the discomfort, infection, illness and pain of animal subjects.

(e) Psychologists use a procedure subjecting animals to pain, stress or privation only when an alternative procedure is unavailable and the goal is justified by its prospective scientific, educational or applied value.

(f) Psychologists perform surgical procedures under appropriate anesthesia and follow techniques to avoid infection and minimize pain during and after surgery.

(g) When it is appropriate that an animal's life be terminated, psychologists proceed rapidly, with an effort to minimize pain and in accordance with accepted procedures.

8.10 REPORTING RESEARCH RESULTS

(a) Psychologists do not fabricate data. (See also Standard 5.01a, Avoidance of False or Deceptive Statements.)

(b) If psychologists discover significant errors in their published data, they take reasonable steps to correct such errors in a correction, retraction, erratum or other appropriate publication means.

8.11 PLAGIARISM

Psychologists do not present portions of another's work or data as their own, even if the other work or data source is cited occasionally.

8.12 PUBLICATION CREDIT

(a) Psychologists take responsibility and credit, including authorship credit, only for work they have actually performed or to which they have substantially contributed. (See also Standard 8.12b, Publication Credit.)

(b) Principal authorship and other publication credits accurately reflect the relative scientific or professional contributions of the individuals involved, regardless of their relative status. Mere possession of an institutional position, such as department chair, does not justify authorship credit. Minor contributions to the research or to the writing for publications are acknowledged appropriately, such as in footnotes or in an introductory statement.

(c) Except under exceptional circumstances, a student is listed as principal author on any multiple-authored article that is substantially based on the student's doctoral dissertation. Faculty advisors discuss publication credit with students as early as feasible and throughout the research and publication process as appropriate. (See also Standard 8.12b, Publication Credit.)

8.13 DUPLICATE PUBLICATION OF DATA

Psychologists do not publish, as original data, data that have been previously published. This does not preclude republishing data when they are accompanied by proper acknowledgment.

8.14 SHARING RESEARCH DATA FOR VERIFICATION

(a) After research results are published, psychologists do not withhold the data on which their conclusions are based from other competent professionals who seek to verify the substantive claims through reanalysis and who intend to use such data only for that purpose, provided that the confidentiality of the participants can be protected and unless legal rights concerning proprietary data preclude their release. This does not preclude psychologists from requiring that such individuals or groups be responsible for costs associated with the provision of such information.

(b) Psychologists who request data from other psychologists to verify the substantive claims through reanalysis may use shared data only for the declared purpose. Requesting psychologists obtain prior written agreement for all other uses of the data.

8.15 REVIEWERS

Psychologists who review material submitted for presentation, publication, grant or research proposal review respect the confidentiality of and the proprietary rights in such information of those who submitted it.

Appendix C

American Counseling Association's Code of Ethics

Section G: Research and Publication

To read the entire statement of ethical principles developed by the ACA, see http://www
.counseling.org/Resources/CodeOfEthics/TP/Home/CT2.aspx.

INTRODUCTION

Counselors who conduct research are encouraged to contribute to the knowledge base of
the profession and promote a clearer understanding of the conditions that lead to a healthy
and more just society. Counselors support efforts of researchers by participating fully and
willingly whenever possible. Counselors minimize bias and respect diversity in designing
and implementing research programs.

G.1. RESEARCH RESPONSIBILITIES

G.1.a. Use of Human Research Participants

Counselors plan, design, conduct, and report research in a manner that is consistent
with pertinent ethical principles, federal and state laws, host institutional regulations, and
scientific standards governing research with human research participants.

G.1.b. Deviation From Standard Practice

Counselors seek consultation and observe stringent safeguards to protect the rights of
research participants when a research problem suggests a deviation from standard or
acceptable practices.

G.1.c. Independent Researchers

When independent researchers do not have access to an Institutional Review Board (IRB), they should consult with researchers who are familiar with IRB procedures to provide appropriate safeguards.

G.1.d. Precautions to Avoid Injury

Counselors who conduct research with human participants are responsible for the welfare of participants throughout the research process and should take reasonable precautions to avoid causing injurious psychological, emotional, physical, or social effects to participants.

G.1.e. Principal Researcher Responsibility

The ultimate responsibility for ethical research practice lies with the principal researcher. All others involved in the research activities share ethical obligations and responsibility for their own actions.

G.1.f. Minimal Interference

Counselors take reasonable precautions to avoid causing disruptions in the lives of research participants that could be caused by their involvement in research.

G.1.g. Multicultural/Diversity Considerations in Research

When appropriate to research goals, counselors are sensitive to incorporating research procedures that take into account cultural considerations. They seek consultation when appropriate.

G.2. RIGHTS OF RESEARCH PARTICIPANTS *(SEE A.2, A.7.)*

G.2.a. Informed Consent in Research

Individuals have the right to consent to become research participants. In seeking consent, counselors use language that

1. accurately explains the purpose and procedures to be followed,

2. identifies any procedures that are experimental or relatively untried,

3. describes any attendant discomforts and risks,

4. describes any benefits or changes in individuals or organizations that might be reasonably expected,

5. discloses appropriate alternative procedures that would be advantageous for participants,

6. offers to answer any inquiries concerning the procedures,

7. describes any limitations on confidentiality,

8. describes the format and potential target audiences for the dissemination of research findings, and

9. instructs participants that they are free to withdraw their consent and to discontinue participation in the project at any time without penalty.

G.2.b. Deception

Counselors do not conduct research involving deception unless alternative procedures are not feasible and the prospective value of the research justifies the deception. If such deception has the potential to cause physical or emotional harm to research participants, the research is not conducted, regardless of prospective value. When the methodological requirements of a study necessitate concealment or deception, the investigator explains the reasons for this action as soon as possible during the debriefing.

G.2.c. Student/Supervisee Participation

Researchers who involve students or supervisees in research make clear to them that the decision regarding whether or not to participate in research activities does not affect one's academic standing or supervisory relationship. Students or supervisees who choose not to participate in educational research are provided with an appropriate alternative to fulfill their academic or clinical requirements.

G.2.d. Client Participation

Counselors conducting research involving clients make clear in the informed consent process that clients are free to choose whether or not to participate in research activities. Counselors take necessary precautions to protect clients from adverse consequences of declining or withdrawing from participation.

G.2.e. Confidentiality of Information

Information obtained about research participants during the course of an investigation is confidential. When the possibility exists that others may obtain access to such information, ethical research practice requires that the possibility, together with the plans for protecting confidentiality, be explained to participants as a part of the procedure for obtaining informed consent.

G.2.f. Persons Not Capable of Giving Informed Consent

When a person is not capable of giving informed consent, counselors provide an appropriate explanation to, obtain agreement for participation from, and obtain the appropriate consent of a legally authorized person.

G.2.g. Commitments to Participants

Counselors take reasonable measures to honor all commitments to research participants. *(See A.2.c.)*

G.2.h. Explanations After Data Collection

After data are collected, counselors provide participants with full clarification of the nature of the study to remove any misconceptions participants might have regarding the research. Where scientific or human values justify delaying or withholding information, counselors take reasonable measures to avoid causing harm.

G.2.i. Informing Sponsors

Counselors inform sponsors, institutions, and publication channels regarding research procedures and outcomes. Counselors ensure that appropriate bodies and authorities are given pertinent information and acknowledgement.

G.2.j. Disposal of Research Documents and Records

Within a reasonable period of time following the completion of a research project or study, counselors take steps to destroy records or documents (audio, video, digital, and written) containing confidential data or information that identifies research participants. When records are of an artistic nature, researchers obtain participant consent with regard to handling of such records or documents. *(See B.4.a, B.4.g.)*

G.3. RELATIONSHIPS WITH RESEARCH PARTICIPANTS (WHEN RESEARCH INVOLVES INTENSIVE OR EXTENDED INTERACTIONS)

G.3.a. Nonprofessional Relationships

Nonprofessional relationships with research participants should be avoided.

G.3.b. Relationships With Research Participants

Sexual or romantic counselor–research participant interactions or relationships with current research participants are prohibited.

G.3.c. Sexual Harassment and Research Participants

Researchers do not condone or subject research participants to sexual harassment.

G.3.d. Potentially Beneficial Interactions

When a nonprofessional interaction between the researcher and the research participant may be potentially beneficial, the researcher must document, prior to the interaction (when feasible), the rationale for such an interaction, the potential benefit, and anticipated consequences for the research participant. Such interactions should be initiated with appropriate consent of the research participant. Where unintentional harm occurs to the research participant due to the nonprofessional interaction, the researcher must show evidence of an attempt to remedy such harm.

G.4. REPORTING RESULTS

G.4.a. Accurate Results

Counselors plan, conduct, and report research accurately. They provide thorough discussions of the limitations of their data and alternative hypotheses. Counselors do not engage in misleading or fraudulent research, distort data, misrepresent data, or deliberately bias their results. They explicitly mention all variables and conditions known to the investigator that may have affected the outcome of a study or the interpretation of data. They describe the extent to which results are applicable for diverse populations.

G.4.b. Obligation to Report Unfavorable Results

Counselors report the results of any research of professional value. Results that reflect unfavorably on institutions, programs, services, prevailing opinions, or vested interests are not withheld.

G.4.c. Reporting Errors

If counselors discover significant errors in their published research, they take reasonable steps to correct such errors in a correction erratum, or through other appropriate publication means.

G.4.d. Identity of Participants

Counselors who supply data, aid in the research of another person, report research results, or make original data available take due care to disguise the identity of respective participants in the absence of specific authorization from the participants to do otherwise. In situations where participants self-identify their involvement in research studies, researchers take active steps to ensure that data is adapted/changed to protect the identity and welfare of all parties and that discussion of results does not cause harm to participants.

G.4.e. Replication Studies

Counselors are obligated to make available sufficient original research data to qualified professionals who may wish to replicate the study.

G.5. PUBLICATION

G.5.a. Recognizing Contributions

When conducting and reporting research, counselors are familiar with and give recognition to previous work on the topic, observe copyright laws, and give full credit to those to whom credit is due.

G.5.b. Plagiarism

Counselors do not plagiarize, that is, they do not present another person's work as their own work.

G.5.c. Review/Republication of Data or Ideas

Counselors fully acknowledge and make editorial reviewers aware of prior publication of ideas or data where such ideas or data are submitted for review or publication.

G.5.d. Contributors

Counselors give credit through joint authorship, acknowledgment, footnote statements, or other appropriate means to those who have contributed significantly to research or concept development in accordance with such contributions. The principal contributor is listed first and minor technical or professional contributions are acknowledged in notes or introductory statements.

G.5.e. Agreement of Contributors

Counselors who conduct joint research with colleagues or students/supervisees establish agreements in advance regarding allocation of tasks, publication credit, and types of acknowledgement that will be received.

G.5.f. Student Research

For articles that are substantially based on students['] course papers, projects, dissertations or theses, and on which students have been the primary contributors, they are listed as principal authors.

G.5.g. Duplicate Submission

Counselors submit manuscripts for consideration to only one journal at a time. Manuscripts that are published in whole or in substantial part in another journal or published work are not submitted for publication without acknowledgment and permission from the previous publication.

G.5.h. Professional Review

Counselors who review material submitted for publication, research, or other scholarly purposes respect the confidentiality and proprietary rights of those who submitted it. Counselors use care to make publication decisions based on valid and defensible standards. Counselors review article submissions in a timely manner and based on their scope and competency in research methodologies. Counselors who serve as reviewers at the request of editors or publishers make every effort to only review materials that are within their scope of competency and use care to avoid personal biases.

Appendix D

Institutional Review Board Research Proposal Format

Your proposal is describing the parameters of the research experiment you are presenting for institutional review. It must describe the design of your research and the methodology to be employed, including the prospective subjects and controls, as well as the equipment, instruments, and regimen(s) you propose to perform on the data you collect. It must also analyze all risk factors and potential benefits for subjects volunteering to participate. It should justify the necessity of research in terms of the potential harm for participants.

Include all of the following information:

Title of the proposed project:

Names and positions of all researchers:

Education and a brief history of past research experience of all researchers:

Objectives of the proposed study or the research questions:

- Provide background data that support the goals and/or objectives of the proposal.
- Describe the purpose of this research project.

Subjects:

- Provide estimated number and description of types of subjects, including their desired demographic category membership (e.g., ethnicity, age, and sex).
- Describe the source of potential subjects.
- What population will your subjects represent or generalize to when the data from them is analyzed?
- Describe your previous or ongoing contact with the source of potential subjects.
- What rewards, stipend, or honorarium (if any) will subjects be given? Are such rewards contingent on the subject's completion of all phases of the study?

- Describe where and how potential subjects will be contacted and what information they will be given about the study prior to obtaining consent.
- Discuss your efforts to prevent subjects from being coerced to participate.
- Provide and justify the specific criteria for eligibility to be a subject in this study.

Research methods to be employed:

- Provide a time frame for this study, or, if data are part of a previously established database, from what era or temporal cohort will the subjects come?
- Describe where the study will be conducted, including all locations or laboratories. Present evidence that all locations are available for your use.
- Describe in detail the procedures that will be followed and describe the sequence of what will be done.
- Describe in detail any equipment that will be employed as part of the study.
- What measurement devices, tests, or surveys will be employed to collect data? What are the qualifications of the researchers to use the measurement devices? What is the evidence of the validity and reliability of the measurement tools?
- What exactly will each subject experience during the study?
- List all potential risks for the subjects from what is most likely to that which is least likely but nonetheless possible.

Benefits to the subjects and the profession:

- In what way is the subject likely to benefit from being a participant in the study?
- How will participation help others in the immediate environment of the participant (e.g., family, co-workers)?
- In what way will participation by the subjects contribute to the profession and or scientific literature?

Risk and possible harm for subjects:

- List all potential risks to the subject if they participate, including physical harm, psychological damage including a loss of self-esteem, social loss including peer pressures, and possible expenses the subject may encounter (e.g., transportation and parking costs, loss of time, income loss).
- Provide an analysis of potential long-range losses that the subjects may experience as a result of participation.
- What steps will be taken to minimize or mitigate possible harm or loss?

Risk-to-benefit analysis:

- Justify the proposed study in terms of the ratio of benefit to risk for the participants.
- What protections will be provided to reduce risk factors for participants?
- Explain how the profession may gain from the completion of this research effort

Informed consent or permission:

- From whom will consent for participation be obtained for each individual (e.g., the subject, a parent or guardian, a guardian ad litem)?
- Describe the protocol to be followed in obtaining consent, including forms used, advertisements employed, and explanations presented. Attach these as appendices to this proposal.
- Describe the steps to be taken for non–English speakers, subjects who are incarcerated, subjects who are cognitively impaired, and subjects who are non compos mentis.
- Document that all forms are understandable by and written at a reading level appropriate for the subjects.

Confidentiality:

- Describe in detail how subject records will be maintained in confidence and the safeguards being employed to prevent individual data from being linked to subjects.
- How long will records be maintained?
- How will they be stored?
- Who will have access to those confidential data?

Glossary

a priori: Existing before an occurrence or experience.

abduction: An informed guess about the cause of a phenomenon based on observation of past occurrences.

abductive logic: Logic involving the process of working back from an observed consequence (or effect) to a probable antecedent (assumed cause). Abduction may entail creatively generating insights.

abscissa: The horizontal axis of a graph, often called the x-axis. On Cartesian graphs, it usually carries the scale of the independent variable.

accidental sample: Any sample selected from that part of the population that is easy to access. That is, a nonprobability sample selected because it is readily available and convenient. *See* **convenience sample.**

accountability: Responsibility to a person, organization, authority for any clinical activity; to be held to account for all actions and outcomes.

achievement test: A test measuring an individual's knowledge of specific facts and proficiency in completing cognitive processes such as problem solving.

action research (AR): Field-based research first described by Kurt Lewin that is designed to solve an immediate, pragmatic problem; participants are engaged with researchers in the problem-solving effort.

active independent variable: Variable used in research that the researcher can manipulate by assigning subjects to one or another level of treatment.

active interview: Use of conversation to draw out a participant's true meaning and beliefs. It may include the use of confrontation.

adjusted mean: In ANCOVA, the statistical removal of variance ascribed to the confounding variable results in adjusted data, the mean of which is the adjusted mean.

alpha: Probability of being in error when rejecting a null hypothesis.

alternate forms over time reliability: Stability (reliability) of test scores from two different forms of the same test administered a two different times.

alternate-form reliability: The correlation that can be obtained when two different but well-matched versions of a measure are administered to the same subjects.

analyses-within-the-case: *See* **embedded analysis.**

analysis of covariance (ANCOVA): A statistical technique for equating groups on one or more variables by adjusting scores on a dependent variable for initial differences on confounding variables, such as pretest performance.

analysis of narratives: Identification of a common theme across the stories of individuals in a study and then restorying those themes to provide the shared perspective.

analysis of variance (ANOVA): Statistical analysis for hypothesis testing that tests whether there are statistically significant differences between group means on scores on a quantitative dependent variable across two or more groups using the test statistic F ratio.

anchor items: Test items used every year that serve to set the difficulty level of newly developed test items for subsequent editions of the assessment. Most high-stakes tests consist of up to 33 % anchor items.

antipositivist: Social science view that the focus of researchers should be to understand the perceptions and interpretations that the individuals being studied have vis-à-vis social actions.

artifacts: Intentionally made objects designed for a particular use or to meet a need of the individual who produced them.

assigned factor: Independent variable in empirical research that is not controlled or manipulated by the researcher (e.g., age, ethnic background, gender, etc.).

assigned independent variable: *See* **assigned factor.**

assumed knowledge: Knowledge we have gained by reading and through others that we have not personally verified but nonetheless assume to be true.

asymptotes: The quality of the normal curve such that the tails never touch the horizontal axis even if continued toward infinity.

average: Generic term for one or all of the following ways of defining the central tendency of a data set: mean, median, or mode.

axial codes: Process in grounded theory of assigning codes identified in qualitative data to related concepts or categories through inductive and deductive reasoning.

axiology: Refers to the philosophical study of goodness and the role of values in inquiry.

bar graph: Cartesian linear graphic data presentation for nominal data where one axis shows classifications and the other frequency of occurrence.

baseline: The plotted record of a series of measurements or a pretest taken prior to the introduction of an intervention. It is used to benchmark how the individual is functioning prior to any change.

bell curve: *See* **Gaussian normal curve.**

Belmont Report: A report published in 1979 by the then US Department of Health, Education, and Welfare that established the basic ethical principles that guide the use of human participants in research involving any direct or indirect federal funding.

beta: The name applied to the probability of failing to reject a false null hypothesis, symbolized as β.

between-groups mean square (BGMS): The expression of variance attributable to the treatment effect in ANOVA and the numerator in the calculation of F ratios.

between-groups sum of squares (BGSS): The total of the squared, summed mean group differences around the grand mean of all group means in ANOVA.

between-groups variance: *See* **between-groups mean square.**

bimodal: Distribution of scores around a central mean that has been flanked by two score clusters that each produce an off-mean mode.

binary: Describes a variable with two distinct levels.

Bonferroni inequality: Statistical correction for potential error brought about by familywise Type I error with a series of hypothesis tests.

bound group: Group or individual selected for having special qualities to serve as the focus of a case study.

brainstorming: A group creativity technique by which efforts are made to find a conclusion for a specific problem by gathering a list of ideas (without critical analysis) spontaneously contributed by participants.

Cartesian graph: Graph composed of Cartesian coordinates defined by equidistant parallel lines meeting along a grid at right angles with a center point of zero.

causal validity: The degree of certainty to which it can be said that an intervention caused the outcome.

causal-comparative: Research to determine the causes for, or consequences of, existing differences in groups of individuals; also referred to as ex post facto research.

cell: Subgroup of participants in an experiment who share a common level of intervention or treatment.

census tract: Census tracts are small, relatively permanent subdivisions of a county established by the US Census.

central tendency: A measure of the "average" performance of individuals. It includes the mean, median, and mode.

chart rounds: Regularly scheduled meeting conducted by various health care professionals working as a team for the benefit of inpatients or clients in therapy.

chi-square (χ^2): Nonparametric test of statistical significance appropriate when data are in the form of frequency counts. It can be used to compare frequencies actually observed in a study with expected frequencies to test whether they are significantly different.

classical measurement theory: Theoretical model explaining the relationship between an obtained score of a subject on a test and the relative amounts of measurement error and true score in the composition of that observed score.

client-centered counseling: Rogerian therapy providing clients with active listening, unconditional positive regard, and empathetic reflection.

coefficient of determination (CD): Mathematical expression of criterion variable variance explained in correlation or in a multiple regression analysis by a predictor variable or a combination of predictor variables.

common knowledge: Assumed knowledge shared by members of the greater community that does not require referencing in written research reports.

comparison group: Research group receiving a different treatment from that of the experimental group, a placebo treatment, or no treatment. It is sometimes referred to as the untreated or control group.

complementary pairing: Strength of mixed method research whereby the strengths of one method compensate for the weaknesses of the other, and vice versa.

computer-adaptive testing (CAT): Testing in which software estimates the ability and background knowledge of each test taker and guides the appropriate selection of test items from a computerized item bank.

concurrent validity: Degree to which test scores are related to the scores on another instrument administered at the same time or to some other criterion available at the same time.

confidence intervals: A parameter linked to a normal curve of probability. It provides two points representing the limits of what obtained scores would have been randomly drawn from a normal population.

confirmability: One dimension in the validation of a conclusion from a qualitative study involving the capability of being tested (verified or falsified) by others on whom the analysis was focused.

confirmatory factor analysis (CFA): Factor analysis to confirm the underlying dimension(s) in an empirical assessment of the internal structure of a scale, instrument, or measure.

consensual qualitative research (CQR): Qualitative research method emphasizing the development of a consensus among all members of a research team at every step in the research process.

construct-irrelevant element: An off-target dimension in a measurement of a construct that detracts from the construct's validity.

construct validity: A validation technique used with variables of hypothetical traits or abilities lacking an operational (observable) definition that involves demonstrating both the legitimacy of the variable and the ability to measure it cleanly.

constructionist: One who believes that each individual organizes his or her own perceptions and sensory input within a personal framework of understanding and interpreting.

constructs: Unobservable abstractions useful in interpreting both qualitative and quantitative data, organizing descriptions, and theory building.

content analysis: The study of particular aspects of the information contained in a document, transcript, film, or other form of communication.

content validity: The fidelity of test items to the topic taught and/or the goals of the curriculum area being measured.

continuing education units (CEUs): Units of inservice education equal to 10 clock hours of instruction.

continuous distribution curve: Probability distribution of a randomly drawn continuous variable. When graphed along an axis with the data's mean in the center, it assumes a characteristic bell shape. When plotted as a cumulative frequency, it graphs as an ogive.

continuous scale: A numeric scale that includes real numbers with equal distances between them.

control group: One of two or more randomly assigned groups in an experiment. The control group does not receive the experimental treatment and provides a point of comparison for the other groups.

control group blind: A control group that is unaware that it is not being given the experimental treatment.

convenience sample: A sample of subjects who are easily accessible. This sample does not represent the whole population and may be chosen because of time, availability, or financial constraints. *See* **accidental sample.**

convergent validity: Degree to which an operation, instrument, or scale covaries with other operations, instruments, or scales to which it theoretically should be similar.

copyright: Governmental registration of the ownership of creative or intellectual property.

core ideas: Emerging themes linking concepts within the domains established during consensual qualitative research.

correlation coefficient eta: Coefficient of universal correlation between two variables that includes all linear and curvilinear components.

covariance: The amount of common variance shared by two different measures, measured as a coefficient of correlation.

covariate: Variable with an association with the dependent variable or criterion variable in an analysis that can present an alternative explanation for outcomes.

credibility: The quality of a research outcome being believable through the use of triangulation and the ability of the researcher.

criterion validity: Degree to which a measuring device predicts an outcome defined by other variables or how well it predicts a measurable outcome.

criterion variable: A variable that is to be predicted in a multiple-correlation (multiple-regression) equation by two or more predictor variables.

criterion-referenced tests: Tests designed to measure how well an individual has learned a specific skill or acquired specified knowledge. The reference is absolute and not dependent on a comparison to other test takers.

critical ethnography: Application of critical theory to the qualitative research method of ethnography.

critical value: Cut score established as the point on a statistical distribution of probabilities where the decision to reject the null hypothesis can be made.

cross-analysis: Step in concensual qualitative research in which team members examine the content of each domain's core ideas and, through consensus building, finalize constructs and then recode the data set using the newly finalized constructs.

cross-sectional data collection: Collecting data at one time that cross several different groups, such as different age cohort groups.

culture: A set of learned beliefs, mores, values, and behaviors shared by members of a society.

Current Procedural Terminology (CPT): Medical codes for physical and medical problems to ensure uniformity in diagnosis and treatments. This facilitates third-party reimbursement to the practitioner.

curvilinear: A vector or line that changes in slope between low and high scores; describes lines defined as quadratic and cubic functions.

cut score: The raw score on a standards-based test that denotes a break between two ordinal levels of success (e.g., proficient vs. highly proficient or pass vs. fail).

decile: One tenth part of a distribution of percentiles.

Declaration of Helsinki: A non–legally binding policy statement of the World Medical Association, first published in 1964, on the ethical parameters guiding research with human subjects.

deduction: Logical model in which specific expectations and hypotheses are based on general principles and/or known truths.

degrees of freedom (*df*): The number of data points in a sample that are free to vary minus the number of statistics that have been calculated in the process of estimating a population parameter.

demographic questions: Background information describing statistical characteristics of human samples (e.g., age, gender, race, income, etc.). These data are typically used as independent variables to answer questions comparing subgroup cohorts using data analysis.

denaturalism: Transcripting only the portion of a conversation or other discourse thought to be central or germane to the area of research interest.

dependability: In qualitative research, dependability is analogous to reliability in empirical research, that is, the consistency of observing the same finding under similar circumstances.

dependent variable: Variable expected to change or otherwise be modified by the introduction of some environmental change (independent variable).

descriptive study: Research that examines in-depth situations as they are, identifying characteristics of observed phenomena and exploring possible associations among phenomena. These types of studies cannot determine causal relationships but can describe the current state of things.

dichotomy: Categorical variable that can take one of two values. Usually, these are coded 0, 1 or 1, 2. For example, gender may be coded as a dichotomous variable with 1 = Male, 2 = Female.

differential item functioning (DIF): Statistical analysis of the items of a psychological test to verify that all subgroups of the population perform equally well on individual items.

direct costs: Actual dollar costs associated with the operation of a program, including all operating and support costs noted on the program's budget.

discriminant validity: Validity showing that a test of a concept is not highly correlated with other tests designed to measure theoretically different concepts.

disordinal interactions: Interaction effect in two-way ANOVA whereby one level of an independent variable affects the presentation of a second independent variable but has a different impact on a second level of that variable.

dispersion: Distribution of data points around some central value such as a mean. The range is a simple example of a measure of dispersion, and variance is a more technical one.

distribution-free: Statistical hypothesis-testing method that makes no assumption about the shape of the distribution of scores or about the measurement precision of the data.

domain: A distinct region of knowledge with certain limits and boundaries.

double-barreled question: Question that lends itself to two concurrent possible responses, making it impossible to answer.

double-blind study: Way of conducting a research experiment, usually on human participants, that eliminates possible bias on the part of both experimental participants and experimenters.

Durbin-Watson test: Statistical test for independence of the data by measuring for possible autocorrelation evidence in the data.

ecological validity: The extent to which the methods, materials, and setting of the study approximate the real-life situation under investigation.

embedded analysis: A study of select individuals or situations within a larger case study.

emic: Understanding the perspective and deep meaning of the behavior of others by assuming their point of view.

empiricism: Pursuit of knowledge purely through experience, especially by means of observation, measurement, and careful experimentation.

endogenous variable: A variable in a causal model (path analysis) that has a value determined by other variables in the model.

enhanced design: Mixed methods research or evaluation whereby one approach to research enhances another approach.

envy: Interpersonal source of a loss of research design validity where members of one group resent and are envious of the treatment received by another group.

EPA: Abbreviation for the three underlying factors found through factor analysis of semantic differential scales: evaluation, potency, and activity.

epistemology: Branch of philosophy that studies the nature of knowledge and its acquisition and validation.

equal-appearing interval scale: Measurement scale with hierarchical descriptors that have been empirically shown to provide equal conceptual intervals between levels.

equal-appearing interval technique: Research conducted with a measurement device composed of an equal-appearing interval scale.

eta-squared: Statistical expression of the treatment effect size statistic that is interpreted as the proportion of variance in the scores on the outcome variable that is predictable from group membership.

ethnographer: Qualitative researcher with the goal of gaining an in-depth understanding of the culture of a group, organization, or society using procedures such as participant observation, interviews, and examination of artifacts.

ethnographic interviewing: Interviewing informants to extract critical information in a low-stress format.

ethnographic research: Research that collects data by direct, real-time observation of subjects in their natural setting in which the researcher may or may not participate as a member of the group being observed.

ethnography: Qualitative research approach for the study of cultures to learn more about their interactions, values, meanings, behaviors, language, and worldview.

eugenics: Pseudoscience based on the theoretical assumption that child growth and development are genetically driven and can be improved by preventing the mentally defective from becoming parents.

event sampling: Observations carried out during a defined and limited time frame (e.g., lunchtime) and focused on the activities and behaviors of one individual.

evidence-based: Selecting a therapy approach to use with clients on the basis of an accurate diagnosis of the nature of the problem and the best available research evidence on treatment effectiveness.

existential philosophies: Philosophical doctrines holding the primacy of the individual and his or her experiences as central to thinking and knowing; proposed by Soren Kierkegaard, Friedrich Nietzsche, and Jean-Paul Sartre.

experimental group: Subjects selected at random to participate in an experiment in which they are provided a special (experimental) treatment.

experimental validity: The assurance that systematic alterations in the independent variable result in observed (or measured) changes in the dependent variable.

experimental variable: *See* **independent variable.**

external validity: Degree to which research results are generalizable to participants, settings, and materials beyond those included in the study.

extraneous factors: Variables correlated with the dependent variable that may pose an alternative explanation (confounding explanation) for a research finding.

face validity: Degree to which it is obvious what attitudes or abilities a test measures from its content and/or the provision of a demonstration of the importance of the measure for those asked to take it.

factor analysis (FA): Analytical procedure involved in estimating a common factor(s) that links the correlations among measured variables. The goal of factor analysis is to simplify a large number of measures into a meaningful few.

factor structure: Identified latent factors and the largest loadings that define them.

factorial: Analysis of variance design with two or more independent variables.

factorial ANOVA: The use of two or more independent variables (factors) in an analysis of variance. Also called factorial analysis of variance.

factors: Independent variables in analysis of variance.

familywise Type I error (FWE): When more than one a priori inference (family of hypotheses tests) is tested on a single data set, the possibility of committing a Type I error increases as the additive sum of all alpha levels involved.

fat tail: Description of a graph of a distribution of platykurtic data.

fidelity: Quality of a quantitative research design linking the treatment effect (independent variable) with the dependent variable in a causal relationship.

first quartile: Lowest 25% of score values in a percentile-ranked sequence.

focus group: Qualitative research approach involving organized discussion with specifically selected individuals to gain unique information about a particular topic.

formative: Any assessment in an evaluation study carried out as the target processes are being presented; provides ongoing feedback and guidance to the primary stakeholder.

formative assessment: An evaluation designed to provide feedback and advice for improving a program and conducted to adjust and enhance interventions in program evaluation studies.

frame: The parameters around a population that define membership of a group from which a sample of participants can be drawn.

frequency: Number of cases, occurrences, or data points that are the same in a population or sample.

frequency polygon: Graphical representation of a frequency distribution.

frequency sampling: Observational method that counts the occurrences of an observed behavior during a particular time frame.

Gantt chart: Chart depicting progress in relation to a timeline for projects, tasks, and schedules across a series of objectives for a project.

gateway drug: Mood-altering drug, such as a stimulant or tranquilizer, that does not cause physical dependence but may lead to the use of more addictive drugs.

Gaussian normal curve: Mathematically defined natural distribution of the occurrence of data from a large set of independent observations. These data assume a characteristic "bell shape" or an ogive; thus, this curve is colloquially known as the "bell curve." The shape implies that most cases occur in the center and few in the high or low fringe areas.

gaze: In conversation analysis, the gaze of individuals is used as a marker of attention and/or the desire to withdraw from the conversation.

gestalt: Cognitive interpretation of a configuration, pattern, or organized field having specific properties different from the summation of its component parts.

getting in: Gaining access during field research to the site and participants needed to provide meaningful data.

goodness of fit: (1) Test of agreement between a theoretical factor structure and one obtained from data. (2) Agreement between theoretical distribution and a distribution obtained from observed data.

grade equivalent score (GES): An ordinal scoring system indicating the average grade level of students who have achieved at a particular level on an achievement test.

grade point average (GPA): The ordinal Type II average obtained by dividing the total number of ordinal grade points earned by the total number of credits taken.

grand mean: The mean for all the scores in an entire study, denoted by $\bar{\bar{X}}$ or M_{grand}.

gray literature: Written documents and reports that are not published in conventional journals and proceedings and are often only accessible from Internet databases.

grounded theory: Approach to theory development that derives constructs and laws directly from the immediate data the researcher has collected rather than drawing on an existing theory.

guest editors: Individuals with deep expertise who volunteer to provide editorial assistance as a peer reviewer of an article for a professional journal.

heritability: Statistically derived value of inherited component in a genetically expressed characteristic, symbolized as h^2.

hermeneutic analysis: Interpretative analysis used in phenomenological analysis of texts and other forms of communication to derive their latent meanings.

hermeneutic circle: Interpretation of a text by the process of alternating between interpreting the deep or hidden meaning of each part of the text and the meaning of the text as a whole.

hermeneutics: Analytical system for the interpretation of verbal and written communications for their deeper meaning.

high-stakes assessments: Any assessment or test with scores that have serious implications for those taking the test.

high-stakes decision: Any measurement-based decision with serious implications for those taking the test.

histogram: A representation of a frequency distribution having rectangular bars of different lengths. The height of each bar represents the score frequency of an ordinal variable.

holistic: Patterns providing an overall understanding of data, including the integration of various perspectives.

homogeneity of regression: ANCOVA assumption requiring that at each level of the independent variable(s), the correlation between the covariate and the dependent variable is equal.

homoscedastic: Having equal variances of scores on one variable at each level of a correlated variable.

humanistic: Worldview centered on the human perspective on interpreting and understanding the environment that seeks to ensure individuals have the freedom to fulfill felt needs and facilitate personal development.

humanistic psychology: Field of psychology started in the 1950s under the leadership of Carl Rogers that emphasizes the study of humanistic applications in personal development and growth and is linked to the philosophy of phenomenology.

Husserl reductionism: Core concept in phenomenology espoused by Edmund Gustav Albrecht Husserl of the centrality of mental conceptualization of objects over an assumed physical reality.

hypothetico-deductive reasoning: Process used in the "scientific method" involving the a priori deduction of a research hypothesis from a theory or conceptual framework.

independent variable: Variable established and controlled (systematically altered) by the researcher to bring about a change in the dependent variable being measured as an outcome.

indirect costs: Hidden costs, including fringe benefits and other fixed expenses, related to the project's operation within an organization.

Individuals with Disabilities Act: Earlier name for the Individuals with Disabilities Education Improvement Act (IDEA). This was a reauthorization of the 1974 Education for All Handicapped Children Act (Pub. L. 94-142).

induction: System of logic in which general principles are derived from specific observations.

institutional review board (IRB): University's or other organization's board of faculty and other stakeholders who review research and thesis proposals to protect the rights of human participants or animal subjects.

instrumental case: Use of a small group of subjects to examine a selected pattern of behavior with the goal of being able to explain the nature and cause of the behavior.

intact group: Group sharing a common reason for being, such as a graduate department, a local church congregation, or clients of a community clinic.

internal validity: The linkage of the research question being asked and research methods employed to answer the question. High internal validity implies that there are no viable alternative explanations for the outcome with the dependent variable.

interpretivists: Researchers employing methods that are subjective and that interpret the context-bound nature of human behavior and thought.

interquartile range: The 50 % of the cases in a percentile distribution that fall between the 25th to the 75th percentile.

interrater reliability: Statistical statement of the degree to which two or more raters (evaluators) agree when rating the same items.

interval sampling: Observational method for data collection involving the timing of intervals between behavioral occurrences, for example, temper tantrums.

interval scale: Measurement scale composed of steps having the same mathematical unit size and based on a standardized data distribution.

interview protocol: Listed sequence of questionnaire items.

interviewer drift: Tendency for interviewers to change their interviewing behaviors as they conduct numerous interviews with participants.

IQ score: Abbreviation for *intelligence quotient*. A score representing mental ability reported in a standardized form where the average is 100 and the standard deviation about 15.

item characteristic curve (ICC): Ogive graphing how a sample of subjects performs on a single test item.

key informants: Individuals who can provide expert opinions or are presumed to have special knowledge about a target population's problems or needs.

Kruskal-Wallis one-way ANOVA: Nonparametric inferential statistic used to compare two or more independent groups to determine statistical significance of differences.

latent factor: Relational factor among several measured variables identified through factor analysis.

law of large numbers: Statistical rule assuming that as the number of samples increases, the average of these samples approaches the mean of the whole population (μ).

least squares regression: Correlation method involving a weighted linear combination of predictors (independent variables) with a single dependent variable (criterion).

leptokurtic: The quality of a normal curve with an excess of score points close to the sample's mean that has a relatively high central peak, low measured variance, and thin tails.

lexiphanicism: The use of unnecessarily large words or pretentious phraseology.

lifespace: Dynamic, ever-changing phenomenological field constructed by each individual in which all values, motives, feelings, ideals, and anxieties are housed.

linear regression: Calculated regressions that do not include curvilinear or interaction terms in the calculation.

lipid-dense: Lipids are one of six types of nutrients recognized by medical science as part of the human diet. Lipid-dense foods are high in fats and cholesterol.

literature: Collected publications of a discipline presenting original research that may be used as primary source material.

log linear regression: Statistical approach for determining the odds of a dichotomous outcome based on categorical predictor variables.

logical positivism: The name of a philosophy, developed by members of the "Vienna Circle" and predicated on the writings of Moritz Schlick, that marked the beginning of an empirical philosophy of science.

longitudinal: Research approach that includes a temporal factor (e.g., development) as a dimension in a research study by repeatedly testing subjects over time.

longitudinal data collection: Data collected from subjects over an extended time frame by employing repeated measurements or observations made on the same group of subjects and analyzed for trends (*See* **longitudinal**).

main effect: Each independent variable in factorial ANOVA.

managed health care: Arrangements to control the costs of health-related services by having a large organization contract with care providers to pay the cost of services for many people's care at reduced costs.

marginal note: Notation of an unusual or telling behavior or response to a survey item during an interview; the interviewer makes the notation in the margin of the survey's protocol.

margin of error: In sampling, the expected difference between the estimated parameter provided by a sample and the actual parameter from the population.

mean: A measure of central tendency referred to as an arithmetic average of a set of scores.

median: The score equal to the center of a rank-ordered data set, the 50th percentile.

mediator variable: Variable that describes how correlational effects will occur by accounting for the relationship between the independent and dependent variables.

meta-analysis: Research method of statistically weighting and combining a number of related research findings into a single reliable statement.

mixed methods research: Research in which the investigator collects and analyzes data, integrates the findings in collaboration with the participants, and draws inferences using primarily qualitative approaches.

mode: The most frequently occurring score or outcome in a distribution of scores.

moderator variable: Variable that changes the correlational relationship between a predictor and criterion variable.

monotonic: The relationship between two variables is monotonic if an increase for one is always associated with an increase for the other, but the relationship is not necessarily linear.

monotonic association: *See* **monotonic.**

mores: Socially agreed-upon patterns for behavior that often provide moral guidance for individuals.

mortality-morbidity (M&M) conference: Committee of clinical professionals who meet on a regular basis to discuss the progress and treatment of patients.

multicultural competence: Core competency in counselor education stating that counselors have an appreciation of other cultures with regard to education, research, and therapy.

multiple case study: Method of strengthening a case study through replication of the case study method with another bounded group.

multiple correlation: The correlation between a variable and a weighted linear combination of predictor variables. This mathematical method is frequently referred to as multiple regression.

multiple reality: Theory in the methods of phenomenological qualitative evaluation that the world is unique to each individual and individuals perceive it in different ways.

multisite case study: Application of case study methods at parallel sites to provide a more generalizable set of findings.

multitrait multimethod method (MTMM): Method employed in establishing construct validity of measures of a new construct in which tests measuring the construct are correlated but measures not theorized to be associated with the construct are not correlated with the construct's measurements.

moot courtroom: Location of a simulated trial court proceeding.

narrative analysis: Qualitative research method focused on the life stories related by participants related to a theme being investigated.

natural philosophy: Precursor of the modern term *science* and its various divisions.

naturalism: Transcription method that makes a written record of every utterance, pause, and gesture. Also the doctrine that the focus of science should be on the natural or material world and researchers should search for physical causes of phenomena.

negative skewness: This occurs in data that have an excess of low scores, causing the mean to be lower than the median of the data.

neo-Freudians: Theories and theorists who followed the teachings of Sigmund Freud before developing theoretical models of their own.

nested design: Focused, small-scale case study research carried out within a larger case study.

No Child Left Behind Act: A revamping of the Elementary and Secondary Education Act in 2002 (Pub. L. 107-100). The goal of the law was to "close the achievement gap with accountability, flexibility, and choice, so that no child is left behind."

NOIR: Mnemonic device, based on the French word for the color *black*, representing the levels of data precision: nominal, ordinal, interval, and ratio.

nominal: Level of measurement precision involving nonsequential, name-only categories.

nominal data: Data from a variable expressed as a series of names or descriptors that are devoid of a mathematical measurement scale.

nominal definitions: Working definitions for ambiguous terms used in research.

nominal scale: A scale composed of mutually exclusive categories that are given names and are not able to be ordered or sequenced.

nomological net (NN): A method for establishing construct validity by identifying and delineating all interrelationships and observable relations among elements of the construct.

nonequivalent pretest-posttest comparison: A quasi-experimental design for research featuring the use of a control group and two samples of convenience.

nonparametric statistics: Statistics not requiring the parametric statistical assumptions that may be employed with ordinal and nominal data.

nonprobability samples: Sampling in which cases are selected not by chance but by some other means.

nonprobability sampling: Method for selecting research participants on a nonrandom basis.

norm group: *See* **normative comparison group.**

normal curve: *See* **Gaussian normal curve.**

normal distribution: *See* **Gaussian normal curve.**

normal distribution of errors: *See* **Gaussian normal curve.**

normative comparison group: A distribution of measurement scores from a group of subjects with known characteristics (age, sex, grade in school, etc.) with whom an individual's performance may be compared; typically selected to represent the range of typical performances on a measure.

normative reference group: *See* **normative comparison group.**

null hypothesis: Research statement that any observed difference between groups is not significant and only represents a chance occurrence.

Nuremberg Code: A set of research ethical principles that came about as a result of the 1947 Nuremberg Tribunal at the end of World War II; it is still used in many parts of the world.

obedience: Personality dimension involving an individual's willingness to follow the orders of those in authority.

observer effect: Also known as the Hawthorne effect, it is the tendency for research subjects to change their behavior when they know they are being observed.

Occam's razor: Maxim that assumptions introduced to explain a phenomenon should be succinct and still explain all cases.

odds ratio: Ratio of the likelihood of an event to the likelihood the event will not occur. The approach used to express outcomes for logistic regression.

ogive: Graph of a frequency distribution curve in which the frequencies are cumulative.

one-tailed null hypothesis: Hypothesis test with *all* possible Type I error occurring either above or below the mean of the probability distribution.

one-way ANOVA: Extension of the independent-groups *t*-test for the analysis of differences between two or more groups.

open coding: The first step in most qualitative data analyses, this involves examining the raw information in minute detail while developing some initial categories or spotting latent trends and directions.

operational definitions: Specific definition of something in terms of the operations by which its effect is evident.

opportunistic samples: Sampling strategy that involves using available subjects who have been grouped for another reason but are conveniently available for the researcher.

oral history: Outcome of qualitative research with transcript analysis of interview data from one or more informed individuals about their lived experiences.

ordinal interaction: Intensity of the effect of an independent variable's varying as a function of a second independent variable. The two independent variables do not move parallel to each other.

ordinal scale: Measurement scale of mutually exclusive categories in an ordered sequence with categories having differing dimensions, making the scale nonparametric.

ordinal type II data: Ordinal data mathematically treated as though the data were truly interval with equal interval size (e.g., grade point average).

ordinate: The vertical axis of a graph, often called the y-axis, depicting the scale of dependent variable in a graph of a simple linear regression line.

orthogonal: Two vectors representing uncorrelated data, often graphed as lines at right angles.

orthogonal factors: Factors identified through factor analysis that are independent of (uncorrelated with) each other.

outlier: Extreme or unusual score relative to the sample distribution.

oversampling: Selecting larger subpopulations than would be normal if strict proportional sampling were employed to better understand small minority groups within the population.

paradigm: Personal worldview for the understanding and interpretation of the environment and human activity.

parameter: A constant linked to a statistical value that is determined by an arbitrarily selected position on a distribution of cases.

parametric: Mathematically derived statistics used to apply inferences from a sample to a population.

path analysis: Statistical procedure, based on regression analysis, that provides a graphic picture of a causal model for understanding relationships between variables.

Pearson product moment correlation (PPMC): Statistical expression of the degree to which two variables covary. The minimum correlation is zero, and the maximum is ± 1.

peer reviewers: Selected experts in a respective field of study who scrutinize and critique scholarly work, studies, or research methods.

percentile: Part out of 100. A 100th part of any group or set of data or objects.

personal field: Hypothetical construct proposed by Kurt Lewin to describe how the human mind creates a framework (field) to understand experiences and make external realities interpretable.

personality inventory: Measure that assesses a variety of personality traits, typically in a self-report in paper-and-pencil format but also as a clinical application of projective assessment methods.

personological variable: Variable that may impact a study's outcome and that cannot be manipulated, such as a trait or characteristic of the subjects being measured.

phenomenologically: Adverb describing a family of qualitative research methods involving interpretative approaches for data analysis.

pictograph: Graphic representation of data through the use of diagrammatic pictures or cartoons.

pilot study: Small-scale study administered before conducting a larger study to reveal possible limitations in the research method.

pilot test: Small-scale evaluation of a data-gathering method to reveal possible problems prior to employing the method with a larger study.

placebo: Literally meaning "I do nothing," an inactive treatment or procedure used to provide comparative data for subjects receiving a real treatment.

placebo effect: When a placebo condition in an experiment seems to have an effect even though it is given as a nontreatment control, the measured change from pre-placebo to post-placebo is described as a placebo effect.

platykurtic: The quality of a normal curve with relatively few score points close to the sample's mean that has relative flatness, large measured variance, and fat tails.

point-biserial correlation: Correlation coefficient used to express the correlational relationship between a dichotomy and a set of continuous scores (parametric data).

population frame: The limits (parameters) around a population of potential subjects describing who will be included in the research sample.

population validity: Delineation of the range of the population to which the findings of a study can be generalized. This is part of external validity.

positivism: Belief in the scientific method, based on direct observation and measurement, as the key to a true understanding as elaborated by the Vienna Circle of philosophers in 1922.

power analysis: Statistical approach to determine the likelihood of not committing a Type II error when rejecting a null hypothesis (Power = $1 - \beta$).

precision: In psychological measurement, the amount of potential measurement error is expressed in terms of precision. Some forms of measurement have a potential for high precision, (ratio scales) and others for lower levels of precision (ordinal scales).

predictive validity: Ability of a test or measure to estimate how well a person will perform a task. High predictive validity implies excellent predictions, while low predictive validity indicates much error in the predictions.

predictor variable: Variable used to predict scores on an outcome or criterion variable.

pre-experiment: Experimental design fraught with many potential problems of validity due to the lack of a control group and no random assignment of subjects to groups.

presentism: Source of historical error involving the use of current moral standards and values to interpret past events and individuals.

primary sources: Report on research written by the researcher who conducted the research and considered part of the literature of the scientific field.

principal component: Central factor in factor analysis providing a single core of communality to the various measures. First used by Charles Spearman in his structuring of the human intellect.

probability sampling: Sampling from a population such that each individual in the population has an equal chance of being selected.

program audit: Abbreviated form of program evaluation frequently conducted by professional societies to monitor members.

projective assessments: Tests that involve the presentation of ambiguous stimuli in which participants are asked to interpret or tell stories about the ambiguous stimulus.

prompts: In questionnaire construction, prompts provide the researcher with a list of possible extra questions to use in eliciting extended answers from respondents.

protected Fisher LSD test: More formal name applied when the least significant difference test is used following a significant ANOVA finding.

proximal similarity: The degree of similarity between the elements of a study and the external elements where the researcher plans to apply the results of the study.

pseudo-evaluation: Ersatz scientific survey or other "evaluation" method designed to push a cause or point of view, not to collect meaningful data.

pseudo-science: Ersatz science for an area of inquiry or practice that has a superficial appearance of being scientific but upon careful inspection can be seen to violate one or more principles of the scientific method or contain fallacies against which the scientific method attempts to guard.

psychoanalysis: Method employed to analyze psychic disorders through various interpretative approaches involving talk therapy.

psychological constructs: Overlapping conceptualizations describing a psychological activity or pattern of behaviors that cannot be directly measured.

purposeful sampling: Nonprobability sample in which subjects are selected for study or observation on the basis of the researcher's judgments.

push surveying: Pseudoscientific survey designed to push the researcher's hidden agenda, not to collect meaningful data.

qualitative research: Research methods assuming multiple dynamic realities that can only be understood in context and interpreted from the point of view of informants.

quality of prevention efforts: In evaluation research, a statement of the efficaciousness of an intervention or treatment.

quantity of services: In an evaluation, the amount of service delivered in terms of number of clients served, hours of therapy provided, or other numerical expression of quantity of effort.

quartiles: In a distribution of percentiles, the points at the 25th, 50th, and 75th percentiles define the four quartiles of the distribution.

quasi-experimental designs: Design for experiments in which participants are not randomly assigned to the experimental and control groups and often are composed of samples of convenience.

quasi-experiment: Experiment employing a quasi-experimental design.

quintile: In a distribution of percentiles, the points at the 20th, 40th, 60th, and 80th percentile define the five quintiles.

quota sample: A group of participants selected to match specified quotas to represent specified subgroups of the population.

random association method: Creativity exercise to increase production of divergent thinking by starting with known associations and identifying new, divergent ways to reformulate the concept.

random cluster sampling: Random sampling from a natural cluster within a population.

random sample: Selection of members or elements to be included in a sample in such a way that each element of the original population has an equal chance of inclusion.

randomly: Method for the selection of the members or elements to be included in a sample in such a way that each element of the original population has an equal chance of inclusion.

randomly select: Select the members or elements to be included in a sample in such a way that each element of the framed population has an equal chance of inclusion.

range: Distance (as measured in data points) between the highest and lowest scores on a distribution that may be found by subtracting the lowest score from the highest.

Rasch IRT: Test statisticians use this method (developed by Georg Rasch) for analyzing each individual item of a test for its functioning with differing groups of test takers.

rater drift: Small changes in the evaluation standards that may occur when raters measure large numbers of outcomes or items; rater drift has the potential to threaten the validity of the ratings.

ratio scale: Mathematically appropriate scale of measurement based on consistent real numbers.

raw score: Number of questions answered correctly on a test or assessment.

reactive measure: Pretest reacts with the subjects so as to directly or indirectly change the outcome posttest scores.

real numbers: Rational numbers along a line extending to infinity above and below zero with all fractions and decimals available between whole integers.

realistic approach: Research method from cultural anthropology in which the researcher assumes a role as a member in the community being studied.

reflection: Operative internal step in making a judgment about a phenomenon.

regression toward mediocrity: Term introduced by Sir Francis Galton that became the modern term **regression toward the mean.**

regression toward the mean: Statistical phenomenon producing a natural variation in the repeated measurement of data that looks like a shift away from the extreme score levels toward the median.

reliability: A statement of the stability and/or consistency of test scores from the administration of a measure or of the findings of a research study.

repeated-measures design: Research design in which each participant is tested on the dependent variable at more than one point in time.

representativeness: Extent to which a sample is identical to the intended population.

research blinds: Research design features that separate research assistants and participants from the details of the research design as a method of controlling bias.

research question: A situation that a researcher wants to find out more about through an organized research study. May also take the form of a specific statement of purpose.

restories: A recasting of the life stories of participants as a step in the narrative analysis research process.

reversal technique: Creativity improvement method that reverses the given assumptions and asks questions based on the opposite premise.

rival hypothesis: An extraneous hypothesis that challenges the main independent-dependent variable relationship.

robust: Having a lack of sensitivity to a departure from an assumption's requirements.

Rosenthal effect: Named for Robert Rosenthal, who documented how humans tend to fulfill their expectations for outcomes even in highly controlled environments.

rubber chicken circuit: A round of luncheons and/or dinners, often featuring chicken, that a lecturer attends to promote a cause or program.

running head: Very abbreviated identification of a written report appearing on the top of each page.

runs test: Nonparametric test procedure that assumes two sets of observations are independent and that there is no pattern to the combined distributions.

sample: A portion of the population from which data are collected and used to estimate various dimensions of the whole population.

sample of convenience: A nonstatistical sample drawn from subjects available to the researcher and not representative of a larger population.

sampling: Process of selecting participants from a framed population for inclusion in a group.

sampling error: Difference between a sample's statistic, for example the mean ($\bar{X}$), and the equivalent parameter of the population (μ).

sandwich generation: Generation of adults with both child care responsibilities and caregiving responsibilities for aging relatives, usually parents.

satori: Word from the Japanese lexicon for "true and total understanding."

saturation: *See* **saturation point.**

saturation point: Saturation occurs in purposive sampling when the addition of more units (e.g., more cases) does not result in improved information. In qualitative research, it is the point at which the meaningful data from a study have been gathered and additional informers are only providing redundant information.

scaled scores: Raw scores that underwent a statistical transformation so that users of the data can better compare scores between individuals.

scatterplots: Two-dimensional (linear-coordinate) graphic presentation of the simultaneous outcome for two variables measured on one group of subjects.

scientific inquiry: Method of adding new knowledge by systematic procedures for the collection and analysis of data.

selective coding: An advanced step in the method of grounded theory in which one category from previous coding is selected to be the core category and all other categories are related to it.

self-esteem: The evaluation made by an individual of his or her self-concept.

semantic differential scale (SD): Rating scale presenting two polar opposite descriptors of an object being evaluated; the descriptors are connected by a number line on which the respondent indicates the strength of his or her opinion.

semilingualism: Stage in learning a second language in which the language learner is losing proficiency in the native language and is not yet fluent in the new one.

semistructured interviews: Interviews using a structured interview guide with predetermined questions that also allows the interviewer to follow leads introduced by participants.

serum analysis: Literally "blood test," this is a biochemical analysis of the contents and makeup of blood.

short-term outcomes: Immediate changes in attitudes/perceptions, knowledge, skills, and/or behavior.

simple effects: Follow-up to a significant interaction effect in ANOVA in which the complex interaction is divided into several smaller, simple tests of effects using a priori methods.

simple random sampling: Sample of individuals drawn by a procedure in which all possible cases in the framed population have an independent and equal chance of being selected.

single-blind study: Research design that prevents subjects from knowing whether they are part of the treatment or control group, thereby reducing possible bias and improving internal validity.

skew: Asymmetry in a distribution of scores such that an unusually large number of cases is above or below the median of the data, resulting in the separation of the mean and the median.

slope: Gradient or inclination of a line that is not horizontal or vertical.

snowball sample: A form of nonprobability sampling in which current research participants are recruited to ask other people whom they know to participate.

social learning: Theory that individuals can learn in social contexts through observation, modeling, and vicarious self-administered rewards.

split-half reliability coefficients: Internal consistency reliability of a measure determined by correlating half of the items with the other half.

split-plot: A term used to describe a repeated-measure ANOVA.

spread of effect: Threat to internal validity posed by treatment group subjects sharing the treatment with individuals in the control group.

stability: Reliability that demonstrates that the scores obtained on a measure by a group of subjects will be correlated with a retest using the same measure and subjects at a later time.

standard deviation: Square root of variance (i.e., square root of the sum of the squared individual variations of scores from the mean score).

standard error of measurement: Statistical estimate of the probable range within which an individual's true score on a measure falls.

standard score: A derived test score expressed in deviation units indicating how far the score is from the mean score of the group.

standardized score: *See* **standard score.**

standards-based assessment: High-stakes tests linked with the approved standards for learning in a particular field.

static group: Nonprobability sample of subjects that usually occurs as a naturally occurring group and is a sample of convenience.

statistical attenuation: Loss of treatment effectiveness or correlational relationship by only examining a limited range of levels of the experimental effect, sometimes known as regression dilution.

statistical power: Probability that a particular test of statistical significance will lead to the rejection of a false null hypothesis. Signified as β.

stochastically: Type of mathematical dominance in which one set of observations is superior to another set on a case-by-case basis.

stratified random sampling: Probability sampling in which a population is divided into groups (or strata) on the basis of characteristics such as gender, age, ethnicity, and so forth; random samples are drawn within each stratum.

structural equation modeling: Hybrid statistical approach for building an explanatory model for an outcome or behavior that may include known variables and latent variables uncovered by the modeling.

subjective: Interpretative method for finding the essence of a thing as opposed to an empirical approach to measuring its properties.

subtraction residuals: When the subtrahend is mathematically subtracted from the minuend, the result is a remainder known as a subtraction residual.

subventions: Monies provided by an external agency (governmental or philanthropic) in support of a program or project.

summative: Ultimate outcome or final products and achievements of a study.

summative evaluation: Evaluation focused only on final outcomes.

systematic sampling: Probability sampling in which every kth unit on a list of the members of a framed population is selected for inclusion in the sample after the first unit is selected at random.

table of specifications: Two-dimensional blueprint for a test. Dimensions are the content of the test and the level of cognition the test items require. This approach ensures the measure will have content validity.

tau-equivalent: Term describing the assumption that all items of a semantic scale have equal variances.

technical manual: Informative manual accompanying a published measure providing normative, reliability, and validation evidence.

telemental: Use of technology to provide mental health therapies, including counseling at a distance.

test-retest reliability: The correlation between the scores from two sequential administrations of a test to one group of subjects. Provides an estimation of test stability.

theoretical sample: Qualitative research approach for selecting participants who best represent the dimensions of a concept across a range of settings.

thick description: Generalizability of qualitative research evidence based on full and complete descriptions of the context and meaning of observed actions, behaviors, and words of those studied.

think tanks: Centers for interdisciplinary research, usually sponsored by a corporation, philanthropy, or university.

third force: Name applied to client-centered, phenomenological approaches to psychotherapy and counseling as developed by Carl Rogers (the first two forces are behaviorism and psychoanalysis).

third-party agencies: Health insurance companies and governmental agencies that pay the cost of an individual's health care.

third-party fee-for-service: Describes health insurance companies and governmental agencies that pay the cost of an individual's health care.

threshold loss: Concept of reliability in criterion-referenced tests such as the NBCC state licensing examination, expressed as the coefficient kappa (κ).

Thurstone scale: Hierarchical format for a measurement scale assessing a psychological affect or attitude.

time sampling: Observational system involving making periodic observations precisely after a pre-selected unit of time has elapsed.

time series designs: Research design in which the dependent variable is measured at a number of points in time, usually including before, during, and following a treatment.

transductive: Logic of small children that moves from particulars to other particulars by which contiguity implies causation.

transferability: One of four hallmarks of the fidelity of a qualitative research study that implies the findings have meaning in other venues and under different circumstances.

transformative mixed methods research: Mixed methods research with the superordinate worldview of one or more dimensions of social justice.

treatment group: Subject group that is presented with the experimental treatment.

triangle of error: When a researcher uses triangulation in designing a study, the parameters of possible error are set by the differences in findings from the research approaches.

triangulate: Use of more than one imperfect data collection alternative in which each option is vulnerable to different potential sources of error.

triangulation: Method used to establish credibility in qualitative social research. It involves using more than two perspectives to determine the accuracy of some aspect of the study and its findings.

triple-blind study: Research design that protects against bias by not allowing participants, research assistants, or data managers to know which participants were in the treatment group(s) and the control group.

true experiment: Research design including two or more groups with randomly assigned subjects and a control group.

trustworthiness: Qualitative research equivalent to the concept of internal validity in empirical research studies. Includes four dimensions: credibility, transferability, dependability, and confirmability.

t-**test:** A probability-based method for testing null hypotheses based on a modification of the Gaussian normal distribution of errors.

two-tailed hypothesis: A hypothesis that a difference exists between two data sets that does not specify the direction of the difference.

two-way factorial ANOVA: ANOVA with two independent variables.

Type I error: Conclusion based on empirical data that a treatment or intervention works when it actually does not; also called a false positive.

Type II error: Conclusion based on an analysis of data that there is no evidence a treatment works when it actually does; also called a false negative.

valance: Directionality of questionnaire items switching between high numbers, representing agreement with a premise, on some items and low numbers, indicating agreement with the same premise, on other items.

validity: In measurement, a statement of both the appropriateness of the test and its components and of the veracity and utility of the test scores and their interpretations.

value-free: In value-neutral research, an effort is made to prevent all personal values of the researcher from impacting the research design or conclusions.

value-neutral: Stance assumed in employing the "scientific method" whereby the researcher attempts to remove all subjectivity and potential for bias from his or her research.

values: Individual standards defining concepts of good and bad and providing guidelines for behavior and living one's life.

variability: Statistical measure of the amount that individual scores on a measurement will vary from, or spread out from, the mean of the data.

variable: A factor, conceptual entity, characteristic, or attribute likely to vary between individuals and/ or within individuals over time.

variance: The average of the sum of the squared deviations of individual scores from the mean.

variance between groups: Also defined as between-groups mean square in ANOVA, where it represents the variance found to be brought about by the effect of the treatment.

variance within groups: Also defined as within-groups mean square in ANOVA, where it represents the variance in the data related to individual subjects' a priori differences and is viewed as error variance.

variance-covariance matrix: Matrix that summarizes all variances and all possible covariances for a list of variables, in which the variances all fall along the main diagonal and the possible covariances in the off-diagonal area.

Venn diagram: Illustration using circles to represent sets (e.g., variance), with the position and overlap of the circles indicating the relationships between the sets (e.g., the commonality of variance from two variables).

vicarious learning: Theory that learning can occur by observing the behavior of others and the outcomes they receive (*See* **social learning**).

voice: Term from literature describing each writer's unique way of expressing his or her ideas.

volunteer samples: Nonprobability sample of individuals who volunteer or otherwise provide prior approval for their participation in a research study.

within-groups mean square (WGMS): The sum of the amount of individual variation within each group or experimental condition divided by the number of subjects less the number of groups.

within-groups sum of squares (WGSS): Component in the calculation of the within-groups mean square.

within-site case study: Method for presenting cogent data drawn from a single case study.

within-subjects design: Component of repeated-measure ANOVA for testing hypotheses that requires the retesting of the same subjects.

working paper: Draft of a document still in development, usually inappropriate for attribution or citation.

writer's block: Psychological condition in which a writer loses the ability to create new work even though his or her desire and ability are unchanged.

Yates's correction for continuity: Correction to chi-square distribution for small samples.

zero-order correlation: A simple Pearson correlation between two continuous variables.

z-score: Standard score with a distribution of continuous data that has a mean of zero and a standard deviation of 1.00.

References

Aanstoos, C. S., Serlin, I., & Greening, T. (2000). History of Division 32 (Humanistic Psychology) of the American Psychological Association. In D. A. Sewsbury (Ed.), *Unification through division: Histories of the divisions of the American Psychological Association* (Vol. 5). Washington, DC: American Psychological Association.

Abbot, N. C., Harkness, E. F., Stevinson, C., Marshall, F. P., Conn, D. A., & Ernst, E. (2001). Spiritual healing as a therapy for chronic pain: A randomized clinical trial. *Journal for the International Association for the Study of Pain, 91*(1), 79–89.

Adler-Baeder, F., Kerpelman, J. L., Schramm, D. G., Higginbotham, B., & Paulk, A. (2007). The impact of relationship education on adolescents of diverse backgrounds. *Family Relations, 56*(3), 291–303.

Aiken, L. R. (1997). *Questionnaires and inventories: Surveying opinions and assessing personality.* New York, NY: John Wiley and Sons.

Akos, P. (2004). Outcomes research on school counseling. In B. T. Erford (Ed.), *Professional school counseling: A handbook of theories, programs, and practices* (pp. 35–42). Austin, TX: CAPS Press/PRO-ED.

Aldhous, P. (2011, November 17). Psychologist admits faking data in dozens of studies. *New Scientist.* Retrieved from http://www.newscientist.com/article/dn21118-psychologist-admits-faking-data-in-dozens-of-studies.html

Alise, M. A., & Teddlie, C. (2010). A continuation of the paradigm wars? Prevalence rates of methodological approaches across the social/behavioral sciences. *Journal of Mixed Methods Research, 4*(2), 103–126.

American Counseling Association. (2003). *Standards for qualifications of test users.* Retrieved from http://www.theaaceonline.com/standards.pdf

American Counseling Association. (2005). *ACA code of ethics.* Alexandria, VA: American Counseling Association. Retrieved from http://www.counseling.org/ethics/feedback/ACA2005Code.pdf

American Evaluation Association. (2005). *About us.* Retrieved from http://www.eval.org/News/news.htm

American Evaluation Association. (2011). *Statement on cultural competence in evaluation.* Retrieved from http://www.eval.org/ccmaterials.asp

(AMHCA) American Mental Health Counselors Association. (2010). *Principles for AMHCA code of ethics.* Alexandria, VA: American Mental Health Counselors Association. Retrieved from https://www.amhca.org/assets/news/AMHCA_Code_of_Ethics_2010_w_pagination_cxd_51110.pdf

American Personnel and Guidance Association. (1961). Ethical standards: American Personnel and Guidance Association. *Personnel and Guidance Journal, 40*(2), 206–209.

American Psychiatric Association. (2012). *Diagnostic and statistical manual of mental disorders* (5th ed.). Washington, DC: American Psychiatric Association.

American Psychological Association. (2010a). *Ethical principles of psychologists and code of conduct.* Retrieved from http://www.apa.org/ethics/code/index.aspx

American Psychological Association. (2010b). *Publication manual of the American Psychological Association* (6th ed.). Washington, DC: American Psychological Association.

American Psychological Association. (2011). Summary report of journal operations, 2010. *The American Psychologist, 66*(5), 405–406. doi: 10.1037/a0023978

American School Counselor Association. (2012). *The ASCA national model: A framework for school counseling programs* (3rd ed.). Alexandria, VA: American School Counselor Association.

American School Counselor Association & Association for Assessment in Counseling (1998). *Competencies in assessment and evaluation for school counselors.* Alexandria, VA: American School Counselor Association & Association for Assessment in Counseling.

Andrews, W. H., & Hammack, T. S. (2003). Food sampling and preparation of sample homogenate. In *Bacteriological analytical manual* (Chapter 1). Washington, DC: US Food and Drug Administration, Department of Health and Human Services. Retrieved from http://www.fda.gov/Food/ScienceResearch/LaboratoryMethods/BacteriologicalAnalyticalManualBAM/ucm063335.htm

Anton, H., Kolman, B., & Averbach, B. (1988). *Mathematics with applications for the management, life, and social sciences.* New York, NY: Harcourt Brace Jovanovich.

Arenson, K. W. (2005, March 22). Faculty panel at Cal faults way to pick Merit scholars. *The New York Times,* p. A14.

AACE (Association for Assessment in Counseling and Education). (2010). *Standards for assessment in mental health counseling.* Retrieved from http://www.theaaceonline.com/AACE-AMHCA.pdf

Association for Humanistic Psychology. (n.d.). *Historic review of humanistic psychology: Humanistic psychology overview.* Tiburon, CA: Association for Humanistic Psychology. Retrieved from http://www.ahpweb.org/

ASPPB (Association of State and Provincial Psychology Boards). (2011). *Information for psychologists teaching professional psychology.* Retrieved from http://www.asppb.net/i4a/pages/index.cfm?pageid = 3479

Ataöv, A., Brøgger, B., & Hildrum, J. M. (2010). An action research approach to the inclusion of immigrants in work life and local community life: Preparation of a participatory realm. *Action Research, 8*(3), 237–265. doi: 10.1177/1476750309335209

Atkins, P., Coffey, A., & Delamont, S. (2001). A debate about our canon. *Qualitative Research, 1*(1), 5–21. doi: 10.1177/146879410100100101

Ayer, A. J. (1952). *Language, truth, and logic.* Mineola, NY: Dover.

Ayers, D. (2002). Mission priorities of community colleges in the southern United States. *Community College Review, 30*(3), 11–30.

Babbie, E. (1995). *The practice of social research* (7th ed.). Belmont, CA: Wadsworth.

Bailey, J. (2008). First steps in qualitative data analysis: Transcribing. *Family Practice, 25*(2), 127–131.

Bailey, S. J., & Deen, M. Y. (2002). Development of a web-based evaluation system: A tool for measuring life skills in youth and family programs. *Family Relations, 51*(2), 138–147.

Baillie, C. (2003). *Enhancing student's creativity through creative thinking techniques.* Unpublished document, Queens University, Ontario, Canada. Retrieved from http://www.uwa.edu.au/__data/assets/pdf_file/0009/825246/Enhancing_studentsrsquo_creativity_through_creative_thinking_techniques.pdf

Balkin, R. S., & Sheperis, C. J. (2011). Evaluating and reporting statistical power in counseling research. *Journal of Counseling and Development, 89*(3), 268–272.

Bamberger, M., Rugh, J., & Mabry, L. (2012). *Real world evaluation: Working under budget, time, data, and political constraints* (2nd ed.). Thousand Oaks, CA: Sage.

Bandura, A. (1976). *Social learning theory.* Upper Saddle River, NJ: Prentice Hall.

Bandura, A., & McDonald, F. J. (1963). The influence of social reinforcement and the behavior of models in shaping children's moral judgments. *Journal of Abnormal and Social Psychology, 67,* 274–281.

Bangert, A. W., & Baumberger, J. P. (2005). Research and statistical techniques used in the *Journal of Counseling & Development. Journal of Counseling & Development, 83*(4), 480–487.

Barlow, D. H., & Hayes, S. C. (1979). Alternating treatments design: One strategy for comparing the effects of two treatments in a single subject. *Journal of Applied Behavioral Analysis, 12*(2), 199–210. doi: 10.1901/jaba.1979.12-199

Bauerlein, M., Gad-el-Hak, M., Grody, W., McKelvey, B.,& Trimble, S. W. (2010, June 13). We must stop the avalanche of low-quality research [Commentary]. *The Chronicle of Higher Education.* Retrieved from http://chronicle.com/article/We-Must-Stop-the-Avalanche-of/65890/

Bauman, S. (2004). School counselors and research revisited. *Professional School Counseling, 7*(3), 141–151.

Baxter, P., & Jack, S. (2008). Qualitative case study methodology: Study design and implications for novice researchers. *Qualitative Report, 13*(4), 544–559.

Beck, A. T., Steer, R. A., & Brown, G. K. (1996). *Beck Depression Inventory: Manual* (2nd ed.). Boston, MA: Harcourt Brace.

Berg, B. L. (2004). *Qualitative research methods for the social sciences* (5th ed.). Boston, MA: Allyn & Bacon.

Berliner, D. C. (2002). Educational research: The hardest science of all. *Educational Researcher, 31*(8), 18–20.

Black, E. (2003, November 25). The horrifying American roots of Nazi eugenics. *George Mason University's History News Network* [Blog]. Retrieved from http://hnn.us/articles/1796.html

Bloom, B. S. et al. (Eds.). (1956). *Taxonomy of educational objectives: The classification of educational goals. Handbook I: Cognitive domain.* New York, NY: David McKay.

Boeree, C. G. (1999–2000). *Wilhelm Wündt and William James.* Unpublished manuscript, Psychology Department, Shippensburg University of Pennsylvania. Retrieved from http://www.ship .edu/~cgboeree/wundtjames.html

Boser, S. (2007). Power, ethics, and the IRB: Dissonance over human participant review of participatory research. *Qualitative Inquiry, 13*(8), 1060–1074. doi 10.1177/1077800407308220

Box, G. E. P. (1953). Non-normality and tests on variances. *Biometrika, 40*(3/4), 318–335. doi:10.1093/biomet/40.3-4.318

Bracht, G. H., & Glass, G. V. (1968). The external validity of experiments. *American Educational Research Journal, 5*(4), 437–474. doi:10.3102/00028312005004437

Bradbury, H., Mirvis, P., Neilsen, E., & Pasmore, W. (2007). Action research at work: Creating the future following the path from Lewin. In P. Reason & H. Bradbury (Eds.), *The Sage handbook of action research: Participative inquiry and practice* (pp. 77–92). Thousand Oaks, CA: Sage.

Bradbury, H., & Reason, P. (2006). Conclusion: Broadening the bandwidth of validity; Issues and choice-points for improving the quality of action research. In P. Reason & H. Bradbury (Eds.), *Handbook of action research* (Concise paperback ed., pp. 343–351). Thousand Oaks, CA: Sage.

Briere, J. (2000). *Cognitive distortion scales.* Lutz, FL: Psychological Assessment Resources.

Brown, T. E. (2001). *Brown-attention-deficit-disorder scales for children and adolescents.* San Antonio, TX: Harcourt Assessment Division, Psychological Corporation.

Brown, W. (1910). Some experiment results in the correlation of mental abilities. *British Journal of Psychology, 3,* 296–322.

Brunswik, E. (1956). Historical and thematic relations of psychology to other sciences. *Scientific Monthly, 83,* 151–161.

Bryman, A. (2004). *Social research methods* (2nd ed.). Oxford, UK: Oxford University Press.

Buchanan, P. J. (2011). *Suicide of a super power: Will America survive to 2025?* New York, NY: Thomas Dunne Books.

Bugental, J. F. T. (1964). The third force in psychology. *Journal of Humanistic Psychology 4*(1), 19–25. doi:10.1177/002216786400400102

Burkert, W. (1991). *Greek religion: Archaic and classical* (J. Raffan, trans.). Malden, MA: Wiley-Blackwell.

Burnard, P. (2004). Writing a qualitative research report. *Accident and Emergency Nursing, 12*(3), 176–181. doi: 10.1016/j.aaen.2003.11.006

Burns, D. (2007). *Systematic action research: A strategy for whole system change.* Bristol, UK: Policy Press.

Cady, S. H., & Caster, M. A. (2000). A diet for action research: An integrated problem and appreciative focuses approach to organizational development. *Journal of Organizational Development, 18*(4), 79–93.

Campbell, D. T. (1957). Factors relevant to the validity of experiments in social settings. *Psychological Bulletin, 54*(4), 297–312. Retrieved from http://campus.murraystate.edu/academic/faculty/mark .wattier/Campbell1957.pdf

Campbell, D. T., & Fiske, D.W. (1959). Convergent and discriminant validation by the multitrait-multimethod matrix. *Psychological Bulletin, 56,* 81–105.

Campbell, D. T., & Russo, M. J. (1999). *Social experimentation* (Sage Classics 1). Thousand Oaks, CA: Sage.

Campbell, D. T., & Stanley, J. C. (1963). Experimental and quasi-experimental designs for research on teaching. In N. L. Gage (Ed.), *Handbook of research on teaching* (pp. 171–246). Chicago, IL: Rand McNally.

CCPA (Canadian Counselling and Psychotherapy Association). (2003). *Accreditation procedures and standards for counselor education programs at the master's level.* Retrieved from http://www.ccpa-accp.ca/en/accreditationmanual/

Carey, B. (2012, February 13). The therapist may see you anytime, anywhere. *The New York Times.* Retrieved from http://www.nytimes.com/2012/02/14/health/feeling-anxious-soon-there-will-be-an-app-for-that.html.

Carroll, M. (2010, October 27). *A professional reader of voters' minds discusses his 'blunt instrument.'* WNYC. Retrieved from http://www.wnyc.org/articles/new-york-vote/2010/oct/27/professional-reader-voters-minds-discusses-his-blunt-instrument/

Carter, E. M., & Carter, M. V. (2007). A social psychological analysis of anomie among National Football League players. *International Review for the Sociology of Sport, 42*(3), 243–270.

Cassell, C., & Symon, G. (1994). Qualitative research in work contexts. In C. Cassell & G. Symon (Eds.), *Qualitative methods in organizational research, a practical guide* (pp. 1–13). London, UK: Sage.

Castro, F. G., Kellison, J. G., Boyd, S. J., & Kopak, A. (2010). A methodology for conducting integrative mixed methods research and data analysis. *Journal of Mixed Methods Research, 4*(4), 342–360. doi: 10.1177/1558689810382916

Centers for Medicare and Medicaid Services. (2012). *Medicare and your mental health benefits.* Baltimore, MD: US Department of Health and Human Services. Retrieved from http://www .medicare.gov/publications/pubs/pdf/10184.pdf

Chandler, D., & Torbert, W. R. (2003). Transforming inquiry into action: Interweaving 27 flavours of action research. *Action Research, 1*(2), 133–152. doi 10.1177/14767503030012002

Charmaz, K. (2006). *Constructing grounded theory: A practical guide through qualitative analysis.* Thousand Oaks, CA: Sage.

Chemyshenko, O. S., & Ones, D. S. (1999). How selective are psychology graduate programs? The effect of the selection ratio on the GRE score validity. *Educational and Psychological Measurement, 59*(6), 951–961. doi: 10.1177/00131649921970279

Christians, C. G. (2005). Ethics and politics in qualitative research. In N. K. Denzin & Y. S. Lincoln (Eds.), *The Sage handbook of qualitative research* (3rd ed., pp. 139–164). Thousand Oaks, CA: Sage.

Chubin, D. E., May, G. S., & Babco, E. L. (2005). Diversifying the engineering workforce. *Journal of Engineering Education. 94*(1), 73–86.

Cicourel, A. V. (1964). *Method and measurement in sociology.* New York, NY: Free Press.

Clark, W., Polakov, W. N., & Trabold, F. W. (2010). *The Gantt chart: A working tool of management.* Ithaca, NY: Cornell University Library/Nabu Press.

Code of Federal Regulations. (2009). *Human subjects research (45 CFR 46).* Retrieved from http://www .hhs.gov/ohrp/humansubjects/guidance/

Coghlan, D., & Brannick, T. (2010). *Doing action research in your own organization* (3rd ed.). Thousand Oaks, CA: Sage.

Cohen, J. (1960). A coefficient of agreement for nominal scales. *Educational and Psychological Measurement, 20,* 37–46.

Cohen, J. (1988). *Statistical power analysis for the behavioral sciences* (2nd ed.). Hillsdale, NJ: Lawrence Erlbaum Associates.

Cole, M., Hood, L. & McDermott, R. P. (1997). Concepts of ecological validity: Their differing implications for comparative cognitive research. In M. Cole, Y. Engeström, and O. A. Vasquez (Eds.), *Mind, culture, and activity: Seminal papers from the laboratory of comparative human cognition* (pp. 49–57). New York, NY: Cambridge University Press.

(COAMFTE) Commission on Accreditation for Marriage and Family Therapy Education. (2005). *Accreditation standards: Graduate & post-graduate marriage and family therapy training programs* (Version 11.0). Retrieved from http://www.aamft.org/imis15/Documents/Accreditation_Standards_Version_11.pdf

Comte, A. (1988). *Introduction to positive philosophy* (Trans. E Ferré). Indianapolis, IN: Hackett. (Originally published 1865)

Conners, C. K., Erhardt, D., & Sparrow, E. (1997). *Conners rating scale—revised: Technical manual.* North Tonawanda, NY: Multi-Health Systems.

Conners, C. K., Erhardt, D., & Sparrow, E. (1999). *Conners adult ADHS rating scale.* North Tonawanda, NY: Multi-Health Systems.

Cook, T. D., & Campbell, D. T. (1979). *Quasi-experimentation: Design and analysis issues for field settings.* Boston, MA: Houghton Mifflin.

Cooley, W. W., & Lohnes, P. R. (1971). *Multivariate data analysis.* New York, NY: John Wiley and Sons.

Corbin, J. M., & Strauss, A. L. (2008). *Basics of qualitative research: Techniques and procedures for developing grounded theory* (3rd ed.). Thousand Oaks, CA: Sage.

Cortese, J. (2007). *Internet learning and the building of knowledge.* Youngstown, NY: Cambria Press.

CACREP (Council for Accreditation of Counseling and Related Educational Programs). (2009). *Standards.* Alexandria, VA: Council for Accreditation of Counseling and Related Educational Programs. Retrieved from http://www.cacrep.org/doc/2009%20Standards%20with%20cover.pdf

CORE (Council on Rehabilitation Education). (2011). *CORE standards.* Schaumburg, IL: Council on Rehabilitation Education. Retrieved from http://www.core-rehab.org/COREStandards/

Cox, J., & Cox, K. B. (2008). *Your opinion, please! How to build the best questionnaires in the field of education* (2nd ed.). Thousand Oaks, CA: Corwin.

Cramer, D., & Howitt, D. (2004). *The Sage dictionary of statistics.* Thousand Oaks, CA: Sage.

Creswell, J. W. (2008). *Educational research: Planning, conducting and evaluating quantitative and qualitative research.* (3rd ed.). Upper Saddle River, NJ: Pearson.

Creswell, J. W. (2012). *Educational research: Planning conducting, and evaluating quantitative and qualitative research* (4th ed.). Boston, MA: Pearson.

Creswell, J. W. (2013). *Qualitative inquiry and research design: Choosing among five traditions* (3rd ed.). Thousand Oaks, CA: Sage.

Creswell, J. W., & Plano Clark, V. L. (2010). *Designing and conducting mixed method research* (2nd ed.). Thousand Oaks, CA: Sage.

Creswell, J. W., & Tashakkori, A. (2007). Developing publishable mixed methods manuscripts [Editorial]. *Journal of Mixed Method Research, 1*(2), 107–110. doi: 10.1177/1558689806298644

Crick, F. (1995). *The astonishing hypothesis: The scientific search for the soul.* New York, NY: Touchstone.

Cronbach, L. J. (1951). Coefficient alpha and the internal structure of tests. *Psychometrika, 16,* 297–334.

Cronbach, L. J., & Meehl, P. E. (1955). Construct validity in psychological tests. *Psychological Bulletin, 52,* 281–302.

Dalrymple, G. B. (1991). *The age of the earth.* Stanford, CA: Stanford University Press.

Dalton, J. (1808). *A new system of chemical philosophy.* London, UK: William Dawson & Sons. Retrieved from http://archive.org/details/newsystemofchemi014416mbp/

Darwin, C. R. (1877). A biographical sketch of an infant. *Mind: A Quarterly Review of Psychology and Philosophy, 2*(7), 285–294. In C. D. Green (Ed.), *Classics in the history of psychology.* Retrieved from http://psychclassics.yorku.ca/Darwin/infant.htm

Davidson, C. (2009). Transcription: Imperatives for qualitative research. *International Journal for Qualitative Research, 8*(2), 35–52. Retrieved from http://ejournals.library.ualberta.ca/index.php/IJQM/article/view/4205/5401/

Dawes, J. (2008). Do data characteristics change according to the number of scale points used? An experiment using 5-point, 7-point, and 10-point scales. *International Journal of Market Research, 50*(1), 61–77.

Dawes, R. M. (1977). Suppose we measured height with rating scales instead of rulers. *Applied Psychological Measurement, 1*(2), 267–273. doi: 10.1177/014662167700100213

Death Penalty Information Center. (2012). *State statutes prohibiting the death penalty for people with mental retardation.* Retrieved from http://www.deathpenaltyinfo.org/state-statutes-prohibiting-death-penalty-people-mental-retardation/

Deis, J. N., Smith, K. M., Warren, M. D., Throop, P. G., Hickson, G. B., Joers, B. J., & Deshpande, J. K. (2009). *Transforming the morbidity and mortality conference into an instrument for systemwide improvement.* Unpublished document, Vanderbilt University Medical Center. Retrieved from http://www.ahrq.gov/downloads/pub/advances2/vol2/Advances-Deis_82.pdf

Delgado, R., & Stefancic, J. (2001). *Critical race theory: An introduction.* New York, NY: New York University Press.

De Moivre, A. (1985). On the law of normal probability. In H. W. Walker (Ed.), *A source booking mathematics* (pp. 75–84). Mineola, NY: Dover. (Originally published 1738)

Denny, T. (2011). Story telling and educational understanding. *Journal of Multidisciplinary Evaluation, 7*(15), 258–271. (Originally published 1978)

Denzin, N. K. (1978). *The research act: A theoretical introduction to sociological methods.* New York, NY: McGraw-Hill.

Derby, K. S., Cuthrell, K., Caberto, C., Carmella, S. G., Franke, A. A., Hecht, S. E., . . . Le Marchand, L. (2008). Nicotine metabolism in three ethnic/racial groups with different risks of lung cancer. *Cancer Epidemiology Biomarkers and Prevention, 17*(12), 3526–3535. doi:10.1158/1055-9965.EPI-08-0424

DeTardo-Bora, K. A. (2004). Action research in a world of positivist-oriented review boards. *Action Research, 2*(3), 237–253. doi: 10.1177/1476750304045938

Dick, B. (2000). Grounded theory: A thumbnail sketch. *Resource papers in Action Research.* Retrieved from http://www.aral.com.au/resources/grounded.html

Dong, Y. R. (2007). Learning to think in English. *Educational Leadership, 64,* 22–26.

Donley, E. A., Claussen, N. R., Cornish, S. L., Roberts, J. L., Cornell, E. A., & Wieman, C. E. (2001). Dynamics of collapsing and exploding Bose-Einstein condensates. *Nature, 412*(6844), 295–299.

Duma, R. J. (1971). First of all do no harm. *New England Journal of Medicine, 285,* 1258–1259.

Duncan, B., Sparks, J., Miller, S., Bohanske, R., & Claud, D. (2006). Giving youth a voice: A preliminary study of the reliability and validity of a brief outcome measure for children, adolescents, and caretakers. *Journal of Brief Therapy, 5*(2), 66–82.

Eagelton, T. (2008). *Literary theory: An introduction* (3rd ed.). Minneapolis: University of Minnesota Press.

Ellis, C. (2007). Telling secrets, revealing lives: Relational ethics in research with intimate others. *Qualitative Inquiry, 13*(1), 3–29. doi: 10.1177/1077800406294947

Ellis, W. D. (1999). *A sourcebook of Gestalt psychology.* London, UK: Routledge, Taylor Francis. (Originally published 1938 in London by Kegan Paul, Trench, and Trubner)

Erford, B. T., McKechnie, J., & Moore-Thomas, C. (2004). Program assessment and evaluation. In B. T. Erford (Ed.), *Professional school counseling: A handbook of theories, programs, and practices* (pp. 303–309). Austin, TX: PRO-ED.

ETS (Educational Testing Service). (2009). *Interpreting your GRE® scores.* Retrieved from http://www.ets.org/Media/Tests/GRE/pdf/gre_0809_interpretingscores.pdf

Exner, J. E., Jr. (2005). *The Rorschach basic foundations and perceptions of interpretation: Vol 2.* Hoboken, NJ: Jonn Wiley & Sons.

Fanning, P. J. (2010). *Influenza and inequality: One town's tragic response to the epidemic of 1918.* Amherst: University of Massachusetts Press.

Farber, N. K. (2006). Conducting qualitative research: A practical guide for school counselors. *Professional School Counseling, 9*(5), 367–375.

Farr, R. M. (1983). Wilhelm Wündt (1832–1920) and the origins of psychology as an experimental and social science. *British Journal of Social Psychology, 22*(4), 289–301.

Feingold, H. L. (1995). *How America and its Jews responded to the Holocaust.* Syracuse, NY: Syracuse University Press.

Feldt, L. S., & Brennan, R. L. (1989). Reliability. In R. L. Linn (Ed.), *Educational Measurement* (3rd ed., pp. 105–146). New York, NY: American Council on Education and Macmillan.

Ferguson, G. A., & Takane, Y. (1989). *Statistical analysis in psychology and education* (6th ed.). New York, NY: McGraw-Hill.

Ferketich, S. A., Figueredo, A. J., & Knapp, T. R. (1991). Focus on psychometrics: The multitrait-multimethod approach to construct validity. *Research in Nursing and Health, 14,* 315–320.

Fern, E. F. (2001). *Advanced focus group research.* Thousand Oaks, CA: Sage.

Ferrance, E. (2000). *Action research.* Providence, RI: Northeast and Islands Regional Educational Laboratory at Brown University. Retrieved from http://www.alliance.brown.edu/pubs/themes_ed/act_research.pdf

Fetterman, D. M. (1988). Qualitative approaches to evaluating education. *Educational Researcher, 17*(8), 17–23.

Fetterman, D. M. (1989). *Applied Social Research Methods: Vol. 17. Ethnography: Step by step* (2nd ed.). Newbury Park, CA: Sage.

Finerman, W., Tisch, S., & Newirth, C. (Producers), & Zemeckis, R. L. (Director). (1994). *Forrest Gump* [Motion picture]. Los Angeles, CA: Paramount Studios.

Fisher, R. A. (1921). Studies in crop variation: An examination of the yield of dressed grain from Broadbalk. *Journal of Agricultural Science, 11,* 107–135. Retrieved from http://digital.library.adelaide.edu.au/dspace/handle/2440/15170/

Fisher, R. A. (1935). *The design of experiments.* London, UK: Oliver and Boyd.

Fisher, R. A. (1973). *Statistical methods and scientific inference* (3rd ed.). New York, NY: Hafner Press.

Fisher, R. A. (1990). *Statistical methods, experimental design, and scientific inference: A re-issue of statistical methods for research workers, the design of experiments, and statistical methods and scientific inference.* New York, NY: Oxford University Press. (Originally published 1925)

Fleischman, H. L., & Williams, L. (1996). *An introduction to program evaluation for classroom teachers.* Arlington, VA: Development Associates. Retrieved from http://teacherpathfinder.org/School/Assess/assess.html

Flynn, J. R. (1987). Massive IQ gains in 14 nations: What IQ tests really measure. *Psychological Bulletin, 101*(2), 171–191.

Fontana, A., & Frey, J. H. (2005). The interview. In N. K. Denzin & Y. S. Lincoln (Eds.), *The Sage handbook of qualitative research* (3rd ed., pp. 695–727). Thousand Oaks, CA: Sage.

Foster, M. (1972). An introduction to the theory and practice of action research in work organizations. *Human Relations, 25*(6), 529–556.

Freedman, E. B. (2003). *No turning back: The history of feminism and the future of women.* New York, NY: Ballantine Books.

Fuchs, M. (2009). Differences in the visual design language of paper-and-pencil surveys versus Web surveys: A field experimental study on the length of response fields in open-ended frequency questions. *Social Science Computer Review, 29*(3), 213–227. doi: 10.1177/0894439308325201

Gabriele, E. F. (2003). The Belmont ethos: The meaning of the Belmont principles for human subject protections. *Journal of Research Administration, 34*(2), 19–24.

Gage, N. L. (1989). The paradigm wars and their aftermath: A "historical" sketch of research on teaching since 1989. *Educational Researcher, 18*(7), 4–10. doi: 10.3102/0013189X018007004

Gall, M. D., Borg, W. R., & Gall, J. P. (1996). *Educational research: An introduction* (6th ed.). White Plains, NY: Longman.

Galton, F. (1883). *Inquiries into human faculty and its development.* London, UK: Macmillan.

Galton, F. (1886). Regression toward mediocrity in hereditary stature. *Journal of the Royal Anthropological Institute of Great Britain and Ireland, 15,* 246–263. Retrieved from http://www.jestor.org/pss/2841583

Ganapathy, K. (2004). Medical accountability in the information age. *Neurosurgical Critical Care Reviews, 3*(1). Retrieved from http://www.wfns.org/pages/read_the_reviews_author/103.php?rid = 12

Gee, J. P. (2010). *An introduction to discourse analysis: Theory and method.* New York, NY: Rutledge.

Geertz, C. (1985). *Local knowledge: Further essays in interpretive anthropology* (3rd ed.). New York, NY: Basic Books.

Gelling, L., & Munn-Giddings, C. (2011). Ethical review of action research: The challenges for researchers and research ethics committees. *Research Ethics, 7*(3), 100–106.

Giddings, L. S. (2006). Mixed-methods research: Positivism dressed in drag? *Journal of Research in Nursing, 11*(3), 195–203.

Glaser, B. G. (1992). *Basics of grounded theory analysis: Emergence vs. forcing.* Mill Valley, CA: Sociology Press.

Glaser, B. G., & Strauss, A. (1967). *The discovery of grounded theory: Strategies for qualitative research.* Chicago, IL: Aldine Transaction.

Glaser, R. (1963). Instructional technology and the measurement of learning outcomes: Some questions. *American Psychologist, 18,* 519–521.

Glutting, J., Sheslow, D., & Adams, W. (2003). *College ADHD response evaluation* (4th ed.). Lutz, FL: Psychological Assessment Resources. (Originally published 1979)

Golden, T. W., Skalak, S. L., Clayton, M. M., & Pill, J. S. (2006). *A guide to forensic accounting investigation.* Hoboken, NJ: John Wiley & Sons. (Originally published 1939)

Gosselin, P. (1995). Le developpement de la reconnaissance des expressions facials des emotions chez l'enfant [The development in the child of facial expressions of emotion]. *Canadian Journal of Behavioral Science, 27*(1), 107–119. doi: 10.1037/008-400X.27.1.107

Goulden, C. H. (2007). *Methods of statistical analysis.* New York, NY: John Wiley and Sons.

Gouldner, A. W. (1980). *The coming crisis of Western sociology.* New York, NY: Basic Books. (Originally published 1971)

Greenburg, D. L., Durning, S. J., Cohen, D. L., Cruess, D., & Jackson, J. L. (2007). Identifying medical students likely to exhibit poor professionalism and knowledge during internship. *Journal of General Internal Medicine, 22*(12), 1711–1717. doi: 10.1007/s11606-007-0405-z

Greene, J. C., Caracelli, V. J., & Graham, W. F. (1989). Toward a conceptual framework for mixed-method evaluation designs. *Educational Evaluation and Policy Analysis, 11*(3), 255–274.

Greene, J. C., & McClintoc, C. (1985). Triangulation in evaluation: Design and evaluation issues. *Evaluation Review, 9*(5), 523–545. doi: 10.1177/0193841X8500900501

Greenwood, D. J. (2002). Action research: Unfulfilled promises and unmet challenges. *Concepts and Transformation, 7*(2), 117–139.

Greenwood, D. J., & Levin, M. (2007). *Introduction to action research: Social research for social change* (2nd ed.). Thousand Oaks, CA: Sage.

Groenewald, T. (2004). A phenomenological research design illustrated. *International Journal of Qualitative Methods, 3*(1). Retrieved from http://www.ualberta.ca/~iiqm/backissues/3_1/pdf/groenewald.pdf

Guba, E. G., & Lincoln, Y. S. (1989). *Fourth generation evaluation.* Newbury Park, CA: Sage.

Guba, E. G., & Lincoln, Y. S. (2005). Paradigmatic controversies, contradictions, and emerging influences. In N. K. Denzin & Y. S. Lincoln (Eds.), *The Sage handbook of qualitative research* (3rd ed., pp. 191–215). Thousand Oaks, CA: Sage.

Gulliksen, H. (1950). *Theory of mental tests.* New York, NY: John Wiley & Sons.

Guskey, T. R. (2007). Multiple sources of evidence: An analysis of stakeholders' perceptions of various indicators of student learning. *Educational Measurement: Issues and Practice, 26*(1), 19–27.

Haft, S., Witt, P. J., & Thomas, T. (Producers), & Weir, P. (Director). (1989). *Dead poets society* [Motion Picture]. United States: Buena Vista Picture Distribution.

Hägglund, G. (2001). Milestones in the history of factor analysis. In R. Cudeck, S. Du Toit, & D. Sorbom (Eds.), *Structural equation modeling: Present and future* (pp. 11–38). Lincolnwood, IL: Scientific Software International.

Haley, A. (1965). *The autobiography of Malcolm X.* New York, NY: Grove Press.

Hambleton, R. K. (2004, June). *Traditional and modern approaches to outcomes measurement.* Paper presented at the 2004 conference of the National Institute of Cancer and the Drug Information Association, Bethesda, MD.

Hannan, A. (2006). *Observation techniques.* Plymouth, UK: Faculty of Education, Plymouth University. Retrieved from http://www.edu.plymouth.ac.uk/resined/observation/obshome.htm

Hansen, G. P. (2001). *The trickster and the paranormal.* Bloomington, IN: Xlibris.

Harris, G. (2011, March 5). Talk doesn't pay, so psychiatry turns instead to drug therapy. *The New York Times.* Retrieved from http://www.nytimes.com/2011/03/06/health/policy/06doctors.html

Hart, A. M., Brennan, C. W., Sym, D., & Larson, E. (2009). The impact of personalized prenotification on response rates to an electronic survey. *Western Journal of Nursing Research, 31*(1), 17–23. doi: 10.1177/0193945908319249

Hausendorf, H., & Bora, A. (2006). *Analyzing citizenship talk: Social positioning in political and legal decision-making processes.* Amsterdam, The Netherlands: John Benjamins.

Hays, D. G., & Wood, C. (2011). Infusing qualitative traditions in counseling research designs. *Journal of Counseling and Development, 89*(3), 288–295. doi: 10.1002/j.1556-6678.2011.tb00091.x

Hayter, A. J. (1986). The maximum familywise error rate of Fisher's least significant difference test. *Journal of the American Statistical Association, 81*(396), 1001–1004.

Healey, J. F. (2010). *The essentials of statistics: A tool for social research.* Belmont, CA: Wadsworth.

Heerwegh, D. (2006). An investigation of the effects of lotteries on web survey response rates. *Field Methods, 18*(2), 205–220. doi: 10.1177/1525822X05285781

Hegel, G. W. F. (1979). *Phenomenology of spirit* (J. N. Findlay, Trans.). New York, NY: Oxford University Press. (Originally published 1807)

Heise, D. R. (1970). The semantic differential and attitude research. In G. F. Summers (Ed.), *Attitude measurement* (pp. 235–253). Chicago, IL: Rand McNally. Retrieved from http://www.indiana.edu/~socpsy/papers/AttMeasure/attitude..htm

Hemingway, E. (1999). *Death in the afternoon.* New York, NY: Scribner. (Originally published 1932)

Henry J. Kaiser Family Foundation. (2011). *Medicare.* Menlo Park, CA: State Health Facts. Retrieved from http://www.statehealthfacts.org/comparecat.jsp?cat = 6

Hertz, R. (1997). *Introduction: Reflexivity and voice.* Thousand Oaks, CA: Sage.

Hevesi, D. (2010, September 25). Robert W. McCollum, who studied rare viral diseases, dies at 85. *The New York Times.* Retrieved from http://www.nytimes.com/2010/09/26/education/26mccollum.html

Hill, C. E., Knox, S., Thompson, B. J., Nutt-Williams, E. N., Hess, S. A., & Ladany, N. (2005). Consensual qualitative research: An update. *Journal of Counseling Psychology, 52*(2), 196–205.

Hill, C. E., Thompson, B. J., & Williams, E. N. (1997). A guide to conducting consensual qualitative research. *The Counseling Psychologist, 25*(4), 517–572. doi: 10.1177/0011000097254001

Hines, T. (2002). *Pseudoscience and the paranormal* (2nd ed.). Amherst, NY: Prometheus.

Hollingsworth, H. H. (1980). An analytical investigation of the effects of heterogeneous regression slopes in analysis of covariance. *Educational and Psychological Measurement, 40*(3), 611–618. doi: 10.1177/001316448004000306

Holloway, I. (1997). *Basic concepts for qualitative research.* Boston, MA: Blackwell.

Holstein, J. A., & Gubrium, J. F. (2004). The active interview. In D. Silverman (Ed.), *Qualitative research: Theory method and practice* (pp. 140–161). Thousand Oaks, CA: Sage.

Honigman, J. J. (1970). Sampling in ethnographic fieldwork. In R. Naroll & R. Cohen (Eds.), *A handbook of method in cultural anthropology* (pp. 266–281). Garden City, NY: Natural History Press.

House, J. D., & Johnson, J. J. (2002). Predictive validity of the graduate record examination advanced psychology test for grade performance in graduate psychology courses. Statistical data included. *College Student Journal, 73*(1), 184–186. doi: 10.2466/pr0.1993.73.1.184

Howe, K. R. (2004). A critique of experimentalism, *Qualitative Inquiry, 10*(1), 42–61.

Howell, M. C., & Prevenier, W. (2001). *From reliable sources: An introduction to historical methodology.* Ithaca, NY: Cornell University Press.

Huck, S. W., & Sandler, H. M. (1979). *Rival hypotheses: Alternative interpretations of data based conclusions.* New York, NY: Harper & Row.

Hughes, E., & Gray, R. (2009). HIV prevention for people with serious mental illness: A survey of mental health worker's attitudes, knowledge, and practice. *Journal of Clinical Nursing, 18*(4), 591–600.

Hume, D. (1961). An inquiry concerning human understanding. In R. Taylor (Ed.), *The empiricists: Locke, Berkeley, and Hume* (pp. 307–430). New York, NY: Anchor Press. (Originally published 1748)

IACS (International Association of Counseling Services Inc.). (2005). *Accreditation standards for university and college counseling centers.* Alexandria, VA: International Association of Counseling Services. Retrieved from http://www.iacsinc.org/IACS%20STANDARDS.pdf

Jacoby, S. B., & Youngson, R. M. (2005). *Encyclopedia of family medicine: Vol. 15.* New York, NY: Marshall Cavendish.

Jamieson, S. (2004). Likert scales: How to (ab)use them. *Medical Education, 38*(9), 1212–1218.

Jefferson, G. (2004). Glossary of transcript symbols with an introduction. In G. H. Lerner (Ed.), *Conversation analysis: Studies from the first generation* (pp. 13–23). Philadelphia, PA: John Benjamins. Retrieved from http://www.liso.ucsb.edu/Jefferson/Transcript.pdf

Jinha, A. E. (2010). Article 50 million: An estimate of the number of scholarly articles in existence. *Learned Publishing, 23*(3), 258–263. doi: 10.1087/20100308

Johnson, R. B., Onwuegbuzie, A. J., & Turner, L. A. (2007). Toward a definition of mixed methods research. *Journal of Mixed Methods Research, 1*(2), 112–133. doi:10.1177/1155868906298224

Joint Committee on Testing Practices. (2005). Code of fair testing practices in education. *Educational Measurement: Issues and Practice, 24*(1), 23–27.

Kalton, G. (1983). *Quantitative applications in the social sciences series: No. 35. Introduction to survey sampling.* Newbury Park, CA: Sage.

Kamata, A., Turhan, A., & Darandari, E. (2003, April). *Estimating reliability for multidimensional composite scale scores.* Paper presented during the annual meeting of the American Educational Research Association, Chicago, IL.

Kane, M. T. (2006). Validation. In R. L. Brennan (Ed.), *Educational measurement* (4th ed., pp. 17–64). Westport, CT: Praeger.

Kellman, L. (2011, June 5). Palin: I didn't "mess up" Paul Revere history. Associated Press in *Anchorage Daily News.* Retrieved from http://www.adn.com/2011/06/05/v-printer/1900385/palin-i-didnt-mess-up-paul-revere.html

Kemper, E., Stringfield, S., & Teddlie, C. (2003). Mixed methods sampling strategies in social science research. In A. Tashakkori & C. Teddlie (Eds.). *Handbook of mixed methods in social and behavioral research* (pp. 273–296). Thousand Oaks, CA: Sage.

Kendall, M. G. (1938). A new measure of rank correlation. *Biometrika, 30*(1–2), 81–93.

Kendall, M. G., & Stuart, A. (1967). *The advanced theory of statistics: Inference and relationships* (Vol. 2). New York, NY: Hafner.

Kimmelman, M. (2011, March 14). In Germany, uproar over a doctoral thesis. *The New York Times.* Retrieved from http://www.nytimes.com/2011/03/15/books/merkels-possible-successor-resigns-in-plagiarism-scandal.html

Kitchener, K. S. (1984). Intuition, critical evaluation and ethical principles: The foundation for ethical decisions in counseling psychology. *Counseling Psychologist, 12*(3), 43–55.

Klenke, K. (2008). *Qualitative research in the study of leadership.* Bingley, UK: Emerald Group.

Knapp, T. R. (1990). Treating ordinal scales as interval scales: An attempt to resolve the controversy. *Nursing Research, 39*(2), 121–123.

Kolen, M. J. (2006). Scaling and norming. In R. L. Brennan (Ed.), *Educational measurement* (4th ed., pp. 155–186). Westport, CT: American Council on Education and Praeger.

Kramer, R. (1995). The birth of client-centered therapy: Carl Rogers, Otto Rank, and "The Beyond." *Journal of Humanistic Psychology, 35*(4), 54–110. doi:10.1177/00221678950354005

Krefting, L. (1991). Rigor in qualitative research: The assessment of trustworthiness. *The American Journal of Occupational Therapy, 45*(3), 214–222.

Krejcie, R. V., & Morgan, D. W. (1970). Determining sample size for research activities. *Educational and Psychological Measurement, 30*, 607–610. Retrieved from http://opa.uprrp.edu/InvInsDocs/KrejcieandMorgan.pdf

Kremelberg, D. (2010). *Practical statistics: A guide to IBM®, SPAA®, Statistics, STATA, and other statistical software.* Thousand Oaks, CA: Sage.

Kruskal, W. H., & Wallis, W. A. (1952). Use of ranks in one-criterion variance analysis. *Journal of the American Statistical Association, 47*(260), 583–621. Retrieved from http://homepages.ucalgary.ca/~jefox/Kruskal%20and%20Wallis%201952.pdf

Kuder, G. F., & Richardson, M. W. (1937). The theory of the estimation of test reliability. *Psychometrika, 2*(3), 151–161.

Kuhn, T. S. (1996). *The structure of scientific revolutions* (3rd ed.). Chicago, IL: University of Chicago Press.

Lamb, T. (2005). *The retrospective pretest: An imperfect but useful tool.* Cambridge, MA: Harvard Family Research Project, Graduate School of Education, Harvard University. Retrieved from http://www.hfrp.org/evaluation/the-evaluation-exchange/issue-archive/evaluation-methodology/the-retrospective-pretest-an-imperfect-but-useful-tool

Lapadat, J. C., & Lindsay, A. C. (1998, April). *Examining transcription: A theory laden methodology.* Paper presented at the annual meeting of the American Educational Research Association, San Diego, CA.

Lawler, P. (1993). A longitudinal study of women's career choices: Twenty-five years later [Preconvention workshop from the annual meeting of the American Association of University

Women]. In *Gender issues in the classroom and on campus: Focus on the twenty-first century* (pp. 187–192).Washington, DC: American Association of University Women.

Laws, G. (1995). Understanding ageism: Lessons from feminism and postmodernism. *The Gerontologist, 35*(1), 112–118.

Leech, N. L., & Onwuegbuzie, A. J. (2010). Guidelines for conducting and reporting mixed research in the field of counseling and beyond. *Journal of Counseling and Development, 88*(1), 61–69.

Lehner, P. N. (1998). *Handbook of ethological methods.* New York, NY: Cambridge University Press.

Lenhart, A., Fallows, D., & Horrigan, J. (2003). *Content creation online.* Washington, DC: Pew Internet & American Life Project. Retrieved from http://www.pewinternet.org/Reports/2004/Content-Creation-Online.aspx

Leob, L. E. (1981). *From Descartes to Hume: Continental metaphysics and the development of modern philosophy.* Ithaca, NY: Cornell University Press.

Lewin, K. (1948). *Resolving social conflicts: Selected papers on group dynamics* (E. W. Lewin, Ed.). New York, NY: Harper Brothers.

Lewin, K. (1975). *Field theory in social science: Selected theoretical papers* (D. Cartwright, Ed.). Westport, CT: Greenwood. (Originally published 1951)

Lienert, T. (2002, Autumn). Doing an action research evaluation. *Stronger Families Learning Exchange Bulletin,* 16–20. Retrieved from http://www.aifs.gov.au/sf/pubs.html

Likert, R. (1932, June). A technique for the measurement of attitudes (Columbia University contributions to philosophy and psychology series No. 140). *Archives of Psychology,* pp. 5–55.

Lincoln, Y. S., & Guba, E. G. (1985). *Naturalistic inquiry.* Newbury Park, CA: Sage.

Linn, R. L., & Miller, M. D. (2005). *Measurement and assessment in teaching* (9th ed.). Upper Saddle River, NJ: Pearson, Merrill, Prentice Hall.

Lombardi, C. M., & Hurlbert, S. H. (2009). Misprescription and misuse of one-tailed tests. *Austral Ecology, 34*(4), 447–468. Retrieved from http://www.bio.sdsu.edu/pub/stuart/2009MisprescriptionOneTailed.pdf

Lundy, P., & McGovern, M. (2006). Action research, community "truth-telling" and post-conflict transition in the North of Ireland. *Action Research, 4*(1), 49–64.

Lunsford, T. R., & Lunsford, B. R. (1996). Research forum: How to critically read a journal research article. *Journal of Prosthetists and Orthodontics, 8*(1), 24–31.

Lynch, A., & Fleming, W. M. (2005). Bystander approaches: Empowering students to model ethical sexual behavior. *Journal of Family and Consumer Sciences, 97*(3), 27–33.

Lynd, R. S., & Lynd H. M. (1937). *Middletown in transition: A study in cultural conflicts.* New York, NY: Harcourt, Brace.

Mabe, M. (2003). The growth and number of journals. *Serials: The Journal for the Serials Community, 16*(2), 191–197.

Macdonald, P. T. (1989). Competing theoretical explanations for cocaine use: Differential association vs. control theory. *Journal of Contemporary Criminal Justice, 5*(2), 73–88. doi: 10.1177/104398628900500204

Mack, J. L., & Patterson, M. (2001). *CERAD behavior rating scale for dementia* (2nd ed.). Durham, NC: Center for the Study of Aging and Human Development, Duke University Medical Center.

Mack, N., Woodsong, C., MacQueen, K. M., Guest, G., & Namey, E. (2012). *Qualitative research methods: A data collector's field guide.* Research Triangle Park, NC: Family Health International. Retrieved from http://www.fhi360.org/NR/rdonlyres/emgox4xpcoyrysqspsgy5ww6mq7v4e44etd6toiejyxalhbmk5sdnef7fqlr3q6hlwa2ttj5524xbn/datacollectorguideenrh.pdf

Manchester, W. (1984). *The glory and the dream: A narrative history of America, 1932–1972.* New York, NY: Bantam.

Mankiewicz, R. (2001). *The story of mathematics.* Princeton, NJ: Princeton University Press.

Mann, H., & Whitney, D. R. (1947). On a test of whether one of two random variables is stochastically larger than the other. *Annals of Mathematical Statistics, 18*(1), 50–60.

Marshall, P., Willson, P., & de Salas, K. (2010). Action research in practice: Issues and challenges in a financial services case study. *The Qualitative Report, 15*(1), 76–93.

May, R. (1994). *The discovery of being: Writings in existential psychology.* New York, NY: W. W. Norton.

Mayo, E. (1949). Hawthorne and the Western Electric Company. In *The social problems of an industrial civilization* (pp. 60–76). New York, NY: Routledge. Retrieved from http://xa.yimg.com/kq/groups/30802428/1886432542/name/elton + mayo + %2B + studiu + de + caz.pdf

Mayo, E. (2003). *The human problems of an industrial civilization.* New York, NY: Routledge. (Originally published 1933 by Macmillan)

McColl, M. A., James, A., Boyce, W., & Shortt, S. (2006). Disability policy making: Evaluating the evidence base. In D. Pothier & R. Devlin (Eds.), *Critical disability theory: Essays in philosophy, politics, policy, and law* (pp. 25-46). Vancouver, Canada: University of British Columbia Press.

McConney, A., Rudd, A., & Ayres, R. (2002). Getting to the bottom line: A method for synthesizing findings within mixed-method program evaluations. *American Journal of Evaluation, 23*(2), 121–140.

McGhee, G., Marland, G. R., & Atkinson, J. (2007). Grounded theory research: Literature reviewing and reflexivity. *Journal of Advanced Nursing, 60*(3), 334–342.

McIntire, S. A., & Miller, L. A. (2007). *Foundations of psychological testing: A practical approach* (2nd ed.). Thousand Oaks, CA: Sage.

McIntyre, A. (2008). *Qualitative research methods: Series #52. Participatory action research.* Thousand Oaks, CA: Sage.

Mcleod, S. (2008). *Simply psychology: Likert scale.* Retrieved from http://www.simplypsychology.org/likert-scale.html

McNiff, J. (2002). *Action research for professional development: Concise advice for new action researchers* (3rd ed.). Excerpt retrieved from http://www.jeanmcniff.com/userfiles/file/Publications/AR%20Booklet.doc

McNiff, J., & Whitehead, J. (2011). *All you need to know about action research* (2nd ed.). Thousand Oaks, CA: Sage.

Mehl, M. R. (2006). Quantitative text analysis. In M. Eld & E. Diener (Eds.), *Handbook of multimethod methodology in psychology* (pp. 141–156). Washington, DC: American Psychological Association.

Mehler, B. (1988). Brief history of American and European eugenics movements. Excerpt from *A History of the American Eugenics Movement* (Doctoral dissertation, University of Illinois). Retrieved from http://www.ferris.edu/ISAR/archives/Brief-History-American-Eugenics.pdf

Merleau-Ponty, M. (1976). *Phénoménologie de la perception.* Paris, France: French and European. (Originally published 1945)

Mertler, C. A. (2012). *Action research: Improving schools and empowering educators* (3rd ed.). Thousand Oaks, CA: Sage.

Messick, S. (1989). Validity. In R. L. Linn (Ed.), *Educational Measurement* (3rd ed., pp 13–103). New York, NY: American Council on Education and Macmillan.

Meyer, G. J. (2007). *A world undone: The story of the great was, 1914–1918.* New York, NY: Delacourte.

Miles, M. B., & Huberman, A. M. (1994). *Qualitative data analysis: An expanded sourcebook.* Thousand Oaks, CA: Sage.

Milgram, S. (1974). *Obedience to authority: An experimental view.* New York, NY: Harper Perennial.

Miller, B. J., Sundre, D. L., Setzer, C., & Zeng, X. (2007, April). *Content validity: A comparison of two methods.* Paper presented during the annual meeting of the National Council on Measurement in Education, Chicago, IL.

Miller, S. D., & Duncan, B. L. (2000). *Session rating scale.* Retrieved from http://www.mgh.org/telehealth/src_handout.pdf

Miller, S. D., Duncan, B. L., Brown, J., Sparks, J. A., & Claud, D. A. (2003). The Outcome Rating Scale: A preliminary study of reliability, validity, and feasibility of a brief visual analog measure. *Journal of Brief Therapy, 2*(3), 91–100.

Mills, G. E. (2007). *Action research: A guide for the teacher researcher* (3rd ed.). Thousand Oaks, CA: Sage.

Moffatt, M. (1989). *Coming of age in New Jersey: College and American culture.* New Brunswick, NJ: Rutgers University Press.

Monahan, T., & Fisher, J. A. (2010). Benefits of "observer effects": Lessons from the field. *Qualitative Research, 10*(3), 357–376. doi: 10.1177/1468794110362874

Morgan D. L. (2007). Paradigms lost and pragmatism regained: Methodological implications of combining qualitative and quantitative methods. *Journal of Mixed Methods Research, 1*(1), 48–76. doi: 10.1177/2345678906292462

Moustakas, C. (1994). *Phenomenological research methods.* Thousand Oaks, CA: Sage.

Murphy, G., & Likert, R. (1938). *Public opinion and the individual: A psychological study of student attitudes on public questions with a retest five years later.* New York, NY: Harper Books.

Murray, H. A. (1943). *Thematic apperception test.* Cambridge, MA: Harvard University Press.

Naglieri, J. A., Dragsgow, F., Schmit, M., Handler, L., Prifitera, A., Margolis, A., & Velasquez, R. (2004). Psychological testing on the Internet: New problems, old issues. *American Psychologist, 59*(3), 150–162.

National Academy of Sciences. (2009). *Tracing similarities and differences in our DNA.* Retrieved from https://koshland-science-museum.org/sites/all/exhibits/exhibitdna/intro03.jsp

National Board of Certified Counselors. (2012). *Study guides for the NCE and the NCMHCE.* Retrieved from http://www.nbcc.org/study/

National Board of Professional Psychology. (2012). *Candidate examination manual for board certification in counseling psychology for the American Board of Professional Psychology.* Retrieved from http://www.abpp.org/files/page-specific/3364%20Counseling/02_Candidate_Exam_Manual.pdf

National Commission for the Protection of Human Subjects of Biomedical and Behavioral Research. (1979). *The Belmont report: Ethical principles and guidelines for the protection of human subjects of research.* Washington, DC: Office of Human Subjects, Department of Health and Human Services. Retrieved from http://ohsr.od.nih.gov/guidelines/belmont.html

Nichols, M. (2011). The social construction of sexuality and perversion: Deconstructing sadomasochism. *Contemporary Sociology: A Journal of Reviews, 40*(2), 153–154. doi: 10.1177/0094306110396847b

Niethammer, D. (2004). Empfehlungen zu forschungs und lehrförderlichen Strukturen in der Universitätsmedizin [Recommendations for research and teaching-conducive structures in university medicine]. Cologne, Germany: German Council for Science and Humanities (*Wissenschaftsrat*). Retrieved from http://www.wissenschaftsrat.de/download/archiv/5913-04.pdf

Nordal, K. C. (2012). Outcomes measurement benefits psychology. *Monitor on Psychology, 43*(1), 51.

North Dakota Center for Persons with Disabilities. (2009). *Mythbusters disability datebook.* Minot, ND: Minot State University Center of Excellence. Retrieved from http://www.ndcpd.org/resources/perceptions/2010%20disability%20final.pdf

North, J., Blackburn, R. A., & Curran, J. (1998). *The quality business: Quality issues and smaller firms.* London, UK: Routledge.

Oakley, A. (1999). Paradigm wars: Some thoughts on a personal and public trajectory. *International Journal of Social Research Methodology, 2*(3), 247–254. Retrieved from http://www.soc.uoc.gr/socmedia/papageo/paradigm%20wars-why%20researchers%20choose%20their%20methods.pdf

Obama, B. (1995). *Dreams from my father.* New York, NY: Times Books/Random House.

O'Cathain, A., Murphy, E., & Nicholl, J. (2008). The quality of mixed methods studies in health services research. *Journal of Health Service Research Policy, 13*(2), 92–98.

O'Connor, J. J., & Robertson E. F. (2003). Karl Pearson. *MacTutor History of Mathematics Archive.* Retrieved from University of St. Andrew, School of Mathematics and Statistics, http://www-history.mcs.st-and.ac.uk/Mathematicians/Pearson.html

Office of the Inspector General. (2001). *The globalization of clinical trials: A growing challenge in protecting human subjects.* Washington, DC: Department of Health and Human Services. Retrieved from http://oig.hhs.gov/oei/reports/oei-01-00-00190.pdf

Ogilvie, J. P. (2011, May 30). Is lowering the drinking age a good idea? *Los Angeles Times.* Retrieved from http://articles.latimes.com/2011/may/30/health/la-he-drinking-age-20110530/

O'Keefe, K. (1993). *American eugenics society 1926-1994.* Retrieved from http://www.all.org/abac/aes.txt

Oliver, D. G., Serovich, J. M., & Mason, T. L. (2005) Constraints and opportunities with interview transcription: Towards reflection in qualitative research. *Social Forces, 84*(2), 1273-1289.

Onwuegbuzie, A. J., & Leech, N. L. (2006). Linking research questions to mixed methods data analysis. *The Qualitative Report, 11*(3), 474-498.

Onwuegbuzie, A. J., Leech, N. L., & Collins, K. M. T. (2010). Innovative data collection strategies in qualitative research. *The Qualitative Report, 15*(3), 696-726. Retrieved from http://www.nova.edu/ssss/QR/QR15-3/onwuegbuzie.pdf

Osgood, C. E., Suci, G., & Tannenbaum, P. (1957). *The measurement of meaning.* Urbana: University of Illinois Press.

Oswalt, P. H., & Lebeau, M. (2011, March). *Hot topics in counselor ethics.* Paper presented at the American Counseling Association Conference and Exposition, New Orleans, LA.

Outten, C. (2011). *Gray literature.* Long Beach: University Library, California State University-Long Beach. Retrieved from http://csulb.libguides.com/graylit/

Oxford English Dictionary (2nd ed.). (2002). New York, NY: Oxford University Press.

Page, E. B. (1975). Statistically recapturing the richness within the classroom. *Psychology in the Schools, 12*(3), 339-344.

Patten, M. L. (2001). *Questionnaire research* (2nd ed.). Los Angeles, CA: Pyrczak.

Patton, M. Q. (1990). Humanistic psychology and qualitative research: Shared principles and processes. *Person-Centered Review, 5*(2), 191-202.

Patton, M. Q. (2002). *Qualitative research and evaluation methods* (3rd ed.). Thousand Oaks, CA: Sage.

Patton, M. Q. (2012). *Essentials of utilization-focused evaluation* (3rd ed.). Thousand Oaks, CA: Sage.

Paulus, T, Woodside, M., & Ziegler, M. (2008). Extending the conversation: Qualitative research as dialogic collaborative process. *The Qualitative Report, 13*(2), 226-243. Retrieved from http://www.nova.edu/ssss/QR/QR13-2/paulus.pdf

Pawson, R., & Tilly, N. (1997). *Realistic evaluation.* London, UK: Sage.

Pearson, K. (1896). Mathematical contributions to the theory of evolution: No. 3. Regression, heredity and panmixia. *Philosophical Transactions of the Royal Society of London, 187,* 253-318. Retrieved from http://www.jstor.org/pss/90707

Pearson, K. (1900). On the criterion that a given system of deviations from the probable in the case of a correlated system of variables is such that it can reasonably be supposed to have arisen from random sampling. *London, Edinburgh, and Dublin Philosophical Magazine and Journal of Science, series 5, 50*(302), 157-175.

Pearson, K. (1901). Mathematical contributions to the theory of evolution. *Philosophical Transactions of the Royal Society of London* [Series A, Containing papers of a mathematical or physical character], *197*(1-2), 443-459. Retrieved from http://o-www.jstor.org.libcat.widener.edu/stable/90841/

Peckham, P. D., Glass, G. V., & Hopkins, K. D. (1969). The experimental unit in statistical analysis. *Journal of Special Education, 3*(4), 337-349.

Peirce, C. S. (1998). *The essential writings* (E. C. Moore, Ed.). Amherst, NY: Prometheus Books. (Originally published 1877)

Peräkylä, A. (2005). Analyzing talk and text. In N. K. Denzin & Y. S. Lincoln (Eds.), *The Sage handbook of qualitative research* (3rd ed., pp. 869-886). Thousand Oaks, CA: Sage.

Pew Internet & American Life Project. (2012). *Trend data (adults)*. Retrieved from http://www.pewinter net.org/Static-Pages/Trend-Data-(Adults)/Online-Activites-Total.aspx

Piaget, J. (1932). *The moral judgment of the child*. London, UK: Kegan Paul.

Piaget, J. (1952). *The child's conception of number*. London, UK: Routledge and Kegan Paul.

Piaget, J. (1955). *The language and thought of the child* (M. Gabain, Trans.). New York, NY: Meridian Books.

Piaget, J. (1960). *The child's conception of the world* (J. Tomlinson & A. Tomlinson, Trans.). Totowa, NJ: Littlefield, Adams.

Piaget, J. (1962). *Play, dreams, and imitation in childhood*. New York, NY: Norton.

Piaget, J. (1965). *The child's conception of number*. London, UK: Taylor & Francis Group.

Piaget, J. (1967). *Foreword to: John Amos Comenius on education*. New York, NY: Teachers College Press.

Piaget, J., & Inhelder, B. (1956). *The child's conception of space*. London, UK: Routledge and Kegan Paul.

Piaget, J., Inhelder, B., & Szeminska, A. (1960). *The child's conception of geometry* (E. A. Lunzer, Trans). London, UK: Kegan Paul.

Piotrowski, Z. A. (1987). *Perceptanalysis: The Rorschach method fundamentally reworked, expanded and systematized*. London, UK: Psychology Press.

Piper, S. (2006). Qualitative theory testing as mixed-method research. *Journal of Research in Nursing, 11*(3), 183–193. doi: 10.1177/1744987106064633

Popper, K. R. (1985). *Popper selections* (D. W. Miller, Ed.). Princeton, NJ: Princeton University Press.

Popper, K. R. (2002). *The logic of scientific discovery*. New York, NY: Taylor-Francis. (Originally published 1935)

Porter, S. R., & Whitcomb, M. E. (2005). E-mail subject lines and their effect on Web survey viewing and response. *Social Science Computer Review, 23*(3), 380–387. doi: 10.1177/0894439305275912

Potter, J., & Hepburn, A. (2005). Qualitative interviews in psychology: Problems and possibilities. *Qualitative Research in Psychology, 2*(4), 281–307. doi: 10.1191/1478088705qp045oa

Price, L., Gerber, P. J., & Mulligan, R. (2003). The Americans with Disabilities Act and adults with learning disabilities as employees. *Remedial and Special Education, 24*(6), 350–358. doi: 10.1177/07419325030240060601

Punch, K. (2005). *Introduction to social research: Quantitative and qualitative approaches* (2nd ed.). Thousand Oaks, CA: Sage.

Puterbaugh, D. (2004, May). Psychotherapy and insurance: The double bind. *USA Today Magazine*, p. 66. Retrieved from http://connection.ebscohost.com/c/articles/13062520/psychotherapy-insurance-double-bind/

Quek, F., McNeill, D., Bryll, R., Duncan, S., Ma, X., Kirbas, C., . . . Ansari, R. (2002). Multi-modal human discourse: Gesture and speech. *Transactions on Computer-Human Interaction, 9*(3), 171–193. doi 10.1073-0516/02/0900-0171

Rasmusson, A. M., Picciotto, M. R., Krishnan-Sarin, S. (2006). Smoking as a complex but a critical covariate in neurobiological studies of posttraumatic stress disorder. *Journal of Psychopharmacology, 20*(5), 693–707. doi: 10.1177/0269881106060193

Repp, A. C., Roberts, D. M., Slack, D. J., Repp, C. F., & Berkler, M. S. (1976). A comparison of frequency, interval, and time-sampling methods of data collecting. *Journal of Applied Behavior Analysis, 9*(4), 501–508.

Reynolds, C. R., Richmond, B. O., & Lowe, P.A. (2003). *Adult manifest anxiety scale*. Torrance, CA: Western Psychological Services.

Riel, M. (2010). *Understanding action research*. Los Angeles, CA: Center for Action Research, Pepperdine University. Retrieved from http://cadres.pepperdine.edu/ccar/define.html

Riel, M., & Lepori, K. (2011, April). *A meta-analysis of the outcomes of action research*. Paper presented at the annual meeting of the American Educational Research Association, New Orleans, LA.

Riessman, C. K. (1993). *Qualitative research methods series No. 30: Narrative analysis.* Newbury Park, CA: Sage.

RMC Research Corporation. (2005). *Using research and reason in education: What is scientifically based research?* Based on P. J. Stanovich & K. E. Stanovich, *Using research and reason in education: How teachers can use scientifically based research to make curricular and instructional decisions.* Jessup, MD: ED Pubs. (ERIC Document Reproduction Service No. ED482973). Retrieved from http://www.nichd.nih.gov/publications/pubs/science_stanovich.cfm

Roediger, H. L., III, & Karpicke, J. D. (2006). The power of testing memory: Basic research and implications for educational practice. *Perspectives on Psychological Science, 1*(3), 181–208.

Rogers, C. R. (1951). *Client centered therapy: Its current practice, implications, and theory.* London, UK: Constable.

Rogers, C. R. (1961). *On becoming a person: A therapist's view of psychotherapy.* Boston, MA: Houghton Mifflin.

Rogers, C. R., & Russell, D. E. (2002). *The quiet revolutionary, an oral history.* Roseville, CA: Penmarin Books.

Rorschach, H. (2007). *Psychodiagnostics: A diagnostic test based on perception.* (P. Lemkau & B. Kroenberg, Trans.). Alachus, FL: Sabine Press. (Originally published 1921)

Roseberry-McKibbin, C., & Brice, A. (2005). *Acquiring English as a second language: What's "normal," what's not.* Retrieved from http://www.asha.org/public/speech/development/easl.htm

Rosenbaum, J. E. (2009). Patient teenagers? A comparison of the sexual behavior of virginity pledgers and matched nonpledgers. *Pediatrics, 123*(1), 110–120.

Rosenthal, R., & Fode, K. (1963). The effect of experimenter bias on performance of the albino rat. *Behavioral Science, 8*(3), 183–189. doi:10.1002/bs.3830080302

Rosenthal, R., & Jacobson, L. (1966). Teachers' expectancies: Determinants of pupils' IQ gains. *Psychological Reports, 19,* 115–118. Retrieved from http://cuiz.cafe24.com/library/etc/Teachers'%20Expectancies.pdf

Rowell, L. L. (2006). Action research and school counseling: Closing the gap between research and practice. *Professional School Counseling, 9*(4), 376–384.

Rubin, A., & Babbie, E. R. (2011). *Research methods for social work* (7th ed.). Belmont, CA: Brooks/Cole.

Ruxton, G. D., & Neuhäuser, M. (2010). When should we use one-tailed hypothesis testing? *Methods in Ecology and Evolution, 1*(2), 114–117. doi: 10.1111/j.2041-2010X.2010.00014.x

Ryser, G., & McConnell, K. (2002). *Scales for diagnosing attention-deficit-hyperactivity disorder.* Austin, TX: PRO-ED.

Sack, K. (2011, September 15). Report finds improved performance by hospitals. *New York Times.* Retrieved from http://www.nytimes.com/2011/09/15/us/hospital-performance-improved-report-finds.html

Salsburg, D. (2001). *Tasting tea: How statistics revolutionized science in the twentieth century.* New York, NY: Henry Holt.

Salthouse, T. A. (2001). General and specific age-related influences on neuropsychological variables. In F. Boller & J. Grafman (Eds.), *Handbook of neuropsychology* (2nd ed., pp. 39–50). Waltham, MA: Elsevier.

Sartre, J. (2001). *Jean-Paul Sartre: Basic writings.* New York, NY: Routledge.

Saukko, P. (2005). Methodologies for cultural studies: An integrative approach. In N. K. Denzin & Y. S. Lincoln (Eds.), *The Sage handbook of qualitative research* (3rd ed., pp. 343–356). Thousand Oaks, CA: Sage.

Sax, G. (1997). *Principles of educational and psychological measurement and evaluation* (4th ed.). Belmont, CA: Wadsworth.

Scambler, G. (2007). Sex work stigma: Opportunist migrants in London. *Sociology, 41*(6), 1079–1096.

Schell, K. L., & Grasha, A. F. (2000). State anxiety, performance accuracy, and work pace in a simulated pharmacy dispensing task. *Perceptual and Motor Skills, 90*(2), 547–561.

Schmidt, L. K. (1996). Recalling the hermeneutic circle. *Philosophy Today, 40*(2), 263–273.

Scriven, M. (2005). *The logic and methodologies of checklists.* Unpublished paper, Western Michigan University. Retrieved from http://preval.org/documentos/2075.pdf

Sevenhuijsen, S. (1998). *Citizenship and the ethics of care: Feminist considerations on justice, morality, and politics.* New York, NY: Routledge.

Shadish, W. R., Cook, T. D., & Campbell, D. T. (2002). *Experimental and quasi-experimental designs for generalized causal research.* Boston, MA: Houghton Mifflin.

Shallcross, L. (2011). Do the right thing. *Counseling Today, 53*(10), 28–34.

Shurkin, J. N. (1992). *Terman's kids: The groundbreaking study of how the gifted grow up.* Boston, MA: Little Brown.

Sieber, S. D. (1978). The integration of fieldwork and survey methods. In N. H. Denzin (Ed.), *Sociological methods: A sourcebook* (pp. 358–385). New York, NY: McGraw-Hill.

Siegel, S., & Castellan, N. J. (1988). *Nonparametric statistics for the behavioral sciences* (2nd ed.). New York, NY: McGraw-Hill.

Skinner, B. F. (2005). *Walden two* (Rev. ed.). Indianapolis, IN: Hackett. (Originally published 1976)

Skinner, K. A. (1978). *The Japanese salaryman in a government bureaucracy: Participant observation study of a public corporation.* Unpublished dissertation, University of Minnesota.

Sklare, G. B. (2005). *Brief counseling that works: A solution-focused approach for school counselors and administrators* (2nd ed.). Thousand Oaks, CA: Sage.

Smart, R. G. (1966). Subject selection bias in psychological research. *Canadian Psychologist, 7*(2), 115–121.

Smothers, R. (1989, December 14). Discipline imposed on a school chief. *The New York Times.* Retrieved from http://www.nytimes.com/1989/12/14/us/discipline-imposed-on-a-school-chief.html

Snow, R. E. (1974). Representative and quasi-representative designs for research on teaching. *Review of Educational Research, 44*(3), 265–291. doi: 10.3102/00346543044003265

Snyder, L. J. (2009). William Whewell. Philosophy of science: Induction. In E. N. Zalta (Ed.), *The Stanford encyclopedia of philosophy* (winter 2009 ed.). Retrieved from http://plato.stanford.edu/entries/whewell/#SciInd

Solomon, R. L. (1949). An extension of control group design. *Psychological Bulletin, 46*(2), 137–150.

Sparks, J. A., Kisler, T. S., Adams, J. F., & Blumen, D. G. (2011). Teaching accountability: Using client feedback to train effective family therapists. *Journal of Marital and Family Therapy, 37*(4), 452–467.

Spearman, C. E. (1910). Correlation calculated from faulty data. *British Journal of Psychology, 3*, 271–295.

Spearman, C. E. (2000). General intelligence, objectively determined and measured. In C. D. Green (Ed.), *Classics in the history of psychology,* http://psychclassics.yorku.ca/Spearman/. (Originally published 1904 in the *American Journal of Psychology, 15*(2), 201–292)

Spies, R. A., Plake, B. S., & Murphy, L. L. (Eds.). (2005). *The sixteenth mental measurements yearbook.* Lincoln, NE: Institute of Mental Measurements.

Spradley, J. P. (1979). *The ethnographic interview.* Belmont, CA: Wadsworth, Cengage.

Spradley, J. P. (1980). *Participant observation.* Belmont, CA: Wadsworth.

Stake, R. E. (1995). *The art of case study research.* Thousand Oaks, CA: Sage.

Stake, R. E. (2005). Qualitative case studies. In N. K. Denzin & Y. S. Lincoln (Eds.), *The Sage handbook of qualitative research* (3rd ed., pp. 443–466). Thousand Oaks, CA: Sage.

StatSoft. (2011). *Electronic statistics textbook.* Tulsa, OK: StatSoft. Retrieved from http://www.statsoft.com/textbook/

Stenius, K., Mäeklä, K., Movsky, M., & Garbhelik, R. (2008). How to write publishable qualitative research. In T. F. Barbor, K Stenius, S. Savva, & J. O'Reilly (Eds.), *Publishing addiction science: A guide for the perplexed* (pp. 82–97). Brentwood, Essex, UK: Multi-Science.

Stepansky, P. E. (2009). *Psychoanalysis at the margins.* New York, NY: Other Press.

Sternberg, R. J., Grigorenko, E. L., & Kidd, K. K. (2005). Intelligence, race, and genetics. *American Psychologist, 60*(1), 46–59.

Stobbe, M. (2011, February 27). Past medical testing on humans revealed. Associated Press. *Washington Post.* Retrieved from http://www.washingtonpost.com/wp-dyn/content/article/2011/02/27/AR2011022700988.html

Storey, J. D. (2002) A direct approach to false discovery rates. *Journal of the Royal Statistical Society, Series B (Statistical methodology), 64*(3), 479–498.

Strauss, A., & Corbin, J. (1990). *Basics of qualitative research: Grounded theory procedures and techniques.* Newbury Park, CA: Sage.

Strauss, A., & Corbin, J. (1998). *Basics of qualitative research: Techniques and procedures for developing grounded theory* (2nd ed.). Thousand Oaks, CA: Sage.

Stringer, E. T. (2007). *Action research* (3rd ed.). Thousand Oaks, CA: Sage.

Stufflebeam, D. L. (1981). A brief introduction to standards for evaluations of educational programs, projects, and materials. *Evaluation News, 2*(2), 141–145.

Stufflebeam, D. L. (2003, October). *The CIPP model for evaluation: An update.* Paper presented at the annual conference of the Oregon Program Evaluation Network, Portland. Retrieved from http://goeroendeso.files.wordpress.com/2009/01/cipp-modeloregon10-031.pdf

Stufflebeam, D. L. (2007). *CIPP evaluation model checklist: A tool for applying the CIPP model to assess long-term enterprises* (2nd ed.). Kalamazoo: Western Michigan University. Retrieved from http://www.wmich.edu/evalctr/archive_checklists/cippchecklist_mar07.pdf

Sue, D. W. (2001). Multidimensional facets of cultural competence. *The Counseling Psychologist, 29*(6), 790–821. doi: 10.1177/0011000001296002

Sue, D. W., Arredondo, P., & McDavis, R. J. (1992). Multicultural competencies and standards: A call to the profession. *Journal of Counseling and Development, 70*(4), 477–486.

Suter, W. N. (2012). *Introduction to educational research: A critical thinking approach* (2nd ed.). Thousand Oaks, CA: Sage.

Sutherland, E. (1937). *The professional thief.* Chicago, IL: University of Chicago Press.

Swan, N. (2010, April 26). Lack of medical ethics—from the 19th century to Nazi Germany [Interview with Professor Paul Weindling; podcast]. Sydney, New South Wales, Australia: Australian Broadcasting Corporation. Retrieved from http://www.abc.net.au/radionational/programs/healthreport/lack-of-medical-ethics---from-the-19th-century-to/3106556

Tabasco Inc. (2011). *What are Scoville units?* Retrieved from http://www.tabasco.com/mcilhenny-company/faqs-archives/

Tashakkori, A., & Teddlie, C. B. (1998). *Applied social research methods series: No. 6. Mixed methodology: Combining qualitative and quantitative approaches.* Thousand Oaks, CA: Sage.

Teddlie, C., & Tashakkori, A. (2009). *Foundations of mixed methods research: Integrating qualitative and quantitative approaches in the social and behavioral sciences.* Thousand Oaks, CA: Sage.

Thomas, S. G. (2009, May 6). Today's tykes: Secure kids or rudest in history? MSNBC.com. Retrieved from http://www.msnbc.msn.com/id/30585984

Thompson, C. L., & Henderson, D. A. (2007). *Counseling children* (7th ed.). Belmont, CA: Thomson.

Thompson, W. E., & Hickey, J. V. (2011). *Society in focus: An introduction to sociology* (7th ed.). Boston, MA: Allyn & Bacon.

Thurstone, L. L. (1927). A law of comparative judgment. *Psychological Review, 3,* 273–286. Retrieved from http://www.brocku.ca/MeadProject/Thurstone/Thurstone_1927f.html

Trochim, W. M. K. (2006). Social interaction threats. *Research methods knowledge base.* Retrieved from http://www.socialresearchmethods.net/kb/intsoc.php

Trochim, W. M. K., & Donnelly, J. P. (2007). *The research methods knowledge base* (3rd ed.). Mason, OH: Atomic Dog-Thompson.

Tufts Managed Care Institute. (1998). *A brief history of managed care.* Boston, MA: Tufts Health Care Institute. Retrieved from http://www.thci.org/downloads/briefhist.pdf

Turner, S. M., DeMers, S. T., Fox, H. R., & Reed, G. (2001). APA's guidelines for test user qualifications: An executive summary. *American Psychologist, 56*(12), 1099–1113. doi: 10.1037/0003-066X.56.12.1099

US Department of Education. (2007). Final guidance on maintaining, collecting, and reporting racial and ethnic data to the U.S. Department of Education. *Federal Register, 72*(202), 59266–59279.

US Department of Health and Human Services. (2010). *Historical highlights: Health and Human Services.* Retrieved from http://www.hhs.gov/about/hhshist.html

Utt, S. A., & Pasternak, S. (2000). Update on infographics in American newspapers. *Newspaper Research Journal, 21*(2), 55–66.

Van Horn, P. S., Green, K. E., & Martinussen, M. (2009). Survey response rates and survey administration in counseling and clinical psychology: A meta-analysis. *Educational and Psychological Measurement, 69*(3), 389–403. doi 10.1177/0013164408324462

Vaterlaus, J. M., & Higgenbotham, B. J. (2011). Qualitative program evaluation methods. *The Forum for Family and Consumer Issues, 16*(1). Retrieved from http://ncsu.edu/ffci/publications/2011/v16-n1-2011-spring/vaterlaus-higginbotham.php

Virginia Association of Clinical Counselors. (2011). *History of VACC: A brief history of VACC.* Retrieved from http://www.vacc.org/index.php/what-is-vacc-about-68/history-of-vacc-about-26/

von Hippel, P. T. (2005). Mean, median, and skew: Correcting a textbook rule. *Journal of Statistics Education, 13*(2). Retrieved from http://www.amstat.org/publications/jse/v13n2/vonhippel.html

Walach, H., & Schmidt, S. (1997). Empirical evidence for a non-classical experimenter effect: An experimental, double-blind investigation of unconventional information transfer. *Journal of Scientific Exploration, 11*(1), 59–68.

Walecki, P., Lason, W., Porebski, G., & Obtukowicz, K. (2005). Abductive logic programming in allergy diagnosis. *Bio-Algorithms and Medical Systems, Journal of the Medical College of Jagillonian University, 1*(1/2), 57–60. Retrieved from http://www.bams.cm-uj.krakow.pl/bams_pdf/57-60_walecki.pdf

Warner, R. M. (2013). *Applied statistics: From bivariate through multivariate techniques* (2nd ed.). Thousand Oaks, CA: Sage.

Watkins, K. E. (1991, April 4). *Validity in action research.* Paper presented at the annual meeting of the American Educational Research Association, Chicago, IL. (ERIC Document No. 334246)

Watson, J. (1913). Psychology as the behaviorist views it. *Psychological Review, 20,* 158–177.

Webb, E. J., Campbell, D. T., Schwartz, R. D., & Sechrest, L. (1966). *Unobtrusive measures: Nonreactive research in the social sciences.* Chicago, IL: Rand McNally.

Wechsler, D. (2008). *Wechsler adult intelligence scale IV.* San Antonio, TX: Pearson Assessment.

Wertheimer, M. (1997). Gestalt theory [Section 1]. In W. D. Ellis (Ed.), *A source book of Gestalt psychology* (pp. 1–55). Gouldsboro, ME: The Gestalt Journal Press.

West, R., & Ussher, M. (2010). Is the ten-item questionnaire of smoking urges (QSR-brief) more sensitive to abstinence than shorter craving measures? *Psychopharmacology 208*(3), 427–432.

Westfall, P. H., Kropf, S., & Finos, L. (2004). Weighted FWE-controlling methods in high-dimensional situations. *Lecture Notes Monograph Series, Institute for Mathematical Statistics, 47,* 143–154.

Wheeldon, J. (2010). Mapping mixed methods research: Methods, measures, and meaning. *Journal of Mixed Measures Research, 4*(2), 87–102. doi: 10.1177/1558689809358755

Whiston, S. C. (2002). Response to the past, present, and future of school counseling: Raising some new issues. *Professional School Counseling, 5*(3), 148–157.

Whitbourne, S. K. (2011, March 8). The end of talk therapy? *Psychology Today: Fulfillment at Any Age* [Blog]. Retrieved from http://www.psychologytoday.com/blog/fulfillment-any-age/201103/the-end-talk-therapy/

Whitehead, J., & McNiff, J. (2006). *Action research: Living theory.* Thousand Oaks, CA: Sage.

Wilcoxon, F. (1945). Individual comparisons by ranking methods. *Biometrics, 1*(1), 80–83.

Wildt, A. R., & Ahtola, O. T. (1978). *Quantitative applications in the social sciences: Series No. 12. Analysis of covariance.* Newbury Park, CA: Sage.

Williams, M. J. (2001). *Problems of knowledge: A critical introduction to epistemology.* New York, NY: Oxford University Press.

Willing, R. (2006, February 1). DNA rewrites history for African-Americans. *USA Today.* Retrieved from http://www.usatoday.com/tech/science/genetics/2006-02-01-dna-african-americans_x.htm

Winer, B. J. (1971). *Statistical issues in experimental design* (2nd ed.). New York, NY: McGraw-Hill.

Wolcott, H. F. (2009). *Writing up qualitative research* (3rd ed.). Thousand Oaks, CA: Sage.

Wong, D. L., Hockenberry-Eaton, M., Wilson, D., Winkelstein, M. L., & Schwartz, P. (2001). *Wong's essentials of pediatric nursing* (6th ed.). Saint Louis, MO: Mosby.

Wright, R. J. (2008). *Educational assessment: Tests and measurements in the age of accountability.* Thousand Oaks, CA: Sage.

Wright, R. J. (2010). *Multifaceted assessment for early childhood education.* Thousand Oaks, CA: Sage.

Wright, R. J. (2012). *Introduction to school counseling.* Thousand Oaks, CA: Sage.

Wright, R. J., & Richardson, L .P. (1977). Response bias in cognitive complexity and course evaluation. *Educational and Psychological Measurement, 37*(1), 177–183. doi: 10.1177/001316447703700117

Wündt, W. (1999). *Introduction to* Grundzüge der Physiologischen Psychologie. In R. H. Wozniak (Ed.), *Classics in psychology, 1955–1914: Historical essays.* Retrieved from http://psychclassics.yorku.ca/Wundt/Physio/wozniak.htm (Originally published 1874)

Yarbrough, D. B., Shulha, L. M., Hopson, R. K., and Caruthers, F. A. (2011). *The program evaluation standards: A guide for evaluators and evaluation users* (3rd ed.). Thousand Oaks, CA: Sage.

Yin, R. K. (2008). *Applied social research methods series: Vol. 5. Case study research: Design and methods* (4th ed.). Thousand Oaks, CA: Sage.

Zhang, Y., & Wildemuth, B. M. (2009). Qualitative analysis of content. In B. Wildemuth (Ed.), *Applications of social research methods to questions in information and library science* (pp. 308–319). Westport, CT: Libraries Unlimited.

Ziegler, M., MacCann, C., & Roberts, R. D. (2012). Faking: Knowns, unknowns, and points of contention. In M. Ziegler, C. MacCann, & R. D. Roberts (Eds.), *New perspectives on faking in personality assessment* (pp. 3–18). New York, NY: Oxford University Press.

Zimbardo, P. G. (2007). *The Lucifer effect: Understanding how good people turn evil.* New York, NY: Random House.

Index

About the Author

Robert J. Wright earned a bachelor's degree in chemistry and secondary education from Kutztown University of Pennsylvania in 1966 and began teaching high school science. A few years later in 1971, he earned a master's degree in school counseling from West Chester University and was employed as a school counselor, first with high school students and later with middle schoolers.

As a full-time fellowship student, he finished a doctorate (PhD) in educational psychology with specializations in developmental psychology and counseling, research, and educational measurement from Temple University. As part of working toward that degree, he completed a clinical fellowship in rehabilitation counseling at Moss Hospital, part of the Albert Einstein Medical Center (Philadelphia). Following graduation, he completed advanced studies in school psychology at Lehigh University and was licensed as a psychologist in Pennsylvania.

Professor Wright has taught counseling and supervised counseling interns and has also taught educational measurement and educational statistics for graduate students in counseling. During his career, he has chaired 114 successful doctoral dissertations and served on many other dissertation-sponsoring committees. Dr. Wright has published four books, the latest being *Introduction to School Counseling* (Sage, 2012). He has also published a dozen articles in the professional literature and presented 60 research papers at the national meetings of professional associations. In the 1980s, he consulted on the construction and standardization of professional licensing examinations, and he has served as the psychometrician for the annual examination of psychiatrists in residency training.

He is a member of: the American Counseling Association, American School Counselor Association, American Psychological Association Division 17 (Society of Counseling Psychology), American Educational Research Association, Association for Counselor Educators and Supervisors, and National Council for Measurement in Education.